Acting Globally

Memoirs of Brazil's Assertive Foreign Policy

Celso Amorim

TRANSLATED BY MICHAEL MARSDEN

Hamilton Books

An Imprint of
Rowman & Littlefield
Lanham • Boulder • New York • Toronto • Plymouth, UK

4501 Forbes Boulevard, Suite 200, Lanham, Maryland 20706
Hamilton Books Acquisitions Department (301) 459-3366

Unit A, Whitacre Mews, 26-34 Stannary Street,
London SE11 4AB, United Kingdom

Printed in the United States of America
British Library Cataloguing in Publication Information Available

Library of Congress Control Number: 2016959346
ISBN: 978-0-7618-6881-1 (pbk : alk. paper)—ISBN: 978-0-7618-6882-8 (electronic)

∞™ The paper used in this publication meets the minimum requirements of American National Standard for Information Sciences Permanence of Paper for Printed Library Materials, ANSI/NISO Z39.48-1992.

To Ana, my loving and patient companion;
To Vicente, Anita, João, and Pedro, who realized the dreams I dreamed;
To all those, young in spirit, who believe in Brazil and its people.

A Note on the Photographs

The cover photograph is a reproduction of a world map produced by Jeronimo Marini in 1512. A drape based upon the map decorates the office of the Brazilian foreign minister in Brasilia. Historical records suggest that this was the first ever map to feature the word "Brasil." Jerusalem, or the region of Palestine, appears in the center. Due to Arab influence, the southern hemisphere appears in the upper part of the map and the northern hemisphere in the lower part.

All the photos in the photospread that follows page 253 are from the author's personal archives, and most of them were taken by his direct collaborators. Every effort was made to identify the photographers and to give them due credit. Where this was not possible, we encourage the possible copyright owners to contact the publisher so that credit can be given in future editions.

Contents

Foreword

These memoirs consist of three narratives relating to episodes in Brazilian foreign policy between 2003 and 2010, when I was foreign minister in the governments of President Lula. The first narrative deals with our attempts to bring about a negotiated solution to the Iranian nuclear issue. I decided to begin with that subject because in 2014, as I was about to start writing the original text of the book,[1] the "Tehran Declaration" regarding the Iranian nuclear program—signed by Iran, Brazil, and Turkey—was back in the news in Brazil due to the resumption of talks between Iran and the P5+1. Later, on the very same day as I wrote the original foreword, I read an interview with the American author Vali Nasr in which a Brazilian journalist asked him if he thought the Tehran Declaration really was a diplomatic victory for Brazil. The persistence of such doubts seemed to provide further justification for my earlier choice of theme for the opening narrative. And in 2016, as this English translation of the book was being prepared, the Iranian nuclear program was still very much in the news.

Recalling the periods when I taught political theory and international relations at Brasilia University, I am now inclined to see the story of the Tehran Declaration as a case study in which the attitudes of countries, and especially their leaders, came to light through the very specific catalyst of the "swap deal"—which was initially proposed as a confidence-building measure in relation to the Iranian nuclear program but was then reneged upon by the proponents themselves, who depicted it as a dilatory maneuver by Iran in which Brazil and Turkey were supposedly victims of Tehran's perfidy. Leaving aside for a moment my role as an actor in this process and donning instead the mantle of scholar, I am tempted to see in this episode a basis for analyzing the foreign policies of the great powers, the tangled web of motives that produce those policies, and the ethical issues involved in the *raison d'État* of each country and in the behavior of certain individuals. It would be even more interesting, of course, to compare my account with those of other participants in the events that culminated in the Tehran Declaration. But I will leave that task for someone else.

The second narrative concerns the evolution of our diplomatic efforts toward the Arab countries (and, as a consequence, Israel) and the rationale behind them. It deals with a region of the world that is, of course, extremely complex and diverse. For me personally there was a long learning process and a series of discoveries whose meaning I have not yet fully grasped. Never, for example, did I foresee the "revolution" represented by the Arab Spring. The difficulty of seeing far ahead with regard to the region is reflected, for example, by something I did in February 2011, when I was no longer foreign minister. I had been invited by Al Jazeera to give a lecture in Doha, and in what appears in retrospect to have been a bout of recklessness, I took the opportunity to travel through the interior of Syria. My main aim was to visit Palmyra, a city that in ancient times, as a great commercial center, was in a certain sense the capital of a vast territory extending from the eastern Mediterranean to the borders of Iran. A month later, that journey would have been impossible for a tourist—indeed, I was probably one of the last Brazilians to see that marvelous ancient site before religious fundamentalists set about destroying it.

Both of the above narratives give prominence to individuals who exerted (and in some cases still exert) a strong influence over the destiny of the Middle East. As far as Brazil is concerned, the narratives also frame a transition from inhibited "middle power," confined to its own region, to global player, a new status recognized and indeed welcomed by a great many countries that interacted with us.

The third and final narrative concerns Brazil's participation in the Doha Round of the World Trade Organization. Our role in these negotiations came to be seen as a central one by our partners and by much of the international media. As with the Iranian nuclear program, the Doha Round is back in the news, even if not always in a positive light. Recently, the tendency to seek alternatives to the multilateral trade negotiations through so-called mega-regional trade agreements (such as the TPP and the TTIP)[2] appears to have drifted into a cul-de-sac. This fact leads me, as an incurable optimist, to think it might still be possible to bring the negotiators back to the multilateral table. The light at the end of the tunnel is indeed faint, but has not yet been extinguished entirely.

I want to thank my editor, Débora Guterman, for her patience and constructive contributions. Three other people were essential in order for me to finish this book: the brilliant young diplomat Luiz Feldman, who always offered valuable suggestions; my competent and dedicated research assistant Mariana Klemig, who systematically corrected the texts, making them more precise, and also enriched them with footnotes; and my wife Ana, who accompanied my writing of these narratives with affectionate attention, notable tolerance, and implacable demands for clarity. I should also express my deep appreciation for the efforts of the translator, Michael Marsden, who was indefatigable in his search for solutions to every difficulty he faced. Thanks to his work, even the next edition in Portuguese, when it appears, will be a much-improved one.

Rio de Janeiro, October 2016

NOTES

1. The original version of the book, in Portuguese, was entitled *Teerã, Ramalá e Doha: memórias da política externa ativa e altiva*. It was published by Benvirá in 2015.
2. The Trans-Pacific Partnership (TPP) and the Transatlantic Trade and Investment Partnership (TTIP).

1. The Tehran Declaration: a Missed Opportunity?

The question mark in the title of this narrative is not purely rhetorical. Although I am convinced that the Tehran Declaration, at the time it was issued, would have helped ensure the dispute over Iran's nuclear program was conducted peacefully, it is difficult to say whether its acceptance would have resulted in a definitive solution to the issue. History, unlike physics, does not allow us to make entirely safe or certain assertions about the consequences of changing a single variable. As will be shown throughout this narrative, it was certainly the case that the rejection of the Declaration meant time was wasted and the context for negotiations became less favorable. Moreover, the economic sanctions caused hardship to much of the Iranian population, who had nothing to do with the orientation of their country's leaders on this or indeed other issues. However, it could be argued that the hardship possibly exerted pressure in favor of changes in the Iranian political landscape, which in turn perhaps facilitated the resumption of negotiations in the context of a broader deal, incorporating reciprocal commitments that were not actually part of the Tehran Declaration. It is a subject that invites endless speculation. But the purpose of this narrative is instead simply to recall—from the perspective of one particular country, one government, and indeed one person—the events and circumstances that together constituted a controversial but also significant chapter in the recent history of Brazilian foreign policy.

BACKGROUND

Of all Brazil's diplomatic initiatives and all the situations our diplomats were involved in during the eight years of the government of President Lula, none illustrates more clearly our potential for political action at the international level—and, at the same time, the limitations of so-called "soft power"—than the process that culminated in the Tehran Declaration of May 17, 2010, through which Brazil, along with Turkey, sought to ensure a peaceful and negotiated solution to the Iranian nuclear issue.

It is always difficult to pinpoint exactly where such a process begins. In this case there were both endogenous and exogenous factors leading the Brazilian government to engage in the search for a negotiated solution. I will discuss the exogenous factors later on. As for the internal motivation, it came from two sources. One was the desire on the part of President Lula to have a truly universal foreign policy, not limited by no-go areas of any kind. This had already been demonstrated by previous initiatives such as the president's trips to Arab countries (including some that the Brazilian media considered out of bounds, such as Syria and Libya).[1] Alongside this impulse was a perception of the political and economic importance of Iran—which, in the case of the president himself, I think came more from his prodigious powers of intuition than from detailed analysis. On more than one occasion, long before the diplomatic maneuvers that led to the Tehran Declaration, he had mentioned to me during interminable flights in the presidential aircraft that he was interested in visiting Iran and initiating a relationship with the country. Aware of the complications surrounding Iran in the international context—and also with quite enough on my plate with controversial issues such as the Free Trade Area of the Americas (FTAA), Venezuela, negotiations with the European Union, and the Summit of South American-Arab Countries (ASPA)[2] —I did not initially encourage what appeared to me to be a premature and risky venture. A lack of time and an already busy foreign agenda meant that any possible initiative with regard to Tehran was postponed.

As the person directly responsible for conducting foreign policy, I had a natural interest in any theme connected with peace and security. That interest had developed particularly during the period when I was Brazil's permanent representative[3] to the United Nations (after my first period as foreign minister in the government of Itamar Franco), when I became personally involved in delicate situations such as the one concerning Iraq. My interest was nurtured by frequent contact with individuals who were themselves closely involved with peace and security, and would ultimately be one of the factors leading to Brazil's participation in the negotiations regarding the Iranian nuclear program between 2009 and 2010. I sensed that, given the circumstances at that time, if Brazil wanted a closer relationship with a state seen as a "pariah," albeit unjustly, it was going to be necessary to legitimize that relationship by making some kind of contribution to addressing the nuclear issue. I already had some experience of disarmament issues, having been president of the Geneva Conference on Disarmament (CD) in Geneva in

1993 and 2000—an experience no one now is likely to repeat, given the expansion of the forum's membership since then. The CD is, in the jargon of the UN, "the single multilateral disarmament negotiating forum of the international community." In the first of those two periods I coordinated the CD response to a report by the UN secretary-general, Boutros Boutros-Ghali, entitled "New Dimensions of Disarmament."[4] It was also during that time that an initial step was made toward the negotiation of a comprehensive treaty on nuclear tests (CTBT). During my second period as president I tried in vain to establish a program of work for the CD. The so-called "Amorim Proposal," the result of those efforts, remained a reference point for many years. I had also participated in commissions that dealt with nuclear disarmament—especially the so-called Canberra Commission, whose proposals had an impact on the discussions but unfortunately did not achieve much in practice.[5] When I chaired the United Nations Security Council (UNSC) "panels" on Iraq in the 1990s, I was able to familiarize myself with the practical aspects of disarmament verification, and also became convinced that Brazil had a role to play in that area. I came to believe, as I still do, that if we dedicated ourselves seriously to the issue, our voice would be heard.

Thanks to those experiences, which predated the Lula government, but also as a consequence of initiatives Brazil had been taking on global issues right from the start of that government, especially with regard to the invasion of Iraq, I had established a good channel of communication with other individuals directly involved in the Iranian issue, notably the High Representative of the European Union, Javier Solana (who had been Spanish foreign minister during my time as foreign minister in the Itamar Franco government), and the director-general of the International Atomic Energy Agency (IAEA), Mohammed El-Baradei. I had come into increasing contact with El-Baradei in the context of the inspections regime that the IAEA applied to Brazil's nuclear program, about which we had been able to agree upon a practical solution, with the necessary technical support, during a visit he made to Brazil in 2007. During my frequent stops in Brussels (most of them related to trade negotiations), where I usually met with Solana, and in meetings such as those in Davos, where I generally spoke both with him and El-Baradei, there were conversations about international affairs in which the subject of Iran always came up. I also had the opportunity to talk to Solana about the Iranian issue at international conferences such as the one on the reconstruction of Iraq in June 2005, or on Afghanistan in January 2006. I was able to stay quite well informed about the proposals that were emerging and the reactions from the Iranian government, which were generally negative. It was sufficient for me to realize, even from a certain distance, that the western "offers" were bound to be rejected because they ignored an essential fact: Iran would never accept a scheme that deprived it of the possibility of enriching uranium—which is a right that the Treaty on the Non-Proliferation of

Nuclear Weapons (NPT), despite all its imbalances, does not deny to "non-nuclear" states (i.e. those that do not possess nuclear weapons). Certain suggestions aimed at "building confidence," some of which came from the European Union (probably with the authorship or co-authorship of my friend Solana) also struck me as unrealistic. One of them stipulated that there would be no new sanctions against Tehran in return for an Iranian commitment not to proceed with its enrichment program—the so-called "freeze-for-freeze" proposal. Even leaving aside the significant issue surrounding the principle of discriminatory treatment, it seemed to me highly unlikely that Tehran would agree to give up a right (or what it perceived as such) merely in order to avoid incurring additional penalties. In a simplistic but graphic comparison, I said to Solana on at least one occasion that the proposal was equivalent to twisting someone's arm and saying: "If you behave yourself, I won't twist your arm any further, so the pain will stay as it is. But if you don't, the pain will get worse." Later events showed that I was right: Iran never took the proposal seriously.

Overall, I became very interested in the issue. As far as I could tell, there was virtual unanimity, at least in the West, about the Iranians having transgressed the rules of the IAEA by not having previously informed the organization of their intention to develop their enrichment capacity. The arguments used by Iran, meanwhile, were not wholly convincing. I remember, for example, an Iranian official coming to my office in Brasilia to discuss the issue. Referring to suspicions arising from the discovery of a certain amount of enriched uranium at facilities in Iran, he attributed the fact to "contamination" caused by a batch of uranium received from an ex-Soviet republic. As for the other arguments Iran used to justify its nuclear program, hinging on some small technical detail in the IAEA rules regarding deadlines and notifications, they were not accepted by the western countries. I lacked a thorough knowledge of the subject that would have allowed me to judge whether Iran was indeed breaking the rules. But, as I said to my western contacts, even if such a violation had indeed taken place, the international community should not be treating Iran as a pariah. Making an analogy with the way credit card companies treat clients who do not pay what they owe, I said the sensible thing was not to "banish" Iran from the community of nations, and especially not from the community of members of the Non-Proliferation Treaty. The prospect of the West permanently adopting a punitive attitude would only strengthen Iran's perception that the penalties it was suffering were due, above all, to the country being Islamic or anti-western (and an adversary of Israel), which would accentuate its sense of being discriminated against. In general my contacts listened carefully, or at least curiously, to what I called my "credit card theory," but without ever taking it seriously enough to be persuaded. The subject also came up in conversations with some of my contacts in developed countries, such as British foreign secretary Jack Straw.

However, as with Ariel Sharon's stance toward the Arabs,[6] Straw believed the role Brazil might play was simply that of persuading Tehran to accept the western proposals, and he tried to convince me in a conversation we had during Lula's state visit to the United Kingdom in 2006. From our point of view, such attempts to involve us in the process as mere auxiliaries to the western approach were clearly a non-starter.[7]

There was also a telephone conversation between President Lula and Chancellor Angela Merkel, on January 26, 2006, in which they talked about diverse issues ranging from the scheduling of bilateral visits and EU-Latin America meetings to the discussions concerning the expansion of the UN Security Council. From Brazil's point of view the main issue in that particular conversation was how to follow up on the WTO Ministerial Conference that had just taken place in Hong Kong. Merkel, however, introduced the topic of Iran, which seemed to be worrying her. She commented that the other members of the European negotiating group (the UK and France)[8] shared her concern. She indicated that Germany hoped the IAEA Board of Governors would arrive at a consensus, and that so too would the Security Council if the matter were put before it. In response, Lula admitted it was necessary to put pressure on Iran to "fulfill its commitments and avoid public statements that could hamper the negotiations," but he reiterated Brazil's understanding that state signatories to the NPT had the "legitimate right" to develop nuclear technology for peaceful purposes. "Dialogue and negotiation," he said, were still the best way to resolve the issue. Lula added that Brazil, as a country committed to achieving peaceful outcomes and yet in this case not "directly connected with the issue," would not only be capable of contributing to a solution but also "entirely willing" to do so. The conversation with Merkel took place about a week before the IAEA Board of Governors' decision, which did indeed refer the matter to the Security Council. Despite this initial dialogue, the Germans would not ultimately become active interlocutors when Brazil became more deeply involved in the issue two or three years later.

Of all my discussions with western officials about the Iranian nuclear program, one of the most productive was with the Swiss foreign minister, Micheline Calmy-Rey. A neutral country with potential commercial interests in Iran, Switzerland was already talking about the issue with Iranian officials, seeking to break the deadlock caused by mutual intransigence. I discussed the matter with Calmy-Rey when I made an official visit to Berne in October 2007, during her reciprocal visit to Brasilia about a year later, and at least once on the phone. On the basis of those conversations, in which we were both seeking a reasonable way of moving forward, I instructed our ambassador to Denmark, Georges Lamazière, who had significant experience in disarmament-related matters, to travel to Berne for talks. However, this well-meaning dialogue did not yield any concrete results.

FIRST MOVES

I made my first trip to Tehran on November 2, 2008, seventeen years after what I believe to have been the only previous visit to the Iranian capital by a Brazilian foreign minister—that of José Francisco Rezek during the government of President Collor. The Iranian government had been giving regular indications of its interest in greater proximity with Brazil. President Ahmadinejad had even been planning to fit in a visit to Brasilia as part of a trip to Latin America following the United Nations General Assembly (UNGA), in which his scheduled stops were in La Paz and Caracas. But, for more than one reason, the inclusion of Brazil in his prospective itinerary, without prior consultation with our government, did not strike me as appropriate. Given the importance of Brazil in both the regional and global contexts, it should have been the centerpiece of his trip, not an appendage. And also, if Brazil were to be included as part of an essentially "ALBA"[9] itinerary, it would unnecessarily aggravate the negativity of our media and the more conservative elements of public opinion toward a possible rapprochement with Tehran. Just to give an indication that my concerns were not unfounded, later on, when the negotiations for the Tehran Declaration were underway, a major Brazilian weekly magazine published an article illustrated by two photos, side by side, of the Iranian president and myself, supposedly united by a shared hatred of Israel. I did my diplomatic best, therefore, to indicate to the Iranian foreign minister, Manouchehr Mottaki, with whom I had not had much contact until then, that it would be better to schedule the visit for another time, in a more appropriate context. I also emphasized that a presidential visit should be well prepared, which meant prior meetings of a technical nature and understandings between the respective foreign ministers. Mottaki agreed, and after further discussion we settled upon the idea that I should visit Tehran in November. This was not mere procrastination; the truth is I wanted to put in place as much "armor-plating" as possible to protect the visit from the kind of media attacks that might even have affected other areas of our foreign policy. Personally I had no preconceived view on Iran, although I had certain reservations about the confessional nature of the ayatollahs' regime. As foreign minister under Itamar Franco I had met my Iranian counterpart at the time, Ali Akbar Velayati, on the sidelines of the UNGA in New York; and I had also come across him once before then, when he visited Brazil during Francisco Rezek's time as our foreign minister, a period in which my position in Itamaraty[10] was concerned with economic affairs. Also, in 1993, when I had been ambassador in Geneva, during my first period as president of the Conference on Disarmament, I mediated (successfully, as it turned out) a disagreement over the coordination of one of the working groups by the Iranian representative, who was suspected of having participated in the invasion of the US embassy in Tehran in 1979. Our diplomatic relationship with Iran was a fluid one. Also during my time as foreign minister under Itamar, it was our embassy in Tehran that took care of the interests of Argentina, at our neighbor's request, in the wake of the 1994 terrorist attack on the AMIA[11] in Buenos Aires, the planning of which was attributed to Iran. With regard to issues of human rights, as ambassador to the United Nations from 1995–1999 I took the position that Iran should be kept engaged in some form of dialogue with the "international community."[12] And as foreign minister it was for that same reason that I resisted pressure, including from some of my (supposedly powerful) colleagues in government, to vote in favor of resolutions condemning Iran in the UN Commission on Human Rights (now the Human Rights Council). The pressure came principally from people linked to the Bahá'í religious community. I instructed our delegation in Geneva to maintain the Brazilian position of abstention but also, when justifying their vote, to issue a criticism of restrictions on religious freedom in Iran.

My thoughts ahead of the Tehran visit were not focused solely on its format. I remained convinced that some kind of initiative on the nuclear issue would contribute to legitimizing the visit, placing it in the context of the international efforts to find a solution to the "problem" of Iran's nuclear program. I therefore insisted that in addition to discussions with my Iranian counterpart and other meetings that were a standard part of the protocol, my stay in Tehran should also include a conversation with the secretary-general of Iran's Supreme National Security Council, Saeed Jalili, who was the main person responsible for the negotiations with the European Union and the IAEA. I also spoke to President Ahmadinejad, who received me with great courtesy, but nothing very substantial came of our meeting.

Before leaving for Tehran I had spoken on the phone with Javier Solana, who once again explained to me the European proposal and updated me on the recent discussions. He asked me to emphasize to the Iranians the importance of a positive response on their part. I may also have spoken with El-Baradei or Calmy-Rey. In Tehran, in my conversation with Jalili, I did indeed convey Solana's message, with an addendum of my own about the advantages of sustaining dialogue and avoiding diplomatic isolation. Our conversation turned toward specific technical issues that I cannot describe properly here; suffice to say I concluded that Tehran would not accept a solution that withdrew its right to continue enriching uranium, and would certainly never do so under the pressure of sanctions.[13] I must admit that Brazil had made a mistake in February 2006, as a member of the IAEA Board of Governors, by accepting that the issue of Iran's nuclear program should be referred to the Security Council.[14] In general my position in relation to such attempts to politicize the issue was one of abstention, partly because I had already seen at close quarters the workings of the Security Council, and I knew there was a risk of setting in motion a chain of actions and reactions that often culminated not only in the use of armed force but also in humanitarian tragedies. Nevertheless, at some point, faced with international pressure and the positions of those countries that tended to vote with Brazil, such as India, I accepted the idea of following the "parliamentary majority," which so frequently serves as a means of circumventing difficult situations. The decision to refer the subject to the Security Council was supported by Russia, as Foreign Minister Sergey Lavrov had told me in advance a few days previously, on the sidelines of a conference in London on the subject of Afghanistan. Egypt and Yemen, among other developing countries, also went along with the majority. Before the vote, Brazil, India, and South Africa had managed to lighten the text somewhat, emphasizing the essentially informative nature of the IAEA's reports to the Security Council, but that did not prevent the Security Council from imposing sanctions on Iran—sanctions that Brazil would support, for the same debatable reasons. In this case South Africa was more coherent, abstaining from the IAEA Board of Governors' vote. Brazil's position certainly was not decisive in allowing the issue to be passed on to the Security Council (and therefore in allowing sanctions to be adopted), and I do not remember Iran ever raising it as an obstacle to our mediation efforts. But our position was still inconsistent with that of valuing the IAEA as a forum and seeking a negotiated solution.

In our meeting in November 2008, Jalili explained his views firmly. Although courteous to the point of accompanying me to the foot of the stairs when I was leaving (which was when I noticed he walked with a limp—the result, I was told, of an injury sustained during the war with Iraq), he did not offer any kind of opening that might allow me to imagine Brazil playing a mediating or facilitating role. He said he would inform me of the response Iran would give to the European Union, and indeed did so a few weeks later. But when I received the document, it did not seem very positive. It wove together general considerations about geopolitics, the rights of states, and the world order, but without stating a clear position on the EU proposal. Over time, the negotiations would take another turn, and the central idea in the European proposal of "building confidence" on the basis of the so-called freeze-for-freeze would be left to one side. As I left the meeting with Jalili, my expectation of Brazil joining countries such as Switzerland in contributing to a negotiated solution of the Iranian issue still seemed a long way from being realized.

In the other meetings, especially the one with my counterpart Mottaki, I dealt with the preparations for Ahmadinejad's visit to Brazil, which was sure to take place sooner or later. Mottaki paid me a visit in Brasilia a few months later, when he reiterated directly to President Lula the intention of the Iranian leader to come in the near future. I think it was then that the visit was formally announced. There were, however, some hitches to overcome during the preparations. The Iranians were unhappy with certain aspects of the protocol, and with criticism from the Brazilian media. At one point I had to explain that because Brazil is a fully democratic state, the government did not have (or wish to have) control over the media, and so we were not responsible for what it published or broadcast. It was anticipated that the visit would take place in the first half of the year, but eventually, with elections looming in Iran, the Iranian government decided to push it back toward the end of the year.

PREPARATIONS FOR THE VISIT

From the moment the visit was announced, the Brazilian media started to pay close attention to everything going on inside Iran. Showing total incomprehension (whether genuine or feigned) of the rules governing relations between countries, the prevailing vision of our principal media commentators seemed to be that in accepting Ahmadinejad's visit to Brazil (or, as some put it, "rolling out the red carpet" for him), we were legitimizing human rights violations and undemocratic practices on the part of the Tehran regime. In my opinion it was undeniable that the Revolutionary Guards and other bodies responsible for internal security committed abuses in clamping down on demonstrations. But that did not make Iran any less important as an interlocutor, whether because of its influence in the region or indeed because of the nuclear issue.[15] In this case, as in others, I was irritated by the unbalanced attitude of the critics. It is worth noting, for example, that they never questioned the two visits President Bush made to Brazil; nor did they ever insinuate that by receiving him we were endorsing the use of torture at Guantanamo or the invasion of Iraq without UN authorization. A hurried statement Lula made to journalists in a hotel lobby in Kazakhstan, expressing support for the electoral process in Iran in the wake of Ahmadinejad's victory, further inflamed the bellicose mood of the section of the Brazilian media that was conducting its own holy war against the scheduled visit. Despite the deplorably repressive measures used against supporters of Mir-Hossein Mousavi (the defeated candidate), the likelihood that the results officially released by Tehran were close to reality was confirmed by a respected North American think tank[16] based on a pre-election survey it carried out in Iran.

Meanwhile, declarations by the Iranian leader in which he denied the Holocaust or said the State of Israel should disappear did nothing to foster a less hostile atmosphere. In a long conversation with Ahmadinejad on the sidelines of the UN General Assembly, about two months before the visit, Lula tried to convince him not only of the historical errors in his assertions but also that such rhetoric was counterproductive. In response, the Iranian president claimed he was not calling for the physical destruction of the State of Israel or its people, but instead the legal dissolution of the Jewish state (or

"Zionist entity," as he put it) and its replacement by a non-denominational state that would be a home for Jews as well as for Palestinians and Christians. As for the Holocaust, he said he did not mean to deny that Jews had been killed in large numbers, but instead wanted to stop the fact being used as justification for the oppression and persecution of the Palestinians. Of course, these awkward explanations, given in private, were not sufficient to improve the public image of the Iranian president.

I think there is space here for some brief comments on Ahmadinejad's personality. I always saw him not as a fanatic imbued with a sense of spiritual or ideological mission, but as an authoritarian and pragmatic populist, always seeking to boost his credentials in the eyes of the religious leaders and strengthen his position with the Revolutionary Guards. Despite his overt obedience to Muslim rituals (during his visit to Brazil he requested, for example, that a space for prayers be arranged for him in our foreign ministry building), he was in my opinion more similar to the Latin American leaders who seek direct contact with the people, bypassing party and institutional structures, than to the ayatollahs in his own country. It is worth remembering that Ahmadinejad was the first president to emerge from a political rather than religious background. He had been mayor of Tehran, and apparently still enjoyed the support of the poorer sections of the capital's population. He clashed frequently with the Shia clergy and even with the Supreme Leader, who on more than one occasion overruled or revoked appointments he had made, including of government ministers. None of that, however, excused his bouts of intemperate language, which were intended essentially to strengthen his position with religious groups or other radical elements such as the Revolutionary Guards.

Although frequently inconvenienced by the Iranian president's verbal outbursts, I believed it was absolutely justified and necessary for Brazil to be seeking closer relations with a country whose importance in regional and indeed global politics seemed indisputable. Indeed, more recently, in the context of the diplomatic efforts concerning Syria, Iran's role has received increasing recognition. The years 2008–09 were a period in which Brazil was increasing its presence in the talks on the Middle East, and in many of my discussions with leaders from the region the importance of Tehran (for better or worse) was quite clear, therefore underlining the advantages of a policy of engagement. Quite apart from that, Iran also offered a promising market for Brazilian products. At one point our annual exports exceeded $2 billion USD (and did not include any arms or dangerous materials; their main component, in fact, was entirely peaceable: chicken). That was the reason why, when I visited Tehran in November 2008, I took with me a sizable group of Brazilian businesspeople,[17] although I must admit that overall I did not feel commercial considerations were decisive. The possibility of Brazil being able to mediate on the nuclear issue—which I had not given up on, despite the many difficulties—would not only contribute to the legitimate objective of strengthening peace but would also be a way of elevating our status on the global political stage.

As previously mentioned, my first visit to Tehran did not yield the kind of results that might have allowed me to envisage Brazil's medium-term participation in the resolution of the central issue in the relationship between Iran and the West. Nor did I perceive, on the part of the United States or other major partners, any clear sign that they might be willing to move beyond simply condemning Iran and embark on a policy of engagement. The most they offered was the prospect of desisting from further punishment of Iran if it gave up the right to enrich uranium for peaceful purposes. What changed my perception was a meeting between Lula and Obama on the sidelines of the expanded G8 summit in L'Aquila, a small Italian town in the Apennines that had just been rocked by violent earthquake, leaving several casualties. In fact the tragedy contributed to Berlusconi choosing L'Aquila as the venue, a decision criticized by many at the time. Looking back at my notes from that period, it is curious that I cannot find more than a passing reference to this meeting between the two leaders, amid brief notes referring to the main aspects of the summit, which concerned climate change. The way my tasks and commitments used to pile up means it is not uncommon for important facts to go almost unmentioned in my notes—but I am still surprised by this particular omission, given the degree of interest I already had in the Iranian issue.

After President Chirac opened (or, should I say, part-opened) the doors of the G8 during its meeting in Évian in 2003, Brazil was invited to all the subsequent summits until 2009, with the single exception of the one that took place at Sea Island in the United States in 2004. It seems appropriate at this point to make a short digression on the efforts to expand, albeit with many restrictions, this informal mechanism of global governance. There is in fact a parallel between what would later take place in the context of Brazil's participation in the discussions on Iran's nuclear program and the ambiguous attitude of the richest and most powerful countries toward the role of so-called emerging nations—at times sharing with them certain responsibilities (or pushing them to accept certain duties), at other times denying them an effective role in major international decisions. This expanded G8 had several different formats, depending on the host country and the circumstances of the moment, but the most common was a G8+5, which consisted of, in addition to the eight richest countries (seven plus Russia, which was included simply because, in the words of the Russian leaders themselves, it had the atomic bomb), China, Brazil, India, South Africa and Mexico. The participation of these five countries was marginal, however, as they were not invited to give their opinions on the most important decisions. In some cases there were documents specific to the G8+5 on a certain subject and yet the official statement emanating from the summit would still be that of the G8 only. That was the case at the Évian summit, and it carried on like that until L'Aquila. It was certainly the case that the G8 members had no desire to involve the developing countries in decisions regarding peace and security. At the ministerial level, the "+5" might be invited to meetings on the environment or transnational crime, areas in which the cooperation of these countries was obviously essential, but not to meetings of the G8 foreign ministers. Although the openness to developing countries' limited participation could be seen as the beginning of a process, and a reflection of some degree of recognition of changes in the international order, the model was obviously unsatisfactory. Lula once remarked about the G8 summits that he was not willing to turn up for a meal and then sit at the table only for coffee. As time went by, there were attempts to improve the form of dialogue, but then the rise of the G20[18] summits rendered those timid efforts almost pointless.

The G8 eventually became less relevant (and has now been reduced to the G7, with the exclusion of Russia). Indeed, I myself asserted in 2009, after a lecture at the University of Paris, that as a forum for deliberating on global issues (if not actually taking decisions itself), the G8 was dead. A few months later President Obama said much the same thing, albeit in more emollient terms. When stressing the importance of the G20 at its Pittsburgh summit, Obama described it as the principal global forum on economic issues. I do think, however, that the conclusion remains valid: just as the dominant powers, especially the western ones, sought to attract large developing countries to their side while keeping them at arm's length from the actual decision-making, so too in the case of Iran, some of them, especially the United States, saw a chance to draw on the support of countries such as Brazil and Turkey for their own benefit, without ever accepting them as "full members" of the exclusive circles in which decisions were taken.

As political meetings taking place at the highest level, however, the expanded G8 summits did have some merits. One was that, aside from the speeches and declarations, they were good opportunities for face-to-face meetings between heads of state and government, relatively free of time-consuming protocol. During the meetings between Lula and Bush on the margins of the G8 summits, once the trauma of Iraq had been put aside, the dominant theme (apart from bilateral issues) tended to be the Doha Round of world trade negotiations, in which Brazil had been recognized as a key player by virtue both of its own economic weight and its role as a leader among developing countries. In L'Aquila, with COP15[19] fast approaching, the pressing issue was climate change, including the discussion about what a maximum acceptable ceiling on global warming by the year 2050 might be. As usual, the issue put rich and poor countries on opposing sides, with the so-called "emerging" countries very much in the spotlight.

Obama had requested a conversation with Lula in L'Aquila. Such bilateral meetings were in fact one of the attractive elements of the expanded G8 summits, whose format was not really conducive to achieving an end result. Indeed, the event inevitably ended up with the media (not only Brazil's, in this case) depicting it as a waste of time and money, and it also featured the usual maneuvering to see who could be made to appear intransigent and who could be blamed for failing to advance a solution to the climate issue. The meeting between the two presidents—also attended by Secretary of State Hillary Clinton and myself, along with a couple of aides—lasted no more than half an hour. According to my diary it took up forty minutes, but that would have included the time spent on greetings and on moving between rooms. Although Lula and Obama did not speak much about the central theme of the summit, they would have mentioned it at some point; and they probably also touched on the Doha Round, which by then had gone into a state of hibernation. But the more important subject, very likely to have been the reason for the meeting in the first place, was Iran.

President Obama perceived, of course, that his stance of openness toward Iran had not been reciprocated by the regime of the ayatollahs. As he put it, his "outstretched hand" had been left hanging in the air. And so the objective of achieving a thaw in relations, which had been frozen ever since the hostages episode following the Iranian revolution, was not achieved. The US president seemed sincere in his desire to reach out to Tehran. Brazil, and especially Lula ("my man," as Obama referred to him at one of the G20 summits, with a mixture of admiration and condescension), could potentially help. What Obama said, more or less, was "We need friends who can talk to countries that refuse to talk to us"—with the nuclear issue obviously looming large in the background. That was the encouragement we needed to engage more deeply on the issue. It is worth mentioning that, at that time, there was already the clear prospect of Brazil being elected as a non-permanent member of the Security Council for the period 2010–11. And, as we had already demonstrated on previous occasions, we were a country that took very seriously Article 24[20] of the UN Charter and our responsibilities when serving on the Security Council.

The L'Aquila summit took place in early July 2009. In the months that followed, leading up to Ahmadinejad's visit to Brasilia, I spoke frequently with my two established interlocutors, El-Baradei and Javier Solana. Both of them, unfortunately, were about to leave their respective posts—a fact that came up frequently in my telephone conversations with the Iranian foreign minister, given the clear and justified assumption that their successors would be more rigid in their approach.[21] Also at that time I received a phone call from the Turkish foreign minister, Ahmet Davutoglu, who was interested to know how we saw the situation ahead of Ahmadinejad's visit. There were also visits to Brazil by US representatives connected with the Iranian nuclear issue. I remember two of them: Gary Samore, an advisor to the National Security Council, whose opinion on such matters is highly respected; and William (Bill) Burns, the successor to another Burns (Nick, from Bush's time), with whom I had a useful dialogue, including on the vexed issue of the reform/expansion of the UN Security Council.

From point of view of protocol, neither Samore nor Bill Burns would be my natural interlocutors. Indeed, both had meetings with their Brazilian counterparts (in Samore's case, a head of department or undersecretary; for Burns, possibly the secretary-general of our foreign ministry). But I was interested in following the evolution of the Iranian issue very closely, particularly in the wake of the L'Aquila conversation between Obama and Lula. Burns, as a high-level official, was someone I from whom I was naturally willing to receive a courtesy visit. My conversation with Samore was more technical; the main thing I remember was his emphasis on the US president's commitment to making progress in the search for a diplomatic solution to the impasse with Iran. Also, he emphasized a desire for Brazil to "help" the matter progress. Burns, by comparison, was more specific and also, as I recall, more emphatic. Indeed, it would not be an exaggeration to say that, more than a mere conversation, my dialogue with the US under secretary of state on that occasion, in the run-up to Ahmadinejad's visit, was a *démarche* aimed at getting Brazil to make Iran see the great advantage in accepting the offer of a "swap agreement" that the P5+1[22] was making through the AIEA, pushed forward principally by the United States.

What did this swap agreement consist of? How had it come about? What I inferred from conversations with various interlocutors—including El-Baradei and Solana, and the US representatives who came to Brazil—was that a few months previously Iran had requested the mediation of the International Atomic Energy Agency so as to acquire on the international market pellets (or rods) containing fuel with 20%-enriched uranium for its research reactor in Tehran (the acronym TRR is often used), which produces isotopes for the diagnosis and treatment of cancer. Two points should be emphasized here. The first is technical: once uranium has been converted into fuel, it cannot (or at least not easily) be converted back again into its original state and be enriched to the higher degrees that would take Iran close to being able to produce an atomic bomb. The second point is a political-legal one: Iran, like any other country, has the right to request that the IAEA help it obtain material for exclusively peaceful use—in this case connected with healthcare for its population. Faced with the Iranian request, I gathered that the western countries—the US, more specifically—had come up with the idea of proposing that Iran paid for the fuel pellets not with money but instead with a proportional amount of low-enriched uranium (LEU), which it was already capable of producing. The ratio would be about ten to one, i.e. to receive one kilogram of 20%-enriched uranium, Iran would give ten kilograms of LEU.

That way, Iran's legitimate request would be granted, and at the same time part of its stock of uranium would be taken away, pushing to a distant future horizon the day when Iran would possess a nuclear weapon (assuming that was actually its intention) or become a so-called "threshold state" (a country with the capacity to produce a nuclear device).

The idea was simple and ingenious. Iran would receive the fuel it needed (the raw material consisted of uranium enriched to 20%) while the western countries could ensure that the LEU remaining in Iran would not be enough to build a bomb, never mind a "nuclear arsenal."[23] But as is so often the case with seemingly simple ideas, at least in politics, there were in fact certain complex issues that needed to be resolved. The first concerned the quantity of 20%-enriched uranium contained in the fuel pellets Iran would obtain, and therefore also the amount (weight) of LEU Iran would hand over in exchange. The approximate ratio between one and the other was, as previously mentioned, one to ten: every kilogram of uranium enriched to 20% and processed into fuel would be treated as equivalent to ten kilograms of LEU (enriched to between 4 and 5%).[24] It is worth pointing out that low-enriched uranium is mainly used to produce electric energy. According to the proponents of the idea, it would be necessary to take about 1,200 kilograms of LEU from Iran in order to prevent the country from developing a bomb in the short term, and so it would also be necessary to convince Tehran to acquire 120 kilograms of the fuel. This in itself was already a problem because, as the Iranian officials repeatedly told me in subsequent conversations, a much smaller amount of fuel would be sufficient for the remaining life of their nuclear reactor. A second difficulty concerned the location where the LEU would be deposited until it was transformed into fuel, or until that fuel was handed over to Iran. On several occasions the Tehran government expressed disagreement with the western proposal that Iran's low-enriched uranium should be sent to another country, which it considered an affront to its sovereignty. Also, based on past experiences dating back to the sudden transition from the Shah's regime to the Islamic Republic, the Iranians harbored a great distrust of the West. They feared that if anything went wrong during the process, their LEU would not be returned. It is not difficult to imagine the degree of insecurity that such fears provoked in the individuals conducting the negotiations. It was in that context that Iran suggested its 1,200 kilograms of LEU should be deposited on the island of Kish, a free-trade area inside Iranian territory. It did accept, however, that the uranium should remain under the supervision of the IAEA. As far as I know, the West never seriously considered this suggestion.

There was also a third problem to be resolved: that of the timing of the different actions involved in the swap deal. Tehran maintained that it would not be fair to proceed immediately with handing over its LEU but to have to wait a long time, probably more than a year, to receive the fuel. In the metaphorical terms in which the proposal had been submitted, there was no reason why Iran should make a "payment" so far in advance. In the negotiations that took place a few months later, by then with the participation of Brazil and Turkey, Iran insisted on the concept of simultaneity: the LEU would only be handed over when the fuel pellets were delivered. Over time, this concept would become more flexible: Tehran reached a position in which it appeared ready to accept a kind of "partial simultaneity," that is, it would release a part of the LEU, probably half, when the agreement was adopted, and the remainder upon receipt of the fuel. But that was not considered acceptable by the proponents on the western side, eager as they were to achieve a substantial and immediate reduction in Iran's existing stock of LEU. I am not sure if all these concerns were raised explicitly in September/October 2009, when the US proposal was made and it was accepted in principle by the Iranian negotiators. But they were to become clearer as Brazil and Turkey became more deeply involved in the issue, seeking to revive the agreement.

During this period there was a hiatus in the P5+1 negotiations that puzzled analysts. Why might a proposal accepted *ad referendum* by the Iranian negotiator end up being rejected by Tehran? Given the nature of Iranian political system, it is difficult to imagine that the country's representative at the IAEA would act autonomously on such a sensitive issue, putting himself in a position where he might be overruled. It is very likely that his position did have the endorsement of the government, including Ahmadinejad. But this endorsement seemed to have been withdrawn at the last minute due to pressure from higher up—including from the Supreme Leader himself, probably. Despite his populist and authoritarian tendencies, everything seemed to indicate that Ahmadinejad was above all a pragmatic politician, interested in freeing the Iranian economy from the heavy sanctions imposed either by the UN Security Council or unilaterally (and indeed this would be confirmed by his behavior in subsequent negotiations). Ahmadinejad knew the sanctions would become more severe if no agreement were reached. This step back on the part of Iran, and the reasons behind it, would become the focus of some of the discussions we had with Iranian officials, especially in Lula's meeting with Ahmadinejad in Brasilia.

Iran's rejection of the swap agreement was a great disappointment for its proponents. As previously mentioned, I had several phone conversations during that period with El-Baradei and Solana. Ahead of Ahmadinejad's visit to Brazil, both of them were hopeful about the role Brazil might be able to play in convincing the Iranian government to accept the proposal, which they saw as an important confidence-building gesture. In the months leading up to the visit, there were other meetings and phone calls. I already mentioned the US representatives who came to Brasilia. As for the phone calls, I spoke to Secretary of State Hillary Clinton at least twice. In those conversations, although issues such as the situation of the ousted Honduran president Manuel Zelaya and the preparations for COP15 also came up, and may even have been main topics, the subject of Iran was always present. In that same period there was a visit to Brasilia by the US national security advisor, General Jim Jones, at the invitation either of our defense minister, Nelson Jobim, or the international advisor to President Lula, Marco Aurélio Garcia. I do not know what was said in his conversations with those two of my colleagues, but presumably they discussed the US military bases in Colombia, a very important issue at the time, and the announcement of the reactivation of the Fourth Fleet, intended to be deployed in the Caribbean and the South Atlantic. In my own meeting with Jones, in addition to those topics, we spoke at length about the situation in the Middle East, particularly the Israel-Palestine conflict. Jones himself had direct experience of the issue, having previously been an envoy to the region, a role in which he had made a positive impression, including among the Palestinians, as a person who took an objective approach and was eager to find a solution. That was also how he came across during our meeting, in which he expressed sensible opinions about the conditions necessary for the resumption of the peace process, which was still suffering the impact of the Israeli attacks on Gaza. Naturally we also spoke about Iran, although I do not have any notes to suggest we addressed in any detail the elements that might be necessary for a solution. Further down the line, Jones would come to be an important interlocutor, above all for my Turkish counterpart.

It was also in this period that I received a visit from Bill Burns. His visit is not recorded in my diary, perhaps because it was arranged at short notice. He came up with various arguments in his attempt to obtain Brazil's support in convincing Iran of the advantages of the swap agreement, one of which struck me as particularly persuasive. He underlined the fact that the P5+1, in proposing a deal involving LEU produced on Iranian territory, was in fact accepting the reality that Iran was enriching uranium. But that went against certain Security Council resolutions—which would therefore have to be "adapted," as he spontaneously put it. The right to enrich uranium for peaceful purposes was, in my mind, an essential element in order for Iran to be able to accept some form of agreement. Indeed, the absence of that element was the main reason for the failure of the previous efforts to engage Iran in an effective dialogue. Although as far as I can remember he did not actually use the words "recognize" or "recognition," Burns' comments seemed to me to contain an important conceptual step forward—and one that, in my opinion, Iran should take into consideration.[25]

Not long afterwards, Ahmadinejad would arrive in Brazil for a visit that was swathed in controversy. Most of the Brazilian media seemed oblivious to the fact that we were working for peace and seeking to contribute to the resolution of a complex political-diplomatic problem, and that in so doing we were actually responding to a request that had been made first, in political terms, by the US president, and then later, in more technical terms, by one of his representatives. It was not merely by chance that Ahmadinejad's visit to Brasilia was preceded, a few days before, by an official visit from the president of Israel, Shimon Peres. This "coincidence" did not go unnoticed by the international media. According to my notes at the time, the *Washington Post* referred to them as "dueling visits." Anyway, the dialogue with the two heads of state, in the space of a single week (to complete this highly symbolic portrait of our universalist diplomacy and its focus on the Middle East, in the same period we also received the president of the Palestinian Authority, Mahmoud Abbas), shows that in our foreign relations we were endeavoring to attain a delicate balance and an attitude of openness to different positions.

THE VISIT

Before describing the sequence of events between Ahmadinejad's visit and the decisive days leading up to the Tehran Declaration, I will give a brief summary of the evolution of the political dialogue between Brazil and the United States, the country that was unarguably the main actor (apart from Iran itself) in the process. Despite differences on a variety of topics, the political dialogue between Brazil and the US during the Lula government remained a good one, contrary to what certain commentators and critics—including former Brazilian foreign ministers and retired ambassadors—might suggest. I could mention, for example, the two visits President George W. Bush made to Brazil in a two-year period between 2005 and 2007. A mental image from one of those visits, during which a memorandum of cooperation on fuel ethanol was signed, is of Bush wearing a Petrobras hard hat—the symbolism of which would previously have been unthinkable for my generation of Brazilians, who grew up with the "the oil is ours" campaign. Various issues were addressed in a friendly atmosphere of mutual understanding, ranging from cooperation with third countries (notably in the Caribbean and Central America, in the case of ethanol; and in Africa, especially Sao Tome and Principe, on combating malaria) to coordination with regard to multilateral trade negotiations.

There was also another meeting, at Camp David in March 2007, which lasted more than seven hours (including the working dinner) and was attended by the principal ministers and advisors from both sides. Bush and Lula talked about highly sensitive issues such as the Middle East and the US efforts in the region that would lead to the convening of the Annapolis Conference later that year. Bush also commented that the US Coast Guard was ready to prevent a massive influx of exiles from Cuba but would also act to thwart any attempt by Miami Cubans to invade the island.

This level of trust also characterized my conversations with Secretary of State Condoleezza Rice. The subjects of Venezuela and Haiti were ever-present, of course, but I also spoke with her frequently about the resumption of the peace process between Israel and Palestine, and Syria's position in the conflict. Condoleezza did not merely pass down messages from on high—a common attitude among US representatives—but was also an attentive listener. For example, when I told her that during a recent trip to the Middle East I had been taken aback by the barriers to the movement of Palestinians, including senior officials, and the fact that children were forced to make huge detours merely in order to reach their schools in the morning, sometimes adding more than an hour on to their journeys, the secretary of state gave me the impression that she was genuinely paying attention.

I will not pretend that such reports from me would have influenced US attitudes toward Israel in any way—after all, similar accounts, or indeed more dramatic ones, were no doubt received from the Palestinians themselves—and yet a few months later the Israelis did relax some of their more severe controls on freedom of movement. Condoleezza Rice also took an interest in the IBSA Dialogue Forum (composed of India, Brazil and South Africa) as a possible mediator in conflicts, as reflected by the fact that the three countries were later invited to the Annapolis Conference (the only non-Middle Eastern and non-Islamic developing countries to have that distinction). Of course, despite our good level of understanding, there were still differences of opinion. Bilateral commercial issues also arose during our face-to-face or phone conversations, such as the possible purchase of US fighter planes by the Brazilian Air Force. Even at the height of the Gaza crisis in January 2009, which buried any hopes of an agreement during Bush's presidency, we spoke regularly on the phone.

Curiously, the only record I have of a conversation with Rice about Iran's nuclear program is some notes from September 28, 2005, in which I refer to a meeting a few days before at the State Department, followed by lunch. In the *tête-à-tête* that preceded the formal meeting, we basically dealt with two subjects: Iran and Venezuela. Afterwards, I wrote the following in my notebook: "On Iran, there is obviously concern [on the part of Washington] about Brazil's abstention in the last vote [in the IAEA Board of Governors] that led the way to the referral to the Security Council, [and] an expectation that we can support the resolution to be presented in November. . . . I explained to her that our position is based in part on our experience of other issues that were taken to the UNSC and the subsequent chain of events, difficult to stop. I asked her . . . if the US did not have 'enough on its plate' with the situation in Iraq. Condoleezza tried to say [Iraq] was moving toward normalization. As for Iran, she said the fear of international isolation would have more impact. She raised the possibility of diplomatic sanctions. I told her something I had said to Solana—that Iran should not be given the impression that it was seen as intrinsically untrustworthy and therefore could never have access to enrichment. It would be better to treat the issue like you treat someone who's lost your trust and needs time to regain it. Condoleezza . . . [did not totally] reject that approach, but didn't seem enthusiastic. I asked her if she had spoken to Sergey Lavrov,[26] and if so, what he said about the issue: 'More or less the same as you,' was her answer—short and meaningful." The subject of Iran, despite already having given rise to Security Council resolutions, had not yet become the main focus of newspaper headlines. Nor had it previously occurred to Washington that Brazil might be able to play the role of intermediary on the issue. After all, Bush—unlike Obama—had never shown the slightest desire to achieve a breakthrough in relations with the regime of the ayatollahs.

The arrival of Barack Obama in the White House and Hillary Clinton at the State Department did not substantially change the pattern of dialogue, at least at first. In the early days of the new administration, Lula was invited to a working meeting at the White House. It was added on to a previously scheduled trip to New York, the main objective of which was to attract investment to Brazil in the midst of the financial crisis unleashed by the bankruptcy of Lehman Brothers. That initial meeting was dominated by financial and trade issues. It was a period in which we still had some hope of reviving the Doha Round, a theme always present in Lula's conversations with Bush. The WTO, however, was not a priority for the new American president, who was focused primarily on domestic issues, such as the reform of the healthcare system, and unwilling to spend political capital on the difficult task of persuading Congress of the benefits of a multilateral trade agreement. During that meeting, economic advisor Lawrence Summers made comments that seemed not to take into account the changes in the global panorama that had taken place in recent years, including the bigger role of the developing countries in the trade negotiations. As far as I can remember, no other foreign policy issue was addressed in greater depth on that occasion. Obama, though affable and smiling, gave me an impression of superficiality. Even his friendliness toward Lula in front of the cameras concealed, in my view, a certain degree of condescension, in contrast to the frank and direct approach of Bush.

The conciliatory presence of President Lula at the Summit of the Americas in April 2009, when Obama met for the first time with a group of South American leaders—including some very critical of the United States, such as Chávez, Morales and Correa—certainly helped ease the mood of the occasion. During the opening session, by chance I found myself sitting next to Hillary Clinton, who was friendly and good-humored, even commenting later to Lula, in a brief bilateral meeting on the sidelines of Obama's meeting with the Union of South American Nations,[27] that she had been "gossiping with your foreign minister." About a month later, in San Pedro Sula, Honduras, at the meeting that discussed Cuba's readmission to the Organization of American States (OAS), I took a moderate line (in contrast to the more inflammatory ALBA countries) even as I argued unequivocally that Cuba's suspension should be revoked. This attitude ultimately helped ensure the resolution adopted was free from any unnecessarily aggressive language about the United States. On the morning of the meeting I had a "bilateral" with Hillary, at her request. And immediately after the lunch offered by our Honduran hosts, she came over to sit by me: "I'll stay here, protected," she said. Aside from diplomatic exaggerations and pleasantries, however, the secretary of state was genuinely counting on Brazil to find a solution that did not leave the US in an isolated position. We therefore worked together toward a consensual resolution, which was eventually adopted (after, it must be said, some bumps in the road). We managed to avoid a confrontation, but without adversely affecting the substantive result of the meeting: the overturning of Cuba's suspension from the OAS.

By using such examples my intention is not to depict Brazil and the United States as having a "special relationship." However, only a significant level of mutual trust can explain, for example, the fact that in 2004 Colin Powell told his advisor Roger Noriega to consult with a Brazilian diplomat about the text of a speech on Venezuela that Noriega was due to give to US senators.[28] Obviously the relationship had its disagreements. Perhaps the most significant came when the Obama/Hillary era had already begun, concerning our divergent views on the removal from office of President Zelaya of Honduras. In practical terms, the US supported (or was at least tolerant toward) the coup that deposed the populist leader, while Brazil gave him "refuge" in our embassy. And yet, throughout that episode, our dialogue with Washington went uninterrupted. Therefore, essentially, when Obama asked for Lula's assistance in reaching out to Iran, which then led to concrete suggestions about how Brazil might participate in the "swap agreement," his attitude was based on a recent history of intense and productive political dialogue, albeit with differences on certain specific issues.

In the period immediately preceding Ahmadinejad's visit to Brasilia, the communications between Obama and Lula, and between Hillary and me, already reflected a reduced level of US optimism in relation to the talks with Iran, and yet also continued to reveal—or so it seemed to me—a great deal of trust in Brazil. On November 22, the eve of the visit, Obama sent Lula a letter in which, among other topics, he devoted four lengthy paragraphs to the Iran issue. Declaring that Lula's meeting with Ahmadinejad was taking place at a crucial moment, Obama reiterated his commitment to diplomacy. Nevertheless, he indicated that sanctions were also a possibility—he referred to it as a "dual-track approach." He said he had no wish to humiliate or isolate Iran, and yet it was clear his mood had changed somewhat since L'Aquila. He concluded by saying he valued Lula's "wise counsel" and hoped to continue working with him "on this and other important global and hemispheric issues."

Immediately before any presidential visit to Brasilia, I always met with Lula to give him a quick briefing. Often these conversations were interrupted by advisors coming in to ask about some aspect of the agenda or detail of protocol. On other occasions, due to a lack of time, the briefing consisted simply of sitting with Lula as he read through the speeches he was going to deliver or the list of so-called "talking points" intended to guide his dialogue with the visitor. In the case of Ahmadinejad, I conveyed to Lula that he would need to spend some time explaining the current state of the negotiations on the nuclear issue; it would not be enough simply to make generic assertions or reiterate positions of principle, although those would also be important. Until that moment, I myself had not needed to give a detailed presentation of the technical (or quasi-technical) aspects of the discussions I had been having with my various interlocutors. Lula began to listen attentively as I embarked on a detailed explanation of the "swap agreement," but then he interrupted me: "Celso, you know the subject. You do the talking." I agreed, although I said it was important Lula himself should introduce the subject, from a political perspective, providing the foundations for what I would go on to say. In fact that was an unnecessary observation, due to an excess of zeal on my part, as there was never any doubt Lula would proceed in precisely that fashion.

As with many previous meetings of presidents in Brasilia, the one between Lula and Ahmadinejad took place in my office in Itamaraty. The presidential palace was being renovated at the time, so the headquarters of the foreign ministry was even more of a natural choice of venue. But there was also a symbolic element in having presidential meetings take place there, as to some degree it reflected Lula's appreciation of the role played by the foreign ministry. At the beginning of the meeting there were various participants. On the Brazilian side, I remember there were the ministers of (or representatives from) Industry and Trade, Agriculture, Mines and Energy, and Science and Technology, along with the president's special advisor, Marco Aurélio Garcia, and our ambassador in Tehran, Antonio Salgado. There might also have been someone from the economic area or the Central Bank, because one of the points of great interest for the Iranians—and for our exporters—was the creation of a payment arrangement that would make it possible to circumvent the trade restrictions imposed unilaterally by the United States and, in some cases, the European Union. Although obviously our interest in dialogue with Iran extended beyond the commercial arena, it is worth mentioning that Brazil's exports to Iran had been growing exponentially. After forty minutes of dialogue on bilateral matters, Lula requested, as he had told me he would, that the discussion be restricted to the two presidents and their foreign ministers; everyone else, apart from the interpreters, would leave the room. The Iranian president agreed, and so we proceeded accordingly.

On the subject of the interpreters, I should mention that on this occasion the translation between Portuguese and Farsi was not being conducted directly. Lula had his own interpreter, who put the president's words into English, at which point Ahmadinejad's interpreter, whose English was excellent, translated into Farsi for the benefit of the Iranian president. This procedure, though indispensable, was also rather time-consuming and increased the risk of misunderstandings. As I had seen happen on a few previous occasions, certain subtleties were, quite literally, lost in translation. Though I do not understand a word of the Persian language, at various moments I found myself repeating in English what Lula (or, occasionally, I myself) had said in Portuguese, because Ahmadinejad appeared to have a passive understanding of the language.

In his "political" introduction, in which he sought to convey an understanding of the difficulties Iran was facing, Lula emphasized the importance of Tehran avoiding international isolation. To preserve Iran's right to a peaceful nuclear program, including the right to enrich uranium, it was necessary to find a formula that would eliminate, or at least alleviate, the doubts of the western countries, thereby avoiding the adoption of new punitive measures (whether just or otherwise). It was also important for Iran to be fully reintegrated into the community of nations. Lula reiterated his willingness to collaborate actively in the search for an agreement that would preserve the rights and dignity of Iran. He indicated that he spoke frequently about the subject with the leaders of several countries involved in the issue. Then he handed over to me, for a more technical explanation of what stage the negotiations were at. I presented the swap agreement as a confidence-building instrument, describing in detail its different elements. I also presented the argument Burns had made to me, according to which, in accepting "payment" for the fuel in the form of LEU produced in Iran, the international community would in effect be recognizing Iran's uranium-enrichment program as an established fact.

Ahmadinejad did not respond directly to that last point. He focused instead on the aspects that had led him to reject the proposal made by the P5+1. He admitted that at first he had actually been inclined to accept the proposal, but then what he described as "western propaganda"—especially on the part of the US, with its declaration that the agreement would delay the Iranian nuclear program by at least one year—provoked a strong negative reaction in Iran, both among its leaders (he was obviously alluding to Ayatollah Khamenei, without referring to him in person) and also among the opposition, as represented by (among others) Mousavi.[29] According to Ahmadinejad, Mousavi himself had said that accepting the proposed agreement would be tantamount to a "capitulation." The Iranian president was quite frank in indicating that apart from the ideological disputes (thought he did not use those exact words) going on in Iran, there was also an intense struggle for power involving several different individuals and groups. In fact I myself had been able to perceive that during my first visit to Iran, and the situation would become clearer still during future meetings with Iranian representatives. I had noticed, for example, that there was tension between the president and the speaker of the Iranian parliament, Ali Larijani, who advocated a more hard-line position on the nuclear issue. Ahmadinejad also made a number of complaints about the behavior of the West. He was particularly critical of France, which he said had never given back nuclear material Iran sent there for enrichment during the time of the Shah. This lack of trust on Iran's part was one of the factors that led it to insist on the concept of "simultaneity" with regard to the swap agreement. Lula spoke again of his intention to cooperate in search of an agreement, though he also underlined the risks involved if Iran were to become isolated. He referred implicitly, with the necessary delicacy, to a point I had made rather less diplomatically in previous conversations with Mottaki and other Iranian officials: if the impasse were to continue or even get worse, it would inevitably jeopardize the prospects for cooperation between Brazil and Iran. Lula conveyed the message that although we disapproved of sanctions, which we considered counterproductive, Brazil had a longstanding commitment to the multilateral system and would not fail to comply with decisions made by the United Nations. As for unilateral measures, we felt no obligation to go along with them. We recognized, however, from a practical point of view, that unilateral measures might also impact negatively on certain important areas of potential cooperation, such as energy and oil, because Brazilian companies with operations in the United States and the European Union were fearful of suffering some kind of retaliation. This was true also for state-owned companies such as Petrobras and Banco do Brasil, as they were guided largely by economic and commercial—not political—considerations.

At some point in the conversation, Ahmadinejad addressed the accusations that Iran had been "hiding" its nuclear reactor at Qom. He stressed it was Iran itself that had revealed the existence of the reactor, and that Tehran's conduct on the matter was in compliance with IAEA regulations.[30] In the midst of his various complaints about his western interlocutors, Ahmadinejad reaffirmed his wish to return to dialogue, despite the internal political problems that might cause him. In contrast to the image projected by the western media (at least in the past), the Iranian political system is far from monolithic. Though there is respect for the figure of the Supreme Leader, the fighting between factions is intense. Conflicts exist not only between the different layers in the power structure, such as the Revolutionary Guards and the clergy, but also inside the religious layer itself. There are ayatollahs who are more liberal, such as the current President Rouhani and one of his predecessors, Khatami; there are pragmatists, such as Rafsanjani; and of course there are the intransigent defenders of the Shia revolution. To an extent, these conflicts reflect movements in Iranian civil society. In that context, Ahmadinejad needed to maintain and indeed widen the popular support he had gained as mayor of Tehran, on the basis of which he had become president. And for that he needed to achieve at least a minimum level of economic stability, which was impossible while international sanctions (whether UN or unilateral) were in place. It was this fact—more than his suave demeanor and permanent smile during the bilateral conversations—that convinced me that he was sincere in expressing his desire for a negotiated solution to the nuclear issue.

Though Ahmadinejad had appeared to pay little attention to Burns' earlier point about the swap agreement constituting tacit "recognition" of Iran's uranium-enrichment program, Mottaki (who, unlike me, had remained silent during the conversation between the two presidents, apart from briefly stressing Iran's good faith and the western interlocutors' lack of credibility) did seem to grasp its symbolic importance. When I made the point to him again later, as we were walking to the function room in Itamaraty where the official lunch would take place (much later than planned), my Iranian counterpart acknowledged that it was indeed significant, although he still came up with some specious arguments about how the deal was even more favorable to the United States and its allies. In the six months or so between then and the Tehran Declaration of May 17, 2010, the issue of achieving balance between concessions would be the subject of many of discussions with the Iranian foreign minister, whether on the phone, during my visits to Tehran, or on the sidelines of the World Economic Forum in Davos.

In a letter dated November 26, President Lula replied to the letter Obama had sent him on November 22. In addition to other topics (COP15, the situation in Honduras, the Doha Round, Haiti, Palestine) he devoted four lengthy paragraphs to Iran, particularly the nuclear program. He described in great detail his conversation with President Ahmadinejad, emphasizing his efforts to convince the Iranian president that he should grasp the opportunity offered by the IAEA proposal so as to improve his country's position vis-à-vis the rest of the world. Lula added that he had even tried to encourage direct dialogue between Tehran and Washington. He conveyed his genuine impression that Ahmadinejad was not closed to dialogue, even though the Iranian president was facing strong internal pressure (especially from parliament, members of the National Security Council, and the opposition). He described how Ahmadinejad was dubious about whether the West would comply with its part of swap agreement—and the need, therefore, to find ways to assuage his suspicions. He also wrote that he had emphasized to Ahmadinejad that "a posture of confrontation or indifference" could lead to new sanctions that would compromise Iran's cooperation with other countries. Stating that there was scope for negotiation, President Lula expressed the conviction that "dialogue should continue, but through back channels, without revealing developments that might be seized upon by the opponents of peace." This was a fairly clear allusion to the "propaganda war" Ahmadinejad had depicted as the reason for Iran retreating from the agreement. Lula concluded by referring to the possibility of "creative solutions" on the basis of the IAEA proposal, such as shortening the interval between Iran's delivery of the LEU and its receipt of the fuel.

On the same day Lula wrote the letter, the text of which was transmitted immediately to the US government, I received a phone call from the secretary of state, who wanted to address three main issues: COP15, the situation in Honduras, and the draft resolution on Iran's nuclear program that was under the consideration of the IAEA. I myself added a fourth topic: Palestine. With regard to the draft resolution, presented by Germany, Hillary said the text had been written in "moderate language," based on findings in the report by the IAEA director-general. She referred to the discovery of the enrichment facility at Qom and mentioned the Iran's "refusal" to accept the proposed uranium-swap deal. She tried to play down the possible negative consequences of the resolution, saying it was not aimed at implementing punitive measures but instead at achieving a "unification of positions [of the members of the IAEA Board of Governors] regarding Iran's obligations." Indicating that she was already aware of Lula's letter to Obama, Hillary concluded her thoughts on the topic by expressing appreciation of the positions Brazil, and Lula himself, were taking.

I responded to Hillary's points one by one. I said our position on the draft resolution would be dictated primarily by our concern not to undermine the dialogue we had initiated with Tehran regarding its nuclear program. I added that Lula "took very seriously" Obama's request, in L'Aquila, for assistance in convincing Ahmadinejad to respond positively to the openings Tehran was being offered. I said our understanding, based on messages received from US government representatives, was that these openings included the proposed "swap agreement." Bearing that in mind, I said it did not strike me as productive to insist on a condemnatory approach that would inevitably limit Ahmadinejad's room for maneuver and push him toward the "easy path" of "radicalization." In response, Hillary said the picture I presented of a power struggle in Iran was useful, and agreed that the proposed swap agreement had a symbolic value in that context. However, she said, it seemed Iran was changing from a theocratic dictatorship into a military one, led by the Revolutionary Guards. She added some arguments in favor of the draft resolution, but her tone was not peremptory.

Three days after Ahmadinejad's visit, Nicolas Sarkozy arrived in Manaus.[31] Given the geographical location of Guiana, a French overseas territory, the French president had been invited to the summit of the Amazon

Cooperation Treaty Organization (ACTO). Sarkozy (like his predecessor Jacques Chirac) saw in the prospect of rubbing shoulders with Lula an opportunity to possibly win over some moderately left-of-center voters. Also, in forging a relationship with the former metalworker and now leader of a major emerging democracy, there was a chance to enhance his own international prestige. Another factor was that the Copenhagen climate conference was not far away and Sarkozy hoped to play a prominent role in it (with a potential positive impact on public opinion back home, obviously). The strategic partnership between Brazil and France had been developing in recent years, driven by a convergence in relation to major global issues (except for the Doha Round, and agricultural subsidies in particular). In the first meeting between Lula and Chirac, in early 2003, there had clearly been a shared perspective on important issues such as Iraq. During 2003 and 2004 the Franco-Brazilian partnership developed a number of different aspects, significant among which was the two presidents' personal involvement in the global campaign against hunger and poverty. It was also from 2003 onward that Paris explicitly supported Brazil's bid for a permanent seat on the United Nations Security Council (until then the French position had been expressed in more general terms, in favor of the presence of the "major countries of the South"). From the point of view of international politics, Chirac was a Gaullist who attached great importance to French sovereignty and the country's active role in world affairs. He was a believer in multipolarity, which naturally gave him a certain affinity with a leader such as Lula who came from a working-class background and was keen for his country to receive greater recognition on the world stage. Sarkozy, despite some serious disagreements with his predecessor on issues of domestic policy, sought to draw on the capital Chirac had accumulated in relations with Brazil. Unlike Chirac, whose image as a *grand seigneur* seemed to evoke the past greatness of France, the new president sought to convey the image of a modernizing leader, which in the popular French imagination corresponds to some extent with the figure of the enterprising and successful American. Perhaps that explains why one of his first moves in the international sphere was for France to rejoin the integrated command structure of NATO, from which General de Gaulle had withdrawn.

On matters of international governance, Sarkozy's statements and attitudes were ambiguous. On the one hand he sounded revolutionary, or at least reformist, when he proposed that the G8 should be expanded through the inclusion of Brazil, India, China, Mexico and South Africa (all already present in the G8+5) along with other countries such as Egypt and Indonesia, with all members theoretically on an equal footing. That issue became the focus of an intense Franco-Brazilian dialogue, including exchanges of letters. On the other hand, his statements on Security Council reform were generally less clear than those of his predecessor. On more than one occasion he stopped short of referring explicitly to Brazil—perhaps so as not to displease Mexico, with which France has important political and economic ties. These omissions were always played down, *a posteriori*, by Sarkozy's efficient diplomatic advisor, Jean-David Levitte.[32] As for Iran and its nuclear program, Sarkozy seemed ambivalent. In his conversations with Lula, and in mine with Levitte, the emphasis was always on the search for a diplomatic solution. But that more open approach contrasted with statements aimed at the domestic audience and with attitudes France adopted in international forums, particularly in the EU, where it frequently advocated a tougher approach, including the expansion of sanctions. It was certainly the case that France's determination to achieve a closer relationship with Brazil on, for example, nuclear and defense issues had a significant commercial component: Paris realized that the "strategic partnership" was a good business opportunity. And there was nothing wrong with that if our respective interests coincided, as they did in the case of the Brazilian submarine program. In general, Paris sought to minimize its differences with Brasilia and to attain some degree of understanding, which in retrospect, was more difficult to achieve than it appeared. In late August 2009 I was invited to Paris by Bernard Kouchner to make a speech to a gathering of French ambassadors at Quai d'Orsay. The day before my speech, Levitte paid me a visit at the Brazilian embassy. He gave me a copy of the speech the French president had just made to the ambassadors: "*Ton ami, Nicolas Sarkozy, m'a demandé de la rendre*." The diplomatic advisor was keen to highlight the parts of the text that referred to Brazil and to President Lula, and in which the French president addressed issues of global governance from a perspective similar to ours. But his main message was about Brazil's possible purchase of French Rafale fighter aircraft, with regard to which he said he hoped an announcement would be made before Sarkozy's forthcoming visit to Brazil.

In Manaus, where the French president's main purpose was to seek an alignment of positions with Brazil ahead of COP15, his conversations with Lula were not only climate-related. They also spoke about the Middle East, especially Iran. France, like the US, hoped Brazil would support the draft resolution presented by Germany in the IAEA Board of Governors. In that context, one of Sarkozy's advisors offered arguments similar to those used by Hillary Clinton in her phone call to me, emphasizing the revelations about the Qom nuclear reactor. I was quick to say, to another of the officials accompanying the French president, that Brazil was not in favor of the kind of condemnatory attitudes that were unlikely to be helpful in reaching an understanding with Iran. This difference in perceptions and attitudes did not prevent Lula—who at the time, like myself, was very hopeful of coordinating our actions with France on this and other issues—from bringing up the subject directly with Sarkozy. Lula briefly described to him the meeting with Ahmadinejad in Brasilia a few days previously. As in his letter to Obama,

Lula emphasized his perception that the Iranian president was genuinely keen to resume a dialogue on the nuclear issue, even though in so doing he would probably face strong opposition, including in the corridors of power in Tehran. Sarkozy said nothing to contradict Lula, but added: "I can only start a dialogue with Iran when the French citizen Clotilde Reiss is freed." He added that as soon as that was achieved, he would be happy to talk to the Iranian leader. With Lula's permission, I asked the French president a direct question: "Should I take it that such a phone call wouldn't just be to express thanks for [Clotilde Reiss's] release, but also to initiate a dialogue?" "*Bien sûr*," replied Sarkozy, without hesitation.

After a brief stop in Quito for a meeting of South American defense and foreign ministers, at which the US military bases in Colombia were the main theme, I left on a Brazilian Air Force plane to Geneva, with stops in Boa Vista and Cape Verde. I was going there for a WTO ministerial meeting at which, as I expected, nothing very important happened. During those few days, however, there were two significant developments with regard to the Iranian nuclear issue: the IAEA adopted the draft resolution[33] in which it once again condemned Iran, but without the support of Brazil or (largely due to our influence, if I remember rightly) South Africa; and then, as a consequence, the Iranian parliament "instructed" the government to begin enriching uranium to 20%, without delay. When I learned of these two developments, which certainly made the possibility of understanding between the two sides more remote, I took the view that given our involvement, which had obviously become more significant with the recent visits, we needed to act in some way. I called President Lula and got his permission to travel again to Iran, where I would try to talk with Ahmadinejad. I called our ambassador in Tehran, who immediately lent his assistance. Very quickly the Iranian president confirmed he would receive my visit. He could not do so in Tehran, however, as he was traveling around the country; instead we would meet in the historical city of Isfahan, famous for its mosques and palaces. This change of destination only increased my desire to depart from Geneva as soon as possible. The Swiss city has a significant population of journalists, including correspondents from Brazil's major newspapers, who are always eager to get hold of a "leak," preferably involving an element of intrigue. It was a minor miracle that I managed, for a few hours at least, to keep my next destination a secret. And the only reason I could get to Iran in time was because, as previously mentioned, I had a Brazilian military aircraft at my disposal.

I arrived in Isfahan at night and was accommodated in a luxurious hotel, a converted *caravanserai* with a beautiful central courtyard and sumptuously decorated rooms—a magnificent example of traditional Muslim architecture that unfortunately I did not have much time to appreciate. The next morning, my time was divided between purely *pro forma* talks with Foreign Minister

Mottaki and visits to the fabulous mosques and palaces of a city that was once the capital of the Safavid dynasty. It was interesting to see that in some of the palaces there were murals that reflect nothing of the puritanism of modern Iran's ayatollahs. Not only do they show human figures, banned by the more radical versions of Islam, but also quite liberal interpretations of romantic encounters between princes and princesses of Persian mythology. It is a rare tribute to the tolerance of the Shia clergy that, unlike the giant statues of the Buddha in Afghanistan when the Taliban took over, these expressions of the artistic creativity of the sixteenth- and seventeenth-century Persian court have not been destroyed or damaged, but instead carefully preserved and included in the cultural itinerary offered to foreign visitors.

My meeting with Ahmadinejad took place at around 7 p.m. in a beautiful hall in one of the old palaces in the center of Isfahan, and lasted about an hour. Mottaki was also present, on the Iranian side, while I was accompanied only by our ambassador to Tehran. It was a long conversation, in which the same interpreter who had been in Brasilia intervened only occasionally, usually when Ahmadinejad had just spoken. The Iranian president signaled right at the start, with a hand gesture, that he did not require translation of what I said in English. I concentrated on three issues, all of them related to the recent developments and to the conversation a few days before between Lula and Sarkozy. Referring to Ahmadinejad's distrust with regard to the West's fulfillment of its part of the deal (or, more specifically, toward France, supposing it were to produce the fuel rods, which was indeed one of the scenarios suggested), I described the French president's willingness to have Lula as a guarantor of the operation, a role the latter would indeed be very keen to play. Ahmadinejad once again expressed his full confidence in the Brazilian president, but said nothing more on that specific point. The second issue I addressed, this one related directly to the decisions taken by the IAEA and also by the Iranian parliament, was the enrichment of uranium to 20%. I told Ahmadinejad that although I could understand his domestic political difficulties, it would be very positive if the beginning of the enrichment process could be delayed for a while, thereby creating space for the negotiations. The Iranian president's reaction to this was curious: he alluded even more frankly than he had done in Brasilia to the political opposition he was facing domestically, while insisting that he himself could not announce publicly that the process was being delayed. Referring to the ministers and advisors from the P5+1, however, he authorized me to tell my "interlocutors," as he put it, that he had given me a "guarantee" that the process would indeed be delayed. I therefore requested—in line with a suggestion from one of my aides—that the beginning of the production of 20%-enriched uranium be postponed by two months. The speed with which Ahmadinejad accepted the idea made me think that perhaps I should have been more demanding. I had the feeling that if I had said three months, or four, his response would have been the same.

But that concession would prove to be of little interest to my P5+1 interlocutors, committed as they already were by that point to the punitive dual-track approach. For example, the then British foreign secretary, David Miliband (whose father, Ralph Miliband, a leftist guru in British academia in the 1960s and 70s, had been my supervisor when I was a student at the London School of Economics) would say simply that Ahmadinejad's offer was a "delaying tactic," as if Iran actually had something to gain from the postponement.

The third issue I raised with Ahmadinejad in Isfahan was that of the young French woman detained in Iran on suspicion of spying. Ahmadinejad initially said the matter was in the hands of the Iranian justice system, and he was unable to interfere. It soon became clear, however, that this difficulty might not be absolute, as he revealed there had in fact been an earlier attempt to resolve the issue, which had been unsuccessful because another country involved had failed to keep the maneuver secret. Ahmadinejad implied there would be scope for negotiation if France was prepared to release an Iranian citizen accused of murdering a former Iranian prime minister, Shapour Bakhtiar, in 1991. It would be a complex operation, full of subtleties; a shadow play in which the two countries would have to agree to a prisoner exchange without appearing to do so. I would later have long telephone conversations about it, both with Mottaki and Levitte. In the end, due to an apparently autonomous decision on the part of the French justice system, circumstances came about that facilitated a solution.

Looking back, I can see that I placed great hopes on the support France might give to our peacemaking efforts, as did President Lula. In addition to the conversations on Iran that had recently taken place, I had good memories from my time on the Security Council of cooperation with my French colleague Alain Déjammet, a fine diplomat of great intelligence with whom I had shared some difficult moments, especially concerning the Iraq issue in the late 1990s, when the discussions had centered on the possibility of the use of armed force against the country if it did not fulfill its obligations. In the context of those discussions I had been seeking a compromise between conflicting positions. Before formally presenting our own position I consulted Déjammet, because I did not want to leave him isolated in the not-always-comfortable company of Russia and China. Déjammet's answer on that occasion was a surprising one: "Whatever's acceptable for Brazil is acceptable for France." The same sense of understanding on international issues had been present in my relationship with French foreign minister Dominique de Villepin during the Iraq invasion of 2003. With regard to Iran, however, my optimism about the French approach would soon prove unfounded, although for some months—and even after the adoption of sanctions by the Security Council, with France's total endorsement—my interlocutor at the Élysée Palace continued to insist that "*Sarkozy est un homme de parole.*"[34]

OPERATION YASEMIN

Throughout the month of December 2009, I continued to have a lot of telephone conversations about the Iranian issue. I spoke to Hillary Clinton, David Miliband and Jean-David Levitte, among others. My contact with other members of the P5+1 included a call to the German foreign minister, Guido Westerwelle, although that did not lead anywhere in particular. I was in touch less regularly with the foreign ministers of the other two members of the group, Russia and China—which in hindsight seems slightly odd, particularly with regard to my Russian counterpart, Sergey Lavrov, with whom I had enjoyed a very good relationship ever since our days as colleagues on the Security Council, working closely together on issues including Iraq and the former Yugoslavia. More recently, on the margins of the UN General Assembly, I had been quick to welcome a proposal from Lavrov that led to the BRICs becoming established as a political forum. As for my Chinese counterpart, a typical member of the Beijing bureaucracy, my relationship with him was friendly but formal.

At the start of January 2010, our involvement with the Iranian issue stepped up a gear. I had arranged a visit to Turkey, where I was to head the bilateral mixed commission alongside the Turkish trade minister, Zafer Caglayan. Once again it proved useful to be wearing two hats—one political-diplomatic, the other that of a trade negotiator. I took the opportunity of my stay in Ankara to accept an invitation from the Turkish foreign minister, Ahmet Davutoglu, to give a lecture to Turkish ambassadors participating in an annual meeting in the city, a privilege that was unprecedented at that time but would later also be enjoyed by my successor Antonio Patriota. It reflected the high degree of affinity, and indeed trust, between Turkey and Brazil in that period. I had working meetings with Davutoglu and President Abdullah Gül in which the Iranian issue featured prominently. As mentioned previously, I had already spoken with Davutoglu on the phone about Iran, before Ahmadinejad's visit to Brazil. But it was during my Ankara meeting with him that the outlines of a joint Brazilian-Turkish action on the Iranian nuclear issue began to be drawn. Comparing our notes on the subject, my Turkish counterpart and I could see there was significant convergence between our respective efforts in pursuit of a diplomatic solution based on the swap agreement originally proposed to Iran by the P5+1. I also mentioned to Davutoglu our attempts to obtain from Iran a moratorium on the production of 20%-enriched uranium. It was around this time that western newspapers were covering the declaration by Mottaki that if the West did not return to the negotiating table, Iran would start producing 20%-enriched uranium "within a month." The declaration—preemptory in tone, as so often the case with the Iranian government—was interpreted by the West as an ultimatum. Perhaps that was precisely the impression Mottaki intended to convey, given Iran's internal divisions on the nuclear issue. Curiously, an Iranian newspaper, considered to be the official mouthpiece of the government, provided the clarification that Mottaki's declaration had in fact been a way of referring positively to a "proposal from a friendly nation"—an obvious reference to my conversation with Ahmadinejad in Isfahan. Davutoglu and I agreed that Turkey and Brazil would begin to coordinate actions on the Iranian nuclear issue. He named this joint action "Operation Yasemin" in an affectionate reference to my grand-daughter Yasemin, whose father is a Turkish diplomat. Our conversations had shown just how closely our objectives coincided. We agreed to concentrate our efforts on closing the gap between what Iran was willing to do and the West was demanding, given that both sides agreed in principle with the concept of a swap agreement.

Closing that gap, however, was a far from simple task. The Iranians, for their part, insisted that the LEU to be delivered to international custody should stay in their territory, even if that meant supervision by the IAEA. Citing its alleged reasons not to trust the West, Iran continued to argue that its giving up of the LEU and its receipt of the fuel should take place simultaneously. Above all—and this was something that became even clearer when I spoke to Mottaki on the margins of the Davos forum—Iran was unwilling to deliver the quantity of enriched uranium demanded by the P5+1 (1,200 kilograms). I was given an insight into an ancient, trade-orientated culture when Mottaki told me that in any commercial transaction it was up to the buyer, not the seller, to decide the quantity to be acquired, in accordance with their needs. The demands on the part of the western countries, for their part, were shifting in the opposite direction. The United States was beginning to show signs that with regard to the quantity of LEU to be handed over by Iran, the terms initially proposed for the agreement might no longer be acceptable, given the additional stocks Iran had managed to build up since October—estimated to be between 600 and 800 kilograms. That was what I inferred from a telephone conversation with General Jim Jones shortly before the trilateral meeting between President Lula, Turkish prime minister Recep Erdogan, and President Obama during the nuclear security conference in Washington in April 2010. Faced with this divergence of positions, evident also in relation to other issues such as the production of 20%-enriched uranium, I started to think that our efforts might not lead anywhere. Davutoglu, however, remained hopeful. My perception, perhaps not entirely correct, was that our Turkish friends—as members of NATO, and having a broader military-strategic dialogue with the US—were more confident than we were about the chances of getting some degree of flexibility from the Americans on some aspect of the three basic dimensions of the swap agreement (quantity, time, and place). This, perhaps, was the expectation that led Davutoglu to present to their interlocutors in Washington (including General Jones) a non-paper, or informal document, which they told us about and for which we expressed support, albeit more out of solidarity than conviction.

Between the meeting in Ankara and the conference in Washington in April, I had many more face-to-face meetings or telephone conversations with my main contacts. I already mentioned the conversation with Mottaki in Davos. It took place in a small, dimly lit room in a hotel in that ski resort which for a few days in January becomes the center of the world's attention. That is when the small Swiss town, previously home to the tuberculosis sanatoriums described so masterfully by Thomas Mann in *The Magic Mountain*, becomes the setting for a kind of festival of economic and political discussion. That year, with the Doha Round seemingly moribund, my attention was mostly on the situation in Haiti in the wake of the terrible earthquake there. Among other events, I took part in a round-table on the issue with Bill Clinton, and a dinner sponsored by the World Food Programme. But I still made time to talk with my Iranian counterpart. From the very start of the meeting I could tell he was fully engaged, and he said he was keen to meet Ambassador Levitte, but he did not bring to the table any significant change from his previous positions.

In telephone conversations with foreign ministers from the P5+1 countries, my "interlocutors" (as Ahmadinejad had put it) were still skeptical about Iran's willingness to reach an agreement or keep its promises. David Miliband, who had become a personal friend through my longstanding connection with his family, and who shortly after he was made British foreign secretary traveled to see me when I was passing through Paris, was particularly distrustful toward Iran's intentions. In the conversation we had at the time of the Washington conference, he again raised doubts he had previously expressed in an article published in the *International Herald Tribune.*[35] In fact he said, perhaps not entirely seriously, that what he had written in article was a message intended directly for me. Equally distrustful was Guido Westerwelle, the German foreign minister, whom I had become very friendly with as a result of our partnership within the G4[36] at the UN. In the period between my meeting with Davutoglu in Ankara and the trilateral meeting in Washington, however, the most important event with regard to Brazil's involvement in the issue was a visit to Brasilia by Hillary Clinton in early March.

THE MAIN PLAYERS

Looking at my notes from the period before the secretary of state visited Brazil, I see a reference to another conversation in my office with Bill Burns, the under secretary for political affairs, who came to Brasilia to make preparations for the visit. His attitude was quite different from the one he had displayed during his previous trip to Brasilia, when he had been looking for support in trying to convince the Iranians that they should accept the swap agreement. This time he was skeptical about the chances of any understanding with Tehran. He implied that the United States was committed to approving new sanctions in the UN Security Council, in addition to those it was already imposing unilaterally. He thought it would only make sense to return to the negotiating afterwards, with Iran in a weaker position. Although I did not think there was much chance of making Burns change his mind, I told him about a proposal the Iranian foreign minister had made to me over the phone a few days before, clearly expecting that the message would be passed on to the Americans. The proposal, a rather complex one, was based on the swap agreement but diverged from it in some important respects (especially those relating to quantity and simultaneity). Although at first I did not understand why, there was also a new element: the idea that the fuel for Iran's research reactor could actually be provided by the United States. Excluding the possibility of there being any economic motive, it seemed the idea might derive from Tehran's desire to obtain a clear commitment from the Americans. This would be consistent with the lack of trust the officials in Tehran had shown, once again, toward other potential suppliers such as France and even Russia. Burns listened politely but gave no indication that Washington might actually consider the Iranians' new suggestion.

My notes also mention a telephone conversation with Mottaki in which he was skeptical about the idea of a face-to-face meeting with an American official (an idea aired by General Jones in a previous phone conversation). "A direct meeting with American officials is a very complex subject and will require many consultations," he told me, giving the impression not only that he lacked the authority to decide on such a matter but that it might also be out of President Ahmadinejad's hands. Basically he was implying that only the Supreme Leader could authorize such a step. This resistance to the possibility of direct dialogue with Washington seemed to me to contradict the suggestion that the fuel for the research reactor should be supplied by the Americans—just one of many contradictions I would encounter as the process went on. I concluded my notes as follows: "And so, on the eve of Hillary Clinton's visit and two and a half months before President Lula's visit to Tehran, my 'professional optimism' is beginning to wear thin in the face of the multiple difficulties I've encountered."

The meeting with Hillary Clinton at Itamaraty, on March 3, lasted about three hours, not including lunch or the press conference. We spoke about various issues, including Honduras, relations with Cuba, and of course Iran. It was an intense dialogue, conducted respectfully but marked by divergences. The differences between our respective approaches were quite obvious in what we said to the media. A few days later, when I was in the presidential plane on the way to Israel, a foreign ministry colleague said a friend of his remarked that I had defended Brazil's position with "firmness and elegance." As for the long conversation in my office with the secretary of state, the friendly tone that generally characterized our dialogue was maintained throughout. I remember that, unlike with most of my visitors, we sat together on the same sofa, which lent a certain air of intimacy to the occasion. But it did not make our differences any less obvious. Although she reiterated that "the doors to an agreement remain open," Hillary made clear that the Americans had already made their minds up. They had spoken before of a "dual-track approach"—that of dialogue and that of sanctions—but now it was clear the latter would take priority over the former. Only later would I come to realize that this was basically because Washington had managed to persuade (or was on the verge of persuading) Russia and China not to veto any draft resolution that took the sanctions route. At various moments the secretary of state emphasized the importance the US attributed to Brazil's position, and tried to convince me of the need for Brazil to support the course of action Washington intended to take in the Security Council. Faced with her insistence on this point, I felt obligated to point out that Brazil was a non-permanent member of the Security Council and therefore did not have the power of veto (nor could I resist referring, somewhat ironically, to our previous discussions about the expansion of the Security Council). This aspect, among others, made it seem strange that there was such keenness to gain Brazil's endorsement. Wondering what the underlying reason might be, I remembered certain situations I had experienced as Brazil's representative on the Security Council. On one occasion, for example, the issue being discussed was Angola, where the civil war between the MPLA and UNITA,[37] under Jonas Savimbi, was still going on. The mere threat of Brazil's abstention was enough to get the resolution modified so as to accommodate our concern that the rebels, who had systematically disrespected the UN's decisions and thereby prolonged that cruel conflict, were being treated too leniently. In the case of Iran, if countries such as Brazil and Turkey were to adopt a favorable stance toward sanctions, it would go some way toward legitimizing the measure, even though they lacked the power to block the adoption of an eventual resolution. Also, the position of such countries could potentially persuade a permanent member to withhold their support—as had happened on certain previous occasions, albeit regarding issues that were not so crucial.[38] In the following days and weeks, statements by both sides revealed the widening gap between them. Ahmadinejad, meanwhile, indulged in some more unhelpful rhetoric. Resuming the bombastic tone he had previously used when speaking about Israel and the Holocaust, the Iranian president stated, at one point, that the September 11 attacks were a "big lie."

It was in this less than auspicious atmosphere that we arrived in Washington for the Nuclear Security Summit convened by Obama.[39] Turkey and Brazil had not given up on Operation Yasemin, despite the difficulties. As previously mentioned, my Turkish counterpart was proactive in the period up to and including April. In our phone conversations Davutoglu gave me details of the non-paper he intended to deliver to the Americans, containing elements of a potential agreement that he, having already consulted Iranian officials, thought would prove acceptable to Tehran. Among the flexibilities suggested in relation to the initial proposal, there was the idea of "partial simultaneity," according to which Iran would initially deliver only part of the LEU; a substantial part (possibly half) would be sent abroad only when Iran received the fuel for the Tehran Research Reactor. I am not absolutely sure, not having kept a copy of the non-paper, but I think the proposal also included other flexibilities and nuances, for example regarding the quantity of LEU to be handed over by Iran. Davutoglu expected that the presence of Lula and Erdogan in Washington would offer an opportunity for a trilateral meeting with President Obama, when these ideas could be discussed substantively.

The trilateral meeting did in fact take place on the margins of the summit, but the circumstances were somewhat unfavorable. Obama (who apparently already knew about the Turkish proposal, and treated it as if it were a Turkish-Brazilian idea) was short of time, and concerned about the outcome of the multilateral meeting. He showed little willingness toward any kind of opening. The tone of his observations switched between impatience and irritation. He said he had other priorities to deal with and that the initiatives aimed at attracting Iran toward a purely diplomatic solution were "naive." President Lula was so troubled by Obama's tone that immediately after the meeting, which lasted no more than twenty minutes, he said he was seriously considering abandoning the summit. In the end, I managed—probably with the help of Marco Aurélio and our ambassador in Washington, Mauro Vieira –to convince him to stay until the end of the event, which was a multilateral one after all.I should also mention that during his meeting with Lula and Erdogan, one of the things Obama said in arguing for the urgency of sanctions, although I do not recall his exact words, was that any delay in adopting them could lead to a military strike by Israel against Iran. I was taken aback by this for two reasons. First, because the president of the world's predominant power was brandishing the prospect of a military attack by another country—his ally, moreover—even though his objective was actually to prevent it from happening. And second, because what he was saying was tantamount to an admission that in the very special relationship between Washington and Tel Aviv, it was the latter, not the former, who called the shots. I remember mentioning this to Lula, who was just as perplexed as I was.

Although unexpected, Obama's assessment was not unfounded. The possibility of Iran becoming a nuclear power or even a "threshold state" was seen by Israel as an "existential threat." During Lula's state visit to Israel, one month earlier, the subject of Iran had come up repeatedly. President

Shimon Peres, Prime Minister Benjamin Netanyahu, and the opposition leader, Tzipi Livni, were all very concerned about our initiatives regarding the Iranian nuclear program. But none of them, I should make clear, showed any distrust toward Brazil. They even went so far as to encourage us in our communications with the Palestinian Authority at a time when, as so often, the relationship between Ramallah and Tel Aviv was in crisis. Even more significant was the fact that, during Lula's visit, Netanyahu asked us to assist in the efforts to resume talks with Syria on the Golan Heights.[40] With regard to Iran, all three of them seemed to agree that pursuing a simple dialogue with Tehran, aimed at achieving a peaceful solution to the nuclear standoff, served to legitimize a regime whose principal objectives included the destruction of the State of Israel.

So real was this concern that the Israeli prime minister suggested I should talk to "specialists" who possessed intelligence information on the allegedly military nature of the Iranian nuclear program. The meeting with these experts took place the next day, in my hotel room. As usual in this type of situation, the "evidence" was far from convincing, in this case based on images which revealed very little. To my untrained eye, the pictures might indeed have been taken during an undercover operation in Iran—or then again they might have been created on a computer anywhere in the world. While listening to the so-called specialists I could not resist mentioning the "evidence" of weapons of mass destruction that was presented to justify the invasion of Iraq and, sad though it is to recall, presented to the Security Council by Colin Powell in February 2003. The conversation became more interesting when it turned to the number of atomic weapons necessary to create a nuclear arsenal. Certainly a single bomb would not be enough—but even to make that, according to the experts, it would be necessary to have 2,000 kilograms of LEU. That amount, coincidentally, was approximately what Iran had at the time. And the figure, quoted as it was by an official who had no apparent reason not to be straightforward, reinforced my belief that the swap agreement would still be worthwhile, given that it would deprive Tehran of about half the LEU it possessed.

The efforts the Israelis made to convince us of the dangers of the Iranian nuclear program demonstrated just how closely they were following our initiatives. It was debatable whether their obsession with the prospect of the Iranians developing a nuclear capacity (ignoring completely their own vast arsenal of atomic weapons) could actually lead them to launch an attack on Iran without Washington's blessing. Quite apart from the supposed evidence that Iran was pursuing a nuclear program for military purposes, the mere possibility of Iran developing the capacity to produce a bomb was clearly intolerable for the Israelis. In that sense, when the American president surprisingly stated during the trilateral meeting with Brazil and Turkey that it was necessary to avert an Israeli attack on Iran at all costs (even, indeed, at the cost of scuppering the possibility of negotiations with Iran), it was a clear sign of the pressure he was under.

Looking back, it is tempting to ask what it was that made the American government change its attitude (in a positive sense) between 2010 and 2013, apart from the fact that Obama was no longer seeking re-election. There were also the elections in Iran, of course, which brought to power a less hostile regime. One might also speculate that Bill Burns' reasoning during his second visit to Brazil was (partially) correct in the sense that Iran became more willing to make concessions when its economy had been further weakened by new sanctions. And yet that is not what various aspects of the "interim agreement" of 2013 seem to imply. A full analysis of those aspects would inevitably extend far beyond the scope of this book, but one element at least deserves to be mentioned. If, at that time, Tehran's possession of 2,000 kilograms of LEU (or slightly more) was a cause for concern, what about the 7,000 kilograms it possesses today?[41] Thinking back, I again recall the moment at the G8 in L'Aquila in July 2009 when Obama told Lula he was frustrated about there not having been a positive response to his attempts at greater openness toward Iran. It was Obama's frustration, indeed, that led him to request Lula's help in the pursuit of rapprochement with Tehran. By April 2010, that already seemed a distant memory.

THE LETTER

On April 20, no more than a week after the meeting in Washington, Obama wrote a letter to President Lula (an identical letter was sent to Erdogan, as I discovered when I visited Istanbul a few days later) that basically reiterated the value of the swap agreement as a confidence-building measure. What could have made the US president change his mind so quickly? More than five years on, I still do not know. It might be argued that when the Nuclear Security Summit took place, Turkey and Brazil were still seeking to introduce "flexibilities" into the agreement that were unacceptable to the Americans. But if that were the case, why not say so, and insist on the terms of the original proposal? After all, neither Turkey nor Brazil was making proposals in a spirit of "take it or leave it," which would have been wholly inappropriate in the circumstances. It is possible that President Obama felt on reflection after the trilateral meeting in Washington that he had been too cool toward the leaders of two countries that were both close to the United States (and one of them a military ally). It is also possible that given Tehran's insistence on seeking, through Brazil and Turkey, changes to the basic elements of the agreement, Obama and his aides concluded after the meeting that the original proposal would probably be rejected by Iran. If that were actually the case, then for the US to seek to resume a relationship of trust with Turkey and Brazil—two friendly countries that were also "emerging powers" and members of the recently formed G20, which at the time was seeking to coordinate responses to the unfolding global financial crisis—would demonstrate a consistent position on its part, and also one that did not entail major political risks. Though I find that a plausible explanation, it is worth pointing out that in this case the Americans' reasoning seems to have been based on an assumption—later proved incorrect—that Iran would not reconsider its rejection of the original terms of the agreement. The assumption would have been, in other words, that Brazil and Turkey were incapable of persuading Iran to change its position. That view would, in turn, have rested partly on the perception that because Brazil and Turkey had no power of veto in the Security Council, their "soft power" had its limits.

Before replying to Obama's letter, Lula waited for me to arrive back from a visit to Iran that had included stops in Moscow and Istanbul. On May 10, Lula wrote to the US president to inform him about my meetings during the trip and the efforts we were making to bring Tehran as close as possible to the original terms of the proposed swap agreement. Lula mentioned the message he had instructed me to convey to Ahmadinejad regarding the "narrowing space for negotiation, [the] progressive isolation of the country, and [the] need for a concrete gesture from the Iranians that will help build confidence." Lula also informed Obama in his reply that during my visit to Tehran there had been "receptivity toward Brazil's suggestions, interest in discussing details, and greater pragmatism."

I believe it was President Lula's reply, with its indications of possible Iranian flexibility, coupled with his imminent visit to Tehran, that prompted the secretary of state to ask to speak to me by phone on May 11. I should mention the rather unusual way her request reached me. I had started the day with a phone call to the Chinese foreign minister, Yang Jiechi; if I remember correctly it was the first time I had ever spoken with him specifically about the Iranian issue. I will return to China's position, and that of other countries, below. I was still getting ready to leave home in the morning when I received a call from my chief of staff, Ambassador Maria Laura da Rocha, who told me the secretary of state wanted to speak to me "right now, in an hour's time, or whenever you can." Anyone acquainted with the high-handed attitude of senior US officials will appreciate that such a request reflected an unusually keen interest on Hillary Clinton's part, which could only be explained by Washington's anxieties about the possible success of the mission we were undertaking. I asked for the call to be arranged for later in the morning, when I would be in my office and could have one of my aides close by. (The only person with me when I was speaking to the Chinese minister was a secretary, the highly efficient Camila Scheibel.) I see from my diary that the conversation took place at 11:45 a.m., almost as soon as I had arrived at Itamaraty. I remember I did not actually get as far as my office; instead, for some reason,

I used the phone in Ambassador Maria Laura's room. My aide Leonardo Gorgulho was probably also there. As we tended not to keeping recordings of our phone conversations (and still do not), it was an established practice in such situations to have colleagues in attendance so they could help reconstruct the conversation afterwards.

I think it is important to provide a summary of certain parts of my conversation with Hillary Clinton that day. As she had done on various previous occasions, the secretary of state emphasized her distrust of Iran's leaders. She said, more than once, that the Iranians were taking advantage of our good faith and making promises they had no intention of keeping.[42] Referring to the suggestions made by Iran to Brazil and Turkey, Hillary told me Tehran was saying things to us or to other countries (she mentioned China) but all the while avoiding formal commitments. "They know what address they should write to," she said, alluding to the IAEA. With regard to Iran's positions, I described the progress I had perceived from conversations during my recent visit to the country. I explained that one of the messages from President Lula I had conveyed to Ahmadinejad was that our solidarity had limits and that Iran needed to give some concrete indication that its nuclear program was genuinely pacific. Iran's acceptance of the swap agreement would be an important and necessary step in that direction. If that step were not taken, Tehran would inevitably become increasingly isolated. I said that those messages, expressed delicately but unequivocally, seemed to have been understood. In various respects I felt Iran was coming closer to accepting the terms President Obama said were essential in his letter to Lula. I recognized there were still gaps to fill, but did not think the difficulties were insurmountable.

I cannot be sure, not least because I was not able to see Hillary's face as we spoke, but I sensed she was listening to me with a certain degree of impatience. Rather than trying to find out more about my recent contact with the Iranians, she interrupted that part of the conversation and turned to two other issues: the increase in Iran's stock of LEU since the proposal had been made (a point General Jones had already raised with me), and its commencement of enrichment to 20%. These were fundamental concerns, regarding very real problems. But I was convinced they could be dealt with at a later stage. The key thing at that point was to get Iran to agree to the terms of the swap agreement—or something very close to them—and thereby build the confidence necessary for the resumption of a fruitful dialogue. This had been the central message in Obama's letter, which at no point referred to the two issues the secretary of state was now raising with me. It was surprising, therefore, to find myself being told about additional requirements that went beyond the conditions stipulated by the president of the United States as being necessary for a breakthrough. I was frank in expressing my astonishment. Indeed, I must have been quite vehement, because there was then quite a long silence on the line, broken only when Hillary changed the subject and started talking about three young Americans who had been detained in Iran: she wanted our help in securing their release. I could only assume either that she was not aware of the precise content of Obama's letter or that she had not paid it sufficient attention. Both hypotheses might seem absurd in a system such as Brazil's—and even more so that of the US—where, even on much less serious issues, decisions are taken only after an intense process of consultation between all the relevant agencies or departments. And in this case, obviously, the other "agency" involved, apart from the State Department, was the president himself!

Initially I leaned toward the hypothesis that Hillary simply did not know about the letter—but, I must say, there is another possible explanation. It was always clear to me that Hillary had her own political agenda. It was to become clearer as time went by that she had her own ideas on the Iranian nuclear issue, so perhaps in this particular situation she was subtly but delibcerately diminishing the importance of what Obama had written. It was certainly the case that both Hillary and Obama expected Lula would fail in his efforts to influence Iran. But my impression in retrospect is that Hillary—unlike Obama—actually feared the possibility that Brazil and Turkey might succeed. If that happened, the US might have to reconsider its strategy of seeking support for sanctions from the other members of the P5. This interpretation is supported by the fact that my previous discussions in Tehran, as described in Lula's reply to Obama's letter, had indeed suggested the Iranians might be adopting a more flexible position. Might Hillary have wanted to introduce extra conditionalities, in addition to those stipulated by Obama, so as to hedge against that possibility? It is a plausible hypothesis. But in any case it is worth pointing out that, with a touch of typical imperial arrogance, the secretary of state wrongly assumed I would not dare point out the contradiction between what she had just told me and the content of the recent letter written by the US president.

There is another consideration I should mention, which I think complements the one above. The United States, like France, was seeking to build a positive relationship with Brazil, driven partly by commercial interests. At that time the US already had a considerable trade surplus with us—indeed, it was one of their biggest. Also, the US was keen for the American company Boeing to be chosen to supply the new combat aircraft that the Brazilian Air Force intended to acquire (a deal worth billions of dollars). This issue had been raised by Condoleezza Rice at a previous stage of the selection process and was now coming up again in communications and negotiations between US and Brazilian officials. At one point, in fact, the secretary of state herself wrote to me on the matter. It was not in Washington's interests to create a situation in which, from the point of view not only of the Brazilian government but also much of Brazilian public opinion, the US appeared to be abandoning us after having initially encouraged our efforts, but eventually that was a situation Washington could not avoid. The ideal outcome for the US would have been to carry on pursuing the strategy of sanctions without any adverse effect on its bilateral relations with Brazil. To achieve that, Washington needed to convince us to abandon our efforts toward Iran. In the end, when it proved impossible to reconcile the two objectives, Washington chose to maintain its hard line on Iran to the detriment of its relationship with Brasilia.

HESITANT PARTNERS

It was against this unclear and uncertain backdrop that we set off for Tehran on May 12, 2010, with stops on the way in Moscow and (for Lula) Doha. Before describing the meetings and negotiations that preceded the adoption of the Tehran Declaration, I should explain the positions of two important participants in the process: China and Russia. Immediately after the Nuclear Security Summit in Washington, Brazil was due to host the IBSA and BRICs summits, scheduled to take place in the space of two days. However, a serious earthquake in China, with many victims, obligated President Hu Jintao to cut short his stay in Brasilia. Therefore we decided to squeeze the two summits, and the various bilateral meetings, into one day, April 15: a logistical and diplomatic *tour de force*. The Iranian nuclear issue arose in every conversation that took place. Our four interlocutors on that memorable occasion (which became the main focus of a documentary made by the Franco-German TV channel Arte, entitled *Le monde selon Brasilia*) were following Brazil's and Turkey's efforts to achieve a peaceful and negotiated solution. To differing degrees they all expressed support for our initiatives.[43]

I will start with China. President Hu Jintao's stance was a curious one. While saying he agreed with Lula on the need for a diplomatic solution, and even stating that sanctions were "essentially counterproductive," Hu seemed to regard the adoption of coercive measures by the UNSC as inevitable, which he attributed partly to Tehran's refusal to fully accept the agreement proposed by the P5+1 and endorsed by the IAEA. But in my view there was something ambiguous or even contradictory about the Chinese position. How could a permanent member of the Security Council, with the power of veto over its decisions, maintain that the sanctions were undesirable but at the same time resign itself to their inevitable adoption? I had the same feelings after speaking on the phone with Chinese foreign minister Yang Jiechi, shortly before leaving for Tehran. He told me he supported our efforts but gave no guarantee that Beijing would veto the request for sanctions, or even that it would abstain in the case of a vote. China is a country that jealously guards its national sovereignty—and which was generally averse to sanctions against developing countries—but it adopted an ambivalent position and ultimately, less than two months on from the BRICs meeting, it would vote in favor of the Security Council resolution. Why? Without wanting to jump ahead to other moments in this process, I think it is relevant here to give my general view of the Chinese position. First, like the other four members of the P5—which, perhaps not by chance, are also the only countries whose possession of nuclear weapons is recognized by the NPT—China has an inherent interest in preventing other countries from developing or possessing nuclear arms. Although Iran has always declared that its nuclear program is for peaceful purposes, the mere existence of doubts about Iran's intentions, and also the "slips" in its compliance with the rules of the IAEA, might have inclined Beijing to take the side of the other nuclear powers. Another noticeable feature of Chinese foreign policy in recent decades has been its pragmatism. Eager to maintain its profitable economic relations with the West, and especially the US, Beijing tries whenever it can to minimize areas of friction, taking firm positions only on issues that directly affect its interests. I do not wish to say there are never exceptions to this rule, particularly when the use of force is involved (as in the former Yugoslavia, or Iraq), but pragmatism seems to be an increasingly prevalent feature of China's diplomacy. Finally, during the process that led to the adoption of sanctions, China (as well as Russia) secured the exemptions it needed to ensure its commercial interests would not be affected—principally its purchases of Iranian oil. None of these factors alone is sufficient to explain the Chinese position, but together they do appear to provide a rationale for Beijing's behavior.

In the bilateral meeting on the sidelines of the BRICs summit, Russian president Dmitri Medvedev seemed to have a somewhat more positive view of the chances of achieving a diplomatic solution. He said Lula's visit to Tehran would be the "last chance" to avoid the imposition of new sanctions against Iran. During a brief stop in Moscow on April 25, during the same trip that took me to Istanbul and Tehran, I had the opportunity to discuss Iran with my counterpart Sergey Lavrov. The meeting was arranged at my request, and at the last minute. I hardly spent half a day in Moscow; my Brazilian Air Force plane landed in the early afternoon, at an airport still semi-covered in snow, and took off again for Tehran before midnight. Lavrov, as I mentioned before, was someone I had worked alongside at the UN, including from 1998–99 when Brazil served on the Security Council. Lavrov had appreciated our partnership particularly with regard to issues surrounding the former Yugoslavia, on which Russia had been left virtually isolated with only China for company. A perception of our political affinities or convergent interests was also expressed, as I mentioned before, in a conversation with Lavrov during the UN General Assembly in 2006, when he suggested to me that the BRICs should become established as a political forum. Despite the friendly way he greeted me in the hall of honor at the

Russian foreign ministry (the place where many important international treaties have been signed, such as the 1963 ban on the testing of nuclear weapon in the atmosphere), and his offer of a working dinner at a time of my choosing, Lavrov did not seem enthusiastic about the Turkish-Brazilian efforts in search of a negotiated solution to the Iranian issue. As I wrote in my notebook: "The conversation with Lavrov was objective, matter-of-fact, but not very inspiring. [He] didn't offer any ideas, nor did he seem to be trying to come up with any, although he did indicate that he was open to suggestions from me. . . . His attitude was basically non-committal. He seemed to be saying: 'If it works, great. If not, we'll follow our path [i.e. that of sanctions], even though we're not very keen on it.' His main concern is to avoid measures that might affect Russian interests, such as the supply of equipment to the Bushehr nuclear power plant. He was also worried about some form of sanctions that might impact indirectly [on Russian interests] or serve to legitimize the unilateral imposition of restrictions." At the end of my notes I added a more personal comment, which reflected my mood of disappointment: "[Lavrov] was friendly, but our closeness during the situations we experienced in New York . . . is a thing of the past."[44]

We would again have contact with the Russians in the context of Lula's visit to Moscow, on the way to Tehran. On that occasion, in addition to a meeting with Russian businesspeople, Lula met with President Medvedev and the then prime minister, Vladimir Putin. In a private conversation between the two heads of state, Medvedev raised the issue of Iran. Lula briefly spoke about his belief in "politics," which is how he often referred to the pursuit of negotiated solutions, and then asked me to explain the details of the proposal we were taking with us to Tehran. By this point, following communications with various interlocutors, Brazil and Turkey had reached the point of telling the Iranians that they must write to the IAEA, expressing their complete acceptance of the proposal made in October. Responding to a question from Medvedev, I explained that the Iranians now appeared to be more engaged in the discussion, and that my impression was that they had not rejected the proposal. Medvedev then mentioned a phone conversation the day before with President Obama. During that conversation Obama had apparently repeated the opinion—by that time familiar to anyone in regular communication with US officials—that the dialogue with Tehran would have greater chances of success if new sanctions were in place.[45] As for the predictable hardening of the Iranian government's position that sanctions would provoke in the short and medium term, not to mention the suffering they would cause the Iranian population, it seemed not to enter the Americans' considerations. When Medvedev asked Lula what he thought, his response was indirect but still made clear his opposition to sanctions, emphasizing the value of dialogue and recalling, for example, the mistakes that had been made in relation to Iraq. The conversation with Putin was little different. I am not sure why, but the Russian prime minister was even more skeptical than Medvedev (it might have had something to do with issues related to Russia's "near abroad," including Transcaucasia and Central Asia, for which he was directly responsible). Also during that visit to Moscow, I remember an interesting moment during the joint press conference given by the two presidents. In response to a question from a Brazilian journalist (after a couple of difficulties in translation), Medvedev said he put the chances of success of our efforts with Iran at "thirty per cent." Lula, keeping to the numerical scale (zero to ten) suggested by the reporter, said "9.9." Another thing worth mentioning, though not related directly to the Iran issue, was a conversation between the two presidents and their foreign ministers on the reform of the Security Council, which took place during the banquet offered by Medvedev. The Russian president was more open to our aspirations than Lavrov, who—typically for a former permanent representative to the United Nations—brought up a number of technical and political difficulties that the envisaged reform might entail. Lavrov's arguments provoked answers on my part that might have been a little too spirited: afterwards, in the car, Lula said, "Gee, Celso, you were very fierce with your friend!" At the end of the meeting, Medvedev repeated what he had said in Brasilia, which was that he saw Lula's visit to Tehran as the last chance to achieve an agreement. As Lula departed, the Russian president wished him "good luck."

In assessing Russia's possible motives, the first factor that comes to mind is the shared position of the P5 countries when it comes to any threat—or even suspicion—of nuclear proliferation. To that I would add the historical rivalry between Russia and Iran, which persists to this day, especially in jostling for influence in the Middle East. One might also suppose that Russia, which has serious frictions with western countries but also depends on them for investment and markets for its products, would have weighed up the various elements of the Iranian issue and concluded that on balance it would not be a good idea to create an obstacle to a course of action which was strongly favored by Washington and also, after all, would not hurt any vital Russian interest. If so, Moscow, like Beijing, was guided by economic and political pragmatism, seeking above all to protect its economic interests. And in that sense Russia was undoubtedly successful: in addition to securing its supplies to the Bushehr nuclear plant, it also managed to exempt some of its companies from the sanctions, even including those imposed unilaterally by the US.[46]

NEGOTIATIONS

From the moment we began to follow more closely the search for a solution to the issue of Iran's nuclear program, we had a continuous and intensifying dialogue with the main actors involved. In the run-up to Lula's visit to Tehran, our discussions with the Iranian authorities became more focused. Even when negative, the feedback we received from the major powers, especially the United States, was one of the factors leading those discussions to concentrate on the essentials. Looking back at Brazil's and Turkey's negotiations with Iran, which culminated in the Tehran Declaration of May 17, it is clear they should not be reduced—as has often been the case in subsequent public discussions—merely to the seventeen hours I spent with my Turkish and Iranian counterparts, along with other Iranian officials and various advisors, in the room in a Tehran palace where the text of the Declaration was prepared. There was, in fact, a slowly evolving process, punctuated by backward steps, in which Iran came gradually closer to the original terms of the agreement, due largely to Brazil's and Turkey's credibility and power of persuasion.

I already mentioned that I visited Tehran at the end of April and that my conclusions from the trip were briefly summarized in the letter President Lula sent to President Obama. However, to give a clearer picture of the evolution of the Iranian position and indeed of our own thoughts, it seems useful to refer briefly to the notes I made during that visit. I arrived in Tehran from Moscow—where I had met with Lavrov—in the early hours of April 26. Later that day I had two important meetings: one with the secretary of the Supreme National Security Council, Saeed Jalili; the other with Ali Larijani, speaker of the Iranian parliament and the previous occupant of Jalili's position. Both conversations were extensive and detailed, despite a few difficulties with the translation from Farsi to Portuguese. Jalili agreed in principle to write a letter to the IAEA (the requirement the western countries constantly insisted upon), but said the letter should be prepared "together with Turkey and Brazil." In it, Iran would announce, without restrictions or conditionalities, its willingness to start negotiations "on the basis of" the proposed terms of the swap agreement. There was, of course, a difference between accepting the proposal and using it as a starting point for negotiations. Also, I was aware that this apparent show of trust might in fact contain a clever ploy of linking Ankara and Brasilia with Iranian positions. There were potential pitfalls. And yet the proposal did represent an advance in relation to previous positions held by Jalili himself. Ever since our first meeting in 2009, I had been impressed by the deep stare and apparently calm demeanor of the secretary of the Supreme National Security Council; he seemed accustomed to operating under all kinds of pressure, and to offering steely resistance. His flexibility on this occasion, although requiring careful attention on our part, showed that something in Iran was moving.

The speaker of the Iranian parliament, Larijani, received me in a large, bright and discreetly decorated lounge. I made a comment about the pleasant surroundings, saying they were conducive to "high thinking." Larijani listened calmly and with interest to my argument about the importance of confidence-building measures. I suggested the possibility that an initial amount of uranium could be deposited in Turkey. I also mentioned that, upon signing the agreement, a declaration of a moratorium on the enrichment of uranium to 20% would help create a climate of trust. Larijani did not reject the ideas but nor did he express agreement; he said merely that they deserved further reflection. It was during this conversation with Larijani that I first ventured a comparison between the three central issues—place, time, and quantity—and concepts in physics, in the sense that they could easily be made subject to verification. Despite the friendly tone of our conversation, Larijani did not fail to criticize the agreement. More specifically, he returned to Mottaki's argument that "the buyer is the one who decides the quantity." He pointed out that given the remaining life of its research reactor, Iran needed only about 60 kilograms of fuel, equivalent to 600 kilograms of LEU. Therefore, he said, the proposed 120 kilograms of fuel in exchange for 1,200 kilograms of LEU did not correspond to Iran's actual needs. Following that line of reasoning, the agreement became unviable. It is worth noting at this point that some of the tough positions the Iranian government had been taking, such as the commencement of enrichment to 20%, originated from Parliament. Larijani, more than anyone, was the public face of this hard-line stance, which was not unconnected with internal struggles for power.

On April 27, I met with the foreign minister and the president. The conversation with Mottaki was longer and more objective than on any previous occasion. He had just come back from a meeting in Vienna with the new Japanese director-general of the IAEA, to whom he had indicated Iran's willingness, as a "gesture of flexibility," to place at the IAEA's disposal 1,000 kilograms of LEU (although it was not yet clear how and where) with a view to it being exchanged for the fuel. In all my conversations until then, the maximum quantity Iran had been willing to part with was 800 kilograms. Although I knew this concession would not be sufficient, I recognized it as a noteworthy step in the direction of an agreement. Friendly and affable as always, Mottaki agreed with my suggestion that we should not prolong the "expanded meeting" in which, accompanied by our respective groups of officials, we were also dealing with the preparations for Lula's visit. In the private meeting, when Mottaki and I were accompanied only by two advisors each (in my case our ambassador, Antonio Salgado, and a diplomat from my office, Leonardo Gorgulho), I stressed the importance of the letter Iran was due to send to the IAEA. On that issue I did not perceive any negative reaction from Mottaki. I mentioned the idea of the LEU (or at least a portion of it) being sent to Turkey before receipt of the first batch of fuel—a proposal aimed at addressing one of the criticisms of the credibility of the agreement expressed in my previous conversations with General Jones, the secretary of state, and President Obama. I said to Mottaki that in this case Iran would be leaving a deposit in advance not with a distrusted rival but with a "trusted friend." If the agreement were to fall through, Turkey would simply send the LEU back to Iran. Mottaki seemed to understand, and asked me to repeat the argument later to President Ahmadinejad. The third point I raised was that of the moratorium on the enrichment of uranium to 20%, once the agreement was signed. Without contesting Iran's rights under the NPT, I insisted that the continuation of uranium enrichment to that degree would be difficult to justify once Iran had received the fuel it needed for its research reactor. Mottaki was silent, which I took to mean that he recognized the force of the argument.

Much of my conversation with President Ahmadinejad focused on the liberation of the French citizen Clotilde Reiss, previously stipulated by France as a precondition of engagement with the Iranian government. I will leave aside the details, but it is worth mentioning again that a positive conclusion would later be facilitated by the timing—coincidental or otherwise—of certain judicial and administrative decisions taken in France, not only in the case of Bakhtiar but also in a delicate situation regarding an Iranian engineer whose extradition from France had been requested by Washington but denied by Paris. In these meetings, it became clear as the talks progressed that Iran's trust in Brazil and Turkey was growing, and indeed that the Iranians were interested in the possibility of the two countries effectively acting as guarantors of the swap operation. At one point one of my interlocutors even suggested the LEU could be deposited with Brazil. This idea was not taken forward, both for political (our relationship with Turkey) and logistical reasons. When Mottaki was saying goodbye to me, shortly after my conversation with Ahmadinejad, he gave another sign of his trust in Brazil. Referring to the Clotilde Reiss situation and the possible release by France of the Iranian prisoner accused of murdering Bakhtiar, he said: "A guarantee from Sarkozy to Lula is enough. It isn't necessary for the French president to speak directly to the Iranian president."

And now back to those decisive days in May. At the end of President Lula's trip to Russia, on May 14, my view was that there was still work to be done in trying to close the gaps between Tehran's positions, even though they were now more flexible, and the original proposal for the agreement, subsequently reiterated by Obama. I suggested that instead of accompanying him to Qatar, his next stop before Tehran, I should head straight to the Iranian capital. He promptly agreed, and put his reserve aircraft at my disposal.[47]

Before turning to the talks that took place in Tehran on May 15, 16, and 17, I should make an observation. Throughout the discussions described above, the precise objective to be pursued in Tehran underwent a slow but progressive process of evolution. It gradually became clear that we—Brazil and Turkey—could not in fact work with any alternative to the basic elements of the proposed agreement. As the reader might already have inferred from the narrative so far, I am not sure when exactly my Turkish counterpart and I abandoned the search for adjustments to the original proposal—which, incidentally, had included certain aspects of potential interest to the western countries (such as the moratorium on enrichment to 20%)—and resolved to concentrate on the four elements contained in the letter from President Obama: 1,200 kilograms; deposit in a third country; immediate dispatch of the LEU; and formal communication to the IAEA. Obama's letter alone was not the turning point, however, as can be seen from the fact that in late April my Iranian contacts and I were still discussing ways in which the terms of the original proposal might be made more flexible. In my case it was a period of reflection in the wake of those conversations that brought about the change of course. It was the same for my Turkish counterpart. As a result, when I landed in Tehran in the early morning of May 15, it was with the firmly established notion that the only way forward was Iran's full acceptance of those four elements, in exchange perhaps for some guarantees and a reaffirmation of certain principles that the Iranians held dear.

On the day of my arrival in Tehran, the ministerial meeting of the G15[48] was also taking place in the city. The G15, which includes Brazil, is a forum that has gradually lost importance over the years—but Iran, permanently under threat of international isolation, attached great importance to the event and to its role as host. The choice of Tehran as the venue had been decided in a meeting in Havana, which I attended. The Iranians had therefore asked us to help with the preparations, aiming to achieve some practical results with at least a little substance. I therefore sent to Tehran our undersecretary for economic affairs, Ambassador Roberto Azevêdo (now director-general of the WTO), who acted as Brazil's high representative at the summit. Azevêdo advised the Iranians in preparing the agenda and probably also the final communiqué. Given the Iranians' trust in us and also our level of professional competence and experience in preparing such meetings, Brazil was one of the few countries Tehran could ask for that kind of assistance. I should point out that Turkey is not a member of the G15.

My first conversation with Mottaki took place on the morning of my arrival. It lasted about an hour and a half but was of little value from the point of view of the nuclear negotiations. My Iranian counterpart informed me that the day before there had been a "very, very important" meeting. From his choice of words and the way he emphasized them, I inferred that the Supreme Leader must have participated. As a result, he said, "the government has been placed in charge of discussing the issue." Such an observation would normally be redundant; the reason for it, I think, is that I had earlier said I was willing to meet anyone Mottaki thought it worthwhile for me to talk to. Implicitly that would include the speaker of the Iranian parliament, Ali Larijani, who I had met during my visit in April. Mottaki thought it necessary to emphasize that the government—not any other organ of the state—had the authority to conduct the discussions. During that same conversation on the morning of May 15, Mottaki said that the talks with Brazil and Turkey, which would take place the next day, would be conducted, on the Iranian side, by himself, by Supreme National Security Council secretary Saeed Jalili, and by the president of Iran's atomic energy organization, Ali Akbar Salehi. All I could extract from this initial conversation were questions of procedure.

The procedural side was not entirely irrelevant, however. I was worried there would not be enough time for meaningful negotiations. Davutoglu, whose presence was essential if the discussions were to yield some result, told me he could not make it to Tehran until the evening of the following day, May 16, which was also when Lula's official visit would take place. I sensed that Turkey's optimism was waning and that perhaps it was now having doubts about the idea, already agreed in principle, of a trilateral discussion between the leaders of the three countries involved in the negotiation. The meeting between Lula, Erdogan and Ahmadinejad was a key aspect of the process: one of the biggest incentives for Iran to accept the agreement would be the presence alongside Ahmadinejad of the leaders of two important developing countries that possessed a high degree of credibility. I was left uneasy, therefore, by what I felt to be Davutoglu's waning enthusiasm. My concern was sharply accentuated on May 15 when a *Washington Post* journalist who was interviewing me asked for my interpretation of Erdogan having "cancelled" his trip to Tehran, which he insisted was the case. It was the first I had heard of it. But, coupled with my impressions from my earlier conversation with Davutoglu, it alerted me to the need to speak to him again as soon as possible. I did so at some point between lunch and the start of the G15 ministerial meeting, and I asked Mottaki to call him as well. Our insistence paid off: Davutoglu said he could arrive the following morning. At such moments, a minister or a negotiator looks for signs in the smallest gestures. Mottaki's prompt agreement with my suggestion that he insist the Turkish foreign minister should arrive earlier than planned appeared to be the first indication (apart from the "very, very important" meeting) that the Iranians were genuinely committed to a successful conclusion.

On the afternoon of May 15, slipping into autopilot mode, I took part in the G15 meeting, where I must have made a speech but do not recall a single word of it. Still, the Iranians appreciated my presence, Brazil being a country whose importance in economic and commercial negotiations had grown significantly in the preceding years. At some point Mottaki suggested that he and I should have dinner with Saeed Jalili that evening, which I agreed to. But they did not arrive at the time I was expecting them, and eventually, deciding not to wait any longer, I made my way to the hotel cafeteria to get a frugal meal (as was my habit, especially in the evenings) from the buffet. At that very moment Mottaki appeared, having decided to pay me a "visit" alone. So we had another conversation, this time for almost two hours, in the slightly cramped lounge area of my suite (the more spacious suite which I had stayed in on previous visits, with a view over the snow-capped mountains to the north of Tehran, had been reserved for President Lula). As usual, the conversation with Mottaki was friendly, vague, and full of circumlocutions. He stressed it was important that if we reached an agreement, it should establish a "general framework" for cooperation between Iran and the international community. It was an idea which struck me as another way of evading discussion of more specific points. Mottaki came across as somewhat slippery, careful to avoid committing himself to anything. I found myself constantly assessing and then reassessing the situation, and could feel my confidence in the success of our endeavors beginning to wane again.

The trilateral meeting of foreign ministers was scheduled for 7 a.m. the next day, May 16. The reason for it being so early was to fit in with Lula's official visit, the ceremonies for which would start at 10 a.m.. The meeting of the three delegations, initially in an "expanded format," took place in a hall in a former palace that I was told had once belonged to the Shah. Mottaki was accompanied by Jalili, Salehi, and various advisors. Davutoglu, for his part, had brought four or five Turkish officials. In my case, my only "technical" advisor was the diplomat from my office who had been dealing with the Iran issue, Leonardo Gorgulho. But to ensure the Brazilian delegation did not consist only of two people, I also took along my press secretary, Maurício Lyrio, whose astute political analysis I held in high regard. My chief of staff, the efficient Ambassador Maria Laura, was unable to be present as she had to take care of the complex task of coordinating my meetings with the schedule of President Lula, who had arrived the night before. Further adding to the drama and emotions that punctuated those few days, the early morning of May 16, after Lula's arrival, was also when the French citizen Clotilde Reiss finally left Iran on a KLM plane bound for Paris. I will return to the significance of her release later.

At the start of the 7 a.m. meeting there were introductions of a general nature that did not provide much indication of whether the negotiations might ultimately be successful. On the table were two draft declarations: one Turkish-Brazilian, the other Iranian. As both documents followed roughly the same methodology, though with differing approaches, the "technical" advisors were able to merge the texts into a single document so as to facilitate discussion of the specific points of divergence. This discussion would take place after lunch, at about 2:30 p.m., when Davutoglu and I returned to sit down again with our Iranian interlocutors.

Between the morning session and the resumption of the ministerial meeting, there was the official arrival ceremony for President Lula, followed by his meetings with Ahmadinejad and the Supreme Leader. Perhaps due to fatigue—after the meeting with Mottaki the night before, I had gone to speak to Lula at about midnight to tell him how the discussions were going, and then had to wake up at 5:30 a.m. for the early meeting—I do not remember much of the conversation between the two presidents, which took place in the presence of ministers and officials. They talked, of course, about issues related to bilateral cooperation, such as trade, investment, and financial relations (a sensitive topic due not only to the UN sanctions but also the unilateral ones imposed by the US and EU). As for the nuclear issue, nothing substantial was said; the two presidents merely expressed positive expectations about the parallel discussions. Had anything significant come up I would have realized immediately, despite my tiredness.

Next came Lula's meeting with the Supreme Leader, Ayatollah Ali Khamenei. With regard to the nuclear negotiations, again nothing was said; the important thing was simply that the meeting in itself had taken place. The Supreme Leader of Iran is an unusual character in contemporary international affairs. He is, simultaneously, both the political and the religious leader of Iran: no other important nation has a comparable figure. It is true, for example, that the British monarch is formally head of state and head of the Anglican Church, but even the most ardent monarchists must acknowledge that Queen Elizabeth, despite the fondness she inspires in some, does not have much power over political or ecclesiastical matters. It would not be true to say there was no precedent for Khamenei's meeting with Lula, but it was certainly uncommon for the Supreme Leader to meet with the heads of state or government of non-Islamic countries. The mere fact that the encounter took place, therefore, was a positive symbol in relation to our efforts. And we knew that the Supreme Leader's receptivity, without which the meeting could not have taken place, would be absolutely essential if those efforts were ultimately to be successful.

This unusual meeting between a labor union leader who had risen to the presidency of a major developing country and the head of the modern world's only important theocracy is certainly worthy of note. Khamenei cut an impressive figure: a venerable old man with a voluminous but carefully maintained white beard, and a look in his eyes that conveyed an impression—perhaps only superficial—of tranquility and self-assuredness. It was hard to imagine that a man of such advanced years (who did not try to hide the fact, unlike certain western leaders) had in fact been responsible for, or at least inspired, the deaths or imprisonment of a large number of Iranian citizens in the aftermath of Ahmadinejad's disputed re-election. Khamenei greeted everyone courteously and with a hint of affection; a demeanor a critical observer might have perceived as vaguely paternalistic. The room in which he received us, in quite a simple house located close to the presidential compound, contrasted with the luxurious halls of the official palaces. It probably measured no more than ten meters by six; the walls, painted white, were completely bare apart from one single adornment (if it can be described as such): a portrait of the great "father" of the Islamic revolution, Ayatollah Ruhollah Khomeini. There was not even a Persian rug: the only color on the floor was provided by a reddish carpet, slightly faded. Some members of our group, including Lula's official photographer, were asked to remove their shoes. Khamenei was dressed very simply, though I noticed his costume, semi-concealed under a white robe, was well cut. On his feet he was wearing slippers.

After the initial pleasantries, I began to fear that the discussion, initiated by quite a long introduction from Lula, was taking on a very official, almost bureaucratic tone. The first things said, by both sides, added very little to what had already been heard on other occasions. The Supreme Leader talked in very broad terms about the current state of international relations, and the need for unity among developing countries. The conversation only warmed up when President Lula began a summary of his life story. At one point he mentioned that he was seven years old when he ate his first piece of bread. "What had he eaten until then?" the puzzled ayatollah asked me. It was quite a task, for the interpreters and me, to explain that Lula had survived on manioc flour mixed with water. Khamenei bade us farewell with the same courtesy he had shown on our arrival, and wished Lula "good luck." It was the same expression Medvedev had used, though the context now was different. Up until that point it was, in fact, the only positive and encouraging reference to the negotiations.

While we were waiting for the technical meeting to end, Ambassador Maria Laura and I were led to a waiting room inside the palace. In fact it was a large hall, half-empty but with some comfortable armchairs. Unlike the cramped room where the conversation between Lula and Khamenei had taken place, this one had a beautiful rug and delicate plasterwork reliefs on the ceiling. We were there for some time, perhaps more than half an hour. Exhausted from the meetings of the previous evening and that morning, feeling I might be about to come down with flu, and knowing that ahead of me lay long meetings that might extend into the evening, I fell asleep. When Mottaki entered the room, Maria Laura (as she later told me) went to wake me up—but then he gestured, silently, that she should let me rest. Thanks to this little act of kindness on the part of my Iranian counterpart, I enjoyed a nap of at least a quarter of an hour, until someone came to call us for lunch.

I was informed by my technical advisors of the purely procedural progress that had been achieved. They also told me there had been an attempt by Turkey, with our support, to include in the text of the agreement a reference to the stock of LEU and also to enrichment to 20%. But the Iranian delegation had promptly rejected both suggestions, and our side had not tried to force the issue. When we met again in the afternoon, the discussions centered on two aspects: the first concerned the three essential elements of the exchange agreement, plus the letter to the IAEA. The other concerned Iran's insistence on referring to wider geopolitical issues such as the right of states to develop nuclear energy (including the enrichment of uranium) for peaceful purposes under the NPT, and the resumption of Iran's cooperation with the international community, including in the nuclear field. It was only then that I fully understood what Mottaki had been saying in our conversation the night before about the comprehensive framework for cooperation. As the negotiations went on it became clear that Iran—particularly Salehi, the head of the atomic energy council—was genuinely interested in international cooperation as a means of overcoming the technical and material difficulties surrounding its nuclear program.

The discussions were long, and occasionally somewhat heated. Most of the time the focus was on practical details, such as the deadline for delivery of the first batch of LEU or precisely how the fuel would be received. The concrete elements that would be necessary for an agreement however, were easy to identify. To sum up the negotiations that took place on May 16, the potential agreement by that stage consisted of the acceptance by Brazil and Turkey of the "conceptual proposals" put forward by Iran (with inevitable adjustments), and the acceptance by Iran of the essential elements of the swap deal (but with certain refinements that would provide the Iranians with a minimum degree of comfort).

In the trio of principal Iranian negotiators, it was obvious that the authority to make decisions lay mostly (though not entirely) with Jalili, the head of the Security Council. I already referred above to his generally saturnine demeanor. During the negotiations he smiled frequently when speaking to me or Davutoglu—but it was almost a rictus grin, making me think it was a way of protecting himself and not appearing hostile when he answered questions in a very direct manner. Often he let other members of the Iranian delegation voice their opinions, including those who appeared not to have the same level of expertise. Their interventions, in general, served only as obstacles. One of these individuals, a relatively young man whose position in the Iranian bureaucracy was not clear (maybe he was close to the Supreme Leader, or the Revolutionary Guards) kept butting in to express quite extreme and unrealistic positions. I thought he might even be an *agent provocateur*, sent to sabotage the negotiations. Short and rather overweight, he was wearing a black shirt that reminded me of the Italian fascists of Mussolini's era, reinforcing the unpleasant impression of a highly ideological functionary. He became so irritating that by about 8 p.m. I had had enough, so I requested that from then onward only the ministers and their equivalents be allowed to speak. That took the wind out of his sails, but only temporarily; soon he was interfering again in the discussion, with undiminished zeal. Ironically, the next day, after we had arrived at a definitive agreement, he would be all smiles, and even quite affectionate when the time came for us to leave. Of the three main Iranian negotiators, it was Salehi who seemed most interested in reaching a positive conclusion. His contributions were generally constructive, aimed at finding common ground. Mottaki, whom overall I had the most contact with during the process leading up to the Tehran Declaration, did not participate much on this particular occasion, though it seemed his stance was closer to that of Jalili—or the short fat guy—than to Salehi.

In the midst of the tough discussions there were some moments of warmth. From time to time we took a break to allow the advisors to write down what had been agreed, and during one of these intervals we went out on a balcony adjacent to the meeting room, under the branches of a huge mulberry tree. Jalili, normally so severe, started picking the berries and offering them to us. Slowly we were advancing toward formulations acceptable to both sides. One of the difficult issues was Iran's demand that the text include an explicit reference to the suspension of sanctions in exchange for the "concessions" they were making. My Turkish counterpart and I were of the opinion that a specific reference to sanctions would devalue the statement as a confidence-building gesture on the part of Iran. Eventually we got round the problem when I suggested, based on years of experience at the UN, the inclusion of a reference not to "sanctions" but to "measures," which is the term used in Chapter VII of the UN Charter. The Iranians accepted the idea.

We had already almost concluded the negotiations on the text when Mottaki—who had returned after being away for about an hour and a half at the banquet hosted by Ahmadinejad for Lula (which I did not attend)—suddenly insisted in a peremptory manner that the word "sanctions" should in fact appear in the text. Mottaki's position as foreign minister was never very secure, and I suspect that at this point he was to some extent playing to the gallery (which I am sure would have included the black-shirted guy). I did not hide my annoyance with this intervention from my Iranian counterpart, and the only reason I did not leave without saying goodbye was because the Turkish delegation offered a meal of lamb with rice to the starving negotiators. Sitting with the Turkish and Brazilian delegations in the makeshift dining area adjacent to the meeting room, Mottaki changed his tone, reiterating his affection and friendship. I told him the feelings were mutual, though I could not resist adding: "I'll continue to be your friend, but I don't know if I can continue to be your advocate."

The negotiating process and tiring discussions of May 16 gave me a better understanding of some of the Iranian representatives' concerns with regard to various sections of their domestic audience. As for Brazil and Turkey, though we could see the legitimacy of certain Iranian concerns (defending the right to uranium enrichment for peaceful purposes, for example), we were focused on the impact the text would have on the other countries involved. Significant advances had been made during that afternoon and evening. We had a text we could present to the heads of government; one that had a good chance of being approved. Although it was still possible that the complex and fragmented Iranian political system might throw up last-minute obstacles, it seemed likely we would reach a consensus the following morning, at the trilateral summit. Around midnight I went to report to President Lula, who was pleased with the developments. "Go and get some sleep," he said. "You deserve it."

Because the negotiations continued through the afternoon and into the evening of the next day, May 17, I was unable to attend any of Lula's official engagements. I heard later that my extended absence generated a certain amount of disquiet among the Brazilian delegation. Apparently the special advisor to the president, always ready with a joke, said I must have been kidnapped. His theory seemed to be confirmed when the Iranian foreign minister turned up at the gala dinner without me at his side.

THE AGREEMENT

"May the 17th, 2010. I thought I'd write the date out in full because, who knows, maybe it will prove to be a historic one." That is how I started the entry in my notebook on the day the Tehran Declaration was adopted. Next I wrote: "It might seem presumptuous on my part to say that, but in fact it was mentioned as a possibility by more than one speaker at the G15 meeting this morning." And indeed, a few days later, *Le Monde* published an editorial that declared: "The history books will record this date, Monday, May 17, when Brazil and Turkey proposed to the UN the agreement negotiated with Iran."

On the evening of May 16 we had arrived at a text that incorporated the points that were important from the point of view of the P5+1, along with the "questions of principle" and certain guarantees requested by Iran. From the very beginning we had known that in order to reach an agreement it was important to recognize the right of all state parties to the NPT to use nuclear energy for peaceful purposes. This was stated in the first paragraph, which contained two important points. One was a direct reference to the Islamic Republic of Iran as a state that does indeed have the aforementioned right. The other was a specific reference to "enrichment activities" being an integral part of that right. The first paragraph also managed to overcome an obstacle that had hindered all previous attempts to engage in effective dialogue with Iran: it included the expression "without discrimination," which was very important to Iran as the country frequently complained of being treated unfairly. The following three paragraphs described the swap deal as a "starting point" and a "positive constructive move forward" that would lead to greater cooperation in the field of peaceful nuclear activities. The fourth paragraph contained the Iranian view that the agreement should lead to the abandonment of the strategy based on sanctions—but to avoid the impression that this was a "bargain" rather than a unilateral confidence-building gesture, the reference to sanctions was rather indirect. What the text actually said, at the end of the fourth paragraph, was that it was necessary to avoid "all kinds of confrontation, abstaining from measures, actions and rhetorical declarations that might adversely affect the rights and obligations of Iran under the NPT." The following paragraphs, five to eight, described the procedures for the deposit in Turkey of 1,200 kilograms of Iran's uranium, and for Iran to notify the IAEA. Those paragraphs also contained the guarantee that Iran would receive the 120 kilograms of fuel for its research reactor "in no later than one year." In order to get the Iranians' acceptance it had been important to include the explicit recognition that "while in Turkey, this LEU will continue to be the property of Iran." Accordingly, the eighth paragraph also stipulated that: "In case the provisions of this declaration are not respected, Turkey, upon the request of Iran, will return swiftly and unconditionally Iran's LEU to Iran."

We therefore went into the trilateral summit on May 17 with a text already virtually approved—even by Saeed Jalili, the negotiator who appeared the most hard-line. It was ready, therefore, to receive the endorsement of the heads of government. The only remaining issue was the one raised by Mottaki, about the use of the word "sanctions" in the fourth paragraph. As it turned out, this point did indeed spark quite a lot of discussion during the morning, even making us think that all our efforts might ultimately come to nothing. Just like his foreign minister the night before, Ahmadinejad, at the instigation of some hard-line advisor or other, requested that the word "sanctions" should be specifically included. Erdogan and Lula, however, duly assisted by Davutoglu and myself, held firm to the position that an explicit reference to sanctions would sound more like a bargain than a "confidence-building gesture." In parallel, both leaders reaffirmed their commitment to continue working to prevent the adoption of sanctions. The Iranian president, after a short break for consultations, and realizing that if he insisted on that point it would genuinely undermine the declaration, accepted our argument. And so we reached the end of the negotiation process for the Tehran Declaration, which was signed shortly afterwards by the three foreign ministers in the presence of their heads of government. For Davutoglu and me, it was the culmination of six months of hard work and intense emotional involvement. Lula and Erdogan, for their part, could celebrate a success few people had believed possible.

When the Declaration was signed, the enthusiasm of those present was clear to see, and duly captured by the photographers. Those pictures provoked a negative media reaction, above all in Brazil. Most critics suggested some kind of unseemly fraternization had taken place, or even that the leaders of two democratic countries—Brazil and Turkey—had signaled their support for President Ahmadinejad, widely considered a modern Shia version of the bloody tyrants who appear all too frequently in twentieth-century history. But, obviously, the scenes that accompanied the signing were nothing of the sort; only someone who had not experienced the tension of the latter stages of the negotiations could arrive at such a conclusion. What we were celebrating was the end of a long process, littered with mishaps and obstacles, in which we had been asked to intervene and had subsequently pursued to the very end. We knew that a successful outcome—which at that point we were very hopeful of—would be an important step toward a peaceful solution of a very complex issue and, equally important, a means of avoiding more suffering for the Iranian people.

In my notes about the events of May 17, written aboard one of the president's reserve aircraft, I made a first attempt at assessing the reasons for the positive result in Tehran. It seems I myself was surprised at the outcome. I wrote as follows: "What factors contributed to [this] positive result, which no doubt some will now try to undermine? The unique optimism of President Lula, which always animated my efforts? The good understanding with Turkey . . . especially in recent months and weeks? The increasing isolation of Iran? The clear messages I took [to Tehran] after the BRICs meeting helped Tehran to realize that some flexibility was needed. The climate of trust between us and the Iranian leaders was also significant." Regarding the steps immediately preceding the Declaration, it was now clear that my decision to head straight to Tehran from Moscow, without going to Doha first, had been absolutely the right one. Without those preparatory conversations in Tehran, which among other things had convinced me of the need to persuade Davutoglu to arrive earlier than planned, it would not have been possible to conclude the negotiations in time.

To use a commercial metaphor, the goods were now ready: all we needed to do was sell them. This task, unfortunately, was to prove more difficult than the negotiations. Before leaving Tehran, at about 1 p.m. (5 a.m. in Washington), I woke our ambassador to the United States, the competent and ever-attentive Mauro Vieira, and asked him to try to schedule a telephone conversation for me with Hillary Clinton during my stop in Madrid on the way back to Brazil. I regarded the call as a necessary gesture of transparency. I should make clear, incidentally, that at this point I had again parted from the presidential delegation in order to deal with more urgent matters. Lula understood perfectly that modern diplomacy often requires a foreign minister not just to be an advisor to the head of the government but also to have their own field of activities. And in this case, between the two options of defending the Declaration and participating in the European Union, Latin America and the Caribbean (EU-LAC) summit in Madrid, a biennial event that had lost some of its previous importance and where in any case there were other people who could advise the president, the former obviously had to take priority.

INITIAL REACTIONS

Even before leaving, while still in the airport VIP lounge, we spoke to Sarkozy, whom Lula was due to meet the following day on the margins of the EU-LAC summit. I say "we" because Lula, after the initial greetings, handed me the phone so I could explain to the French president, in his language, the principal aspects of the agreement. Sarkozy seemed very receptive, even saying he would make a public statement in support of Lula's efforts. Ever the optimist, I told him it would be important to mention in the statement not only the efforts made but also the progress achieved. Sarkozy agreed to do so, though his words suggested he had doubts about whether Iran would indeed fulfill the commitments made in the Tehran Declaration. I also had a brief phone conversation with the Russian foreign minister, Sergey Lavrov, but I do not have any written record of it; I vaguely recall that the connection was terrible and that we agreed to talk again later.

Immediately upon arrival at Torrejón air base, where some of my advisors were waiting, having arrived as the advance guard ahead of the meeting in Spain, I asked my spokesperson Liliam Chagas to arrange the phone conversation with Hillary Clinton. The call went through without delay. The secretary of state made no attempt to hide her perplexity—or indeed her disappointment—with the result of the Tehran meeting. In my opinion she feared the Tehran Declaration was an obstacle to the approval of sanctions by the Security Council. More than once during the conversation she made a point of saying that the United States was already counting on the support of the P5 and would therefore continue trying to get a Security Council resolution that condemned Iran and imposed new sanctions. She repeated her all-too-familiar opinion that "Iran can't be trusted." Also, seeking to justify her tough stance, she referred to a statement made by an Iranian government spokesperson that seemed to interpret the Tehran Declaration as a means to continue producing 20%-enriched uranium. That particular statement would subsequently be corrected by the relevant Iranian officials. And in any case, the issue of enrichment to 20% had not even been the object of detailed discussion between the three countries, and certainly did not feature, either explicitly or implicitly, in the Declaration. I reminded Hillary that the points raised by President Obama in his letter to Lula had been adequately dealt with. I also pointed out that the Declaration included commitments the Iranian government had never previously accepted even verbally, never mind in writing. All the ambiguities and complications surrounding the "swap location" and the "simultaneity," along with the attempts to reduce the quantity of LEU to be handed over, had been expressly resolved in the text of the Declaration. Once again, just as in the telephone conversation that had preceded my trip, I said I was well aware that there were other issues to address but that the objective of the agreement, as stated by the US president himself in his letter to Lula, was to "build confidence." Our expectation was that the text would be read in that light.[49]

I knew very well that my arguments were not going to convince the secretary of state, but I made a point of saying clearly that Brazil now felt it had greater backing in continuing to seek a peaceful, negotiated solution. Those arguments were presented more formally in a letter President Lula sent to President Obama on May 24. Lula wrote that "the Declaration involved the country's most senior leaders ... despite the well-known internal resistance." He concluded the letter as follows: "For all these reasons, I am convinced, more than ever, that the swap deal can be a gateway to a negotiated solution to the Iranian nuclear issue as a whole."

I also took the opportunity of the stop-off at Torrejón to speak to Lula, who was already in the hotel in Madrid. He told me he had spoken to Medvedev and that the next day he would talk to Hu Jintao and Sarkozy. He said Medvedev thought sanctions were no longer appropriate, given the progress that had been achieved. I have always suspected that this version of what the Russian president said—the optimistic version, perhaps—was in fact due to an error of translation, and later events would prove I was right to be skeptical. My main concern at that moment was to return quickly to Brazil and make the necessary phone calls: to the members of the Security Council, including the non-permanent ones; to the high representative of the European Union; to the UN secretary-general; and, of course, to Ahmet Davutoglu and Manouchehr Mottaki, whom I needed to stay in close contact with as events relating to Tehran Declaration unfolded.

I arrived in Brasilia early in the morning of May 18. Around 11 a.m. I made my first call, to Sergey Lavrov; later I phoned other foreign ministers including China's Yang Jiechi. The following day I spoke to the EU representative, Catherine Ashton, and to Katsuya Okada of Japan. The telephone marathon would continue for the rest of the week. I spoke to my counterparts from the member countries of the Security Council or/and the P5+1, one by one, or to other officials who had some degree of influence over those bodies' decisions. The majority of them recognized the value of Brazil's and Turkey's efforts. Nothing they said, however, gave me hope that they would vote against sanctions, or even abstain. I knew that while I was making my calls, and no doubt Davutoglu was making his, the US State Department's powerful political-diplomatic machine was already clicking into gear. Indeed, I imagine that is precisely why it was difficult to get hold of certain ministers, particularly those of the less powerful countries. Clearly they were trying to avoid talking to me, and probably also my Turkish counterpart, about the Iranian issue. Eventually, however, my persistence paid off and I managed to speak to all of them.

Looking at my diary for the days following the Tehran Declaration, I see my time was spent not only on those phone calls but also on trying to communicate what we had achieved both to the public (in Brazil and abroad) and to members of Congress. This was vital because as I knew only too well, above all from my experiences in the WTO, how the media can be used to construct and consolidate versions of events that best suit the interests of the major powers. In the midst of otherwise negative news coverage, some foreign papers did publish positive interpretations of the agreement. An important *Financial Times* journalist, Philip Stephens, supported the Brazilian-Turkish initiative.[50] Roger Cohen wrote in the *New York Times* that in criticizing the agreement and declaring it to be insufficient, Washington was moving the goalposts.[51] At the end of May, in Brazil, the *Jornal do Brasil* published a long interview with Mohamed El-Baradei,[52] the former director of the IAEA and Nobel Prize winner, in whose office the original terms of the swap deal had been drawn up. There was no one more authoritative or impartial on the issue of what had been achieved in Tehran. El-Baradei said that to reject the Tehran Declaration, as the US and other countries were doing, was contradictory to say the least. As he put it, they were "refusing to take yes for an answer."[53] Meanwhile, I took the opportunity to insist that my Iranian counterpart, whom I had spoken to twice during the preceding days (according to a note in my diary on May 21), should send the letter to the IAEA as quickly as possible. The letter was in fact sent on the last day of the timeframe set out in the Tehran Declaration.

As the days went by, I was losing hope that the Declaration might serve as a confidence-building instrument capable of persuading the UN Security Council not to adopt sanctions. On July 4 I received a copy of the document that would be delivered to the IAEA by the Vienna Group.[54] This *aide-mémoire* was, in my opinion, a jumble of ill-thought-out criticisms and half-truths, purporting to identify the shortcomings of the trilateral agreement. It referred to issues that, in our understanding and also that of El-Baradei (as expressed in the aforementioned interview), were supposed to be discussed at a later stage. The letter from the Vienna Group also contained observations on procedural issues that were only of secondary importance and could easily be resolved on the first day of any discussions. One example, taken from my notes, is that the letter said it was not clear when the one-month period in which Iran would deliver the LEU would actually begin. Such petty objections made clear the ill will with which the text of the declaration had been analyzed. It seemed the instruction to the writers of the *aide-mémoire* must have been: "Find as many problems as you can." In the case of Russia, such an attitude was surprising. Also, the intransigence of the Vienna Group raised doubts, to say the least, about the sincerity of the statements I had heard from the French president, reiterated by his aides, about their willingness to "engage" with Iran as soon as certain conditions were met—principal among them being the release of the young French woman Clotilde Reiss, which took place early in the morning of the day Lula arrived in Tehran.[55]

Toward the end of the same day, July 4, there was more bad news: the conversations at a technical level in the Security Council had come to an end and the text of the draft resolution was going to be voted on the following week. In all these actions it was clear that the United States and its allies felt they were racing against the clock, their aim being to avoid any facts arising that might get in the way of the approval of new sanctions.

THE SANCTIONS

It is unsure whether May 17 will come to be regarded as a historic date, as *Le Monde* declared in its editorial, but June 9 certainly will be. That was the day when, for the first time ever (my assistants reliably inform me), a UN Security Council resolution was adopted but with Brazil voting against it. On previous occasions Brazil had registered its disagreement with approved resolutions (for example on Haiti in 1994) by abstaining. But the Iran issue went deeper. Together with Turkey, Brazil had been committed to bringing about a peaceful and negotiated solution that we believed would open the way to a useful dialogue with positive implications for the stability of the Middle East as a whole. Quite apart from that, Brazil, like Turkey, had been encouraged—urged, in fact—to contribute to finding just such a solution. Merely to abstain would not have been sufficient to express our disagreement and—I see no reason to mince my words—indignation. And so, on June 9, together with Turkey, Brazil voted against the draft resolution that established new sanctions against Iran.[56] Those were the only two votes against. Lebanon abstained. Our position was decided upon after various phone conversations and other communications during the weekend and right up until the morning of June 9, when there were calls between Lula and Erdogan. The last of those calls took place just as the Security Council session was starting. Less than a fortnight earlier, during a meeting on the margins of the Alliance of Civilizations Forum in Rio de Janeiro, the Turkish prime minister and Lula had agreed that if a draft resolution with sanctions were put forward, Turkey and Brazil would vote against. "It's a question of honor!" Erdogan had said. But in the days preceding the vote I had the impression that Turkey, or at least some of its diplomats, was wavering. The truth is that the pressure Washington was exerting on Ankara was stronger than that experienced by Brazil. Although it was unprecedented for Brazil to express disagreement by means of a negative vote on a resolution that was bound to be approved by the Security Council, we were generally seen by the US government as a country not easily pushed into alignment with the positions of the dominant power. This "rebellious" attitude manifested itself mainly in forums on economic and commercial issues, but it was also present with regard to sensitive issues addressed by the UNSC. From the US point of view, this could be uncomfortable, but it was not a serious problem. However, in the case of Turkey—a NATO member, strategically located between the Middle East and Europe, and also close to Russia—a rebellious stance was less tolerable. In the run-up to the vote, Erdogan received a call from Obama, and also an appeal from the Lebanese prime minister, Saad Hariri, who feared the vote might upset the political balance in his country between pro-western and pro-Iran factions. It would be understandable, therefore, if sectors of the Turkish government hesitated over voting "no" to a US proposal on an issue Washington deemed to be of great strategic importance. With the Security Council session about to start or already underway, it was the phone call between Lula and Erdogan, in which the words spoken in their conversation two weeks previously were recalled, that sealed the two countries' vote against the draft resolution. Davutoglu and I were listening in on the call, which was interrupted a few times to allow Erdogan to speak to the Iranian president.

That same morning, I spoke at length both with Lula and our ambassador to the UN, Maria Luiza Viotti. Maria Luiza showed great character and conviction. She gave a great speech, which she herself had written with the assistance of her aides and a few small alterations and extra suggestions from me. One of those suggestions actually stemmed from a request from Lula that the issue of "honor" should be mentioned. Ambassador Viotti found an elegant way to do so, by stating that Brazil was "honoring the proposals that inspired the efforts that resulted in the Tehran Declaration of May 17." I watched the Security Council proceedings on the BBC, which gave live coverage to the first three explanations of vote. The first was that of Brazil, read with great calmness by our representative. Her serene but firm tone contrasted with that of the Turkish ambassador, who seemed rather ill at ease during his speech. The next speech was given by the US representative, Susan Rice, whose speech was also broadcast live by the BBC. Next on the list of speakers was the British ambassador, but interestingly, just as he began his address, the voice of the BBC commentator cut in, leaving him mouthing his words silently on the screen. The moment seemed to reflect a perception on the part of the BBC that in certain cases the positions of two non-permanent members of the Security Council can be more significant than those of members of the P5, even including the broadcaster's home country.

The explanation of vote read by the Brazilian ambassador presented the reasons that had led us to take our unprecedented position. One of those points concerned the haste with which the countries that have the decision-making power on the Security Council acted in this case. The same eagerness to engineer a *fait accompli* had been evident on the part of the secretary of state in my phone conversation with her during my stop-over in Madrid on the way back to Brazil a few hours after the Tehran Declaration had been signed. The unspecific nature of her criticisms, her return to arguments such as "Iran can't be trusted," her insistent reiteration that the strategy of sanctions would not be altered: it all smacked of an attitude that could be summarized as: "I haven't read it but I don't like it." Further evidence of this undue haste was the absence of anything like a reasonable interval between the presentation by the Vienna Group of its comments on the Tehran Declaration and the Security Council session at which the sanctions were approved. My aides calculated that in fact, taking into account the different time zones, little more than six hours elapsed between the delivery of the *aide-mémoire* and the beginning of the UNSC meeting. What that meant in practice is that even if Iran had accepted all the criticisms and capitulated in the face of all the Vienna Group's demands, there still would not have been time to halt the process set in motion in the Security Council. To use a legal analogy, seldom has expediency prevailed in such an arbitrary way over the legitimate right to a defense.

In her explanation of vote, as well as criticizing the excessive acceleration of the procedures, Ambassador Viotti pointed out the inefficiency of sanctions as an instrument for securing Iran's cooperation, which was indispensable in trying to ensure that the country's nuclear program was exclusively peaceful in nature. She drew attention, very appropriately, to the suffering of the Iranian people as a result of the sanctions, and also reminded her audience of the tragic consequences of the economic restrictions previously imposed by the Security Council in the case of Iraq. She conveyed the essence of the Tehran Declaration in saying that it combined two equally important objectives: recognition of Iran's right to use nuclear energy for peaceful purposes, and in return, full verifiable assurances that the country's nuclear program did not have any non-peaceful purpose. When she said that the "Tehran Declaration showed that dialogue and persuasion can do more than punitive actions," Ambassador Viotti summed up the thinking that had inspired all our efforts.

Ambassador Viotti also signaled our "grave concern" at the absolute lack of transparency that had characterized the internal consultations between the permanent members of the Security Council. There was something paradoxical and difficult to explain in the fact that while commissions and working groups composed of UN member states went about their work of trying to improve the functioning of the Security Council, when a concrete case arose which had implications for the entire multilateral system, the P5 demonstrated their unwillingness to share with the other members of the Security Council the decision-making process on matters of strategic interest to them. It was only due to Brazil's and Turkey's insistence that, on the eve of the adoption of the resolution condemning Iran, an open session was held in which our arguments could at least be heard.

I think it is appropriate to finish this section by reproducing some notes I made on June 5, four days before the UNSC vote: "The process is coming to an end. The arrogance of the P5, including China and Russia, which negotiated exemptions in accordance with their own exclusive interests, has prevailed over the conciliatory efforts of two outsiders. The global political system is still incapable of absorbing the changes [that have taken place] in the geometry of power. But inevitably that will happen, even if [the wait] lasts twenty or thirty years. And [when it happens] it will help bring peace to the world."

IMPACT AND DEVELOPMENTS

Brazil's involvement in the search for a peaceful and negotiated solution to the issue of Iran's nuclear program had reached a climax with the Tehran Declaration. In a way, this high-point was maintained, albeit in a painful way, right up until the adoption of sanctions. From that moment, the question hanging over us—which I remember was put to me directly by, among others, the Brazil correspondent of the *Financial Times*—was whether we would still have a role to play in the new reality created by Security Council Resolution 1929 (2010). It was not an easy question to answer. The episode had certainly left some wounds; it would take time for them to heal. I did not respond, therefore, when the secretary of state sent the message, through a spokesperson, that Brazil could still have a role to play in a future resumption of dialogue with Iran. Nor was I receptive to the repeated attempts by the diplomatic advisor to President Sarkozy, Jean-David Levitte, to involve Brazil in a possible initiative alongside France in that direction. At one point Levitte, who seemed not to realize how disappointed we were with the sinuous behavior of the French government during the whole episode, actually proposed, through an intermediary, a Franco-Brazilian initiative at the G20 summit set to take place in Toronto in late June. I politely replied, through my chief of staff, that it was not the right time for such joint ventures. But a few days later, when I was in Bulgaria as part of a European trip during which I had the chance to discuss Iran with various interlocutors and also at three public lectures, Levitte called me and raised the issue again. He told me, in a confidential tone, that the Vienna Group was intending to request that IAEA director-general Yukiya Amano convene a technical meeting with Iran in which there would be a joint review of the Tehran Declaration and of the *aide-mémoire* with the Vienna Group's comments. Levitte asked me if I agreed with the idea. Maintaining the friendly tone that characterized my dialogue with him, I said I had nothing against it but that the opinion that mattered in this case was not Brazil's: it was Iran's. There were other, similar moves in the days and weeks that followed. When I returned from Europe I told President Lula about these attempts to prolong our role in the Iran issue even after the adoption of sanctions. Lula agreed with my thoughts. "We'll only get involved again if it's at Iran's request," he said.

During my tour of countries in eastern and central Europe, which included a stop in Vienna, I continued to have contact with Davutoglu and Mottaki, though no longer at the frenetic pace of the period preceding the Tehran Declaration. Even if only for the sake of my own conscience, I felt I should test the willingness of Iran to resume some kind of dialogue with the countries of the Vienna Group, and did so in a coordinated way with my Turkish counterpart. To my surprise, Mottaki's reaction was not negative. He insisted only that any meeting with the United States, France and Russia should be preceded by a meeting with Brazil and Turkey, which in his words were "co-owners of the Tehran Declaration."

There was a reason why, in public statements during my European trip, I wanted to bring up the Iranian issue even though the period of negotiations and talks had been brought to a close with the adoption of sanctions. Opinions on the Tehran Declaration and the preceding diplomatic efforts were divided. There were important voices highlighting the value of what had been achieved thanks to Brazil's and Turkey's efforts. The endorsements came from different quarters. The positive assessment made by El-Baradei had been gratifying; indeed, it was quoted, with his permission, by Brazil's permanent representative during the aforementioned "open debate" in the Security Council on the eve of the sanctions vote. Thomas R. Pickering, who had been under secretary of state for political affairs and ambassador in Moscow (besides being one of the most respected names in the US in the field of international disarmament and arms control), was among those who pointed out the importance of the Declaration in the context of the Iranian issue.[57] Former French and British ambassadors to Tehran welcomed the progress represented by the Declaration while expressing disappointment at their countries' negative reaction. The Organization of the Islamic Conference, whose membership includes countries that are certainly no allies of Iran, issued a positive statement regarding the Turkish-Brazilian initiative. On Brazil's role in the world, a BBC article on June 9 quoted the views of academics and other experts, among them the president of the Inter-American Dialogue, Michael Shifter, and a professor of Middle Eastern and Islamic Studies at New York University, Zachary Lockman, both of whom noted that the actions Brazil had undertaken with Turkey on such a delicate issue reinforced our position as a "major player" on the international stage.

To say the least, however, not all assessments were favorable. In Brazil, there was a clear attempt on the part of the opposition parties and sections of the media to depict the Security Council vote as a "defeat." In order to clarify our position and offer a realistic view of what had happened, I readily accepted an invitation to attend a hearing of the foreign affairs committee of the Chamber of Deputies,[58] which actually took place on the same day as the vote itself. The hearing began at 2:30 p.m., less than two hours after the sanctions had been approved. After that, there was quite a long press conference at Itamaraty, and I also gave one-to-one interviews to various Brazilian and foreign journalists. In the same vein, I felt I should take advantage of public events during my European trip due to begin on June 11, which would take place at three different forums: the Conference on Disarmament (CD) in Geneva, the Diplomatic Academy of Vienna, and a round-table discussion in Paris organized by the *International Herald Tribune*. On those occasions, in addition to describing the Tehran Declaration and giving a general sense of the Brazilian-Turkish initiative, I very deliberately drew attention to certain points. In the CD, for example, I concluded my presentation by emphasizing that "when the parties decide to return to the negotiating table, they'll face an even bigger challenge." A cursory comparison between the agreement the P5+1 and Iran arrived at in Geneva in November 2013 and the situation at the time of the Tehran Declaration shows, unfortunately, that I was right. I referred earlier to the fact that whereas in May/June 2010 Iran had a stock of 2,000 kilograms of LEU or slightly more, by the time of the interim agreement with the P5+1 in 2013, it possessed more than 7,000 kilograms (and that amount will continue to grow). To my mind this is just one example of the negative consequences—including from the point of view of the western countries themselves—arising from the rejection of the "confidence-building gesture" that the Declaration represented.[59] I also tried to make clear during those European lectures that Brazil could no longer engage in discussions on the issue on the basis of ambiguous encouragement from the P5+1 countries: an absolutely clear position on their part would be necessary in order for us to get involved again.

That the Tehran Declaration was not entirely absent from our agenda was clear in the references made to the issue in talks between President Lula and the leaders of other countries who made visits to Brazil. At the end of June we received a visit from the Italian prime minister, Silvio Berlusconi, who is now in disgrace following various scandals. The then Italian leader, who Lula had visited in 2008, had participated in the G8 and G20 summits in Canada. The latter summit, in fact, had been seen by Levitte as potentially the occasion for launching the Franco-Brazilian initiative—a suggestion I had rejected. Lula, busy dealing with severe floods in the northeast of Brazil, did not attend. In the private part of the meeting, held at the headquarters of the São Paulo industrial federation, the main topic of discussion, at Lula's instigation, was Iran. Before Lula could describe Brazil's position, Berlusconi said that the Tehran Declaration had been the subject of discussions on the margins of the G8 summit, the final statement from which had made a positive though somewhat condescending reference to "the efforts of Brazil and Turkey."[60] Interestingly, Berlusconi said that certain leaders, especially Obama and Sarkozy, had described the Brazilian initiative as "naive." Assuming

Berlusconi was telling the truth (and what reason did he have to lie?), this diminished even further the credibility of the overtures toward Brazil that Levitte had outlined just a few days before. The next day, Lula received a visit from the Syrian president, Bashar al-Assad,[61] who mentioned the Tehran Declaration as an example of how Brazil's credentials as an international mediator had been bolstered.

On July 4, while accompanying Lula on another African tour, I received a call from Davutoglu. He told me briefly about a conversation that had taken place a few days before between Erdogan and Obama, and one he himself had had with General Jim Jones. In fact, our ambassador in Washington, Mauro Vieira, who was in quite close contact with Turkey's ambassador, had already outlined what he had heard about the Erdogan-Obama encounter, describing it to me as "a kind of catharsis, with both of them giving reasons for their opposing attitudes on the Iran issue." Davutoglu was very frank during our phone conversation, telling me that the US president had expressed disappointment at the Turkish vote. As for General Jones, he had told my Turkish counterpart that in principle he was positively disposed toward the possibility of further participation by Brazil and Turkey in a future dialogue with Iran—but it seems he was speaking more out of politeness than conviction, for neither Jones nor any other US official did anything to follow up on that idea. Davutoglu also seemed more optimistic than I was about the French position. During our phone conversation we spoke about the idea, broached by Mottaki, of a trilateral meeting in Tehran. Davutoglu was more cautious about that. We agreed that such a meeting, on Iranian soil, could only take place after some kind of clear sign from the Vienna Group. Iran, for its part, was still determined to demonstrate its flexibility. Days earlier, the chairman of the foreign relations committee of the Iranian parliament had stated that the country could stop producing 20%-enriched uranium if it were to receive the fuel for its research reactor in accordance with the Tehran Declaration. Amid these vaguely positive gestures, however, came a statement from Lavrov that poured cold water on any renewed optimism that might have been building up. My Russian counterpart asserted that Brazil and Turkey would not participate in the negotiations between the Vienna Group and Iran. To this day I do not quite understand why he was so peremptory in anticipating a likely US veto of such participation. Perhaps it reflected an unwillingness to see other powers (albeit only "middle" ones) getting involved in a region where Russia has always exerted influence. His view was consistent, however, with what Mottaki said he was hearing from other interlocutors. One of them, I suppose, would have been Levitte, who made a point of telling me, in a positive tone, about the conversation that finally took place between Sarkozy and Ahmadinejad, more than two months after the release of Clotilde Reiss and the Tehran Declaration.

In the first couple of weeks of July I had frequent contact with my Iranian and Turkish counterparts. It was during a phone call to Mottaki that I first raised, with the necessary tact, my concerns following the news that an Iranian woman, Sakineh Mohammadi Ashtiani, had been condemned to death by stoning, allegedly for having committed adultery. Humanitarian issues were to become increasingly prominent in my communications with Iranian leaders; at no point had they been entirely absent, in fact. In addition to the Clotilde Reiss situation, I remember that prior to the Tehran Declaration I had mentioned to Mottaki the imprisonment of an Iranian filmmaker, who was eventually released after a substantial bail payment. And on various occasions I brought up the situation of the three American hikers Hillary Clinton had told me about in our conversation just before I left with Lula for Iran. One of these adventurers (suspected by Tehran of being spies), Sarah Shourd, would be freed in September 2010. Shortly afterwards, during the UN General Assembly, she came to the Brazilian mission to thank me for Brazil's interest in the case (she was accompanied by the mothers of the other two detainees, who at that point had not yet been freed). When I met Ahmadinejad on the sidelines of that same UNGA, a few months after the aforementioned phone conversation with Mottaki, he showed he was aware of Lula's concerns regarding Sakineh's predicament and tried to clarify the legal situation. Although I must say he did not entirely reassure me, as doubts remained about what would actually happen to Sakineh, the fact that the Iranian president himself brought up the subject was recognition of the legitimacy of our concerns.[62] That in itself was uncommon in Iran, where the government's prickliness toward foreign interference had been exacerbated by the number of international resolutions on the human rights situation in the country. At our meeting in September, Ahmadinejad referred to the Tehran Declaration as "the only solution" to the nuclear stand-off. He also said he was willing to look at the case of the two Americans who were still detained, and instructed one of his aides to discuss the matter directly with the two mothers. A few months later, with the help of certain other factors, both were released.

In one of our phone conversations in late June or early July, Davutoglu and I agreed to meet on July 25 in Istanbul, where I would make a stop on the way to Israel. In principle it would be a bilateral meeting, but with the possibility that Mottaki might join us. The main destinations scheduled for that trip—Jerusalem, Damascus and Ramallah—showed that the Iranian issue was already becoming secondary in my agenda. As it turned out, the bilateral meeting with Davutoglu was indeed dominated by other subjects, including Turkey's relations with Israel in the wake of the incident with the Gaza Freedom Flotilla.[63] After the meeting, in which it was again evident that our positions coincided, Davutoglu and I were joined for lunch by Mottaki. This trilateral meeting, the first since the signing of the Tehran Declaration, had to be quite short because of my scheduled departure for Israel, where I was due to meet Prime Minister Benjamin Netanyahu. But it nevertheless had some symbolic value, showing that the three countries were still engaged in the pursuit of dialogue, and that the cautious approach of Brazil and Turkey following the sanctions in no way implied passivity or indifference. We reiterated our shared conviction that the Tehran Declaration continued to be a useful tool for negotiation, even in the new situation following the sanctions. At the same time, Brazil and Turkey reaffirmed their willingness to continue supporting dialogue, if that was the wish of all the parties involved. Davutoglu and I tried to emphasize to Mottaki the importance of Brazil and Turkey continuing to be seen as potential facilitators, not as part of a "bloc" that was opposed to the P5+1. The latter misconception seemed at times to permeate the suggestions made by our Iranian counterpart, so we felt we had to be clear on the issue. Furthermore, we insisted that if any future negotiations did indeed make progress toward a peaceful solution, Iran should respond by ceasing to enrich uranium to 20%. We also spoke about practical steps, including a possible meeting between Saeed Jalili and EU representative Catherine Ashton, who seemed increasingly involved in the Iranian issue (indeed, I had spoken to her about it in Madrid during the preparations for the summit of the EU-Brazil Strategic Partnership). Also during that lunch in Istanbul, which took place in one of the elegant Ottoman palaces beside the Bosphorus, Mottaki announced that the following day Iran would respond to a communiqué from the IAEA that had relayed the comments of the Vienna Group. Contrary to what he had indicated during earlier telephone conversations, Mottaki did not disclose the contents of that response. Given my haste to leave, I suggested that Davutoglu should speak in my name at the press conference to follow, because after our earlier bilateral meeting I had already conveyed publicly most of what I felt I needed to say. Mottaki was not keen on the suggestion, fearing my absence might be interpreted by the media as evidence that Brazil was backing off from the issue. The solution I suggested was that the three of us should leave together, thereby creating a good opportunity for the photographers.

If I said that those two meetings in Istanbul were the last act in the drama (if I can use that word to describe Brazil's involvement in the Iranian nuclear issue), it would probably feel like an anticlimactic end to this story. But essentially it would be true. From that point onward Brazil did not participate in any meeting or other event that was in any way related to the negotiating process. That is not to say, however, that Iran disappeared altogether from our agenda. I carried on speaking about the Tehran Declaration at conferences such as the one held by the Institute for Strategic Studies in Geneva, and at public debates such as the one I had with Thomas Friedman when I went to Washington to receive an award from *Foreign Policy* magazine.[64] It was on that occasion, in fact, that I heard the then Senator John Kerry express recognition of the Turkish-Brazilian efforts, albeit in the rather patronizing tone by then familiar from so many statements by western leaders. Moreover, his praise was accompanied by threatening words toward Tehran. I also dealt with the Iranian issue on more formal occasions, such as the address to the opening session of the UN General Assembly; and again, although this time rather more subliminally, at a high-level meeting of the UN Security Council on September 23, during Turkey's temporary presidency.[65]

Even after I left the post of foreign minister at the end of President Lula's second term of office, I continued to receive invitations from important institutions that wanted to hear Brazil's perspective on the Iranian nuclear issue. They included one from the Carnegie Endowment for International Peace, which asked me to be the key-note speaker at its conference on nuclear policy on March 28, 2011.[66] Researchers of various nationalities continued to show an interest in the Brazilian view.[67] Interest on the part of the Brazilian media was further sharpened by the understandings reached between the P5+1 and Iran in 2013, which inevitably gave rise to comparisons between the terms of the "interim agreement" and those of the Tehran Declaration.[68] I myself was asked to make that comparison, which is certainly not a simple exercise. Whereas the Tehran Declaration, although the result of laborious negotiations, was essentially a unilateral confidence-building gesture on the part of Iran, the current understandings are the result of a bargain entailing reciprocal concessions. The interim agreement of November 2013 was a very positive step and should be welcomed as such. All those who sincerely want a peaceful solution to the issue—which for years has tested the "international community" and its capacity for negotiation—must support the agreement and hope that in time it becomes a definitive instrument.[69] The fact remains, however, that when they discarded the opportunity presented by the Tehran Declaration in 2010, the members of the P5+1, especially the US, showed a lamentable preference for sanctions as a means of resolving disputes. The option they chose not only led to unnecessary hardships for the Iranian people but also wasted a chance to achieve an agreement on more favorable terms. To focus on just one aspect, and to adopt the reasoning of those who are most fearful a nuclear-armed Iran, it should be noted that whereas at that time Iran had sufficient LEU to produce one bomb, today (March/April 2014) it possesses enough to build, in theory, three or four such weapons. It is true that, in part, this can be compensated for by more stringent inspections—but that possibility also existed at the time of the Declaration. Indeed, following on from the confidence-building measures, stringent inspections would naturally and logically have been carried out in exchange for the alleviation and potential lifting of sanctions.

I do not share the fear that Iran is seeking to build a nuclear arsenal, even though I acknowledge that one of its possible objectives is to arrive at the "threshold" of such a capacity. We cannot forget that the region includes a state—Israel—that is known to possess a powerful nuclear arsenal. That is why we have insisted that a lasting solution to the issue lies in an agreement to make the Middle East a zone free of nuclear weapons. Comparing the negotiations of 2013–2014 with those of 2010, the change in position on the part of the P5+1 countries only serves to underline their haste and inflexibility at the time of the Tehran Declaration. But beyond the clauses on certain specific aspects, the biggest contribution Brazil and Turkey made through the Tehran Declaration was to show, despite the disbelief on the part of most of those involved, that the path of dialogue is an option that can be pursued successfully, as long as there is good faith and persistence on all sides. It was that belief that led Brazil—and Turkey—to insist on a path that seemed to many to have become blocked after the phone call from Hillary Clinton on May 11, 2010. As for me personally, I have always believed that the pursuit of diplomacy involves deliberate optimism, even when the chances of success seem low. Often it is necessary to "bet" on a negotiated solution, even though it might involve a degree of risk. Brazil and Turkey were well aware of that risk, but still chose to stick to the peaceful path.[70]

As for the impact of our joint efforts with Turkey on Brazil's international prestige, so frequently the subject of negative evaluations from the Brazilian media, I should also mention an article in the *Economist* on Turkish foreign policy,[71] in which Brazil was mentioned more than once in the context of the Tehran Declaration. Though critical of the Declaration, the article referred to Turkey's association with a "diplomatic giant": Brazil. The most curious aspect of this little piece of flattery is that the magazine had previously criticized many of our initiatives and attitudes on the international stage, whether on economic (FTAA, WTO) or political issues (Mercosur/UNASUR, and indeed the Middle East itself). Many of those criticisms from the *Economist* reflect positions adopted by influential journalists and public figures in Brazil, who in turn tend to be influenced by the foreign media. And so one might ask, with a touch of irony, how a succession of supposed "failures" resulted in this elevation of our status in the international arena. This is a question that deserves some thought if we wish, as naturally we do, to have some influence over the course of the events that shape our world.

BRAZIL AND "THE GREAT GAME"

During this narrative I have referred more than once to the fact that the Brazilian media, in general, have been more critical of our positions than their counterparts elsewhere—including the media in countries that might well have felt challenged by some of our initiatives. The issue I have not addressed is why such an attitude exists in the first place. There is, of course, the so-called "mongrel complex" that Nelson Rodrigues[72] talked about; and there are those who will go in search of Freudian interpretations of that complex. For my part I would rather limit myself to political-diplomatic considerations. In July 2011 the Council on Foreign Relations in the United States recommended that Washington undertake a policy review in relation to Brazil, taking into account the new status the country had achieved.[73] The group that drew up the report included distinguished figures from academia and individuals connected with US diplomacy, such as Nick Burns and David Rothkopf. The report singled Brazil out among Latin American nations and expressed support for our bid for a permanent seat on the UN Security Council. In an article I wrote shortly afterwards for the Brazilian magazine *Carta Capital*, I said it was strange that the report had aroused little interest in Brazil—especially because it focused on a subject frequently discussed by Brazilian journalists, who were generally critical of our diplomatic ambitions.[74]

More than any other diplomatic initiative of recent years or indeed decades, our efforts—alongside Turkey—to negotiate a peaceful path for Iran's nuclear program brought us closer to what might be described as "The Great Game" of international politics. That was the expression Rudyard Kipling used in his novel *Kim* to describe the jostling between the two great empires of the second half of the nineteenth century, the British and the Russian, particularly with regard to what the former considered the jewel in its crown, India. For Britain it was a question of containing Tsarist expansionism, whether in the Middle East or Central Asia, and denying Russia access to the Indian subcontinent. "The Great Game" today is different, obviously, and yet in a way it still takes place in the Middle East, a region in which, like it or not, Iran plays a major role.

Perhaps an aversion to participating in this game explains why our initiatives were received with such hostility by a large part of the Brazilian media. Those initiatives were often misrepresented in a way that suggested Brazil was eagerly seeking proximity with a regime considered to be despotic and a serial violator of human rights, or wanting simply to "provoke" the North American giant. We were doing nothing of the sort, as the comments from foreign experts and my own analyses throughout this narrative make very clear. Outside Brazil, even those commentators who disagreed with our positions did so with seriousness and respect.

In nearly half a century as a diplomat, I have been able to observe that in most countries the government's participation in efforts to address major international political and economic issues, even those that do not impinge directly on domestic matters, tend to elicit satisfaction and pride. It intrigued me that in Brazil, however, our initiatives were generally considered an unnecessary and dangerous intrusion into issues that did not concern us. I wondered (and still wonder) about the reason for this attachment to a secondary and dependent position that seems to be so deeply rooted among our media commentators. In a way it is as if we are afraid of shouldering the burdens that are a natural corollary of growth and maturity, and prefer instead to hide in the shadow of a bigger power, real or imaginary, even if that means discarding opportunities and sacrificing our interests. But perhaps I should leave that question to sociologists and other students of collective psychology.

In considering these issues, an observation made by San Tiago Dantas[75] about independence in foreign policy comes to mind. Reflecting on the criticism that came his way in response to the positions Brazil adopted during his time at the helm of Itamaraty, San Tiago said: "It was natural to find rising up against [our] political position the incomprehension of some, the challenged interests of many, and the exaggerated zeal of those who are afraid to displease powerful friends, although in general those friends are more understanding than they are toward Brazil's positions. . . . The people, however, applauded, and quickly incorporated it into their political outlook."[76] The relevance of these reflections to Brazilian diplomacy in the case of the Tehran Declaration is really quite striking.

Before he took office as foreign minister, in the speech he made upon leaving the Chamber of Deputies in 1961, San Tiago left us with a lesson that still seems not to have been properly learned, and one that is also a fitting way to bring this narrative to an end:

> And so, today, our country is no longer as it might have appeared to the idealistic generation who participated in the hopes and failures of the League of Nations: a secondary country, destined in world politics to play the role of mere accomplice, albeit often an illustrious one. Our responsibilities today are already those of a country that can speak for others. Today, above all, we are able to make an impartial contribution not only to solving problems in which we find ourselves directly implicated, but also to solving other problems which we contemplate from a distance but which we, like any other mature people, feel a responsibility to deal with in a positive way.[77]

July 2014[78]

NOTES

1. See also the narrative on Brazil and the Middle East.

2. The Summit of South American-Arab countries—or ASPA, to use its South American acronym—is a bi-regional forum made up of twelve South American countries and the twenty-two in the Arab League. The first ASPA summit, in 2005, also recognized as members the Arab League and the Union of South American Nations (UNASUR). The creation of ASPA is described in detail in the narrative on Brazil and the Middle East.

3. Permanent representatives to international organizations (such as the UN in New York and the WTO in Geneva) normally also have the more formal title of "ambassador." Throughout this book the two terms are used interchangeably.

4. The full title of the report by Boutros-Ghali was: *New Dimensions of Arms Regulation and Disarmament in the Post-Cold War Era: Report of the Secretary-General on the Occasion of Disarmament Week,* 1992 (UN Doc. A/C. 1/47/7).

5. The conclusions of the Canberra Commission were later taken up again, to a certain extent, in the drawing up of the thirteen steps toward disarmament stated in the final document of the sixth meeting of the Review Conference of the Parties to the Treaty on the Non-Proliferation of Nuclear Weapons , in 2000 (NPT/CONF.2000/28, Parts I and II). On that occasion I was leading the Brazilian delegation, which had a significant role in the context of the so-called "New Agenda Coalition."

6. See the narrative on Brazil and the Middle East.

7. Javier Solana and El-Baradei were not, therefore, the only individuals I talked to about Iran. I had a dialogue with the US secretary of state, Condoleezza Rice, who appears later in this narrative. And during a visit to Moscow, in October 2005, I discussed the matter with Russian foreign minister Sergey Lavrov and with his predecessor, Igor Ivanov, who at the time was secretary of the Security Council of Russia. Lavrov seemed to agree with the idea I had already brought up with certain other contacts, which was that Iran had the right to complete a full nuclear cycle but needed to win back trust. Interestingly, Lavrov revealed to me that Iran wanted to replace the EU-3 (France, Germany, and the UK) with a broader group that would include Russia, China, India, South Africa, and Brazil.

8. The European negotiating group was sometimes called the "EU-3" or "troika." And on more than one occasion the grouping that would come to be known as the P5+1 (see later in this narrative) was referred to as the "E3+3" (denoting the three European countries plus the US, Russia, and China).

9. The Alianza Bolivariana para los Pueblos de Nuestra América (ALBA) is the Spanish name for the group of countries led by Venezuela. At the time of the events recounted here, it was composed of Bolivia, Cuba, Dominica, Nicaragua, and Venezuela. Its ideological position was critical of the capitalist system.

10. Brazil's foreign ministry. The word "Itamaraty" is widely used in Brazil to refer both to the ministry and its headquarters at Itamaraty Palace in Brasilia.

11. Asociación Mutual Israelita Argentina, a Jewish community center. The explosion of a car bomb killed eighty-five people and injured another 300.

12. I use the term "international community" with some reluctance, because often it is employed merely to denote the opinions of a small group of western countries that are members of the UN Security Council.

13. By that time Iran had already been subject to three rounds of sanctions imposed by the Security Council. See Resolution 1737 (2006), 1747 (2007), and 1803 (2008).

14. Resolution of February 4, 2006, by the IAEA Board of Governors (GOV/2006/14).

15. Some years later, it was interesting to see how political commentators in the West suggested that with the conclusion of the Joint Plan of Action on the nuclear issue, Iran might become an important supporter of the peace efforts in Syria.

16. The survey was carried out by Ken Balley and Patrick Doherty for the think tank Terror Free [*sic*] Tomorrow: the Center for Public Opinion, in association with the New America Foundation. Their findings were published in the *Washington Post* on June 15, 2009.

17. In an article about a trip to Iran by a commission of Brazilian parliamentarians in 2014, the Brazilian newspaper *Folha de São Paulo* reported that Brazil-Iran trade declined from $2.4 billion USD in 2011 to $1.6 billion in 2013. It attributed the drop to the sanctions the Iranian government was enduring and a supposed lack of interest in the bilateral relationship on the part of Dilma Rousseff's administration, in contrast with the Lula government. (*Folha de São Paulo*: "*Irã cobra 'retomada' de relação com o Brasil*," February 17, 2014.)

18. The group of major economies. Not to be confused with the G20 of developing nations, the trade negotiations bloc that I refer to frequently in the narrative on the Doha Round.

19. COP15: the 15th Conference of the Parties to the United Nations Framework Convention on Climate Change, which took place in Copenhagen from December 7–18, 2009.

20. Article 24.1: "In order to ensure prompt and effective action by the United Nations, its Members confer on the Security Council primary responsibility for the maintenance of interna-

tional peace and security, and agree that in carrying out its duties under this responsibility the Security Council acts on their behalf."

21. In the case of the IAEA, my pessimistic expectations regarding its new director-general, Yukiya Amano of Japan, proved entirely justified. He took no active role in the events that followed the Tehran Declaration, serving merely as a carrier pigeon between the so-called "Vienna Group" (the US, Russia, and France) and Iran in the period between the Declaration and the adoption of sanctions. During a visit he made to Brazil in relation to our own nuclear program, we had a meeting in which he appeared to conform to his image as an international bureaucrat without any inclination to take an independent stance in relation to the major powers, especially the United States. As for the EU, my friend Catherine Ashton of the United Kingdom would initially take a somewhat timid approach in her role as High Representative for Foreign Affairs and Security Policy. I remember only a long conversation we had in Madrid, after the Tehran Declaration, in the context of preparations for a summit of the EU-Brazil Strategic Partnership, in which she listened attentively but did not engage in the search for a solution. This inhibition was probably due to her being new to the job, and contrasts with her positive role, according to news reports, in the more recent talks between the P5+1 and Iran.

22. The group composed of the five permanent members of the United Nations Security Council, plus Germany.

23. The differences between these two things will be addressed further on in the text, when I describe conversations that took place in Israel a few months later.

24. At this point I should provide a very brief explanation of the concept of enrichment. Uranium in its natural state is composed of two isotopes: U-235 and U-238. The former is unstable and therefore suitable for nuclear fission; it can be used both to produce energy and to make a bomb, as well as having other possible uses (medical, for example). Enrichment essentially consists of increasing, by means of isotopic separation, the proportion of U-235. The process most often used in enriching uranium is that of centrifugation. It is considered that for the purpose of producing electric energy, "low"-enriched uranium is sufficient. For research purposes, this degree of enrichment is higher: generally 20%. For an explosive device, the uranium needs to be enriched to above 80%. According to the experts, making the jump from 4% or 5% to 20% is more complex and difficult than going from 20% to 80%.

25. This de facto acceptance on the part of the P5+1 was one of the aspects of the 2013 interim agreement with Iran.

26. A career diplomat, Sergey Lavrov was ambassador to the UN from 1994 to 2004, when he became Russia's foreign minister in place of Igor Ivanov.

27. The organization is much more commonly known by its acronym in Spanish (UNASUR) or Portuguese (UNASUL).

28. This episode is referred to in some detail in my book *Breves narrativas diplomáticas*, published in Portuguese (Benvirá, 2013) and in Spanish (Taeda, 2014).

29. Mir-Hossein Mousavi Khameneh was Iran's prime minister from 1981 to 1989. He was a presidential candidate in 2009, in the controversial election won by Ahmadinejad. During the protests that followed the announcement of the results, Mousavi played a leading role in the opposition to the government.

30. Having closely followed the international media coverage of this "discovery," which took place during the UN General Assembly two months earlier and was taken as evidence that Iran was acting in bad faith, I cannot fail to note in retrospect that the subject of Qom virtually disappeared from public debate as soon as the P5+1 re-engaged with Iran in 2013. Previously, however, it had been an important issue, and arose again in other conversations I had at that time.

31. A large city in northern Brazil, in the Amazon region. It is the capital of the state of Amazonas.

32. Levitte, who had earlier served both as France's ambassador to the United Nations and to Washington, was to become my principal interlocutor on the Iran issue. It is worth noting that in this period, unlike previously, there was an unofficial division of labor between the diplomatic advisor to the French president, who dealt with issues of a strategic nature, and the French foreign ministry (Quai d'Orsay), which was headed by the likable and media-friendly

Bernard Kouchner, best known for his humanitarian actions at the helm of Médecins sans Frontières and as UN special representative in Kosovo.

33. The resolution was adopted by the Board of Governors on November 27, 2009. It was entitled *Implementation of the NPT Safeguards Agreement and Relevant Provisions of Security Council Resolutions 1737 (2006), 1747 (2007), 1803 (2008) and 1835 (2008) in the Islamic Republic of Iran.*

34. Among the recent surveillance revelations by Edward Snowden, I noticed a comment made during the period described above by a French official, according to whom there was no reason for Washington to worry about France's "understandings" with Brazil on the Iranian nuclear issue. I was rather taken aback by the official's assertion that France's underlying motive in that particular dialogue was simply to keep us engaged in the parallel conversations about our purchase of Rafale fighter aircraft for the Brazilian Air Force.

35. "Averting the Iranian Nuclear Flashpoint," published on March 27, 2010.

36. A group composed of Brazil, India, Germany, and Japan, the four most obvious would-be permanent members of the UN Security Council in the case of a reform.

37. These are the acronyms in Portuguese for the Movimento Popular para a Libertação de Angola, which formed the government, and União Nacional para a Independência Total de Angola, the armed opposition.

38. In 1994, in votes on Haiti, Brazil's abstention certainly had a bearing on China's decision also to abstain.

39. The Nuclear Security Summit took place in Washington from April 12–13, 2010, with the principal aim of strengthening security around countries' stocks of nuclear materials so as to prevent them falling into the hands of terrorists. Forty-seven countries took part, including Brazil.

40. See the narrative on Brazil and the Middle East.

41. By the time of the eventual nuclear agreement between Iran and the P5+1 in July 2015, most experts estimated Iran was in possession of about 10,000 kilograms of LEU.

42. It is particularly interesting here to compare, on the one hand, the secretary of state's idea of the Iranian regime (and government) as intrinsically malevolent and always inclined toward deception and false promises, and on the other, the view President Obama conveyed in an interview with a Bloomberg journalist a few years later, which was much closer to our own perception. On that occasion, when asked about Shia extremism, Obama said: "[The Iranians] are strategic, and they're not impulsive. They have a worldview, and they see their interests … They are a large, powerful country that sees itself as an important player on the world stage, and I do not think has a suicide wish, and can respond to incentives." The interview was quoted by Trita Parsi in an article entitled "Pivot to Persia," published on the website of *Foreign Policy* magazine on June 16, 2014.

43. There was a clear convergence of positions at the IBSA summit, as shown by the fact that the Iranian nuclear issue was mentioned in the countries' joint declaration. The positions of Russia and China were more ambiguous and the joint declaration at the end of the BRICs summit did not mention the issue.

44. Four years later, in July 2014, during a lunch offered by President Dilma Rousseff to Vladmir Putin at Itamaraty, Lavrov and I were both seated at the main table. Though we were some distance from each other, he interrupted a conversation he was having with the Brazilian foreign minister, Luiz Alberto Figueiredo, on the understandings between the P5+1 and Iran, and spoke directly to me: "Do you remember, Celso, the agreement Brazil and Turkey negotiated? If it had been accepted [by Washington], we would have saved a lot of time."

45. In a recent conversation I had with Lula, he speculated that Obama's call to Medvedev and another call he made to the Emir of Qatar (ahead of Lula's stop in Doha en route to Iran) were aimed principally at getting the two leaders to persuade Lula to call off the trip to Tehran. If that really was Obama's intention, it was very presumptuous on his part.

46. See, among others, Baker, P. and Sanger, David E.: "US makes concessions to Russia for Iran Sanctions," *New York Times*, May 21, 2010.

47. I should also mention a curious episode from a few days before. Shortly after my trip to Iran at the end of April, I told Lula I might have to go back there again to try to push forward the negotiations. Although he gave his consent, the trip never took place—due principally to

scheduling difficulties arising from the fact that I wanted the Turkish foreign minister also to be present at the Tehran meeting. However, amid my various other commitments, I forgot to tell Lula I was no longer going. This carelessness on my part was responsible for a comment Lula made to the press that could have been misinterpreted as a slip on his part. In an interview shortly before our departure, Lula said I had made a second trip to Iran during the preceding weeks, which was not in fact the case.

48. The G15 was established in 1989 at the Ninth Non-Aligned Movement Summit Meeting in Belgrade. One of its long-term objectives was to be recognized as a platform for dialogue with the G7 group of highly industrialized nations.

49. In an article entitled "*O diplomata*" published in the Brazilian magazine *Piauí* (no. 80, May 2013), the journalist Cláudia Antunes quotes Ambassador John Limbert, who was dealing with the Iranian dossier at the time when the Tehran Declaration was adopted. According to the journalist, Limbert, who was in Germany when the Declaration was signed, said he was "surprised" by the secretary of state's immediate decision to reject it and that her reaction was not in line with normal diplomatic procedure. The normal response, he suggested, would have been to say: "That's interesting, we need to take a closer look. . . ." The article goes on to say that in the ambassador's opinion, "the agreement matched 85 to 90% of the proposal the United States had approved seven months previously. . . . It also followed the suggestions in the letter sent not long before by Obama to President Lula and to the Turkish prime minister Recep Erdogan." According to Limbert, the agreement arrived at the wrong moment because, after months of trying, Washington had obtained the consent of China and Russia to new UN sanctions.

50. Stephens, Philip. "Rising powers do not want to play by the West's rules," *Financial Times,* May 20, 2010.

51. Cohen, Roger. "America moves the goalposts," *New York Times*, May 20, 2010.

52. Duarte, Joana. "*Sanções vão polarizar hemisférios, diz o Nobel Mohamed El Baradei,*" *Jornal do Brasil*, May 29, 2010.

53. In an article published in *Foreign Policy* on May 17, 2010, Trita Parsi used the same expression in examining the likelihood of the western powers recognizing the Turkish-Brazilian agreement ("The Turkey-Brazil-Iran Deal: Can Washington Take Yes for an Answer?"). He argued that the world's center of geopolitical gravity had shifted and that the Tehran Declaration was important in order to build confidence, which the West had not yet managed to do. Other voices also came to share the opinion that the declaration was a valuable step. One person in particular deserves a mention because at the time she was director of policy planning in the US State Department: Anne Marie Slaughter. In an article published in the *Financial Times* on November 9, 2011, entitled "Diplomacy is the Least Damaging Option with Iran," Slaughter argued that the western powers should "turn back to Brazil and Turkey." She briefly summarized the agreement and stated that its rejection by the western powers represented an opportunity for cooperation with Iran discarded in favor of coercion.

54. The Vienna Group, composed of the United States, France and Russia, can be seen as the "hard core" of the P5+1. It was frequently this smaller group that conducted the negotiations.

55. A few days after her arrival in Paris, the young French student telephoned me in Brazil to express her thanks for our successful efforts.

56. United Nations Security Council Resolution 1929 (2010).

57. "The five permanent members of the UN Security Council plus Germany (P5+1) should take advantage of this opportunity as the first step in a broader dialogue that could include further confidence-building measures." Pickering et al.. "US shouldn't dismiss Turkish-Brazilian nuclear deal," *The Huffington Post*, June 1, 2010.

58. Brazil's lower house of Congress.

59. Even two years on from the Declaration, its importance as a "confidence-building gesture" continued to be stressed by various important figures. See, for example, the article "The Only Option on Iran" by Carl Bildt and Erkki Tuomioja, the foreign ministers of Sweden and Finland respectively, published in the *New York Times* on March 20, 2012. Concerned by the escalating rhetoric about armed intervention at that time, they wrote that: "There is, in our opinion, little doubt that we would be in a better position now had we further explored the diplomatic opening made by Turkey and Brazil in the spring of 2010."

60. See the section "International Peace and Security" of the Final Statement of the G8 summit held on June 26, 2010 in Muskoka, Canada.

61. The main topic on the agenda during Assad's visit was the possibility of Brazil playing a mediating role on the issue of the Golan Heights. For more on this, see the narrative on Brazil and the Middle East.

62. Sakineh was eventually pardoned and released in 2014.

63. The Gaza Freedom Flotilla was organized by the Free Gaza Movement and the Turkish organization Foundation for Human Rights and Freedoms and Humanitarian Relief. Its six vessels were carrying materials to be used as humanitarian aid for the population of the Gaza Strip when they were intercepted by Israeli military forces on May 31, 2010, and prevented from reaching their destination. Nine Turkish activists were killed and others were seriously injured. The incident provoked a strong public reaction in Turkey and had a significant negative impact on Turkey-Israel relations.

64. The awards ceremony for the "Top 100 Global Thinkers" of 2010 took place on November 30. *Foreign Policy* had placed Davutoglu and me in sixth and seventh place respectively, with our participation in the Tehran Declaration clearly a major factor in their decision. During the same trip to Washington I also took part in a debate entitled "The New Geopolitics: Emerging Powers and the Challenges of a Multipolar World" at the headquarters of the Carnegie Endowment for International Peace.

65. 6389th Meeting of the United Nations Security Council, September 23, 2010. (Document: S/PV.6389.)

66. The transcription of my speech, and those of the other participants, can be found on the Carnegie Endowment's website.

67. In 2013 I was interviewed by the academic researchers John Tirman, of the Massachusetts Institute of Technology, and Malcolm Byrne, of the National Security Archives. On the subject of Brazilian nuclear policy I particularly recommend *Brazil's Nuclear Kaleidoscope: An Evolving Identity* by Toghzan Kassenova (Carnegie Endowment for International Peace, 2014), which includes a chapter on the Tehran Declaration. Other books covering Brazil's efforts with regard to the Iranian nuclear issue include *A Single Roll of the Dice* by Trita Parsi (Yale University Press, 2013); *Going to Tehran* by Flynt and Hillary Leverett (Metropolitan Books, 2013); and *The Dispensable Nation* by Vali Nasr (Anchor, 2014).

68. *Folha de São Paulo* columnist Clóvis Rossi, for example, wrote two articles: "*O acordo Irã-Lula era o correto*," on October 15, 2013; and "*O acordo Irã-Lula era o melhor*," on November 26, 2013. For a comparative analysis of an academic nature, also in Portuguese, see "*Iran Talks: das Palavras aos Atos. A Declaração de Teerã e o Plano de Ação Conjunto de Genebra em Perspectiva*" by Pérola Pereira and Antonio Jorge Ramalho da Rocha, published in *Contexto Internacional* in 2014.

69. On July 14, 2015, the P5+1 reached agreement with Iran on a Joint Comprehensive Plan of Action.

70. Even after I had finished writing this narrative, the Tehran Declaration continued to be mentioned as an example of the search for peaceful solutions to international disputes. In a speech he made on October 14, 2014, to the UN Committee on the Exercise of the Inalienable Rights of the Palestinian People, the great thinker Noam Chomsky deplored the rejection of the Tehran Declaration by the US as a sign of arrogance. He characterized the US attitude as: "How dare [Brazil and Turkey] do this!" A few months earlier, in an interview with the Chatham House publication *The World Today* (June 2014), Chomsky said that one way to pursue the goal of stopping Iran acquiring nuclear weapons "would have been to have pursued the agreement between Brazil, Turkey and Iran in 2010. . . . As soon as Brazil and Turkey and Iran reached that agreement, they were bitterly denounced by the White House, and of course the press followed along."

71. "Is Turkey turning its back on the West?" (*The Economist*, October 21, 2010).

72. Nelson Rodrigues (1912–1980), a famous Brazilian playwright and journalist, coined the expression "mongrel complex" ("*complexo de vira-lata*") when describing the negative evaluations of the Brazilian media in relation to the country's soccer team during the 1950s.

73. Council on Foreign Relations: *Global Brazil and U.S.-Brazil Relations*. Independent Task Force Report no. 66, July 2011.

74. The article, entitled "*O complexo de vira-lata,*" was published in the edition dated July 25, 2011. I was not serving as a government minister at the time.

75. Francisco Clementino San Tiago Dantas was Brazil's foreign minister between September 1961 and July 1962. He is associated with the pursuit of an "independent" foreign policy in which Brazil would not automatically be aligned with any country or bloc.

76. Dantas, San Tiago. *Política externa independente* (Civilização Brasileira, 1962).

77. Annals of the Chamber of Deputies, August 25, 1961.

78. English translation completed in October 2016.

2. Brazil and the Middle East

TOWARD THE ASPA SUMMIT

First steps

"If the soul is infected with partisanship for a particular opinion . . . it accepts without a moment's hesitation the information that is agreeable to it. Prejudice and partisanship obscure the critical faculty and preclude critical investigation."[1] This observation by the great Arab historian and philosopher of the fourteenth century, Ibn Khaldun, serves quite well as a warning to anyone venturing to study the relations between Brazil and the Middle East during the last ten years.

Despite the immense demographic, cultural and economic contribution that Arab immigrants have made to our society,[2] Brazilian foreign policy tended to keep its distance from issues related to the Middle East and North Africa until the final decades of the twentieth century. Even the presence of a Brazilian military battalion in Suez during the UN peacekeeping operation after the 1956 crisis can be attributed less to a direct interest in the region than to the perception, after the Second World War, that we should contribute to collective security. During the Cold War, greater proximity to the Arab countries was not seen as a priority by those in Brazil who favored special relations with one of the superpowers.[3] A possible exception to this approach was the decision by the elected president Jânio Quadros to include Egypt, under Nasser, in a foreign trip he undertook before taking office. Brazil already had some diplomatic missions in Arab countries (and also in Tel Aviv). Others were opened in the Maghreb in the early 1960s, when countries in that sub-region were gaining their independence.

Until the 1970s it was rare indeed for a Brazilian position on issues related to the Middle East to come to public attention. Brazil simply never used to express opinions on matters that transcended South or Latin America—apart from declaring support, when necessary, for the position of the superpower that we were tied to by hemispheric agreements. Except for the participation of Osvaldo Aranha, as president of the UN General Assembly, in the process through which the State of Israel was created, for 30 years after the Second World War there was no significant Brazilian involvement in the pursuit of solutions for issues in the Middle East. This timidity was consistent with the constraints imposed on our diplomacy during that long period of East-West confrontation. And although we stayed out of the Korean War, thereby avoiding a costly alignment with the United States, it was also the case that apart from during Jânio's brief period as president, Brazil at no point made any gesture that could have been interpreted as a step toward the "neutralist" stance embodied by leaders such as Nehru, Sukarno, and Nasser. The latter, responsible for the nationalization of the Suez Canal, was undoubtedly the greatest and most important leader in the Arab world. In the period when Brazil pursued an independent foreign policy, our diplomacy was decidedly in favor of decolonization, as reflected by the famous speech by Araújo Castro at the UN General Assembly in 1963,[4] and we also took other positions that indicated a desire to act independently on the international stage. And yet, despite that, we almost always remained distant from the major issues that periodically shook the Arab countries.

In the wake of the oil crisis of 1973, Brazil expanded its diplomatic presence in the region through increasing commercial ties, spurred largely by our dependence on Arab oil. During the presidency of Ernesto Geisel, from 1974 to 1979, Brazil began to take a firmer position in favor of the Palestinians' right to self-determination. In 1975, authorization was given for the Palestine Liberation Organization to have a representative in Brazil. In the following years there was increased diplomatic contact with the Gulf countries, especially on economic and energy-related issues. The flows of trade and investment between Brazil and the Arab countries of the Maghreb and the Gulf increased significantly. In Mauritania and Iraq, Brazilian companies built roads and irrigation wells. In Iraq, our companies planned major building projects while Brazilian-made cars circulated on the streets of Baghdad—they were easy to spot in TV footage filmed shortly before the invasion of Kuwait in 1990. In the wake of the First Gulf War in 1991, however, the Brazilian presence in Iraq virtually came to an end, with our companies incurring significant losses.[5]

Brazilians maintained strong personal connections with countries such as Lebanon and Syria, where the vast majority of our Arab immigrants had come from. On my travels, from the 1990s onward, I would frequently hear Arab interlocutors make reference to Brazilian politicians and businesspeople. And the reverse was also true, with various high-profile figures in Brazil mentioning their family ties with Lebanon (and sometimes Syria), where often they had relations still living in small villages in rural areas. However, these personal ties were generally not reflected by any intensification of our political dialogue, which continued to be lukewarm. Even taking into account the relatively low number of foreign trips undertaken by Brazilian presidents before the advent of "presidential diplomacy," it is still surprising that although Brazil has about ten million people of Arab ancestry, Lula in 2003 became the first Brazilian leader to visit the region since Emperor Dom Pedro II in the nineteenth century.

Despite this apparent lack of interest on our part, decision-makers in the Arab world were not unaware of the affinities between Brazil and certain Arab countries, or the balanced positions Brazil adopted in the UN. One noteworthy event took place in 1994, during my first period as foreign minister, when President Itamar Franco was the only Latin American leader to be invited to the signing of the peace treaty between Israel and Jordan. I had the honor of representing the president that day, October 26, at the border crossing point of Wadi Araba, in the desert not far from the Gulf of Aqaba, whose waters lap the coastlines of Israel, Egypt and Jordan. Also in attendance, apart from the heads of state and government of Israel and Jordan, were UN Secretary-General Boutros Boutros-Ghali, President Bill Clinton, and several heads of government and foreign ministers from countries in the region. With one or two exceptions, my contact with Arab foreign ministers and other Middle Eastern leaders, which would prove useful later, began on that day. On the eve of the signing ceremony, the then Crown Prince of Jordan, Hassan bin Talal—a cultured man with a humanistic outlook, who despite that (or because of it) would later be passed over when it came to the succession, offered a dinner for a few foreign ministers in the palace where he had his residence. At the end of the banquet Prince Hassan presented me with a book he had written about early Christianity in the East, which in a way was an interesting introduction to the foundations of what would later become known as the "Dialogue Among Civilizations" (or "Alliance of Civilizations").[6]

From Jordan I was due to head directly to Casablanca, where an ambitious conference was taking place on economic relations in the Middle East and North Africa. The objective, in addition to attracting investment and promoting trade, was to initiate a series of meetings in which both the Arab countries and Israel would participate, taking advantage of the positive momentum created by the agreements in Oslo[7] and the peace treaty that had just been signed by Amman and Tel Aviv. At the time there was a certain amount of optimism about those relations; there was even talk of a free-trade area that would include Israel and some Arab countries. As part of that process, a number of conferences were held in the 1990s, but ultimately the initiative would not survive the successive impacts of the First Gulf War and the Second Intifada.[8] The process did not achieve the hoped-for results, but it is worth noting that Brazil was one of the few Latin American countries invited to participate in the inaugural event.

During the Casablanca Conference, my second visit to Morocco as foreign minister (I had been in Marrakech a few months before, to sign the agreement that created the WTO), I met with King Hassan II, to whom I delivered a letter from President Itamar Franco. Before the meeting, which took place in the imperial palace in Casablanca, I had to sit quite a long time in the lobby of my hotel, gradually overcoming the effects of a violent stomach upset I had suffered soon after arriving. While waiting to be told I could leave for the palace, I received a visit from a minister connected with Morocco's internal and external security, who was interested in closer cooperation with Brazil in the area of intelligence. I found it a curious coincidence that someone should seek to talk to me on such matters in the city where the famous film by Michael Curtiz, with Ingrid Bergman and Humphrey Bogart, was set.[9] Anyway, I noted down the minister's suggestions for future discussion, but I do not know if the issue was ever pursued further. In the conversation with King Hassan II, in addition to bilateral matters I brought up the issue of UN Security Council reform. The fact that my *démarche* was positively received (albeit without any firm commitment) would later lead me to adopt a more cautious position than we had done previously on the unresolved issue of Western Sahara. That dispute, which also involves Algeria and Mauritania, explains why Morocco, a full member of the Arab League, is not formally part of the African Union—a situation which years later would force us into some diplomatic juggling when organizing summits involving South American and African countries. I remember that, at the time, I had some difficulty persuading our mission to the UN to tone down our support for the Polisario Front. I confess that I did so with a certain discomfort, recognizing as I did the legitimacy of the struggle of the Sahrawi people. Later, as permanent representative to the UN, I would again have to confront this particular issue, trying as far as possible to maintain a balance between the conflicting positions. It is a complex problem that defies easy solutions, as demonstrated by the countless plans (the most famous of which was drawn up by Secretary of State James Baker) that ended up on the shelves of the UN Secretariat. Anyway, it was not the only case in which national interest prevailed over sympathies and affinities when it came to taking foreign policy decisions.

To get from Amman to Casablanca I had to change aircraft in Beirut and then in Paris (at that time our air force did not have planes capable of flying such a distance non-stop). When he found out I would be passing through Beirut airport, the Lebanese foreign minister, Farès Boueiz, insisted on transforming my brief stop into an official visit. Beirut still bore the scars of the terrible civil war that had ended only a few years previously. Most of the buildings lining the road between the airport and the city center were in ruins. In some cases I could see, even from afar, families going about their domestic lives in homes without external walls, in buildings supported only by a few pillars; it was almost as if they were characters in a play. I was particularly taken aback by the fact that those buildings had been destroyed, either totally or partially, by gunfire, with bullet marks still clearly visible on the walls left standing. In the city center there was the same bleak vista. It seemed a miracle that the old European-style palace housing the foreign ministry was not only still standing but, as far as I could tell, undamaged. This was the first time I had had a personal and direct view of the complex problems that marked the Middle East (and still mark it today, of course—perhaps to an even greater degree). On the way back to the airport after about two hours with my Lebanese counterpart, I asked his chief of protocol, a tall man with graying hair who spoke impeccable French, how a conflict that had lasted so long and claimed so many victims had eventually come to an end without a clear victor. His answer, which might also apply to certain situations we are witnessing today (and, in a way, offers hope), was simple and direct: "The opposing sides just got tired." My brief stop in Beirut did not only allow me to speak to an interlocutor from the region about a subject I had had little involvement with until then: it also gave me the opportunity to announce, in an interview I gave on the front steps of the foreign ministry building, Brazil's support for the UN Security Council resolutions calling for the national integrity of the Lebanese state to be respected.[10]

It was not always major issues of world politics or economic interests that led me to seek contact with leaders from the Middle East. In 1994, there was—and had been for some time, in fact—a Brazilian woman, Lamia Marouf, in prison in Israel, accused of being part of a group that had kidnapped and killed an Israeli soldier. Her imprisonment had provoked a strong reaction in some sections of the Arab community in Brazil, and indeed in Congress. Airton Soares, an experienced congressman who had fought for the return of democracy during Brazil's military dictatorship, led the movement and was someone I spoke to frequently. Petitions were drawn up, urging the Brazilian government to take an aggressive stance in demanding Lamia's release. We acted in several ways. We sent a special envoy, Ambassador Pedro Paulo Assunção, director of Itamaraty's "Near East" department, to Tunis, where the PLO had its headquarters. He was carrying a letter from President Itamar Franco to Yasser Arafat, in which the former requested that Lamia's name be added to a list of prisoners Israel should release as part of the goodwill gestures in the context of the Oslo and Washington agreements. For my part, I arranged a meeting with Farouk Kaddoumi, the PLO "foreign minister," on the margins of the UN General Assembly in September 1994. That same day, coincidentally, I also met the Israeli foreign minister, Shimon

Peres. This was just a few days after the signing in Washington of the agreement between Israel and Palestine, which therefore gave both meetings a special flavor. But the main issue on my agenda, in both cases, was the Brazilian prisoner. Just as Arafat had done, Kaddoumi responded positively to our request, even though, given the limited number of prisoners to be released, meeting our request would entail changing the order of priority of the potential beneficiaries. Shimon Peres—who had taken the initiative to asking to meet me—said that because the day our aides had arranged for the meeting was a Jewish holiday, it would not be possible for him to go to UN headquarters. He therefore asked if I could pay him a visit at his hotel on Park Avenue, not far from the Brazilian mission to the UN on Third Avenue. To make the proposal more enticing he added that, despite the religious holiday, he would be offering me a "glass of wine." When I arrived, it seemed he had already guessed what I wanted to talk about. For him it was a sensitive issue, because from the Israeli perspective it involved my compatriot's participation in a "bloody crime" that was being dealt with by the Israeli justice system. In fact, Peres did all he could to shift our conversation to other subjects, such as the role of "moderator" that Brazil might play with the Arabs; his various visits to Brazil; and his friendship with Brazilian leaders who were members of the Socialist International, including the then governor of Rio de Janeiro, Leonel Brizola. I did not refuse to discuss any of those issues—especially the first, which was of genuine interest to us, although we probably viewed it differently. But I made it clear that a closer relationship between Brazil and Israel (including the acceptance of his invitation for me to visit Tel Aviv) depended upon the satisfactory resolution of the Lamia Marouf case. At one point in the conversation he even tried to convince me to discreetly drop the issue: "I understand you have a problem with Brazilian public opinion on this matter. But I too have a problem with public opinion, and also with the Israeli justice system, which is independent. So let's do this: you tell the press you raised the issue with me, and I won't say anything to the contrary." But in the end, seeing that I was not going to give up, Peres very reluctantly agreed to receive the *aide-mémoire*[11] I was carrying and said he would study it, but without making any promises. Lamia Marouf ended up being released sometime later, during the government of Fernando Henrique Cardoso, when I was no longer foreign minister, but our efforts back then had not been in vain.

During my first period as foreign minister, from mid-1993 to the end of 1994, when Brazil was a non-permanent member of the Security Council, the issue of Iraq did not give rise to any controversy that I personally was involved in. The world at that time was still living under the umbrella of what we might call "consensual unipolarity," in which US hegemony went unchallenged. But even during that time, in which an apparent consensus prevailed in international relations, Brazil showed signs of its independence by seeking closer ties with Cuba and abstaining from resolutions on Haiti that were supported by the United States.[12] In the economic arena, the idea of the South American Free Trade Area was launched so as to counter—preventively—what would later become the FTAA initiative. Also under consideration was a possible association between Mercosur and the European Community, first discussed on the margins of a meeting in São Paulo in April 1994 between the Rio Group[13] and European countries. It was seen as potentially providing some balance in the face of the attempts to bring about hemispheric integration that would place us in a situation of political and economic dependence upon the "only remaining superpower." Apart from our actions in the context of the recently concluded Uruguay Round,[14] after which the multilateral world trade negotiations went into an extended state of hibernation, our diplomatic initiatives were quite limited. Also, the recent memory of Iraq's invasion of Kuwait, and Saddam Hussein's use of chemical weapons against the Kurds, were factors that discouraged any attempt to prevent Baghdad being punished.

The Iraq-related issues that continued to come up in the Security Council (protection of the Kurds and Shias; no-fly zones) did not actually cross my desk as foreign minister: instead they were dealt with by our competent and respected ambassador to the UN, Ronaldo Sardenberg. Nevertheless, the perception that Brazil adopted a balanced position, and was particularly sensitive to the suffering of the Iraqi civilian population caused by the sanctions, possibly influenced the decision by the Iraqi foreign minister, Said Sahaf, to visit Brasilia in the second half of 1994. In one of the two UN General Assemblies I attended as foreign minister under Itamar Franco, I also had the opportunity to meet with Tariq Aziz, an experienced diplomat who, unfortunately for him, would still be occupying the position of deputy prime minister when the 2003 invasion took place. Aziz, a Christian (which in itself showed that, at least from a religious point of view, the Baghdad regime was far from sectarian or monolithic), made a good impression on me, seeming to possess clarity of thought and a serene temperament.

On the subject of Libya, which was obviously also of interest to the Arab countries as a whole, Brazil expressed concern at the lack of alternatives to the sanctions regime. Specifically in relation to those sanctions, our representative at the UN said that "such acts must be specifically prepared by the [Security] Council so that the state on which the sanctions will be imposed can know in advance, without any doubts, that those sanctions will be lifted as soon as the specific requirements are met."[15]

"What's good for Brazil will also be good for France"

Between March 1995 and April 1999, I was Brazil's permanent representative to the UN. Even before Brazil returned to the Security Council as a non-permanent member in 1998, I had some involvement with the Iraq issue, especially regarding sanctions. Shortly after arriving in New York I was chosen to chair a sub-commission of the General Assembly that dealt with the effects of on the civilian populations of the economic measures adopted by the Security Council.[16] I was chosen for the position by Nabil Elaraby, the Egyptian ambassador, who chaired the "umbrella commission" on various aspects of the "Agenda for Peace" proposed by the Secretary-General, his compatriot Boutros Boutros-Ghali. Elaraby, with whom I had a friendly and productive working relationship throughout my time in New York (he was also part of the Canberra Commission on the elimination of nuclear weapons, mentioned in the first narrative), would go on to be a judge in the International Court of Justice, Egyptian foreign minister (for a brief period only, although it coincided with a visit I made to Cairo shortly after I left the post of foreign minister), and secretary-general of the Arab League.

The great privations suffered by the Iraqi people as a direct result of the punitive measures imposed in the wake of the First Gulf War were already of concern to many countries, especially developing ones—including, of course, the Arab nations, regardless of what they thought about the Baghdad regime. The Iraq situation provided the backdrop to much of the work carried out by the aforementioned sub-commission.[17] In the same period, 1995–1999, the inspections carried out by UNSCOM,[18] in a highly intrusive manner, provoked constant clashes with the government in Baghdad, raising the possibility of force being used. That was especially the case after Rolf Ekéus, a Swede, was replaced as UNSCOM director by Richard Butler, an Australian, in July 1997. The discussions about UNSCOM's actions came to my attention, and that of the Brazilian delegation, even in the period when we were not part of the Security Council.

Our level of involvement with the subject obviously increased from January 1998, when we rejoined the Security Council as a non-permanent member. As early as February, the Security Council had to deal with a potentially explosive situation. It needed to clearly define the status of Saddam Hussein's so-called "presidential palaces": were they subject to weapons inspections, and if so, what procedures should be established? Brazil gave its full support to the initiative of UN Secretary-General Kofi Annan, which sought to engage with Baghdad and find a mediated solution. That met with strong opposition from the United States and the United Kingdom, the two fiercest opponents of any appeasement of the Iraqi regime. Annan returned from Baghdad with a memorandum signed by the government, with the personal backing of Saddam Hussein. But the story did not end there. To incorporate the memorandum into the legal framework of the UNSC, it was necessary to adopt a resolution stipulating what would happen in the event of non-compliance by Iraq. And on that point there were two opposing positions. On one side, led by the US and the UK, were those who believed that failure to comply with the resolution should automatically give the members of the 1991 coalition the right to "take all necessary measures" (a euphemism for the use of force). On the other side, the other permanent members, Russia, China and France, insisted on the need for a new Security Council resolution to determine whether Iraq had indeed committed a transgression, and if so, to explicitly authorize the use of armed force. This discussion would take place again, in much the same way, in 2002–03, in the period preceding the Iraq War culminating in the decision by the US and UK (with the support of some other countries) to act unilaterally.

In February 1998, three and a half years before 9/11, Washington tried to avoid an explicit break with the terms of the Charter of the United Nations. I can say without hesitation that Brazil played an important role in the search for a negotiated solution, based on the terms of the resolutions from 1991, which allowed for a decision by consensus. The "unity of the Council" had an almost mythical status in that period, marked as it was by the illusion of a "benign unipolarity."[19] There is no space here to go into the minutiae of the wording that allowed the agreement to be adopted. But it is pertinent to mention two things, one of them concerning the position of France and its excellent UN ambassador, Alain Déjammet. With the UNSC split over whether there was "automaticity" with regard to the use of force, the Brazilian delegation, which I led, had basically adopted a position alongside Paris (and also, in a way, Moscow and Beijing), despite some contradictory noises when Bill Richardson[20] had visited Brasilia. February 27, a Friday, was the day the ambassador of Gabon departed from the Security Council, with the permanent representative of Gambia due to take his place at the start of March. At a cocktail party hosted by the Gabonese mission, I remarked to the French ambassador that I was seeking a "creative" solution to the impasse. The next morning, Saturday, the Japanese ambassador, who for some reason (probably the unreliability of his Gambian counterpart) had been put in charge of consultations on the subject, called me to a meeting at UN headquarters. On my way, in the car, I called the French ambassador, not wanting my "creative ideas" to undermine the French position, given that essentially we were in agreement. Déjammet listened to me attentively and said: "Go ahead. What's good for Brazil will also be good for France."

I therefore presented the idea, which my aide Achilles Zaluar and I had written together, to Ambassador Hisashi Owada,[21] who received it coolly. I even had to listen to him lecture me on the responsibilities that a candidate for permanent membership of the Security Council such as Brazil (and Japan) should be ready to assume. At the time I was left in doubt as to whether those responsibilities meant the acceptance of the use of force in certain situations, or the need to always agree with dominant power. It is quite possible he meant both. I returned home frustrated, feeling I had already tried everything. My spirits sank further when I received sad news about a much-loved member of my family. About an hour later, the US ambassador, Bill Richardson, phoned me to say he had heard about my suggestion that had been summarily rejected by the Japanese ambassador. He encouraged me to carry it forward, with certain adjustments, as in his opinion it could form the basis of an agreement—and in fact, after long negotiations that lasted the whole of the weekend and Monday morning, that is what happened.

The language we used in the document—borrowed, with some alterations, from 1991 (the "ceasefire resolution")[22] —established that the Security Council would continue to deal with the issue ("remain seized of the matter") and would take whatever actions were necessary. It recognized, implicitly, that there would be no automaticity in the use of force. After some clarifications during the "informal consultations,"[23] the text was accepted by all members and approved by consensus in the formal meeting of the Security Council.[24] This conciliatory role on the part of Brazil, performed without moving away from our positions of principle, allowed the work of the weapons inspectors in Iraq to resume. It also gave us the necessary credentials to play a prominent role in an even more complex situation about a year later.

In January 1999 I was faced with the challenge of chairing the Security Council at a critical juncture following "Operation Desert Fox"—the bombing of Iraq in December 1998 by the United States and the United Kingdom, without the Security Council's permission. The military action, triggered by a report from UNSCOM director Richard Butler that the Security Council did not even have time to examine, was fiercely opposed by France, Russia, and China, and also criticized by other members, including Brazil. The split between the five permanent members not only made any rational discussion of the Iraqi issue impossible, but it also ended up adversely affecting the work on every other subject on the Security Council's agenda. Some weeks after the Anglo-American attack took place, Brazil took over the presidency of a Security Council whose entire agenda (including the ongoing civil war in Angola, the conflict between Ethiopia and Eritrea, and the repression of the independence movement in East Timor) was effectively stalled.

It was up to me, as president, to move the agenda forward again. I managed to do so essentially by separating the Iraq issue from all the others. With the support of the other members, particularly the non-permanent ones, I proposed that commissions ("panels") should be created to deal with the two most controversial aspects of the issue: disarmament; and the humanitarian situation, which had become genuinely grave because of the sanctions. The extent of the restrictions imposed on Baghdad can be gauged by one example related to so-called dual-use (i.e. civil and military) materials: imports of pencils were subject to controls because they contained graphite, which could supposedly be used as a moderator in Iraq's nuclear facilities! And this was despite a declaration from the International Atomic Energy Agency that Iraq had already ceased all activities in that field. The more complex matter, however, was obviously that of disarmament. In accordance with the way the resolutions had been drawn up in the wake of the 1991 ceasefire, the inspectors' activities were in two areas: one was concerned with disarmament itself, which is to say the proven destruction of chemical, biological and nuclear weapons (or materials that could be used to make them). Also to be destroyed were components for missiles ("means of delivery") with more than a certain range. The other area of activities was referred to as "continuous monitoring," which would continue indefinitely, even after the "disarmament" stage was complete. Only when the ongoing monitoring stage had been reached in all four categories relating to weapons of mass destruction would Iraq be eligible for the lifting of sanctions. Much of the controversy that preceded the December attack had to do with this distinction between the two stages; it was a subtle one but had great practical consequences for Iraq. Also, the Baghdad regime was faced with an obligation which was virtually impossible to fulfill, based upon what could be described as "negative proof." In other words it was up to Iraq to prove that it *did not* have any of the prohibited materials. Meanwhile, it was also the case that Iraq resorted to all sorts of maneuvers to hinder the work of the inspectors, hiding behind the argument (albeit often justified) that its "sovereignty" and "integrity" (words that appeared in most of the resolutions from 1991 onward) needed to be respected.

To stop the Security Council going around in circles, I suggested that the "panel" on disarmament could examine the issue from a new perspective, in the form of what I called a "reinforced monitoring regime." Ideally this regime would create a bridge between the two stages ("disarmament" and "ongoing monitoring")—and, if there was the necessary political will, make possible the gradual alleviation of economic sanctions. After discussions that went on until the last day of Brazil's temporary presidency of the Security Council (Saturday, January 30), the creation of the panels was approved. At the request of Bahrain, which at the time was a UNSC member—and was in this case speaking on behalf of Kuwait—a third panel, dealing with prisoners of war and Kuwaiti property that had disappeared during the Iraqi occupation, was added to the two previously mentioned. All three panels were to be chaired by Brazil, which is to say by me, as permanent representative. A timeframe of sixty days was set for the results of the panels' work to be presented.[25]

As coordinator of the panels, perhaps one of my most difficult tasks was to decide who should sit on them. The participants had to reflect the different currents within the UNSC, and to include specialists from each of the five permanent members (some of whom were well known to have connections with their intelligence services) and from international organizations in the area of arms control, along with individuals whose names would lend credibility to the panels' work while also reflecting at least a degree of geographical balance (always a concern in the UN). In this chess game of personalities and interests, the most delicate question was what to do with the director of UNSCOM, whose behavior—excessively aggressive and, according to many, far from impartial—lay at the root of the impasse between the members of the Security Council. I recall that the UN secretary-general, whose blessing I thought I should seek as soon as the panels had been created, asked me outright: "What do you intend to do with Butler?" I responded with a metaphor absolutely typical of the UN: "I think I'll put him in brackets." And that, indeed, is what I did, by not nominating him for the disarmament panel and leaving him on the sidelines of the discussions. It is more than likely that my decision contributed to his resignation a few months later.

It would be tedious to describe in detail the work of the panels and the conclusions they arrived at, but it is worth noting that a few months after the submission of my report on March 30 and some interventions I made in the Security Council in April (before leaving on May 1 for my next post, in Geneva),[26] the Security Council would approve a resolution based largely on the basic concepts in that report. The panel's verdict on the humanitarian situation, pointing to a direct link between the sanctions and the privations suffered by the Iraqi people, was conveniently pushed to one side.[27] Therefore, the connection between the conclusions arrived at by the two panels, which in my view was essential in order to find a peaceful and definitive solution to the Iraq issue, as indeed I explained to the Council, was not considered.

Some progress had been achieved, however. The UN special commission (UNSCOM), seen by most as unnecessarily hostile toward Baghdad, had been transformed into a more flexible mechanism: the United Nations Monitoring, Verification and Inspection Commission (UNMOVIC).[28] The idea of a more gradual approach to Iraqi disarmament was also introduced, although for various reasons it did not achieve practical results. It was under the auspices of UNMOVIC that Hans Blix would attempt to find a solution to this complicated issue,[29] and the reasons for his "failure" go far beyond the competences of the inspectorate. Our engagement showed that dialogue was possible, as long as there was good will on the part of all the actors involved.[30]

I think it is worth mentioning a curious episode that provides a little insight into the way the great powers act on issues that are of direct interest to them. Soon after the adoption of Resolution 1284 (1999), there arose the problem of deciding who would head the new commission. The names initially suggested included my own. Another potential candidate, Rolf Ekéus of Sweden, the first director of UNSCOM, was vetoed by Moscow and also, I believe, by Beijing. Ekéus was an experienced diplomat who had served on the Disarmament Commission; when his name was put forward for UNMOVIC he was Sweden's ambassador in Washington. His time at the head of UNSCOM, though inevitably marked by some difficulties, was not nearly as troubled as that of Richard Butler. Maybe, however, he seemed too compromised by the previous inspections regime, and therefore ineligible in the eyes of those countries that had been most critical of UNSCOM. France, Russia and China, therefore, settled on my name. After all, my role on the panels had attracted praise from diverse quarters, including from the US representative to the UNSC at the time when UNMOVIC was created. The UN secretary-general, Kofi Annan, asked me through an aide if I agreed with my name being included in the consultations he was carrying out with the P5. In fact I had already heard rumors that this was being considered while I was on vacation in Rio de Janeiro for a few days at the end of the year (1999), immediately after the turbulent WTO ministerial conference in Seattle.[31] In early 2000, I received a call from Kofi Annan's aide. I told him I was willing to take on the role—after having been largely responsible for its creation—as long as the Secretary-General could see there was a genuine consensus in favor of my name. I wanted to avoid the same fate as Ekéus, although in his case the veto had come from another member (or members) of the P5. One strong supporter of my being appointed was the French ambassador on the UNSC, Alain Déjammet, who told me in a phone conversation that I had to accept the role: "*C'est le seul nom*," he said. As it turned out, however, I would not have to endure the embarrassment suffered by of Ekéus. A few days after the phone call from the Secretary-General's aide, I was approached by the US permanent representative in Geneva, an African American who would later find himself in the embarrassing position of trying to block a Brazilian initiative condemning racism.[32] He had been instructed to convey to me the following message from Washington: that the US government had great respect for me and did not want to create any ill-feeling with Brazil, so it was requesting that I should not let my name be formally presented as a candidate—or else the US would be obliged to veto it. By way of further explanation for his government's attitude, he said that it was difficult for the US to accept the nomination of a figure from a developing county for a position it considered to be "strategic." He added: "You know, we're in an election year." I felt like saying that even in moments of paranoia, I never dreamed I might have some impact on a US election, but instead I held my tongue and just thanked him for his frankness. I do not know what would have happened had I actually been nominated. At the time I was somewhat frustrated, since the UNMOVIC role would have been a huge but stimulating challenge and, in a way, an extension (as well as recognition) of my work on the panels. But now, recalling how Hans Blix suffered due to the pressures of his work, I can perhaps conclude that my time in the role would have been even shorter, that the cause of peace would not really have been advanced, and that I might have suffered damage to my political reputation (and indeed my health) that would have reduced my chances of being appointed as foreign minister under Lula.

I will finish these recollections with another episode that took place around the same time. Together, I think the two cases illustrate what the French call *géométrie variable*. Also in January 2000, after the debacle of Seattle, there were some countries that wanted to put my name forward to chair the agriculture committee of the WTO. The role was especially important at that time because the issue of agriculture had been the chief villain in Seattle. Unlike in relation to my possible nomination for UNMOVIC, to which Itamaraty reacted rather coolly, in this case there was enthusiasm back at "headquarters" in Brasilia. This time, however, the veto came from France (via the European Union), while Washington was an enthusiastic backer of my appointment!

Another topic in which Brazil had significant involvement were the sanctions against Libya, imposed some years previously in response to the terrorist acts carried out against civilian aircraft over Scotland (Lockerbie) and Niger. Concerned principally by the humanitarian impact of the sanctions, and disappointed by the way the subject had become stalled in the so-called "informal consultations," Brazil proposed an "open debate" in the Security Council. One of the perverse aspects of the workings of the Security Council, not only in the case of Libya, was the fact that once sanctions had been imposed on a country, they could only be lifted by means of a new resolution, for which it was necessary to have a consensus on the part of the permanent members. The use of the veto is inverted, in other words. In fact, to prevent the lifting of the sanctions, the power of veto did not even need to be exercised explicitly. Once the subject was presented for informal consultation, if it was clear there would not be a consensus, this fact was communicated to the president without the need for a public discussion. The idea of an "open debate" was therefore a dangerous innovation from the point of view of those who preferred, lamentably, to keep the situation unchanged and opaque. It would represent the breaking of a taboo. Unsurprisingly, the suggestion was at first vigorously resisted by the US and the UK. France, in this case, said little. Washington even made formal requests in Brasilia that we desist from the idea. As the months went by, the situation evolved, partly due to pressure from the Arab League and possibly also because a potential solution was glimpsed with regard to the compensation to be paid by Libya. Brazil's legalist approach in seeking to deal with the subject in a fair and balanced way was much appreciated by the Arab countries as a whole, regardless of their feelings toward the Libyan regime. I believe it would not be incorrect to say our stance on Iraq provoked largely the same reaction. Much more than a supposed desire to assist the Baghdad regime, our impartial attitude, reflecting a legitimate concern about the suffering of the Iraqi people, was seen as evidence of a sensitivity the Arabs perceived only rarely on the part of most other countries, particularly western ones.

When President Lula took office in January 2003, the invasion of Iraq by the so-called "coalition of the willing" was already looming on the horizon. Lula's first bilateral visits were to France and Germany. Among the western countries, President Jacques Chirac and Chancellor Gerhard Schröder were leading the opposition to the war. Having been invited to return to the post of foreign minister, in the first few months of Lula's government I also visited another country vehemently opposed to the use of force against Baghdad: Russia. Brazil expressed in very clear terms its confidence in the inspections regime led by Hans Blix, although I was well aware of the difficulties he faced. We tried to coordinate our position with various partners and interlocutors, from the UN secretary-general to the president of Chile, which at the time was a non-permanent member of the Security Council. Throughout the period leading up to the attack on Iraq, and even after the start of the invasion, Brazil's diplomacy maintained an intense rhythm. The bombing, which started on March 19, was a sobering reminder of the persistence of unilateralism and the readiness to use force. In 2002, while still serving as ambassador in London, I wrote an article on the subject in the *Folha de São Paulo*.[33] As foreign minister I was now faced with a brutal breach of international norms. The day after the US attack on Baghdad, President Lula made a forthright statement condemning the invasion and the illegal use of violence.

After the war, Brazil continued to take an interest in the situation in Iraq. I had meetings in the first half of 2003 that helped broaden the horizons of our diplomatic activities. The instability and uncertainties caused by the war against Iraq ended the illusions of a peaceful and benign international order in the post-Cold War world, and reinforced the need for a more balanced international system. A reform of global governance was no longer merely desirable or convenient: it was imperative. And it needed not only to include the institutions concerned with peace and security, as Brazil had been advocating for more than ten years, but also entities in the fields of trade and finance. We had a clear understanding that such changes would not come about merely as a result of actions taken in international forums, however important those might be. What they required was a new conception of Brazil's foreign relations, based on a diversification of our partnerships and on the creation of new regional and inter-regional mechanisms.

"New economic and political geography"

Early in the Lula government, during one of my first foreign trips with the president, he told me about his idea of a summit between Brazil and the Arab nations. In his view, such a meeting would be a step toward a "new economic and political geography." His perception that the world did not consist only of the United States and Europe (plus, of course, our neighbors) would be fundamental in building an unprecedented relationship with the Arab world.

Initially, the objectives of this "pivot to the Middle East" seemed primarily commercial, but there was also a political dimension that certainly had not escaped the president's attention. A search for new markets and an effort to consolidate multipolarity were added to Brazil's aspiration to play a more active role in issues related to world peace. From a foreign policy perspective, the expansion of our relationship with the Arab world, which until then our diplomacy had explored in only a limited way, opened new avenues for addressing issues that were of great interest to Brazil, such as the WTO negotiations and the reform of the UN Security Council.

The political will was there; the challenge, obviously, was to give shape to it. I suggested to Lula that rather than "convene" a summit between Brazil and the Arab countries, we could propose a meeting between the heads of state and government of South America and their Arab counterparts. No doubt this wider focus would introduce some complications, but it would have the advantage of strengthening our policy of regional integration by giving South America an external face. The president agreed. The preparations for the Summit of the South American-Arab Countries (later to be known by the acronym ASPA) led to a multiplication of bilateral contacts with the Arab countries, and with the Arab League itself. They also prepared the ground for Brazil's greater involvement in issues connected with the Middle East—and also, paradoxical though it might appear, contributed to an intensification of our relations with Israel.

In June 2003, during a trip to Évian (a French resort on the shore of Lake Geneva) to attend a meeting of the expanded G8, President Lula met the Crown Prince of Saudi Arabia, Abdullah bin Abdulaziz al-Saud (who in August 2005 would ascend to the throne). The discussion was mostly about economic matters. On the Brazilian side, I remember that in addition to the ministers from the economic area there was at least one other politician (from the opposition, incidentally; in those days it was still on good terms with the government) whose goal was to secure investment in an oil refinery in his state. Lula also spoke to the Algerian president, Abdelaziz Bouteflika, who was seeking our help in assisting the victims of a natural disaster. Bouteflika had been an iconic Third World leader during a long period as foreign minister of his country in the 1960s and 70s, so his discussion with Lula naturally embraced international political issues. These meetings certainly contributed to consolidating the idea of closer ties with the Arab countries, and to the holding of the summit.

During my first visit to Arab countries as foreign minister in the Lula government, I explored the idea of the summit with my interlocutors, including the Arab League secretary-general. At the end of that month, we sent special envoys to deliver invitations to the leaders of the Arab League countries. My chief of staff, Ambassador Mauro Vieira, went to Palestine with a letter from Lula to Yasser Arafat, then living virtually under siege in the

Muqata complex in Ramallah.[34] To go there, Mauro needed to get the approval of Tel Aviv,[35] which was only granted after what he later described to me as a lengthy "sermon" from an undersecretary in the Israeli foreign ministry about the position Brazil adopted in the UN on the Palestinian issue.

As foreign minister, I took every available opportunity to strengthen ties with the Arab countries. Cairo, Beirut and Amman were among my principal official visits during early 2003. In June, reflecting the positions we had taken on Iraq issue, I was invited to a meeting on the Middle East held in Jordan (by the Dead Sea) under the auspices of the World Economic Forum. Among other activities, I took part in an interesting round-table with representatives from Israeli and Palestinian civil society. It was also there that I met, for the first time, King Abdullah II of Jordan, who would become a frequent interlocutor during future trips to the region. To him and to the leaders of the other countries I visited, I took messages from President Lula conveying Brazil's desire for closer relations and reiterating our invitation to the summit.

In Cairo I met President Hosni Mubarak and his foreign minister, Ahmad Maher; I also visited the Secretary-General of the Arab League, Amr Moussa. I was accompanied by our ambassador, Celso Marcos Vieira de Souza, a longtime friend whom I had worked under in the early 1980s when he was chief of staff to the education minister and I was CEO of Embrafilme.[36] Maher, the foreign minister, an intelligent and witty man, offered me a dinner in his office at the foreign ministry, an old building by the Nile. He interspersed our conversation with anecdotes that made me laugh a number of times. In that relaxed atmosphere we talked about various bilateral and also international matters. We discussed the reform of the Security Council—an issue on which, as I already knew from my time as ambassador to the UN, Egypt's position was different from ours. Despite some occasional oscillations, Egypt was identified with the positions advocated by the so-called "Coffee Club," alongside countries such as Italy and Mexico. This group, which years later would adopt the somewhat misleading name of "Uniting for Consensus," rejected any expansion of the number of permanent members, giving political reasons based on the principle of equity and an opposition to "privileges." In fact, these countries' attitude stemmed mainly from the realization that, despite exercising some influence over international relationships within their respective regions, they themselves did not possess the geographic, demographic or economic attributes that would, in the eyes of the other members of the UN, make them eligible for a permanent seat on the UNSC.

During the lively discussion with my Egyptian counterpart, I was able to explain in detail our ideas for UNSC reform, including procedures for selecting the new members (election by the General Assembly), equitable geographic distribution, acceptance of a review mechanism after a certain period, and abdication of the use of the veto. I do not think I was able to convince him, however. I also perceived, on his part, a subtle nuance with regard to the proposed summit. Without rejecting the idea, whose merits he acknowledged, he hinted that a possible meeting of heads of state should include Mexico. I later found out that Mexico's ambassador in Cairo had raised the idea. (I will digress very briefly at this point to note that Mexico is a great country with an admirable people, but that its strong economic ties with the United States have the effect of limiting its autonomy. While avoiding actions that might displease its giant neighbor and partner to the north, such as the initiatives Brazil was proposing in this particular case, it also showed a persistent inclination to put obstacles in the way of any attempt to strengthen collective South American identity.)[37] Ahmad Maher was Egyptian foreign minister until 2004, when he was replaced by Ahmed Aboul Gheit. Despite the differences that had surfaced in our first meeting, we kept up a friendly relationship. At least once during my later trips to Cairo he visited me at the residence of the Brazilian ambassador (in 2008, I believe), and as a former rather than serving minister showed himself to be much more sympathetic toward our positions and initiatives. In contrast to his earlier skepticism, he praised our leadership in pursuing closer links between South America and the Arab countries. By that time he had also become very critical of the ambiguous attitude of the Egyptian government toward Israel. I was sad to hear that he died not long after my last meeting with him.

Also in Cairo, I visited the Arab League. I was informed at the time that it was the first ever visit to that institution by a foreign minister from Latin America. The Secretary-General, Amr Moussa, quickly grasped the positive potential for the Arab world in strengthening ties with another group of developing countries. As an experienced and astute diplomat (he had previously been Egypt's foreign minister for many years), he saw the value of a stronger relationship with South America not only from an economic and commercial perspective but also in terms of strengthening alliances around Arab causes, particularly the Israeli-Palestinian conflict. I had first met Moussa about ten years before, at a summit of the G15 in Delhi, in which we had participated as representatives of our heads of state. Since then we had developed a good camaraderie, boosted by meetings on the sidelines of the UN General Assembly. Our relationship had continued during the period in which, as permanent representative, I had been present at the bilateral meetings between the Brazilian and Egyptian foreign ministers. Moussa became a very enthusiastic backer of Brazil's proposal for a summit. His support, along with that of countries such as Lebanon, Syria, Morocco and Algeria, and also from the Palestinian Authority, made it possible, about a year later, for the heads of state of the Arab League to approve a resolution favorable to the staging of the ASPA summit. The good response to my visit and to the messages I had conveyed gave rise to an invitation, before the end of 2003, for Brazil to become an observer state in the Arab League. We were the first Latin American country ever to be given that status—one for which, I later learned, there was not even any provision in the organization's statutes. Also in 2003, the Arab League expressed the intention to reopen its diplomatic mission in Brasilia.[38] In April 2005, Moussa would visit Brazil.

The last of my visits in June 2003 was to Beirut, where I met with Lebanon's principal leaders, President Emile Lahoud and Prime Minister Rafik Hariri, and also the foreign minister, Jean Obeid. Hariri, who had been in Brazil a few weeks before, was very receptive to the messages from Lula that I was carrying; so too was President Lahoud, who would make a state visit to Brazil in February 2004. Lebanon was one of the first countries to express support for the summit initiative. Over the years it would also give backing on several occasions to Brazil's bid for a permanent seat on the UNSC. During my brief stay I did not have chance to talk at any length about the sectarian conflicts afflicting a country linked to Brazil by so many family and emotional ties, but the complexity of the political balance between the various Lebanese factions was immediately obvious: the president was a francophone Christian with westernized manners, but allied to Damascus; while the Prime Minister was a Sunni Muslim who had close links with Saudi Arabia. The speaker of the Lebanese parliament, Nabih Berri, was a Shia, and the leader of the Amal Movement.[39]

In December 2003, President Lula embarked on a journey that would take him to Syria, Lebanon, the United Arab Emirates, Egypt and Libya. Since the very beginning of his presidency he had shown a strong desire for greater proximity with the Arab countries, principally for economic motives. Government ministers in the economic field were keen to find openings to new markets and also to attract investment, and their approach was supported by businesspeople and politicians of various stripes. At each stage of the trip, business seminars were organized in parallel with the official visits: all of them were well attended. In Dubai, in the UAE, a big trade exhibition was held. Despite the differences between our respective approaches to other topics, these events were marked by fruitful cooperation between Itamaraty and the Ministry of Development, Industry and Trade. It was also clear, both to the supporters and the critics of this shared endeavor, that in defiance of certain preconceived views, we were breaking new ground by forging relations with countries of varying tendencies and alignments in the international context.

In the bilateral meetings with his fellow leaders and also in his public statements, President Lula made no attempt to evade delicate political issues. He addressed the need to create a Palestinian state, the Israeli occupation of the Golan Heights, and the reconstruction of Iraq under United Nations coordination. He deplored the disastrous effects of the US intervention. He raised, when appropriate, the issues of Security Council reform and the WTO Doha

Round, highlighting the role of the G20 group of developing countries that had emerged as a force in the multilateral trade negotiations at the Cancún conference. In relation to the rise of that group, Lula declared in one of his speeches that: "The developing countries have to convince themselves that it is within their power to change the economic and commercial geography of the world. . . . That's what we tried to do in the WTO with the G20." And he added: "That's what we're also doing through our contacts with other countries and regions." Of course, he also reiterated to the heads of state and to the Arab League the earlier invitation to the ASPA. Lula always made a point of emphasizing that the ASPA was not only a Brazilian initiative and that our South American neighbors were also very much involved, which is why his delegation of ministers, politicians and businesspeople also included a former president of Argentina, Eduardo Duhalde, who had been nominated a few months before to chair the committee of permanent representatives of Mercosur.[40]

The first stop during that trip was Damascus, where Lula was received by President Bashar al-Assad. In the Brazilian press, the meeting in itself was sufficient to provoke criticism. Seen by Washington as hostile to Israel and uncooperative with regard to US initiatives in the region (although it had been a US ally in the Gulf War), the Syrian government also attracted criticism because of its indisputably authoritarian character. But in that respect, Syria was not an isolated case. Virtually all the Arab states exhibited political restrictions that placed them at a distance from the western model of democracy (and still do today, despite the Arab Spring), regardless of their alignments and inclinations in the field of international politics. In reference to that Syria trip, I was rather astonished to be asked by a Brazilian journalist if we had consulted the White House beforehand. The same ideologically charged question, indicative of an attitude of submissiveness toward a foreign power, would be asked about the visit to Libya. I should point out that these concerns about authoritarian regimes do not arise when the country in question is an ally of Washington.

In the meeting in Damascus, despite the drowsiness that the Brazilian delegation succumbed to after such a long journey, the dialogue between Lula and Assad took place in a very friendly atmosphere. In his speech during the banquet hosted by the Syrian president, Lula said it was not by chance that Damascus had been chosen as the "first destination in the trip . . . to the Arab world," and drew attention to Brazil's vote in the UN in favor of the "resolution calling for the return to Syria of the Golan Heights,"[41] which represented a change from our previous position of abstention. During the private dialogue there was extensive discussion on the situation in the Middle East, and particular attention was given to the issue of the expansion of the UNSC. The Syrian president agreed with the need to make the UNSC more legitimate and representative, and seemed receptive to Brazil's bid for a permanent seat. That position would be consolidated over the years to come, partly as a result of Syrian recognition of Brazil's balanced approach to Middle Eastern subjects, some of them of direct interest to Damascus. Aside from the issue of the occupation of the Golan Heights, Syria would appreciate Brazil's independent stance on the allegations of Syrian interference in Lebanon's internal affairs,[42] and on the involvement of Damascus in the assassination of Lebanese prime minister Rafik Hariri. Syria's positive attitude toward Brazil's positions was also reflected in its support for the ASPA summit.[43]

President Lula and I were very tired after an almost sleepless night on the plane. The words of the Syrian president, in Arabic, seemed almost to be lulling us to sleep, and it is possible that one or both of us dozed off for a brief moment at some point. The translation into Portuguese, performed by a Brazilian interpreter of Syrian or Lebanese ancestry who had been hired by the president's office, slowed the flow of the dialogue. And although the interpreter was fluent in Arabic, unfortunately he knew nothing of geopolitics or international relations; one particular expression he kept using made no sense to me, until eventually I realized he was referring to the UN Security Council.

During the visit to Lebanon, the emphasis was on commercial and cultural matters, which were discussed during President Lula's talks with Prime Minister Rafic Hariri and President Émile Lahoud. Several agreements were signed. Like the Syrian officials, the Lebanese leaders expressed full support for the holding of the summit. Lula also, of course, expressed his support for the Road Map and the Arab Peace Initiative.[44] In the statement he made before the Lebanese parliament—presided over by the speaker, Nabih Berri—Lula called for "a Palestinian state that is independent, democratic, secure, cohesive and economically viable." But on that, as on other subjects, he always sought to maintain a balanced position. He therefore underlined the importance of guaranteeing "the conditions for the State of Israel to live in peace and security within its borders." Indicating the need for United Nations involvement in an issue usually handled only by a limited number of participants, Lula said that "peace between Palestinians and Israelis is a task for all the community of nations." Although they might seem innocuous, these statements were very deliberately intended as a warning against the appropriation of the Middle East issue by a small group of countries, and as a reiteration of the need to preserve the role of the multilateral system in the search for a just and comprehensive solution to the region's conflicts. Similarly, in relation to Iraq, Lula said "the extensive experience and credibility of the United Nations are indispensable." Looking again at the president's speech, I see that apart from a brief reference to "the right [of Lebanon] to fully exercise sovereignty in the territories belonging to it under international law," which was certainly important in the context of the disputes with Israel,

Lebanon's internal problems were hardly mentioned. "Lebanon's experience in achieving lasting peace," however, was pointed to as an inspiration for the region. Unfortunately, the optimism expressed in that speech, which I was involved in crafting, would be punctured fourteen months later by the shock of Rafik Hariri's assassination and the long political crisis that has continued almost uninterrupted to this day, aggravated now by civil war in Syria.

The visit to the United Arab Emirates (UAE) had two main elements: one political, in the form of a meeting with the Emir of Abu Dhabi, who holds the position of president of the federation; and the other economic, in the form of a business seminar and trade fair in Dubai. I do not recall much of the conversation with the emir, Sheikh Zayed bin Sultan al-Nahyan, who was clearly in poor health and would die the following year. At the banquet I sat next to another member of the royal family, much younger than the emir. Unlike the other representatives of the Emirates, who were all wearing traditional Bedouin clothing, he was in military uniform. We talked about Brazilian armaments, including missiles, and training aircraft, which were clearly of great interest to him. I later reported the details of the conversation to Itamaraty's trade promotion department, but as far as I know there was not any immediate follow-up. At the time of writing (May 2014), the Emir of Dubai (who is also the prime minister of the UAE) has just visited Brazil, and as a minister in Dilma Rousseff's government I signed a cooperation agreement in the area of defense.

I remember from a few things President Lula said during the inauguration of the "Brazil Week" in Dubai that the aged president of the Emirates had a particular interest in agricultural projects. As for the political issues we discussed with the other leaders, they were also raised in Abu Dhabi, though not with any great emphasis. At the business seminar, Lula referred indirectly to possible collaboration between the Gulf Cooperation Council (GCC) and Mercosur. The two entities would later sign a framework agreement on trade liberalization during the ASPA summit in Brasilia. I should point out, however, that the benefits of the agreement were mainly indirect, to the extent that they contributed to a closer relationship between the business sectors of the two groups of countries. Later, on more than one trip to the GCC headquarters in Riyadh, Saudi Arabia, I would try to make the framework agreement more concrete, but without much success. The lack of institutional progress, however, did not prevent a significant expansion of trade and investment between Brazil and the Gulf countries. Between 2003 and 2013, for example, our exports to the UAE increased almost fivefold, from $550 million to $2.6 billion USD.

Because our departure from Dubai to Cairo was delayed, and President Mubarak had a travel commitment that Egyptian officials told us could not be postponed, his meeting with Lula was rather short, and their conversation restricted to generalities. Some bilateral agreements were signed, and the

Brazil-Egypt Business Council created. The most significant aspects of the Cairo visit, however, were not bilateral in nature.

President Lula visited the Arab League, and also received a visit from the foreign minister of the Palestinian Authority, Nabil Shaath, in the old palace where we were staying, which had been the residence of King Farouk. To meet Lula, Shaath had traveled by road to Egypt from the West Bank, passing through several Israeli checkpoints on the way; he told us the journey took nine hours. In addition to conveying President Arafat's support for the ASPA summit, Shaath made two suggestions that Brazil would readily accept: the opening of a representative office in Ramallah, and the appointment of a special envoy for issues related to the Middle East. In his conversations with me and President Lula, he was very enthusiastic about greater Brazilian participation in the search for a solution to the Israeli-Palestinian conflict. He talked at length about the Road Map and the actions of the Quartet. It became clear that, for him, Brazil's interest in the Middle East came as a welcome breath of fresh air in a largely stagnant process. Later, at other moments during our dialogue with Palestine, Shaath would prove to be a key interlocutor by virtue of the key positions he held.[45]

During his stay in Cairo, President Lula made a speech at the Arab League headquarters. This was an important event, not only because it was unprecedented (no previous Brazilian head of state had ever addressed that forum) but also because of what he said. Rereading the text of the speech, I notice Lula's concern with placing Brazil's desire for greater proximity with the Arab world in the broader context of closer cooperation between the countries of the South. He therefore spoke in some detail about his personal contacts with and visits to the countries of South America and Africa during his first year in office. He noted the historical ties between Brazil and the Middle East, and highlighted the potential for economic cooperation not only with Brazil but also Mercosur and South America as a whole. On Palestine, he reiterated Brazil's position in support of a sovereign Palestinian state. He went on to say that "in 2004, with a new mandate as a non-permanent member of the UN Security Council, Brazil will support [the Palestinian cause] even more vigorously . . . just as we also strive, as far as we can, to find peaceful and diplomatic solutions to the Iraqi crisis." Lula referred to Brazil's admission to the Arab League as an observer, which he described as a "significant step in order for Brazil to keep track of the positions of the Arab world on the most important issues on the international agenda." He expressed the expectation that the Summit of South American-Arab Countries would create a "new framework for cooperation and dialogue between our regions" and pointed out that "the coordination of positions in multilateral forums and closer ties between countries of different regions that share similar views" would be helpful in creating a "healthy multipolar environment."

Multipolarity, and ways to strengthen it, would also feature in the dialogue between Lula and Muammar Gaddafi that took place in the Libyan leader's tent in the desert outside Tripoli. I have some rather vivid mental images of the occasion—for example the irksome presence of large numbers of flies, which led Gaddafi to use a kind of fan, made from vegetable fibers, in an effort to disperse them. Initially I took his abrupt movements to be a form of religious self-flagellation; only when I myself felt the insects attack, causing me to slap my leg rather violently, did I realize what was going on. The problem continued throughout the meeting, there apparently being nothing we could do about it. Rows of chairs had been arranged inside the tent, with the two leaders seated at the front, facing their "audience." As he had done on previous occasions, Lula commenced the dialogue by underling the potential of the relationship between the Arab world and South America, particularly in economic terms. Gaddafi soon interrupted, embarking on a lesson in geopolitics for the benefit of the Brazilian delegation. In this world according to Gaddafi, the Arab League and the countries that comprised it were not of great importance—apart from Libya, of course. The Libyan leader attached much greater importance to Africa. He understood little of the realities of Latin America and the Caribbean. He did not realize, for example, that the strong economic ties Mexico and Central America have with the United States tend to restrict not only the attempts at regional integration but also any South-South initiatives involving other parts of the world. His prioritization of Africa, meanwhile, reflected the influence he wished to exert (and in many cases already exerted) over African countries through significant amounts of financial aid. In his enthusiasm for closer ties between Africa and Latin America, Gaddafi went so far as to suggest the creation of a political (and possibly military) organization that "would counter NATO." Faced with these extravagant ideas, which contrasted with our rather more pragmatic initiative (though it still had a political dimension), Lula was quick to respond. He took from Gaddafi's hand the baton he had been using to point at a world map, and began to talk about his own vision of greater South-South cooperation, based on concrete initiatives in areas such as trade, science, and culture. The Libyan leader, judging from his facial expressions and gesticulations, was not convinced. Although in the end Libya would be represented at the Brasilia summit by an important minister, it would be fair to say that Gaddafi's enthusiasm for a process he did not initiate himself and could not control was rather limited.

The visit to Libya was also marked by a number of minor incidents and potential pitfalls. Before we even arrived, a Brazilian journalist who had landed in Tripoli without a visa had been arrested and detained by the authorities, meaning that much of our energy during the early part of the stay was devoted to securing his release. The episode served to exacerbate the Brazilian media's negative perception of the visit; the same kind of criticism we had heard during the visit to Damascus was aired again, but now with aggravating factors. How could the leader of a democratic country, who had come to power through free elections, allow himself to be received by a host who headed a notoriously dictatorial regime? But, as in the case of Syria, what really concerned our press was not so much the authoritarian or dictatorial nature of the regime but the lack of prior consultation with Washington. Paradoxically, the same media organizations did not bat an eyelid when Colin Powell went to Damascus, and reacted either positively or with indifference when the prime ministers José María Aznar and Tony Blair visited Libya soon after Lula's trip.

I do not underestimate Brazilians' sensitivity toward the nature of political systems and the importance we attach to human rights, having ourselves spent almost twenty years under an authoritarian regime. I confess that I myself had doubts about the inclusion of Libya in this first presidential tour of Arab countries, but I do not remember having expressed them to Lula, who had high expectations of economic cooperation with Libya given its oil wealth and its willingness to invest in developing countries. The goal of creating closer ties between South America and the Arab world seemed more important. Nor was I unaware of the principles of political realism and the role of national interests in the international arena. About a year and a half later, when President George W. Bush visited Lula at Granja do Torto (the modest Brazilian replica of Camp David on the edge of Brasilia), the irritating presence of swarms of flies reminded me of our trip to Libya, and prompted me to remark to Secretary of State Condoleezza Rice that I had visited somewhere she had probably never been: Gaddafi's tent. But Condoleezza was quick to reply: "I'm going there sooner than you'd imagine!"

Gaddafi was not an easy person to deal with, as was already obvious from that memorable dialogue between him and Lula about their differing geopolitical visions. As is so often the case with closed regimes, our hosts had various little tricks up their sleeves. At one point, under the pretext that the Brazilian delegation was being taken to visit the grave of Gaddafi's father, the Libyan officials dragged us off to lay flowers at the memorial to the victims of US air strikes in 1986. I feared this would be seized upon by our critics, but to my surprise the episode went almost unnoticed by the media. Another interesting moment was the banquet Gaddafi hosted for Lula. Seated at the head table were various leaders from the radical fringes of Third Worldism between the 1960s and 80s, including the Nicaraguan Sandinista leader Daniel Ortega (who would return to power not long afterwards) and the former Algerian president Ahmed Ben Bella, who I must confess I had imagined already to be dead. Based on the support Gaddafi had given to some of these figures when they were either in exile or opposition, he adopted a posture toward them that was that was a mixture of paternalism and arrogance. The same attitude was perceptible in the demands he made in relation to the schedules and formats for his own visits abroad. This might explain why, despite his declared admiration for President Lula and the relationship the two leaders had in the past, Gaddafi never visited Brazil. In fact, the respectful treatment foreign heads of state and government receive in Brasilia was not enough for him: he wanted to be welcomed differently, in ways that would have been compatible neither with the norms of our protocol nor with Lula's natural tendency to treat all heads of state as equals, whether they represent great powers or small nations. By the way, it is interesting to note that the countries that would later participate actively in Gaddafi's overthrow—and, to some extent, in his brutal killing—were prepared to meet some of his bizarre demands. An example of this ambivalence was France, which allowed Gaddafi to pitch his tent in the middle of the Champs-Élysées.[46] Berlusconi's Italy, which would also participate in the NATO attacks on Libya, albeit in a more reticent way, saw fit to dispense similar treatment to the Libyan leader.

If 2003 was the year new ideas for our relationship with the Arab world were launched, 2005 was when they really took shape. As for 2004, it was devoted mainly to preparatory and backstage work. Rereading my notebook, I see that on the first day of the year I wrote down a short list of "issues to be dealt with immediately from January 6." Alongside a reference to the Summit of South American-Arab Countries, I wrote: "Define more clearly the summit's objectives; meeting of senior officials; agenda/dates/logistical details; consultations with South America; Argentina." The last item in the list was "special ambassador to the Middle East." To put these plans into action I intended to take the opportunities offered to deepen our dialogue with the Arab world. Parallel moves were made toward our South American neighbors, who in general welcomed the idea. We were always concerned with achieving a good degree of coordination with Argentina. To that end, we were later pleased to have the enthusiastic support of former Argentine president Eduardo Duhalde, who at the suggestion of Buenos Aires had been appointed chairman of the Committee of Permanent Representatives of Mercosur.

At the end of January, on the way back from a trip to India with President Lula, I took advantage of a stop in Geneva to meet with the Arab countries' permanent representatives to international organizations. In May I returned to Cairo, again with a message from President Lula to President Mubarak, this time inviting him to participate in the Mercosur summit scheduled to take place in Brazil in December. The Egyptian leader did not attend the summit in the end, but my visit nevertheless allowed me to meet again with key contacts such as the foreign minister, Ahmad Maher, and my friend Amr Moussa. Thanks to the latter I was able to have a working lunch with the Arab League foreign ministers. In an interview I gave to the Egyptian-Brazilian journalist Randa Achmawi of the French edition of the *Al-Ahram* newspaper, I expressed my optimism regarding the ASPA summit, presenting it in the context of fostering South-South relations. In that same interview I made clear our strong support for a Palestinian state and urged the Quartet to continue working on the basis of the Road Map. One of the journalist's questions referred to the Palestinians' well-known desire for Brazil to play a more "dynamic" role in the peace negotiations: in my answer I took the opportunity to reiterate our willingness to work together with the main players toward that objective. I should mention that during the visit, as would be the case when I made other stops in Cairo, I also discussed issues related to the WTO. Egypt was an active member of the G20[47] and its trade minister at the time, Youssef Boutros-Ghali, an important interlocutor in the discussions with the rich countries. Brazil's leadership in that group of developing countries in the WTO was an important catalyst for alliances and associations that extended well beyond the field of trade.

Also in May, I returned to Jordan to attend another meeting organized by the World Economic Forum, and repeated my invitation for the country's representatives to attend the ASPA summit. In September, on the margins of the UN General Assembly, there was a first meeting of Arab and South American foreign ministers, following an understanding Amr Moussa and I had arrived at during our meeting in May. It turned out not to be a straightforward meeting, however. There were moments when there seemed to be major differences among the Arab ministers themselves. Occasionally these divergences were expressed rather harshly, but gradually I realized they had little to do with Brazil's proposal: essentially they reflected disputes and rivalries between members of the Arab League, or between the members and the secretariat. The foreign minister of Oman was especially forthright in his criticism of the organization, and for me, a newcomer to those issues, his words sounded unusually aggressive. After a few moments of anxiety, Amr Moussa (who was sharing a table with me) managed to restore calm, and the proceedings took a positive turn. It was during this meeting that a schedule of preparations for the summit in Brasilia, in May 2005, was established. It was also agreed that a preparatory meeting of foreign ministers would take place two months before, in Marrakech. In the meantime, meetings would be held between senior officials and deputy ministers at the Arab League's headquarters. Over the course of 2004, a lot of work was done to put flesh on the bones of the summit. Initiatives in the areas of culture, science, and business were planned under the guidance of Itamaraty's Undersecretary for Political Affairs, Ambassador Vera Pedrosa. Later on, it would also fall to her to draw up the declaration to be issued by the heads of state and government, a task requiring great dedication and diplomatic skill. A few days after the meeting of foreign ministers at the UN, Brazil hosted the Seminar of South American-Arab Countries on Arid Lands and Water Resources in the northeastern coastal city of Fortaleza. The focus of the event was itself already a concrete example of the potential for cooperation between the two regions.

That same year, two Arab leaders visited Brazil: President Émile Lahoud of Lebanon, in February, and King Mohammed VI of Morocco, in November. Both of them expressed support for the ASPA summit. The year 2004 was also marked by the death of Arafat. Lula was represented at the funeral by his chief of staff, José Dirceu. The loss of the great leader would be a further complication in dealing with the Palestinian issue.

The grand Arabian tour

"February 18, 2005, 7:15 a.m.. The bright sun illuminates the dust-colored buildings of Ramallah. Sitting at a desk in my hotel room, I look toward Mecca. The silence and calm of the streets contrast with the image we're used to seeing. Here, the sun also rises!" It seems a significant coincidence that the notes I wrote during a journey that encompassed ten Arab countries in ten days begin with a description of a scene in Palestine. Although the initial and stated aim of the trip was to ensure the highest possible attendance at the Brasilia summit, Palestine had already come to occupy a central place in my thoughts. As I would learn during my visits there, the unresolved issue of a state for the Palestinian people was—and still is—at the root of most of the problems afflicting the Middle East. The existence of a power struggle between two rival factions (Fatah and Hamas) generated alignments that, for example, placed Syria in opposition to Egypt and Saudi Arabia, and accentuated splits within countries such as Lebanon. Moreover, the presence of large numbers of Palestinian refugees in Lebanon, Syria, and Jordan contributed significantly to a situation of instability. That was certainly my early impression, when I was just beginning to delve into the political issues of the region.

The Embraer[48] Legacy aircraft that took me from Suriname—where I had accompanied the president on an official visit and a meeting with CARICOM[49] —to the Middle East landed first in Amman, which I was visiting for the third time since the beginning of the Lula government. In a meeting with Jordanian foreign minister Hani Mulki, I emphasized our eagerness for Jordan to be present at the summit (it would be represented by a member of the royal family) and heard about recent political developments in the region. The journey from Suriname to Amman had taken about fifteen hours. Nevertheless, soon after my conversation with Mulki, I set off for Ramallah. I crossed the border between Jordan and Palestine in the Jericho region. With me as I crossed the famous Allenby Bridge was a small entourage consisting of Affonso Ouro-Preto, formerly my chief of staff during the Itamar government, now acting as special representative to the Middle East; Bernardo Brito, the head of our diplomatic mission in Ramallah, opened in September

2004; Antonio Patriota, my chief of staff (later to become foreign minister in Dilma Rousseff's government); Sarkis Karmirian, director of Itamaraty's "Near East" department; Ricardo Tavares, Itamaraty spokesperson; and two personal assistants (Andrea Watson and Alexandre Ghislene). The Israeli guards controlling the border between the territories of two Arab entities were polite but over-scrupulous. Usually in these situations the visa comes on a separate piece of paper, but in the case of at least one of us (Ricardo Tavares) the guards put the stamp inside the passport itself, which would end up causing problems at certain moments during the trip. In Ramallah I was greeted almost as if I were a head of state. I had meetings with the president of the Palestinian Authority, Mahmoud Abbas (also known as Abu Mazen), the prime minister, Ahmed Qurei, and the foreign minister, Nabil Shaath. I placed flowers at the Yasser Arafat Memorial, built next to the Muqata, where the Palestinian leader spent his last days. All the conversations were very positive and the meetings took place in a distinctly warm atmosphere. The Prime Minister offered me lunch. At the end of each meeting I was asked to give an interview to the press, with my interlocutors, including the president, accompanying me each time. The conversation with Shaath was the most in-depth: we spoke about Brazil's participation in the peace process; the ASPA summit, which Shaath said was of "strategic importance" to Palestine; and bilateral cooperation. During our joint press conference, when a journalist asked if the fact that Brazil had relations with Israel would be detrimental toward our involvement in the peace process, Shaath said simply: "We trust Brazil." At the end of the long day of meetings, Shaath insisted on offering us a magnificent dinner of lamb roasted in the traditional Arab style. When we arrived back at our hotel, my colleagues and I celebrated our "historic day" with cups of mint tea. Our rooms were basic but clean, and I slept soundly. The only uncomfortable moment came early the next morning when I opened the door and there was a Palestinian policeman outside with a submachine gun. Eventually, over the course of my travels to the Middle East, I would become used to such scenes.

The landscape of the West Bank, both natural and human, made a strong impression on me. The checkpoints that prevented simple, direct travel between cities and villages—thereby separating families or greatly prolonging children's journeys to and from school—were in stark contrast with the highways that crisscrossed the country. Some of the expressways looked like they had come out of a science-fiction movie—and the local population was not permitted to use them. On the way back to Jordan I was accompanied by a deputy foreign minister who put me through on the phone to a former colleague from New York, Nasser al-Qudwa, a nephew of Arafat, who had just been appointed foreign minister. My friend Nabil Shaath, whom he replaced, was to become deputy prime minister. My impressions from the journey led me to write in my notebook: "Judging by their leaders, [the Palestinian people] are not bitter, despite their suffering. They even exude a certain tranquility, as if adversity has instilled in them a great deal of patience, which should not be confused with fatalism."

According to the schedule, which had been prepared by my aides in coordination with our various embassies, the next stop should have been Lebanon, but the assassination of Prime Minister Rafik Hariri, just before I left Brazil, forced me to change my plans. I gained a rest day in Amman. Not far from the capital, I visited the Roman ruins of Jerash (or Gerasa, in ancient times), which served as a reminder that good ideas, including in artistic creation, always have an antecedent. The design of the main temple, a large oval surrounded by columns that enclose it like two hands, struck me as a foretaste of what the Italian master Bernini created for St. Peter's Square; no doubt both were intended to convey the same sense of embracing the faithful.

After that brief cultural distraction, I set off for Damascus. It was a sensitive moment to be arriving in Syria, with the government suspected of having participated in or even planned the assassination of the Lebanese prime minister. Suspicion would give way to an open accusation on the part of the United States, which withdrew its ambassador from Damascus. For me, in the context of planning the summit, contact with the Syrian government was very important. But there was also another issue which had made my stop in Damascus virtually obligatory: I hoped to secure the cooperation of the Syrian intelligence agency, said to be highly effective, in locating and potentially freeing a Brazilian engineer, João José Vasconcellos, who had been abducted in Iraq about a month earlier. The fate of our compatriot, who was eventually found to have been murdered, was a constant theme during the trip, especially in those countries with particularly capable intelligence services.

In Damascus I was received by the foreign minister, Farouk al-Sharaa, whom I had met during the presidential visit in December 2003. We had a long and interesting conversation in which the main subject, inevitably, was the assassination of Hariri, in the context of the wider issues of the Middle East and the pressures to isolate Syria. In a friendly tone, and taking every precaution to avoid giving any impression of intrusion, I ventured the opinion—based largely on my experience with Iraq—that Syria should not reject Security Council Resolution 1559, from 2004.[50] An uncooperative attitude, I said, would be used by the country's opponents to blame Damascus, and could even trigger increasingly aggressive actions by certain permanent members of the UNSC. It was an intense conversation, and difficult to some extent, but still essentially friendly. My interlocutor realized my intention was to help find a solution, on the assumption that the Syrian government—or at least its highest levels—was not actually involved in the assassination. "You're a good man," Sharaa told me, in a tone that seemed spontaneous and sincere. The next day I had an audience with President Bashar al-Assad, who received me with great courtesy and profuse expressions of appreciation for President Lula. He carefully read the two letters I gave him: one specifically concerning the ASPA summit, the other about the bilateral relationship and also multilateral issues such as Security Council reform. Assad was particularly keen to discuss the latter. He made positive comments about Brazil and India, but was more reticent in relation to Germany: "It isn't a totally independent country," he said. He listened attentively to my observations on the "possible reform" (the way new members could be chosen, how many there could be, etc.). He referred to a conversation he had had with Putin on the issue, in which apparently they had agreed about the need for new permanent members such as "Brazil and India." Actually I was surprised by how interested the Syrian president was in the subject: he asked me several specific questions about the positions of the current permanent members on reform, their attitudes toward the veto, etc.. It would be no exaggeration to say our discussion on UNSC reform took up almost half the meeting, which lasted about an hour.

At the end of the conversation I introduced, indirectly, the subject of Lebanon. Assad told me categorically that "Syria wants to comply with Resolution 1559." At that time, of course, there was no way I could judge whether he was being sincere. On this and various other occasions when I had contact with Assad, I was always left with an ambiguous impression. On the one hand he presented himself as a rational and pragmatic man, willing to solve problems. On the other, reading between the lines (and also listening to certain other interlocutors), it seemed he remained the prisoner of sinister forces from which he was trying to break free. These would have been inherited from his father, Hafez Assad, who ruled Syria for nearly thirty years: Bashar appeared at times to have some success in shaking them off, with positive consequences for the Lebanese situation, but all too often his fleeting successes disintegrated in the midst of new crises. The elusive and puzzling nature of Assad's true intentions was emphasized by the contradictory analyses I would hear during the remainder of the trip. For example, Brazil's honorary consul in Jeddah, a prosperous businessman who also happened to be a half-brother of Osama bin Laden, said he did not believe Syria was involved in Hariri's assassination—a view not shared by, among others, our ambassador in Beirut or, as I will describe below, the Qatari foreign minister.

From Damascus I left on board the Legacy—my "flying office," as I called it—for Saudi Arabia. These flights in the in the company of my aides brought to mind Winston Churchill's liking for long train journeys, which according to one of his biographers[51] derived from the fact that they provided him with opportunities for reflection. In my case the thought process was generally collective. I had the benefit of the wide historical and political knowledge of our special envoy, Affonso Ouro-Preto, and the analyses offered by my closest collaborators such as Patriota and Neiva Tavares. Often, as during the flight from Damascus to Jeddah, I used these periods of relative isolation to reread speeches I was due to make. In Jeddah, where we would stay only a few hours, I was due to participate in the Economic Forum, where there would be several well-known figures from the Arab world and further afield. I thought I should not miss an opportunity to address an audience whose opinions might influence, in some way, the undertaking I was involved in.

During the forum there was a curious coincidence: the person who addressed the audience immediately before me was former US Secretary of State Madeleine Albright, who had been my colleague at the United Nations. During the period we served together there, our relationship was very cordial and friendly. I have kept to this day a photo with a dedication from Albright "in memory of a good meeting": in the foreground appear presidents Fernando Henrique Cardoso and Bill Clinton, with the two of us behind them. The brief meeting in question had taken place in the lounge situated behind the foyer of the UN General Assembly, where speakers wait their turn to be called. It was arranged largely upon my initiative, thanks to the improvisational skills of my colleague Antonio Simões. Cardoso gave Clinton a volume of memoirs by Roosevelt's secretary of state, Cordell Hull, which recall the president's desire to see Brazil included as permanent member of the UNSC. Albright would later refer to the gesture as proof of the competence of Brazilian diplomacy. Such were our relations back then. Later, however, when she was the head of US diplomacy, Albright more than once complained directly, or through the US embassy in Brasilia, about positions I adopted toward the tough line on Iraq. In our brief meeting in Jeddah, my former colleague, her head partially covered by a shawl out of respect for Islamic traditions, was very affectionate and suggested that I should visit her when I was next in Washington. In fact I would not see her again until after Obama's election, on the occasion of a G20[52] summit in the US capital, when she was given the role of welcoming the foreign delegations as they arrived. On that occasion, as witnessed by some of my colleagues, Madeleine's reaction when she saw me was to throw her arms around my neck and wrap me in a warm embrace.

As on other occasions, although I had already gone through the text of the speech I was due to deliver in Jeddah, which had been prepared by my staff, it still contained too many "UN-isms," which I tried to replace with more direct and affirmative language. Part of the speech was on issues related to social and economic development of Brazil. I spoke about Brazil's efforts, led by President Lula, to put the issue of combating hunger and poverty on the international agenda, especially at the meeting of leaders that took place in 2004 on the margins of the UN General Assembly.[53] I referred to the Doha Round of trade negotiations, emphasizing the need for coordination among developing countries through closer ties between the G20 and the G90.[54] As usual, I explained Brazil's view of the need for Security Council reform, with new permanent members from the developing world. I referred to initiatives we had taken in search of new partnerships with countries of the South, and highlighted the potential of the economic relationship between South America and the Arab world—the context in which I also introduced the subject of the proposed ASPA summit. In an attempted rhetorical flourish, I said the event would be "the first meeting of heads of state of two major regions of the developing world since the conferences of African and Asian countries that gave rise to Non-Aligned Movement." But more important at that particular moment, following a mention for Sérgio Vieira de Mello,[55] was my insertion into the text of a solemn appeal for the release of the Brazilian engineer kidnapped in Iraq. I was under no illusions that my public message would have any impact in practical terms: it was my private conversations on the matter, such as the one in Damascus and the others that would shortly take place in other capitals, that I really hoped would achieve concrete results. In fact, in including the appeal in my speech, I was aiming partly at Brazilian public opinion. I knew an emotional issue such as that one, quite apart from its intrinsic importance in human terms, needed to be handled with special care and attention if it was not to be used as a pretext for criticizing the conduct of our foreign policy. That is why, when I had first learned of the kidnapping, a few weeks before the start of the Middle East tour, I had called a meeting of my principal aides in my office in Itamaraty, even though it was during the weekend. Vice President José Alencar also made a point of attending. The meeting went on into the evening and I made sure the lights in the building were on. It was a way of saying to potential critics: "You see, we're doing all we can to save our compatriot."

Regarding the media's coverage of the case of the abducted Brazilian, I think it is relevant to jump ahead slightly and transcribe some notes I made on April 3, when any hope of finding him alive had already virtually disappeared: "Discouraging news, almost definitive, on the Brazilian engineer kidnapped in Iraq, a subject always difficult to deal with. The conservative press . . . is trying maliciously to exploit the situation. [A newspaper] has even published an article with the headline 'Itamaraty sends diplomat-painter to Iraq.' [That was a] spiteful reference to the irrelevant fact that Sérgio Telles (who, by the way, conducted himself with great courage and patriotism) is also an artist. Fortunately, the family [of the engineer] has been supporting our approach."

After my speech at the economic forum I set off for Riyadh, arriving in the Saudi capital at night. I immediately called my Spanish counterpart Miguel Ángel Moratinos, a recognized expert on Middle East issues. I should point out that I did not intend to conduct my political talks with Arab leaders in isolation: on the contrary, whenever possible and appropriate, I sought to share the content of those conversations with relevant colleagues. Moratinos, who had recently visited Brazil with Prime Minister José Luis Zapatero, had given me useful information about some of the figures I would be meeting during the trip, along with detailed analyses of the relations between the Arab countries. It was natural that I should reciprocate his kindness, so I briefly filled him in on my conversations in Syria.

In Riyadh I took part in a business seminar at the headquarters of the Chamber of Commerce, which on the Brazilian side was attended by Banco do Brasil, Petrobras and some trading companies. Even though our efforts to boost trade with Saudi Arabia were still in their early stages, it was already possible to note an improvement. Our exports to the kingdom in 2004 showed a 26% increase in relation to 2003, reaching $800 million USD (and would reach $3.5 billion in 2011). My notebook makes clear my optimistic reaction to that development. From an economic point of view, my most important meeting in Riyadh was with the secretary-general of the Gulf Cooperation Council (GCC), Abdul Rahman bin Hamad al-Attiyah, a Qatari whom I had met before on some occasion or other, possibly at the United Nations. Al-Attiyah had certainly done his homework, revealing quite a detailed knowledge of our diplomatic positions and initiatives. He even surprised me by knowing the name of our special envoy to the Middle East, "Ambassador Affonso." He was sympathetic to the possibility of Brazil becoming a permanent member of the Security Council; indeed, he described it as a "necessity." He himself spoke at length about the importance of the proposed summit in Brasilia—which gave me the opportunity to formally invite him, as our ambassador, Luiz Sérgio Figueira, had suggested I should. We swapped ideas on a Mercosur-GCC framework agreement, and at his request I promised to push forward the necessary work so that such an agreement could be signed during the summit, which indeed would be the case.[56] That same afternoon I called my good friend Leila Rachid, the foreign minister of Paraguay, who at that time held the presidency of Mercosur. She offered her help with the idea. During our conversation Al-Attiyah referred spontaneously to the "positive role" Brazil could play in the peace process. When leaving the building at the end of the meeting, I could not help noticing the huge scale of the GCC headquarters—a rather brutal contrast with the modest rooms housing the Mercosur Secretariat in Montevideo.

My main mission in Saudi Arabia was to deliver to the prince regent, Abdullah bin Abdulaziz al-Saud—who would soon become king—two letters from President Lula to the monarch. In retrospect I can see that although strictly speaking it was correct in terms of protocol to address the letters to the ailing King Fahd bin Abdulaziz al-Saud, and therefore it was not a diplomatic gaffe, the gesture was unnecessarily punctilious. Fortunately I do not think it caused offence to Prince Abdullah, the de facto ruler, or affected the Saudi response. One of the letters specifically concerned the summit; the other was on bilateral and also wider Middle East issues, in which the importance of the Arab Peace Initiative, proposed by the Saudis in 2002, was naturally highlighted. At the meeting with the prince I explained the reasons that had led Brazil to take the initiative of organizing the summit. A few times during the conversation I had to correct the interpreter, who in translating "South America" came up with a term in Arabic which I took to mean "Latin America." The subtle error served merely to confirm something I already knew, which is that "South America" is a rather difficult concept to establish, not just within our region itself but also outside. The prince, who was more than 80 years old, seemed to respond sympathetically to my comments but remained monosyllabic. When I emphasized how keen President Lula was for him (rather than the king) to participate in the Brasilia summit, His Highness restricted himself to saying "*Inshallah*!" But he did so with a smile that gave me some hope. In the end, Saudi Arabia would be represented at the summit by its experienced foreign minister Prince Saud bin Faisal (at the time the oldest of all the world's foreign ministers, if I am not mistaken), who had gained notoriety for his criticism of the invasion of Iraq, widely reported in the international media.

While in Riyadh I was accompanied by an efficient and—in comparison with the prince regent—loquacious deputy foreign minister. This senior official, who according to our ambassador was the individual who in reality ran the foreign ministry, told me that Saudi perceptions of the summit were developing very favorably and that Prince Abdullah's own opinion was very positive. I inferred that my companion had arrived at that conclusion on the basis of contact he had had with Prince Abdullah after the meeting—which was pleasing and also, I confess, something of a relief. Because of the economic power Saudi Arabia possesses on the basis of its fabulous oil reserves, and given its "aura" as guardian of the Islamic faith, its attitude would have a great bearing on the success, or otherwise, of the summit. Although Riyadh of course participated in the consensus decision taken by the Arab League, I had my doubts about what position the country would eventually take. This uncertainty, due to the lack of clear signals from the Saudi government, was increased by an unfortunate scheduling problem that had prevented President Lula from including the country in the trip he made in December 2003. Nothing was ever said officially about it, but in my mind there was a persistent worry that the Saudis might have felt offended because they were not consulted in advance about the trip. The words of the deputy minister, added to the benevolent smiles of His Highness during my audience with him (and his positive reaction to the presidential letters, again expressed more in gestures than in words), made me believe my fears were unfounded.

There was, however, a detail of protocol that could have been interpreted negatively. Unlike two and half years later, when King Abdullah—by then established as Protector of the Two Holy Cities—would receive me promptly and with great courtesy in his sumptuous tent in desert, in 2005 the prince regent made me wait for several hours at the hotel where official guests were accommodated. Was this a way of signaling displeasure at that "misunderstanding" in 2003? Despite the tension that inevitably arises in such situations, I chose not to interpret it that way. I should also mention a sociological aspect of the visit to Saudi Arabia: during that whole tour of Arab countries it was the only place where my aide Andrea Watson had to use an *abaya* that covered her from head to toe, leaving not a single strand of hair visible. Some stories we had been told, including one involving a female former Brazilian ambassador, had made clear the need for prudence on the part of visitors, the country of course being marked by profound discrimination against women.

From Saudi Arabia I left for Oman. The inclusion in my itinerary of Muscat—a beautiful city by the Indian Ocean, with white-painted houses and the remnants of fortresses built by our Portuguese ancestors—was due largely to the insistence of Nabil Shaath, who—like Amr Moussa—would be a valuable source of advice throughout the preparations for the summit process. Shaath suggested the small sultanate in the south of the Arabian Peninsula would be one of the countries disinclined to participate in the meeting of leaders. Actually I had already witnessed the somewhat distrustful attitude of the Omani foreign minister in two meetings with his counterparts from the rest of the Arab League—one in Cairo, the other at the UN. This rather unfavorable impression was reinforced by one particular aspect of his traditional attire: he always carried on his waist a menacing-looking ceremonial dagger. But my meetings in Muscat completely changed my perception. It became clear, as indeed I had sensed at the meeting in New York, that the apparent reticence in relation to the summit was due less to the Brazilian invitation in itself than the internal rivalries of the Arab world. My meetings in the Omani capital were with Prince Sayid Assad bin Tareq, the sultan's cousin, and the foreign minister, Yusuf bin Alawi. Both were very receptive toward our idea. The prince made a point of explaining that the Sultan, on whose behalf he was receiving me, was not in the capital. He spoke freely about a number of topics and came across as well informed and modern in his attitudes, in contrast to the traditionalism of his clothing and the surrounding *décor*. There were also some picturesque moments during my audience with him. In addition to the large quantity of coffee with cardamom that I sipped with pleasure every time it was served (which was very often: only later was it explained to me that to indicate I did not want more I had to subtly jiggle the cup), there was also a large bowl containing a kind of sweet paste made with honey and spices. But there was no spoon, or indeed any similar utensil. It was then that I realized I should use my fingers, just as His Highness was doing. I believe it was during this trip to Oman, where at the time we did not yet have an embassy, that a diplomat based in Dubai, Sergio Abi-Sad, presented me with the book *Travels with a Tangerine* by the English author Tim Mackintosh-Smith, a travel diary in the footsteps of Ibn Battutah, a kind of Arab Marco Polo of the fourteenth century. I had the impression that besides stimulating my traveler's instinct, my colleague wished to stress the importance of adapting to local habits—which is what I endeavored to do in sharing the tactile experience of the delicacy placed in front of me. The foreign minister and I also covered, in a separate meeting, more conventionally diplomatic issues such as the peace process, the crisis in Lebanon, Iraq, etc.. On the subject of Security Council reform, he said he regarded Brazil (and India) as a "natural candidate" for a permanent seat. He also referred positively to the summit, as indeed did the prince.

There was only a short journey between the sultanate of Oman and my next stop, the emirate of Qatar. In Doha—which I had visited once before, as ambassador in Geneva, to attend the launch of the trade round that bears the city's name—time restrictions meant my agenda consisted only of meetings with the foreign minister and deputy prime minister, Sheikh Hamad bin Jaber al-Thani, an old friend from the days when I was foreign minister under Itamar Franco. Al-Thani had visited Brazil in January 1994, when we signed a document committing our two countries to the reciprocal opening of embassies.[57] We met again at a historic moment: the inauguration of Nelson Mandela as president of South Africa. That was an occasion marked by strong emotions but also some logistical hitches. Before the start of the ceremony, the assembled guests had to wait a long time in a large grandstand, exposed to the sun. I had suffered three attacks of diverticulitis over the preceding years (one of them, in fact, contributed indirectly to my becoming Itamar's foreign minister)[58] and was therefore anxious to avoid going a long time without eating or, more important, drinking. My Qatari counterpart, who was sitting one or two rows behind me, perceived my distress and duly came to my rescue. His aides, accustomed to life in the desert, were equipped with several bottles of mineral water, and Sheikh Hamad offered me one. Needless to say I recalled the incident and reiterated my immense gratitude as soon as I met him again in Doha.

When I arrived, I learned from our representative in Abu Dhabi (who at that time was also accredited to the government of Qatar) that a Brazilian business mission had been in the country the day before. A contract to supply 400 buses had been signed: a good sign for our economic relations with a country which, although small, is open to the world and also very rich. The meeting with Sheikh Hamad took place at his residence, a palace built in a style similar to some of the others I had visited. Actually, it was a working dinner, which is to say a political dialogue conducted while we sampled various delicacies. The conversation was absolutely candid. The deputy prime minister, who belongs to the same family as the emir, told me he had personal investments in Brazil, which were "doing well." We talked about economics, the WTO, the ASPA summit, UNSC reform, the kidnapped Brazilian, and the situations in Iraq, Palestine, Syria, and especially Lebanon. The conversation felt uninhibited and informal. I also noticed that his aides were at liberty to offer their own opinions and comments, which I had not seen anywhere else during the trip. Sheikh Hamad did not hold back from describing recent episodes regarding Iraq and the relations between Qatar and the US. At one point, implying he was privy to inside information, he said the Iraq invasion had been planned "even before Bush's election"—clearly he enjoyed displaying intimate knowledge of the corridors of power in Washington. He was also surprisingly frank about Saudi Arabia, "whose difficulties could lead to a crisis in the short to medium term." As for the situation in Lebanon and whether Syria was involved in Hariri's murder, he did not mince his words. He said he was not sure if Bashar had ordered the assassination or even if he had known it was being planned, but he confidently asserted that Syrian groups with interests in Lebanon ("the cow they get their milk from") were behind the attack. He believed the only solution to the political situation in Lebanon was the resignation of President Émile Lahoud and the calling of new elections. I should mention at this point that, based on information received from the Brazilian ambassador in Lebanon, I had decided to include Beirut in the trip, and had scheduled the visit to follow the brief stop in Kuwait that would take place the day after the dinner in Qatar. What Sheikh Hamad told me, however, put a doubt in my mind about whether that was a good idea. Upon reflection, I decided the visit to Beirut should go ahead, not only because of the ASPA summit but also because I was counting on the assistance of the Lebanese and Syrian intelligence services to find and perhaps even rescue the Brazilian engineer José Vasconcellos.

I also took advantage of my brief stop in Doha to give an interview that was published by the Qatar-based newspaper *Al-Rayah* and reproduced by the Arab newspaper *Al-Ahram* in its Cairo, Beirut, Damascus, and London editions. This was part of a communications effort intended not only to advertize our positions on various issues of interest to the countries I was visiting, but also to create understanding of what our objectives were in launching the ASPA initiative. The interview covered various aspects of the relations between Brazil and the Arab countries, with special emphasis on the Brasilia summit. The journalist was well aware of the political changes taking place in South America, and his questions allowed me to explain how the integration process was evolving. The Doha Round negotiations also aroused great interest in Qatar, for obvious reasons. In my reply to a question on that subject, I highlighted the role of the G20 in seeking to bring about a balanced conclusion to the negotiations. The reporter also asked me questions related to Middle East issues, including one on Palestine and the possible role of Brazil in the peace negotiations, to which my answer was as follows: "During my visit [to Ramallah], last week, President Mahmoud Abbas insisted that Brazil should be ready to play an important role in the matter. He suggested the creation of a quadripartite committee composed of Brazil, South Africa, India and Turkey in order to assist the existing Quartet. Of course, our role would not be to provide magic solutions, but to assist in the process."

I have often said that without one's own aircraft it is impossible to conduct foreign policy, or at least the active foreign policy we wanted to make a feature of the Lula government. I think my conviction was proved correct on the day after the working dinner with Sheikh Hamad. On February 23, my delegation and I had breakfast in Qatar, lunch in Kuwait, and dinner in Lebanon. As far as I can remember, I did not have another day like that until very recently, when as defense minister I repeated the feat with South Africa, the Democratic Republic of Congo, and Angola. I spent only a few hours in Kuwait, where I had a meeting lasting a little over an hour with the Prime Minister, Sheikh Sabah al-Ahmad al-Sabah, and the foreign minister, Mohammed al-Sabah. In one of the Security Council panels on Iraq I had had the opportunity to deal with Kuwaiti interests, and had tried to do so as impartially as possible. Therefore, although I had never set foot in the country before, the Kuwaitis knew who I was. This time, however, I did not discuss Iraq at all: I was well aware of local sensitivities around the subject. The main topic, instead, was the ASPA summit. This small, oil-rich country, which Saddam Hussein tried to annex as Iraq's "nineteenth province," had made some significant investments in Brazil in the 1980s, but they had not worked out well. Perhaps that was why the prime minister, who had previously been foreign minister for many years, expressed a certain amount of skepticism toward the summit in his response to my presentation of the idea. He insisted on the importance of achieving "concrete" results. The foreign minister, meanwhile, seemed to regard our proposal more favorably, frequently nodding his head in approval. Gradually the prime minister accepted my arguments about the likely positive impact of the summit not only on business but also on other aspects of the relationship between Brazil and the Arab world. After the meeting, my Kuwaiti counterpart traveled with me in the same car to a lunch with businesspeople. As we were leaving the Bayan Palace, where I signed a cultural agreement that had been pending for at least two decades, he told me in what sounded like a sincere tone that I had been "very persuasive." He also asked me some questions about the summit, giving me the impression he wanted to have arguments of his own to defend the project. In my notebook I registered the conviction that Kuwait would not go unrepresented at the event.

The Kuwaiti foreign minister also asked me about Security Council reform, an issue I had touched on only briefly during the conversation with the prime minister. He wanted to know how we saw the issue of the veto. I gave him a quick explanation, after which he said he favored the option of having new permanent members that included an Arab country. I said Brazil did not see a problem with that, although of course the existing permanent members would have their objections to any "excessive" expansion. Just to see how my interlocutor would react, I ventured the opinion that the permanent member from the Arab world could be Egypt, which would not be regarded as a third African country and therefore would not provoke opposition from other regions.[59] As far as I remember, my Kuwaiti counterpart made no comment. Such conversations about UN reform punctuated my dialogues with various different interlocutors, and they all responded with some degree of sympathy or, in certain cases, expressions of outright support for Brazil's bid. When appropriate, I also brought up the WTO and Brazil's initiatives against world hunger. Therefore, though my grand Arabian tour was motivated principally by the ASPA summit, it also served certain other diplomatic objectives.

I was able to follow the route between Kuwait and Lebanon on a small screen in the cabin of the Legacy that showed our position on a map. The pilot carefully avoided entering Iraqi airspace. Shortly before we landed, I wrote in my notebook: "The faithful Legacy is approaching the Lebanese coast and the city of Beirut. I'm thinking about the delicate moment at which this visit is taking place. I'm spending only one night in Beirut. In principle my schedule is limited to a meeting with President Lahoud and the foreign minister since October 2004, Mahmoud Hammoud, who'll probably be together. I'll be giving them Lula's message. I've been thinking about a suggestion made by our ambassador, Marcus Vincenzi, who would like me to meet someone from the opposition to the regime. The name suggested to me was Carlos Eddé, a Lebanese-Brazilian, grandson of a former president of the country. I think that, at the moment, the gesture could be misinterpreted. My priority is to get as many Arab countries as possible (hopefully all of them) to attend the summit. But I told the ambassador I would be willing to meet with an independent figure, provided there was no chance of the Lebanese government seeing it as a provocation."

I ended up having two meetings during the evening of February 23. The first was the official meeting with the president and foreign minister, who once again confirmed Lebanon's participation in the Brasilia summit. I also spoke about the internal situation. As I had done in Damascus, I stressed the need for compliance with UN Security Council Resolution 1559. I pointed out that gestures perceived as positive by the international community would help stabilize the political situation in the country. Making a somewhat bold comparison, I referred to the case of Venezuela, where the presence of foreign observers during the recall referendum had served to strengthen the position of President Chávez. Lahoud listened carefully and did not seem offended by my having ventured an opinion on his country's internal affairs. Bearing in mind some of the observations I had heard elsewhere, particularly the previous day in Qatar, I found the Lebanese president surprisingly relaxed. He shared anecdotes about his relationship with his predecessor, laughing openly at various moments.

With my official mission accomplished, I went off to follow the ambassador's suggestion, albeit only partially. At the ambassador's residence I met the former Lebanese foreign minister, Jean Obeid, who was already a familiar face from my two previous visits in 2003. Obeid, like Lahoud a francophone Christian, had moved away from the president politically. What he told me reinforced my impression that Lahoud did not fully grasp the situation in his own country. I was struck by a reference Obeid made to the parliamentary elections due to take place a few weeks later. He said that looming over the vote were two corpses: that of Hariri, who despite being dead was still present in everyone's minds; and that of Lahoud, who despite being alive was already dead politically. Later that night I called President Lula to tell him about the progress that had been made.

The Lebanese issue—with all its ethnic, religious and geopolitical ramifications—was a constant theme throughout that tour of the Middle East in 2005. I am able to say I acquired a more realistic perception (although certainly still incomplete) of the struggle between the different factions. The assassination of Hariri allowed me to see more clearly the complexity of the power play in the country. I knew that the very creation of Lebanon as an entity separate from Syria had come about largely to suit the interests of the two great European powers (France and Britain) in the wake of the dissolution of the Ottoman Empire. It had been part of the famous Sykes-Picot Agreement.[60] But it was only during the journey that I came to appreciate the depth of feeling around the issue, both in Lebanon and in Syria. I must confess I had not previously been aware that Damascus—which had played a dominant role in Lebanese issues ever since the Taif Agreement of 1989 had ended the civil war—did not even have a diplomatic mission in Beirut, because it disagreed with the very idea of an independent Lebanese state. I also came to realize that the simplistic idea of the main division in Lebanon being between Muslims and Christians—with the former friendlier toward the West than the latter—did not correspond to reality. Hariri, a Sunni Muslim leader who preferred to speak English in conversations with foreign interlocutors, had been a friend and, according to some, "partner" of Jacques Chirac. President Lahoud, a former military man with westernized manners, was Christian and a francophone, but had the support of Syria (according to some in the region, he was a mere puppet) and, via Damascus, the Shias of Hezbollah. Some Christian groups strongly opposed the president and allied themselves with the Sunnis. My background knowledge came, one could say, from on-the-job training, and would give me a better appreciation of the concessions made by one side or the other that would make possible, about two years later, the formation of a coalition, thereby giving the country a period of relative stability that would ultimately prove illusory. After the death of Hariri, during the coalition government led by Fouad Siniora, Lebanon would have to endure the war of 2006 waged by Israel in retaliation against attacks by Hezbollah.

After the visit to Lebanon, the last two stops on the tour were Tunis and Algiers. In Tunisia, my only meeting was with the foreign minister, Abdelbaki Hermassi, who was new to the job (he had previously been culture minister). By that time, my "pitch" to my various interlocutors, on the summit and other subjects, had started to sound a bit like a stuck record—both to me and my aides, who did not spare me their honest appraisals. It was the same again in Tunisia. I met the foreign minister after a quick visit to the ruins of Carthage and a longer walk around the famous Bardo Museum, which had the most impressive collection of Roman mosaics I had ever seen. I must also mention our ambassador, Sergio Telles, whom I would post to Iraq a few weeks later. It was at his residence in Tunis that I heard that Pascal Lamy (with whom I had had a close relationship when he was EU trade commissioner, and even more so when became WTO director-general), had made an inappropriate comment about environmental preservation in the Amazon. At that time Lamy was a candidate for the WTO job and one of his rivals was a Brazilian, Luiz Felipe de Seixas Corrêa. I quickly made a statement, by phone, in which I said Lamy should keep his distance from issues of national sovereignty. I added a comment to the effect that his remark, typical of the arrogance of the developed countries, was a bad omen with regard to how he might conduct himself if chosen to head the WTO. This little incident shows that, throughout my tour of the Arab countries, I also had to keep an eye on other developments.

The conversation with my Tunisian counterpart was pleasant but did not bring up anything new. Apart from a brief discussion of bilateral subjects, particularly in the cultural field, and the decision to convene the joint committee of our two countries in the near future, I spoke about the usual subjects: the UNSC, the WTO, Lebanon, and above all, the summit. Hermassi, who was particularly keen on issues with a cultural aspect, said the idea of the meeting between South American and Arab leaders was "ingenious," and assured me that Tunisia would be represented. However, my stop in Tunis did not include a meeting with President Zine El Abidine Ben Ali (whose overthrow would later mark the beginning of the Arab Spring): one had been arranged, sufficiently in advance, but it was then cancelled. That was rather frustrating, of course, but it did not shake my confidence in Tunisia's participation in the summit.

On February 26, I watched dawn break over the Bay of Algiers. It was a rainy morning, but from the top of the hill where official guests are accommodated in a building very much in the socialist style, I could still see several large ships. Most of them were oil and gas tankers, an indication of Algeria's main source of wealth. Any feelings of disappointment at the cancellation of the meeting with the Tunisian president would be largely offset by the attentions I would receive in Algiers, including a long conversation with President Bouteflika. The day before, the foreign minister, Abdelaziz Belkhadem, had gone to the airport to welcome me—a courtesy less frequent among foreign ministers these days because of the sheer number of visits (indeed, during that tour, the only other time it happened was in Lebanon). Belkhadem was an interesting character. Dressed in the traditional clothing of his region (in contrast to the western attire of his ambassadors and other officials), he cut an elegant but unusual figure, reminding me of the figures depicted by European Orientalist painters in the second half of the nineteenth century. Often his face would contort into a severe expression, apparently indicating dislike for something I had just said, but then a moment later it would crease into a broad smile, suggesting heartfelt agreement. We talked at length in the car on the way from the airport, and during dinner in the restaurant at the accommodation for official guests. At his request, I spoke a lot about the WTO. Algeria was still in the process of acceding to the organization, and he wanted to know more about the details of the negotiations. As for the ASPA summit, Belkhadem left me in no doubt that Algeria would be represented "at the highest level." As in the other countries I had visited, the situation in Lebanon also came up. We agreed on the need for compliance with Resolution 1559, although Belkhadem also insisted there were double standards at work, comparing the Syrian occupation in Lebanon with the presence of the US in Iraq and Israel in Palestine.

Before starting my journey back to Brazil, I was received by President Abdelaziz Bouteflika (who at the time of writing has just been re-elected for another term—his fourth—at the head of the Algerian government). I had met him once before, briefly, when accompanying President Lula to the expanded G8 summit in Évian in June 2003. He greeted me warmly but also made some demands during our conversation, referring to various bilateral agreements that had been proposed by Algeria but were, he said, still awaiting a reply. Not having at my disposal the information that would allow me to explain Brazil's lack of response, I limited myself to saying that Bouteflika's state visit to Brasilia—an invitation Lula was extending to him—would be a good opportunity to "get the bureaucracy into gear." Bouteflika, physically diminutive and bright-eyed, is a former revolutionary who held the post of foreign minister for sixteen years during the height of Algeria's anticolonialist fervor. He retained some of the rhetoric from that period, but it was tempered by an attitude of pragmatism toward the West and in particular the old colonial power, France. Bouteflika told me that a "miracle" was taking place in Algeria under the stewardship of his government, though he diluted his pride with a touch of Islamic humility by attributing the phenomenon to God. He was referring to the end of the carnage that had blighted the country for several years, caused mainly by the fundamentalist Islamic Salvation Front (FIS). Civil and political institutions were gradually being rebuilt. Nevertheless, during my brief stay—and again during subsequent visits—I did have the feeling of being in a tightly controlled society, not unlike Hungary or Yugoslavia in the period immediately preceding the end of communism.

Early on during our conversation, Bouteflika began talking at length about the reform of the UN Security Council. I had known since my time as permanent representative at the UN that Algeria's positions did not coincide with ours, so I was not actually intending to raise the subject myself. But Bouteflika had obviously studied (in surprising depth, for a head of state) the report by the commission ("blue-ribbon panel") convened by Kofi Annan.[61] Indeed, he said he had identified "failings and gaps" in it. He criticized the so-called "Option A" presented in the December 2004 report, which proposed six new permanent members without the power of veto (the proposal favored, with certain adjustments, by Brazil and the other members of the G4).[62] His criticisms were based on the perception that Algeria—despite having been so politically proactive in the decades preceding the long years of internal conflict—was unlikely to be included among the six new members. Obviously the president himself did not put it like that; instead he made some conceptual observations about the feasibility and fairness of the proposal. After a long and friendly discussion, punctuated by meanderings and digressions, Bouteflika told me, with apparent sincerity, that he could support Brazil's candidature. India also seemed a natural candidate, he said, "despite the difficulties with Pakistan and the Muslim world in general." He considered it a mistake, however, for Brazil and India to have tied their fate to that of Japan and Germany, whose inclusion would in his opinion only increase the influence of the developed world in the UNSC. Bouteflika said more than once that his own country could not give up its candidature for permanent membership "every time an opportunity appears." So as to better explain our own position, I mentioned the idea, which we supported, that the reform should be reviewed after a certain period, so as to correct any errors or distortions. I also told him that the procedures we had in mind for the choice of new permanent members would not prevent any country from coming forward as a candidate, and that it would be up to the General Assembly to make the final decision, in accordance to the basic criteria of balance between regions and developed/developing countries. At various moments during our cordial dialogue, Bouteflika expressed appreciation toward Brazil and President Lula. At the end of the conversation, whether out of politeness or otherwise, he requested a non-paper setting out Brazil's vision of Security Council reform.

Bouteflika and I also touched on some delicate issues. The president was very candid about all of them: the relations between Lebanon and France ("Chirac and Hariri were Siamese twins"); the presence of Syria in Lebanon

("You can help more than we can"); and Palestine ("Brazil has to have a role"). At various moments the Algerian president stressed Brazil's leadership role, which according to him constituted a continuation, in modern form, of the Third World causes for which, he said, Algeria "had sacrificed its own progress and well-being." Bouteflika was keen to know more about the Doha Round and the G20. He asked questions about Venezuela and Cuba, and listened to my explanation of the difference, from a geopolitical point of view, between South America and Latin America. In a reprise of some of his old revolutionary jargon, he requested very directly that Algeria be admitted to the "political *bureau* for combating hunger and poverty." Referring to the New York summit on that issue on the margins of the UN General Assembly in 2004, he showed he was an astute observer by recalling the "reticent attitude" of President Thabo Mbeki. I promised him I would give due attention to all those issues, and also convey to President Lula his opinions and concerns. We were together for more than two hours—the longest conversation I had ever had with any head of state, with the sole exception of my meeting with Fidel Castro in 1994.

The next morning, on the flight back to Brazil, I wrote in my notebook: "We had lunch at the hotel-residence and at about 2 p.m. we left for Paris, bringing to an end a veritable marathon of ten countries (eleven cities) in as many days." I had set off for the Middle East with the main objective of raising awareness among Arab leaders of the importance of the summit scheduled for May in Brasilia. But the conversations with my various interlocutors had provided a mosaic of impressions that in fact went far beyond that goal. Bilateral relations in the political, economic and cultural fields, the Doha Round negotiations (and, in that context, the candidature of Ambassador Seixas Corrêa for the post of WTO director-general), UN reform, and the internal situations in various countries: all of those subjects had been addressed to an unprecedented extent, which I am sure was a turning point in our relationship with the Arab world. As foreign minister I had acquired a more direct knowledge of the political forces at work in complex situations, such as Lebanon and its relations with Syria. I had a better appreciation of the diversity of opinions, even within smaller groups such as the GCC. Even the individual tragedy of a kidnapped (and, as we would later discover, murdered) Brazilian citizen had been addressed in the midst of discussions about trade and geopolitics. The summit was still to come, but in our efforts to build multipolarity I felt we had already managed to lay a brick or two.

"Crimes committed by the colonialists"

On March 16, about a month after the beginning of my Arabian tour, I set off on another long journey that would take me to India (G20), Algiers and Marrakech. In notes written on the plane shortly after leaving Brasilia, I summarized the development of the summit idea up to that point. I recalled that the initial impulse had come from President Lula, and that it had then been up to me give the idea shape and take it forward. Perhaps the most interesting thing I recorded in my notebook concerned the US attitude toward the summit initiative: "At first the project went almost unnoticed, but as it has taken shape it has been causing concern [in Washington], recently conveyed by Condoleezza Rice to Lula's chief of staff, José Dirceu. Not being able to stop the initiative, the US gave up on criticizing it and instead began to seek to influence the agenda ('it would be good if the issue of democracy were raised at the meeting'). You have to ask what they mean by 'democracy,' and how to achieve it. Is Iraq the model?" In retrospect, those notes are doubly interesting. First, they record Washington's desire to undermine the meeting by molding its content. The democratization of the Arab countries was certainly a desirable goal in itself—but also extremely difficult to achieve, as would be evident years later during the Arab Spring. And to make that an item on the agenda would certainly have been regarded as a provocation by those countries, almost all of which were autocracies tightly controlled by their rulers. Second, in referring to the secretary of state's phone call to Dirceu, my notes show how the US government operates, seeking whenever possible to bypass our foreign ministry and talk directly to people whom Washington regards as having influence over government decisions. In this case the maneuver did not work, because Dirceu himself told me about the call. The most curious thing is that Condoleezza Rice, with whom I would later develop a good relationship, had phoned me soon after her appointment as secretary of state and expressed her commitment to a frank and direct dialogue. But on subjects such as these, Lula always listened to my opinion, rendering futile any attempt to circumvent Itamaraty. During her visit to Brazil at the end of April 2005, just before the summit, Condoleezza and I spent almost six hours together (including moving from one place to another, and press conferences), and she resumed the friendly tone of her phone call to me in January. In my notes about that meeting, I wrote: "We spoke extensively about Haiti, Africa, and the Middle East. Always from an angle of understanding, and even the possibility of cooperation. In short, a positive agenda." At one of the press conferences that day, when a journalist asked the secretary of state how she saw the ASPA summit, she took great care in her reply to avoid any criticism of our initiative.

In the second half of March, after the G20 meeting in Delhi, I made my second trip to Algeria in less than a month. This time it was in response to an invitation from the Algerian government, which held the presidency of the Arab League, to address the organization's summit in Algiers. Along with some other non-Arab representatives (the UN secretary-general, the Spanish prime minister, and a few foreign ministers) I had been invited to address the member countries' heads of state, which was an unusual distinction for Brazil. With the ASPA summit fast approaching, I certainly was not going to turn down such an opportunity. The opening session, on March 22, was a long one. Gaddafi made an interminable speech in which he vehemently criticized the two-state solution to the conflict between Israel and Palestine. He thereby placed himself in clear opposition to the majority position, and collided head-on with the Arab Peace Initiative, the Saudi proposal that continued to inspire all the Arab League's official statements. The Libyan leader's long-winded speech was sufficient to rid me of any illusion of unanimity among the Arab countries on the issue of Palestine. In fact, there were evident differences on several of the region's political issues (Lebanon, Iraq, Palestine); I had already noticed that was the case during my long journey the month before, but this was the first time I had heard a divergent position expressed so emphatically in a forum that was essentially Arab although it included a few "outsiders" such as myself. Nevertheless, Gaddafi's speech fitted perfectly with the "lesson" we had endured in his tent in 2003, and indeed helped explain its content.

The length of the speeches made by several of the participants led me to worry that the chair of the meeting, my friend Abdelaziz Bouteflika, might have to cancel the speeches by the invited foreign ministers. If that happened, my visit to Algiers would be rendered pointless. In the end Bouteflika appealed to the speakers to be more concise. I spoke immediately after the French foreign minister, Michel Barnier, and the high representative of the European Union, Javier Solana. I followed the example of both by speaking only for three minutes, but I still covered everything that was important: the objectives of the ASPA summit; Palestine; and UN reform. On the latter point I thought I should make a positive gesture toward the audience by expressing support for a permanent seat for an Arab country, "without prejudice to the two permanent seats for Africa." I could see that was not enough to satisfy my Egyptian counterpart Ahmed Aboul Gheit, however. I pointed out that the ASPA summit was going to take place at a moment when South American integration had received major boost with the official launch of the Community of South American Nations (CASA) in Cuzco about three months before. The summit between the South American countries and the Arab League would therefore be the first event involving this newly created community and another region of the developing world. To my delight, Bouteflika and Amr Moussa mentioned the summit in their own speeches. I took advantage of the closing ceremony to complete my exercise in public relations.

A few other details are worth mentioning. Before the start of the summit (which took place in a convention center by the sea, guarded by an impressive detachment of cavalry), as I reached the front of the line of visiting dignitaries, Bouteflika greeted me with four kisses, two on each cheek. According to our ambassador, Isnard Penha Brasil, that was indicative of "great friendship." Several Algerian newspapers reported positively on the "presence of the Brazilian minister" at the event and also made reference to the forthcoming Brasilia summit. During the dinner offered by Bouteflika, I scribbled a few notes in the margins of the menu: the only really interesting one concerned the Algerian ambassador to Cairo, a former combatant in the war of liberation, who commented that a distinction should be made between "terrorism" and "resistance to foreign occupation." This point would prove one of the most difficult in the meeting of South American and Arab foreign ministers that took place in Marrakech over the next few days.

My visit to Algiers, given the extended schedule of the Arab League summit, allowed me to gain a better understanding of the historical development of Algerian culture from its Numidian origins, through the vestiges of the Roman presence, up to the recent struggle for independence. Especially interesting was the visit I made, accompanied by the *Wali* (mayor) and an impressive number of security guards, to the Casbah, the old city whose white-painted houses and narrow alleyways surround what was once the residence of the *Dey*[63] (governor) of Algiers. The area was still considered "dangerous," and it needed some persuasion from our ambassador before the Algerian authorities consented to my request to see it. Our guide—a man of apparently humble origins, but extremely eloquent and also so animated that I thought he might have ingested some kind of stimulant—described to me in detail the *coup d'éventail*, or slap with a hand fan, that the *Dey* administered to the French envoy in 1827, which served as a pretext for the start of the colonial adventure by Charles X. He punctuated his descriptions with keen invitations to take photos (so I could show people in Brazil evidence of "the crimes committed by the colonialists") and repeated expressions of deference, including a ceremonial form of address (*votre honneur*) that I had never heard before. The experience served to demonstrate, if I was not already aware, that alongside the pragmatism of the country's rulers there is a strong current of resentment among the Algerian people about their history of forced submission to imperialist rule—a sentiment that further complicates the task of governing a country divided by tribal and linguistic loyalties. My foray into the Casbah also allowed me a direct experience of the houses and streets, with their intricate secret passages, that provided the backdrop to Gillo Pontecorvo's famous film about the Battle of Algiers, the event which marked the "beginning of the end" of the French colonial adventure in Algeria.

"Who knows, maybe the next pope will be from Argentina?"

On March 25, the preparatory ministerial meeting for the ASPA summit took place in the historic, culturally important, and much-visited Moroccan city of Marrakech. It was there, eleven years previously, that in the name of Brazil I had signed the famous agreement that marked the end of the Uruguay Round and created the WTO. This was my first time back in the city, although I had already visited Morocco that same year for a major conference in Casablanca. So there were extra emotions added to my sense of expectation as I prepared to co-chair the meeting with Moroccan foreign minister Mohammed Benaissa. A positive aspect was the high number of South American representatives (including nine foreign ministers) who would be attending: our diplomatic efforts in our neighbors' capitals had paid off. To try to ensure the support of my South American counterparts, I gave them as much attention as I could. In the few hours between my arrival and a meeting (followed by dinner) with my Moroccan counterpart during which we would agree on the details about how to conduct the ministerial meeting the following day, I spoke to the foreign ministers of Venezuela, Alí Rodríguez, and Suriname, Maria Levens. The meeting with Levens was simply a formality aimed at maintaining the good atmosphere created by President Lula's recent visit to our little Amazonian/Caribbean neighbor. Rodríguez, consistent with a habit I was already accustomed to from CASA meetings, wanted to propose radical changes to the text of the declaration, which had already been the subject of laborious discussions among senior officials and deputy ministers. Regardless of their possible merits, such alterations would have added enormous complications to a debate on subjects which were very delicate and complex. Rodríguez, an orthodox Marxist and lover of dialectics who nevertheless retained a sense of political priorities, was kind (or sensible) enough to discuss his suggested alterations with me before the plenary session. I agreed to a couple of amendments that would not change the structure of the draft declaration and my Venezuelan counterpart was happy with that, at least for the time being. Further down the line, on the eve of the Brasilia summit, during a ministerial meeting to finalize the text of the declaration, Rodríguez would again put extra work on my plate, as indeed would Chávez during the meeting of heads of state.

One of the few South American foreign ministers not present was Rafael Bielsa of Argentina, our close and strategic partner in Mercosur. Despite our best efforts to accommodate the interests of our neighbors (efforts that provoked criticism from the media and business leaders, as well as a few clashes with Itamaraty colleagues), some of the attitudes adopted in Buenos Aires during the first year and a half of Kirchner's government were highly disturbing (later the situation would improve). To describe them here, never mind explain them, would require an extra chapter, so I will limit myself to reproducing some notes I made about two weeks afterwards. My comments were directly relevant to the preparations for the Brasilia summit, and also suggest, in one particular aspect, that I had acquired remarkable powers of premonition: "Difficult moments in our relationship with Argentina. In addition to the repeated statements against Brazil on the issue of [the reform of] the Security Council, including an absurd reference [in the discussions in New York] to regional instability, and a lack of support for Seixas [in his candidature for WTO director-general], we're faced with frequent signs that Argentina is distancing itself from us: doubts about whether Kirchner will come to the summit with the Arabs, Bielsa's absence from the Marrakesh ministerial meeting, and now from the CASA meeting. The question is: what can we do? If what's behind all this is basically jealousy . . . what's the solution? Even the timeframe for UNSC reform is something we have no control over. Should we involve them more in our initiatives? That's what we've been trying to do since Lula's trip to India . . . our support for Duhalde, etc. *Who knows, maybe the next pope will be from Argentina?* But that's for the Holy Spirit to decide. . . ."

The main objective of the Marrakech meeting was for the assembled foreign ministers to approve the draft of the declaration that would be made at the Brasilia summit. We worked on the basis of texts already negotiated by the representatives of the two groups of countries in preparatory meetings, during which the Brazilian delegation had been headed by Ambassador Vera Pedrosa. Despite the progress made, there were still issues to resolve, the most delicate of which concerned Palestine and the concept of terrorism. I will return to those points later, when I describe the summit itself. After discussions that were not always easy, we arrived at formulations that were acceptable to all. In addition to the two co-chairs of the meeting (the foreign ministers of Morocco and Brazil), a place of honor was reserved for the Algerian foreign minister, given that his country held the presidency of the Arab League and that Bouteflika would be co-chairing the summit in Brasilia alongside Lula. Also seated at the top table were the Arab League secretary-general, Amr Moussa, and the chair of the committee of Mercosur representatives, Eduardo Duhalde. Adopting a suggestion made by Moussa, we named the forthcoming gathering in Brasilia the "summit of hope." In an improvised speech I made during media interviews, I referred to the Brasilia summit as "a seismic movement that future historians won't fail to register."

Despite the positive results obtained in Marrakech, I knew certain issues would be raised again in Brasilia. For delegates accustomed to negotiating texts at the United Nations, it was not easy to grasp that the meeting of leaders of the two groups of countries was not the culmination of the process but instead a starting point. The fact of bringing together heads of state and government of two regions of the developing world, most of whom had never spoken to each other, was highly significant. For me, in a way, the summit declaration was almost of secondary importance. But of course I did not fail to recognize that, particularly from the point of view of the Arabs, establishing a consensus on important issues was in itself valuable.

"Why wasn't this summit organized before?"

A few days after the meeting in Marrakech, Arab League secretary-general Amr Moussa visited Brasilia—the first time such a senior official from the organization had come to Brazil. We had a very wide-ranging conversation about the summit and various topics on the international agenda. As usual I gave a lot of attention to Security Council reform, a subject on which some Arab countries held positions different from Brazil's. Countries that were very active in the United Nations, such as Egypt and Algeria, were resistant to the idea of new permanent members (despite the positive opinions expressed by Bouteflika). Moussa himself, in his previous role of Egyptian foreign minister, had been critical of it. Now, as Arab League secretary-general, he certainly had a broader view, and so I raised the issue with him, reiterating what I had said in my speech in Algiers about the importance of an Arab country occupying a permanent seat. I knew my constant efforts to accommodate legitimate interests in a balanced way with Brazil's own positions would probably come up against the resistance of some permanent members of the UNSC to what they saw as "excessive expansion." My notes do not record Moussa's reaction, but I imagine that despite listening to me carefully, he did not commit himself to any position.

During his stay in Brasilia, the Arab League secretary-general was received by President Lula and awarded the Order of the Southern Cross in recognition of his endeavors in support of our initiative. Moussa also had meetings with members of Congress, and traveled to São Paulo and Rio to meet members of the Arab community in both cities. I can recall certain moments from the joint press conference we gave at Itamaraty on April 4. Moussa praised Lula's vision in conceiving of the South American-Arab Summit. He referred to the progress achieved in Marrakech and emphasized the positive effects our efforts had already had on trade relations. In response to a journalist who asked whether the summit would be "another opportunity for Arab countries to speak out against Israeli policy," Moussa recalled the Arab Peace Initiative of December 2002. He reiterated that the summit was not directed against anyone. It was a meeting, he said, "between two groups, between two major regions of the world." In his closing remarks, the Secretary-General highlighted the strong impression my own diplomatic activities had made on the Arab world, because of the determination with which the proposal had been pursued and the political will that clearly underlay it. The same journalist asked me whether I understood the concern on the part of the US that the summit might become a big anti-Israel forum, and whether I still adhered to the Brazilian government position that there would be no observers at the event. On the first point I repeated what I had said in Algiers about the issue of Palestine, and reiterated that Brazil had—and wished to maintain—good relations with Israel. I repeated Moussa's own words about the name given to the event ("summit of hope"), and suggested it could also be regarded as a "summit for dialogue," a meeting that would look to the future and aim toward peace. On the issue of observers, I pointed out that at meetings of two regions, such as those between Mercosur and the European Union, it was not common practice to invite third parties. And I added: "Much of [the summit] will be public, so anyone who wants to observe can just turn on the TV and do so." In response to a question about what "concrete actions" would be taken, I pointed out the remarkable increase in trade that had already taken place, which would certainly receive a further boost from the business forum set to take place during the summit. In that respect, I said, the summit was already a success before it had even happened. I also mentioned the scientific seminars and the various cultural events and projects that were part of the overall program. It is interesting to compare these questions with the evolution of perceptions in the Arab press. During one of my first trips to Cairo, a skeptical Egyptian journalist had asked me: "What's the point of this summit, after all?" In contrast, after the ministerial meeting in Marrakech, the question I heard was very different: "Why wasn't this summit organized before?"

As part of our communications strategy aimed at Arab public opinion, a week later I gave a long interview to the journalist Ibrahim Nafei from the Egyptian newspaper *Al-Ahram*. My interviewer brought up the differences between the draft declarations prepared by the Arabs and those drawn up by the South Americans. He referred specifically to the same points the Algerian ambassador to Cairo had raised at the dinner hosted by President Bouteflika: the condemnation of terrorism, and the legitimate right of resistance to foreign occupation. I replied that an understanding had been reached in Marrakech on those and other issues, and that I did not foresee any major problems that might prevent the draft declaration from being ratified by the heads of state in Brasilia. In fact, I added, the only point still to be agreed concerned the follow-up mechanism for future summits (frequency, next venue, ministerial meetings, technical groups, etc.)—an issue I had discussed with Amr Moussa and which would be satisfactorily resolved in Brasilia. My interviewer revealed he was aware of recent episodes in South America, including a meeting in Puerto Ordaz, Venezuela, attended by the leaders of Brazil, Colombia and Spain (in addition, of course, to the host country), at which a call for a "new international political map" was issued. I took advantage of that particular question to speak about the need for reform of the UN—including, of course, the Security Council (again I mentioned the idea of an Arab country as a permanent member), but possibly more comprehensive than that. I specifically mentioned the importance of a mechanism that would fill the existing gap with regard to the reconstruction of countries recovering from recent conflicts.[64] Such a mechanism, I said, could even prove useful to Palestine. Following on from that, I emphasized the importance of a future Palestinian state being able not only to exercise its right to sovereignty but also to guarantee a decent life for its citizens. I alluded to my recent trip to the West Bank, which had given me a vivid idea of what "human dignity" actually means.[65] There is, after all, a huge difference between reading about a situation and seeing it with one's own eyes.

The last of the preparatory ministerial meetings for the ASPA summit took place on May 9. The most difficult substantive matters had already been resolved in Marrakech; the only remaining issue concerned the follow-up mechanism. Certain foreign ministers revealed a subconscious resistance to the whole process by proposing long gaps between the future meetings of heads of state; nor were they very enthusiastic about sectoral meetings of government ministers. The Chilean foreign minister, Ignacio Walker, was among those who objected to the idea of more regular encounters. Although I was aware of the importance Chile attached to other processes of cooperation and/or association (two years earlier the country had signed a free-trade agreement with the US), I still found Walker's attitude troubling and to some extent surprising, not least because on other subjects, such as the Community of South American Nations (CASA), we worked well together. Eventually, after some discussion, we arrived at an agreement expressed in item 13.1 of the Brasilia Declaration[66] In my welcoming speech I tried to draw attention to the economic, commercial and cultural dimensions of the initiative. I referred to the business seminar, which 1,200 businesspeople had already registered to attend (250 Arabs, 650 Brazilians, and 300 from the other South American countries)—an obvious indication of the potential of our relationship. I also mentioned the opening of the photographic exhibition, *Amrik*, on Arab immigration in South America, which had been carefully organized by Itamaraty's cultural department and whose images were a moving testament to the role of Arabs in our own cultural development. The exhibition was later taken to a number of Arab and South American countries, and also to the UN headquarters in New York.

On May 10, the summit began. In his brief opening speech at the meeting of heads of state, President Lula referred to democracy and human rights—the themes the critics had said were going to be conspicuously absent from the event. When he got on to his favorite subject—the attempt to create a new political and economic geography—he said: "This effort will only be rewarded if we know how to transform the fruits of development into effective tools for reducing social inequality, promoting human rights, and improving democratic institutions." He added: "We're not gathered here only to seek economic and commercial advantages. We stand for the democratization of the international organizations, so that the voice of the developing countries can be heard." The issue of democracy came up when Lula spoke to journalists immediately after the summit, just as it did in all the interviews I participated in. In our answers, Lula and I pointed out the specific references to human rights and democracy in the text of the declaration, especially in the context of the situations in Iraq and Somalia. We also emphasized that because the declaration involved more than twenty countries from two regions in different geopolitical contexts, it had to reflect a compromise between different points of view. More importantly, we stressed the Brazilian view that the best way to support democracy is through dialogue and example, not by trying to impose it. If anything could influence political processes in the Arab world (in which there were significant differences between countries), it would be the opportunity to contemplate the South American experience. This is a firm belief that I still hold today.[67] One aspect of democracy that was not referred to in the declaration, a serious omission that curiously enough failed to provoke comment in the Brazilian media at the time, was the issue of gender equality.[68]

Another controversial point, which came up in the post-summit interviews, regarded the condemnation of terrorism. It had already proved to be a thorny issue during the preparation of the declaration, particularly in the context of the right to resistance against foreign occupation. The solution eventually reached is expressed in paragraphs 2.16 and 2.17 of the declaration. The former leaves no doubt about the need to combat terrorism "in all its forms and manifestations," calling for international cooperation to that end. On the other hand, the right to resistance was also recognized in the declaration, with certain qualifications. According to the text, that right must be exercised "in accordance with the principles of international legality and in compliance with international humanitarian law." There were also allegations that the text was deliberately unfavorable or even hostile toward Israel. On that point, both President Lula as I pointed out that the expressions used in the Brasilia Declaration were based on the language of UN decisions and resolutions. More importantly, before the opening of the summit it was announced by Itamaraty that I had accepted an invitation to Israel and that the visit was scheduled for the end of the month.

The formal meeting of leaders consisted mostly of a succession of speeches. Some were longer than others, as in the case of President Chávez. The only surprise in the proceedings, if I can call it that, was when the Venezuelan leader intervened to say he wanted the declaration to include an explicit condemnation of the overthrow of Saddam Hussein by force. Such a reference, although in itself justified, would never have obtained consensus. Not only would the Iraqi president have objected but so too would the leaders of countries that had supported the US invasion, albeit in some cases only tacitly. This minor hitch was overcome with a call for understanding. The summit was briefly interrupted. Eventually, Chávez and Talabani[69] emerged together from this "coffee break" as if they were two old friends.

Apart from the aforementioned themes and the various aspects of the cooperation between the two regions, the Brasilia Declaration also expressed shared views of international issues. It emphasized the need for effective action aimed at universal adherence to the Treaty on the Non-Proliferation of Nuclear Weapons (NPT) and called for the creation of a nuclear-weapon-free zone in the Middle East. It advocated the establishment of an independent Palestinian state and the withdrawal of Israel from all occupied Arab territories, back to its 1967 borders. The declaration expressed concern about unilateral US sanctions against Syria. On Iraq, it emphasized that the United Nations should play a central role in rebuilding the country. Finally, the text reaffirmed the need for comprehensive reform of the UN, with a view to making its principal organs "efficient, democratic, transparent and representative." The wording of this last point, obviously, represented the lowest common denominator, compatible with the various individual positions on the issue. Despite of all the difficulties and compromises, the Brasilia Declaration stands as a landmark in building consensus between two geographically distant continents that, until then, had also been politically remote from each other. In that sense, as President Lula said in his opening speech, it symbolized "the courage to break with established models."

The first ASPA summit also provided an opportunity for separate meetings between heads of state and foreign ministers. The official visit by the Algerian president took place the next day, helping to revive our bilateral relations with that important country in the Maghreb. Many of the pending agreements Bouteflika had complained about during my first visit to Algeria were finally signed, setting in train a process that would be marked by high-level visits and closer relations in all areas: political, economic-commercial, and cultural. Especially noteworthy was the unprecedented meeting between Lula and President Mahmoud Abbas of the Palestinian Authority. In the light of their conversation, Lula inserted a reference to Abbas into his closing address, emphasizing the Palestinian leader's "wisdom and . . . tranquility in knowing that peace is above all a game that requires patience, like a game of chess." He then added: "Although we're in a hurry to achieve [peace], we have to be patient in order to build the political opportunities to bring it about."

Every country in South America and the Arab world was represented at the summit. With only one exception (Yemen), whose delegate was a deputy foreign minister, the chiefs of delegation were either heads of state or government (a total of nine, plus a member of one of the royal families), or foreign ministers. The first visit to Brazil by the Iraqi president, Jalal Talabani, was of special significance not only because his country was still in the throes of internal strife but also because Brazil had vehemently opposed the US attack that resulted in the new Iraqi government coming to power. In the words of the Tunisian foreign minister: "It's very rare to see so many Arab leaders together." The event had a significant impact internationally and generated headlines in newspapers such as *Le Monde* and *El País*, which described it as "historic" and "unprecedented." Some commentators referred to the creation of a new "South-South axis" and a "meeting of two worlds." As the president of Djibouti (where, as I found out during the summit, a Brazilian company was modernizing the port infrastructure in partnership with a company from another Arab country), Ismaïl Omar Guelleh, put it during his bilateral meeting with Lula: "An opening has been made in the wall that will never be closed again."

In my notes from May 15, I observed that the Brazilian newspapers were still focusing their attention on the summit. That same day, in the light of the event, the ombudsman (public editor) of the *Folha de São Paulo* dedicated much of an article to the shortcomings of the newspaper's coverage of Brazilian foreign policy. Also in the *Folha*, columnist Eliane Cantanhêde contrasted the foreign policy we were pursuing, which she considered bold and audacious, with that of previous governments.[70] From my point of view, despite the verbal bullets fired in my direction, one of the merits of the initiative was to place foreign policy at the center of the national agenda. Personally I attached enormous importance to the summit, which I saw as a climactic "end of the first act" because it coincided, more or less, with the half-way point in Lula's term of office (at that point I was choosing not to take into account the possibility of a second term). After the change of course that we had managed to bring about in the trade negotiations (FTAA and Doha), and the boost to South American integration with the creation of the CASA, the ASPA summit represented, in terms of our foreign relations, a major step—albeit not without risks—toward a world order that would be less rigid and hierarchical. And in that respect, whatever the remarks emanating from the most conservative sections of Brazilian society, it was also a triumph of our "assertive" foreign policy.

FROM JERUSALEM TO RAMALLAH

Jerusalem

On May 29, about two weeks after the ASPA summit, I began my visit to Israel. It was ten years since one of my predecessors, Luís Felipe Lampreia, had visited the country. At that time I had been permanent representative to the UN, and I remember the foreign minister's enthusiastic descriptions of the trip and the manner in which he was received. But now the situation was different. Our initiatives in relation to the Arab world had pricked the sensibilities of the Israeli government, whose reaction was greatly amplified by the Brazilian media. There was also Brazil's influential Jewish community to think about. Also, if we wished to play a role in trying to achieve peace in the Middle East—as had been asked of us by, among others, the president of the

Palestinian Authority—we needed to preserve and even deepen our relationship with Israel.

One of the aims of the visit was to remove any doubts about the true aims of the ASPA summit and to reaffirm the traditional ties of friendship between Brazil and Israel. The reaction of the Israeli government when the summit had been convened, as reflected by comments by diplomats and others in the foreign ministry, merited our attention. I certainly did not want the meeting with the Arab countries to be interpreted as an anti-Israel stance on our part. Nor indeed did President Lula, who never missed an opportunity to express his appreciation for and solidarity with Brazil's Jewish community, for example by attending ceremonies in memory of the victims of the Holocaust. Even before the summit took place, therefore, I had been keen to arrange an official visit to Israel, which would prove to be the first of five during my tenure. Contrary to the acerbic criticisms and warnings from our media, the Israeli officials were very receptive. They guaranteed at the outset not only that I would meet my counterpart, Silvan Shalom, but also the president, the deputy prime minister, and Prime Minister Ariel Sharon.

So it was that on the morning of May 30, before any of my official commitments, I found myself on the balcony of my hotel suite, contemplating the Walls of Jerusalem, made of light gray stone, and beyond, the domes of the temples of the three great monotheistic religions. It was a view that brought to mind the magnificent description by Eça de Queiroz in *The Relic*. The day before, I had met members of the Brazilian community, almost all of whom were living permanently in Israel. They included scientists, engineers, doctors, businesspeople, and intellectuals. A professor of literature (unfortunately I did not make a note of her name) had taught at the very high school in Rio de Janeiro where I myself had studied. A musician, Myrna Herzog, "the greatest viola da gamba player in the world" according to our ambassador Sérgio Moreira Lima, gave me a CD of her renditions of pieces by Villa-Lobos and Dorival Caymmi. An architect, a disciple of Oscar Niemeyer who had lived in Israel for fifty years, presented me with a beautiful book. It was a heart-warming experience to meet men and women who had chosen to make their lives in Israel but still had strong emotional and family ties with Brazil. For them, being in the company of Brazil's foreign minister in the country they considered to be that of their ancestors mattered far more than any scratches incurred by the political-diplomatic relationship between Tel Aviv and Brasilia, which in any case would prove to be less deep than some in Brazil wanted to believe. In a press conference afterwards, attended by Brazilian correspondents as well as Israeli journalists, the questions were not provocative. The subject of greatest interest was actually the commercial initiatives between Brazil and Israel, including those involving Mercosur. One journalist asked if my visit to Jerusalem and Tel Aviv might cause discomfort in the Arab capitals, and if so, how much I cared about that. The question gave me the opportunity to reaffirm the complete independence of Brazilian foreign policy—an independence which, I stressed, "applies to all sides."

The backdrop to my visit was the withdrawal of Israeli forces from Gaza, a situation which added an extra element of interest to my talks with government officials. My first meeting, on May 30, was with President Moshe Katsav, who was about my age and—a detail I recorded in my notebook—had been born in Iran. Although in theory only a formality, my conversation with the president was not devoid of interest because he raised a number of political issues. After the greetings and the usual photos, we soon got talking about the relations between Israel and Palestine. He said there had never been a situation more conducive to reaching an understanding, although he acknowledged that a "derailment" could always occur at any moment. He praised the positive attitude of Mahmoud Abbas but feared the president of the Palestinian Authority would not be able to exert control over Hamas, "whose power and popularity are growing." He recognized that Israel should work to strengthen the Palestinian leader's position, but complained about the lack of more stringent measures from the PNA to curb terrorism. He made no mention of the ASPA summit or our relationship with the Arab countries, but his frankness in addressing sensitive issues showed he had confidence in Brazil. Quite soon afterwards, President Katsav would become involved in a scandal that ultimately led to his resignation. Apart from the content of our dialogue, what most impressed me during the meeting was the number of security personnel who surrounded him. In fact, the security apparatus was an ever-present feature of my visit—such as when I opened the door of my hotel room to find an Israeli soldier standing outside with a machine gun. I must say it did not make me feel any safer. Curiously, the only other time I had felt similar disquiet was three months before, in Palestine.

Of all my meetings in Israel, perhaps the least interesting was with the foreign minister, Silvan Shalom—who years later, as deputy prime minister, would sit next to me at the official banquet during Lula's state visit. During our working lunch, Shalom obviously wanted our conversation to have a professional/diplomatic rather than political tone. He had a list of topics on a written agenda in front of him, and he seemed keen not to linger too long on any of them. Like the president, he made no mention of any issue related to the ASPA summit, even though I deliberately indicated I was willing to discuss the subject. I referred, for example, to Lula's conversation with the president of the Palestinian Authority, and to the dialogue between Chávez and Talabani. Shalom mentioned, in a measured tone, Israel's "discomfort" at positions taken by Brazil in certain votes at the UN, but then immediately changed tack by expressing gratitude for our participation in the initiative on anti-Semitism. After a brief foray into bilateral topics (trade, scientific cooperation, cultural projects), the conversation turned back to the Palestinian issue. Shalom referred to it in terms similar to those used by President Katsav, although perhaps in a slightly more negative tone. He revealed he was concerned about Hamas gaining strength, though he considered it "a bigger problem for the Palestinian Authority than for Israel." And he added: "[Hamas] can cause a death here or there, but it doesn't threaten the State of Israel."

The most interesting conversation that day was with the trade minister and designated acting prime minister (a deputy prime minister, effectively), Ehud Olmert, who a few months previously had met President Lula in Brazil during a visit initially characterized as primarily commercial. In fact, on that occasion, it was Brazil's industry and trade minister, Luiz Furlan who had taken Olmert to meet Lula. Interestingly, there was no reference to the meeting in my official diary, presumably because I had not been told about it in advance. It was not the only occasion when I did not get an invitation to a meeting that, although primarily economic in nature, had obvious political implications.

My meeting with Olmert in Jerusalem began with quite a comic episode. I had agreed to include in my delegation one of the leaders of the Jewish community in Brazil, Rabbi Henry Sobel, with whom I had had a good relationship ever since my first period as foreign minister—starting in 1994, in fact, when Rabin and Arafat were awarded the Nobel Peace Prize in the wake of the Washington Agreement. At the time, responding to a suggestion from our ambassador in Washington, Paulo Tarso Flexa de Lima, I sent compliments not only to the foreign ministers (and, of course, arranged for President Itamar to do the same with the two leaders) but also to the leaders of Brazil's Jewish and Arab communities. Since then, Sobel and I had kept up a valuable dialogue. But in agreeing to his presence in a delegation that was otherwise essentially governmental, I made clear that there were certain meetings he would not attend, such as the one with Sharon. But, in a fit of liberalism, I consented to him coming with us to meet some of the other Israeli officials. After leading us to the Wailing Wall, where I left my prayer on a small, rolled-up piece of paper,[71] the rabbi somehow became separated from our party. Therefore, when I met Olmert, I was accompanied only by my aides. But before we sat down at the conference table where our discussion would take place, Sobel, wearing a kippa similar in color to a Catholic cardinal's skullcap, burst breathlessly into the room. Olmert was momentarily stunned. Then he asked me with a smile: "Do you travel with your own rabbi?"

The conversation with Olmert continued in that relaxed tone, although we dealt with serious issues. Initially we discussed economic subjects, including Embraer aircraft, ethanol, and generic drugs. But after a quarter of an hour, the deputy prime minister said: "Now let's talk politics." He spoke, quite objectively, about relations with the Palestinians, highlighting the positive attitude of President Mahmoud Abbas. He emphasized the "historic gesture" by Sharon in proceeding with the unilateral withdrawal from Gaza, despite protests from members of the governing coalition and even his own party, Likud. He did not hold back from criticizing those who, on the pretext of defending the settlers, opposed the departure of the Israeli security forces. His reasoning followed a line very similar to what I would hear the following day from Sharon. Olmert said Israel would not hesitate to use force to ensure the security of Israeli citizens. Like Sharon (who would suffer a severe stroke in 2006, after which Olmert took over from him), the deputy prime minister could not be described as a "dove." And yet he fully understood the importance of dialogue with the Palestinians. Referring to Gaza, he said he did not expect any "reciprocal gesture" from the Palestinian Authority ("except a firmer attitude in relation to terrorism"). Nor did he insist that the withdrawal from Gaza would be the "end of line." He knew that the dialogue with the Palestinians would, sooner or later, involve difficult reciprocal concessions.

Olmert listened attentively to my thoughts about the importance of strengthening the leadership of Mahmoud Abbas through concrete actions that could be "shown" to the Palestinians. He mentioned, still in relation to Gaza, details about the destruction of the settlers' homes and the specific problems regarding the "Philadelphia Route."[72] The last part of our conversation was lighter in tone: we spoke about cinema; our sons, who are moviemakers; and the actor Richard Gere, a friend of Olmert whom he was due to see again in the near future and whom I myself had met in Davos at the start of the year. "Give him a hug from Vicente's dad," I said (Vicente being the eldest of my moviemaker sons, and also a friend of the famous actor). Olmert and I agreed that our dialogue had been rich and productive. He said as we parted: "If we're still alive 25 years from now [why 25, I do not know], we'll remember this conversation."

According to our ambassador, it would have been feedback from Olmert that secured my audience with the prime minister, Ariel Sharon, the following day. Before that, I met with Shimon Peres, who also held the position of deputy prime minister (I am not sure how many there were in total). I went to see him at the headquarters of the foundation that bears his name (which works to bring Israeli and Palestinian children and young people closer together), a modern building in Tel Aviv. He received me in quite a small meeting room. I will reproduce the notes I made afterwards, which reflect my optimistic (but, as it later proved, rather naive) outlook at the time: "I recalled that we'd met before, in 1993 . . . right after the celebrated Oslo/Washington agreements. . . . I praised his efforts [aimed at] reconciliation between Palestinians and Israelis. At his request I spoke a little about [the recent development of] the Brazilian economy. On the Palestinian issue, when I asked him what he thought the prospects were, his response was encouraging. Now more than 80 years old, Peres takes an almost philosophical view of the situation, but is still committed to working for peace. He praised the current Palestinian leadership. . . . We also talked about civil society; the meetings between the families of [victims on both sides]." I added to my notes my impression that Peres was genuinely committed to achieving peace with the Arabs.[73] But I also wrote: "Given the vagaries of history, perhaps it will fall to another person, someone who's always been a truculent hawk [I was thinking of Ariel Sharon], to take the most important concrete step." After the meeting, which lasted about an hour, Peres repeated in front of the TV cameras something he had already said to me in private: "Brazil is the most tolerant country in the world, which in itself makes it an important player in the Middle East." After a participating briefly in a business seminar alongside some leading entrepreneurs and former Brazilian agriculture minister Marcus Vinícius Pratini de Morais, I returned to Jerusalem, where in the late afternoon I visited a sports project run by the Peres Center for Peace. I handed out medals to Palestinian and Israeli children, and submitting to a demagogic impulse, allowed evidence of my soccer skills to be photographed.

My meeting with Ariel Sharon had been scheduled for midday on May 31, at the Knesset. After some uncertainty—eagerly monitored by the Brazilian journalists—it was rescheduled for 5 p.m. at the prime minister's office, one of the most heavily protected buildings in the country (and indeed the whole world). Only two people went with me: Ambassador Moreira Lima and our special envoy to the Middle East, Affonso Ouro-Preto. I did not have high hopes for the conversation; imprinted in my mind were Sharon's provocative actions that had triggered the Second Intifada. I referred in my notebook to the fact that Sharon—unlike Peres, of the Labor Party, or Omert, his co-religionist in Likud—was a hard man, a warrior, and a general, rather than a politician or a diplomat. However, after a wait in an unusually busy room, like the command center of a country at war, the old general greeted me in a manner that was not merely courteous but positively friendly.

Sharon made a fleeting reference to the ASPA summit that struck me as somewhat derogatory. Later in the conversation I managed to return to the subject, attempting to convey the vision that had inspired that "summit of hope" and my conviction that the initiative would eventually prove to have been successful. Sharon responded calmly. He focused mostly on the subject of Gaza, expressing determination to continue the withdrawal: it was a decision that had already been taken, he said. He told me, more emphatically than Olmert had done, that it was necessary to reduce the terrorist attacks "by one hundred percent," though he still acknowledged the need for dialogue. When I commented that the Palestinian leadership seemed to be pragmatic, Sharon, perhaps out of courtesy, did not disagree. Courtesy might also explain his sympathetic response when I mentioned the possibility of Brazil contributing to the dialogue between Israel and Palestine. For my part, I praised the courage of the Israeli decision on Gaza, which I knew had cost the prime minister the support of part of his political base. With regard to that particular issue, I thought (but of course did not say) that the advantage of having a hard man like Sharon—who, by the way, referred more than once during our conversation to Israel's "Biblical rights"—in charge of such a process is that the decisions taken are subsequently difficult to reverse (the case of Richard Nixon and China comes to mind). Sharon had some friendly words of appreciation for Brazil. He said our role should consist essentially of convincing the Arabs of Israel's "good intentions." The conversation also included some relaxed moments: at one point the prime minister recalled his meeting with Pope John Paul II, who apparently told him that Jerusalem was considered part of the "Holy Land" by the three great monotheistic religions but had been "promised" only to the Jews. In short, Sharon came across as a man of deep-seated convictions who had no empathy toward his opponents, but who nevertheless understood the need, for the sake of Israel's security, to arrive at some kind of deal with them. Contrary to predictions—including my own—the meeting ended in a pleasant atmosphere, with the two of us showing each other photographs of our grandchildren.

I returned from Israel with the feeling that those two men (one of whom would become physically incapacitated soon afterwards, while the other would later become involved in a financial scandal that ultimately cost him his job), without giving up their firm convictions, would be capable of pursuing dialogue and carrying forward the peace process with some chance of success. That was what Olmert would try to do, for example, at the Annapolis Conference, before he was forced to leave the government. Also, equally important, I saw during my frank dialogue with both of them that the highest levels of the Israeli government regarded Brazil as a valid interlocutor, capable of contributing to the solution of a conflict that continues to claim lives and to bring uncertainty to all the inhabitants of the Middle East. Later it would be confirmed on various occasions that this initial impression was correct, for example when I was the bearer of messages to the Israelis from Bashar al-Assad, or vice versa.

Our balanced approach earned us recognition

In June 2005, in Brussels, I took part in a meeting on the reconstruction of Iraq. As the main theme of the meeting was the cancelation of Iraq's debt and there was no way of recovering what the country owed us, I came up with an idea that seemed ingenious to me at the time: the debt could be converted into capital in an ASPA bank, the creation of which had been proposed by President Talabani during the summit. As it turned out, neither the bank nor the conversion process got off the ground, but the idea demonstrated our commitment both to helping in the reconstruction of Iraq and to strengthening our relationship with the Arab countries, including in the financial sector. In my short speech I tried to convey a vision for the future, with an emphasis on reconciliation between the various factions, the consolidation of the political process, and greater United Nations involvement in Iraqi affairs. The reference to the UN was sufficient for parts of the Brazilian media to assume I wanted merely to criticize the United States. That was not, however, the perception of the US secretary of state, with whom I had a lively conversation before the start of the meeting (as recorded in photographs in several newspapers). In my speech I announced our intention to reopen the Brazilian embassy in Baghdad, which had closed in 1991. On December 19, 2006, our ambassador, Bernardo Brito, based at an office in Amman (a separate entity from our embassy in the Jordanian capital), would present credentials to President Talabani. Due to bureaucratic obstacles, however, it was only in 2012 that our embassy in Iraq would finally be up and running.

Between May 2005 and July 2006 I was focused on other areas: the preparations for the WTO ministerial conference in Hong Kong, the consolidation of the CASA, and the inevitable problems with or between our South American neighbors. We received a visit from the US president in 2005, while other initiatives such as the IBSA forum and our policy of pursuing closer ties with Africa followed their course. Equally important—and requiring constant monitoring—was the situation in Haiti, where under the command of a Brazilian general and the banner of the United Nations, our soldiers were helping to maintain security. We nevertheless managed to keep an eye on events in the Middle East, issuing official communiqués whenever the occasion demanded. With regard to Lebanon, even before the ASPA summit the Brazilian government had already made statements on the beginning of the withdrawal of Syrian troops from the country, echoing my diplomatic efforts during my visit to Damascus. Developments in Gaza in 2005, including the withdrawal of Israeli forces, were the subject of three Itamaraty communiqués. Nor did we fail to express our repudiation of terrorist attacks against civilians. And in mid-December, our special envoy to the Middle East spent two days in Israel at a critical moment in the Palestine situation, meeting with government officials and also members of the Quartet.

My schedule during the UN General Assembly of 2005 reflected the importance Brazilian diplomacy continued to attach to the Arab countries. In addition to various one-to-one conversations (with the Arab League secretary-general and the Moroccan foreign minister, among others) I endeavored to keep the flame alive by participating in the follow-up meeting to the ASPA summit. During the same General Assembly, Lebanese prime minister Fouad Siniora[74] requested to meet me—a highly significant indication of how Brazil's role in Middle East issues was being perceived. That same year, Brazil would adopt an independent and balanced position during the discussions about the draft that resulted in Security Council Resolution 1636 on the situation in the Middle East in the wake of Rafic Hariri's assassination. The resolution, adopted unanimously at a ministerial meeting of the Security Council on October 31, concerned the work of the Investigation Commission established by Resolution 1595 in April, which had also been adopted unanimously. In my explanation of vote I made clear that Brazil would not have been able to support the draft resolution originally submitted by France, the United Kingdom, and the United States, which sought to impose sanctions on Damascus (with predictable consequences). In particular I criticized the language of the document for failing to follow the principle of presuming the innocence of the accused, almost all of whom were Syrians or linked to Syria. I also said Brazil would not support a text whose goals extended beyond the investigation in itself. I stated our understanding that Chapter VII of the UN Charter, referred to in the text, did not authorize the adoption of measures against Syria, and added that the assessment of the findings of the Investigation Commission should be carried out by the Security Council itself. I considered it important to avoid a situation in which the sponsors of a draft resolution considered themselves entitled to adopt measures in the event of Syria's non-compliance (real or perceived) with its provisions—as had been the case with Iraq. I concluded my statement with a warning about "hasty decisions" that could lead to an escalation of tensions in the region.

Throughout this affair, my coordination with the Algerian foreign minister, Mohammed Bedjaoui, was particularly important. Algeria, like Brazil, had abstained on Resolution 1559 in September 2004. Our two countries' understanding was that the situation had changed with the murder of Hariri and with the report by the Investigation Commission, headed by German prosecutor Detlev Mehlis. I think Brazil's position, indicating that we would abstain if no changes were made to the text in order to address our concerns, certainly helped our Algerian friends to maintain a firm position. And the converse was also true. The "threat" of abstention was communicated subtly to one of the sponsors of the draft resolution, the French foreign minister Philippe Douste-Blazy, with whom I had a fluid relationship in the context of the Lula-Chirac partnership on combating hunger and related initiatives: I told him we would not feel comfortable about voting differently from the only Arab country on the Security Council. Brazil's role during the discussions was certainly appreciated by Syrian foreign minister Farouk al-Sharaa, who embraced me warmly at the end of the meeting. Meanwhile, Condoleezza Rice, one of the individuals primarily responsible for the draft resolution, made a point of thanking me for attending. Somehow, our balanced approach earned us recognition from both sides in the dispute.

From 2006 onward, Brazil became increasingly involved in "donor conferences," especially those concerning Lebanon and Palestine. Not only did we start participating more frequently in the relevant meetings but we also substantially increased our contributions. When I was not able to attend the meetings myself, another senior Itamaraty official went in my place—normally the undersecretary for cooperation, Ambassador Ruy Nogueira. There was an increase in the number of joint governmental commissions with Arab countries, usually chaired by the foreign ministers, while the business missions also became more frequent. The Arab Chamber of Commerce in São Paulo was a frequent interlocutor. Important trade missions went to the United Arab Emirates and Saudi Arabia in November, following up on the business seminar held during the May summit. As for the negotiations between Mercosur and the GCC, the first technical meeting was held in November, with promising results. But despite the initial enthusiasm on both sides, the negotiations ran into difficulties regarding the list of products, mainly due to Brazilian resistance to the inclusion of petrochemicals. The Gulf countries, for their part, wanted to put restrictions on certain products that were important for our agro-industrial sector. Although it was not possible to arrive at an agreement on tariff preferences, the flow of trade and investment still increased steadily.[75] There was also frequent cooperation in the academic field, again following up on initiatives launched at the ASPA summit.[76]

I will digress briefly at this point to reproduce some notes I made on February 1, 2006, on a subject indirectly linked to our participation in the aforementioned conference on Iraq. They concern Afghanistan, which of course is in Central Asia rather than the Middle East, but whose predicament is connected with that of Iraq in more than one way. After all, it was in Afghanistan—a complex country with a large number of ethnic groups, each with their own loyalties—that the attacks of 9/11 originated. My notes are self-explanatory: "From Geneva [where I stopped on the way back from Davos] I went to London, where I attended an international conference on Afghanistan convened by [Tony] Blair and Kofi Annan. The US and the European Union, particularly [Javier Solana], took prominent positions. [Brazil was] the only Latin American country invited. Although the time [for speeches] was very limited . . . I think it was worth it. It is important to make clear that our interests are global and that our capacity to provide assistance, whether political or technical, extends beyond our immediate region. The universalism of our foreign policy is useful for [our aspirations with regard to the] Security Council, but it also has intrinsic merit: gradually we have to 'open the minds' of the Brazilian public to the role that our country—given its size, ethnic composition, and cultural variety—can play in the world." I should also note that in my two most important meetings that day—with Russian foreign minister Sergey Lavrov and the high representative of the European Union—the main subjects were Iran and Palestine (especially the situation with Hamas). Our willingness to participate, albeit to a modest degree, in the reconstruction of Afghanistan (a genuine crossroads between different worlds, both literally and figuratively) would later be reflected in various kinds of technical assistance, and would culminate in 2010 in the decision to open an embassy in Kabul—although that has still not been implemented, due apparently to budgetary problems. Afghanistan, for its part, moved more quickly in opening its embassy in Brasilia.

The rescue

On July 14, 2006, in response to Hezbollah attacks on Israeli territory, the Israel Defense Forces bombed southern Beirut, initiating an armed conflict that would last about a month. My first notes on this "undeclared war," dated July 22, were made during a flight to Paris, en route to Geneva to attend an important WTO meeting. To be able to make the trip I had needed President Lula's permission to miss a Mercosur summit in Córdoba. Despite being deeply involved in trade issues, I was still thinking a great deal about the Arab world. In fact, in my notes that day, I made a reference to a passage from the writings of Ibn Khaldûn on the importance of "group feeling" (which today could perhaps be translated as patriotism) for the survival of societies.

That was the state of mind in which I wrote the notes I will reproduce below. Despite some inaccuracies arising from the limited information available to me at that moment, they clearly reflect my concern about the Israeli attacks on Lebanon: "Not going to Córdoba made it possible to deal more closely and directly with the tragedy in Lebanon, which has already claimed the lives of seven Brazilians (there are doubts about the condition of one other woman, the mother of one of the children who were killed). [This is] the largest number of [Brazilian] civilians killed in a conflict since the Second World War. Whether to obtain direct assistance [for the Brazilians], to request restraint on the part of the Israelis, or to argue for an immediate ceasefire—in line with the proposal by the UN secretary-general—I spoke to Condoleezza Rice, Turkish foreign minister Abdullah Gül, and Canadian foreign minister Peter MacKay, as well as with Kofi Annan himself. I made a point of summoning the Israeli ambassador to my office to emphasize the potential damage to our relations, which had been getting closer since my 2005 visit." My notes continue: "As well as the predicament of the Brazilians [it is necessary to consider] the situation of Lebanon itself, whose fragility is again evident. It is hard to say what will result from the Israeli offensive. In addition to the possible spread of the conflict—although that seems unlikely, given the lack of appetite on the part of the other Arab countries—there will be many deaths and much destruction. . . . The internal divisions [in Lebanon] could be exacerbated, with the risk of the country being plunged back into civil war. Or the most radical tendencies will be strengthened. . . . These issues, previously somewhat abstract and distant, are now very much present on my agenda and in my feelings."

Two days later, in Geneva, in the midst of another crisis of the Doha Round, I wrote further notes: "What a day. Alongside the rather unedifying discussions [in the WTO] I had to deal with the situation in Lebanon. From logistical issues—such as the possible hiring of a plane and sending money to our consulate in Beirut—to delicate political discussions with the Israeli government [especially the foreign minister, Tzipi Livni] to try to ensure a convoy of Brazilian refugees [on their way] from the Bekaa Valley to Syria aren't bombed by mistake. . . . I called Condoleezza Rice, who was herself about to set off for the Middle East. . . . After those conversations with the Israeli government and the secretary of state, it remains to be seen how the dice will fall for our compatriots, who are mostly poor people from the countryside. We can only hope common sense prevails on the part of those in Israel who are commanding the operations, and therefore a tragedy can be averted." Most of the Brazilian refugees headed north toward Turkey, passing through part of Syria. We advised the inhabitants of the Bekaa Valley also to take that route, despite it being longer and more complicated, but instead most of them opted for the route to Damascus, which was shorter but also much more likely to be bombed.

That same day, the president called me. He was being kept up to date by Ambassador Everton Vargas, chief of staff to Itamaraty secretary-general Samuel Pinheiro Guimarães, who I had left in charge of practical arrangements. In one of his conversations with Everton, Lula said he wanted to "adopt a firmer tone with Israel." This expression had been used by the newspapers in referring to the positions I myself had adopted. But there was a dilemma: on the one hand, from a political perspective, it was natural and fair that we condemn Israel's disproportionate actions; but on the other, as I wrote at the time, "the top priority at the moment is to get the Brazilians out, and for that we need the goodwill of the Israelis. I have to take that into account." The rescue of the three thousand Brazilians in Lebanon was an unprecedented operation for our foreign ministry.[77] As well as making political arrangements, we had to organize a complex logistical procedure that included mobilizing the Brazilian Air Force (FAB) along with private aviation companies, obtaining fuel for about twenty trips, and the constant involvement of our embassies and/or consulates in Beirut, Damascus and Ankara. We also created an office (a temporary consulate, in effect) in Adana, the Turkish city that a large proportion of our refugees headed for.

I decided I had to go to Adana and see for myself the situation our compatriots were experiencing, take note of their needs, and give them moral and material support. And so, after another frustrating stay in Geneva (to discuss the Doha Round), during which I also had the unhappy experience of seeing Brazil eliminated from the World Cup, I traveled to Turkey on July 25. I arrived in Adana the next day. That same night, 120 refugees were due to leave for Brazil on board an FAB 707; another 100 would fly out the next day. About 200 had already left Turkey by their own means. In my notes I referred to the support given by the Turkish government and in particular by the then foreign minister (and later president), my friend Abdullah Gül.[78] I recall that one of our greatest concerns was finding places to stay for the Brazilian families arriving from Lebanon, and in that respect Turkey's assistance was very important. As I was able to see for myself, the families were placed in various different hotels across the city, in accommodations that were perfectly adequate.

During my stay in Adana, the bombing in Lebanon continued non-stop. Brazilians continued to leave the country in convoys organized or financed wholly or partially by Itamaraty. With the Lebanese banking system paralyzed, even sending money to Beirut was difficult. But the biggest problem was ensuring a minimum degree of security for the refugees while they were on the move. Our contact with the Israeli authorities was not limited to a political-diplomatic dialogue. The head of the FAB's office in Tel Aviv gave the Israelis detailed information about the refugee convoys, some of which displayed Brazilian flags intended to be visible from the air. But the most we ever got in response was the less than reassuring statement that the information would be "taken into account." An official in the Israeli military command even told an FAB officer: "You know, some pilots are very young." My anxiety had further increased when, on the eve of my arrival in Adana, I received the news that a Red Cross convoy had been attacked.

In the morning of July 26 I visited three hotels where Brazilians were waiting to be called to board the FAB plane. Among them were women and children—some with visible signs of malnutrition—but also men who looked like successful businesspeople or professionals. Others, however, were clearly not so affluent; they were probably the people from the interior of Lebanon. Anyway, the scene was nothing like the refugee camps we are accustomed to seeing on television. Despite the suffering many of them had recently experienced, the majority had certainly kept their dignity. The situation of the Brazilian refugees who had fled to Syria was more difficult, as many of them had to be accommodated in the soccer stadium. One woman, I heard, gave birth in Damascus. In Adana, many of the women had western clothing but several others wore a *shador*. One of them, a slender young woman with a beautiful face, had five small children with her, the oldest a girl of about ten. They had all spent several days in a basement, sheltering from the bombing.[79] The young mother told me that after they had reached safety the children were still so traumatized that they did not want to eat anything for days. I could see, however, from her facial expressions and the way she spoke, that she was regaining hope. An older woman, part of a group rescued by a Canadian ship, said it was the third time in her life that she had fled from a war, and added: "But this is the first time I had help from the Brazilian government."

There were emotional moments. I gave and received many hugs. Not even the women covered in the *shador* held back from physical demonstrations of affection. There was quite a thick-set teenage boy, wrapped in a Brazilian flag, who was vaguely reminiscent of the Brazilian soccer player Ronaldo: I took advantage of that to make a few jokes and generally try to alleviate the tension of waiting. Later I went on board the FAB 707 to say goodbye to my compatriots who were either returning to Brazil or, in some cases, going there for the first time. I was greeted with applause, and cries of "*Viva* our minister!" I responded with "*Viva* Brazil!" and "*Viva* Lebanon!" Moments like those are rare in the routine of a foreign minister, which is generally characterized by cold diplomatic calculation and administrative planning. Even when negotiations give rise to feelings of tension, relief or (more rarely) satisfaction, there generally is not the human element that I experienced so strongly in that aircraft. I left the airport at about 10 p.m.. Afterwards I gave interviews to Brazilian and Turkish TV channels, and had meetings with local officials. I ended my day with a call to President Lula, who listened carefully to my report, then asked me, as he so often did: "When are you coming back?" When I answered the question, he said: "Ah, so you won't be accompanying me to Peru!"

The next day I started my journey back to Brazil, via Istanbul and Paris. In my notebook I wrote: "I would have liked to go to Syria, where there are also lots of Brazilian refugees, but the logistical difficulties and the need to be in Brazil on Saturday for a meeting with [US Trade Representative Susan] Schwab make that impossible. Too bad. Maybe I'll find a way to return soon." Back in Brasilia, after the meeting with Schwab in Rio de Janeiro, I continued to deal with two emergencies: the crisis in Lebanon, including the situation of the Brazilians; and the need to revive the Doha Round. On August 2 I attended a hearing at the Senate, where I spoke about both issues. For more than three hours I replied to questions and comments from the senators, but unlike on other occasions (such as a recent statement I had made on the subject of Bolivia),[80] the mood was friendly. Indeed, there was no lack of praise for Itamaraty's response to the Lebanese crisis.

Two days after the hearing, I gave a lecture at the Rio Branco Institute[81] in which I spoke again about the situation in Lebanon. I was critical of the inertia on the part of the UN, drawing a contrast with its hasty response in certain other situations. I mentioned a phone call I had made to the secretary-general, Kofi Annan, in which I expressed support for his appeal for a cease-fire, agreeing that the most urgent thing was to stop the killing. I also looked at the situation from the perspective of the humanitarian operation we were involved in. I pointed out to the students that it showed the truth of a phrase I used to repeat when teaching political theory (and which, I later learned, came originally from Arnold Toynbee, although some say it can be traced all the way back to Pericles, the Athenian statesman): "You might not take an interest in politics, but that doesn't mean politics won't take an interest in you." In fact, our response to the Lebanon crisis was unusual in the sense that it combined two different sides of diplomacy—our adoption of a political position in relation to the Israeli attacks, expressed in official government statements[82] and telephone calls to the foreign ministers of the countries involved;[83] and our responsibility to protect Brazilians abroad.[84] And at the time, in addition to the tensions arising from the Lebanese crisis and the Doha Round, I also had to endure the frustrations of a daily struggle with bureaucracy. In writing my notes I appear to have been letting off steam: "Yesterday, for example, I had to appeal to President Lula to get 'our' Petrobras to release the [aviation] fuel required for the evacuation of the Brazilians in Adana and Damascus. A similar situation, though this time without the need for intervention from higher up, was the FAB's reluctance to allow one of our old 707s to pick up . . . our nationals who are stranded in Damascus. They were worried because it was a 'high-risk area'!"

"Un ami du Liban"

On August 14, I found myself heading back to Istanbul, and from there to Adana. I never imagined that in the space of just over a fortnight I would find myself making two visits to a city in southern Turkey whose existence I had previously been only vaguely aware of, due to the US military presence there. During the hearing in the Senate I had been pleasantly surprised (in view of our tendency toward a certain isolationism) to realize that some of senators—especially Pedro Simon, a democrat and a nationalist with whom I had close relations—were keen for Brazil to get more involved in the search for a solution to a conflict that was, in a very concrete sense, bringing the troubles of the Middle East to our doorstep. And so I had decided I should return to Lebanon, despite the continuation of the hostilities. Before undertaking that rather risky mission (or so it seemed to me), I had a week's vacation in Geneva, with my daughter and grandchildren, and in Venice, where my wife Ana and I went in search of some valuable relaxation and esthetic contemplation. During that week, my chief of staff, Maria Nazareth Azevêdo ("Lelé"), worked very hard on preparing the trip, which of course was not a simple task. As various practical obstacles arose, Lelé removed them one by one. They included the question of how I was actually going to get to Beirut. Given that the airport had been damaged by Israeli bombing, and commercial flights suspended, the only way to reach the Lebanese capital—in order to deliver donations from the Brazilian government and the Arab community in our country—was to use an FAB transport aircraft (a Hercules C-130). Again we had to overcome a certain hesitance on the part of our air force. I said I had informed the Israeli foreign minister of my intended trip, and obtained a promise that due care would be taken, but still the FAB's top brass were not convinced. In the end, defense minister Waldir Pires had to intervene to authorize the Hercules to fly to Adana with the donations and then, with me on board, to continue to Beirut. When the trip was agreed, the Israeli bombing of Lebanon, including Beirut, was still very intense. Although negotiations were ongoing, there was obviously no guarantee that the violence would be brought to an end. But finally, on the day I returned from Venice, UN Security Council Resolution 1701 (2006) established a ceasefire. However, it only came into force on the day I left Geneva for Adana, from where I would set off for Beirut less than twenty-four hours later.

My journey to the Lebanese capital began promptly at 9 a.m. on August 15. The interior of the C-130 looked like a huge workshop. Under an enormous Brazilian flag were crates containing medical supplies and blankets, all of which had been donated. At the back, seats had been fixed to the floor to accommodate the small number of passengers. In addition to my chief of staff I was accompanied only by Ambassador Ouro-Preto, a personal assistant, and a young diplomat from Itamaraty's public affairs section. Also on board were teams from TV Globo and Radiobrás. The flight took about an hour and a half. It was necessary to avoid the airspace of Cyprus, which is in permanent dispute with Turkey. We flew over the eastern Mediterranean, part of Syria, and then the sea again, before descending toward Beirut airport. I was standing in the cockpit during the last part of the flight. There were few clouds, and visibility was good. Even from a distance it was possible to see smoke rising from various parts of the Lebanese capital.[85] As we approached the runway, which had been reduced to half its normal length, we could see craters caused by explosions. On the ground, after we had landed, I could see only one other aircraft, a military plane with what I think were Qatari markings. The Lebanese foreign minister, Fawzi Salloukh, was waiting for me outside the plane, along with our ambassador, Eduardo Seixas, and other officials. After passing quickly through the VIP hall, where my Lebanese counterpart memorably said to me "Welcome to *your* country,"[86] we went outside again for the delivery of the donations.

I was the second foreign minister to arrive in Lebanon after the ceasefire: Massimo D'Alema of Italy had visited the day before. But the difference was that Brazil did not have a fleet in the Mediterranean (today, at least, we have a frigate, the flagship of the UNIFIL task force). As prearranged, I started my visit in the south of Beirut, in the Shia neighborhood that had borne the brunt of the Israeli aerial bombardment. Most of the bombs had actually fallen in the period between the declaration of the ceasefire and its entry into force, a fact that added a particularly cruel twist to the tragedy. Strangely, the UNSC resolution had not stipulated a precise time for the violence to end. In fact the bombing stopped at 8 a.m. on August 14, but that was a unilateral Israeli decision. Salloukh informed me that during the weekend the air attacks had actually been more intense than at any previous time during the conflict, and our ambassador later confirmed that was the case. Never before had I been so close to a war zone, or seen such destruction and evidence of recent deaths. In various places there was excavation work still going on, in search of dead bodies or possibly even survivors. Many people were wearing masks to protect them from the dust or, very likely, the stench of corpses. Here and there, adding to the emotional impact of the scene, I spotted little Brazilian flags or the shirt of the Brazilian soccer team—worn in most cases by passers-by, but in a few cases also half-buried in the rubble. Looking at the wreckage of so many buildings, I wondered how many families must have been killed or injured. And how many of the dead would actually have belonged to Hezbollah, the declared enemy of Israel? When our convoy of vehicles finally emerged from the tangle of small streets (where traffic and pedestrians were beginning to reappear, and daily life stubbornly recommencing), we followed a route along broader, quieter roads toward the Lebanese foreign ministry, which I had been to a few times since my first visit to Beirut in 1994. On the way I noticed several viaducts destroyed by bombs, presumably for no reason other than to damage the country's infrastructure.

The foreign minister, Fawzi Salloukh, had previously been a career diplomat, and then more recently the director of the Islamic University of Beirut. A Shia, he was linked to the faction that supported President Lahoud, and thereby also had a connection with Syria. This fact represented an important shift in the balance of forces inside the Lebanese government. At the time of my earlier visits to Lebanon during the Lula government, the country's foreign ministers had generally been Christians (Jean Obeid, for example) who, although critical of Israel, adopted positions closer to the West. As we walked through the building together, Salloukh made comments about national unity, the Lebanese army, and the composition of the international force that all seemed consistent with the mental framework generally attributed to the Shias and the president. In the formal meeting, in the presence of other officials, Salloukh read out some points that had been written by hand: he criticized the bellicose actions of Israel; asserted that the abduction of Israeli soldiers was merely a pretext for a military operation planned in advance with the "consent" of the US; made references to the Shebaa Farms;[87] and expressed the conviction that the Lebanese issue could only be resolved in the context of a comprehensive settlement of the problems of the Middle East that included, above all, the Palestine situation. He also warmly expressed Lebanon's gratitude toward Brazil (and would do so again later, during the press conference).

Bearing in mind that the bombing had ended little more than twenty-four hours before my arrival in Beirut, I had a remarkably full schedule of meetings. I was received by the speaker of the Lebanese parliament, Nabih Berri; Prime Minister Fouad Siniora; and President Émile Lahoud (declared politically dead by Jean Obeid about eighteen months earlier). Some of the positions they set out coincided: the importance of preserving national unity, repudiation of Israeli aggression, and the need for help and engagement from the international community. But there were also differences of perspective that were more than mere nuances. Of all the interlocutors, Nabih Berri struck me as the most secure and—surprisingly, given the circumstances—optimistic. He told me that despite all the suffering, privations and countless deaths, Lebanon might actually have a "golden opportunity" to begin wide-ranging negotiations with Israel. Referring indirectly to the position of strength gained by Hezbollah during the armed conflict, he said that Tel Aviv should now understand, once and for all, that the military action was "no longer an option." The leader of the Amal Movement, always sounding very sure of himself, stressed Lebanon's desire for peace and also emphasized, as had Salloukh, the central role of the Lebanese army. The international force should merely provide assistance and be limited to a "maximum" (a word he repeated several times) of fifteen thousand men. When we turned briefly to Lebanon's internal affairs, Berri said that the country's different religious denominations (seventeen in total, according to one of the other deputies) should be able to live together. Like all my other interlocutors he had kind words for Brazil, which he had visited more than once. Before the conflict with Israel erupted, Berri had been seeking to establish a national dialogue. Given his leadership role among the Shias and his apparently close relations with Hezbollah, I had the impression he might be better placed than other political figures to lead the reconciliation process that would be essential in order to bring about stability and reconstruction. In fact it would not turn out like that, but the Shia politician with the westernized ways (in contrast to the other deputies I saw) did continue to play a fundamental role in all the attempts to create a stable government in Beirut.

My conversation with the prime minister was the longest and, in a sense, the most interesting. Siniora was frank and loquacious, rarely stopping talking during the hour or so we were together. Sometimes he seemed to lose his thread, so I stepped in with a few brief remarks to keep the dialogue on track. He was very effusive about Brazil, saying that our solidarity and assistance, both in humanitarian and political terms, were of great value "at this moment of suffering and pain." He said he would be in favor of Brazil's inclusion in any core group of countries that came together to deal with the Lebanese issue, and that he would endeavor to bring that about. One element that distinguished Siniora's position from those expressed by the foreign minister and the speaker of the parliament was his obvious concern about the attitudes of Iran and Syria. Regarding the former, he said: "Iran needs to understand that Lebanon is a pluralistic state." He continued: "I'm a Muslim, but Lebanon is not and cannot be an Islamic state." As for Syria, he said it was necessary to make the regime in Damascus understand that "Lebanon is not and does not want to be a satellite state." In order to secure those two objectives, which were obviously interconnected, Lebanon hoped to receive the support of the international community, including Brazil. At that point I told Siniora that I would soon have to return to Brazil, but that our special envoy to the Middle East would be staying in the region and seeking to arrange meetings in Tehran and Damascus, among other capitals. The prime minister said that sounded like an important mission and expressed his best wishes for its success.

Siniora—who displayed sincerity and some signs of a sense of humor, along with a little insecurity—grew in political stature during the conflict with Israel. Much more than President Lahoud, he was the "face" of Lebanon as far as the outside world was concerned. But, as I noted at the time, his task was one of the most complex, and eventually it would prove impossible. Although internationally the prime minister's image had been bolstered, internally it was Hezbollah and its leader Hassan Nasrallah who gained most in strength by having led the military resistance to the Israeli forces. And the stimuli Hezbollah continued to receive from Iran and Syria certainly were not conducive to moderation, or at least not in the sense of the word that Siniora understood. The prime minister and I embraced at the end of the meeting, exchanging words of mutual affection. At the exit to the building where his office was located, I told him, not without some emotion in my voice, that Lebanon could rely on Brazil for support, both humanitarian and political. And indeed, at the donor conference held in Stockholm on August 31, we made an initial contribution, admittedly modest, of $500,000 USD toward the reconstruction effort. In October Brazil would send two missions to Lebanon with the aim of expanding the cooperation efforts. On January 25, 2007, I attended the Paris International Conference in Support of Lebanon, where I announced an additional donation of $1 million USD.[88]

My last official meeting in the Lebanese capital was with my old acquaintance, President Emile Lahoud. Given his precarious political situation and my lack of time (we needed to fly out before nightfall), I tried to steer the conversation away from any in-depth analysis. On Israel and the internal situation, Lahoud said more or less what I expected. As on other occasions, he spoke warmly about Brazil and had words of friendship and admiration for President Lula. As the Prime Minister had done, he accompanied me to the door of his palace, and told me as I was leaving that I was "*un ami du Liban*."

In my notes on the meetings that took place during the seven or eight hours I spent in Beirut, I noticed that none of my interlocutors had suggested Brazil should participate in the international peacekeeping force that was the subject of so much discussion at the time. That could be understood in a number of different ways. At the time I assumed the "omission" was because Beirut did not want to get involved in—and thereby appear to legitimize—a decision arising in response to Israeli demands, backed by the US, to "securitize" the south of Lebanon. Years later, however, with the full support of various Lebanese senior officials and factions, and as I myself was able to see during a visit to Beirut in 2012 as Brazil's defense minister, a Brazilian frigate would be the flagship of the UNIFIL naval task force, which itself was under the command of a Brazilian admiral. My stay in Beirut ended with a brief visit to the Brazilian consulate, where I thanked the staff for their excellent work and spoke to community leaders from the Bekaa Valley. All of them were very grateful to the Brazilian government, and to Itamaraty in particular. At about 5 p.m., the Brazilian Air Force C-130 took off for Adana. Curiously, taking into account the FAB's initial reluctance, the commander of the plane, a lieutenant colonel whom I would later meet again on a flight to Antarctica, was very happy: "It was the riskiest mission the FAB has undertaken since the Second World War," he told me, bursting with justified (if somewhat exaggerated) pride.

Throughout the conflict I kept in close contact with the Arab community in Brazil, particularly the Lebanese groups. My meetings with them continued after the ceasefire. Less than a fortnight after my return, on September 26, at the Monte Líbano club in São Paulo, there was a big get-together followed by a dinner in my honor. It was attended by the governor of São Paulo, Claudio Lembo, parliamentarians, academics, religious leaders, and other representatives of Lebanese organizations. In my speech I recalled my impressions during my two trips to Adana and my quick visit to Beirut, and tried to convey a hopeful vision for the future of Lebanon. I recalled what all my interlocutors had told me, regardless of their political party or religious denomination, about the importance of maintaining Lebanese national unity. I said that despite the suffering caused by the conflict and the problems that remained, I had noticed "a sliver of optimism." Today, looking back, I think that was felt more by me than the Lebanese officials I spoke to. But, at the time, I did believe there existed "a window of opportunity [arising] from exhaustion [in relation to the conflict]." I said I could not see a "solution to the Middle East without resolving the issue of Palestine." In that regard I underlined the importance of a broad dialogue and emphasized the role Brazil could play in building peace "in Lebanon and the Middle East." I referred to the speech President Lula had made just a few days before at the UN General Assembly, in which he said that for many years the Middle East had wrongly been left to the major powers to deal with, without a solution having been found. I said it seemed the moment had arrived to invite to the table other countries, such as Brazil, whose societies were based on a "substratum of solidarity and humanism, which are indispensable means for survival." I ended my speech by mentioning the passage from Ibn Khaldun that appears at the start of this narrative, and its relevance to the initiatives Brazil was taking in Lebanon and elsewhere in the Middle East. Those initiatives, I said, could be seen as part of an effort to overcome preconceptions and create understanding, based on the conviction that "the truth doesn't push us apart, the truth brings us closer together."

Annapolis

On November 27, 2007, a major international conference on the Middle East peace process took place in the small city of Annapolis, Maryland, the headquarters of the United States Naval Academy. Among the countries invited to attend, Brazil was one of three developing countries that were neither Arab nor Muslim, nor a permanent member of the UNSC. The other two were our IBSA partners: India and South Africa. After repeated representations to Washington, Mexico was also admitted, but not as a full participant. No Mexican minister was invited, and the country's representative (an undersecretary from the foreign ministry) sat next to our ambassador in a seat that would normally be occupied by an aide.

For some time, Brazil's initiatives with regard to the Middle East had been making clear our interest in participating more actively in the peace process. Lula's aforementioned proposal at the UN General Assembly in 2006 can obviously be seen in that context. This interest was reciprocated by Arab leaders, including the president of the Palestinian Authority, who I knew had been the main proponent of Brazil's presence at the Annapolis Conference. But the receptivity toward Brazil on the part of countries such as Lebanon and Syria (the latter agreed only reluctantly to participate in the conference) certainly helped ensure that the invitation was issued. Our ability to conduct a dialogue with opposing factions was clear in various situations.[89] And the fact that we maintained a good dialogue with Israel, even while condemning many of its actions, must also have weighed in our favor, as it was hard to imagine Washington inviting us to the conference without having consulted Tel Aviv. Nor do I think it was a coincidence that the three IBSA countries were invited. In the narrative on the Tehran Declaration I mentioned that the US secretary of state had already taken an interest in this group composed of three multicultural, multiethnic democracies from the developing world. The BRICs grouping, whose potential was beginning to be explored at meetings of foreign ministers on the sidelines of the UN General Assemblies, might also have been a helping factor. Our dialogue with Moscow and Beijing was fluid, as were our political contacts with the other permanent members of the Security Council. The idea of a broad conference, with Brazil among the participants, had already been discussed on various occasions with French and British officials (particularly the former). The Annapolis Conference constituted recognition of the need to bring greater transparency to the proposals that until then had been dealt with only within the ambit of the Quartet, and to secure greater international support for them.

For a long time we had argued that the debates conducted by the Quartet were in need of "fresh air," and our participation in the donor conferences had already provided solid evidence of our desire to contribute to peace and development in the region, so it was natural for Brazil to be invited. Also, our pursuit of closer ties with the Arab countries might also have counted in our favor with other governments that had some influence over the process.[90]

Over the course of 2007, the Brazilian and US governments spoke on various occasions about the Middle East. On March 9, President George W. Bush made a quick visit to Brazil in the context of cooperation on the use of ethanol as a source of energy. Before the meeting of the two presidents at a Petrobras terminal near São Paulo, I had breakfast with Secretary of State Condoleezza Rice. There were various subjects for us to deal with, but I remember the Middle East was one of five points I had noted down in advance. My conversations with Condoleezza were always very frank and I was impressed by how she always seemed to be paying close attention, even though she probably disagreed with much of what I said. Around that time, one of the aspects I used to emphasize to her was the need to involve Syria in the dialogue. Far be it from me to claim that my words had much influence on the US decision to invite Damascus to the Annapolis Conference—and yet I would say, based on the perception that all the actors with influence over the process should be seated together around the table, that Syria's inclusion proved to be a positive aspect of the US initiative of relaunching the peace process.

I met again with the secretary of state on March 30, in Washington, to prepare the presidential meeting that would take place the following day at Camp David. Much of our conversation concerned ethanol, trade relations, and South American politics. But other subjects also came up, such as cooperation with third countries (especially in Africa and the Caribbean), the rise of China, and UN reform. The Middle East was also one of the items on the informal agenda drawn up for the presidential meeting, which took place without any ceremonial formalities. President Bush initiated the discussion on the Middle East by asking Lula what role Brazil thought the UN should play in the peace process. In reply, while emphasizing the importance of UN involvement, Lula took the opportunity to explain the historical and cultural reasons that led Brazil to take a continued interest in the search for a solution to the problems of the Middle East. The statistics concerning Syrian and Lebanese immigration in Brazil never failed to impress. Lula also spoke of the frustration caused by the lack of practical measures, "despite the agreements of the past." But rather than expand upon our well-known position in favor of greater UN participation, Lula turned the question around, asking Bush what role he himself could play, as US president, and "how Brazil can help." Bush was forthright in replying that Brazil's involvement would be positive. Speaking in direct and sometimes rather simplistic terms, the US president said it was important to understand what the prerequisites for peace were. It was necessary, he said, to achieve a definitive solution to the issue of the borders, and at the same time improve the living conditions of the Palestinians. He lamented the fact that Hamas had won the election without having renounced its objective of destroying Israel.[91] After making what struck me as a harsh comment about the late Yasser Arafat (whom he accused of having "betrayed" President Clinton while ostensibly favoring peace), Bush asserted that he himself was "the first US president to clearly support the creation of a Palestinian state." The gratuitous reference to Arafat reminded me that on one occasion, during a dinner at the Americas Summit in Monterrey, Mexico, Secretary of State Colin Powell had told me that "as long as those two stubborn old mules [Arafat and Sharon] are in power, we won't manage to move forward." At that time Washington's approach had been to try to strengthen the Palestinian prime minister, Mahmoud Abbas. In 2007, with the two old "mules" out of the picture (one dead, the other disabled), Bush and Rice still pursued a strategy of supporting Abbas, now president of the Palestinian Authority, to the detriment of Hamas. But this was complemented by the idea of a referendum, in which the question about the creation of the Palestinian state would presuppose its coexistence alongside Israel. "Condi is already working on that [not only with the Palestinian Authority, but also with Israel]," Bush said. Finally, he asked for help from the Brazilian government in carrying out that strategy.

For the next part of the conversation, Lula handed over to me. I started by saying that Brazil did not have any "illusions of power," but we had "good relations with both sides." I recalled my trips to the region, including the visit two years before to Ramallah, Jerusalem and Tel Aviv. I added that in order to advance our dialogue on the subject, we had appointed a special envoy who would shortly be having talks with the assistant secretary of state, David Welch. During that conversation, I hoped, both officials would be able to identify how we could help with the pursuit of peace. Bush referred to the assassinations in Lebanon, criticized the inflexibility of Bashar al-Assad, and indicated that the speaker of the House of Representatives, Nancy Pelosi, would be paying the Syrian president a visit: "Although she's a Democrat, she'll be reporting back to me," he added. As far as the US president was concerned, there were only three democracies in the region: Israel, Lebanon, and Iraq. Regardless of those positions, the US government's inclusion of the Middle East on the agenda and the frankness of the discussion were, as far as I know, unprecedented in a US-Brazil presidential dialogue. Equally unprecedented was the US request for help from the Brazilian government. The Middle East issue did not appear in the joint statement. However, a few months later, the invitation to participate in the Annapolis Conference showed that Bush's request was not purely rhetorical.

"You're a man of peace"

On November 26, in Washington, on the eve of the Annapolis Conference, I wrote in my notebook: "The opening represented by the invitation issued to Brazil and other developing countries . . . needs to be consolidated and built upon. So I tried to prepare a speech . . . that would contain clear and strong messages, along the lines of what the Palestinians want, but without creating resistance [on the part of] Israel or the United States itself." Even though it was not very clear what role Brazil might actually play in the conference, apart from being present and conveying a message, I was eager to continue giving signs of our engagement. For that reason I had already agreed with President Lula that at the next donor conference, due to take place in Paris, we should commit ourselves to making a substantial financial contribution of about $10 million USD. There was also the possibility of undertaking projects in association with other countries, such as Turkey or our IBSA partners. Coordination with the latter struck me as particularly important, so I invited the two other representatives from IBSA countries who were going to attend the conference—South Africa's foreign minister, my friend Nkosazana Zuma; and India's science and technology minister, Qepil Sibal—to an "IBSA lunch" that same day at the residence of our ambassador, Antonio Patriota.

The next entry in my notebook was on November 29, by which time I was in Mexico City for a bilateral meeting. I wrote: "Annapolis had a positive outcome, although everyone recognized that the greatest difficulties still lie ahead. Brazil's participation was positive. Condi, who was chairing the conference, put me in an appropriate position in the order of speakers. I was able to make my speech calmly [i.e. without the stress that arises when time is running out]. In fact . . . I had to adapt the speech to refer to what had already taken place: the understanding announced by Bush and the pronouncements by Abbas and Olmert. . . . [I raised] ideas that need to be followed up: participation in the donor conference, IBSA, meetings of civil society." The most important part of my speech, which I made in English, was as follows:

> Land for peace continues to be a guiding principle for a negotiated and lasting solution. This should lead to a sovereign, democratic, cohesive, and economically viable Palestinian state, within a credible timeframe. Peace must also include efficient measures to protect and defend Israel against acts of violence. . . . The negotiations should be comprehensive and inclusive [and] must be accompanied by efforts in good faith to resolve, definitively, outstanding issues between Israel and its Arab neighbors (Syria and Lebanon) based on the pre-1967 borders and the UN resolutions. . . . Only solid, tangible results in the peace process will give the moderates the support they need from their political bases.

I also expressed concern at "the continuing deterioration in the living conditions in the occupied territories, particularly the Gaza Strip," where "we see deprivation, poverty and frustration." I mentioned projects financed by Brazil, and others by the IBSA Fund, aimed at mitigating "those dismal conditions." I referred to Brazil's support for the efforts by the special representative of the Quartet, Tony Blair, to stimulate the Palestinian economy and consolidate the process of developing Palestinian institutions, and I underlined the importance of dialogue between the Israeli and Palestinian civil societies. I also said that "given its experience of friendly coexistence on the part of our Arab and Jewish communities," Brazil would be ready to host inclusive meetings aimed at promoting adherence to the "values of peace and coexistence in the Middle East." I praised the way the conference had brought about the "expanded participation" of the international community, noting that this corresponded to the ideas we ourselves had been advocating. Finally, I emphasized the need for follow-up to the process initiated in Annapolis, and expressed support for Russia's proposal to hold a conference in Moscow in 2008.

In pursuit of peace in the Middle East, Brazil put its chips on the process launched in Annapolis. President Lula himself would refer to it in speeches and in conversations with other leaders. As I said to Israeli foreign minister Tzipi Livni a few months later, Annapolis had created an opportunity—which should not be wasted—to legitimize, on the international level, decisions taken in smaller groups. More than that, in allowing the discussion to take place in wider circles, Annapolis would eventually exert some positive influence, albeit limited, on those same decisions. Also, the format avoided the creation of the "automatic majorities" that Israel always objected to in the more "politicized" environment of the United Nations. I recognized that Annapolis did not constitute an ideal form of inclusive multilateralism—but it was the multilateralism possible in the circumstances. And Brazil was ready to participate in it.

Having already described my good relationship with the Arab community in Brazil, I should also mention an incident that illustrates the favorable perception of my role on the part of many Brazilian Jews. A few days after the Annapolis Conference, I went to São Paulo with my wife to celebrate my youngest son's thirtieth birthday. In the late afternoon, on a Friday, we went to have a coffee and visit a bookstore. On the way back home we crossed paths with a group of four or five orthodox Jews: they had dark suits, black wide-brim hats, and long beards (I do not remember if they also had sidelocks). Just after they had walked past us, I heard one them whisper: "Is that Amorim?" I turned round to greet them. Excitedly, they asked me: "How was Annapolis? Are we going to get peace?" Before I could answer, one of them said: "We probably are. Because you were there, and you're a man of peace."

The Protector of the Two Holy Cities

Imbued with the spirit of Annapolis, in early February 2008 I set off on another Middle East tour, taking in Saudi Arabia, Syria, Jordan, Palestine, and Israel. On the way to Riyadh, taking advantage of the days of carnival and the need to stop off in Europe, I made an official visit to Spain. During my stay in Madrid—although my attention was largely focused on the eruption of a new crisis between Venezuela and Colombia, which led me to have a fruitful exchange of views with the secretary-general of the Ibero-American Forum, Enrique Iglesias[92] —the issue of the Middle East also featured prominently. My Spanish counterpart Miguel Angel Moratinos, an expert on the Middle East, had just come back from Egypt, where he had accompanied King Juan Carlos on state visit. I should mention that at that time, unlike after the outbreak of the Arab Spring, the Egyptian leader was still referred to by the international media (and, by extension, the Brazilian media) as a "president," not as a "dictator." For the king of Spain to visit him was therefore uncontroversial. Some Brazilian newspapers, however, appeared to anticipate the Arab Spring by starting to call Mubarak a dictator as soon as he agreed to make an official visit to Brazil (which in the end did not take place).

Unlike most European foreign ministers, Moratinos had good relations with the Syrian government, including with his counterpart Walid al-Muallem. At the time of my visit to Spain, the Palestinian issue was still dominated by the rupture between Fatah and Hamas, which had occurred the previous June.[93] Since then, Hamas—which is linked to the Muslim Brotherhood and generally considered more radical than Fatah, and indeed classified as "terrorist" in certain quarters—had established a position of dominance in the Gaza Strip, from where it launched rocket attacks against Israel quite regularly. Combined with other factors, especially the vulnerability of the PNA leadership due to the lack of concessions from Israel, the rift between the two Palestinian factions and the Hamas attacks on Israel had a negative impact on the Annapolis process. The Spanish foreign minister was critical of Israel and distanced himself from the opinion of most western foreign ministries on Hamas. By advocating some form of dialogue with the movement he placed himself in open opposition to Washington and Tel Aviv, who wanted to isolate it through sanctions. And so, a little more than two months on from the Annapolis Conference, Moratinos perceived the process as already being in crisis (from which, in truth, it would never recover). Aside from the Fatah-Hamas conflict, which was politically undermining the Palestinian Authority even in the West Bank (theoretically under Fatah control), my Spanish counterpart said that among the Arab countries there was a widespread feeling that, contrary to the earlier optimistic expectations, Bush had not taken advantage of his visit to the region to put pressure on Israel.[94] Moratinos believed, however, the Annapolis process might still be "saved." My own purpose in visiting the Middle East at that time was precisely to show Brazil's willingness to make a contribution, however small, to those salvage efforts.

Before leaving Spain, I visited Toledo with my wife Ana and our ambassador to Madrid (and former defense minister), my good friend José Viegas. The city, like no other, symbolizes the coexistence of the three great monotheistic religions (or "peoples of the book," as Muslims say) during the period of Arab domination of the Iberian Peninsula. Naturally I visited the great gothic cathedral, built during the *Reconquista* era, but also went inside an ancient synagogue, now a museum, and saw the remains of a mosque and "baths" from the Muslim era.

I arrived in Riyadh on February 9, almost exactly three years after my previous visit, which had been in preparation for the ASPA summit. The next morning I met with the secretary-general of the Gulf Cooperation Council, the friendly Abdul al-Attiyah, with whom I made another attempt to revive the Mercosur-GCC negotiations, which had become somewhat bogged down. At the suggestion of our ambassador, Isnard Penha Brazil (formerly Brazil's representative in Algiers), I also went to see Prince Khalid al-Faisal, who took a particular interest in cultural relations and at the time was preparing an exhibition of paintings in São Paulo.[95] I learned that he was the son of the famous King Faisal, who was killed by a fanatic apparently for having a Turkish wife whom, in contravention of Saudi habits, he treated as a true "queen." Among other interests, Prince Khalid ran an important foundation to support the arts and also funded a university. He venerated the image of his father, who was the subject of a photographic and iconographic exhibition that he was keen to show me in detail. I wrote in my notebook that he was "a relationship to be cultivated." And indeed, two and a half years later, I would find myself writing to the prince, by then elevated to the status of governor of Mecca, to request his intervention so as to secure the release (eventually achieved) of a Brazilian who was working as an interpreter for a soccer coach and had been arrested for assaulting a referee!

Early in the afternoon of February 10, King Abdullah, whom I had visited in 2005 when he was still crown prince, received me in his tent in the desert. The monarch's official title is "Protector of the Two Holy Cities" (Mecca and Medina), which in itself illustrates the semi-theocratic nature of the Saudi regime. This "tent"—actually a vast palace composed of trailers and other dismountable constructions, set in the midst of camel-breeding farms about an hour from the capital—that the king usually rests during the Saudi "winter" (when temperatures average about 30 degrees). While waiting to be seen by His Majesty, I was taken to one of the trailers. Remembering my previous visit, I prepared myself for a long wait. Very quickly, however, I was led to the "royal tent," which consisted of various rooms, all decorated with oriental rugs and beautiful curtains. The king received me in a hall that looked like the kind of space in which an ambassador might present credentials. I handed him a letter from the president and verbally reiterated the respectful greetings it conveyed; in response the king asked about Lula and spoke about him with affection and admiration. I soon realized the atmosphere was friendlier and more relaxed than during my previous visit. Then, however, I noticed something that initially left me somewhat perturbed: we were not the only delegation the king was receiving that afternoon. Not far away was a British group, members of the Conservative opposition in parliament, led by the shadow foreign secretary. Unsure how the situation would turn out, I concentrated on conveying the most important messages I had brought with me: concerning reciprocal state visits, the continuation of the ASPA process, etc.. Later, however, I realized that my anxiety was unwarranted.

His Majesty led us into another room, opposite the entrance hall, where a sumptuous banquet had been prepared. After washing our hands in basins of perfumed water, we proceeded to the buffet, which was presented in silverware. The king pointed me in the direction of the tastiest dishes and often served me himself. The long table, at which the other guests were already seated, was in the form of a rectangle with one side missing, or a "U" with two right-angles. The king sat in the middle chair on the shortest side; I was immediately to his right, the leader of the British group to his left. As we sat down, there was another surprise: right in front of us was a large television, which the king turned on. The size of the screen actually made it impossible to see the back of the room, so I was not sure which of my aides were participating in the meal. In particular I was worried that my chief of staff, Ambassador Maria Nazareth Azevêdo, might have been excluded because of her gender (she had already suffered a certain amount of discourtesy on the part of some of the lower-ranking Saudi officials who were accompanying us), but fortunately that turned out not to be the case. While we were eating, the conversation consisted of little more than pleasantries. The questions from His Majesty on everyday matters, his comments on the various different ways to cook a lamb, the TV (although no one was watching it): it all conveyed the clear message that the lunch was a courtesy, a way for the king to share a moment of relaxation with his guests. I understood that a political discussion would not have been appropriate in that atmosphere, but I hoped there would still be an opportunity to deal with more serious matters. The lunch, in fact, did not last very long.

Leaving behind his other guests, King Abdullah led our delegation into a smaller room at the very far end of the huge tent, putting an end to my anxieties about having to share his attention with another visitor. All the members of my delegation were present, including the less senior ones. On the Saudi side there were various other members of the royal family—all male, obviously. I was accompanied by our special envoy to the Middle East, Affonso Ouro-Preto; the ambassador in Riyadh, Penha Brasil; my press officer, Ricardo Tavares; and a secretary. Also present was Ambassador Maria Nazareth, dutifully "protecting" herself with an *abaya*. As I spoke, the Protector of the Two Holy Cities seemed to be listening with interest. He laughed a lot when, in response to one of his questions, I drew a similarity, perhaps a little unfairly, between Chávez and Gaddafi, saying they were both very fond of their own ideas. I was quick to add that Chávez was more open to listen to the ideas of others, and that he enjoyed a high level of popularity. I talked about the role of Saudi Arabia in the Middle East, indulging in a little attempt at seduction by comparing my host's leadership in the region with that exercised by Lula in South America. That was obviously an awkward comparison, not least because there was no overlap whatsoever between the two most important sources of Saudi influence among the Arabs, namely petrodollars and religious legitimacy (arising mainly from custody of the holy cities), and the two main reasons for the fascination exerted by Lula, namely his life story and his extraordinary abilities as a communicator. But I think the praise must have contributed to His Majesty's subsequent positive reaction to my idea of a "strategic partnership aiming at peace and development." The king also appeared particularly pleased with comments I made about the Arab Peace Initiative. He showed an interest when I spoke in general terms about the potential for cooperation in nuclear energy, and he asked me about the sources from which Brazil generates its electricity. He reacted favorably to the idea of reciprocal state visits, albeit implying he had no plans to visit Brazil in the short term: "I will be very pleased to receive President Lula in Saudi Arabia," he said. More than once I emphasized Brazil's willingness to contribute to peace in the Middle East—but I tried to do so with the requisite humility, carefully acknowledging that "we must learn from those who have more experience and knowledge." Enthused by the direction of the conversation and the apparently positive mood, I suggested we might consider a partnership for the benefit of the poorest countries in Africa, specifically mentioning Guinea-Bissau (whose population is forty percent Muslim) as a possible beneficiary. More through his frequent questions than his rare affirmations, King Abdullah kept the conversation alive for almost an hour. I then took the initiative of bringing the meeting to a close so as not to take up any more of my royal host's time. He was, after all, 84 years old. The king said goodbye to me and my entourage in a very affectionate manner, escorting me to the adjacent hall, close to the exit.

During the car journey and before lunch, I spoke to the interim foreign minister Nizar bin Obaid Madani, an intelligent and pragmatic man who, despite wearing a costume similar to the other Saudi officials I spoke to that day, exhibited straightforward political reasoning and spoke in the manner of any western diplomat or politician, without recourse to the colorful metaphors and other rhetorical flourishes typical of many Arab leaders. We spoke about international issues, particularly those related to the Middle East. In very frank fashion, Madani offered his opinions on Lebanon (highlighting the country's institutional fragility and the "negative influence" of Syria), Iraq (emphasizing its political instability and the Shia-Sunni rivalry) and Iran (seen as a very real threat and a factor disturbing the peace in the region). I assumed from what he said about Lebanon that, despite the strong rivalry between Riyadh and Damascus, talks were probably taking place behind the scenes and that an understanding might even be reached that would bring a minimum level of stability to that deeply divided country. Before my departure, on February 11, I had a meeting with the finance minister, Ibrahim bin Abdullah al-Assaf, in which we talked about opportunities for trade and investment between Brazil and Saudi Arabia. One year and three months later, those opportunities would constitute the main focus of President Lula's visit.

A woman with a sharp, penetrating gaze

My next destination was Damascus. My first meeting, in the late afternoon of February 11, was with the minister for expatriates (responsible for communication with Syrian communities abroad), Bouthaina Shaaban, a woman whose sharp, penetrating gaze suggested a strong character and firm convictions. Her beautiful face, with its well-defined features, reminded me of dramatic actresses of 1940s European cinema such as Anna Magnani, who played the role of a heroine and victim of the Nazis in Roberto Rossellini's *Rome, Open City*. The minister requested that the meeting take place in the hotel where I was staying. Although the formal reason (the pretext, one might even say) for our conversation was the large Syrian community in Brazil, Bouthaina wanted to talk politics. Her position was decidedly anti-Israel (or anti-Zionist) and she was an open critic of the two-state solution, which was the essence of the Annapolis process and indeed of various other peace efforts, including the Arab Peace Initiative of 2002. In relation to Lebanon, Bouthaina made no attempt to hide her feelings. She was very upset about the weakening of Syria's role in the country, which had come about as a result of the attitude of foreign powers (as expressed, for example, by the previously mentioned Security Council resolutions). She had a very pessimistic outlook, believing that conflict was inevitable between the United States and its allies (notably Israel) on the one hand, and the "national liberation forces" of the Arab countries on the other. Given her very forceful tone, I found myself wondering if the incursion into my hotel of a minister with one of the lower-profile portfolios was intended to send a message about what I could expect in my other political and diplomatic meetings in Damascus. Bouthaina Shaaban's persona was impressive nonetheless. A few months later she became a direct advisor to Assad, and therefore I would meet her again on subsequent visits to Syria. In 2011, in the early stages of the rebellion against the regime, she would act as government spokesperson—a rare example of a high-profile female among the politicians of the region. During those terrible days, seemingly still without end, she appeared to be adopting a moderate position, in contrast to the impression she had conveyed during our first encounter.

Next on my agenda was a dinner offered by the Syrian foreign minister, Walid al-Muallem. I had met him during my visit in 2005, when he was deputy minister and accompanied me on a few car journeys around Damascus. An experienced diplomat whose previous posts included that of ambassador to Washington, Muallem had also participated in the Marrakesh ministerial meeting as the principal Syrian negotiator of the document that became the Brasilia Declaration. I distinctly recall that despite the hard-line position of his country on some issues, Muallem played a positive role on that occasion, exerting a moderating influence and seeking consensus. The dinner took place in a former Ottoman palace that had been converted into a restaurant; not only was the food excellent but there was also an impressive performance by whirling dervishes. Whether due to sheer tiredness or because Muallem did not want to overload a social occasion with weighty issues, I do not remember much of our conversation apart from a vague impression of pessimism in relation to the Annapolis process and the political situation in the Middle East, although expressed in a tone less dramatic than that of my interlocutor earlier in the day.

The next morning, I had an audience with President Bashar al-Assad. Three points were discussed in broad terms: the situation in Lebanon; the Iraq issue; and, at my instigation, the relationship with Israel. On Lebanon, the president said Syria was willing to have conversations with third countries in search of a solution. He specifically mentioned Saudi Arabia, whose foreign minister Saud bin Faisal had made a "secret" visit to Damascus just the day before. This willingness to conduct a dialogue with Riyadh was in itself a positive factor. Assad spoke about the different options that, in his view, might solve the problem of the Beirut government's composition. One way or another, all of them revolved around the number of representatives each faction had in the government and the number of votes necessary for decisions to be approved, so that the minority faction could retain the power of veto. That would be the way to ensure the influence of the Shias, especially Hezbollah. The Syrian president also envisaged that new elections might take place. I realized that a more flexible approach on Lebanon was taking shape in Damascus, which I interpreted as a result of greater control by the president over the Syrian security apparatus. In fact, a few months later, on May 21, the Lebanese factions would reach an agreement brokered by the Emir of Qatar. It is highly unlikely that could have happened without some kind of signal from Damascus to its Lebanese allies. More importantly, in August 2008, Syria would abandon its longstanding resistance to recognizing the Lebanese state and establish diplomatic relations with Beirut.

Bashar al-Assad spoke at some length about the situation in Iraq. He expressed concern about the very large number of Iraqi refugees in Syria (about 1.5 million, or one tenth of the Syrian population). Making a prediction that would prove accurate, he said a civil war between Iraqi factions was a real possibility, but added, "We're not there yet." I told the Syrian president I was due to visit Israel and asked if he wanted to convey a personal message through me to Prime Minister Ehud Olmert. Without hesitation he replied that the Israeli leader needed to know Damascus was still open to triangular discussions ("proximity talks") with Israel—to be mediated by Turkey, which at the time had good relations with both Tel Aviv and with Damascus (a situation that would later be dramatically reversed as a result of the episode involving the so-called Gaza Freedom Flotilla and then the Syrian version of the Arab Spring). That was the most important point to come up during our conversation, and it would have practical consequences. Later, Muallem would say more on the subject, emphasizing that in order to have a chance of success the talks would have to be based on the elements previously agreed ("during ten years of discussions"). Muallem made reference to a document, which he referred to as a "deposit," delivered to President Clinton by the then Israeli prime minister, Ehud Barak. Two years later, during the visit by Bashar al-Assad to Brazil, I finally gained a better understanding of the contents of that "deposit"—it is a subject I will return to later. At the time, the information I did have was sufficient to carry out the task the Syrian president had requested of me.

After the meeting with Assad I went to see the vice president, Farouk al-Sharaa. He had been foreign minister when I visited in 2005, and I had met him again at UN headquarters during the vote on Resolution 1636, when I was the object of explicit expressions of gratitude and affection on his part. Looking at my notes, I see that I noticed a difference in tone between the words of Bashar al-Assad and those of his deputy. The latter seemed more hard-line, especially in relation to the situation in Lebanon, in contrast with the president's openness to dialogue and seemingly pragmatic, flexible attitude. I imagined that Al-Sharaa, whose appearance and way of speaking reminded me of the Russian *apparatchiks* of the Soviet era, represented more traditional currents within the regime, perhaps linked to the late Hafez Assad. The thought even occurred to me that he might have been appointed to his position so that Muallem, a more natural negotiator with more of a feeling for western manners, could take charge of foreign affairs. It would therefore come as something of a surprise to me that during the early stages of the rebellion against Assad, in mid-2011, Al-Sharaa appeared as a "moderate voice" of the regime.

Following my conversation with Al-Sharaa I went to have another meeting with the foreign minister, who came across as much less negative than during dinner the night before. I attributed the change to the relative optimism and the capacity for problem-solving displayed by the president. In this second meeting with Muallem we agreed on some details of how I should go about the *démarche* with Olmert. I left for Amman in the early evening.

"A lot of history and not much geography"

My first meetings with the Jordanian officials during this "second tour" of the Middle East took place the next morning, when I met the foreign minister, Salah al-Bashir, and the prime minister, Nader al-Dahabi. Beforehand, I also had a brief conversation with our ambassador to Jordan, Antonio Coelho da Rocha, and another, somewhat longer chat with Ambassador Bernardo Brito, accredited to the government of Iraq. Based provisionally in Amman, Brito traveled regularly to Baghdad; the journeys sounded nightmarish from a security point of view. He told me he hoped to move to the Iraqi capital by the start of 2009, which—as previously mentioned—ended up not being possible, despite my personal interest in the matter. As a young diplomat, Brito had performed important roles with competence and dedication. Later, after a period of relative ostracism, I appointed him as our first representative in Ramallah, after which he volunteered for the role of ambassador in Baghdad.

My meeting with the foreign minister, Salah al-Bashir, a successful young lawyer who already had experience of dealing with trade issues for the Jordanian government, was much more interesting than my conversation with Prime Minister Al-Dahabi. The latter struck me as having more of an administrative profile, with apparently little feeling for the subtleties of politics and diplomacy. As I saw it, this was in tune with the nature of the position of head of government in Jordan. Although Jordan is not an absolute monarchy in the style of Saudi Arabia, and it has a government theoretically rooted in parliament, it is the king who deals—personally and directly—with the most important issues, particularly those concerning foreign relations, defense and security. Moreover, as I had already noted on previous visits, the ministerial positions in the Jordanian government tended to change hands quite frequently, which contributed to weakening the role of the prime minister. Although we dealt with some bilateral themes and did not fail to raise the political issues of the region, my meeting with the prime minister was valuable more as a demonstration of consideration toward Brazil than because of its actual content.

At my request, Al-Bashir conveyed to me his thoughts about the peace process. The foreign minister was clearly very concerned about the situation in Palestine and the erosion of Mahmoud Abbas's leadership. He said Abbas had not been able to show concrete results from the path of peaceful negotiation that he had chosen, in contrast to the path of total confrontation that Hamas was pursuing. Jordan, which has a very large population of Palestinian origin (including refugees, who do not enjoy full citizenship), is naturally worried about the risk of "contamination" by movements linked to the Muslim Brotherhood. In the past, many Palestinians had opposed the very existence of the Hashemite kingdom. I myself remembered that many decades earlier, when I had been studying at the Diplomatic Academy of Vienna, a young Jordanian student, Akram Barakat, made a big impression on me because of the maturity of his political thinking. Although he was the holder of a diplomatic passport issued by Amman, he said he had Palestinian nationality, attributing the creation of the Jordanian kingdom to a "moment of drunkenness" on the part of Winston Churchill.[96] (Curiously, our paths crossed again, many years later, when he was Jordanian ambassador to Switzerland.) Al-Bashir was very critical of Israel, accusing it of deliberately placing obstacles in the path of the Annapolis process, which was "strongly supported by Jordan." I told him some of the details of my meetings in Syria, especially those regarding the situation in Lebanon. On that point, Al-Bashir, though intelligent and open-minded, expressed opinions not dissimilar to many others I had heard from Arab government officials, which struck me as rather simplistic: it all came down, he said, to the choice Damascus would have to make between Iran (perceived as a major threat) and the Arab world. During the car journey between the foreign ministry and the prime minister's office, Al-Bashir told me that Amr Moussa had been in Lebanon a few days before and was due to travel again to Beirut, which he took to be a hopeful sign. I said that in my opinion—as an apprentice in Middle Eastern affairs—the discussion about the composition of the Lebanese government (the distribution of positions, etc) concealed another, equally important issue that was directly relevant to the security of both Lebanon and Syria: the status of Hezbollah, and whether it might be integrated into the Lebanese army. I could still clearly recall conversations that had taken place just a few days after Hariri's assassination. During that period of great tension, concerns about Syria's security had featured prominently in my discussions with my interlocutors, including the then foreign minister (now vice president) Al-Sharaa. All of them—with the significant exception of President Bashar al-Assad—had shown reluctance to comply fully with UN Security Council decisions.

My last meeting was in Jordan with King Abdullah II. He received me in his palace, accompanied by the foreign minister and an aide. With me were the Brazilian ambassador and our special envoy to the Middle East. I spoke briefly about bilateral matters, including the invitation I was carrying for the king to visit Brazil.[97] Reflecting his past as a military pilot, Abdullah II expressed great interest in the aircraft manufactured in Brazil, especially the

Super Tucanos. He was also aware of the design of an Embraer aircraft built for transport and refueling (the KC-390, as it came to be known). His Majesty replied without inhibitions when I asked him about the Middle East, and made two observations that I considered especially noteworthy. One of them concerned the Syrian president. Bashar al-Assad, he said, had consolidated his hold on power over the previous eighteen months. This more or less confirmed my own impression, but contradicted the prevailing view that Bashar was still dominated by the old guard he had inherited from his father. The king's other comment, made with great conviction, was that Ehud Olmert (unlike Tzipi Livni, to whom he attributed a tougher attitude) was in favor of maintaining the timetable of the Annapolis process, including the ministerial meeting scheduled to take place in Moscow. The king himself also wanted the follow-up conference to take place, an opinion he said he had conveyed to Putin during a trip to Russia the day before. A relatively young monarch, he spoke with authority and objectivity on all topics. Even his habit of blinking his eyes quite often did not detract from the weight of his words. During my visit to Israel, Olmert would tell me that he held the Jordanian monarch in very high regard, and also that he agreed with his opinion about the Syrian president.

After a pleasant lunch hosted by Al-Bashir at his private residence, I set off by car to the West Bank with my little entourage. Again we crossed the Allenby Bridge (known in Jordan as a King Hussein Bridge), this time with simpler and quicker border procedures than in 2005. We had been informed that President Abbas was away on a trip and that the prime minister, Salam Fayyad, was not in Ramallah either: he had gone to Washington to lobby the US Congress for the release of the $300 million USD pledged at the Paris conference. So in terms of protocol the visit to Ramallah—the centerpiece that the rest of the Middle East trip had been scheduled around—was somewhat diminished. Partially compensating for that, however, was the long meeting I had with Saeb Erekat, the most visible face among the Palestinians negotiators during their dealings with Israel. I went to his office on the morning of February 13. Erekat spoke almost non-stop, and in a very emphatic tone. He was so didactic that at one point I had to interrupt and tell him he was preaching to a converted. But he was engagingly frank, and made a number of interesting remarks. He spoke of the positive climate between the Palestinian and Israeli negotiators, and conveyed the impression that progress was being made. In general, and contrary to what I had heard from other Arab interlocutors, he seemed to be leaning toward a moderately optimistic position. He admitted to being aware that in a final settlement between the PNA and Israel on the creation of a Palestinian state, the latter would not have any armed forces. This was the first time I had heard a Palestinian with influence in the decision-making process express acceptance of that particular Israeli demand—one which in my view constituted a limitation on the sovereignty of the state to be created. It represented, without doubt, a major concession to Tel Aviv. Erekat insisted firmly that the negotiations should be bilateral. That position, which implicitly reduced the importance of multilateral processes, appeared to me to be contrary to Palestine's own interests, but I understood that it would have stemmed in part from Erekat's own role as a negotiator, the preeminence of which he seemed keen to preserve. Responding to a question about whether the PNA would have popular support for an agreement, even in the face of Hamas opposition and its echoes in the West Bank, Erekat was adamant: "If we do a good deal, we'll submit it to a referendum and we'll win." He politely expressed gratitude for Brazil's participation in the Annapolis process and the donation we had made at the Paris conference. Overall, Erekat gave me the impression of being a determined man with a profound knowledge of his dossier, and certainly very committed to the Palestinian cause, but also—like most people from the academic world (he made a point of alluding to his studies at British and American universities)—a little too proud. I made a comment about the difficulties arising from the weight of history on both sides (at the time the Israelis were saying they were unable to cede a piece of land claimed by the Palestinians because "Rachel's Tomb" was located there). "You have too much history," I said. In reply, the Palestinian negotiator came up with a clever phrase that I ended up using as a chapter title in one of my books: "A lot of history and not much geography."

The chief Palestinian negotiator made two requests which, curiously, would not be repeated by the foreign minister, Riyad al-Maliki. The first was his wish for Brazil to host a meeting of the Committee on the Exercise of the Inalienable Rights of the Palestinian People, which we were hesitant about, given the possible repercussions that might affect Brazil's participation in the Annapolis process. I was always very clear that our participation in the process should not affect our positions on matters of principle. Consistent with this attitude, we supported the convening of several special sessions of the UN Human Rights Council and continued voting in favor of the resolutions on Palestine. However, in relation to the point raised by Erekat, the question was whether, in those circumstances, a meeting of the Committee—seen by Tel Aviv, fairly or unfairly, as an "instrument of propaganda"—would help advance the process. I thought it would be more productive to organize meetings between Israeli and Palestinian civil society organizations. I had alluded to this idea in my speech in Annapolis and would later mention it to more than one interlocutor in Israel. But the feeling that we were disappointing the Palestinians was still uncomfortable. The issue posed a dilemma that I had not been able to resolve, and the situation was cast in a sharper light by the fact that Erekat was quite insistent in his request. His second point concerned the rules of origin applicable to products from the Israeli-occupied territories, with regard to the recently signed free-trade agreement between Mercosur and Israel. We had been careful to follow previous examples, especially the agreement made with Tel Aviv by the European Union, which had not provoked any negative reactions in Palestine as far as I knew. The issue would be satisfactorily resolved (at least from the legal point of view) during the process of ratification by the Brazilian congress, and it did not come up again in bilateral conversations with the Palestinians during my time as foreign minister.[98]

The foreign minister, Riyad al-Maliki, had arrived that morning from a meeting with the European Union in Malta. Al-Maliki, whom I was in constant contact with throughout my time as foreign minister and indeed afterwards, is a man of mild manners with a background in civil engineering. Like most Palestinian militants, he had spent time in Israeli prisons. My conversation with him was valuable, above all, as an illustration of the difficulties and humiliations imposed by the Israeli occupiers on the Palestinian population. He told me, for example, that on one occasion, when he was walking between his home and the university where he worked as a professor (the distance was small but the two locations had been cut off from each other), an Israeli soldier, "almost a boy," stopped him and began looking through his documents in an arrogant manner. Al-Maliki decided to stare at him intensely. The young soldier's reaction was to tell Al-Maliki, who was old enough to be his father, "You can't look at me. You have to look down." The story reminded me of another one, with a bitter Kafkaesque flavor, that I had heard the day before from the Jordanian foreign minister (himself descended from Palestinians on his father's side), concerning the contents of a letter written by a Palestinian prisoner in Israel to his mother. The letter, which the minister had in his possession and kept on his desk, began more or less like this: "Mom, you might think I'm going crazy, but I'm starting to talk to the insects."

Paradoxically—given the fact that, in theory, there was a peace process underway—the situation in Palestine felt tenser than during my previous visit three years before. The Israeli military presence was more obvious. Unlike before, when a Palestinian vehicle picked me up at the border between the West Bank and Jordan, my aides and I were taken in an Israeli convoy almost to the very edge of Ramallah. Only there, in a place surrounded by high walls and protected by huge, electronically controlled steel gates, were we handed over to the Palestinian convoy; it felt almost like a prisoner exchange. During the night I spent in Ramallah, the Israeli forces detained 56 Palestinians; I was told it was the biggest operation in two years. Three of the Palestinians were arrested just a kilometer from our hotel (the same one as in 2005). I mentioned this fact both to Tzipi Livni and Ehud Olmert, who made no comment.

During my visit to the West Bank, an agreement was signed to establish political consultations between Brazil and Palestine. Before leaving Ramallah for Jerusalem, I visited the building housing our diplomatic mission, led at that time by Ligia Scherer (now ambassador in Mozambique), the highly skilled successor to two experienced ambassadors, the aforementioned Bernardo Brito and Arnaldo Carrilho. Accompanied by the foreign minister, the culture minister and the mayor of Ramallah, I took the opportunity to inaugurate the exhibition *Amrik* at the city's cultural center, an artistic touch that brought to an end my stay in the administrative center of Palestine (the capital, of course, is Jerusalem!).

"Nothing is agreed until everything is agreed"

I arrived in Israel at about 5 p.m. on February 13. My accommodation was a comfortable apartment inside one of the principal hotels in Tel Aviv. At 6:30 p.m. I went to a dinner hosted by the foreign minister, Tzipi Livni,[99] whom I had met twice before: the first time, at her request, on the margins of the 2007 UN General Assembly; and later, fleetingly, at social events around the Annapolis Conference. Livni, a middle-aged woman, had pleasant and occasionally pretty face, despite her grave demeanor. A strand of hair often fell over her forehead, covering part of her right eye; she kept swiping it away with a brusque movement that an observer might wrongly have interpreted as a sign of nervousness. The conversation during dinner was very objective, totally devoid of pleasantries. First, she asked what impressions I had gained from my trip. She was particularly curious about Saudi Arabia, which was precisely the place where I had had the fewest in-depth conversations. But I also commented on what I had seen and heard in Syria, Jordan, and above all, Palestine. Livni listened attentively, without making any comments herself. Then, in a very affirmative tone, she spoke about certain aspects of Israeli policy toward Palestine. She emphasized her country's concern with security, in particular in the areas close to Gaza. She described, to a degree of detail I had not heard before, the porous nature of the border between Gaza and Egypt: elevators inside houses that connect with tunnels, which in turn connect with other elevators, etc.. Moreover, she said, the Egyptian army, which was supposed to police the border, was "corrupt and inefficient." She revealed some sympathy and even a degree of fellow feeling toward the Palestinian negotiators, thereby confirming the "positive atmosphere" that Saeb Erekat had referred to. She alluded several times to the possibility of Israeli military action in Gaza, with a particular emphasis on the "Philadelphia Corridor." So frequently did she return to that point that I wondered if she might deliberately be testing the water to see her interlocutors' reaction (with me as one of the guinea pigs). In that context, I said an Israeli attack on Gaza would have disastrous consequences and would be unanimously condemned by the Palestinian leaders, not just Hamas. Livni came back with a somewhat surprising reply: "That's not what I hear when I'm alone in a room with a

PNA representative." Whom, I wondered, might she be referring to? Saeb Erekat? Or was it just a piece of rhetoric aimed at underlining the rivalry between the political factions in Palestine? No answers were forthcoming. I spoke about the "humiliation" of teachers, doctors, and elderly people, all subject to the whims of Israeli soldiers who were only sixteen-year-old boys. "Eighteen," she retorted. Livni acknowledged the difficulties of day-to-day life for the Palestinians, but did not mention any concrete measures that might actually improve the situation. The way my interlocutor referred to her relations with the negotiators in Ramallah suggested some real progress had been made, but she gave no details. She told me the basic principle of the negotiations was that "nothing is agreed until everything is agreed." Her choice of words inevitably brought to mind the minutiae of the WTO negotiations—not a good omen, given the absence of an agreement on the Doha Round. Even with regard to Jerusalem, Livni acknowledged the possibility of a negotiated solution, although the location of two holy places (one for Jews, the other for Muslims) on the same rock made the issue particularly difficult. The harsh tone of my Israeli counterpart contrasted with a certain degree of flexibility on substantive issues. She said the only genuinely non-negotiable point among those always cited by Palestinians was that of the refugees, whose return, she said, "would be incompatible with the Jewish character of the State of Israel." At that point in the conversation we made a brief digression to discuss whether the term "Jewish" referred to a religion or a people. Later, with that question still in mind, I looked for the text of the resolution that created the State of Israel, also known as the "Partition Plan."[100] It was only then that I learned that the text does in fact refer to the "Jewish State."

During our conversation, Livni seemed to be listening to my comments attentively and with interest, even though she frequently disagreed with me. Despite her somewhat abrupt manner, she was more communicative than dogmatic. Accompanying her words with expansive hand gestures, which appeared to indicate sincere concern, she said she could "understand" the problems of the Palestinians, and there were moments when she seemed genuinely interested in solving them. "I have young children and I want them to live in peace," she said at one point. But she kept coming back to the issue of security, which seemed almost to be an obsession. I asked her how she viewed the Annapolis process and the meeting scheduled to take place in Moscow. Corroborating the impressions I had heard from other interlocutors, including the king of Jordan, Livni seemed unenthusiastic about the meeting. She said it was necessary first to achieve further progress in the bilateral negotiations. As always in such cases, the stronger party prefers to conduct discussions bilaterally, thus avoiding the moral pressure of a large group of countries (although curiously and somewhat paradoxically in this case, the "weaker party," Saeb Erekat, had also expressed a preference for the bilateral approach). I made the observation that this "moral pressure" could also be exercised with regard to issues that were in Israel's interest, such as "good governance" in Palestine and the preference for the political approach backed by the PNA rather than the military option pursued by Hamas. Following a similar line of reasoning, I also commented that the format of Annapolis could contribute to giving "multilateral legitimacy" to an eventual agreement without the disadvantages routinely depicted by Tel Aviv with regard to the UN General Assembly and its "automatic majorities." It would also help ensure, I said, that the provisions of the agreement were respected in future. Livni did not disagree, but nor did she seem persuaded.

My meeting with the Israeli foreign minister lasted an hour and a half, with no let-up in the rhythm or pauses for small-talk. Livni was in a rush because she was about to take a commercial flight to the US to participate in a ceremony in honor of a recently deceased US congressman, a great defender of Israel. But there was still time for us to sign a cultural agreement. As she was leaving, she told me she had appreciated the conversation and wanted to continue it on another occasion. Despite the harshness of her tone over the previous ninety minutes, I had the impression she was being sincere.

The next day, February 14, I met Prime Minister Ehud Olmert in his office in Jerusalem. It was another long conversation, but the dialogue was an effective one. It was less rigid, both in tone and content, than with Tzipi Livni. At no point did Olmert allude to the possibility of a military solution in Gaza (although, a year later, that was the route Israel would opt for). He acknowledged the validity of my concerns regarding the daily lives of the Palestinians, and admitted that those difficulties impacted negatively on the position of the Palestinian Authority. His reasoning seemed to be based on considerations that were more political than humanitarian. The constant concern with security, although he expressed it less obsessively than the foreign minister had done, was obvious in his comment that any analysis of those everyday issues had to take into account the need to minimize the risks that would arise, he said, from greater freedom of movement for the Palestinians in the West Bank. Olmert was clearer than Livni in expressing his appreciation of the role played by Brazil. At the end of the meeting I asked him to request that our aides, on both sides, leave the room. When we were alone, I passed on the message from Bashar al-Assad about Syria's acceptance of the "Turkish channel" for proximity talks with Israel, which would focus principally on the Golan Heights. I explained that the Syrian president had told me he would be willing to move on to direct negotiations as soon as the basis for them had been clearly established. The prime minister reacted positively to Assad's message about Turkish mediation and agreed, without going into details, that it would not make sense to return to issues that had already been discussed.[101] Olmert added, however, that the problem with Syria "isn't so much the map, but the support for Hezbollah and for Hamas."

I also met with President Shimon Peres. Our conversation lasted over an hour, but I did not glean anything new from it. In his role as head of state (rather than head of government), Peres adopted the demeanor of a wise old man, discoursing philosophically about globalization, the primacy of the economy over politics, etc.. He referred kindly to Brazil as a "pioneer in valuing difference, which is essential in the modern world." At his instigation, I spoke about UN Security Council reform, the G4, and the G8+5. To my surprise, much of the conversation took place in front of the cameras and microphones of the media. Occasionally the journalists would ask questions, introducing an unusual element into the encounter. I even feared briefly that I might have walked into some kind of trap, but soon I realized that was not the case. I mentioned to Peres a conversation I had had that morning in Tel Aviv with the great novelist Amos Oz, in which we had explored the idea of a meeting of Palestinian and Israeli educators. That elicited further musing from the president: "At the end of the day, who are the true educators? We have a lot to learn from the young." Such reflections were certainly interesting, but did not contribute much to the pursuit of my objectives.

My meeting with Amos Oz deserves more than a fleeting reference. At some point before my trip I had expressed an interest in meeting him—either through our ambassador or, more likely, Israel's highly active representative in Brazil, Tzipora Rimon. I had read two of Oz's novels, including the autobiographical *A Tale of Love and Darkness*, an unbiased but also highly personal account of the journeys undertaken by Jews who went to live in Palestine between the end of the nineteenth and the early twentieth century, up to the creation of the State of Israel. I was also aware of his criticism of certain decisions by the Israeli government, including the disproportionate response—causing many civilian casualties in Lebanon—to the attacks by Hezbollah. I had been told the novelist was willing to travel from his home near the Dead Sea to meet me in Tel Aviv, but I confess I did not really expect him to do so. It was a pleasant surprise, therefore, to be told on the morning of February 14 that the writer was waiting in the lobby of my hotel. Amos Oz is a short man with blue-green eyes and a serene countenance. We talked a little of his books and his trips to Brazil. He himself raised the subject of the peace process, which he supported. He outlined, objectively and unromantically, the elements of what he considered a possible peace deal. I said it seemed important for there to be interaction between the Israeli and Palestinian civil societies, including intellectuals. Oz underlined the contribution made by "educators," and said he would be willing to be participate in some kind of dialogue along those lines. Before we parted he said we should resume our conversation at some future point. His exact words were: "To be continued."

On the way back to Brazil, I stopped in Madrid. At the Torrejón air base I phoned the Syrian foreign minister, Al-Muallem, to tell him about Olmert's reaction to the message from Assad. During my trip I had met two kings (of Saudi Arabia and Jordan), two presidents (Syria and Israel), two prime ministers (Jordan and Israel), a vice president (Syria), as well as foreign ministers, deputy prime ministers, and negotiators. I had also met other figures who were known internationally, such as Amos Oz, or within their own countries, such as the Syrian minister for expatriates, Bouthaina Shaaban, who I would later discover was also a writer. Perhaps one of the most important impressions I had gained from this latest immersion in the Middle East was of the receptivity toward Brazil in all the countries I visited. This time, unlike during my tour in 2005, I had not been seeking positive responses to an invitation to participate in a Brazilian initiative. The fact that my objective was essentially political, part of the work of following up on the Annapolis process, lent greater significance to the good reception I had been given. Beyond the standard courtesies of protocol, I had perceived that my interlocutors were genuinely interested in hearing our positions and conveying their own analyses. All the dialogues had flowed quite naturally, without any expressions of surprise or discomfort, whether direct or indirect, at Brazil's involvement. My carrying of messages between the Syrian president and the Israeli prime minister on such a sensitive issue as the resumption of negotiations over the Golan Heights was a clear illustration of the degree of trust placed in Brazil. Whether due to the characteristics of our people, highlighted by Shimon Peres, or our political attitudes, appreciated by Arabs and (to a large extent) also Israelis, or our recognized influence in Latin America and the Caribbean, and indeed the developing world in general, I could see that Brazil was regarded as an important actor on the international stage, capable of exerting a positive influence in the search for peace in the Middle East. I returned to Brazil feeling keen to deepen our relations with the countries I had visited, and more broadly, to consolidate our position in the process initiated in Annapolis.

"Il n'y a qu'un brésilien qui puisse dire cela"

On February 20 and 21, less than a week after my return from the Middle East, Buenos Aires hosted a meeting of South American and Arab foreign ministers in preparation for the second ASPA summit, scheduled to take place in Doha, Qatar, in 2009.[102] Ever since 2005, Brazil had been working on the follow-up to the initial summit. As well as encouraging and promoting various sectoral initiatives, we appointed a special representative for ASPA affairs, Ambassador Arnaldo Carrilho, who visited fifteen Arab countries to convey messages about the importance of developing the relations between the two regions. Between February 17 and 19, before the meeting of foreign ministers in the Argentine capital, the Egyptian foreign minister, Aboul Gheit, made an official visit to Brasilia. The journey between South America (and, specifically, Brazil) and the Middle East was becoming part of the international diplomatic route network. During Aboul Gheit's visit, bilateral matters such as trade and technical cooperation were addressed. There was also an exchange of views on international and regional (i.e. South American and Middle Eastern) issues. Though initially Egypt had been somewhat reticent toward our initiatives, it was now beginning to advocate Brazil's greater involvement in its region, especially with regard to Palestine. My Egyptian counterpart had an audience with President Lula, who thereby reciprocated the treatment I had received in Cairo. There was talk, again, of a possible visit by Mubarak to Brazil, which for one reason or another was always being postponed. On the subject of the ASPA preparatory meeting, I made the following note: "The ministerial meeting [of South American countries] with the Arabs represented a positive development. An 'offspring' of Lula's foreign policy—one of those most criticized by the political right [in Brazil], but also one that has attracted the most attention internationally—is starting to have a life of its own. . . . At the press conference, alongside the foreign ministers of Argentina and Saudi Arabia, as well as the secretary-general of the Arab League and the deputy foreign minister of Bolivia (representing UNASUR!), [I said that] the new trade geography and international politics that Lula talks about are now taking shape." As usual, the meeting provided opportunities for numerous bilateral conversations. In my speech at the opening session of the ministerial meeting, I reiterated the well-known Brazilian positions, illustrating them with impressions gained from my recent Middle East trip. I gave special attention to the ASPA follow-up mechanism, mentioning the various ministerial meetings (economic, cultural and social fields) that had already taken place. I emphasized that it was important to see the ASPA not as a substitute for the United Nations General Assembly or a reproduction of it on a smaller scale, but as a forum for cooperation aimed at bringing together the countries of the two regions. I pointed to figures, both for trade and cultural initiatives, that gave encouragement to our efforts. I finished with a reference to the relationship between Brazil and our hosts. I think it was the first time I stated publicly that the relationship with Argentina was "the most strategic of our partnerships." It is worth noting the contrast between this assertion and my perception at the time of the first ASPA summit, to which I referred earlier. Despite the inevitable commercial disputes, the Brazil-Argentina relationship had been evolving in a very positive way during the previous few years, as reflected in our increasing cooperation on regional and global issues (UNSC reform continued to be the exception, but even in that context our differences were being expressed less stridently). The ASPA foreign ministers' meeting, chaired by my Argentine counterpart Jorge Taiana, was a good example of this convergence. And that, for me, was a source of genuine happiness.

There were important visits to Brazil during 2008, including those by King Abdullah II of Jordan—preceded by a preparatory visit from his foreign minister, Salah al-Bashir—and the foreign minister of the Palestinian Authority, Riyad al-Maliki.[103] In addition to the practical benefits for our bilateral relations, these visits were also useful in another way: they allowed President Lula, who always took a great interest in the Middle East, to hear for himself, directly from important interlocutors, realistic assessments of the situation and possible ways forward. Despite my admiration for Lula's political intuition, I did occasionally think that his belief in the ability of leaders to influence the course of events went slightly too far. That was my opinion, for example, about his repeated suggestion regarding a soccer match between Palestinians and Israelis, inspired by the successful example of the "peace game" between Brazil and Haiti in 2004, shortly after the arrival of our troops in that country as the largest contingent in the UN peacekeeping mission (MINUSTAH). I had nothing against the idea in itself, which was in line with our plans for greater contact between the two civil societies, but it seemed to me that such an event could only take place when the peace process was more advanced. My arguments were not always convincing. The sober thinking of leaders in the region would carry greater weight.

Between June 22 and 26, I visited Algeria, Morocco and Tunisia, continuing the high-level contact with those three countries that had been established over the previous years.[104] In those countries of the Maghreb, the predominant themes were those to do with bilateral cooperation. But of course international issues, especially those concerning the Middle East, also came up. Relations between Rabat and Algiers had been tense for a long time because of the issue of Western Sahara. It was a situation that required me and my aides to perform something of a diplomatic balancing act when it came to writing communiqués, especially since the Moroccan government gave clear signs of support for Brazil's bid for a permanent seat on the Security Council. Part of the reason for my visit to Algiers was to participate in the closing ceremony of the third meeting of the Brazil-Algeria Joint Commission (the second meeting had taken place in Brazil in April 2006). There were also many economic issues to discuss, including Embraer's interest in selling civil and military aircraft to Algeria, which was the context in which I met the minister with responsibility for defense-related issues, Abdelmalek Guenaïza. There was also a lot of interest in Algerian government projects on the part of Brazilian construction companies. Some of those subjects came up in the meeting I had with Prime Minister Abdelaziz Belkhadem, whom I had met on previous visits when he had been foreign minister. Again, my most interesting dialogue in Algeria was with President Bouteflika. The Algerian head of state had been kind enough to invite me to a lunch in honor of the French prime minister, François Fillon. Also at the banquet, which took place in the beautiful Ottoman-style hall where Bouteflika had received Lula two years before, were other French ministers including my "friend" (as I referred to her in my notebook at the time) Christine Lagarde, with whom I exchanged pleasantries and smiles. I sat between Prime Minister Belkhadem and the foreign minister, Mourad Medelci. We discussed bilateral relations, the Algerian economic situation, and—very discreetly—the presidential succession, which appeared to be in the offing at that time. On the latter two issues, which were obviously connected, the Brazilian ambassador, Sérgio Danese, had showed me some figures that pointed to growing popular dissatisfaction with the government and the resurgence of fundamentalism. His analysis was that the prosperity brought by oil was not reaching the majority of the population. Indeed, during both of my previous visits, in 2005, I had been struck by the large numbers of apparently unemployed men on the streets of Algiers. None of that, however, would prevent Bouteflika securing another term of office.[105]

Shortly after lunch, Bouteflika invited me for a private meeting in a small room decorated in a style similar to that of the hall where we had eaten. As I already knew from my previous visits, Bouteflika liked to discuss international issues. So, after some brief comments from me on the Brazilian economy, and some words of appreciation from him for President Lula, we embarked on global issues such as multipolarity and the international order. The president was quick to say he favored a reform of the Security Council that incorporated Brazil and India ("*Personne ne peut s'y opposer*") and also included a "solution for Africa." As he had done in previous meetings, he said he did not agree with the idea of permanent seats for Germany and Japan. I could see, in that respect, a certain irony in way the discussions on reform had evolved, given that they had been initiated in the 1990s by a desire on the part of the US to see those two developed countries—potential providers of financial assistance to operations such as the First Gulf War—enter the Security Council. Provocatively, I told my interlocutor that a loud and clear statement from a leader of his standing would certainly have an impact on the course of the discussions on the subject at the United Nations, but Bouteflika did not take the bait. The Algerian president spoke animatedly about various world leaders. He highlighted Lula's pragmatism—reflected in good relations with both Chávez and Bush; Thabo Mbeki's mixture of timidity and pride; and the charisma of former Nigerian president Olusegun Obasanjo. For my part, I suggested that the likely successor to Mbeki, Jacob Zuma, seemed "more authentically African," to which Bouteflika replied in an approving tone: "*Il n'y a qu'un brésilien qui puisse dire cela.*" As we parted, Bouteflika said goodbye to me with the four kisses customary "between brothers." Later I recorded in my notebook: "Fortunately the lips don't quite reach the face; the intention is enough."

My host in Rabat was the foreign minister, Taïeb Fassi Fihri. He had recently taken over from the veteran diplomat Mohammed Benaissa, with whom I had chaired the Marrakesh conference at which, in the run-up to the ASPA summit, the outlines of the Brasilia Declaration had been decided. Like his predecessor, Fassi Fihri proved to be a competent interlocutor. We had a good conversation about the Middle East and issues on the bilateral agenda. Regarding Western Sahara, he realized the embarrassment it would cause to Brazil if we produced a joint statement with language that directly went against the position of Algeria, but I was not sure how insistent the Moroccan negotiators would be. I recall that my preoccupation with this sensitive issue led me to send a message to my aides, who were negotiating over the text of the communiqué in another room, in an attempt to establish how far we could go. Regarding the Security Council, Fassi Fihri's position was very positive. The minutes of our meeting contain words that had actually already appeared in a letter from King Mohammed VI to President Lula, in which the monarch expressed "understanding of Brazil's legitimate aspiration." But later, in front of the media, Taïeb (he was quick to suggest we dispense with surnames) went further: he took the initiative of interpreting the phrase as being indicative of "strong support" for Brazil's bid. Taïeb made a point of demonstrating he was a modern man, unencumbered by the excessive concerns with protocol that characterize many other Arab ministers. He invited me to lunch at his private residence and drove me there himself, in a latest-model Mercedes-Benz belonging to the foreign ministry. The day before, I had met the prime minister, Abbas El Fassi (no relation to the foreign minister, apparently), who also addressed the issue of Western Sahara. Like the foreign minister, he had not pressured me to adopt a position against Algeria. We had also spoken about bilateral economic issues that would later feature in meetings with the mines and energy minister and the finance minister. Both seemed very keen on the possibilities for cooperation with Brazil: dams, water management, biofuels, investment, and trade. I was told there was already some cooperation between Petrobras and a Moroccan institute in the area of oil shale, and that the Brazilian subsidiary of the company Bunge was involved in phosphate mining in Morocco. We also spoke about the prospects for negotiating a preferential trade agreement between Mercosur and Morocco during Brazil's presidency of the bloc, which was about to commence.[106]

In the late afternoon, at the ambassador's residence, I received a visit from André Azulay, an advisor to King Mohammed VI who represented the Moroccan Jewish community, which had once been very numerous. I had met Azulay on the occasion of the king's visit to Brasilia, and our brief conversation that day had aroused my curiosity. This time, in Rabat, we delved into the issue of the Middle East. My interlocutor provided a detailed analysis of the situation, leaving me with a feeling I might summarize as: "Even without the Americans and without Annapolis, something can still be done." Azulay's comments led me to consider the possibility of reviving the idea of a visit by Lula to Israel and Palestine that same year. As it turned out, however, that visit would occur only in 2010, against a backdrop made even more complex by the attacks on Gaza and the paralysis of the negotiations. Listening to Azulay, I also became more convinced of the importance of organizing a meeting between intellectuals and/or educators, which I had discussed with Amos Oz during my visit to Israel in February.[107] In my notebook, my evaluation of the visits to Algeria and Morocco was as follows: "Our relationship with the Maghreb is putting down roots. For the first time I felt a real engagement, which might bear fruit in various fields [such as UNSC reform, and economic and cultural relations]. Even on the difficult issue of Western Sahara, the interest of both parties in having a deeper conversation with us—not just indulging in propaganda—reveals a positive perception of Brazil's role on the international stage." To those same notes, made in Tunis, I added: "Tunisia seems to be the weakest link [in our relationship with the Maghreb]."

The visit to Tunisia was not without interest, however. My host Abdelwahab Abdallah, the foreign minister, proved to be an affable man with a good sense of humor. We spoke at length about the Middle East, though I could tell he did not necessarily know more than I did about the most recent developments. When I touched on the issue of Western Sahara, Abdallah was direct: "Don't try to help." I replied: "I don't want to help, only to understand." We spoke about Annapolis, the attitudes of the Israelis and Hezbollah, and Iranian influence in the region. Abdallah made an assertion I would later hear again from other interlocutors, but which at the time left me not merely surprised but dumbfounded. He said Israel would bomb Iran during the period of the US elections, when Washington's capacity to act would be reduced. Fortunately this macabre prediction would prove incorrect, although it remained on the radar for a long time. Naturally we also spoke about the bilateral issues that were being dealt with by the Joint Committee,[108] which would also arise in my conversation with Prime Minister Mohammed Ghannouchi. One of the key points was the possibility of Brazilian investment in phosphate prospecting and processing. The subject would come up again during my visit to Tunis in 2009, but I do not know if there was any subsequent progress. An interesting meeting was the one I had with the defense minister, Kamel Morjane, who apparently had met me before in Geneva, where he had been permanent representative and UN assistant high commissioner for refugees, as well as a friend of my compatriot Sérgio Vieira de Mello. I must admit I remembered neither his name nor his face, but that did not stop me hugging him, diplomatically, as if we were old friends. I had the impression that our meeting might bear fruit in future. During my journey to the Maghreb I was pursued constantly by WTO-related issues. I spoke with Roberto Azevêdo, Clodoaldo Hugueney, and Pascal Lamy, learning that there was probably going to be a ministerial meeting on July 21. My premonitory entry in my notebook was: "It will be the last chance."

In November 2008 I returned to the Middle East to participate in a United Nations conference on financing for development. The event took place in Doha, under the auspices of the Emir of Qatar. It was very well attended, with various presidents and prime ministers present. Among the people I met there was President Mahmoud Abbas, though I do not remember if it was at my request or his. He looked haggard and downcast; I even thought he might be in poor health, although that was not in fact the case. What was decidedly sickly, however, was the peace process itself. It was suffering the ill effects of a lack of strong initiative from the United States or the other members of the Quartet, and the unending disputes between Palestinian factions. Political crises in Israel—with the weakening of the position of Prime Minister Ehud Olmert, who was embroiled in financial scandals—aggravated the situation.

Gaza

For me, the main event at the end of 2008 should have been the visit to Brazil by the French president, Nicolas Sarkozy, when the "strategic partnership" between the two countries was made concrete with the signing of several agreements. However, the short period of calm did not extend far beyond Christmas. From December 28, the Israeli bombing of the Gaza Strip began to demand my attention.[109] At first I did not think there was scope for us to do anything, apart from merely issue condemnatory statements.[110] Incidentally, I was not satisfied with the first of those communiqués, drawn up by aides when I was away in Rio de Janeiro: in trying to be "balanced" it had been too lenient toward Israel. Soon afterwards, as the attacks continued, we issued a stronger statement, referring to the disproportionate response by Tel Aviv. The president himself gave signs that he wanted something more vigorous from us. The Itamaraty secretary-general, Ambassador Samuel Pinheiro Guimarães, who was in Brasilia, conveyed to me a question from Lula about the chances of a "special meeting" in the context of the Annapolis process—a suggestion which, although well intentioned, would certainly have fallen on deaf ears. But I myself was already thinking that issuing statements was not enough. In the absence of a more concrete idea, I vaguely considered some kind of initiative with France, in the light of the good understanding generated by the strategic partnership. I traveled to Brasilia on December 30 and contacted the president, who was indignant about the passivity of the international community in the face of such "carnage." I told him I had returned to Brasilia precisely in order to have phone conversations with several key players, starting with French foreign minister Bernard Kouchner. That seemed to ease Lula's concerns somewhat.

Between December 30 and January 2, I talked to Kouchner, Egyptian foreign minister Aboul Gheit, Palestinian president Mahmoud Abbas, US secretary of state Condoleezza Rice, UN secretary-general Ban Ki-Moon, and the secretary-general of the Arab League, Amr Moussa. From those conversations I concluded that the focus at that moment was on obtaining a ceasefire. Realistically, I imagined that would not come about until Israel had completed what it understood as the "cleansing" of all the "terrorist elements," which would probably entail a land invasion and certainly many civilian casualties, including women and children. Through those conversations and also through contact with our mission to the United Nations, I knew that the Arab countries were trying to get a Security Council resolution so as to bring about the ceasefire. I also realized that our interest in the situation was being well received. But between this favorable attitude toward Brazil's involvement and the actual convening of a conference, there was obviously a big gap. As Lula was spending a few days with his family on an island resort off the northeast coast of Brazil, I decided to wait until he returned to Brasilia to discuss my impressions with him.

Before the outbreak of the Gaza crisis, I had arranged a trip to Portugal that was going to be a mixture of vacation and relatively light work commitments. The most important of the latter was a lecture to a gathering of Portuguese ambassadors. I would also be meeting President Cavaco Silva and Prime Minister José Sócrates, in addition, of course, to my counterpart Luís Amado. Between these bilateral conversations and some brief periods of relaxation, there were numerous phone calls and also interviews with the Brazilian media on the situation in Gaza. I spoke to, among others, the foreign ministers of Spain, Israel and Turkey: Miguel Ángel Moratinos, Tzipi Livni, and Ali Babacan. I also had another conversation with the US secretary of state. Tzipi Livni returned a call I had made to her in Brasilia: our conversation stayed within the bounds of politeness, but was very tough. Interestingly, with regard to our statements, she did not complain about our condemnation of the Israeli attacks, and said she "appreciated" our criticism of Hamas. She listened without any obvious emotion when I gave my opinion on the disastrous consequences the attacks were having for civilians. "We're doing everything possible not to hit the civilian population," was all she said. I got the impression, in fact, that she was repeating in automatic fashion a response she had already given to other interlocutors. Her phone call to me, in response to mine to her, was little more than a diplomatic courtesy. Livni told me that Israel continued to support Annapolis, which is to say the path of dialogue, but strangely she seemed not to see a connection between the actions that were being perpetrated and the peace process. I mentioned, *en passant*, President Lula's suggestion of a conference on the subject of Gaza, but my Israeli counterpart showed no openness toward that or any other, equivalent initiative.

Taking advantage of the good dialogue I had already established with Condoleezza Rice, I requested that she exert her influence to restrain the Israeli aggression. Through my Turkish counterpart and our ambassador to the UN, Maria Luiza Viotti, I was aware that the attempts by the Security Council to adopt a resolution or even a presidential statement had failed. In reaffirming to Condoleezza our willingness to help in the search for dialogue, I was quite forthright: "Israel might think it's destroying its arch-enemy, Hamas, but in fact it's destroying the political base of the interlocutor it claims to value, the Palestinian Authority." Unlike on previous occasions, she did not come up with counter-arguments. She said the United States also wanted a rapid cessation of hostilities. She did not even reject the oblique reference I made to the need to involve all the factions in order to achieve a ceasefire. On the contrary, she mentioned the role Brazil and other countries would have in the reconstruction of Gaza. The attitude of the secretary of state contrasted with that of Livni, who two days earlier had been peremptory: "It isn't possible to have a dialogue with Hamas."

My conversations with the Turkish foreign minister, Ali Babacan, gave me good insights into the mood in the region. For some months Ankara had been involved in the proximity talks between Israel and Syria, now interrupted by the Gaza attack. Turkey was also trying to play a facilitating role in the mediation efforts Egypt was conducting between Fatah and Hamas. Babacan insisted that if I were to embark on another journey to the Middle East, I should also visit Turkey.[111] Motivated in part by my Turkish counterpart's references to Syria, I decided to talk to the Syrian foreign minister, Walid Muallem, who had recently participated in meetings with Sarkozy and Kouchner in Damascus. When I spoke to Muallem, he was even more emphatic in suggesting I should visit the region: "It will be a way to demonstrate Brazil's solidarity with the Palestinian people." Having already been inclined to make the trip, I readily accepted the suggestion and asked my aides to make the necessary plans. However, deciding whether or not to go was not the only issue: I also needed to strike an appropriate balance between the capitals to be visited. Damascus was obviously an important destination, but there was the problem that the principal leader of Hamas, Khaled Meshaal, lived there. It seemed equally important to visit Israel, but to do so while the military assault was still going on would not be a trivial undertaking either. Between deciding to make the Middle East trip and leaving Lisbon, I had a brief excursion to the island of Madeira, the political base of my host Luís Amado and also, coincidentally, the birthplace of my maternal grandfather. My arrival at Funchal airport inevitably caught the attention of journalists, who were curious to know what my next destination would be. I told them innocently that I was going to visit some countries in the Middle East. The next morning, the island's main newspaper published a story—alongside a photo of me and other visitors, including my wife—with the headline "Madeira on the route to peace."

I have no wish to hide the fact that as I boarded the Legacy that would take me to Damascus, and from there to other Middle Eastern capitals, I was asking myself a question: Why was I getting so involved in this subject? Could Brazil contribute effectively to a peaceful solution to the conflicts that had plagued the Middle East for decades? Or, despite the tragic nature of the situation, might our efforts be no more than a brief "vacation," a short period before I was again enveloped by the issues of South America and the WTO? These were not easy questions to answer. In addition to my previous experience, such as with the Iraq panels, and the feeling that the pursuit of peace is an obligation of all countries, I was motivated by the positive response that Brazil's demonstrations of interest in the Middle East had elicited from the countries of the region and also from some of the major powers. Was it not the case that Tzipi Livni had originally sought me out to talk about the Israel-Palestine conflict, even before Annapolis, on the margins of the United Nations General Assembly? Was it not true that ever since my first visit to Ramallah, in 2005, Mahmoud Abbas had been emphasizing Brazil's potential role? The invitation to Annapolis had itself been a form of recognition of our capacity for dialogue, as subsequent conversations with the US secretary of state had confirmed. Those expectations about the positive role Brazil could play had been reiterated, explicitly or implicitly, in frank dialogues with Middle Eastern leaders on issues such as Palestine and Lebanon. Finally, how could Brazil, increasingly integrated into the global economy, ignore a crisis that sooner or later would have repercussions for the well-being of our own citizens? And so, albeit not without a few uncertainties, I understood—and in this I had the full support of President Lula—that we could not just stand aside from the collective effort aimed at restoring the peace process that was being so severely shaken by events in Gaza.

In principle, my itinerary was going to be similar to that of the trip I had undertaken about twelve months earlier: Damascus, Jerusalem, Ramallah, and Amman. But, during the course of the trip, I decided to extend it with a visit to Cairo as well. Coincidentally, my point of departure was again the Iberian Peninsula, where the Islamic, Christian and Jewish cultures had mixed with each other so deeply. But the situation in the Middle East had changed significantly. In 2008, despite the difficulties, the Annapolis process had still been arousing positive expectations, including on the part of those most directly involved. Now, however, my trip was taking place after two weeks of Israeli bombing in Gaza, predictably accompanied in recent days by a ground invasion. During the flight between Lisbon and Damascus, on January 10, I wrote as follows: "The day before yesterday (or yesterday in the very early morning) the Security Council adopted, with 14 votes in favor and one abstention (the US), Resolution 1860 (2009), which calls for an "immediate and durable ceasefire."[112] The second adjective would certainly have been demanded by Israel, via the United States, with the support of the UK and France. But [the addition] was not sufficient to allow Condoleezza Rice, whom I had spoken to again on the eve of the resolution, to vote in favor. In fact, there are contradictory aspects to the US abstention. On the one hand, not using their veto shows that [Washington] is beginning to acquire some sensitivity when faced with virtually unanimous repulsion at the barbarity of the Israeli attacks, which caused the deaths of more than two hundred children and women. On the other hand, it shows the inability [of the US] to give a clear signal to Israel, contrary to the expectations of those, such as our ambassador to the UN, who closely followed the long negotiations that resulted in the text of the resolution." On the basis of my conversations with Condoleezza, I myself had thought the US might support the resolution, which was certainly naive on my part. I asked myself whether the US abstention was a result of the strength of the Israeli lobby; a reflection of the obsession with terrorism (Hamas, in this case) on the part of the group around the Vice President Dick Cheney; or even—and this would be a very bad sign—an indication of the position of the next administration.[113] I was reminded, incidentally, of a conversation with Luís Amado during our trip to Madeira. My Portuguese counterpart, a good political analyst with broad view of international relations, had referred to certain episodes in the Europe-US relationship on the basis of which he was convinced that Condoleezza, with whom he had developed a friendly relationship, was impotent in the face of Cheney's radically conservative positions. Amado's comment suggested the second of my hypotheses might be correct. In fact, during my own conversations with the US secretary of state on the draft resolution, at no point had she tried to contradict my argument that the attacks on Gaza would have negative effects for Israel, or that the civilian deaths were debilitating for the Palestinian Authority ("an authority that runs the risk of not having any authority," in the words of President Lula during a phone conversation an hour before I left Lisbon).

That phone call to Lula was actually valuable as a blessing for the course of action I had decided to adopt. Although those actions were inspired to a large extent by the president's own indignation, clearly my choices as to whom to call and which cities to visit were entirely my own. It was important—partly because of certain voices inside the Planalto[114] that were more "understanding" toward Israel—for the president to have a clear understanding that Syria was a key player not only by virtue of its own weight but also because of the influence I perceived it could have over Hamas. On the other hand, certain other voices inside the Planalto were sometimes the source of scathing declarations about the "state terrorism" practiced by Israel. Such assertions were perhaps correct and fair, in themselves, but they did not help us in the task we had set ourselves of contributing to the resumption of dialogue. It was clear, however, that I also had to avoid falling into the trap of the pseudo-neutrality preached by those who, consciously or unconsciously, sympathized with the attitude of Tel Aviv or simply wanted to avoid displeasing Washington. These crisscrossing opinions—present in the Brazilian media, in Congress, and inside the government itself—obliged me to proceed carefully and caused me some moments of significant tension.

I left Lisbon on the afternoon of January 10 and arrived in Damascus just before midnight. It was not purely by chance that Syria was my first destination on this latest Middle East tour. In truth, when calling Muallem from Lisbon, I had been almost certain he would invite me to Damascus, and his invitation helped me make a difficult decision. My hesitation had stemmed from doubts about whether my visit would be positively received in a region in the midst of a conflict, and also from a certain reluctance to visit Israel—an inevitable stop on any tour of the region—while the killing of civilians in Gaza was still going on. Once I had decided to make the trip, the priority given to Syria derived partly from the its relationship with Hamas, which would have to be involved as an interlocutor, even if only indirectly, in any effort to return to the path of negotiations. This was true both in the long run, with regard to a lasting peace process, and in the short term, so as to make viable a ceasefire.

The morning after my arrival in Damascus, I met with President Bashar al-Assad. As before, he received me with great courtesy in his hilltop palace: an imposing and sumptuous residence with a blend of modern and neoclassical architectural styles, including an abundant use of marble—reminiscent, in fact, of presidential palaces in the former Eastern Europe. In rather didactic fashion, Assad described his vision of the situation resulting from the Israeli attacks in Gaza (especially the ground invasion). I will reproduce here some of his assertions, or at least how I remembered them three days later when writing my notes during the flight back to Brazil. He described the invasion of Gaza as a "huge setback," but did not think it was necessarily the case that "all is lost." He made a point of emphasizing the need to preserve the advances that had been achieved—although I confess that, being familiar with the Syrian criticisms of the Annapolis process, I did not really know what advances he meant. Certainly there were parallel conversations going on through other interlocutors (including the proximity talks mediated by Ankara), and they would have been affected by the negative atmosphere in the wake of the Gaza attacks. As for the prospect of a ceasefire, Assad argued that it should be "short" and quickly followed by negotiations on the withdrawal of Israeli troops and the opening of the access routes to Gaza. I interpreted his conception of a brief ceasefire as less than wholly innocent, as at the end of that brief period Hamas would presumably be free again to pursue its war of liberation—unless, of course, the movement was called to the negotiating table and became directly involved in the political process.

The president told me Mahmoud Abbas had been to Damascus three times since the beginning of the crisis—a fact he deemed to be significant, given the difficult relationship with Fatah. Abbas, however, never wanted to meet Khaled Meshaal, which Assad said was "regrettable." A possible explanation was that a meeting between the PNA president and the Hamas leader could only ever take place in the latter's hiding place in Damascus—because, in the words of foreign minister Muallem in the conversation we would have later, "if Meshaal goes to the West Bank, he'll certainly be killed by the Israelis." On the other hand, Abbas probably thought that to go to Meshaal's hiding place would somehow imply recognition of the latter's leadership. Assad reiterated his interest in continuing the talks with Israel concerning the Golan Heights, but added that he could not do so while the bombing of Hamas (or Gaza) was going on or—in reference to the forthcoming elections in Israel—"while we don't have a genuine interlocutor in Jerusalem."

As I started this latest Middle East tour, there was a dispute going on between the Palestinian factions about the duration of Mahmoud Abbas's term of office as PNA president. In that regard, Assad was keen to stress that Syria was exerting a "moderating influence" on Hamas. Some Hamas leaders were arguing that due to certain legal technicalities Abbas's mandate had already expired and that therefore his position was no longer legitimate.[115] I myself had heard that one of the most important figures in Hamas, resident in Lebanon, had made a strongly worded statement to that effect. According to Assad and Muallem, the message from Damascus to Hamas was that "this is a time for unity." Although the Syrian government acted on the basis of self-interest rather than any natural instinct for moderation, this was nevertheless an important development, and one I did not fail to mention to other interlocutors in the region. According to President Mubarak, perhaps the most strident critic of Damascus among all those interlocutors, there was also another reason for Syria's "moderation": "It's because if Hamas or Hezbollah attacks Israel, Jerusalem will retaliate directly against Syria." That reasoning would also explain Hezbollah's unwillingness to claim responsibility for the few attacks against Israel that came from southern Lebanon during the assault on Gaza.

It was clear to me that Syria wanted to put an end to the political and economic isolation it had endured for many years, and from which it was beginning to emerge. President Assad told me that before our meeting he had received a visit from a group representing a US think tank, the International Peace Institute, linked to former president Jimmy Carter. Assad had high hopes for the Obama administration—hopes seen as illusory almost everywhere else I visited in the Middle East. The desire for a new relationship with the West led the Syrian rulers, especially the president, to take a pragmatic approach, with potentially positive consequences. Among my interlocutors, Moratinos and Babacan agreed that Syria's engagement was essential in order to achieve peace in the region, but like me, they saw that there were limiting factors. Despite the setback suffered by the "hard-liners" on the Lebanon issue, Assad was still constrained by the Syrian security apparatus. Another factor was Syria's military and economic dependence on Iran, a country that was being shunned by western leaders (it had not participated in the Annapolis Conference, for example). Tehran's strategy toward the region did not seem to consider any accommodation with Israel. Finally, even if the Syrian government wanted to adopt a pragmatic attitude toward Tel Aviv, it was careful to avoid any impression of "selling out" Hamas. As Muallem put it, in a confessional tone tinged with irony: "After all, we too have public opinion to think about."

From Syria, I headed to Israel. The aerial route the FAB intended to take struck me as bold, to say the least. A direct flight between the capitals of two countries technically at war made little sense to me, but I finally accepted the flight plan on the basis that the Israeli authorities had supposedly given their consent. Later I found out that an executive jet carrying former British prime minister and Quartet representative Tony Blair had been intercepted by Israeli aircraft on a similar route. In the airspace above this region of "a lot of history and not much geography," I soon became aware that our Legacy was not taking the direct route that had earlier been chosen, but instead was in Jordanian airspace and flying around in circles. After some prodding on my part, the pilot, who was visibly stressed, admitted he was not being given authorization to land at Ben Gurion airport in Tel Aviv. And our prior permission to make a landing in Amman applied to the following day. Obviously my thoughts turned rather quickly to how much fuel we had on board. Trying to calm my nerves, the pilot said: "We could always head back to Damascus." After at least half an hour of tension, communication between the cockpit and our embassy in Jordan (through what medium, I do not know) secured permission for an unscheduled stop in Amman. Waiting for news from Israel, I did not even get off the plane. And the tension was not only due to flight-safety issues: there was also a political dimension. I had a meeting scheduled with the Israeli foreign minister, the only government official I was due to meet, and it looked like I was going to miss it. It was not difficult to imagine how the Brazilian media would seize upon the cancellation of a meeting with my Israeli counterpart. Finally, after half an hour on the ground in Amman, we got the green light from Tel Aviv. But I was only able to relax when I heard that Tzipi Livni herself was also running late because of a session in parliament (or perhaps a meeting of the governing council); Israel, after all, was a country at war.

Waiting for me at the airport in Tel Aviv were our ambassador, Pedro Mota Pinto Coelho, and our representative in Ramallah, Ligia Scherer, who updated me on developments in their respective countries. They were accompanied by a senior official from the Israeli foreign ministry. The welcome extended to me by the Israeli authorities was especially courteous; indeed it surpassed the standard requirements of protocol. As I descended the steps from the aircraft I was greeted by an array of Brazilian flags; I was taken to West Jerusalem in an armor-plated vehicle with a small motorcade; and I was given the presidential suite in the famous King David Hotel. It all served to ease any concerns about the earlier imbroglio concerning the authorization to land at Ben Gurion, which I began to assume must have been caused simply by some confusion (possibly linguistic) on the part of the pilots.

My conversation with Tzipi Livni was respectful, but marked by glaring differences of opinion. Responsibility for the Gaza conflict, she said, lay entirely with Hamas, which had not stopped launching rockets at Israeli territory, and with countries such as Syria and Iran that provided Hamas with support. As in our earlier phone conversation, she avoided accepting responsibility—indisputable in the eyes of the whole world—for the civilian casualties in Gaza. She did, however, regret the "loss of life," which was "politically damaging" for Israel. By that time the number of victims was in the hundreds; about half of them, according to reliable reports, were women and children. Livni no doubt understood that the mere abstention by the United States during the recent vote on the Security Council resolution, though deplored by those who expected a firmer stance, was nevertheless an unusual indication of Washington's discomfort in the face of the public reaction to the massacre (both at home and, above all, abroad). On that point Livni made a comment that surprised me, as it corresponded with something I myself often said to Israeli interlocutors who displayed some degree of sensitivity: "I know Israel needs to help those friends who want to help us." She was implicitly including Brazil among those "friends" of Israel. Nevertheless, she insisted on the need to destroy the military capability of Hamas—a view she said was shared, albeit not openly, by the "moderate Arab countries" (whatever she meant by that) and the Palestinian Authority. Despite this attempt to totally obliterate the weapons of Hamas, Livni feared Syrian and Iranian rockets were continuing to arrive in Gaza via the Rafah Crossing, and even asked for Brazil's assistance in that regard. She also expressed appreciation for our ideas and offers of assistance, including that of facilitating the dialogue with Syria, which could be a moderating influence with regard to Hamas. Rather surprisingly, given Israel's evident discomfort regarding our contacts with Iran,[116] Livni suggested—whether ironically or otherwise, I do not know—that Brazil could contribute to a lasting ceasefire by asking Tehran to "stop sending rockets to Hamas." The attention she devoted to me, in the midst of a conflict, was in part recognition of Brazil's weight and influence, as recently demonstrated by our support for the convening of a special session of the Human Rights Council (which certainly had some influence on the position of other countries) and the subsequent vote condemning Israel's military actions. I think she was also aware of our fluid relations with Tel

Aviv in the economic, cultural and technological fields. Indeed, when I mentioned that the attacks on Gaza might create difficulties in implementing the trade agreement between Mercosur and Israel, her response was emphatic but also friendly: "You don't need to tell me that!" The dialogue with the Israeli foreign minister was valuable, first and foremost, for having shown that Brazil was willing to talk, without discrimination, with all sides involved in the conflict. Our ambassador, for his part, said he thought the conversation was "more engaged" than the one he had witnessed a year before. But perhaps he just wanted to please me.

The next morning, through the broad window of my room in the King David, I watched the sun rise from behind the historic walls of Jerusalem. But as if to cut short any historical reverie and bring me back sharply to the troubled context of the present day, my breakfast was served by a young man in military fatigues and then consumed in the presence of a bodyguard provided by the Israeli government to "protect" me. That morning, I took advantage of my brief stay in Israel to phone German foreign minister Frank-Walter Steinmeier, who had made an official visit to Brazil in 2006 and with whom I had had frequent contact in the context of the expanded G8 and the discussions on the reform of the UNSC. Steinmeier himself had just been in the Middle East. It was clear to me that despite Germany's understandable inhibition when it comes to criticizing Israel, our analyses of the situation were convergent. There was an urgent need to achieve a ceasefire. I had similar conversations with Moratinos and Babacan. And from my comfortable suite in the hotel—once the target of an Irgun bombing in which Tzipi Livni's father participated—I also called my Egyptian counterpart, Ahmed Aboul Gheit. If I wanted to get a balanced overview of the different standpoints in the conflict and see all the most influential actors, to omit Cairo from my itinerary would be inexcusable. Aboul Gheit responded positively to my intention to visit Egypt, saying not only that he would me more than willing to receive me but also that he would make every effort to arrange a meeting for me with President Hosni Mubarak.

That same morning I left for Palestine, where I would be spending only a few hours because I needed to be in Jordan the next day to attend a ceremony for a Brazilian humanitarian donation to the suffering population of Gaza via the Jordan Hashemite Charity Organization, which as its name indicates, is linked to the Jordanian royal family. Curiously, I found the administrative capital of the West Bank looking more prosperous than on previous visits. This would have been due to the continuing arrival of donations, and possibly also to a more lenient attitude—if one can call it that—on the part of the Israelis toward the transfer of tax revenues to the Palestinian authorities. But I found myself wondering if the relative prosperity might be limited to a certain section of the Palestinian population (principally government employees and those members of the middle class who were involved in commercial activities), thereby further sharpening the contrast with conditions in Gaza. The gap between the two communities was getting wider, hindering the dialogue between the Palestinian factions. Perhaps that was the true objective of Israel and, who knows, some Arab governments too.

In Ramallah I met the prime minister, Salam Fayyad, and the foreign minister, Riyad al-Maliki. Contrary to Tzipi Livni's prediction, both were very critical of Israel's actions, although neither seemed inclined toward a frank dialogue with Hamas, which in the words of one of my interlocutors was an "arm of the Muslim Brotherhood, embedded in Palestine." Al-Maliki also seemed skeptical about any involvement on the part of Turkey, "an ally of the Brotherhood," in the mediation efforts being undertaken by Egypt. However, he did not seem averse to Syrian involvement in the "management" of the ceasefire. From Jerusalem I called Mahmoud Abbas, who apologized for not being in Palestine at the time. I told him about my conversations in Damascus, with emphasis on Syria's "moderating influence" over Hamas. While making clear the central importance of Egyptian mediation, the Palestinian leader seemed to recognize the importance of dialogue with Bashar al-Assad; he pointed out that he had visited Syria three times but "wasn't able to" meet with Khaled Meshaal. I told Abbas that President Lula was following developments in Gaza closely and "with indignation." I recalled that Abbas himself had suggested holding a conference, possibly in Paris, to discuss the Palestinian issue, an idea in line with Lula's own thoughts on the subject. The Palestinian leader had spoken to me about the idea when we met on the margins of a UN conference in Doha, before the attacks on Gaza began. In the present circumstances, obviously, the need for such a conference was greater still. Abbas said he was "still thinking about it."

Originally, the main reason for my visit to Jordan had been the Brazilian humanitarian donation to the population of Gaza. As there was no way to send our donations directly to the territory controlled by Hamas, I had decided that I should instead make use of the Jordan Hashemite Charity Organization. The delivery ceremony took place in a large warehouse belonging to the organization, in the midst of lots of large crates, at around noon on January 13, just before I left for Cairo. I remember we were driven to the warehouse in a minibus bearing the Brazilian flag, and that many people in the street, including children and teenagers, waved happily when they saw our national symbol. I took it as a further testament to the positive image of Brazil among the peoples of the Middle East—due in no small part to soccer, I should point out. I made the formal delivery to the secretary-general of the organization, a young and friendly member of the Jordanian royal family (and son of "ex-crown prince" Hassan bin Talal) who had been in Brazil not long before, accompanying King Abdullah II. A Palestinian minister responsible for social issues had come specially to attend the ceremony. The symbolic handover of the donations was duly filmed and the images sent back to Brazil, but it is very likely they were only shown on the government's own TV channels.

My first political meeting in Jordan had taken place the evening before. Having been informed of my rather restrictive dietary requirements, which prevented me from accepting the invitation to dinner, the friendly and jovial foreign minister, Salah al-Bashir—whom I had met for the first time a year before, and again during the UN General Assembly—insisted on visiting me at my hotel. Al-Bashir was keen to hear my impressions of what I had seen and heard during my trip, so I told him in as much detail as possible about my visits to Damascus, Tel Aviv/Jerusalem, and Ramallah. He took such an interest in the attitude of the Syrian government that the next day, during my meeting with the king, he "reminded" me of what I had told him about the "moderating influence" Damascus was seeking to exert over Hamas in relation to the issue of Mahmoud Abbas's term of office.

As I mentioned in the context of my visit in 2008, most of the population of Jordan is of Palestinian origin. It was in Jordan that the great uprisings of the early 1970s took place, forcing Arafat to leave the country. Demonstrations by the Muslim Brotherhood and other popular organizations had been taking place since the start of the Israeli attacks on Gaza. Amman, which has had diplomatic relations with Israel since 1994 (I was present at the signing of the peace agreement between the two countries), naturally had a great interest in a quick solution to the Gaza situation, quite apart from the humanitarian dimension. In addition to commenting on what I had heard in the three capitals I had visited so far, I also said that on the basis of those conversations it was important for there to be a strong movement in favor of the prompt adoption of Security Council Resolution 1860 (2009). I also mentioned President Lula's suggestion of a conference (maybe even a summit) in order to give greater momentum to the efforts toward peace. Abdullah II made observations that were in line with my comments, and did not rule out the idea of a summit. In fact he was more incisive than that: referring directly to what I had said, the king expressed the opinion that there should be no more talk of a "peace process," with inevitable connotations of delay and procrastination, but instead "peace negotiations," which would be more likely to produce quick results. He did not explain how that might come about, but implicit in his reasoning was the concern that if no agreement were reached within a short period of time, further crises would be inevitable, and even those points already agreed following the Annapolis Conference might become unviable (in accordance with the general rule that "nothing is agreed until everything is agreed"). The Jordanian monarch also addressed bilateral issues, some of which had been discussed during his visit to Brazil the previous October, such as the construction of public housing and cooperation in security and defense. This was the fourth or fifth trip I had made to Jordan during the Lula government, so I was one of His Majesty's more frequent interlocutors. This contributed to the conversation flowing easily in a relaxed and unhurried atmosphere; indeed, when the official in charge of protocol appeared in the room to indicate that my time was running out, he had to stand waiting by the door for a good ten minutes. Similarly unusual was the king's gesture in accompanying me to the door of the palace as I was leaving. Our ambassador later assured me that, according to a Jordanian foreign ministry official he had spoken to, such a gesture on the part of the monarch was "totally uncommon." Well, I thought, ambassadors always say such things.

On the morning of January 14, in Cairo, I had an audience with President Hosni Mubarak. My first meeting in the Egyptian capital had been with the Arab League secretary-general, Amr Moussa, at about 7:30 p.m. the previous day. It was my fourth visit to the organization's headquarters. Despite the fatigue following my long day in Jordan, I was able to convey some of the details of my dialogues in the other capitals. Perhaps the most important aspect of the conversation was an observation by Moussa that coincided, in essence, with what I had heard from the King of Jordan, which was that the basic elements of the "final settlement"[117] between Israel and Palestine had already been discussed. There was no reason, therefore, to prolong the "peace process." Moussa and I agreed on the urgent need for a ceasefire, the fundamental importance of dialogue between the Palestinian factions, and the need to involve all actors who could exert influence over the situation. Despite his Egyptian nationality, Moussa conveyed an impression of impartiality toward the arch-rivals Cairo and Damascus. Soon afterwards I returned to a hotel near the airport to meet with the foreign minister, Ahmed Aboul Gheit. My very first meeting with Aboul Gheit, a career diplomat and former ambassador to the UN, had been during my second period in Geneva as representative at the Conference on Disarmament, when Brazil and Egypt were both involved in the "New Agenda Coalition." Later I had met him again on various occasions, including at ASPA meetings and when he visited Brazil in early 2008. This was our first encounter in Cairo, however. Incidentally, one those previous meetings, at his request, had been on the margins of a UN General Assembly, and it was not the fondest of memories. On that particular occasion he had a string of complaints about the IBSA and the G4, groups from which he alleged that Egypt had been "deliberately excluded," and said he could not understand how countries such as Brazil and India could disregard "a nation with five thousand years of history, and a capital that is a beacon in the Middle East." In subsequent meetings he clearly made efforts to remove that rather unfavorable impression. Once, after elections had taken place in Egypt, he made a point of coming to talk to me in my suite at the Waldorf Astoria, as an alternative to the popular but small and uncomfortable "booths" in the corridors of the UN. In the fast-paced environment of UN General Assemblies, that was a sign of special consideration on his part.

So too, in fact, was the content of our latest conversation, in which he brought me up to date on the political process in his country, seeking to demonstrate that there were developments in a more democratic direction. In our conversation in Cairo on January 13, which took place shortly before he boarded a flight, I did most of the talking, but Aboul Gheit nevertheless condemned Israel, expressed concerns about Hamas, and was distinctly negative about Syria—as President Hosni Mubarak would also be when I met him the next morning.

As I mentioned earlier, Mubarak at that time was not yet treated in the West as a dictator, as he would be when the Arab Spring erupted. From the waiting room I could see the flurry of activity among his aides as they prepared for the visits that would follow mine. As I arrived I met my Spanish counterpart, Miguel Ángel Moratinos, with whom I was only able to exchange a few words before I was whisked off to the presidential office. And upon leaving I bumped into the UN secretary-general, Ban Ki-moon, who had only just arrived in the region (the rather late timing of his visit was difficult to explain, given the seriousness of the crisis). Unlike on previous occasions, including his brief meeting with Lula in 2003, President Mubarak's demeanor was far from imperial (or should I say pharaonic?). He was keen to know what conclusions I had come to on the basis of the time spent in the other capitals, and was particularly inquisitive about Damascus. I briefly described my various impressions, pausing to emphasize Syria's attitude toward Hamas, which I thought might actually have the effect of encouraging the latter toward dialogue with Fatah. I was careful, however, not to convey too positive an evaluation—not only because I did not want to appear naive in relation to what I had been told in Damascus, but also because I did not want to give President Mubarak the impression I had any pro-Syria leanings. Such an impression, even if accidental, would have been very unhelpful in relation to the resumption of dialogue between Cairo and Damascus. I recalled that Bashar al-Assad had been cautious in his evaluation of the situation created by the Israeli attacks Gaza, avoiding any apocalyptic conclusions. In short, I emphasized Assad's perception that it was an enormous setback but also that there was no reason to assume that what had already been gained would now necessarily be lost. Unlike the Palestinians, the King of Jordan, and even to some extent Tzipi Livni, Mubarak questioned both the meaning of Assad's comment and Syria's underlying intentions. Even before I could give my own interpretation, the Egyptian president launched into a tirade of criticism of Damascus in which he returned to certain issues of the past. He mentioned the hostility of Hafez Assad, Bashar's father, toward the negotiations between the PLO and Israel at the time of the Oslo agreements. Hafez had been upset about not being consulted in advance regarding the content of the negotiations—whereas Mubarak, who also had not been informed in advance, had accepted the understandings between Arafat and Rabin without complaint. That particular episode reflected a tendency on the part of Syria to put its own interests (probably regarding the Golan Heights) before the goal of peace between Palestinians and Israelis. Mubarak seemed not to acknowledge the real influence Damascus had over Hamas, and therefore attached little value to the "moderation" I had alluded to. He did reveal some admiration for Hafez's political acumen—mainly, I think, so as to depict Bashar as "inexperienced" in comparison. "During the time of Hafez," he said, "Syria used to manipulate Iran. Now it's the other way round." Yet again in a conversation with an Arab leader, I was hearing concerns about Iran. Mubarak referred to the need for an immediate end to the bloody assault on Gaza. The solution, he said, would have to combine a ceasefire, the withdrawal of Israeli troops, and the lifting of the blockade. On those points there was no significant difference between his view and what I had heard in Damascus and Amman. As for the Rafah Crossing, with regard to which I had heard comments from Syrian officials indicative of an intention to increase the participation of Hamas, Mubarak was forthright: "Rafah is Egypt's concern. A proposal coming from Syria, however good it might be, will never be accepted!" Those might not have been his exact words, but it was the crux of his message. There could have been no clearer illustration of the rivalry between the two great capitals of what was once the United Arab Republic.

The Rafah Crossing seemed to be one of the issues at the heart of the dispute between the two Palestinian factions. Even if the issue could be dealt with through cooperation between Egypt and Israel—which was not going to be easy, given Tzipi Livni's fears about the route being used to smuggle Iranian weapons—there was still the problem of who would control the crossing *on the Gaza side*. The suggestion from Damascus was that Hamas should be involved. I had heard a similar view from Moratinos, who would certainly have been reproducing something Muallem had said to him. But both the PNA and Cairo were firmly against the idea, which would in practice result in some degree of international recognition of Hamas. Looked at from that angle, the question of who would be present at the border took on great importance. Aboul Gheit had told me: "It hardly matters if the Palestinian Authority controls the border, because it's Hamas that controls all the rest of Gaza." However, the issue impinged directly on the chances of obtaining a ceasefire, which in my view (and that of many of my interlocutors) would be impossible without the consent of Hamas. Mubarak also made an ironic comment about the role of Turkey, which he referred to as the "little friend" of Hamas: "If the Turks start meddling, they'll soon be quarreling with the other factions." Mubarak was well aware of how important it was for the Palestinian factions to reach an understanding, but he believed that could only come about through a long-term dialogue. The question of a ceasefire, meanwhile, was universally recognized to be of the utmost urgency. There was therefore a basic contradiction at the root of the situation. And with those disputes still unresolved, the killing went on.

The conversation with the Egyptian president was sufficiently relaxed to allow me to clear up a doubt in my mind about the position of Qatar. The emirate, diminutive in territory but rich in petrodollars, behaved in way that was contradictory or at least inconstant on the international plane. On the one hand, it hosted US military bases. On the other, its television station, Al-Jazeera, was one of the few media organizations to have covered the Iraq War in an objective way. Qatar was known to have close relations with Hamas, and yet that did not stop it being one of the few Arab countries to have a trade office in Israel (the other two were Jordan and Egypt, which maintained diplomatic relations with Tel Aviv). This office only closed when the Israeli attacks on Gaza took place. In my own analysis, no doubt rather superficial, I attributed those contradictions to the two Qatari figures with whom I had had the most contact: the emir himself, Sheikh Hamad bin Khalifa, who conveyed an impression of relative impartiality in relation to the positions of different countries in the region, for example by maintaining a dialogue with Damascus and Tehran; and my old acquaintance Hamad bin Jassim, in the dual role of prime minister and foreign minister, who was more focused on economic and trade issues, seemed to have a closer relationship with the US, and was also extremely critical of Syria and Iran. So I asked Mubarak: "Who's basically in charge in Qatar?" He replied without hesitation: "Sheikha Mozah," referring to the second of the emir's three wives. With that quip he neatly sidestepped my question. And yet in fact, within the next couple of years, I would see for myself the very real influence of the sheikha, witnessing her role in international forums such as the Alliance of Civilizations in Istanbul and Rio de Janeiro.

On the way back to Brazil, my trusty Legacy made a stop-over in Algiers. I had considered staying overnight in the Algerian capital, not so much for convenience reasons as for the opportunity to meet briefly with members of the government. But I decided it would be too complicated to change my existing plans, which centered on meeting between President Lula and President Evo Morales on the Brazil-Bolivia border—so I thought I would just make a phone call to the foreign minister, Mourad Medelci, from the air base. That was not necessary, however: my Algerian counterpart was already there waiting for me, keen to hear my latest news. His interest was sharpened by the meetings of Arab countries that were about to take place in Kuwait and Qatar (the first meeting was due to focus primarily on economic issues, but attention would inevitably turn to Gaza). I spoke to Medelci about what I saw as the need for international mobilization in order to obtain a ceasefire and to end the blockade on Gaza (including by opening the crossings on the border with Israel), and the complexities around the issue of the Rafah Crossing, with its implications for intra-Palestinian dialogue. Medelci, who seemed less well informed than I was, wondered if it might be possible for the Palestinian Authority and Hamas to exercise joint control over the Rafah Crossing. I told him it was easier to imagine a form of administration for the crossing in which neither faction was directly represented. That might be obtained, I said, by some sort of joint control by the European Union and Turkey. In short, there were two ideas aimed at ensuring some degree of neutrality: "*l'un et l'autre*," and "*ni l'un ni l'autre*." The latter seemed more feasible to me. Again it was clear that Brazil had become a valuable interlocutor for a member of the Arab League, not only because of our potential contribution as a mediator but also—extraordinarily, I thought—as a source of information. Indeed, I believe, although I have no way of proving it, that alongside just a few other European or North American foreign ministers, I had attained a degree of access to the most important figures in the region (kings, presidents and prime ministers) that was not offered to the representatives of the Arab countries not directly involved in the conflict. There was the obvious advantage that we were able to speak to all sides. In fact, during the tour I had just undertaken, Israel was the only country in which the most senior person I met was the foreign minister. And that had been quite deliberate on my part, not only because of the unstable situation in which the Israeli government found itself (it was effectively without a prime minister) but also because of the attacks on Gaza, which made formal meetings at the highest level less desirable.

I should include one final observation on the humanitarian situation, the severity of which was even greater than I had imagined. Both the secretary-general of the Jordan Hashemite Charity Organization and the Arab League diplomats who were present at my meeting with Amr Moussa provided details that made up an extremely alarming picture. Certain factors were reducing the effectiveness of the day-to-day efforts to assist the population, from issues concerning the way food and clothing was being distributed to problems when it came to preparing the food itself. I heard that even the doctors sent to Gaza by the Red Crescent (or the Red Cross) had nothing to eat. With these images passing through my mind, I set off back to Brazil.

The Middle East issue would continue to figure prominently in conversations with government representatives who visited Brazil, such as Chinese foreign minister Yang Jiechi, and meetings in Davos, for example with Kofi Annan, the former UN secretary-general. Annan agreed with me on the need to involve Hamas if there was to be any chance of achieving a lasting solution, and mentioned that he had been in contact with the organization while at the helm of the UN, which I had been unaware of. The subject also took up part of my first phone conversation with the new US secretary of state, Hillary Clinton, who made a courtesy call to me shortly after taking up her post. During that conversation I praised the appointment as special envoy to the Middle East of George Mitchell, who had already been a very effective mediator on the Northern Ireland issue. The secretary of state was aware of my recent tour and expressed appreciation for the role Brazil might play. A solution to the Gaza crisis, however, would remain elusive.

I will mention an episode that illustrates the passions aroused by the conflicts of the Middle East—feelings certainly not limited to the Israel-Palestine conflict but also aroused by political and personal rivalries, as well as tensions between different religious or ethnic communities. In late January I was in Davos for the World Economic Forum, having been invited to participate in a working lunch at which the theme for discussion was "Brazil, The New Power Broker." The focus of the meeting was mainly on economic issues, particularly the Doha Round, which by then had slipped into a state of profound lethargy. While waiting to enter a press conference in the main building, I saw Raghida Dergham, an experienced journalist working for a major Arab newspaper published in Lebanon, whom I knew from my time in New York. We had got on well together in those days, particularly in the period of the Iraq panels. She had always taken a positive view of the positions adopted by Brazil, including with regard to some very controversial issues. I told her briefly about my recent Middle East trip, and expressed the opinion—as I did to all my interlocutors at the time—that "all the important actors" should be involved in the negotiations. That did not go down very well, however. The journalist launched into a furious tirade against Hamas and Syria: "You [I think she was referring to me and Moratinos, among others] are totally wrong! What you have to do is demand that Syria stop interfering in the affairs of Palestine." The cascade of criticism would have continued had I not mentioned an urgent commitment and made my escape. But the passion and virulence of what I heard, from a person who had always struck me as very open and well disposed toward our approach, left a lasting impression. The incident underlined the message that when it comes to the Middle East, one needs to walk carefully: it is a minefield in more than one sense.

In early March I went back to Cairo to participate in the ASPA ministerial meeting, the preparatory event for the ASPA summit due to take place at the end of the month in Qatar. On the eve of the meeting I attended a cultural event in celebration of an initiative that was being launched jointly by the EU and Arab countries, four years on from our first ASPA summit. In my short speech at the meeting, I could not resist a reference to our pioneering role: Brazil (and South America) had joined with the Arab world to launch the "alliance of civilizations" *avant la lettre*. The preparations for the second ASPA summit were not the only reason for my trip to Egypt. On March 2, in Sharm el-Sheikh, I took part in the Gaza Donors' Conference and announced that Brazil would be giving $10 million USD to the reconstruction effort—before leaving Brasilia I had confirmed with President Lula that a bill to that effect would be signed into law. The conference, apart from raising funds, also provided a stage for declarations of support for the Palestinian Authority. These statements served as a message to Tel Aviv as the new Israeli government was taking shape. But it was also clear that the majority of speakers wanted to express criticism of Hamas. I spoke shortly after the representative of the Quartet, Tony Blair, who emphasized the need to strengthen the PNA politically. Speaking without notes, I said that the prospects for bolstering the PNA depended above all on the situation on the ground, by which I meant the improvement of the living conditions for the Palestinians in the West Bank. I stressed the importance of alleviating the suffering and disruption endured on a daily basis by ordinary citizens in Palestine, and said that "dignity is just as important as material welfare." I argued that it was important to ensure the full implementation of Resolution 1860, adding that "humanitarian aid and legitimate trade [goods and services] should be able to move freely in Gaza." Alluding to statements from the Israeli government, I said that "setting preconditions for the fulfillment of a Security Council resolution is not acceptable." I lamented the way new obstacles were continually being placed in the path of the peace negotiations, referring specifically to Israel's expansion of the settlements. With a choice of words I hoped would be simultaneously subtle and clear, I referred to the need to involve the various different forces in the political process. I said "all relevant actors in the region who are prepared to act constructively" should be called to the negotiating table. That way, no one would be excluded *a priori*. But it should be made clear to all participants that their conduct needed to be compatible with the two-state solution, which Brazil supported. In the same vein, I conveyed the Brazilian government's satisfaction with the willingness (albeit more theoretical than practical, at that time) of the Palestinian political forces to pursue a path that might lead to a government of reconciliation, and I praised the role of Egypt in that process. Finally, I reminded the audience that developing countries outside the region could usefully be incorporated into the discussion, and said that Brazil hoped to see a conference convened as a follow-up to Annapolis. As I stated Brazil's financial contribution, I also mentioned that my Indian counterpart would be announcing a donation from IBSA. It was a way of showing that the solidarity between developing countries was more than merely rhetorical.

The Sharm el-Sheik conference also provided opportunities for bilateral meetings. In one of them, with President Mubarak, I reiterated Lula's invitation for him to visit Brazil. The Egyptian foreign minister, the official host of the event, was overflowing with courtesy. He came to find me during lunch and took me to what was effectively the "top table," after the presidents had left their seats. Still seated there were the UN secretary-general, Ban Ki-moon; Secretary of State Hillary Clinton, not long in her new job; and also the representative of the Quartet, Tony Blair. Pronouncing "Celso" in a somewhat amusingly British way, Blair joked that I should come and solve the Middle East problem—"but only after solving the Doha Round." The former British prime minister was so effusive that I could hardly pay any attention to the head of the UN. In one of the corridors I bumped into the British foreign secretary, David Miliband, who took the opportunity to invite me to a dinner with "half a dozen" other foreign ministers during the G20 summit, scheduled for April 2. To increase the appeal, Miliband mentioned that Hillary Clinton would be among the other guests. I learned that my Russian counterpart, Sergey Lavrov, had been looking for me in the area where the Brazilian delegation had been seated during the conference. I later wrote in my notebook: "Maybe now's the time to visit Moscow again?"

A good visual metaphor

On March 31, the second Summit of South American-Arab Countries (ASPA) took place in Doha, Qatar. One noteworthy aspect of the event was the good level of attendance on the part of South America's representatives, who had needed not only to travel a huge distance but also to overcome the habitual inertia. The presidents Cristina Kirchner, Michelle Bachelet Fernando Lugo, Evo Morales, Hugo Chávez, and Ronald Venetiaan[118] were all there. So too were the vice presidents of Uruguay, Peru and Colombia. Guyana and Ecuador were represented by their foreign ministers. Attendance on the Arab side was also good, helped by the fact that the summit of the Arab League had taken place just the day before. There was also a business seminar with a healthy number of businesspeople from both sides. All in all, the ASPA initiative that we had put so much effort into was being consolidated at a critical time, in the midst of the financial crisis triggered by the bankruptcy of Lehman Brothers. President Lula, in his speech, did not fail to point out the impressive extent of South-South cooperation and its growing importance in the current global economic context.

The most significant moment in the event was the opening, which took place in a large hall decorated with a mass of arabesques that just about stayed within the boundaries of good taste. Displayed on a huge screen was the image President Michelle Bachelet, a prominent female leader in our region, speaking on behalf of UNASUR to a group of South American presidents and a number of monarchs, presidents and other leaders from the Arab world: it was a good visual metaphor for the value South America attached to gender equality, which of course was still a sensitive issue for many of the countries present. Peru offered to host the next ASPA summit.[119] Whatever the future developments, our boldness in convening an unprecedented summit had already been rewarded. Besides the increased trade and the technical and cultural cooperation projects, the ASPA initiative had led to closer and more active ties between our continent and the Arab countries. It had also contributed to the dramatic raising of Brazil's profile in a geographically distant region—a degree of change that had been unimaginable just a few years before.

The relationship with the Arab countries did of course have certain complications, arising only partly from the Israel-Palestine conflict and the ongoing instability in Lebanon. There was also the constant "policing" carried out by the Brazilian media with regard to our supposed tolerance toward regimes that failed to respect human rights. This vigilance, needless to say, was far from consistent or impartial. Regimes relatively close to the West (to Washington, more specifically), such as some of the Gulf monarchies, were regarded more leniently; the media referred only rarely to their repression of opponents, affinities with fundamentalist movements, or treatment of women. Immediately before the second ASPA summit, one of the problems we had to deal with was our participation in the event alongside Sudan, after the International Criminal Court[120] had issued an arrest warrant for the country's president, Omar al-Bashir. Brazil was well aware of the serious problems surrounding Sudan in that respect. We knew about the violence committed in Darfur, while also noting the less-than-constructive maneuvers by some of the exiled opposition leaders. One year earlier, skeptical about the effectiveness of a merely condemnatory stance, we had contributed to the UN Human Rights Council adopting by consensus a resolution calling on the government in Khartoum to cooperate with the Council's mechanisms, which was a more discreet (and probably more effective) way of expressing our concern over the issue. But that was not enough to pacify certain sections of the media. The indictment of the Sudanese president by the ICC, in early 2009, was perceived by the African countries, and even more so by the Arab world, as further evidence of discriminatory treatment. After all, where were the indictments in response to Guantanamo, or the criticism of Israeli attacks on civilians in Gaza? In the latter case the ICC did not hear the accusations, based on the fact that Palestine was not a state and Israel was not a member of the institution. Irrespective of the validity of such technical arguments, the decisions taken by the ICC were perceived by African and Arab countries as proof of the court's bias against poor and underdeveloped nations. The Arab League certainly was not going to accept Bashir's indictment. And regardless of the merits of the arguments for and against him, his presence at the ASPA summit presented us with a practical problem.[121] I went so far as to call Amr Moussa to see if I could get him to exert some moderating influence over Bashir, who had decided to "retaliate" against the ICC by expelling NGOs working in Darfur. I also tried, through our ambassador to the United Nations, to encourage some kind of measure on the part of the Security Council that would allow the issue to be dealt with in a non-confrontational way—a kind of *sursis* that would maintain the pressure on the Sudanese president while also giving the African Union time to act. After all, those most affected by the human rights violations were members of non-Arab African tribes in Sudan.

At the ASPA summit, my main fear was that Lula would be placed right next to the Sudanese president (either by chance or otherwise) when the official photograph came to be taken. Obviously that would have been a gift to the opponents of the ASPA initiative in Brazil. As it turned out, Lula did indeed find himself sitting next to Bashir at the lunch for the heads of state, despite my earlier warnings to the member of our party who was responsible for protocol. I do not remember exactly what triggered Lula's decision not to stay for the meal. Whether he sensed the risk or was just impatient to eat something elsewhere (the banquet took a long time to be served), the fact is that he made his excuses and left the room. No inconvenient photographs were taken.

The human rights issue was not the only one to provoke noisy criticism of our relations with the Arab countries. Sometimes there was also "friendly fire" coming from members of Congress who usually supported our foreign policy, or from other parts of the government that had specific interests with regard to certain issues. I see from my notes that one such situation was on my mind when flying to Riyadh as part of the entourage accompanying Lula on the state visit to Saudi Arabia. Because they are of interest in a political sense, I will transcribe a few sections: "May 15, 2009: nothing significant in the last few days with regard to foreign policy, apart from the raised voices around the candidatures for [the position of director-general of] UNESCO.[122] The story is more or less as follows: almost a year ago, Egypt declared the candidature of its culture minister, Farouk Hosni. . . . Around the same time, I was approached by Senator Cristovam Buarque, with whom I've had a good relationship ever since he was dean of Brasilia University, [governor of Brasilia], and more recently, education minister. Cristovam expressed an interest in applying for the position himself. [As well as his undeniable credentials] he would have support from various quarters. . . . I told him that . . . the government's decision would have to be guided by *raison d'État*, and therefore . . . that we would have to give consideration to a candidature backed by the Arab countries, given our policy of pursuing closer ties with the region." Cristovam made clear that he would understand if Brazil did ultimately go along with the Arab consensus candidate, but he also speculated that the Arab countries might become "split on the issue."

Meanwhile, another Brazilian candidate emerged: Márcio Barbosa, who in fact already occupied the position of UNESCO deputy director-general, and with whom I also had a friendly relationship. He said he had the support of several delegations, which was probably true, given that he was competent and above all very skillful politically. He was also said to be the candidate favored by the outgoing director-general. And various governments, especially western ones, might well have preferred a Latin American technocrat to an Egyptian minister who had in the past made clumsy statements about Israel. Unlike Buarque, Barbosa seemed unhappy with my argument about the political need for Brazil to support the potential consensus candidate from the Arab world. The creative imagination of the Brazilian media, possibly stimulated by one of the candidates (I will never know, and do not really care), established a supposed link between our support for Farouk Hosni and the soon-to-be-vacant directorship of another UN agency, the IAEA, in relation to which there had been rumors—totally without my knowledge, much less my consent—that my name might be put forward. Given my extensive experience in international organizations—including in the areas of trade, disarmament, labor issues, and health—it was far from unprecedented for such rumors to arise. I had become used to dismissing them as quickly as possible. Senators of various political stripes, including some from parties allied with the government, bombarded me with questions about the candidatures for the UNESCO job. I took the opportunity to state categorically that I was not a candidate for any position in any international organization (I happened to think that being the foreign minister of Brazil was far more important and interesting), and that our decision about the UNESCO situation (I say "our" because I had been careful to discuss the matter with President Lula) was based solely on the wider interests of Brazilian foreign policy.[123]

This digression was justified, I think, for one good reason: it shows how in diplomacy the "macro" and "micro" often become mixed up, causing perceptions and analyses to become confused.

"We must fear the man who does not fear God"

On May 16 and 17, President Lula was in Saudi Arabia as part of a tour that also included China and Turkey. It could be considered part of an effort to "consolidate partnerships" with developing countries that were members of the G20, the grouping that emerged in the wake of the Lehman Brothers crisis. In Riyadh, after a brief visit to the headquarters of the Gulf Cooperation Council, the president attended a banquet hosted by King Abdullah "in his private quarters" (as one of the monarch's aides was keen to point out). In fact it was a large hall, in the middle of which was a kind of pool or artificial lake, filled to the brim with water. I imagined the unusual decorative feature might be intended to symbolize the opulence of the ruler of a country in which water is the scarcest resource. Thankfully no member of the Brazilian delegation either took a dip or fell in by accident. This was my third visit to Saudi Arabia, and each time I had been received in a different location: the palace where most business was done (the equivalent of a president's office); the king's tent in the desert; and now, in the company of Lula, the royal residence. There is not space here to describe the banquet in detail, but I must mention that in one particular aspect the scene was reminiscent of a James Bond movie. Behind the main table, instead of a wall, there was a gigantic aquarium. It contained various species of fish from the Gulf (Persian or Arabian, depending on the point of view), including some sharks that I guessed were "adolescents" on the basis of their being about one meter in length. Although I was seated immediately to the left of the king, I deliberately did not participate in his conversation with President Lula, which covered topics such as energy, the chemical industry, agriculture, and education. In accordance with royal protocol the person to my left was a senior member of the Saudi nobility, but I have no recollection of his name or face. In fact I was surprised not to have been seated next to the Saudi foreign minister, Prince Saud bin Faisal, whom I had been looking forward to speaking to. After dinner we went into the king's private office (a further example of distinguished treatment, according to another of his courtiers), where my attention was particularly caught by the images of two mosques (Mecca and Medina, presumably) carved in wood—what Italians call *intarsia*. Lula and Abdullah sat in two huge armchairs, some distance apart from everyone else. Their conversation was mediated by translation between Arabic and Portuguese via English. I strained to hear what they were talking about. It seemed they were again discussing economic issues. Thinking it was important that they should get on to politics at some point, I wrote a note for Lula on a small piece of paper and passed it to him as discreetly as I could. It was a suggestion that he praise the famous (and by that stage somewhat worn-out) "Arab Peace Initiative." The king was visibly pleased with Lula's remark. With a rare gleam in his eyes he started talking animatedly about the state of affairs in the Middle East. He was critical of Israel, saying that by not allowing the peace process to advance it was debilitating the leadership of Mahmoud Abbas and the Palestinian Authority. The consequence—a worrying one, from the perspective of Riyadh—was the strengthening of Hamas. In the Middle East's complex patchwork of political and religious factions, Saudi Arabia is itself home to movements that could be described as fundamentalist at least in religious terms, foremost among which is Wahhabism. At the same time, the Saudi monarchy is horrified by groups that could be described as representing populist Islamism, such as the Muslim Brotherhood or Hamas.[124] In Riyadh, a comparable degree of antipathy is reserved only for Iran, and the Shias in general. Abdullah said the breaking of the Mecca Agreement[125] had been a "great disappointment," the earlier efforts to conclude the accord having caused the foreign minister, Prince Faisal, to go "three nights without sleep." Abdullah had no hesitation in blaming Hamas, which he (if his interpreter conveyed his words correctly) accused of simply having lied. Brimming with apparently sincere indignation, the king asked: "How is it possible to break an agreement equivalent to an oath, sworn upon the sacred ground of the Prophet?" To that, he added an Arab proverb: "We must fear the man who does not fear God." On a more worldly note, we completed the visit with various agreements—which I signed with my Saudi counterpart, the sleepless Prince Faisal (who incidentally had represented his country four years earlier at the first ASPA summit)—and meetings with businessmen. My only memory of those meetings is a member of the Saudi government describing plans to build fifteen—yes, fifteen—new cities in the desert.

In the first half of 2009, after Lula's visit to Riyadh, there were no further noteworthy events related to the Arab world. In July, Egyptian foreign minister Ahmed Aboul Gheit again visited Brazil. In his press conference he was keen to highlight Brazil's role, saying that two of my trips to the Middle East had taken place at "critical" moments (the end of the war in Lebanon, and during the Israeli attacks on Gaza). As for the intra-Palestinian dialogue, my Egyptian counterpart implied that it was inconclusive but that tempers were subsiding to some extent, particularly on the part of Hamas. I noticed Aboul Gheit was adopting a less rigid position than during my last visit to Cairo. He revealed a certain degree of hope with regard to the mediation efforts by the US envoy, George Mitchell. He wondered if President Obama might make a concrete proposal, containing new elements, at the UN General Assembly in September, and did not discount the possibility that such a proposal might include a summit. He said if that were the case, he "would expect Brazil to be invited." The visit by the Egyptian foreign minister—the second in about eighteen months, and this time only to Brazil—was a clear signal from Cairo of its desire for closer relations with Brasilia. The minister brought with him a letter from President Mubarak in which he reiterated his wish to visit us in the near future. In his letter Mubarak also requested Brazil's support for greater participation by Egypt in global forums such as the G20, and thanked us for the endorsement, in L'Aquila, of Egypt's inclusion in the dialogue mechanism of the expanded G8. Mubarak also reiterated Cairo's intention to obtain some form of association with IBSA and the BRICs.

Aboul Gheit's visit to Brasilia (during which, besides the talks with me, he was also received by President Lula) came a week after a visit by Avigdor Lieberman, the first by an Israeli foreign minister since 1987. I remember little of my conversation with Lieberman, a politician of rough manners and extremely conservative views who had no empathy whatsoever for the Palestinian people, not even their more moderate representatives. At one point he seemed to be implying that he would like there to be no Palestinians whatsoever in the West Bank. It was clear to me from the very start that useful dialogue was impossible with such a man. And yet the fact that even an unrepentant hard-liner like him considered it necessary to initiate a conversation with Brazil was significant in itself. The issues of the Middle East continued to come up in my meetings with other foreign ministers and government officials—for example with Moratinos in July and with General

Jim Jones in August. They were also present in my discussions with my Moroccan and Tunisian counterparts in their respective capitals during visits or stop-overs in September. In October, in Stockholm, on the margins of the Brazil-European Union Summit, I had an interesting conversation on the Israeli-Palestine issue with Carl Bildt, the foreign minister (and former prime minister) of Sweden. Although Bildt was a member of a center-right coalition, when it came to international affairs we had convergent views on a number of issues. A year later Bildt would be one of the few European foreign ministers to show a keen interest in the Tehran Declaration. Toward the end of 2009, issues closer to home, which I could never ignore, would once again take up much of my time. I was very involved in the preparations for the second summit of the Community of Caribbean and Latin American States, which required me to attend a ministerial meeting in Jamaica. Also, the "Zelaya saga" was still dragging on and required frequent conversations, including with the US secretary of state and the former Chilean president, Ricardo Lagos, who had been appointed by the OAS as mediator for the Honduran crisis.[126] On November 4, nevertheless, I wrote: "This will be the month of the Middle East."

The "Road Map" now seemed to include a stop in Brasilia

On November 11, President Shimon Peres came to Brasilia. It was the first visit to Brazil by an Israeli president since 1966, therefore generating significant interest in the media. And it attracted even more attention by taking place in the same month as visits by the presidents of the Palestinian Authority and Iran. The convergence of the three visits was depicted in the international media as a "dispute" between conflicting forces that were all seeking Brazil's support. Even if only figuratively, the "Road Map" now seemed to include a stop in Brasilia. Peres gave a speech to Congress and had a joint press conference with President Lula. At one point he called on Lula, "who created the 'Light for All' program,"[127] to take the same "light" to the Middle East. It was not actually the best moment for metaphors involving electricity, as there had recently been a power outage or "blackout" across much of Brazil. Still, his words were warmly applauded. President Peres requested that I pay him a visit at his hotel on the morning he arrived, so that we could have a less formal conversation. He expressed concern about the fate of Mahmoud Abbas, who seemed increasingly debilitated politically. The Israeli president said he "valued" the role of Brazil and, when I deliberately led the conversation in that direction, that he did not necessarily reject direct dialogue with Syria. Nor was he opposed to "friendly countries" having contact with Hamas, as long as it was to encourage them to take the "peaceful path." He mentioned the work of the Socialist International in encouraging Anwar Sadat during the Camp David agreements, and more recently, in the

1990s, its similar role with Yasser Arafat during the Oslo process. Peres seemed to be implying that something similar might be achievable with Hamas. He was, however, very critical of President Ahmadinejad, and skeptical about the chances of reaching any kind of understanding with Iran. In his conversation with President Lula, the need to reinforce the leadership of the Palestinian Authority was again discussed. I touched on the issue of the Jewish settlements in the West Bank (and the housing projects in East Jerusalem), which in my view were one of the two factors (alongside the Gaza situation) responsible for the ebbing away of President Mahmoud Abbas's political authority, which Peres himself so lamented. The Israeli president responded by taking the conversation in a slightly different direction. Requesting that what he was about to say be kept secret, he suggested that instead of "leveling down" (a ban on the expansion of Israeli/Jewish settlements), there should instead be a "positive compromise" that would allow the Arabs in East Jerusalem to build more homes (while, presumably, the Israeli settlers did the same). Neither Lula nor I commented on the idea. In fact, I did not quite understand why it should be treated so confidentially. As far as I could see, such a gesture would be unlikely to have a significant positive impact on the negotiations. It certainly was not something Mahmoud Abbas could present to the Palestinians of the West Bank,[128] never mind those in Gaza, as a "concession" on the part of Israel. With his usual frankness, President Lula argued that "all the political forces" (including Hamas, therefore) should participate in the negotiations. He criticized the fact that the peace process was restricted to just a few players, and suggested that new interlocutors—including Brazil, obviously—should take part. Exuding confidence in the power of "political will" and intrinsic human goodwill—which has always been one of his most striking characteristics—Lula said: "Let's put the world's five best foreign ministers in a room and get them to come up with a plan that both sides can accept."

On November 19 and 20, Lula met with Mahmoud Abbas. During his visit to Brazil the president of the Palestinian Authority also met the Arab communities in Salvador[129] and Porto Alegre. Our choice of Salvador as the venue for the meetings with Abbas had to do with the fact that Lula was in Bahia state for the Black Consciousness Day celebrations, which the Palestinian leader also attended. In his conversations with Abbas, Lula received an update of the situation on Palestine and did not fail to mention the Brazilian donations to the population of the West Bank and the IBSA-funded project for the construction of a sports center in Ramallah. During dinner at the residence of Bahia state governor Jacques Wagner—a *carioca*[130] Jew with a progressive outlook—and the work session the next day, Abbas referred to the difficulties he was facing. He mentioned the US hesitation in dealing with Tel Aviv, and the discord inside the Israeli government. With surprising candor for a political leader, he admitted he was "tired" and said he would not run again in the next elections if he had nothing to show for his efforts by then. When Lula asked him if his decision was "strategic" or "tactical," Abbas replied that it was "firm." But in somewhat contradictory fashion, or so it seemed to me, the Palestinian president also said he was hopeful that elections might take place in June 2010. This appeared to presume there would be some positive outcome from the talks with Hamas sponsored by Egypt, which I doubted. When he spoke to the media, Abbas said he was keen for Brazil to be actively involved in the dialogue on the Middle East.

It was obvious that Abbas's purpose during this visit was to obtain support from Brazil and also from groups we were part of—particularly IBSA, which was mentioned several times during the meetings in relation to possible concrete steps toward self-determination for the Palestinians. However, as to how to achieve that goal, Abbas—who was accompanied by his affable foreign minister, Riyad al-Maliki, and severe negotiator, Saeb Erekat—was not specific. Earlier on, there had been some speculation about a possible unilateral declaration of the creation of a Palestinian state, but neither the president nor any other member of his party made any explicit reference to that. Abbas merely alluded to a possible proposal from the Arab League to the UNSC, reaffirming certain elements (already present in previous resolutions—regarding borders, Jerusalem, etc.) that would constitute the basis for a Palestinian state. In the context of this "gradualist" approach, Al-Maliki requested that the status of the Palestinian mission in Brasilia be formally raised to that of a fully fledged embassy (which in practical terms it already was). Lula was very receptive to the request, gesturing in my direction and assuring Abbas that I would be able to address the issue before the presidential visit to Israel and the West Bank, scheduled for March. In his statement to the media, Lula reaffirmed Brazil's support for a Palestinian state. He also took the opportunity to criticize the expansion of the Israeli settlements.[131]

The official part of the Palestinian president's visit came to an end on a Friday. The following Monday, President Ahmadinejad arrived, thereby introducing a new dynamic into our treatment of questions related to the Middle East. Until then, we had focused principally on issues such as Palestine and Lebanon, but now they would have to cede some space (and time) to the Iranian issue. On November 26, responding to a letter from President Obama dated November 22, President Lula referred both to the Israel-Palestine situation and to Iran. He mentioned the recent visits by the by Israeli and Palestinian presidents, and the fact that we had made clear to both of them our willingness to help overcome the paralysis of the negotiations. Lula reiterated that the peace process needed "fresh air" in the form of new participants, highlighting the importance of finding interlocutors capable of talking frankly with all the political forces in the region. He mentioned the discouraged demeanor of President Abbas, and added that only concrete concessions from Israel could restore some faith in the peace process. In that context, Lula stressed that a freeze on new settlements would be especially important.

On the same day as his letter was dispatched to Obama, Lula made similar arguments in a bilateral meeting with the French president, Nicolas Sarkozy, in the northern Brazilian city of Manaus, on the margins of a meeting of "Amazonian" countries on the issue of climate change. Sarkozy was present as a special guest because the French overseas territory of Guiana was among the participants.[132] Lula said he hoped Sarkozy would confirm the high-level meeting on the Middle East in Paris, as previously suggested by the French president. Such an initiative, he said, "could give new life to Abbas." Sarkozy reiterated his intention to convene the meeting but said he still needed to "convince" Obama. "If the meeting does happen, we would like Brazil to participate," he added. Seeming to read Lula's thoughts, the French president also said it would be important to include the Syrians in the negotiations, given their influence over Hamas. "After all," he said, "the person in charge of Hamas is Khaled Meshaal, who's living in Damascus under Syrian government protection."

I think I should say a little about the conviction with which Lula embraced the idea that "all the forces," including Hamas and Syria, should participate in the negotiations aimed at a peaceful solution to the Israel-Palestine conflict. It is more than likely that I myself expressed that opinion during conversations with Lula in preparation for meetings and phone calls. However, despite the trust Lula placed in me, any influence on my part is not sufficient to explain his assurance in making that case. And on that particular issue (unlike on others, such as those concerning Latin America), nor do I think it was the case that he regularly sought the opinion of other advisors. During the presidential tour of the Middle East five or six years before, the issue of who should or should not participate in the talks was hardly mentioned. I believe that, given his evident interest in everything to do with international politics, Lula would have closely followed the election in Palestine and the ensuing problems that culminated in the Israeli attacks on Gaza. I certainly mentioned my most recent Middle East trip and my conclusion—shared, for example, by the Spanish foreign minister—that there would be no solution to the problems of Palestine without the participation of Hamas. Whether or not that view contributed to shaping the president's own thoughts, it is certainly the case that Lula, based on his political experience and indeed his own life story, always believed that inclusive and wide-ranging dialogues were the best way to tackle the thorniest issues.

A villain in a spy movie

I began the year of 2010 on a ship cruising down the Nile, accompanied by my wife Ana and daughter Anita. At 7:30 a.m. on New Year's Day, neither the crew nor any of the other passengers had roused themselves following the celebrations of the night before. From the deck of the *Radamis II* I could see the city of Aswan, the end point of our calm and smooth journey. Elsewhere on the river, *feluccas*, small boats with triangular sails, skirted the various islands, the largest of which was the site of the ancient city of Elephantine. I was in Egypt at the invitation of the government. It was a gesture intended by my counterpart Ahmed Aboul Gheit to mark the forging of closer relations with Brazil. The visit had begun with a good day's work in Cairo on December 27. I had a bilateral with Aboul Gheit in which we signed an agreement on a strategic dialogue that would entail annual meetings of foreign ministers or their deputies. For Egypt this was part of a "diplomatic offensive" aimed at making up for lost time in its relationship with the largest country in Latin America, whose influence on the international stage, including with regard to the Middle East, was increasingly visible and indeed welcomed. Aboul Gheit offered me lunch in one of the lounges inside the foreign ministry building beside the Nile. We were joined by three other members of the cabinet: the ministers for foreign trade and international cooperation, both of whom I had met before, and the minister for agriculture. The trade minister, Rachid Mohamed Rachid, had been my partner in the G20 group of developing nations in the context of the WTO negotiations (as indeed had been the case with his predecessor, Youssef Boutros-Ghali), playing a constructive role by making pragmatic suggestions and generally showing good sense. A successful businessman—who, like so many others, would face problems after the fall of Mubarak—he was also Brazil's honorary consul in Alexandria. As a minister he had visited Brazil more than once, and made a significant contribution to advancing our bilateral relations. Unlike so many other trade ministers, obsessed with balancing exports and imports in any bilateral commercial relationship, Rachid took the view that Egypt's trade deficit with Brazil was not a problem "provided that it's accompanied by investments." The international cooperation minister, Fayza Abul-Naga, who had been the Egyptian permanent representative in Geneva during my time there, was interested in involving Brazil in exploring forms of trilateral cooperation for the benefit of African countries.

As usual in Cairo, I devoted some of my visit to speaking to the press, this time in the cozy little library in the residence of the Brazilian ambassador, Cesário Melantonio.[133] In a conversation with journalist Randa Achmawi from the *Al-Ahram* newspaper, who ever since my first visits had been following the evolution of our relations with the Arab countries and Egypt in particular, I emphasized Brazil's commitment to making a positive contribution to the peace process by actively participating in the possible conference in Paris, frequently alluded to by President Sarkozy, and in our role as a non-permanent member of the Security Council for the two-year period of 2010–11. Speaking to *Folha de São Paulo* correspondent Marcelo Ninio, who had traveled from Jerusalem to interview me, I made clear that I did not think Brazil had any "magic formula" to unblock the existing impasses, but stressed that we and other developing countries could help in the search for solutions to specific problems by adopting a fresh approach, unencumbered by specific interests of our own or past baggage. When the *Folha* correspondent asked me how our greater involvement had been received in the region, I illustrated the positive reaction by referring to a suggestion made by President Mubarak—which still needed to be studied—that Brazil should participate in the multinational force monitoring the Egypt-Israel border.

I ended the day with an interesting meeting, almost an hour long, with Egypt's intelligence minister, General Omar Suleiman, the person directly responsible for conducting the intra-Palestinian dialogue. I think the idea that I should meet him had come from Aboul Gheit. A military man with a hard stare who conveyed little empathy, Suleiman said he remained optimistic about the talks between Fatah and Hamas, under Egyptian auspices, though he did not give any reasons to justify that feeling. I say the conversation was "interesting" mainly because of his surprisingly frank assertion about the high chances of a US military attack on Iran's nuclear facilities. "It will happen around October, when it has become obvious the sanctions are having no impact," was more or less what he said. With a nervous smile beneath his thin mustache, which made him look like a villain in a spy movie, he said a "surgical strike" would enjoy international support. Later in the conversation, after I had said something about the likely reaction of the populations of the Islamic countries to such an attack, he retreated slightly from that bellicose opinion and recognized that it would be necessary to take into account the feelings on the "Arab street" (the expression often used to denote public opinion in the region, often far removed from the positions taken by the Arab governments).

Earlier that day, in the morning, I had met once again with President Hosni Mubarak. Though more cautious than his intelligence minister, Mubarak also referred to a foreseeable attack on Iran. But he thought it was more likely to come from Israel than the US. He said, for example, that the significance of Israeli prime minister Benjamin Netanyahu inviting Tzipi Livni to rejoin the cabinet (she did not accept, at that point in time) was that it was part of an attempt to form a "government of national unity," which would be more able to face up to criticism in the wake of an attack on Iran. In fact, as I gathered from subsequent conversations, Netanyahu's invitation to the former foreign minister might also have been linked to a possible resumption of negotiations with Palestine, and to the risk that his far-right allies, such as Avigdor Lieberman, might abandon the government. What the Israeli right particularly feared was that the conversations with the Palestinians might include the status of Jerusalem. Incidentally, the two explanations for the attempt to lure Livni were not mutually exclusive.

Mubarak backed up his view about the likelihood of an attack on Iran with references to information he had received from Russian intelligence, including through former prime minister Yevgeny Primakov. Mubarak had apparently been told that Washington was exerting great pressure on Moscow to cancel, or at least delay, the delivery of any military equipment to Tehran. Mubarak referred to the issue in some detail, suggesting that Israel would seek to use Azerbaijani airspace for its possible attack—a somewhat far-fetched scenario and yet not one that could be dismissed out of hand. Doing so would allow Israel to carry out the strike without the permission of the United States, avoiding the need for its planes to overfly Iraq. My meetings with President Mubarak and General Suleiman made clear that political thinking in Cairo at that time was dominated by the possibility of a military attack on Iran. Well aware of the profound rivalry between several Arab countries (including Egypt) and the regime of the ayatollahs, I found myself wondering whether the frequent predictions of an Israeli or US military attack against Iran—which would be catastrophic, in my opinion—might not be in fact a form of wishful thinking.

On the last evening I spent in Cairo, my Egyptian counterpart Ahmed Aboul Gheit visited me at my hotel—the same one, next to the airport, where we had met the year before. The conversation was brief, as he did not really have anything new to tell me, but it was curious nonetheless. He was keen to hear my impressions from my journey along the Nile, not so much from an archaeological but from a socio-political perspective. Before I could tell him, however, he gave me the benefit of his own views, which in fact were not dissimilar to some of what I was going to say. He referred to the striking contrast between the chaotic dynamism of Cairo and the languid backwardness of rural Egypt, which is to say the narrow strip alongside the Nile. He also alluded to the huge social disparities and widespread poverty. He depicted those contrasts, possibly unconducive to national unity, as an explanation for the "centralized rule" (I do not think he used the word "authoritarian") that has been a feature of Egypt's various political systems ever since the time of the pharaohs—passing through the Mamluk dynasties, British colonial rule, and Nasserism. In short, Aboul Gheit's short excursion to my hotel had a didactic element: to demonstrate that for Egypt, democracy as understood by the West—and, more importantly, adopted as a "model" by the IBSA countries—was something of a problematic proposal. Over the following days I would maintain phone contact with my Egyptian colleague, principally with regard to the evolution of the intra-Palestinian dialogue.

From Egypt I flew to Turkey, where my conversations with President Abdullah Gül and his foreign minister focused mainly on issues related to Iran. But the president also made an observation about Hamas. He mentioned that he had spoken Hamas leader Ismail Haniyeh immediately after the movement's election victory in 2006, suggesting to him that he should follow a moderate path. At first, Gül said, Haniyeh had made conciliatory statements, but they were never translated into concrete acts. Although we were not able to discuss the issue in depth, I did notice that there was some convergence between the Turkish approach and our own. Over time I came to appreciate that Turkey's inclination toward Hamas did not derive only from a pluralistic vision: it was also connected with the fact that the ruling AKP party, of moderate Islamic bent, had some affinity with the Muslim Brotherhood.

From Ankara I traveled to Geneva, and then to Paris for a seminar opened by President Sarkozy and Prime Minister José Sócrates of Portugal, interestingly but perhaps misleadingly entitled "New World, New Capitalism." The political conversations in Paris once again centered on the Iranian issue. In Geneva I met again with the Palestinian foreign minister, Riyad al-Maliki, to continue the dialogue initiated in Brazil by Lula and Abbas. I had sensed in my phone conversations—not only with Aboul Gheit but also with the newly appointed foreign minister in Jordan, Nasser Judeh—that things might actually be moving with regard to the Middle East. Both Aboul Gheit and Judeh had recently been to Washington for meetings. Al-Maliki, for his part, was mildly optimistic because of what he perceived as a change of attitude on the part of Netanyahu, albeit one that "still needs to be proven in practice." The Israeli prime minister had been in Cairo shortly after my visit there. There was a feeling in the air that the US was exerting significant pressure on Israel to make some kind of concession to the Palestinians. Based on my various conversations, however, I understood that Washington's motivation was not entirely pacific. If there were progress on the Israel-Palestine question, the US would have greater freedom to act against Iran, whether in the form of new sanctions or by carrying out a military attack (or allowing Israel to do so). Al-Maliki again expressed a strong desire to see Brazil take a more active role in the Middle East. He mentioned the possibility of a ministerial meeting (possibly in Cairo) that would include representatives from IBSA and also other countries such as Turkey and Indonesia.[134] The goal, again, was to consolidate support for the basic elements necessary in order to establish a Palestinian state. I told Al-Maliki that Brazil was ready to cooperate in that regard and that I had already spoken to the Turkish foreign minister, Ahmet Davutoglu, who had responded positively to my suggestion of a "support group" for the Quartet. At the end of the meeting Al-Maliki and I gave a joint press conference in the dining room of Mont-Riant, the residence of the head of the Brazilian delegation to the UN agencies in Geneva, which had previously been my own "home" during two separate periods. An answer I gave to one of the journalists' questions, in which I said Brazil would be open to the possibility of communicating with Hamas if we thought that would contribute to the pursuit of peace (and also stressed that if that were to happen, the Palestinian Authority could rest assured we would proceed "with complete transparency") provoked another storm of criticism in the Brazilian press. One of the contributing factors to the media's reaction was the Palestinian foreign minister's obvious reticence toward Hamas. Indeed, in that respect he appeared less flexible than Abbas had done about six weeks before.

I arrived back in Brasilia on Friday, January 8, and that same day made a few calls to my Middle Eastern interlocutors. From January 12, however, much of my time would be taken up by another catastrophe, in the most literal sense: the terrible earthquake in Haiti. Directly affecting hundreds of thousands of people, in addition to the tens of thousands who lost their lives, the natural disaster not only created an urgent humanitarian situation but also threatened to destroy all the political capital Brazil had invested in the country. I should note, nevertheless, that on the eve of my departure for Port-au-Prince, the Emir of Qatar made an official visit to Brasilia. Several accords were signed, including an aviation agreement for the start of direct flights between Brazil and the Gulf emirate.

The road to Damascus

The following sections in this narrative will recount the final acts in the saga of our efforts during the Lula government to forge a closer relationship with the Middle East. They are based largely on notes I wrote during March 2010, a month that included presidential visits to Jerusalem, Ramallah, and Amman, and in which I also made a highly significant trip to Damascus. Shortly before our departure, I was approached by an important Brazilian politician, a great enthusiast with regard to our foreign policy, who requested a private meeting with me at his residence. He expressed concerns about what might be said in public during the trip and the negative reaction that any intemperate statement might provoke on the part of the international media, with an obvious knock-on effect in Brazil. He even commented that it was important to maintain the good image of the Brazilian government on the international stage as a counterweight to the criticism it was receiving at home. Interestingly, he did not mention the subject of Iran, which had been an obvious bone of contention during the recent visit to Brazil by the US secretary of state. What he was particularly worried about was the reaction of Israel to whatever we might say on the Palestine issue. This episode illustrates, I think, the profound ramifications that foreign policy can have for domestic issues. And that is never more relevant than in the year of a presidential election, as was the case in 2010.

On the night of March 13, a Saturday, we left for Israel. We knew it was going to be a difficult trip. As well as the usual problems surrounding the Israel-Palestine question, the attempt to re-establish a dialogue between the two sides, with US mediation, had been seriously undermined by the announcement that Israel was going to build 1,600 new homes for Jewish settlers in East Jerusalem. Apparently the decision had been taken by the interior minister without formal authorization from the cabinet, but the prime minister must have given it his blessing (or at least not objected). As if to underline that the decision was a deliberate provocation, it was announced during a visit to Jerusalem by US vice president Joe Biden, who responded by vehemently condemning it. On March 10, during a press conference in Brasilia with German foreign minister Guido Westerwelle, I had said I considered the Israeli announcement "deeply" regrettable, and attributed it to "people who don't want peace." Wishing to avoid any negative repercussions with regard to the impending presidential visit, I was more restrained than would normally have been the case. I was also anxious to know what President Lula himself would say on the subject, as he was due to address the Knesset. There would certainly also be statements to the media in Israel and Palestine. Some criticism of the Israeli government's announcement seemed inevitable, but we needed to find the right tone.

We arrived in Jerusalem on the afternoon of March 14. The next morning we had a work session with the president that was attended by Governor Jacques Wagner, who had come with us at Lula's invitation and who had received Mahmoud Abbas at his residence just a few months before; Lula's press secretary, Franklin Martins; our ambassador in Tel Aviv, Pedro Motta; and one of Lula's aides, Clara Ant, who had strong family and emotional ties with Israel. At Lula's request I attempted to give a brief overview of what was happening, including the severe tension between Israel and the US as a result of the announcement about the new settlements. I emphasized the messages that I thought the speech in the Knesset should contain. With so many interlocutors in the room it was not an easy task, but I managed to convey to Lula the essence of what I wanted him to say. It was a particularly difficult moment: the talks brokered by the United States—already a backward step in relation to the direct negotiations that had taken place post-Annapolis—were under threat. Even in Israel there seemed to be a strong reaction to the provocative gesture of expanding the settlements. A significant proportion of Israeli politicians understood the danger of alienating the country's principal ally. Terms such as "insult" and "offense" had been used by several American spokespersons, although President Obama himself, as far as I knew, had made no comment.

On the afternoon of March 15, President Lula made his speech to a packed Knesset. It was a sober address, featuring references to the Holocaust and quotations from thinkers of Jewish origin such as Albert Einstein. There were also, of course, several references to the contribution Brazil's Jewish community have made to the country's development. Lula also pointed to the harmonious coexistence of Arabs and Jews within Brazil's borders. As for the substance of the problems faced by Israelis and Palestinians, Lula reiterated Brazil's diplomatic positions: that the solution should consist of two states living together side by side, and that direct negotiations and dialogue needed to be resumed. Not wishing to skirt around the sensitive issues of the moment, he said he would address them "with respect and frankness." He condemned "unilateral initiatives that hinder [the negotiations], such as the announcement of the construction of homes in Jerusalem." He also called for greater United Nations involvement—contrary to the Israeli preference for dealing with the Palestinian issue bilaterally or in very restricted forums. Lula's appeal for peace and his declaration of friendship toward the Jewish people were perceived by the members of the Knesset as sincere and, of course, much appreciated. The Brazilian president achieved the feat of receiving a warm ovation from the Israeli parliament while also having conveyed all the most important messages that needed to be given at that moment.

That same day, March 15, Lula met with President Shimon Peres and Prime Minister Benjamin ("Bibi") Netanyahu. Both were very friendly and made a point of expressing their appreciation of Brazil's potential role as a facilitator of dialogue with the Palestinians. In the case of the prime minister it was a long conversation that covered a number of substantive issues—but it also seemed to me that his conception of what the dialogue with the Palestinians should consist of would be unacceptable to Ramallah. Referring to examples from the past involving Egypt and Jordan, Bibi insisted that the important thing was to start talking, without preconditions. That way, he said, the Palestinians would have much more to gain. That comment—coming at a moment when the whole world, including the US, was in shock at the decision to go ahead with expanding the settlements—would have sounded naive were it not a clear indication of the Israeli government's blinkered and self-interested approach. Nevertheless, Netanyahu did appear open toward Brazil's involvement. So too, in a later meeting, did the leader of the opposition, Tzipi Livni. The former foreign minister was emotionally committed to a resumption of negotiations with the Palestinians, and very critical of the Israeli government. I was pleasantly surprised by a comment she made to Lula about me: "I respect your foreign minister very much," she said, which made me realize that her apparent attentiveness during our previous conversations had not been just a formality.

Both the Israeli president and prime minister referred to possible Brazilian mediation so as to revive the negotiations with Syria concerning the Golan Heights, which had been paralyzed since the Gaza invasion. Netanyahu, in fact, was quite explicit, requesting that Brazil take an active role in helping with the discussions, to which Lula replied that he would dispatch me "promptly" to Damascus. That mission, which would follow the visit to Jordan, would be organized with great speed and efficiency by my aides, one of whom made the good suggestion that we name it "Operation Anabella" in reference to my newborn granddaughter. On the night of March 15, Lula was honored with a gala dinner hosted by President Shimon Peres. The banquet, which featured various musical performances (including from a Brazilian singer who was living in Israel), took place in a pleasant atmosphere. I found myself sitting next to the deputy prime minister, Silvan Shalom, whom I had first met during my visit to Jerusalem and Tel Aviv in 2005, when he had been foreign minister. This time he was much more talkative. He spoke at length about a project that, in his view, could be of interest to Brazilian companies—an aqueduct that would carry desalinated water to Israel across Jordan.

The next day, before leaving for the West Bank, President Lula visited the Yad Vashem museum, dedicated to the victims of the Holocaust. I had been there once before, during my first trip to Israel. While Lula was at the museum, I received a visit from Israeli experts who presented me with information about the Iranian nuclear program.[135] That same morning, Lula had an interesting meeting with Israeli and Palestinian civil society organizations that were working to encourage dialogue and increase the chances of peace between the two communities. Overall, the visit was very positive and received a lot of media coverage in Brazil. There was even an unexpected positive element in the form of Netanyahu's request for mediation with regard to Syria, a country with few trusted interlocutors either in or outside the Middle East. There was one minor episode, however, that was exploited unfavorably. Following political guidance from me and other advisors, and with Lula's consent, our protocol department had declined the Israeli suggestion that the visit should include the laying of flowers on the tomb of Theodor Herzl, the founder of the Zionist movement. The monument had been inaugurated just a few months before. At a time when the settlements were expanding to the detriment of Palestinians, I thought such a tribute could have been seen as an unnecessary provocation. None of the Israeli officials we met even mentioned the issue, which was dealt with by diplomats at a lower level, but Israeli foreign minister Avigdor Lieberman, with an eye on his own domestic supporters, took advantage of the situation to make a demagogic gesture: he refused to attend the state dinner hosted by Shimon Peres. Lieberman was well known for his hard-line positions and openly anti-Palestinian attitude, so his "boycott" did not carry much political weight. However, the Brazilian media did not miss the opportunity to criticize what it referred to as a "diplomatic gaffe" on our part.

In the early afternoon we went to Bethlehem, where there was an official ceremony marking our arrival in Palestine. Bethlehem, which is under the administration of the PNA, is practically adjacent to Jerusalem, but to get there we had to cross the Rachel Checkpoint, which had the same depressing characteristics of the other crossings I had seen on the border between Israel and the West Bank. But it did cross my mind that it was useful for the other members of our party, and perhaps also Lula himself, to see with their own eyes the wall that separates Jerusalem from the Palestinians. They could get an idea of the difficulties facing those who live in the West Bank but work in the territory under the control of Israel. Lula was received by Mahmoud Abbas in the "presidential palace" in Bethlehem, which I gathered was used mainly on ceremonial occasions. During my previous visits I had always been in Ramallah, and indeed had not even known of the existence of a Palestinian official building so near to Jerusalem (and yet, simultaneously, so far away). This initial meeting consisted of little more than an exchange of pleasantries, with expressions of thanks from Abbas to Lula. Afterwards I took the opportunity to visit the historic Church of the Nativity (the building of which began in the fourth century, having been commissioned by Emperor Constantine the Great and his mother Saint Helen). There was also a bilateral meeting of businesspeople, valuable mainly as a symbolic gesture toward Palestine. In the evening we returned to the presidential palace for a dinner hosted by Abbas and also attended by the prime minister, Salam Fayyad.

As if to illustrate that diplomacy tends to bear out the Baroque conception of the world, in which there are no empty spaces, even my fleeting cultural excursion ended up having practical results. The guide who took us to the Church of the Nativity was a likable Palestinian middle-aged woman who had lived in Chile (the country with the biggest community of Palestinian origin in South America), and afterwards we went with her for an "Arab" coffee in a hostel run by Franciscan priests. While we were there, her daughter arrived: a girl of about sixteen who played in the Palestine women's national soccer team at youth level. Thanks to that fortuitous encounter, I had the idea of organizing a soccer "internship" in Brazil for young Palestinian female players, which would indeed take place not long afterwards at Santos Football Club near São Paulo, the team of the legendary Pelé.

The most important part of the visit to Palestine was the private conversation between Lula and Abbas, which took place the next morning in Ramallah. My Palestinian counterpart and I were the only two other officials present. Lula asked me to talk about my impressions from the visit to Jerusalem, so I briefly described our conversations there, emphasizing the willingness toward dialogue on the part of Shimon Peres (although, in truth, he did not have much influence) and, up to a point, Netanyahu himself. Abbas said that in principle he too was willing to negotiate, but stressed how difficult it was, in political terms, to resume talks in the wake of the Israelis' authorization of the new buildings in East Jerusalem. The PNA president also focused on a point that had been mentioned by Fayyad the previous day: the efforts being made to improve security in the West Bank in response to the constant demands from Tel Aviv. He remarked, rather surprisingly, that the Palestinian Authority was having more success in clamping down on disturbances in the West Bank than the Israelis were in Jerusalem. I myself had noticed the significant police presence along the route we had taken. Incidentally, on the subject of the route between Bethlehem and Ramallah, I should mention what the Palestinian ambassador to Brazil had told me the previous evening: he said that due to the restrictions imposed by the Israelis, it would take him two hours to make a journey we would complete in little more than twenty minutes. Responding to a remark by Lula on the importance of involving Syria in the negotiations regarding the peace process (due mainly to its influence on Hamas), Abbas said that he had been working to improve relations between Damascus and Washington, and recalled that it was he who had insisted Syria should participate in the Annapolis Conference. He added that the rapprochement between the two countries was in progress, offering as an example the fact that Washington had recently appointed an ambassador to Damascus. The PNA president also mentioned that he was trying to help with a relatively prosaic matter that nevertheless had some political implications: the provision by the US of spare parts for the Syrian presidential aircraft. In fact I was already aware of the issue, as concerns about his plane were delaying Bashar al-Assad's acceptance of the invitation to visit Brazil. At some point Lula mentioned Brazil's commitment to contributing to a positive solution to the Iranian nuclear issue. On that issue Abbas was ambiguous. He avoided criticizing our efforts but said it was important that President Lula should go to Tehran himself, and that he should use the visit to convince the Iranian regime to stop giving active support to Hamas. In the prevailing circumstances, to nurture such a hope struck me as very naive to say the least.

Lula's stay in the West Bank had all the characteristics of a "state visit." In addition to the political meetings, the president laid flowers at Yasser Arafat's mausoleum (the Muqata) and inaugurated a thoroughfare—Brazil Street—in a ceremony attended by a sizable crowd. This was the fourth time I had been to the West Bank, and I could see that the economic situation was continuing to improve. This was due in part to foreign aid, but the general opinion was that it could also be attributed to good administration on the part of Prime Minister Salam Fayyad, a technocrat with a background in economics who had already held an important position at the World Bank. The widening of the economic gulf between the West Bank and Gaza was worrying, however, as it certainly hindered reconciliation between the Palestinian factions, despite the confidence in Egypt's mediation efforts expressed once again by Abbas. During our meetings the PNA president was energetic and in good spirits, despite having suffered a fall the day before during a visit to Tunisia. Abbas seemed less tired, or less despondent, than during his trip to Brazil four months earlier. Nevertheless, he reiterated that he did not intend to stand again for election (a declaration that needed to be taken with a pinch of salt, because at that stage it was not at all clear when the elections might take place).

All these factors led me to reflect upon the lack of popularity of the Palestinian leadership in the West Bank, despite the improvement in economic conditions. During our visit to Jordan, Prince Hassan, the uncle of King Abdullah II, would make the interesting observation that due to the lack of progress in the peace process, the Iranian president currently enjoyed greater support among the Arab "masses" than most of the leaders of their own countries. It was a remarkable comment, coming as it did from a member of the Jordanian royal family, albeit an intellectual who liked to adopt an independent stance. In fact, it seemed his analysis might go some way to explaining the behavior of Ahmadinejad, who was constantly making inflammatory statements about Israel, questioning its right to exist as a state on a number of occasions.

Little that was new came up during President Lula's private meeting with King Abdullah II on the afternoon of March 17, or even during the expanded meeting that followed. The visit, with which Lula reciprocated the one to Brazil by the Jordanian monarch in 2008, concentrated on subjects related to bilateral cooperation. Lula certainly brought up the issues of the Middle East, but did not elicit any comments from the king that aroused my curiosity or were genuinely noteworthy. My relative lack of interest was due partly to the fact that some of the analyses were by now very familiar, and partly also because I was already looking ahead to the trip I would be making to Syria the next day, at the request of Netanyahu. In that context I anticipated that the meeting with the Jordanian foreign minister, Nasser Judeh, would be more productive. Already aware of my impending mission to Damascus, Judeh came to visit me at our hotel the following morning, and provided some insights on the situation in Syria. He mentioned the continuing influence of the "old guard" in the Baath party, the rivalry with Saudi Arabia, and the dependence of Damascus on Tehran. None of it was new, but at that particular moment it helped me gather my thoughts.

At the dinner for President Lula hosted by Abdullah II, I was seated next to Queen Rania, who made an immediate impression on me with the beauty of her face and her bearing, reminiscent of a model in a Parisian fashion show. She very soon also impressed me with her intelligence and by clearly being very well informed. No sooner had we sat down than she asked me about my visits to Israel and the West Bank. Of Palestinian origin herself, the queen followed the political developments very closely. She commented on the intransigence of the Israeli government, Obama's lack of firmness in dealing with Tel Aviv, and the surprisingly muted reaction of the Christian population of Jerusalem to Israel's deliberate policy of increasing the city's Jewish population. She also showed great interest in education as a tool for development, and asked how I thought the theme could be included in the G20 discussions. I gave her some ideas based on my previous experience in relation to similar efforts conducted by the director-general of the International Labour Organization, Juan Somavia, and suggested that the new director-general of UNESCO, Irina Bokova, might be a good intermediary. I pointed out that President Lula himself attached great importance to the subject of education, and would certainly be a good ally. That observation led the queen to speak directly to Lula, who was seated to her left (and directly to the right of the king, of course). And so my dialogue with the enchanting first lady was brought to an abrupt end, leaving me to pursue a less interesting conversation with one of the royal secretaries.

The trip to Damascus had been arranged at very short notice and we managed to keep it secret. It was only just before I was due to depart that the Brazilian press, who were closely following the presidential visit, found out where I was going. To avoid speculation I took the initiative of announcing that I was separating from the presidential party in order to go to Syria. There were, however, logistical complications. The Brazilian Air Force plane that was due to pick me up in Amman was delayed due to a bureaucratic hitch involving Algerian airspace. Finally the problem was resolved, but not soon enough to allow me to arrive in Damascus on time. After some doubts and hesitation, we decided to travel by car instead. Shortly after 11 a.m., immediately after a largely ceremonial meeting between Lula and the president of the Jordanian senate, I set off on—literally—the road to Damascus, accompanied only by a few aides.We reached the Syrian capital at 2 p.m., fifty minutes before my meeting with President Bashar al-Assad. The main objective of my trip, arising from the conversation between Lula and Netanyahu, was to explore the possibility of resuming talks between Israel and Syria on the Golan Heights, and that of course was the focus of my conversation with the Syrian president. But I also briefly addressed other issues such as Palestine and Iran. Assad was extremely courteous, as he had been on previous occasions, and listened carefully to the message I conveyed. In reply, he said he was open to the prospect of recommencing the negotiations at the point where they had stopped. Moreover, the Syrian president said he had no wish to insist that progress on the Palestine situation should be a precondition of fresh talks on the Golan Heights. It is important to remember, in that respect, that the "proximity talks" mediated by Turkey had been interrupted precisely because of the Israeli attacks on Gaza. For understandable political reasons, Assad said it was not an appropriate moment to enter into direct dialogue with Israel: instead he insisted that Ankara should continue in the role of mediator. But he said that Brazil could help relaunch the process by wielding its "influence" with Netanyahu. The Syrian president also made a few comments about the Israeli leaders. The foreign minister, Avigdor Lieberman, was in his opinion a "lost cause," although also "very powerful." As for the pragmatism of the head of the government, Assad portrayed it in less than flattering terms: "The main objective of Prime Minister Netanyahu is to remain prime minister," he said, implying that ideology and principle played lesser roles in shaping his behavior. While this pragmatism *à outrance* could have some advantages from the point of view of the negotiations, it also placed Netanyahu at the mercy of more conservative forces, which he depended upon to stay in power. The essential purpose of my mission had been achieved. The message had been delivered and, with certain qualifications, the reaction had been positive. My trip to Damascus aroused the curiosity of the Brazilian journalists, one of whom managed to follow me to Damascus and interview me by phone. The resulting newspaper article attracted a lot of attention, in fact.

Back in Brazil, I had a busy week. I took part in the UN-Habitat conference, where the recent tragedy in Haiti was the main focus of attention. The country's prime minister, Jean-Max Bellerive, was among the participants. During the event I also had several bilateral meetings (accompanied by Lula in some cases), for example with the presidents of Belarus and Uganda. That same week, I received a visit from the new director-general of the International Atomic Energy Agency, who besides wanting to get a close-up view of Brazil's nuclear program, also brought with him some less than encouraging news on the subject of Iran. On March 25, seven days after my lightning visit to Syria, I telephoned the Israeli prime minister. Netanyahu himself had told me to do just that: he clearly wanted to avoid the foreign ministry getting involved. In fact I spoke first to one of the advisors whose names I had been given, but then I was put straight through to Netanyahu himself. As far as I could tell, he listened carefully to my brief account of my meeting with Bashar al-Assad. I told him the Syrian president was willing to resume discussions, as long as their format would be maintained and the progress already made would be preserved. "That's very helpful," said Netanyahu, adding that he would think about how to proceed. I ended the call with a quick mention of possible dates for the Israeli prime minister's visit to Brazil, which had been agreed in principle during his meeting with Lula.

The phone call to Netanyahu brought to an end the cycle of meetings and conversations related to President Lula's visit to three Middle Eastern countries. Without detriment to our positions of principle—expressed on several occasions, including during Lula's speech to the Israeli parliament—we had put together what could be described as a "balanced" trip, mostly without exposing our flanks to criticism from the political opposition in Brazil, who were becoming increasingly excited with the presidential election campaign looming on the horizon. Moreover, Brazil's status as a "valid interlocutor" had been strengthened, with several expressions of interest in our participation in discussions related to the pursuit of peace in the region—not least the request from Netanyahu, who had reversed the direction of my role of two years previously, when I had been the intermediary for President Assad's *démarches* with the then prime minister of Israel, Ehud Olmert. Now it was necessary to await the outcomes of these contacts. In the meantime, we dedicated much of our energy to cooperating in the search for a peaceful solution to the issue of Iran's nuclear program.

A month after Lula's Middle East tour, Palestinian foreign minister Riyad al-Maliki came to Brazil to participate in a working breakfast with the foreign ministers of the IBSA countries, cementing his frequently expressed interest in involving India and South Africa in the peace process.[136] Also in the first half of 2010, we received a visit from the president of Lebanon, Michel Sleiman. As with any visit by a Lebanese head of state or government, Sleiman's presence in Brazil had the symbolic value of strengthening the ties between the two countries. In his speech, Lula emphasized the period of (relative) stability in Lebanon since the presidential election of 2008 and the parliamentary elections of 2009. Lula also underlined the importance of the Lebanese president having visited Damascus, stressing that a peaceful relationship with its neighbors, especially Syria, was essential in order to maintain Lebanon's stability. He referred to the increase in trade, driven by business missions such as the one that had traveled to Beirut just a few weeks before, with industry and trade minister Miguel Jorge among the participants.

On June 30, Bashar al-Assad was received by President Lula in Brasilia. It was the first time a Syrian president had ever visited Brazil. The main theme of the meeting was peace in the Middle East, with regard both to Palestine-Israel and Syria-Israel. A particular focus, naturally, was the Golan Heights, occupied by Israel since the 1967 war. Assad again expressed his interest in the prospect of Brazil playing some kind of mediating or facilitating role. It appeared to me that, since my latest visit to Damascus, the value Assad attached to such possibility had actually increased. He said repeatedly that Brazil had grown in stature on the international stage. "Brazil today," he told Lula, "is not the same as when you were in Damascus in 2003." He praised our independent stance, demonstrated recently in the context of Iran's nuclear program. Given Assad's enthusiasm for greater Brazilian participation in the Middle East—to which Lula responded positively—I suggested that his foreign minister, Walid al-Muallem, should spend an extra day in Brasilia while Assad had meetings with the Arab community in São Paulo. That way, Muallem and I could have a deeper conversation, discussing details that do not really belong in a dialogue between presidents. Assad readily agreed.

The next day, therefore, I received my Syrian counterpart in my office. Despite a tight schedule due to pre-arranged meetings (including one with Lula himself) about urgent topics of direct interest to Itamaraty, I was able to have a very fruitful conversation with Muallem. He described to me in detail the evolution of the discussions regarding Israeli withdrawal from the Golan Heights, from the Madrid conference of 1991 to the recent proximity talks mediated by Turkey (in the relaunching of which I had played a part, however small). Muallem clarified certain aspects of the issue that had been mentioned in my previous conversations with him and Assad. He explained, for example, that the so-called "deposit," which was frequently alluded to, was a document President Bill Clinton had "keep in his pocket." I gathered that it consisted of no more than one piece of paper, and included a summary of the progress made on the issue in the 1990s. According to Muallem it also contained an explicit acceptance on the part of Israel of a return to the previous borders of June 1967, as long as certain conditions were met by Syria. During the period of Turkish mediation, much more recently, there had been some progress on the demarcation of the border, with the then prime minister, Ehud Olmert, having agreed to "two of the six reference points on the Syrian maps." Muallem revealed some curious aspects of these negotiations that had been going on for twenty years, in which he had been directly involved first as Syria's ambassador in Washington and then as foreign minister. He mentioned a mediation attempt by one of the leaders of the American Jewish community, Ronald Lauder, during the first Netanyahu government. On that occasion, important concessions on the part of the Israeli prime minister were blocked by his foreign minister, Ariel Sharon. The retreat in the face of Sharon's intransigence forced Lauder to abandon his mediation efforts. Although Muallem did not say so explicitly, I inferred that he himself had landed in hot water because of the episode and was called back to Damascus by Hafez Assad, Bashar's father. As for how Brazil could help in the negotiations with Israel, my Syrian counterpart was quite straightforward: during Netanyahu's scheduled visit to Brasilia, he wanted us to try to convince the Israelis to formally reaffirm their acceptance of the pre-1967 border.[137] If they did so, it would be sufficient to restart the proximity talks. Muallem even indicated that Brazil's participation might help "soften" Israel's reticent attitude, which he attributed in part to the recent deterioration of relations between Israel and Turkey. Even before the incident with the Freedom Flotilla, Tel Aviv had been uncomfortable with criticism from Ankara on the subject of Gaza, and with the Erdogan government's presumed sympathies toward Hamas. If, during the proximity talks, Netanyahu were to agree with Syria's six reference points for the border between the two countries, Damascus would then be ready to proceed to direct negotiations. And those negotiations would be "accompanied" by several countries, including Brazil.

Assad's request to Lula, presented to me in detail by Muallem, required some reflection on our part. It would obviously mean deeper and more concrete Brazilian involvement in the Middle East than at any previous moment. Moreover, the Golan Heights was an extremely complex and politically charged issue; one in which forward steps had always been followed by setbacks, as Muallam himself had made clear. It was obvious, however, that Syria's approach to Brazil was a consequence of Netanyahu's earlier request to Lula, three months earlier. I concluded that we should go ahead with the dialogue with Syria and Israel, while taking care not to provoke any kind of "jealousy" on the part of Turkey.

My meeting with Muallem, during Assad's visit to Brazil, took place on July 1. Soon afterwards, Lula embarked on a long African tour that included novelties such as the first ever Brazil-ECOWAS[138] summit, which took place in Cape Verde. I accompanied the president on the trip (which, by the way, we commenced in a bad mood after Brazil had been eliminated from the World Cup by the Netherlands). When I returned to Brasilia there was a summit of the Brazil-European Union Strategic Partnership and then, a few days later, I received visits from the Algerian foreign minister, Mourad Medelci, and from my old acquaintance Nabil Shaath, formerly the Palestinian foreign minister and now the official responsible for international affairs on behalf of Fatah. The meeting with Medelci, who had come to participate in the fourth meeting of the Brazil-Algeria Joint Commission, focused mainly on bilateral cooperation, although we did speak about major issues such as the deteriorating situation in Somalia and the problems in Sudan, where there was shortly to be a referendum on the independence of South Sudan.

Nabil Shaath and I spoke in my office for more than two hours. Later that day, when he was received by Lula, their conversation—at which I was also present, as usual—lasted much longer than most visitors' audiences with the president. Shaath conveyed a perception different from what we had been used to hearing from the Palestinian Authority, especially in relation to the possibility of dialogue with Hamas. He told me about a meeting two months earlier, in Gaza, with Ismail Haniyeh, the Hamas "prime minister." On that occasion, according to Shaath, Haniyeh had come very close to agreeing that it was necessary to find a negotiated solution with Israel. Shaath's perception was that the difficulties in attracting Hamas toward a unified Palestinian position were created mainly by leaders living outside Gaza. He also said the Egyptian mediation had made possible certain advances, and that the remaining issues would be easily resolved as soon as Hamas made the political decision to negotiate. One noteworthy point was Shaath's suggestion, albeit indirect, that Brazil should make contact with Hamas. Referring to the sumptuous seafood banquet Haniyeh had offered him when they met, Shaath described it as "better than any restaurant with three Michelin stars." When I asked if he was trying to tempt me on purely gastronomical grounds or if I should read something else into his words, Shaath smiled but avoided giving me a direct answer. Later, in the meeting with Lula, the former Palestinian foreign minister said the PNA was "ready to negotiate with Hamas on all the essential points." He then added: "You can tell Hamas that, if the opportunity arises." I asked if Fatah (and therefore the Palestinian Authority) would prefer the message to be passed on to Hamas in Gaza or Damascus. "It doesn't matter," our interlocutor replied. "The important thing is that either on the way there or the way back, you stop in Ramallah."

Shaath also had with him a letter from Mahmoud Abbas. There was nothing new in the message, but it was very noticeable that, in contrast to the expectations expressed by Shaath, the PNA president's tone was almost one of despair. Naturally Abbas again requested Brazil's support for the Palestinian cause, without making clear what concrete gesture he expected from us. Shaath was more explicit: he made several criticisms of US mediation and the intransigence of Israel, which he said had not even presented a concrete proposal to the mediator, George Mitchell. Then, verbalizing what Abbas would not have dared communicate in a written document, Shaath requested that Brazil formally recognize Palestine as a state. Lula's immediate response, positive in tone, was to promise he would analyze the matter with me ("I'll talk to Celso.") Lula went on to say that in principle he was in favor of granting the request, but gave no indication of how or when. In fact, Shaath had made the same request in his conversation with me a few hours earlier; I had said that personally I would be favorably inclined toward Brazil's recognition of Palestine, although it would be necessary to proceed cautiously because of the presidential election campaign. I expressed my feelings to Lula that same day, before his own meeting with Shaath, but he seemed less worried than I was about the risk of any negative political repercussions.

Against this backdrop, two days later, I left on another trip to the Middle East—my last as foreign minister under President Lula[139] —with a stop beforehand in Luanda to attend a summit of the Community of Portuguese-Speaking Countries. On the day of my departure, July 22, another Arab visitor arrived in Brazil: the prime minister of Kuwait, Nasser al-Mohammed al-Ahmed al-Jaber al-Sabah, who met with President Lula and then moved on to São Paulo with a sizable business delegation. Our industry and trade minister, Miguel Jorge, a good ally in our efforts to strengthen business links with the Arab world, took good care of our Kuwaiti visitor. Between Luanda and Istanbul (where the main topic of discussion would be the aftermath of the UN Security Council resolution on Iran)[140] I made a stop in Libya. In fact I had done so on some previous occasions, taking advantage of the country's position on the route between Brazil and the Middle East or India to break my journey and meet with government ministers, mainly to talk about economic-commercial matters. (Exactly the same was true of Tunisia; in fact I tended to alternate between Tripoli and Tunis.) These stop-overs were generally arranged not long in advance, so in the case of Libya it never occurred to me to request an audience with Gaddafi. On one occasion I had been received with great courtesy by the prime minister. This time, my only meeting was with the international security minister, Abuzaid Omar Dorda, with whom I had developed a friendly relationship during my time at the United Nations, especially when Brazil had been a non-permanent member of the UNSC in 1998–99. Dorda, in fact, had been very grateful for Brazil's role on the Security Council—as described in the first section of this narrative—in helping to remove the sanctions that had been imposed on his country after Lockerbie. His previous ministerial posts had included infrastructure and international intelligence. According to our ambassadors in Tripoli, on more than one occasion he had assisted in fostering Brazilian-Libyan economic relations. And about a year after my brief visit, in the midst of the rebellion that would ultimately overthrow Gaddafi, our ambassador would inform me that Dorda was instrumental in securing the release of a Brazilian journalist detained by the regime.

I arrived in Istanbul on July 24. The next day, before a trilateral lunch with the Iranian foreign minister,[141] I had a long talk with my Turkish counterpart Ahmet Davutoglu. We discussed Turkey's relations with Israel, which were in a profound state of crisis following the incident with the Gaza Freedom Flotilla. Davutoglu was very frank, even requesting that "as a good friend and valid interlocutor" I convey to Netanyahu the Turkish perspective on the gravity of the situation. He said Ankara could only restore relations with Tel Aviv if certain preconditions were met. These included an apology, compensation, and the return of the boats. Davutoglu also suggested that an international commission should investigate the incident, and said the blockade of Gaza had to be lifted. He made clear, however, that of all those requirements, the most important for unlocking the dialogue would be the Israeli apology. A few days before, Davutoglu had had a private conversation with the Israeli trade minister, Binyamin Ben-Eliezer, but a leak to the media had made it impossible to continue their discussion. Davutoglu attributed the leak to Ehud Barak, Ben-Eliezer's rival within the Israeli Labor Party. I also described the diplomatic efforts we were developing in relation to the Golan Heights question, at the request of both Israel and Syria. My Turkish counterpart said he considered it "natural" for Brazil to step in to provide assistance in that respect—partly indeed because Turkey was preoccupied by assuaging the anger of its own people in the wake of the flotilla incident. The mediation efforts had been given a lower priority. Davutoglu thanked me for my transparent approach and reaffirmed his complete trust in Brazil.

My meeting with the Israeli prime minister was scheduled for 5 p.m. that same day, July 25. The journey from the Ciragan Palace, on the banks of the Bosphorus, to the airport normally took almost an hour, but this time, thanks to the efficiency of the Turkish motorcycle outriders, I arrived in a record time of less than twenty minutes. After the short flight to Tel Aviv, I arrived at Netahnyahu's office at 5:15 p.m., a quarter on an hour late. This small lapse in punctuality certainly did not curtail our meeting, as Netanyahu and I were able to speak for over an hour and a half. I later found out that while we were talking, defense minister Ehud Barak—allegedly responsible for the "leak" mentioned by Davutoglu—was kept waiting outside in the hall. It was the third time I had been in the office of the Israeli prime minister, not counting the occasion when I had accompanied President Lula. Sharon and

Olmert had received me in a room decorated with personal touches, such as photos and other pictures, whereas with Netanyahu I sat at a large table in a rather austere room—the same one I had been in with Lula, in fact. I was carrying a letter from Lula, repeating the invitation to the Israeli prime minister to visit Brazil. Netanyahu read it and politely said he still hoped to be able to make the visit a reality. But it was quite clear he was more interested in hearing about my conversations in Syria.

Netanyahu listened carefully to my account of my conversations with Assad and Muallem, and asked me several questions about specific aspects. At one point he requested a writing pad from one of his aides and began to take notes. He said that he himself wanted to follow the "track of peace." His body language was neutral for most of the time, but he seemed to grimace slightly when I told him that as far as Assad was concerned, a resumption of the dialogue on the Golan Heights did not depend on progress being made on the Palestine issue. I referred to the two elements the Syrians did consider essential, although I was careful to avoid characterizing them as preconditions: Israeli acceptance, in principle, that the border should return to the line of June 4, 1967; and compliance with the six points ("benchmarks") on the demarcation line. The former demand would be important to ensure the resumption of "proximity talks," while the latter would be related to the beginning of the direct talks. Netanyahu asked me for details regarding the six points. I told him what I knew on the basis of what the Syrian foreign minister had told me: they were two points on the northernmost part of the border, two in the center, and two along the southernmost part. According to Muallem, during the sixth meeting within the framework of the proximity talks, held in Turkey shortly before the attack on Gaza, Olmert had agreed with the middle two of the six points on the line, but the other four were unresolved. Netanyahu did not appear to be very well informed on the issue. He consulted with his security advisor, Uzi Arad (a burly, slightly overweight middle-aged man in shirtsleeves; he looked more like a former member of the special forces than an intelligence officer). The Israeli prime minister did not show much interest in the cartographical details. He spoke about the need for certain "guarantees" in order to secure peace: I think he was referring principally to Syria's support for Hamas and Hezbollah. He also made an oblique reference to the relationship between Damascus and Tehran, suggesting the close ties between the two capitals were unhelpful in the context of the efforts to arrive at an understanding between Israel and Syria. Although repeatedly emphasizing his openness to dialogue, Netanyahu mentioned the difficulties surrounding the proximity talks, thereby implying a preference for direct communication with Damascus. "The Turks," he said, "are close to the region, but at the moment they're incapacitated." As for Brazil, it would be a suitable interlocutor, "but it's far away." Nevertheless, the Israeli prime minister did seem interested in continuing to explore possible steps forward.

We talked a little about the relations between Israel and Turkey. Netanyahu showed no inclination whatsoever to make the gestures Ankara was asking for. He also seemed completely unaware of a fact that I had discovered through Davutoglu—namely that in the Turkish foreign minister's previous role as international advisor to Prime Minister Erdogan, he had been personally involved in efforts to try to ensure that the Israeli soldier Gilad Shalit, kidnapped by Hamas, would not be executed. This apparent ignorance of important facts, whether real or feigned, reminded me of something else Davutoglu had told me: that Israeli cabinet ministers often fail to share information with their colleagues and successors, behaving instead as if their files are their own personal property. I talked to Netanyahu again, by phone, on July 27. My motive in calling was to find out if he had any other message or further thoughts that I should convey to Damascus, where I had meetings scheduled for the following day. However, I also hoped that Netanyahu might comment on the situation of the kidnapped soldier, which would give me an extra motive to meet with the Hamas leadership in Syria. On a previous trip, in fact, I had discussed the possibility of making contact with Hamas in a conversation with our efficient ambassador in Damascus, Edgard Casciano, but I remained hesitant, all too aware of the negative reaction the move would certainly provoke in the Brazilian media. As it turned out, Netanyahu did not take the bait, and I remained hesitant, so the meeting with Khaled Meshaal did not take place.[142] Over the phone, replying to a question I posed on the subject of the dialogue with Syria, Netanyahu was not very direct. When I asked him whether or not he would accept the resumption of the proximity talks on the basis of the elements formulated by the foreign minister, he responded with a question of his own (one, in fact, that he had already asked during our meeting on July 25): if Israel were to agree to enter again into proximity talks, who would be the facilitator? He went on to say, again, that Turkey was not a viable interlocutor.

My official meetings in Israel took place on July 25 and 27. The unusual scheduling was due to Avigdor Lieberman inviting me to a working lunch with him on the latter date, the eve of my departure for Syria. I interpreted the invitation from the Israeli foreign minister not only as an effort to "keep up appearances"—it was obvious that my purpose in visiting Israel had been to meet the prime minister, and the foreign minister did not want it to look as if he had been bypassed—but also as a way of erasing the negative impression caused by his intemperate and demagogic attitude at the time of President Lula's visit. In fact the schedule turned out to be useful because it allowed me, on July 26, not only to make a trip to Ramallah but also to meet with intellectuals and members of civil society in East Jerusalem. On the evening of July 25, after the meeting with Netanyahu, I called the diplomatic advisor to President Sarkozy, Jean-David Levitte; I have no written record of the conversation but I am sure it must have been about Iran.

On the morning of July 26 I was awakened in the King David Hotel in Jerusalem by the bells of the Abbey of the Dormition, not very far away. I took it to be a good omen for my activities over the next few days. After breakfast in the hotel's spacious dining room in the company of my closest advisors, including my chief of staff Maria Laura da Rocha ("Laurinha"), I left for Ramallah, which had become an essential stop on any visit to region. As President Abbas was away, I met with Prime Minister Salam Fayyad and Foreign Minister Riyad al-Maliki. According to many analysts, neither was an important figure in the PNA's decision-making process with regard to the key issues in the peace process. Those issues were dealt with mainly by the Fatah leaders, one of whom, Nabil Shaath, had recently been in Brasilia. The conversations were not without interest, however. I could clearly see that the Palestinian leadership was in a state of bewilderment, and to some extent paralysis, because of the dismal state of the peace process, having put its chips on the US mediation efforts ever since the days of George Bush and Condoleezza Rice. Both verbally and through concrete initiatives such as the Annapolis Conference, Bush and Condoleezza had committed themselves to supporting the "moderate Arabs" (a concept I had always considered rather artificial and hard to grasp). But now the Palestinian Authority felt that the new US president, in whom they had placed great hopes, was pulling the rug from under their feet. Obama probably wanted to be able to point to some progress on the peace process ahead of the 2010 mid-term elections, but because he had not succeeded in extracting any significant concessions whatsoever from Israel, instead he had to seek signs of progress merely in the format of the negotiations. Shortly before my visit, Washington had suggested a transition from discussions brokered by a facilitator to direct talks between Palestinians and Israelis. But for the PNA to accept that change would mean abandoning the position they had clearly expressed, which was that direct talks could only take place when certain preconditions had been met. In Ramallah, I ventured an opinion on the subject, both with the prime minister and the foreign minister. I suggested that the Palestinian Authority should focus on a single prerequisite: a clear and firm commitment from Israel to stop expanding the settlements. Concentrating on that point, I said, would give greater legitimacy to the Palestinian position. To state additional preconditions could be interpreted as a desire to achieve their goals before the negotiations had even started. My interlocutors seemed to be listening carefully, albeit without giving any clear sign that they agreed with me. The next day, still in Jerusalem, I was told what the PNA spokesperson had said when commenting on my visit: "Brazil always brings good ideas."

In Ramallah, in the office of Brazil's diplomatic mission, I had a meeting with Mustafa Barghuthi, the leader of a third Palestinian party (neither Fatah nor Hamas) that had received twenty percent of the votes in the most recent presidential elections. Barghuthi, whom I had spoken to briefly on the phone during a previous visit, was very pessimistic about the peace process. Though affable and calm in his demeanor, he was nevertheless very didactic in depicting the progressive undermining of any possibility of a cohesive Palestinian state. Referring to maps he had brought with him, he traced the continual expansion of the Israeli settlements—a graphic demonstration of the fragmentation of the territory that remained for the Palestinians.

I also received a visit from the young members of the Palestinian women's soccer team that had spent time in Santos (the city where I was born, incidentally) for a training internship, an initiative of mine inspired by my previous visit to Palestine. It provided a pleasant and relaxed interval between the intense conversations of that morning and the ones I was scheduled to have later that day in East Jerusalem. At the American Colony[143] I had meetings with the respective director-generals of the Geneva Initiative, Gadi Baltiansky, and the "Peace Now" movement, Yariv Oppenheimer. I also had a conversation with an influential figure in the Palestinian community in Jerusalem, Hannah Siniora. All three of these civil society representatives were encouraging toward Brazil's participation in the peace efforts. Some of what they said connected with ideas that had arisen during my previous trips, such as during my conversations with Amos Oz and André Azulay. I also met my ex-counterpart (both as Palestinian foreign minister and ambassador to the UN) Nasser al-Qudwa, now president of the Arafat Foundation and a member of the PLO Central Council. Before that particular meeting, a question came to mind: Why would the former Palestinian foreign minister, a nephew of Yasser Arafat, prefer to meet me in East Jerusalem and not in Ramallah? His choice of venue, along with some carefully expressed observations he made during the conversation, led me to the conclusion that he had a critical stance toward the PNA's position, which I inferred that he found excessively moderate.

The next morning, I went to Tel Aviv to meet with Tzipi Livni. I also gave two interviews that reached quite a sizable audience: one to the Israeli-Brazilian journalist Guila Flint, of BBC Brasil; the other to José Levy, of CNN's Spanish-language channel. Livni, the leader of the opposition in the Knesset, was emphatic in expressing her skepticism about the chances of an agreement with the Palestinian Authority while the coalition led by Netanyahu remained in power. She was also downbeat about the prospects of fruitful negotiations with Syria, but nevertheless asked me for my views on the subject, which I was careful to give without going into details that might compromise any future negotiations. I asked her about the possibility, mentioned occasionally in the media, of her Kadima party being invited to join Netanyahu's coalition.[144] She said that would only be possible if she was convinced the prime minister genuinely wished to pursue the path of peace with the Palestinians. Of course, as she herself made clear, when she spoke of the Palestinians in that context she was referring only to Fatah. When I mentioned that during Nabil Shaath's visit to Brazil I had perceived possible changes of attitude that might facilitate progress in the dialogue between Fatah and Hamas, Livni made no attempt to hide her opinion that unity between the Palestinian factions "isn't in Israel's interests." In a quick *tête-à-tête* at the end of our meeting, Livni described certain aspects of a conversation she had had with Netanyahu, and what they implied about his attitude toward the peace process. What the prime minister had told her, she said, suggested that changes in the composition of the governing coalition were unlikely "unless the political damage to the Labor Party is such that it decides to abandon the government."

Also on July 27, as scheduled, I had lunch with the Israeli foreign minister, Avigdor Lieberman. It was not the most enjoyable of experiences. His body language during the meal, sprawled in his chair, reminded me of the coarse-mannered *mujiks* in stories by Gogol. And his views, devoid of any subtlety, matched his physical demeanor. After about fifty minutes of lukewarm conversation, Lieberman started criticizing Brazil's positions and making all sorts of complaints. Such was his tone that eventually I had no option but to interrupt him. Making no attempt to hide my annoyance, I said that in Rio de Janeiro I often walked along the main oceanfront avenue in Copacabana, a neighborhood with quite a large Jewish community. Often, I said, Brazilian Jews stopped me to talk about the Middle East, encouraging me to maintain Brazil's participation in the efforts to achieve an understanding between Israel and Palestine. Sometimes, I added, in addition to their messages of support, my Jewish compatriots not only expressed disagreement with certain Israeli policies vis-à-vis the Palestinians, but also said some of the government's attitudes made them feel "ashamed." It was a blunt reaction on my part, but a necessary one in the face of Lieberman's behavior. At the end of the meal we parted without any further courtesies, dispensing with a joint press conference. It was a less than edifying ending to my visit to Israel, but I knew it would have no adverse effect on my dialogue with the prime minister. From Tel Aviv I left for Damascus, this time having taken the care to pre-arrange a stop in Amman and thereby avoid the in-flight stress that the same route had caused us in 2009.

The talks in Damascus were very positive. President Bashar al-Assad thanked us for our diplomatic efforts that had not only prepared the path toward a potential resumption of negotiations but also helped maintain, as he put it, a "good atmosphere." That was important, he said, because it had a "preventive effect" in relation to the ever-present danger of an armed conflict in the region. I recall, incidentally, that during Assad's visit to Brazil, Fidel Castro—whose political and literary creativity was at its peak, reflected in the copious "letters" he wrote in *Granma*—had sent the Syrian president a message, supposedly based on intelligence reports, to the effect that he should return home as quickly as possible because preparations were underway for a military action that could result in a "world war." (During a visit I would make to Havana a few months later, Fidel's brother, President Raul Castro, asked me with a slight smile what the "effect" of the message had been.) Exaggerations aside, there were indeed constant rumors about the possibility an Israeli attack on Syria, due to the constant skirmishes with Hezbollah. Assad said during our meeting that he would send me a short document consisting of five paragraphs, which had been handed to the then Senator John Kerry at the end of May In fact, later that day, Syrian foreign minister Walid Muallem would give me a copy of the document with the Senator's name handwritten at the top. The paragraphs were suggestions of principles that might guide future negotiations with Israel. The first consisted of the suggestion of a peace treaty between Syria and Israel that would include provisions on the border in the Golan Heights, returning it to the line of June 4, 1967. However, very significantly from the point of view of Israel, the same paragraph also stipulated that neither party should give assistance or "comfort" to any state or non-state actor that threatened the security of the other. Although worded so as to apply to both sides, it was obviously a commitment on the part of Damascus to stop supporting the actions of Hamas and Hezbollah against Israel. Other points concerned the termination of the state of war between Syria and Israel; the normalization of diplomatic relations, including the opening of embassies; and support for the Arab Peace Initiative, for agreements between Israel and Palestine, and for the normalization of relations of between Tel Aviv and the members of the Arab League. Later, when I read the copy of the document Muallem gave me, I could not help remembering Ehud Olmert's reaction when I had conveyed Assad's message to him two and a half years before. On that occasion the then Israeli prime minister had seemed flexible, in principle, toward the issue of the delimitation of the border with Syria (although we did not enter into details), and much more concerned with the support Damascus was giving to Hamas and Hezbollah. My own view was that if the five points in the document delivered by Syria (by Bashar al Assad himself, presumably) to Kerry were accepted and complied with by both sides—which might require the participation of third countries as "guarantors"—they would constitute a good basis for progress toward a possible peace agreement between the two countries.

Assad authorized me to tell Netanyahu about the existence of the document and, of course, its contents. He said this would "buy time" while the question of mediation was still being resolved. The Syrian president's concerns about buying time and "maintaining a good atmosphere," which he expressed to me more than once, were somewhat surprising because at that time, Fidel Castro's apocalyptic visions notwithstanding, I did not have the impression that an armed conflict might be imminent.

During the excellent lunch Muallem offered me in a restaurant in the Old City of Damascus, he provided details on the exact point at which the proximity talks mediated by Ankara had been interrupted. With this information I would in principle be able to advance the conversations with the Israeli prime minister. "In practice," Muallem said, "Brazil is already acting as a facilitator." Between my meeting with the president and lunch with the foreign minister, I had time to go to our ambassador's residence, where I called my Turkish counterpart Ahmet Davutoglu to bring him up to date on my conversations in Damascus.

Soon after my return to Brazil, on a Sunday, I called Prime Minister Netanyahu from my home in Brasilia to convey what I had been told in Damascus. The call had been arranged for 1:30 p.m. in Brasilia, so in Jerusalem it was already evening. However, because of a meeting of Israeli ministers, the call had to be delayed slightly. When one of my aides, Leonardo Gorgulho (who had come to my house to connect the call), did put me through to Netanyahu's office, the message was that he was still in the meeting. Also, a little disconcertingly, his secretary seemed not to know about the scheduled conversation, which made me think it might end up not taking place. And from the Monday onward it was going to be difficult to speak to Netanyahu because I had a heavy schedule of commitments, most of them outside Brazil. Leonardo and I were still considering what to do next when the secretary called back, on my cell phone, to say Netanyahu was now ready to receive my call. After the Israeli prime minister had graciously apologized for the delay (which was only twenty minutes, in fact), I described my conversations in Damascus in some detail, stressing that I considered them quite positive. I explained that President Assad wished to keep open the channel of communication, with me as the intermediary, but that discretion was important. It would not be possible for Damascus openly to abandon Turkey's mediation efforts,[145] although it was clear to all sides involved that those efforts were currently "frozen." Based on the information Muallem had given me, I referred to the question of Syria's replies to Israel's questions about security. These responses would have been transmitted (or delivered) to Prime Minister Erdogan, to be communicated to Tel Aviv as soon as Syria considered that the Israelis had responded satisfactorily to its demands regarding the six points ("benchmarks") on the border. I also told Netanyahu that upon Assad's instructions, Muallem had shown me a document containing five points, which had been given to Senator John Kerry in late May. I chose not to mention that my Syrian counterpart had actually given me a copy. I said that I thought this "non-paper" dealt adequately with Israel's security concerns, including in its commitment not to support movements hostile to Tel Aviv. Although, as previously mentioned, the paper given to Kerry was worded so as refer to a mutual commitment, it was clear to me that the reference to "state and non-state actors" referred not only to Hamas and Hezbollah but also to Tehran. Over the phone it was obviously difficult to tell whether or not Netanyahu was surprised by that. He seemed more interested in confirming that Syria was indeed willing to sign an agreement with Israel, even before the conclusion of the peace process with Palestine. I said that as far as I could tell, that was the case. Because the phone connection was not very good, at one point I asked the Israeli prime minister if he was managing to follow what I was saying. "Every word," he replied, adding that the information I had given him was "very valuable." He said he would reflect upon what I had told him, and then talk to me again on the subject as soon as possible. However, soon after the end of the conversation, with a lingering doubt about whether I had indeed been sufficiently clear, I asked Leonardo to call Netanyahu's security advisor just to reiterate my perception of Syria's willingness to pursue an agreement. The following week, at the earliest opportunity, I called Muallem to pass on the details of my conversation with the Israeli prime minister. Those two telephone conversations completed what were potentially the initial stages of Brazil's mediation of an Israel-Syria dialogue. I wrote in my notebook: "It's like throwing a pebble into water: you wait and see how far the ripples spread."

As it turned out, the ripples did not travel very far. As previously mentioned, Israel's internal political problems, coupled with the election campaign in Brazil, prevented Netanyahu's visit from taking place. Nor did I have other opportunities for detailed conversations with my Syrian interlocutors. Brazil's potential facilitation role therefore remained on hold, waiting for an initiative that in practice could only be taken after the end of President Lula's term of office. Unlike the Israeli government officials who, I was told, jealously keep for themselves any documents relating to their period of office, I made sure all the documents related to our incipient mediation role would remain available for the public in the future. Above all, the copy of the non-paper delivered to John Kerry, given to me at the request of President Assad, was carefully placed in the appropriate Itamaraty file. There it will stay, awaiting favorable circumstances for a resumption of our initiatives. As a side note, I should perhaps mention that our pursuit of closer ties would be extended to the economic field by the end of 2010, with the signing of the Mercosur-Syria Framework Agreement.[146]

Ramallah

The most important developments in the second half of 2010 were those concerning Palestine. Before discussing them I should mention that our relations with Egypt were evolving positively in the period immediately before the main players on Cairo's political scene were swept away in the Arab

Spring. On August 2, on the margins of the Mercosur Summit in San Juan, the Mercosur-Egypt Free-Trade Agreement was signed, the culmination of negotiations that had started in 2004. It was the second extra-regional free-trade agreement signed by Mercosur (the first, in fact, was with Israel). During the UN General Assembly I met again with the Egyptian foreign minister, Ahmed Aboul Gheit, whose main concern at the time was Sudan, where a referendum on South Sudan's independence was due to take place in three or four months. He said there was a risk of major instability, with potential repercussions for the rest of the region. Unlike in our most recent meetings, he was very pessimistic about the Palestine situation. He even suggested Lula should call Shimon Peres. "Don't underestimate Brazil's influence," he told me. In the end that phone call was not made, but Brazil did adopt positions on the Palestine question that were to have important international repercussions.

We had been closely following the forward and backward steps of the Israel-Palestine peace process—although, given what was actually happening on the ground, perhaps the word "peace" was less than apt. In response to the resumption of direct talks between the two sides on August 25, our official communiqué was cautious in tone: it said simply that the Brazilian government had "received with interest" the announcement that direct talks between Israelis and Palestinians would resume in September. It also referred to "Palestinian expectations" regarding a freeze on further Israeli settlements. Then, significantly, came a public statement by Saeb Erekat that the PNA would like to see Brazil involved in the discussions. In fact he also mentioned China, Norway, Turkey, and the United Arab Emirates—but only the reference to Brazil was genuinely new, given that two of the other countries are part of the region, China a permanent member of the Security Council, and Norway, since the Oslo Accords, already a participant in the peace process. A diplomatic advisor to Mahmoud Abbas had called our ambassador in Ramallah, Ligia Scherer, to tell her in advance about the content of the statement. However, I was somewhat disheartened to learn from our ambassador in Washington, Mauro Vieira, that the United States, which was strongly backing the resumption of direct talks, did not intend to invite the countries mentioned by Erekat to the first meeting in the new phase of negotiations. Apart from those directly involved, participation would be restricted to the Americans themselves, Jordan, and Egypt, while Tony Blair would represent the Quartet. In other words there would be no resumption of the Annapolis process, at least in the short term. On September 28, the day after I had heard the Egyptian foreign minister's pessimistic prognosis at UN headquarters, the Brazilian government issued another communiqué, this time expressing our concern about Israel's failure to extend the moratorium on settlement expansion. A few days earlier, when making the opening speech of the UN General Assembly, I had devoted five paragraphs to the Middle East. I mentioned the need for a Palestinian state that would ensure a decent life for its citizens, and reiterated the importance Brazil attached to a freeze on further settlements. I also referred to the urgent need to lift every form of blockade from Gaza. In a somewhat veiled reference to the resumption of direct talks, I said: "It is not the form of the dialogue that will determine whether there will be results. What matters is the determination of the parties to reach a just and lasting peace. This will be easier with the involvement of all interested parties."

Brazil's decision officially to recognize the State of Palestine had been made some time before. There had in fact been a slow but steady progression in that direction, culminating in the impact of the visit to Brazil by Nabil Shaath. In retrospect it became clearer to me that Mahmoud Abbas, in his letter, had avoided making an explicit request for Brazilian recognition so as not to provoke a negative reaction from the United States. But it was clear that this was his wish. On December 1, returning from Washington where I had attended *Foreign Policy* magazine's awards ceremony (where I was seated at the head table with John Kerry, who remarked about a need for "effective action" with regard to Iran, making me fearful that a military attack might indeed take place), I jotted down a few notes about the commitments awaiting me in Brasilia later that day. One of them, curiously, was a meeting with the Israeli deputy prime minister, Silvan Shalom, who was quoted in the press as saying he was coming to Brazil "to see the foreign minister." But a more important task was to talk with President Lula to decide how to proceed with our recognition of the Palestinian state. With Brazil's presidential election already behind us, and government candidate Dilma Rousseff victorious, I saw no reason not to press ahead, even though voices of protest might be raised here and there in the Brazilian media. What I wrote at the time was: "It's better to do it now than leave the problem for [President Rousseff]."[147]

We had previously suggested to the Palestinian authorities that their request for recognition from Brazil should be expressed in formal terms. Our aim in doing so was to prevent those who opposed the move from being able to allege it was just a gratuitous gesture directed against Israel. In response, Abbas wrote a letter to Lula dated November 24, which Lula replied to on December 3. That same day, a communiqué was issued with the full text of both letters. Because of its historical value, I think I should quote the central paragraph of Lula's letter to Abbas: "Considering that the request you presented is fair and consistent with the principles upheld by Brazil with regard to the Palestinian issue, Brazil, by means of this letter, hereby recognizes the Palestinian State based on the 1967 borders." Lula's letter was careful to reiterate the conviction that "only dialogue and peaceful coexistence with its neighbors will truly advance the Palestinian cause." Just as Ramallah predicted, Brazil's gesture set off a chain reaction in Latin America. Argentina and Uruguay were the first to follow Brazil's lead, before others did the same.[148] On the same day, *Foreign Policy*, always quick off the mark, said the following on its website: "In their last month in office, President Luiz Inácio Lula da Silva and his transformative foreign minister Celso Amorim are still making news, announcing today that Brazil has recognized the Palestinian State based on the 1967 borders."

Our recognition of the State of Palestine completed a long cycle in the relations between Brazil and the Arab countries, driven by our pursuit of closer political, economic and cultural ties. We took that approach without harming our good relationship with Israel, whose most important leaders, unlike some hard-liners in the right-wing parties, gave us several indications of their consideration and trust.[149] Although many of our initiatives did not come fully to fruition, we sowed the seeds of greater Brazilian participation in a region where, more than in any other part of the world, global peace is at stake. This in itself is important, even if one is aware that in many cases only the passage of time, coupled with a determination not to retreat, can produce long-lasting results. In our economic relations with the Arab world, these results are already there to be seen. In other fields, the delicacy and complexity of the issues will require continued action and determination. This, in turn, will imply trust in our own objectives. The same trust already shared by most of our interlocutors in the Middle East.

July 2014[150]

NOTES

1. Ibn Khaldun. *The Muqaddimah: An Introduction to History* (Princeton University Press, 1989).
2. Arab immigrants' integration into the societies of South America was the subject of a photography exhibition and a book, *Amrik*, during the first ASPA summit in Brasilia in 2005.
3. A notable exception to this conservative outlook was Hélio Jaguaribe, who in 1958 argued that Brazil and Argentina should support the struggle of the Arab countries during the process of decolonization. Jaguaribe also believed that the two South American countries should act together to mediate the rivalry between the superpowers. See his book *O nacionalismo na atualidade brasileira* (Educam, 2005).
4. On September 19, 1963, Brazilian foreign minister João Augusto de Araújo Castro made a speech to the United Nations General Assembly that later gave rise to the expression "the three Ds." His argument was that the international agenda should not be guided only by the concerns of the superpowers. He said the UN, instead of allowing itself to be limited by the logic of bipolarity, should focus on three fundamental issues: disarmament, development, and decolonization. Thirty years later, when I was foreign minister in the Itamar Franco government and made the opening speech at the UN General Assembly, I returned to Araújo Castro's three Ds, but with "decolonization" replaced by "democracy."
5. In 1991, under the auspices of the Security Council, the United Nations Compensation Commission was created with the purpose of paying compensation for losses and damage arising from the Iraqi invasion of Kuwait. The case of Brazil was analyzed by the Brazilian diplomat Anuar Nahes in his thesis "The Reparations for the Gulf War and their Implications for Brazil: the United Nations Compensation Commission" (2003).

6. In 2000, at the United Nations, Iranian president Mohammad Khatami proposed a "Dialogue Among Civilizations" with the objective of increasing understanding between peoples of different origins. The initiative was expanded in 2005 with the creation of the "Alliance of Civilizations," the result of a proposal by Spanish prime minister José Luiz Rodriguez Zapatero aimed at combating extremism and strengthening dialogue and cooperation. Rio de Janeiro hosted the third Alliance of Civilizations Forum in 2010.

7. The Oslo Accords were signed in 1993. They rested upon the idea of "land for peace": Israel would permit the creation of a Palestinian state, which would involve withdrawal from the occupied territories and a return to Israel's original borders. The Palestinians, for their part, would recognize Israel's right to exist, thereby establishing a relationship of coexistence. It was through the Oslo Accords that the Palestinian National Authority was created.

8. The First Intifada, in 1987, was a Palestinian uprising against Israeli occupation that spread from the Gaza Strip to the West Bank. The Second Intifada began in 2000, triggered by a declaration Ariel Sharon made when visiting Temple Mount in Jerusalem, very close to the Al-Aqsa Mosque. Sharon, who was running for leadership of the Likud party, repeated the words of a famous radio message from the Six-Day War of June 1967: "The Temple Mount is in our hands." Violent clashes ensued between Palestinians and Israelis in the area alongside the Wailing Wall.

9. I remember once mentioning the movie *Casablanca* in the unlikely context of a meeting of the GATT, when the trade policy of the European Community was being discussed. In criticizing the GATT's tolerant attitude toward European protectionism, it seemed pertinent to recall a piece of dialogue between the American expatriate Rick (played by Humphrey Bogart of course) and the head of the local police (played by Claude Rains), in which the former is asked why he came to live in Casablanca and comes up with a surprising answer: "for the waters." When the police chief points out that the city is in the desert, Rick replies nonchalantly: "I was misinformed." The GATT was supposed to be a defender of free trade, but in reality the major economic powers continued to be protectionist.

10. Resolution S/RES/425 (1978), which established UNIFIL, calls for "strict respect for the territorial integrity, sovereignty and political independence of Lebanon, within its internationally recognized borders." Several other resolutions repeat this demand and quote directly from Resolution 425.

11. Although the story of this *aide-mémoire* and how it ended up in my possession in Shimon Peres's hotel suite deserves to be told, there is not enough space for it here. Suffice to say the document had become a kind of passport to the meeting with Peres, and that three of my most brilliant colleagues, Affonso Ouro-Preto, Fernando Reis, and Mauro Vieira, were involved in the goings-on surrounding its delivery. The whole episode took place under the serene and good-humored observation of our ambassador to the UN, Ronaldo Sardenberg.

12. S/RES/940 (1994); S/RES/944 (1994); S/RES/948 (1994).

13. The Rio Group was an informal mechanism of Latin American and Caribbean countries created in the 1980s to help solve political conflicts in the region. It was also used as a platform for political and economic dialogue with countries or groups from other regions. Unlike Mercosur, it lacked negotiating capacity. In recent years it has been superseded by the Community of Latin American and Caribbean States.

14. The Uruguay Round was the eighth round of multilateral trade negotiations conducted within the framework of the old General Agreement on Tariffs and Trade (GATT). Its name derives from the fact that it was launched in the Uruguayan coastal resort of Punta del Este in 1986. It ended in 1994 with the Marrakesh Agreement, which established the World Trade Organization (WTO). Comments on various aspects of the Uruguay Round appear in the third narrative in this book.

15. Speech by Ambassador Ronaldo Sardenberg in a meeting of the UN Security Council, November 11, 1993. His cautionary words were also fully applicable to Iraq, as I myself saw from 1995 onward.

16. Richard Falk, who from 2008 to 2014 was the special rapporteur of the UN Human Rights Council on the situation in the occupied Palestinian territories, has stated that the measures adopted against Iraq at the end of the Gulf War represented "the most punitive peace imposed upon a defeated country since the burdens accepted by Germany in the Treaty of

Versailles after the First World War." According to Falk, in the decade following the Gulf War as many as 700,000 Iraqi civilians died because of the sanctions. See his article "The New World Order?" (2014) in his blog *Global Justice in the 21st Century*.

17. The conclusions from the work can be found in the report *Informal Open-Ended Working Group on an Agenda for Peace: Subgroup on the Question of United Nations Imposed Sanctions* (July 1996).

18. The United Nations Special Commission (UNSCOM) was established in 1991 by Security Council Resolution 687, with the aim of ensuring Iraq fulfilled its obligations to eliminate its arsenal of chemical and biological weapons, and to cooperate with the International Atomic Energy Agency in eliminating nuclear weapons. In 1999 it was replaced by the United Nations Monitoring, Verification and Inspection Commission (UNMOVIC).

19. "Benign unipolarity" is a term I have often used to describe the functioning of the collective security system in the period immediately after the end of the Cold War. The beneficiaries of this system, namely the US, preferred to refer to the supposed "assertive multilateralism" of the "new world order." Richard Falk, in his aforementioned article, makes some interesting comments in that regard.

20. Ambassador Bill Richardson came to Brasilia on February 5, 1998, to explain the US position on Iraq's allegedly serious violations of its obligations under the Security Council resolutions. Richardson said the US was contemplating the possibility of using armed force. The statement issued by Itamaraty the next day, though reaffirming Brazil's preference for a peaceful response, said that "given the gravity of the situation and the provisions of the United Nations Charter, the Brazilian government believes that all options remain on the table." This was interpreted as acceptance, in principle, of the use of force, and provoked much comment in the Brazilian media.

21. Hisashi Owada, a career diplomat, was the father-in-law of the Crown Prince of Japan and would later be a judge in the International Court of Justice.

22. S/RES/687 (1991). The last paragraph reads: "[The Security Council] decides to remain seized of the matter and to take such steps as may be required for the implementation of the present resolution and to secure peace and security in the area."

23. Apart from in exceptional situations, the issues to be decided upon by the Security Council are first discussed by its members in a smaller room, away from the media and the other members of the UN. These discussions, which aim to arrive at a decision by consensus (although that is not always possible), are the so-called "informal consultations."

24. S/RES/1154 (1998).

25. The Security Council's decision is set out in the document S/1999/100. My report, with annexes, was incorporated into the document S/1999/356.

26. In his book *The New Asian Hemisphere: The Irresistible Shift of Global Power to the East* (Public Affairs, 2009), the Singaporean diplomat and academic Kishore Mahbubani comments on the circumstances of my departure from New York. He refers to US pressure to accelerate my departure and a conversation in which French president Jacques Chirac urged Brazilian president Fernando Henrique Cardoso to keep me in my post. Although I do not doubt Mahbubani's account, I should mention that I had no knowledge of these events at the time.

27. On the impact of the sanctions on the Iraqi population, see Hans von Sponeck's *A Different Kind of War: The UN Sanctions Regime in Iraq* (Berghahn, 2006). At the author's request I wrote the preface.

28. UNMOVIC was established by UN Security Council Resolution 1284 (1999).

29. Blix, Hans. *Disarming Iraq* (Pantheon, 2004).

30. I dealt with this issue in greater detail in an article I wrote for the Brazilian newspaper *Folha de São Paulo* on September 25, 2002: "*Guerra contra o Iraque e evitável.*" A more comprehensive analysis can be found in Gisela Padovan's *Diplomacia e o uso da força: os panéis do Iraque* (FUNAG, 2010).

31. The WTO Ministerial Conference in Seattle was supposed to launch a new round of trade negotiations (the "Millennium Round"). The attempt ended in failure in the midst of riots in the streets and discord among the delegations.

32. Entitled "The Incompatibility between Democracy and Racism," this Brazilian project was adopted by the UN Commission on Human Rights as Resolution 2000/40. Though the US and the other developed countries initially resisted its adoption, it was eventually approved by consensus.

33. See note 30.

34. Formal relations between Brazil and Palestine date back to 1975, when the Palestine Liberation Organization was authorized to appoint a representative in Brasilia, using the premises of the Arab League mission to Brazil. In 1993, Brazil agreed to the opening of a Palestinian Special Delegation, with diplomatic status similar to that of the representatives of international organizations. This decision was formally conveyed to the head of the PLO political department, Farouk Kaddoumi, on November 18 of that year. In 1998, our diplomatic treatment of the delegation was made equivalent to that of a foreign embassy.

35. Brazil, like many other countries, does not recognize Jerusalem as the capital of the State of Israel. Therefore, when referring in this book to the headquarters of the Israeli government, I mean Tel Aviv.

36. Embrafilme was a state company, linked to the Ministry of Education and Culture, which existed to promote Brazilian cinema. I was its CEO from 1979 to 1982, when the military dictatorship was gradually beginning to relax its grip on the country. Nevertheless, I was forced to resign for having supported the production of a movie (*Pra frente, Brasil*) that dealt with torture.

37. Having been foreign minister under Itamar Franco (1993–1994), I had direct experience of this from the process of trying to accommodate Mexico's membership of NAFTA to the clauses of the Treaty of Montevideo, which created the Latin American Integration Association (ALADI).

38. The Headquarters Agreement between Brazil and the Arab League, signed on April 23, 2007, was enacted by Decree 6,733 of January 12, 2009. This made possible the physical reopening of the Arab League mission in Brasilia.

39. A Lebanese political party associated with the Shia community. It was founded in 1974.

40. Duhalde would also be part of the Brazilian delegation during the state visit to India in January 2004. The presence of the former Argentine president alongside Brazil's head of state was an eloquent demonstration of the importance Brazil attributed to including South American integration in the broader strategic movements of our diplomacy.

41. A/RES/58/23, adopted by the General Assembly on December 3, 2003, coincidentally also the day of the official dinner in Damascus.

42. As a member of the Security Council from 2004–05, Brazil stated its position on the treatment that should be applied to Syria in response to those criticisms and condemnations. Brazil abstained, for example, on Resolution 1559 (2004), which among other things called for the withdrawal of "foreign and remaining troops" from Lebanon. It was an obvious allusion to the Syrian security forces. Nevertheless, as will become clear later in this narrative, Brazil stood in favor of full compliance with the resolution.

43. President Lula referred to the initiative, and to Syria's endorsement of it, in a speech during the gala dinner at the presidential palace in Damascus on December 3, 2003: "I am convinced we must use our joint voice, our potential as consumers and as public opinion, to make ourselves heard by the richest countries. . . . I am grateful for the support . . . for the proposal to hold the Summit of South American-Arab Countries in Brazil in 2004." In fact, of course, the summit would take place in May 2005.

44. The "Arab Peace Initiative" was proposed by Saudi Arabia and endorsed at a meeting of the Arab League in March 2002. In essence it was an attempt to normalize relations between the Arab countries and Israel, based on Israel's withdrawal from the occupied territories, a "just solution" to the Palestinian refugee problem, and Israeli acceptance of the creation of a Palestinian state. In 2003, the so-called "Road Map" was proposed by the Quartet (the UN Secretariat, the United States, Russia, and the European Union), aiming at the resumption of the dialogue between Israel and Palestine. According to the Road Map's original timeframe, the priority in the months of January–June 2003 would be a ceasefire between the two sides; and from June–December the political negotiations would be intensified with a view to staging a

peace conference between Israel and the Arab countries in 2004 or 2005, at which the Palestinian state would be formally established.

45. Nabil Shaath was foreign minister and later deputy prime minister of the Palestinian Authority, and also a member of the Fatah Central Committee.

46. The tent was erected in Paris when Gaddafi made an official visit there in December 2007.

47. In this context, as in several other places in the book (particularly the narrative on the Doha Round), G20 refers to the bloc of developing countries in the WTO trade negotiations.

48. A Brazilian conglomerate—currently the third biggest aircraft manufacturer in the world.

49. The Caribbean Community (CARICOM) is made up of fifteen countries, most of them former British colonies. It was established in 1973 with the aim of promoting economic integration among its members.

50. Resolution 1559, adopted by the Security Council on September 2, 2004, was sponsored by the United States and France. It demanded the restoration of Lebanese sovereignty over its territory and, in reference to Israel and Syria, the withdrawal of foreign forces. The resolution also called for "free and fair" elections to be held.

51. Jenkins, Roy. *Churchill* (Macmillan, 2001).

52. Not to be confused with the G20 of developing nations in the WTO negotiations.

53. The "World Leaders' Meeting on Action against Hunger and Poverty"—an initiative shared with presidents Jacques Chirac of France and Ricardo Lagos of Chile, and Prime Minister José Luis Rodríguez Zapatero of Spain—took place on September 18, 2004, on the sidelines of the UN General Assembly. About fifty heads of state and government attended. With such a large number of leaders and delegates crammed into the room, I happened to overhear a French diplomat say to a colleague: "*Le Brésil embrasse le monde.*"

54. Like the G20, the G90 emerged at the Cancún WTO Ministerial Conference in September 2003, with the objective of facilitating coordination among developing countries. Its members include countries from the African Union, the so-called ACP (Africa, Caribbean and Pacific), and the Least Developed Countries. See also the narrative on the Doha Round.

55. Vieira de Mello, a Brazilian, had a long and illustrious career as a United Nations diplomat, in positions including high commissioner for human rights. In August 2003, while serving as UN representative in Baghdad after the invasion of Iraq, he was killed in a bomb attack.

56. The Framework Agreement on Economic Cooperation between Mercosur and the Gulf Cooperation Council (GCC) was signed on May 10, 2005. The GCC is comprised of Saudi Arabia, Bahrain, Qatar, the United Arab Emirates, Kuwait, and Oman.

57. Qatar opened its embassy in Brasilia in January 1997. However, given what turned out to be the lack of reciprocity on the part of the Brazilian government, it closed in 1999. Brazil would finally establish an embassy in Doha on May 8, 2005, two months after my visit to Qatar and a few days before the summit. Qatar reciprocated the gesture in 2007.

58. The circumstances leading to my appointment as foreign minister in the Itamar Franco government are worthy of a chapter by Machado de Assis. The person chosen by Itamar to succeed Fernando Henrique Cardoso as foreign minister was José Aparecido de Oliveira. He, in turn, appointed me to the post of Itamaraty secretary-general. I came back to Brazil with the intention of spending a week receiving instructions from the new minister and consulting with the outgoing secretary-general. However, a bout of diverticulitis prevented me from returning to Geneva for the usual farewell party. As José Aparecido himself was ill for a long time, it is possible to reflect that the developments related to his replacement might have turned out differently if I had not been unable to leave Brazil.

59. In some of the proposals for UNSC reform it was envisaged that Africa would have two permanent seats, but there was an implicit assumption that both of those new permanent members would come from sub-Saharan Africa.

60. The Sykes-Picot Agreement, which owes its name to the negotiators Sir Mark Sykes of Britain and François Georges-Picot of France, was signed in May 1916. Initially kept secret, the agreement basically divided certain Arab regions of the collapsing Ottoman Empire into

spheres of either British or French influence. These provisions took effect at the end of the First World War.

61. In 2003, UN secretary-general Kofi Annan convened a commission of sixteen experts, the High-Level Panel on Threats, Challenges and Change. In December 2004 the panel submitted the report *A More Secure World: A Shared Responsibility*, which identified the principal challenges that needed to be faced. For Security Council reform there were two options: Option A, consisting of six new permanent seats and three non-permanent seats with two-year terms; and Option B, in which there would be no new permanent seats but instead a new category of eight seats with four-year terms (with the possibility of re-election) and one seat with a two-year term (no re-election). In both cases the Security Council would have a total of 24 members.

62. The G4, composed of Brazil, India, Japan, and Germany, was created to discuss UN Security Council reform. The four members are all candidates for a permanent seat.

63. *Dey* was the title given to the governors of the Regency of Algiers during the era of Ottoman rule.

64. In a sense, this gap was filled by the creation of the Peacebuilding Commission (PBC) in 2005. Brazil had been concerned about the issue for some time. During our 1998–99 term as a non-permanent member of the Security Council, inspired by Article 65 of the UN Charter, which recommends coordination between the Security Council and the Economic and Social Council (ECOSOC), I proposed the creation a mechanism for this purpose. This concern was subsequently shared by the High-Level Panel and resulted in the creation of the PBC.

65. Dignity (*karama*) was very much at the center of the revolts of the Arab Spring, the initial spark for which was the suicide of a Tunisian vegetable seller, Mohamed Bouazizi.

66. "13.1 In order to ensure the follow-up to the decisions contained in this Declaration, [the Heads of State and Government of the South American and Arab Countries] agree that:

The Second Summit of South American and Arab Countries will take place in Morocco, in the second quarter of 2008;

The next meeting of Ministers of Foreign Affairs of South American and Arab Countries will be held in Buenos Aires, Argentina, in 2007;

Extraordinary meetings of Ministers of Foreign Affairs may be convened, as necessary;

A meeting of High-Level Officials of Ministries of Foreign Affairs will take place in November 2005 at the Headquarters of the Arab League, in Cairo." As is usually the case, the dates and locations were later changed.

67. It is interesting to note that in the interregnum between the fall of Mubarak and the election of Morsi, South American personalities were invited to participate in forums in Egypt with the specific purpose of conveying our own experience of democratic transition. One example was the Cairo International Democratic Transitions Forum on June 5, 2011, which I attended as a keynote speaker alongside President Michelle Bachelet of Chile. It is worth reproducing the words of Prime Minister Essam Sharaf of Egypt during the opening ceremony: "We look forward to hearing the contributions of participants in this distinguished forum. While the details of democratic transitions will differ from one country and one historical moment to another, there are similarities and lessons learned which can guide us."

68. On that particular point, however, nothing was more eloquent than the female president of Chile, Michelle Bachelet, speaking on behalf of the South American countries at the second ASPA summit in Qatar on March 31, 2009.

69. Jalal Talabani, the Iraqi president from April 2005 to July 2014, is also one of the country's main Kurdish leaders, and the founder of the Patriotic Union of Kurdistan (PUK) party. Quite apart from its political aspects, the ASPA summit presented us with numerous issues in terms of logistics, protocol and security. With regard to the latter, I breathed a sigh of relief when informed that the plane carrying Talabani had departed safely.

70. Cantanhêde, Eliane. "*Volta ao mundo*," *Folha de São Paulo*, May 15, 2005. Among other comments that went against the grain of most media coverage, she wrote: "The Lula government is systematically criticized for not pursuing the same old economic policy, for a lack of political coordination, and for inefficiency in dealing with social issues. But in foreign policy, whether or not you like the paths being taken, the government cannot be accused of sameness, a lack of coordination, or inefficiency. On the contrary, in its foreign policy there is

boldness and a degree of coordination that existed neither during previous governments nor in other areas of this administration."

71. A photo capturing this moment of ecumenical religious devotion was published by the Brazilian newspaper *Valor Econômico*, accompanying an article about Rabbi Sobel's rather eventful past.

72. The "Philadelphia Route," also known as the "Philadelphia Corridor," refers to a strip of land, fourteen kilometers in length, located between the territories occupied by Israel and Egypt. It was established in 1979 in order to control the movement of people between Egypt and the Gaza Strip. The area was controlled by Israel until 2005, when it was handed over to the Palestinian National Authority. Tensions in the area increased when Hamas took control of Gaza in 2007.

73. The same cannot be said of his attitude toward Iran, as would be seen years later.

74. Fouad Siniora was finance minister under Rafic Hariri, and then prime minister from July 2005 to November 2009.

75. Brazil's exports to the member countries of the Gulf Cooperation Council grew from $2.4 billion USD in 2005 to $6.3 billion in 2010.

76. An example of the involvement of the academic world was the trilingual edition—in Portuguese, Spanish and Arabic—of the book *Deleite do estrangeiro em tudo o que é espantoso e maravilhoso*, which contains descriptions by an Iraqi imam, Al-Baghdadi, of a journey he made to Brazil in the nineteenth century. It was published in Brazil by the Fundação Biblioteca Nacional. The project, organized by Daniel Farah, inaugurated Bibliaspa, an academic initiative launched during the summit. The book was reprinted in 2009 in Brazil, Algeria, and Venezuela.

77. In a press release on August 17, 2006, with about one hundred Brazilians still to be repatriated, Itamaraty stated that 2,950 of our compatriots had been successfully evacuated.

78. In addition to providing logistical support, the Turkish authorities were also cooperative in assisting Brazilians, and above all their Lebanese relatives, in situations involving documentation. Due to a mutual exemption agreement our nationals were able to enter Turkey without a visa. But the same was not true of the non-Brazilian members of their families. In dealing with them, however, Turkey showed goodwill and indeed great flexibility. An especially kind gesture on Gül's part was to put at my disposal a diplomat from his office—none other than Murat Esenli, who was married to my daughter Anita and is the father of my two grandchildren, Yasemin and Omar.

79. Although it does not give a detailed description of the kind of suffering this woman and her young children would have endured, a quote from the book that earned writer Anthony Shadid the Pulitzer Prize does give an idea of a similar situation. Describing people sheltering in the ruins of a bombed hospital, Shadid writes: "'Oh sir!' cried the sexagenarian Saadeh Awada, jumping up from the shredded cushion. 'May God stop the bombs!' Her piercing screams made the children cry louder, with the heat [from the explosions] seemingly getting closer." Shadid, Anthony. *House of Stone* (Houghton Mifflin Harcourt, 2012).

80. The decision by President Evo Morales to nationalize the exploration of gas gave rise to protracted discussions between Brasilia and La Paz, with the opposition parties in Congress and much of the media accusing the Brazilian government of being "too soft" on our neighbor.

81. Brazil's diplomatic academy, in Brasilia.

82. Itamaraty issued several press releases about the escalation of the conflict. On July 12 and 13, the Brazilian government expressed "vehement" condemnation of "the attacks carried out by the Lebanese movement Hezbollah against areas in the north of Israel," and added: "The attack perpetrated by the Israeli forces . . . constituted a disproportionate reaction and has led to the loss of innocent lives among the civilian population. Brazil reiterates its opposition to acts of reprisal that only contribute to worsening the delicate situation in the region."

83. In addition to the aforementioned conversations, I spoke on the phone with my counterparts in France (Philippe Douste-Blazy), the UK (Margaret Beckett), and Lebanon (Fawzi Salloukh).

84. In addition to the efforts to assist our compatriots in Lebanon, there were two other cases involving Brazilians abroad that received a great deal of media coverage: the death of Jean Charles de Menezes in the United Kingdom, and the kidnapping of João José Vasconcellos

Junior in Iraq. In June 2007, Itamaraty created the General Sub-Secretariat for Brazilian Communities Abroad (SGEB). A series of "Brazilians Abroad" conferences was initiated, and a Council of Brazilian Representatives Abroad (CRBE) established.

85. For a vivid description of the destruction carried out by the Israelis in the final days of the conflict, see Anthony Shadid's *House of Stone* (Houghton Mifflin Harcourt, 2012). Shadid's book was given to me by an ex-colleague, the diplomat/academic Filipe Nasser.

86. I later described this episode when I went to meet representatives of Brazil's Lebanese community at the Monte Líbano club in São Paulo on September 26. I said that I had taken the Lebanese minister's words to mean "Brazil is part of Lebanon and Lebanon is part of Brazil." Without realizing it at the time, I came very close to quoting the great Brazilian writer Milton Hatoum, who once said: "Lebanon is very Brazilian and Brazil is very Arab." Perhaps that was never truer than during the summer of 2006.

87. The Shebaa Farms is a small strip of land on the Syria-Lebanon border in the region of the Israeli-occupied Golan Heights. All three countries claim ownership. UNSC Resolution 1701 called for Lebanon's international borders to be delineated "especially in those areas where the border is disputed or uncertain," with specific reference to the Shebaa Farms.

88. In my speech to that conference, which was chaired by Jacques Chirac, I reiterated our unconditional support for Resolution 1701 and expressed appreciation for the efforts by the prime minister to protect the multi-faith identity of the Lebanese state. I took the opportunity to recall President Lula's suggestion during the 2006 UN General Assembly that there should be an international conference, with the participation of some countries from outside the region, to discuss the resumption of the Middle East peace process.

89. One example was on January 23, 2007, the day I left for the International Donor Conference for Lebanon in Paris. I received a call from Lebanese prime minister Fouad Siniora, who was worried about the strong opposition he was facing from Hezbollah (which was allied, paradoxically, with right-wing Christian forces). The day before, coincidentally or otherwise, President Lula had received a visit from an envoy of the Syrian president, keen to put an end to his country's isolation.

90. In a press release dated September 21, 2007, Itamaraty stated that "the National Committee for Refugees decided in May 2007 to resettle in Brazil a group of Palestinian refugees from the Ruweished camp in Jordan, about 70 kilometers from the border with Iraq, where they had been living since 2003." A total of 117 refugees were resettled in Brazil.

91. In January 2006, Hamas won the parliamentary elections in Palestine. A coalition government of Hamas and Fatah was created in March 2007, but in June that year the conflicts in Gaza intensified and the coalition split. Since then, Hamas has been in control in Gaza. At the time of writing there are renewed efforts to form a coalition Palestinian government, in the face of strong opposition from Israel.

92. Iglesias and I agreed that the situation between the two countries was critical, to the extent that even an armed conflict was possible, and that perhaps the only way to alleviate the tension would be for Fidel Castro to intervene and talk to Chávez. I do not know if Iglesias took any practical measures. For my part, very soon after returning from the tour of the Arab countries, when I was in Buenos Aires for the meeting of foreign ministers in preparation for the second ASPA summit, I spoke on the phone with the foreign minister of Cuba, Felipe Pérez Roque, who fully understood my purpose in contacting him and said he would take action. Over the following weeks there would be a "de-escalation" of the crisis.

93. Despite our close relationship with the PNA, we did not reject a dialogue with Hamas. Our representative in Ramallah, Arnaldo Carrilho, went to Gaza to meet Ismail Hanyieh, the Hamas prime minister.

94. In the first fortnight of January 2008, President Bush visited the Middle East to follow up on the conclusions from the Annapolis Conference. He met, among others, the leaders of Israel, Ehud Olmert, and the Palestinian Authority, Mahmoud Abbas.

95. The Saudi Arabian cultural events in Brazil would continue, in fact. Recently, when writing this narrative, I was pleasantly surprised to read an article in *O Globo* by Rasheed Abou-Alsamh about an event in São Paulo entitled "Saudi Arabia Cultural Days," organized by the kingdom's Ministry of Culture and Information.

96. According to Frank Jacobs, in an article entitled "Winston's Hiccup" published in the *New York Times* (March 6, 2012): "In his later years, [Churchill] liked to boast that in 1921 [when serving as secretary of state for the colonies] he created the British mandate of Trans-Jordan, the first incarnation of what still is the Kingdom of Jordan, 'with the stroke of a pen, one Sunday afternoon in Cairo.'"

97. King Abdullah II would make a state visit to Brazil in October 2008.

98. In December 2010, Mercosur signed a framework agreement with Palestine, followed a year later by a free-trade agreement. Although of greater symbolic than practical value, these agreements would nevertheless serve, among other things, to "rebalance" the bloc's relationship with the region.

99. Tzipi Livni was Israel's foreign minister from 2006 to 2009. Her father, Eitan Livni, was a leader of the anti-British armed movement Irgun, responsible for attacks including the famous bombing of the King David Hotel, which caused the deaths of several civilians. Eitan Livni was tried and sentenced to fifteen years in prison by the British authorities. Until 1947, Irgun was considered a terrorist organization.

100. On November 29, 1947, the United Nations General Assembly, in a session chaired by the Brazilian Oswaldo Aranha, adopted Resolution 181, setting out the Partition Plan for Palestine. On May 14, 1948, David Ben-Gurion, the leader of the Zionist movement, unilaterally declared the existence of the State of Israel.

101. Olmert was referring, as Bashar al-Assad had done, to the understandings between the governments of Israel and Syria in 1999 and 2000, under the auspices of President Bill Clinton, which ultimately didn't come to fruition.

102. The Brasilia Declaration foresaw that the second summit would take place in Morocco in 2008. But after some procrastination, for reasons I am still unaware of, Rabat decided not to host the event.

103. Salah al-Bashir was in Brasilia on July 15 and 16. The visit was marked by an emphasis on bilateral issues and took place only a fortnight after the signing of a framework agreement on free trade between Mercosur and Jordan. The visit to Brazil of King Abdullah II, on October23 and 24, was the first by a Jordanian head of state. Very soon after the king's visit, Palestinian foreign minister Riyad al-Maliki arrived. We discussed, among other issues, new ways to achieve greater Brazilian engagement in the peace dialogue and in socio-economic development initiatives in the Palestinian territories.

104. My period as foreign minister saw important exchanges of visits and meetings between Brazilian officials and those of Algeria, Morocco and Tunisia. In February 2006, President Lula reciprocated the state visit Bouteflika had made to Brazil in 2005. Also in 2006, Algerian foreign minister Mohammed Bedjaoui visited Brazil for the second meeting of the Brazil-Algeria Joint Commission. The commission had its third meeting in 2010, with the visit to Brazil of foreign minister Mourad Medelci. The foreign minister of Morocco, Mohammed Benaissa, was in Brazil in April 2004. In November of the same year, King Mohammed VI made an official visit. I went to Morocco in 2005; Benaissa returned to Brazil in 2006 and 2007; and I was in Morocco again in 2007, 2008, and 2009. I went to Tunisia in February 2005 as part of the tour in preparation for the ASPA summit. In January 2006, Brasilia hosted a meeting of the Brazil-Tunisia Joint Commission, with the participation of foreign minister Abdelwahab Abdallah. I went again to Tunisia in September 2009, and met one more time with my Tunisian counterpart when he came to Brazil in December of that year.

105. Nor would it prevent President Bouteflika from repeating the feat in 2014, shortly before this book was first published.

106. The framework agreement between Mercosur and Morocco was signed in 2004. The first round of negotiations took place in April 2008, slightly before the journey I describe above.

107. My successor as foreign minister, Antonio Patriota, further developed the idea of contact between the Israeli and Palestinian civil societies, making certain adjustments and introducing new elements. In July 2012, in Brasilia, he organized an initiative entitled "Side by side—building peace in the Middle East: the role of the diasporas." The event brought together Middle Eastern intellectuals and members of the Jewish and Arab communities in Brazil and

the other Mercosur countries, seeking ways to strengthen the dialogue between the two sides in the conflict.

108. In January 2006, following my trip to Tunisia in 2005 in the context of the preparations for the ASPA summit, the second meeting of the Brazil-Tunisia Joint Commission took place. It had been fifteen years since the first meeting, in 1991!

109. The situation between Israel and Gaza, under the administration of Hamas, was always tense. There was a truce in June, in exchange for promises from Israel about the relaxation of the blockade. Hamas suspended the attacks on Israeli territory it had been carrying out using Qassam rockets. On December 19, claiming that the crossings between Israel and Gaza had been closed, Hamas declared the truce to be over. On December 27 the Israel Defense Forces began large-scale retaliation.

110. In a statement dated January 3, 2009, Itamaraty declared that "the Brazilian government deplores the Israeli military incursion by land into the Gaza Strip, which has the effect of further aggravating the Israeli-Palestinian conflict. Reiterating previous statements calling on both sides to refrain from acts of violence, the Brazilian government supports the efforts, including those of the UN Security Council, aimed at achieving an immediate ceasefire, so as to allow the prompt resumption of the peace process."

111. A few months later, Babacan also hosted the "Alliance of Civilizations" forum, at which he treated me with special distinction. But only in early 2010 would Brazil and Turkey begin to develop a true diplomatic partnership, with regard to the issue of the Iranian nuclear program.

112. Apart from the "immediate and durable ceasefire," the resolution called for the prompt withdrawal of Israeli forces from Gaza and the opening of humanitarian corridors for the transportation of essential supplies for the population. The resolution omitted to mention Chapter VII of the United Nations Charter—the reason for which, no doubt, is because the situation involved Israel.

113. Obama's inauguration took place just a few days later.

114. The presidential palace in Brasilia. Like "Itamaraty," which denotes the foreign ministry, the word "Planalto" is used in Brazil to refer either to the institution (of the presidency) or the building (the palace).

115. Mahmoud Abbas's term of office ended in January 2009 but was extended for another year, the argument being that this was permitted by certain constitutional provisions. Hamas took the view that Abbas's period in office should already have ended. Even after the end of the one-year extension, Abbas would remain in power.

116. As described in the first narrative in this book, I had visited Tehran in October/November 2008 in preparation for the visit to Brazil by President Ahmadinejad.

117. According to Article 1 of the Road Map, "The destination [of the negotiations] is a final and comprehensive settlement of the Israeli-Palestinian conflict by 2005." Among the elements of the final settlement were some of the most difficult questions, such as the status of Jerusalem and the refugees. (See: U.S. Department of State, Office of the Spokesman, April 30, 2003.) Even though the deadline of 2005 was obviously not met, the main substantive elements of the Road Map remained valid for the ongoing negotiations.

118. Ronald Venetiaan was president of Suriname from 2000 to 2010.

119. The third ASPA summit took place on October 2, 2012, after a delay caused by the political changes in the wake of the Arab Spring. An Itamaraty press release announcing President Dilma Rousseff's attendance at the summit highlighted the progress that had been made in terms of cooperation between the two regions in the cultural, scientific-technological, and economic-commercial fields. The text noted that: "South America and the Arab countries have an aggregate GDP of $5.4 trillion USD and an estimated total population of 750 million. Between 2005 and 2011, trade between the two regions grew by 101.7%, from $13.6 billion USD to $27.4 billion. During this period, total trade between Brazil and the Arab countries grew by 138.9%, from $10.5 billion USD to $25.1 billion."

120. The International Criminal Court was created by the Rome Statute in 1998, and began functioning in 2002. About 120 states signed and ratified the statute. The United States is among the non-members.

121. There is no space here for a detailed discussion of human rights. I addressed the issue in an article entitled "*O Brasil e os direitos humanos: em busca de uma agenda positiva*," published in the journal *Política Externa* (vol. 18) in 2009.
122. United Nations Educational, Scientific and Cultural Organization.
123. In the elections for the post of director-general of UNESCO, held in September 2009, the winner was the Bulgarian candidate Irina Bokova. The following month, Rio de Janeiro was chosen to host the 2016 Olympic Games, with massive support from the Arab countries.
124. I should point out that this narrative was written before the explosion of *Daesh* (Islamic State), whose especially radical form of Wahhabism has made the political and religious mosaic even more complex.
125. The Mecca Agreement between Hamas and Fatah was signed on February 8, 2007, when the parties agreed to cease their military clashes in Gaza and to form a government of national unity. Although warmly greeted at the time, the agreement was not fully implemented.
126. Manuel Zelaya, the constitutional president of Honduras, was deposed by a military coup on June 28, 2009. When he returned to Tegucigalpa he "took refuge" in the Brazilian embassy, as described in my book *Conversas com jovens diplomatas*.
127. Light for All (*Luz para Todos*) was a Brazilian government program aimed at providing electricity to every home in Brazil, even in very remote areas.
128. It was during the visit by President Peres that I became aware of a curious and significant linguistic quirk: the Israelis do not refer to the "West Bank" but instead use the biblical term "Judea and Samaria," a subtlety frequently lost in translation.
129. A large city in northeast Brazil, capital of the state of Bahia. Of all Brazil's major cities, Salvador has the highest proportion of people with African ancestry.
130. The term commonly used in Brazil to refer to natives of Rio de Janeiro.
131. On November 19, Itamaraty issued a statement criticizing the Israeli decision to expand the settlements in Gilo, East Jerusalem. The Brazilian government considered that "the decision by the Israeli government to expand the settlement situated in Palestinian territory violates United Nations Security Council resolutions on the issue, and is contrary to the obligations undertaken by Israel within the framework of the 'Road Map.'"
132. The Manaus meeting between the two presidents is referred to in the narrative on the Tehran Declaration.
133. During my time as foreign minister in the Lula government, there were three Brazilian ambassadors to Cairo: Celso Marcos Vieira de Souza, Elim Dutra, and Cesário Melantonio. Given the timing of my visits to the city, I had more contact with the first and the third. Cesário Melantonio had already been our representative in Tehran and Ankara, and was therefore becoming something of a specialist in the Middle East. Indeed, after my departure, he replaced Affonso Ouro-Preto as Brazil's special envoy to the region.
134. A meeting between the foreign ministers of the IBSA countries, along with the Indonesian foreign minister and also Riyad al-Maliki, took place on September 22 on the margins of the UN General Assembly.
135. This encounter is described in the narrative on the Tehran Declaration.
136. On April 15 the IBSA group issued a statement about the meeting with Al-Maliki. In addition to reiterating the previously expressed position in favor of a Palestinian state coexisting peacefully with Israel, the statement condemned the settlements policy in the occupied territories and East Jerusalem.
137. Scheduled for August, Netanyahu's visit to Brazil did not take place in the end. That was due both to internal factors in Israel and the fact that President Lula was nearing the end of his term of office, which obliged him to concentrate on domestic matters.
138. The first summit between Brazil and the Economic Community of West African States (ECOWAS) took place on July 3, 2010, in Cape Verde. The joint statement issued at the summit established a strategic dialogue between Brazil and the group.
139. I returned to Doha and Damascus in a private capacity in February 2011, and paid a working visit to Lebanon as defense minister during President Dilma Rousseff's first term of office.
140. S/RES/1929 (2010).
141. See the narrative on the Tehran Declaration.

142. On a curious personal note, I met fleetingly with Meshaal years later, when accepting an invitation from Ahmed Davutoglu, by then Turkey's prime minister, to attend a congress of his party, the AKP. Meshaal was also there. He embraced me as if we were old friends (or at least as if we knew each other), which made me think that perhaps he had followed some of my visits to Damascus on TV.

143. "The American Colony" was a settlement established in 1881 by members of a Christian utopian society. Now a hotel in East Jerusalem, it is still known by the same name.

144. In 2013—by which time she was the leader of another party, Hatnuah—Livni entered Netanyahu's coalition as justice minister, a role in which she was responsible for the negotiations with the PNA. But in 2015 she left the Israeli cabinet due to differences of opinion with Netanyahu over the peace process.

145. The fact that the Assad government was so anxious to avoid offending Ankara made it all the more surprising that, from mid-2011 onward, Turkey became such a militant supporter of the Syrian rebels.

146. The framework agreement to create a free-trade area between Mercosur and Syria was signed on December 16, 2010, in the southern Brazilian city of Foz de Iguaçu.

147. The government of Dilma Rousseff would maintain the same line in support of a Palestinian state. In November 2012 Brazil voted in favor of Resolution A/RES/67/19, which granted Palestine the status of Non-Member Observer State at the United Nations.

148. In late 2010 and early 2011, Argentina, Bolivia, Chile, Ecuador, Peru, Paraguay, and Uruguay all followed Brazil in recognizing the Palestinian state. By the time the first edition of this book was published, Colombia was the only South American country not to have done so.

149. Brazil's capacity to play the role of mediator or facilitator, which presupposes trust on all sides, was emphasized by Noam Chomsky in a speech to the UN Committee on the Exercise of the Inalienable Rights of the Palestinian People on October 14, 2014. Chomsky said that if the negotiations were to recommence, "they should be conducted by a neutral party, perhaps Brazil." See also note 70 in the narrative on the Tehran Declaration.

150. English translation completed in October 2016.

In January 2010, at the invitation of the Turkish foreign minister, Ahmet Davutoglu, I addressed a conference of Turkish ambassadors in Ankara. During our bilateral meeting, Davutoglu and I agreed to coordinate efforts to persuade Iran to accept the "swap agreement" in relation to its nuclear program, originally proposed by the P5+1. Photo credit: personal archives

In March 2010, Secretary of State Hillary Clinton made an official visit to Brazil. The main subject of our lengthy discussions was the Iranian nuclear program. This photo was taken when she paid a courtesy call on President Lula. Photo credit: Ricardo Stuckert

In preparation for what would become the Tehran Declaration, I made several visits to Iran. In late April 2010, I took with me a letter from President Lula in which he confirmed his visit to Tehran one month later. President Ahmadinejad was clearly very happy with the news. Photo credit: personal archives

On the eve of the signing of the Tehran Declaration, the Supreme Leader, Ali Khamenei (far right), received President Lula for a rather lengthy audience. This gesture was perceived as a "blessing" in relation to the Brazilian-Turkish efforts to find a peaceful solution to the issue of the Iranian nuclear program. Also in the photo are Manouchehr Mottaki (far left), Saeed Jalili (in the gray suit), and an attentive President Ahmadinejad, who remained silent throughout the meeting. Photo credit: Ricardo Stuckert

The secretary-general of the Arab League, Amr Moussa, was a staunch supporter of the idea of a summit of Arab and South American countries. This photo, in which I appear beside my wife Ana, was taken during the ceremony in Brasilia in which Moussa was awarded the Order of the Southern Cross. Photo credit: personal archives

The Summit of South American-Arab Countries (ASPA summit), in May 2005, brought together leaders from those two regions of the developing world. Besides political discussions, the summit also offered an opportunity for dialogue on cultural and economic matters. This photo shows the foreign ministers of Mercosur and the leading officials of the Gulf Cooperation Council (GCC) celebrating the signing of a framework agreement on trade. Photo credit: personal archives

Two weeks after the ASPA summit, I made an official visit to Israel. I had a substantive dialogue on Israeli-Palestinian relations with Prime Minister Ariel Sharon in the aftermath of the decision to withdraw Israeli settlers from Gaza. Photo credit: personal archives

The existence of a large Lebanese community in Brazil and the presence of a sizable number of Brazilians in Lebanon were important factors in the strengthening of Brazilian-Arab relations. This became more obvious during the conflict between Israel and Lebanon in 2006, when three thousand of our nationals had to be evacuated with the help of the Brazilian government. I visited Beirut, whose airport was functioning precariously, one day after the ceasefire. Photo credit: personal archives

Brazil also began to have a more proactive role in donor conferences in support of Lebanon, a fact illustrated by our participation in the conference convened by President Jacques Chirac of France. Photo credit: personal archives

During President George W. Bush's second term, the dialogue between Brazil and the United States on global issues gained strength. The Palestinian question constantly came up in my meetings with Secretary of State Condoleezza Rice. With Rice's support, Brazil was one of the few non-Arab developing countries to be invited to the Annapolis Conference on the Middle East. Photo credit: personal archives

In early 2008, following the Annapolis Conference, I visited several Arab countries with the objective of reinforcing Brazil's presence in the region. This photo shows King Abdullah al-Saud of Saudi Arabia receiving me in his "tent" in the desert. Photo credit: personal archives

During my visits to Israel, I enjoyed frank and open conversations with Shimon Peres (first when he was deputy prime minister, later when president). When he made a state visit to Brazil, Peres requested a private conversation with me in preparation for his meeting with President Lula. Photo credit: personal archives

My tours of the Middle East included several visits to Jordan. In addition to the dialogues with the Jordanian foreign ministers, King Abdullah II was also a frequent interlocutor. Photo credit: personal archives

In October 2015, five years after leaving the foreign ministry, I received the Palestinian Authority's highest civilian award, the Star of Jerusalem, from President Mahmoud Abbas. Cited among the reasons for the award were my role in strengthening the relations between Brazil and Palestine, my actions in favor of peace in the Middle East, and my "indefatigable" support for the Palestinian people in "their struggle for freedom and independence." Photo credit: Thaer Ghanayem/Palestinian National Authority

After the impasse at the WTO ministerial conference in Cancún in 2003, the Doha Round of multilateral trade negotiations gained positive momentum with the so-called "July Framework" (2004). Between July 2004 and June 2007, the nucleus of the negotiations was the G4 (composed of the US, the EU, Brazil, and India), which replaced the former Quad (US, EU, Canada, Japan). This new role for big developing economies was a direct consequence of the creation of the G20 of developing countries in Cancún. With me in this photo are, from left to right, Peter Mandelson, Kamal Nath, and Rob Portman. Photo credit: personal archives

In December 2005, a WTO ministerial conference took place in Hong Kong. The most important achievement was the establishment of a final date for the elimination of export subsidies in agriculture. This was made possible by the coordinated action involving almost all the developing countries that were WTO members, including the so-called emerging economies and the Least Developed Countries. Appearing in the photo, from left to right, are the ministers of Indonesia, India, Mauritius, Zambia, and Egypt, with Brazil at the center. Photo credit: personal archives

In June 2006, six months after the relatively successful ministerial conference in Hong Kong, Susan Schwab replaced Rob Portman as USTR. During President Bush's visit to Brazil in 2007, Lula said that Susan and I should be locked in a room until an agreement between Brazil and the US in relation to the Doha Round was reached. Photo credit: Marcello Casal Jr./ Agência Brasil

At the WTO ministerial conference in Geneva in July 2008, the trade talks collapsed. I was the first to leave the meeting room and speak to the press. On the spur of the moment, I dispelled illusions about an early resumption of the negotiations. I referred to some of the "crises" of the previous years (energy crisis, food crisis, etc.). "New crises will come," I said, adding that they would distract world leaders from the Doha Round. Two months later, the bankruptcy of Lehman Brothers unleashed a profound financial crisis. Photo credit: personal archives

In April 2010, on his way to a meeting of the Cairns Group (which I did not attend), WTO director-general Pascal Lamy made a brief visit to Brasilia to discuss the chances of resuming the multilateral trade negotiations. In this photo, taken in my office in the foreign ministry, Lamy appears between Roberto Azevêdo (then Brazil's ambassador to the WTO in Geneva) and me. Our informal attire attests the fact that our meeting took place on a Saturday morning. Four years later, Azevêdo would be elected to succeed Lamy. Photo credit: personal archives

The confidence that President Lula placed in me as his foreign minister was essential to Brazil's diplomatic initiatives during his two terms of office (2003–2010). In this photo, taken in Davos in 2007, we were making final adjustments to a speech he was due to deliver. During the actual speech, as was so often the case, the president probably added spontaneous comments of his own. Photo credit: Ricardo Stuckert

3. Doha: the Crucial Years

FROM GENEVA TO HONG KONG

By way of introduction

The subject that permeated almost all of my time as foreign minister in the Lula government, alongside that of South American integration, was the Doha Round, officially known as the Doha Development Agenda. There were various reasons for that. First, the negotiations initiated in 2001 under the auspices of the World Trade Organization (WTO) offered a preferable alternative to the pressures toward bilateral and regional negotiations—especially those in which one power exerted hegemony, as was the case, for example, with the United States in the Free Trade Area of the Americas (FTAA). For the Doha Round to fulfill its potential, however, it would be necessary to strengthen its development dimension and give due emphasis to the issue of agricultural subsidies. When the Round was launched, the results obtained in the discussions on intellectual property and health showed that in dealing with trade issues there was scope for a shift toward an approach that would give greater prominence to the interests of developing countries. Although the Doha agenda included several aspects that caused Brazil concern, the power play in the multilateral forum of the WTO allowed for the formation of strategic coalitions such as the G20,[1] and tactical alliances with the main players such as those we entered into with the European Union and the United States, depending on the situation. By their very nature, those actions would not have been viable in a bilateral or regional context. The importance I attributed to the Doha Round did not only reflect a formal attachment to multilateralism on my part. I also saw the Round as offering an alternative to the consolidation of areas of political and economic influence. The concentration of power was incompatible with our vision of a multipolar world. After what I have referred to elsewhere as "the great failure of July 2008,"[2] however, the so-called "MTN" (multilateral trade negotiations) came to merit less attention than before, due to a loss of dynamism caused by the feeling that success was increasingly unlikely. Among Brazil's diplomatic activities, these negotiations were pushed into the background by other priorities such as the creation of UNASUR, the Tehran Declaration, and our involvement in the Middle East. I have also written about the Doha Round in other books.[3] In this narrative, to the extent that my memory and my notes allow, I will attempt to describe the advances and retreats that took place after 2004. I will also try to give an idea of the complex ways in which the diplomatic work of ministers and ambassadors interconnected with the conversations between presidents and prime ministers that took place bilaterally and at forums such as the G8 summits (at which the major developing countries were also represented).

"A defeat is a defeat"

Brazil's proactive role at the Cancún Ministerial Conference in 2003 attracted a lot of attention. I gave several interviews to the international media, including quite a long one to the BBC in which my interviewer was Clare Short, a former minister in the British government who before her resignation had been, one might say, a "progressive voice" in Tony Blair's cabinet due to her disapproval of the Iraq invasion. An article published in the *Financial Times* at the start of the conference illustrates the perception of the pivotal role Brazil played. Entitled "From Amorim to Zoellick: Who's Who in Cancún," the piece quoted four individuals: those representing the United States, the European Union, India, and Brazil. Our central role became even more obvious during the conference, and was increasingly acknowledged, albeit grudgingly, by the other participants. The process that led to the "July Framework"[4] helped to consolidate our prominent position. The role of Brazil and the G20 in achieving that positive outcome was acknowledged publicly by United States Trade Representative (USTR) Robert Zoellick, with whom I had engaged in some tough discussions in Cancún, and EU trade commissioner Pascal Lamy. In a bilateral conversation in Cancún, New Zealand's[5] representative, Tim Groser, described the G20 as "a masterpiece of economic diplomacy." The years that have passed since then, and the obstacles that have still not been overcome, might give the impression that the understanding reached in July 2004 was not particularly important, but at the time it was celebrated both by the participants and, in general, the media. More than a year later, when I was in the office of Bob Zoellick, who by then had become US deputy secretary of state, he pointed with satisfaction to a shelf where there was a photo from the meeting of the Trade Negotiations

Committee (TNC) during which the July Framework had been formally agreed: it showed the two of us smiling in celebration at the achievement, alongside the EU trade commissioner and India's trade minister.

Throughout 2005, and indeed until July 2007 in Potsdam, the nucleus of the Doha Round discussions was the G4, a group composed of Brazil, India, the United States, and the European Union. Prior to that, the negotiations had been centered on a grouping called the "Five Interested Parties" (FIPS), which led the discussions culminating in the July Framework. In the WTO, informal groups tend to be created to deal with specific problems. Very often they break up as soon as the necessary work has been completed, although in some cases they are later revived. The composition of the FIPS, with the participation of Australia, had to do with the fact that the discussions were centered on agriculture, seen as the main stumbling block for the progress of the Doha Round as a whole. With the agricultural hurdle having been overcome, at least temporarily, the composition of the core group had to be adjusted so as to reflect, in a more balanced way, the forces at play. This explains the emergence of the G4, with two participants from the developed world and two developing countries. Occasionally the G4 would meet in an expanded format, becoming a G6 with the inclusion of Australia, the leader of the Cairns Group,[6] and Japan,[7] one of the world's major economies. I should note at this point that until the Geneva meeting in July 2008, China kept a relatively low profile, whether due to pragmatism, based on its own specific interests, or caution, due to the country only recently having become a member of the WTO. That did not prevent China from joining the G20 or "sponsoring" a mini-ministerial meeting (in Dalian), however.

In the months that followed the July Framework, the attentions of the WTO members turned to another topic, connected only indirectly with the negotiations: the process of choosing a new director-general to replace, in 2005, Supachai Panitchpakdi of Thailand. Three candidates quickly came forward: Pascal Lamy of France, Carlos Pérez del Castillo of Uruguay, and the foreign minister of Mauritius, Jaya Krishna Cuttaree, who had the formal (but not effective) support of the African Union. Lamy, as well as enjoying the powerful backing of the European bloc, also had the endorsement of Washington as a result of his previous close cooperation with the USTR.[8] Pérez del Castillo had been president of the WTO General Council in the period preceding Cancún, a role in which he had been responsible for presenting the document on which, theoretically, the negotiations at the conference were going to be based. The rejection of that document was one of the processes through which the G20 came together as a group, Castillo having been excessively lenient toward the defensive interests of the US and the EU in the agricultural sector. The nominal African candidate, meanwhile, was not a strong contender. In this context, Brazil came up with an alternative. The name of Luiz Felipe de Seixas Corrêa, our permanent representative to international organizations in Geneva, was a natural choice from our perspective. He had been directly involved in the preparations for Cancún (together with Itamaraty's undersecretary for economic affairs, Clodoaldo Hugueney) and had therefore contributed to the creation of the G20. I saw the presentation of a Brazilian candidate as an opportunity to reaffirm the positions we had advocated as coordinators of the G20 in Cancún, and in the subsequent discussions. It seemed to me at the time that a Brazilian candidate would have the power to catalyze collective action on the part of the developing countries. The other South American candidate, Pérez del Castillo, had been tainted by an attitude widely seen, including by the members of the G20, as overly shaped by the interests of the rich countries. As for the Mauritian candidate, it seemed he did not even inspire enthusiasm among the African countries.

But my assessment, and that of my advisors, underestimated the difficulties that our late entrant into the race would face, especially in relation to the other Latin American. I also failed to take into account the lack of transparency that generally characterized the decisions of the WTO on such matters. In retrospect I am surprised by my own attitude at the time, which now I can only attribute to my incurable optimism. As permanent representative in Geneva in the period 1999–2001, I had witnessed all sorts of machinations in favor of the candidature of Mike Moore of New Zealand at the expense of the developing country candidate, Supachai Panitchpakdi of Thailand. After strong opposition from the countries supporting Supachai, which included Brazil, the new director-general's term of office, which was supposed to be four years, ended up being divided equally between the two candidates, who served for three years each. So, as they say, I should have known better. Another factor that led to the failure of the Brazilian candidature was connected with domestic politics. At almost exactly the same time as Seixas Corrêa was nominated for the WTO, the Brazilian government, driven by pressure from its political base, put forward the name of the economist João Sayad for the presidency of the Inter-American Development Bank (IDB). Sayad had excellent professional credentials and also enjoyed the support of the Workers' Party (PT), having previously been economic secretary at São Paulo city hall under PT mayor Marta Suplicy. Like Seixas Corrêa, Sayad also faced a strong Latin American rival, in this case Luis Alberto Moreno of Colombia, who had been his country's ambassador in Washington (a factor that counted in his favor from the very start). One of my aides recalls that in a conversation on the subject with President Lula, I said: "Even if we withdraw one of the two candidates, I don't know if the other can win. But if we don't give up on one, both are sure to lose." And that is exactly what happened. After a few months of a campaign in which, in addition to the efforts of Seixas himself and the Itamaraty diplomatic machine, I was personally involved, raising the issue whenever I could in bilateral meetings, our candidate's name was eliminated in the first round of consultations, before the final appointment was made. I knew in advance that this would happen, both from information I received from the WTO itself and from how the questions asked by the committee responsible for conducting the consultations were framed. Not taken into account, for example, was the fact that overall, according to most indications, Seixas was the second preference among WTO members, which indicated that he was regarded quite favorably even by those members whose first choice was one of the other candidates. I was not able to hide my disappointment. As I said to a Brazilian journalist: "A defeat is a defeat." But there was consolation in the fact that, throughout the campaign, we had been able to disseminate our ideas about the democratization of the WTO and the effective participation of developing countries in the negotiations. In an attempt to rationalize what had happened, I even depicted our bid as a kind of "anti-candidature," following the example of the Brazilian politician Ulysses Guimarães during Brazil's military dictatorship.[9] Our leadership role among developing countries and our prestige among WTO members suffered no ill effects, as demonstrated by the active role we maintained throughout the negotiation process.

"Agriculture is the engine"

In the months following the agreement of the July Framework, there were no further WTO activities at ministerial level. The political meetings only recommenced in early 2005. In January, as usual, the World Economic Forum in Davos was the stage for a meeting of ministers responsible for conducting their countries' trade negotiations, the organization of which had become something of an annual ritual for the Swiss hosts. The gathering, which included a lunch, was attended by about twenty ministers. Nothing of any great significance was said. Also in Davos, following a tradition dating back to Cancún, I chaired a meeting of the G20 ministers who were present. And Bob Zoellick, whose imminent departure from his USTR post had already been announced, invited a small number of countries to an informal meeting over coffee—I remember there was Australian trade minister Mark Vaile; Mandisi Mpahlwa of South Africa; a delegate from Hong Kong; the new EU trade commissioner, Peter Mandelson; and the WTO director-general, Supachai Panitchpakdi. Another regular participant in that kind of meeting was Singaporean trade minister George Yeo, who had chaired the agriculture group in Seattle, Doha, and Cancún. Yeo would later be promoted to foreign minister, becoming an important interlocutor not only in our bilateral relationship but also in the efforts to achieve a closer relationship between Mercosur and the Association of Southeast Asian Nations (ASEAN).[10] This get-together of ministers representing countries seen by our American host as having a "constructive" attitude took place at the Flüela hotel, and gave rise to a short-lived group of the same name. I remember that the group met for a second time in May, during the annual conference of the OECD (to which Brazil and other emerging countries were regularly invited), and that another meeting took place in Zurich in October, again convened by the US. That year the World Economic Forum also offered an opportunity for several bilaterals. The most important of them, from my point of view, was with Zoellick himself; we spoke mostly about the FTAA, which by then was in its death throes.[11] Strangely there is no mention in my notebook of a conversation with Peter Mandelson, who would become one of my principal interlocutors during the next four years: I imagine either that I failed to record it or, more likely, that our respective schedules did not give us an opportunity to meet.

In the July Framework we had established the main parameters for the agriculture negotiations, explicitly stating the need for the removal of export subsidies (and certain other support measures). We had also created rules for the so-called "blue box," a category that included subsidies that also distorted trade but, in the eyes of the WTO members, not sufficiently to justify their inclusion in the "amber box" of subsidies earmarked for a total ban.[12] The July Framework had also addressed, albeit not in much detail, the issue of access to agricultural markets. In this context, upon India's initiative, the issue of the "Special Safeguard Mechanism" (SSM)[13] for developing countries, and the idea of "special products" (SP), also featured. Now it was necessary to translate these parameters into quantifiable concepts that could serve as a basis for negotiations. In the WTO, these quantifiable concepts (or numbers), which precede the drawing up of the lists setting out each country's commitments ("schedules"), became known by the curious name of "modalities." In addition to the modalities in agriculture, it would also be necessary to make progress in other areas in which Brazil's positions were basically "defensive," such as NAMA (Non-Agricultural Market Access).[14] These two sets of themes, as well as the further opening of the markets for services (and also "trade facilitation," which had been among the so-called "Singapore issues"),[15] were the subject of ambitious presentations by the developed countries at the meeting organized by the Swiss in Davos. The plan was that the "modalities" regarding agriculture and NAMA should be agreed at the next WTO ministerial conference, due to take place in Hong Kong at the end of the year.

The next stop on the road to Hong Kong would be a "full mini-ministerial" (i.e. not just a brief meeting or a lunch, as had been the case in Davos) at a vacation resort on the coast of Kenya, close to Mombasa, a city mentioned by Camões in the *Lusíadas*. The ruins of a Portuguese fort continue to be the main tourist attraction in the city, which was once part of the Sultanate of Oman. The meeting would be the first of its kind since Montreal in 2003, shortly before Cancún. I was skeptical about its value, based on previous experiences in Tokyo, Sharm el-Sheikh, and Quebec, but other influential participants insisted it would be worthwhile. I remember, for example, that Zoellick (who would not be present in Mombasa) mentioned that the mini-ministerial meetings held before the Doha Ministerial Conference of 2001 had contributed to the "good result" achieved there. The Mombasa mini-ministerial was scheduled for March 3–4. But due to commitments in Montevideo, where I accompanied President Lula to the inauguration ceremony for President Tabaré Vázquez, and in Rio de Janeiro, where I attended a public event at which I was one of the recipients of an important prize awarded by the newspaper *O Globo*, it was already the early hours of March 3 before I left for Africa. Regarding the award ceremony, I wrote in my notebook as follows: "Ironically, in my case, the awards were presented by Miriam Leitão, one of the most assiduous critics of foreign policy under Lula, alongside her fellow columnist Ancelmo Gois. It is also curious that I received the award for having "made a difference" in the economic arena, given the amount of criticism we got from the business sector for our foreign policy, regarded as being Third Worldist, ideological, etc. Among the reasons given for my receipt of the prize were the disputes in the WTO, our positions in Cancún, the G20, South America, and—the biggest surprise of all—our successful efforts to change the course of the FTAA negotiations." Incidentally, the latter subject—despite the evidence of an insuperable impasse between Mercosur and the United States, underlined by the valedictory comments Zoellick had made to me in Davos[16] —continued to hover over us, as I learned in Montevideo when informed of a meeting that had just taken place between our representative to the FTAA negotiations, Adhemar Bahadian,[17] and Deputy USTR Peter Allgeier. Still, I left for Kenya in good spirits, boosted by my award, and even more so by the reasons given to justify it.

I flew to Africa in the president's reserve aircraft, an aging Boeing 737. After a refueling stop in Libreville, which I used as an opportunity for a brief bilateral with Gabon's interim foreign minister, I landed in Mombasa around midnight. My aide Antonio Simões was waiting for me at the airport. Upon arrival I received the good news of our victory in our WTO dispute with the US over cotton subsidies.[18] Besides the pleasure of victory, our success in this case demonstrated the value of the multilateral forum of the WTO for resolving trade disputes. As I have said on various occasions in interviews and during lectures to students at the Rio Branco Institute, the positive outcomes achieved on the issue of cotton with the US and sugar with the EU would not have been possible in the kind of dispute-resolution forum that might have been created under the FTAA, or in the context of a bi-regional EU-Mercosur agreement.

To reach the Kenyan resort, my aide and I climbed into an SUV and embarked on a journey that probably lasted only about an hour but seemed interminable. We drove along a poorly paved road bordered by the kind of makeshift homes that were common in the rural interior of Brazil half a century ago. At one point we had to cross an area of water on a small ferry (or perhaps that was on the way back, by a different route). The shacks with zinc sheeting for roofs, and the rudimentary roadside stores (some were no more than tents), provided stark evidence of poverty and deprivation. So too, in fact, did the condition of some of the buildings in which government bodies had their headquarters. Upon arrival, exhausted by the journey, I went straight to bed, pausing only to hang up the mosquito net that had been provided. I only managed to get to sleep shortly before dawn, however. In the morning I had coffee with Itamaraty's undersecretary for economic affairs, Hugueney, and our permanent representative in Geneva, Seixas Corrêa. I learned that the day before, Clodoaldo had been involved in a heated discussion with Mandelson about the glaring lack of balance between the Europeans' excessive demands in the area of services (and possibly also NAMA) and their meager offers with regard to agriculture. By the time I began my participation in the mini-ministerial, on the second day, tempers had cooled thanks to a conciliatory intervention by the Kenyan trade minister, Mukhisa Kituyi, who was coordinating the meeting. I limited myself to a brief intervention that was political rather than technical in nature, emphasizing that in accordance with its original mandate the Doha Round was supposed to have a "development dimension," and that therefore agriculture was of paramount importance. This was the occasion on which I first referred to the agriculture negotiations as the "engine" of the Round. Later I wrote in my notebook that I had "tried to shake up the excessively technical tone of the meeting, and to create a counterweight to the unbearable condescension of the Europeans." I received positive feedback from some ministers and delegates, including those from Zambia, Bangladesh, and China. And the next day in Nairobi, during the bilateral visit that followed the Mombasa meeting, Kituyi said in reference to my speech: "Brazil always expresses the interests of the developing countries in a more vigorous way. As for India and China, their voice is more muffled."

"Under pressure from Brazil, the European Union gave way . . ."

Apart from the not insignificant fact that it was an opportunity for the voices of the less developed countries (particularly those of Africa) to be heard, the results obtained in Kenya mainly concerned procedural issues. Major advances were never going to be made at a meeting where Washington was represented only by an interim USTR.[19] Nevertheless, as with previous mini-ministerials—and this perhaps had been Zoellick's point—the meeting provided a setting in which those with political responsibility for trade negotiations could engage with issues usually discussed only by their countries' permanent representatives in Geneva. Among the technicalities discussed was a somewhat esoteric issue that would be a focus of attention throughout the first half of 2005: the so-called AVEs. The acronym, which stands for "*ad valorem* equivalents," refers to the way in which specific tariffs (set according to the weight or other measurable characteristic of the goods in question) are converted into *ad valorem* tariffs. It was on the basis of the latter that the reductions to be agreed during the negotiations would be calculated. Again drawing on their inexhaustible creativity in inventing new acronyms and appellations, the negotiators at WTO headquarters, probably repeating an assessment by the European Commission[20] technicians, had identified the AVEs as a "gateway issue," which is to say an issue that constituted an entrance point into the negotiations on market access in the agriculture modality. As is so often the case, lurking behind the technical complexities were economic interests. The European Commission, always imaginative in discovering new forms of protectionism, came up with a method of calculation that would substantially reduce the concessions it would make during the negotiations. I am unable to dissect the mathematical intricacies (nor could I do so at the time), but the purpose of the maneuver was very clear. In response, our own technicians in the G20 proposed an alternative formula, more favorable to our interests. Only at the meeting on the margins of the OECD[21] conference in Paris in May 2005 was the issue finally resolved, after a heated clash between Brazil and the European Union. That was the first of many vigorous discussions I would have with Peter Mandelson in his role as EU trade commissioner, but we would also have several productive dialogues. On the flight back to Brazil from Paris, I wrote: "The outcome of the meeting was satisfactory. Although the issue we discussed (AVEs) was to a large extent technical, we made a step forward that could contribute to unblocking the negotiations. . . . *Le Monde* says in a sub-heading [of an article it published on the subject of the meeting] that 'under pressure from Brazil, the European Union gave way and threw some ballast overboard.' Not bad." The *Economist*, on May 5, referred to the outcome as "progress, at last." In fact, when Mandelson and the EU agriculture commissioner, Mariann Fischer Boel, no longer had any arguments left, they resorted to the old ploy of saying they would have to go away and consult with the twenty-five member countries that had previously agreed with the European formula. At that moment the G20 again proved its worth, even through most of its representatives were not in the room. "And I'll have to consult with the members of the G20," I replied, "so I think we'll have to suspend the meeting," My threat (to some extent a bluff) made it possible for the two sides to arrive at a compromise formula and hence draw this *vexata quaestio* to a close. Returning to the subject of Mombasa, I should mention that despite the frank exchange of views between Mandelson and my colleague on the first day, and the obvious divergences on important aspects of the Round, I was able to have a formal meeting with the EU trade commissioner that was very friendly in its tone and in which we agreed on the outlines of an agenda for another Mercosur-EU ministerial meeting. In fact the idea for the meeting came from Mandelson himself, who was obviously very keen to reach an agreement between the two blocs. He suggested that when the summit took place, both sides should return to the table with the "best offer" among those they had previously made—although what that was would be difficult to determine, given the informal and conditional way in which the offers had been presented on previous occasions. I very soon began to suspect that in fact this might be another crafty maneuver on the part of the European Commission technicians. One of them, Karl Falkenberg of Germany, was particularly well practiced in a wide range of artifices, often leaking information to the media or making statements that distorted the facts and put us in awkward situations. On government procurement, for example, he continually tried to change the terms of the understanding, even though I had already agreed them in principle with Pascal Lamy during his time as EU trade commissioner. The negotiations on government procurement were supposed to be limited to the issue of transparency, and therefore not include concessions on access. Nevertheless, I agreed with Mandelson's idea of a Mercosur-EU meeting. We even came up with a possible date, May 2, which the Europeans would confirm with the *pro tempore* president of Mercosur, Paraguayan foreign minister Leila Rachid.

Allow me at this point to make a brief digression concerning the dynamic relationship between the multilateral Doha Round negotiations and the parallel bilateral or regional trade negotiations, in particular the discussions between Mercosur and the European Union. If I had ever had any doubts about that connection, something Pascal Lamy once said to me would have been sufficient to remove them. In early 2003, in Athens, during a meeting with Mercosur on the margins of a meeting between the EU and the Rio Group,[22] Lamy referred to the issue of market access for agricultural products. He used a graphic metaphor to tell me that any concessions the EU made in an agreement with Mercosur would have to be subtracted from Doha, and vice versa: "I only have one bank account," he said. Unlike what happened with the FTAA, whose death had already been announced but whose burial would prove to be a prolonged affair, the Mercosur-EU negotiations were still alive. In 2004, at a meeting in Brussels, there had been an agreement in principle on a mutually acceptable framework that eliminated from the negotiations complex and sensitive issues such as rules on investment, intellectual property, and access to government-procurement markets. In other words it had been possible, with less difficulty than in the FTAA, to limit the scope of the negotiations to issues that did not impact directly on our ability to draw up our own rules for important aspects of economic policy, thus preserving what is known in the jargon of the UN (especially the UNCTAD)[23] as "policy space." The differences between the two sides' demands and offers (whether in agriculture or in industrial goods and services) were nevertheless considerable, meaning there was no prospect of an early conclusion to the negotiations. At a meeting I attended at the headquarters of FIESP,[24] even some of Brazil's leading businesspeople showed a marked reluctance to move toward an agreement with the EU. This attitude contrasted with future complaints about the priority given by the Brazilian government (and Itamaraty in particular) to the WTO, supposedly at the expense of the Brazil-EU relationship.[25]

In April 2005 I accompanied President Lula on a tour of five countries in West Africa, during which we received several compliments from those countries' presidents about Brazil's leadership role in the WTO, with special mentions for the G20. President Olusegun Obasanjo of Nigeria was particularly emphatic. He was one of the African leaders who said they would support our candidate for the post of WTO director-general, although by that point I no longer had high hopes of success in that regard. Indeed, it was upon returning from that trip that I received the news of Seixas Corrêa's elimination from the selection process. On April 18 I made some notes in which I reflected upon the course of events and also referred to a phone conversation with the EU trade commissioner—two subjects that were in a way connected. I wrote: "Nothing of great importance has happened since I returned from Africa . . . apart from the announcement that our candidate in the WTO is now out of the running. It was a predictable defeat. . . . As the transparency [of the WTO] is almost zero, we will never know [the true circumstances]. To what extent this setback will influence our ability to lead the [G20] isn't clear. . . . On Saturday I had a long and friendly phone conversation with Peter Mandelson. [Mercosur's] negotiations with the EU aren't going well. There are real difficulties . . . but it's important not to play the blame game. . . . I insisted that [therefore] . . . a future meeting should be at ministerial level. We also spoke about the Doha Round. [Mandelson] said he had been 'struck by' my observation in Mombasa that we needed to make progress in many areas but that agriculture would continue to be the engine. Obviously he made that comment as a precursor to asking for improvements to the offer Brazil and India had made in NAMA and services. [Mandelson] is attaching great importance to the meeting on the sidelines of the OECD."[26]

"Alors, vous êtes un homme de sacrifice!"

Between the mini-ministerials in Mombasa and on the sidelines of the OECD in Paris, there was a ministerial meeting of the G20 in New Delhi in March 2005. The idea that the ministers should meet in India was actually mine (or perhaps I enthusiastically adopted a suggestion from one of my aides). Although Brazil was coordinating the group, it would be useful to "share parental responsibilities." I felt it was not convenient for the G20 to be seen as an exclusively or essentially Brazilian venture, because that would only encourage the developed countries to seek to discredit the group if there was another impasse such as the one in Cancún. When the agriculture negotiations became more specific and the rich countries began to exert pressure with regard to issues such as services and NAMA (which was already happening, in fact), maintaining the unity of the G20 would become a complex but essential task.

On the way to Delhi, I realized this would be my fourth trip to India in just over two years as foreign minister under President Lula. I had already been there on a bilateral ministerial visit; to accompany Lula when he was guest of honor at the celebrations on the anniversary of India's independence; and at a ministerial meeting of the IBSA group (India, Brazil, and South Africa). On those trips I had worn at least two different "hats": that of foreign minister, trade negotiator, and even international security advisor. I had met with members of the Indian government and also the opposition. For example, even after the fall of the BJP[27] I received a visit from my colleague in Cancún, Arun Jaitley (who would resurface years later as the influential finance minister in the Modi government). On one of those previous visits, the great interest the Doha Round aroused among the Indian public had led me to give lectures and participate in discussions with industrial associations. The varied aims of those different undertakings had been mutually reinforcing, helping to cement an increasingly solid alliance. Such was the increasing proximity between the two countries that on the sixtieth anniversary of India's independence, at an event in New York that coincided with the UN General Assembly, I shared with Henry Kissinger the privilege of being the only non-Indian invited to speak. When it came to the Doha Round, however, the close relationship between Brazil and India (although an important factor in the agreement of the July Framework in 2004) would not ultimately prove sufficient to avoid the collapse of the negotiations in 2008.

The G20 ministerial meeting in Delhi went smoothly. It was hosted by Kamal Nath, the minister for commerce and industry, who opened the meeting and immediately delegated the coordination duties to me. I do not know if he did so in recognition of Brazil's leadership or because he wanted greater freedom to speak as a member of the Indian government. For my part, despite not having been informed in advance of my allotted role, I considered it positive that our position at the heart of the process had been underlined. I would later be given the same responsibility at G20 meetings in China and Pakistan. With the help of Hugueney and Seixas Corrêa I managed without too many difficulties to get the assembled ministers to approve the platform for the agriculture negotiations that had previously been drawn up at a meeting of senior officials.

I should point out that achieving consensus within the group was not always a simple proposition. Despite the shared interests that had motivated its members since Cancún—namely, forcing the developed countries to eliminate or, in some cases, reduce measures that were harmful to trade in agricultural products—the G20 was far from being a monolithic bloc. There were frequently tensions between members with highly competitive agricultural sectors (such as Argentina, Uruguay, and Chile) and others more focused on protecting their domestic markets (as was the case with India, some other Asian countries including Indonesia, and even countries in Latin America such as Venezuela and Cuba). Ensuring that those differences did not become insurmountable contradictions required constant coordinating efforts at various levels (permanent representatives in Geneva, senior officials in the national capitals, and ministers), otherwise we would be faced with the prospect of returning to the pre-Cancún situation in which the divisions between developing countries played into the hands of the United States and the European Union.

In addition to its political role, the G20 also carried out studies and technical analyses. Before Cancún there had been few activities of that kind on the part of developing countries, and it was rarer still for such initiatives to be shared. I remember that during my first period in Geneva as permanent representative, from 1991–93, just before the conclusion of the Uruguay Round, my advisors and I had often approached the Australian permanent mission to the GATT[28] not only in order to coordinate positions but also to "learn" from the analyses and studies carried out by the country that was the leader of the Cairns Group. And essentially it was still the same picture almost a decade later, when I returned to Geneva as Brazil's representative at the WTO ahead of the Seattle Ministerial Conference of 1999 (at which the "Millennium Round"[29] was supposed to be launched) and then Doha in 2001. Although by then Brazil had become more able to identify and pursue its own interests, in the area of agriculture there was still a glaring lack of coordination between the different groups of developing countries, which was of course exploited by the Brussels negotiators. For example, unless my memory fails me, at no point in that period did I have a meaningful dialogue with my Indian counterpart on any agriculture-related topic, although we did coordinate on other issues such as TRIPS, TRIMs, and implementation.[30] So when the G20 came into being, it is no wonder that the New Zealand representative described it as a "masterpiece." The technical studies (carried out primarily in Geneva, but with significant assistance from diplomats in Itamaraty's economic department in Brasilia, as well as from officials in other ministries and experts from the private sector), added to those undertaken by other countries, allowed us not only to fine-tune our positions but also to present proposals that would form the basis for multilateral negotiations.

Based on my previous experience of the GATT/WTO system, I can confidently say that nothing of the kind had ever been seen before.[31]

I have only a vague recollection of the contents of the platform approved in Delhi, so numerous were the proposals that arose only to be discarded, or "subsumed" into other documents, soon afterwards. But it is certainly the case that it contained more refined proposals on the part of the G20 with regard to export subsidies, domestic support, the Special Safeguard Mechanism (SSM), and special products (SP). The latter two issues were the most contentious for the group, and would remain so until the breakdown of July 2008. The platform approved in Delhi also included some more specific ideas regarding market access for agricultural goods (also known by the acronym AMA), on which little progress had been made since Cancún. On that particular subject the work of the G20 would result in an intermediate proposal between the "extreme" positions of the European Union (protectionist) and the US (in favor of liberalization, but with certain exceptions where its own specific interests were concerned). The G20 platform would make possible some progress on AMA following the mini-ministerial in Dalian about three months later. The meeting in Delhi also proved to be an opportunity for informal discussion of ideas about NAMA and services, thus breaking the taboo according to which those issues were beyond the remit of the G20.[32] Another important aspect of the meeting was the participation of representatives of other groups of developing countries (the African group, the LDCs, some members of CARICOM, etc.), almost on an equal footing with the members of the G20. India deserved to take most of the credit for that initiative. Based on its tradition of non-alignment, India was at that point more proactive than Brazil in communicating with the Asian and African countries. That would change, however, as our policy of pursuing closer ties with Africa and the countries of the Caribbean began to take shape. The good understanding with the members of those groups would prove crucial at the Hong Kong conference, especially with regard to export subsidies.

Before describing the meeting in Dalian, which was the next stop on the road to Hong Kong, I want to mention a couple of memorable things related to the G20 meeting in Delhi. The evening after the meeting, Kamal Nath insisted that I should attend a reception at his home. He said there would be lots of his Indian friends there, including many members of the business community. Always mindful of my travel schedule and also my dietary requirements, I hesitated before accepting his kind invitation, but eventually decided I could not turn it down. Kamal suggested that I make use of one of the ministry's cars, an old Tata model that reminded me a little of the vehicles that used to be manufactured in the Soviet Union or the Trabants of the former East Germany. Beside me on the back seat was the trade minister of Zambia, Dipak Patel, who was at that time the coordinator of the LDCs and with whom I would go on to develop a friendly working relationship that would yield positive results in Hong Kong. The short journey to the home of the Indian minister (and afterwards to the airport) was not without moments that set our pulses racing, the driver setting off at high speed and with blithe disregard for the dividing line between the two sides of the road (not uncommon among motorists in India, as I would discover years later during a vacation there). Our emotions were heightened by the discovery that the Tata's features did not include seatbelts for backseat passengers. After leaving the center of Delhi and the expressway that links it to the airport, we drove through a very poor area where the shacks looked quite similar to those in some Rio de Janeiro *favelas*, before reaching what was clearly an upper-class neighborhood and entering the condominium where the Indian minister lived. Kamal's spacious home was decorated in eye-catching style and, some might say, with debatable taste. In that respect, in fact, it was not dissimilar to many of the houses in the so-called *áreas nobres* of Brasilia. But there was also a surprise in store. The backyard, where the reception was taking place, was dominated by what were clearly the ancient but well-preserved remains of a huge stone cistern supported by sober but elegant columns. This imposing object had originally been part of the water-supply system for a *caravanserai* at the beginning of the era of Muslim rule in northern India. When, years later, I read the trilogy describing the fourteenth-century journeys by Arab explorer Ibn Battutah[33] —specifically the second volume, mostly covering his foray into the Indian subcontinent—the surprising discovery at Kamal's home came naturally to mind. In brief conversations with some of the Indian businesspeople who were present, it quickly became obvious that they knew virtually nothing about Brazil. This made me think that the fixed preference agreement between Mercosur and India, which Kamal and I had signed just hours before, was no more than a statement of intent that would take a long time to yield concrete results.[34] The only exception to this almost total lack of knowledge was a writer, Gita Mehta, whose books had been translated into Portuguese and published in Brazil.

At the end of the G20 meeting in Delhi, I had a very gratifying encounter with a representative of Oxfam, Céline Charveriat, whom I had previously met a few times in Geneva. In general I was always willing to talk to NGOs, whether Brazilian or foreign, as my perception was that they tended to be genuinely interested in pursuing a dialogue. In Brazil, for example, I had already had many meetings with NGO representatives, labor union leaders, and directors of business associations, all of whom were among the Lula government's frequent interlocutors. Among them, for example, was the dynamic figure of Fátima Melo, from REBRIP,[35] a Brazilian umbrella organization comprising various groups concerned with the social impact of trade liberalization. At times she and I disagreed, but always in a civilized manner and in the context of a dialogue conducive to greater mutual understanding. There was frequent contact with civil society on the subject of the Doha

Round, just as there was in relation to the FTAA and the Mercosur-EU agreement. In the case of Oxfam, the well-known UK-based organization that operates internationally to combat hunger and extreme poverty, there was already a dialogue (encouraged by me, but pursued mainly by our negotiators in Geneva) that had been yielding good results. Indeed, Oxfam was an important ally, its good reputation further legitimizing our campaign against the agricultural subsidies used by the rich countries. Thanks in part to that dialogue, Oxfam understood the G20 position that—contrary to the simplistic current view, duly exploited for political gain by the Europeans—agricultural subsidies aggravate food insecurity and harm small farmers in poorer countries. Céline, friendly as ever, reiterated Oxfam's support for the G20's efforts and gave me a copy of the press release written by the NGOs that had attended the meeting as observers. Before she left, I mentioned to her that next I would be heading to Algeria to participate as an invited guest in a summit of the Arab League. This caused her to exclaim: "*Alors, vous êtes un homme de sacrifice*!" I replied (with, I must admit, a demagogic flourish): "When you have a good cause, it's a pleasure to fight for it." My interlocutor's gushing reply was: "*Vous êtes admirable*!" I had no reason to suppose she was not being sincere. And so, brimming with positive thoughts, I left in the early hours of the morning for Paris. In the French capital, taking off the hat of trade negotiator and donning that of foreign minister, I took a plane to Algiers.

The G20 becomes the "center of gravity" of the Doha Round

From July 6–8, 2005, a G8 summit took place at Gleneagles, Scotland. Six developing countries were also invited: Brazil, India, China, South Africa, and Mexico (the five who would become part of the "G8+5"), along with Ethiopia. A few days later I wrote: "On the same day as the G8—during which there were terrorist bomb attacks in London, with many dead—I attended a dinner with Peter Mandelson, Rob Portman, and Kamal Nath. It is in effect a new Quad,[36] formed to monitor the progress of the Round and, potentially, lead the negotiations. The purpose of the meeting was analysis and evaluation. It was basically political, not really dealing with the details of the negotiations." This "new Quad" would become known as the G4 after a meeting at the Brazilian embassy in Paris in September of the same year. Later in that same section of my notes, I mentioned that the meeting had helped give me a clearer idea of the kind of agreement that might eventually be possible. But there were still many unknowns: "How far will the US be willing to go on domestic support (their crown jewels)? What maneuvers might the EU come up with to dilute their offer on market access [in agriculture]? And will we ourselves be able to move forward on industrial goods?" To these musings, I added: "The Indians seem increasingly concerned about protecting their subsistence farming." I concluded my notes with the observation that the meeting had taken place in a good atmosphere and had prepared the ground for the Dalian mini-ministerial a few days later.

As previously mentioned, China kept a relatively low profile in the Doha Round negotiations in relation to its economic weight. I think it would have been the proximity of the ministerial conference in Hong Kong (a territory economically autonomous but still subject to the sovereignty of Beijing, under the precept of "one country, two systems") that led Chinese trade minister Bo Xilai—who years later would be convicted in a high-profile corruption scandal—to convene a meeting of the principal WTO participants in the city of Dalian, once known in the West as Port Arthur. Bo, who occupied one of the most important positions in the Chinese Communist Party, conducted himself with great assurance, as I had already seen during a bilateral visit to Brazil by Hu Jintao in November 2004. The Dalian mini-ministerial began with a meeting of the G20. Just as Kamal Nath had done in Delhi, the host offered a few words of welcome before handing over to me for the coordinating work. Jet-lagged and short of sleep, I only managed to perform my task thanks to the assistance of ambassadors Hugueney and Seixas Corrêa. The G20 approved Brazil's proposal of a press release on the subject of the Round that would reiterate the group's positions on export subsidies and domestic support, and also launch new ideas regarding access to agricultural markets. The European position on AMA had hardly changed since Cancún. The EU continued to insist on a methodology used during the Uruguay Round, based on an average and a minimal cut in tariffs, which would imply very limited reductions overall. The United States, meanwhile, was advocating an ambitious model for AMA, with bigger cuts to higher tariffs, as part of a "harmonizing formula" similar to what was being proposed for industrial goods. The G20 attempted to find a compromise between these positions by means of a methodology based on "tariff bands." Our proposal for AMA did contain an element of harmonization, as the tariffs on the products in the higher bands would be reduced more significantly than those on the products in the lower bands, but its impact would be less dramatic than that of the US proposal. I should point out that in proposing a middle way, the G20 was taking into account divergences within the group itself, namely those between the major agricultural exporters and the countries concerned with avoiding a "flood" of imports that would have an undesirable impact on local production.[37] The US negotiator, Rob Portman, said the G20 proposal was a good, constructive "base" on which to proceed with the negotiations. The Europeans did not reject the idea either, although they tried to twist it to their own advantage by proposing alterations that would further lessen the impact of the tariff reductions. In general the initiative was received positively. Besides highlighting the unity of the group, the tabling of the proposal underlined the fact that the G20 was proactive (not merely defensive) in its operations. After Dalian, when I was in Paris to accompany President Lula during the celebrations for the anniversary of the French Revolution, I read a *Financial Times* interview with Peter Mandelson in which he said the G20 had become the "center of gravity" of the Round. Later, responding to questions from Brazilian journalists regarding that same quote, I recalled La Fontaine's fable about the fox and the crow, in which the French author exposes the often devious objectives of flatterers.[38] Inwardly, however, I could not help feeling a certain satisfaction, particularly bearing in mind all the negative things that had been said about the G20 at Cancún. Since those earlier accusations of "obstructionism," a long road had been traveled, including in terms of the group's image.

My next notes about the Doha Round are in reference to another G20 meeting, in Pakistan, on September 9 and 10. Shortly before that, on September 2, there was a European Union-Mercosur meeting in Brussels—relevant because of the interconnections between the multilateral, regional, and bi-regional negotiations. The most important outcome from Brussels was that we managed to "bury" the methodology of "best offers" that the EU had proposed. It was a proposal that contained, in my view, several pitfalls. In its place I suggested that we should conduct an overview, or "reality check," of the current state of the negotiations. My choice of words was adopted by other participants and ended up denoting certain areas on which attention was particularly focused, such as the prospects for improving the offers on agriculture and services, and for achieving greater flexibility with regard to tariff elimination on industrial goods. An observation I made during this period indicates where my concerns lay: "Finally, we have not only a road map but also [some] content for the different stages on the route. A modest advance, but an advance nonetheless. It will allow us to continue to balance the various negotiations and, in case of the failure (or postponement) of the WTO round, we won't be left only with the FTAA."

Following the Brussels meeting, I returned to Brazil for the Independence Day ceremonies on September 7 and the reception for President Obasanjo of Nigeria, the first African leader to participate in the celebrations as a guest of honor. But on the afternoon of Independence Day itself, even before the bilateral meeting between Lula and the Nigerian president had taken place, I set off for Pakistan. In convening a meeting of the G20, Pakistani trade minister Humayun Akhtar Khan was keen for the event not to stand in the shadow of the one previously hosted by his Indian counterpart. The chosen venue was Bhurban, a hill station to the north of Islamabad, not very far from the border with Kashmir. To get there, the car carrying me and my chief of staff followed a road that wound snake-like around the foothills of the Himalayas, including some exceedingly dangerous bends. Along the route—or often, it seemed, in the middle of it—I noticed elderly men with long but carefully trimmed white beards, women with their heads veiled (and often also their faces), groups of children walking to or from school, old buses painted in an array of bright colors, and donkeys laden with bundles of firewood. The hilly and verdant backdrop completed the picture. There was no shortage of picturesque elements to the journey, although our contemplative reverie was frequently interrupted by violent swerves or reckless overtaking maneuvers.

The format of the meeting included a "retreat" session in which the ministers were free to talk more informally and swap ideas. This took place in a lounge with extremely comfortable armchairs. I had to make an enormous effort not to fall asleep. The conversations were very generic, revolving around the familiar theme of the importance of G20 unity. In my notes, the only reference to this stage in the proceedings is a brief comment that it was "not completely devoid of interest." As for the formal meeting, which again I coordinated, it culminated in the issuing of a lengthy communiqué that had been drafted beforehand by senior officials. The text emphasized points such as a five-year timeframe for the elimination of "all forms" of export subsidies, and the idea, already presented in Dalian, of cutting agricultural tariffs in accordance with a system of bands. It also highlighted the need to devote special attention to the disciplines for domestic support measures used by the developed countries.[39] Due prominence was given to special products (SP) and the Special Safeguard Mechanism (SSM) in agriculture, which were important for India and the other members of the G33. The document also dealt at some length with the need for coordination with the other developing countries grouped together under the umbrella of the G90.[40]

My principal interlocutors at the Bhurban meeting were the ever-present Kamal Nath and the host, Humayun Akhtar Khan. The latter, a pragmatic politician from a business background, would prove to be an important ally at future G20 meetings in Geneva. There were many occasions when he came to my rescue to ensure the debates stayed within realistic parameters. Although I myself sometimes came up with sound bites that I knew would be picked up by the media, and hoped might subsequently have an impact on public opinion, I was anxious for the group not to lose sight of its objectives and start spending most of its time indulging in rhetoric, as was the case with many other coalitions of developing countries. Unfortunately Khan would leave his position in the context of political change in Pakistan in November 2007. I would miss his support during the decisive days of July 2008. More than anything else the G20 meeting in Bhurban served to reaffirm the unity of the group and to give political guidance to the technical work being done in Geneva.[41] During the Bhurban meeting the G20 ministers also had the opportunity to pay a courtesy visit to President Pervez Musharraf, who was sojourning at a country house not far from the place where we were staying. More than a mere protocol gesture, the visit was a sign of the importance many heads of state attributed to the Doha negotiations.

In the evening of the same day, after another memorable car journey through the Himalayan foothills, I had a working dinner in Islamabad with Pakistan's foreign minister, Khurshid Kasuri. Although the WTO hardly came up at all, there were two interesting aspects to the occasion. As part of my permanent efforts to keep the Argentines involved in our diplomatic initiatives, I invited the head of their delegation, Alfredo Chiaradía, to accompany me. Our hosts were a little surprised (it would have been difficult for them to imagine a similar gesture from their powerful neighbor and rival), but agreed to Chiaradía's inclusion among the guests. For my colleague, whose position was that of trade secretary in the Argentine foreign ministry, I think it was an interesting opportunity to hear a politician from the region comment on burning issues such as Afghanistan and Iran. The other memorable moment was Kasuri's assessment of President George W. Bush, who would visit Brazil a few weeks later: "A guy who attacks Afghanistan, invades Iraq, and now wishes to invade Iran needs to have his head checked."[42]

With Hong Kong looming on the horizon, we needed to interweave the relatively large meetings, such as Dalian, with those that took place in smaller groups, where specific issues could be discussed in greater depth. This, in a way, was the role the FIPS had played in the period preceding the July Framework. The forum for these pre-negotiations, which served as a test for what it might be possible to "sell" to the rest of the WTO members, was now the so-called new Quad or G4—the small group that had met on the margins of the G8 summit at Gleneagles, just before Dalian. In one of my conversations with Peter Mandelson, either by phone or during the European Union-Mercosur meeting in early September, the EU trade commissioner asked me to organize a meeting of the G4. I managed, with great difficulty, to find a date acceptable to all (September 23) that did not clash with my own commitments (in Washington, at the UN, and in Haiti). The purpose of this G4 meeting was to give political impetus to the Doha Round negotiations, in which there had been no progress since the Paris meeting at which the AVEs issue had seemingly been resolved.

In terms of the G4 "choreography," apart from the presence of two major developing countries at the core of the negotiations being a novelty in itself, the interest on the part of the world's two biggest commercial powers in having a close dialogue with Brazil was certainly noteworthy. Also significant was the fact that the venue for the meeting was the Brazilian embassy in Paris. The truly extraordinary aspect of the occasion, however, was the keenness of both Mandelson and Portman to have separate private conversations with me. Indeed, there was a point when they and their respective aides seemed to be competing for my attention: the USTR's assistant even complained to a member of my delegation that I was giving more time to Mandelson than to her boss! These separate meetings took place between about 6 and 9 p.m. on September 22, the eve of the G4 meeting, at the residence of the Brazilian ambassador, Vera Pedrosa. Soon afterwards, Pascal Lamy arrived for a *tête-à-tête* over dinner. It was the first time the new WTO director-general had left Geneva after taking office. In my notebook I wrote: "Without wishing to be boastful, I believe I can say we have never been so close to the very center of the trade debate." But I added: "This requires an extra effort in order to keep up with all the technical details, or at least those that are essential in order to be able to address the political issues."[43]

The trade ministers of the European countries did not participate directly in the WTO negotiations conducted by the European Commission. With regard to the Doha Round their role was limited to participating in closed meetings of the EU itself. Therefore they greatly valued any opportunity to talk to ministers from other, non-European countries who happened to be visiting their capitals. That was the case, for example, with the UK's secretary of state for trade and industry, Patricia Hewitt, whom I met a few times not only in London but also in Davos. And it was no different in Paris. Given her subsequent career trajectory, I think it is interesting to transcribe a reference in my notebook to the French trade minister, written on the day of the G4 meeting: "On the desk where I'm writing these notes, there is a small brown bag. Inside it is a card with a message written, for some reason, in English: 'Very sorry to miss you this time! Welcome to beautiful Paris. This is just a small pleasant token from La Maison du Chocolat. All the best, Christine Lagarde, Ministre Déléguée au Commerce Extérieur.'"

The Paris meeting of the G4 did not produce concrete results. Nor was that its principal goal; instead the main aim had been to convey a positive message of engagement on the part of four participants who had the greatest influence over the Doha Round negotiations. The Brazilian media's description of the meeting as a "failure" simply did not correspond to reality. Perhaps the most appropriate headline was that of a Chinese news agency, which referred to the negotiations making gradual progress ("inches forward"). It was agreed that the G4 would meet again, and that it would also hold meetings with other countries and groups. The occasion had also served to give a clearer picture of the limits of each of the four participants. From my point of view, it was important to criticize the European maneuvers that were making it difficult to agree a formula for access to agricultural markets. And I also made clear that the US could not expect to have "a blank check" for their domestic support program (referred to as being "countercyclical" because it aimed to compensate for price fluctuations), which Washington wanted to see included in the "blue box." On board the Brazilian Air Force 737 en route to Washington, I wrote: "Out of the dialectic between the difficulties the Europeans are creating with market access and those of the US with domestic support, a creative solution needs to be born that will allow us to advance. Mandelson seems to clearly understand the elements of the game, but faced with the more protectionist countries in the European Union, his power is limited. Rob Portman has to deal with the US Congress, and says he can't 'rewrite' the Farm Bill.[44] At various moments I had to call attention to Paragraph 14 of the July Framework, which states that the criteria for the new blue boxes 'will be negotiated.' The game of alliances is more or less this: Brazil and the EU, with some support from India, against the United States when it comes to domestic subsidies; and the United States and Brazil, without the explicit support of India, against the EU when it comes to market access."

In the same section of my notes I made some observations about my fellow negotiators: "Mandelson is intelligent but doesn't have a complete grasp of the issues. He doesn't make any move on agriculture unless Mariann Fischer Boel, the agriculture commissioner, is by his side. (And by the way, it was curious to see how quickly the room emptied as soon as we finished the agricultural discussions.) Rob Portman is somewhat reminiscent of some classic descriptions of the 'quiet American' (such as the one by Graham Greene). He doesn't have the strategic vision of Zoellick. He speaks on behalf of the commercial interests of different sectors of the US economy and tries to strike a balance between them, never losing sight of how those interests are expressed through votes in Congress.[45] Kamal Nath has a strategic interest in the G20, but always takes a defensive stance on agriculture. His interventions often seem confusing, or too generic. Lately he has been talking a lot about services."[46] Later, as I gained a more complete (and more complex) view of my partners, some of these impressions would be confirmed and others would change to a certain degree.

"You're the one in the eye of the storm"

On October 10, in Zurich, USTR Rob Portman convened an informal ministerial meeting of the members of the Flüela Group.[47] By far the most important aspect of the meeting was the presentation by the US of a proposal on domestic support. It was the first time this had happened. One of the central points of the proposal was the establishment of a ceiling for the "blue box" of 2.5% of the average total value of agricultural production during the period in question. Another important aspect was the fixing of a maximum level for the various forms of trade-distorting domestic support. The total support allowed in the case of the US would be reduced by 53%, which would result in a ceiling of $23 billion USD. Brazil and the G20 countries welcomed the US proposal, as it introduced the concept of an "overall ceiling" for all the different forms of subsidy. But, at the same time, we said it was insufficient. In describing it, I availed myself of an expression I had heard US negotiators use when seeking to exert pressure in areas such as intellectual property and information technology: "a step in the right direction." The phrase, which evidently contained an element of irony, was repeated by, among others, the

New York Times. The main criticisms from me and other G20 ministers (and also from the EU trade commissioner, at a meeting of the FIPS[48] that same evening) concerned the absolute amount of US domestic support that would be permitted, which would actually be higher than the total sum of trade-distorting subsidies in the immediately preceding years. Although careful to express recognition of the positive aspects of the proposal, I also pointed out the absence of disciplines for the "new blue box" that had been foreseen in the July Framework. In response to that point, the US said that in reducing the ceiling for the blue box from the 5% stipulated in the July Framework to 2.5%, such disciplines would become unnecessary. We did not agree with that argument and were able to demonstrate that the lower ceiling would still leave ample scope for the expansion of countercyclical payments. At the meeting of the FIPS, the shifting alliances I referred to above were evident again. We joined the United States in pressing the European Union for better market access in agriculture, while also allying ourselves with the Europeans in demanding improvements in the US proposal on subsidies. India generally adopted the same positions as we did, although always with a certain amount of caution in relation to market access. The other member of the FIPS, Australia, although considering itself a champion liberalizer of agricultural trade, was muted in its criticism of the United States. Between October 10 and 12, the G20 ministers met several times in Geneva and formally approved a revised version of the proposal we had agreed in Bhurban.

On October 13 I left Geneva for Moscow in order to prepare for an imminent visit by President Lula to Russia. But less than a week after my departure I was back in the Swiss city for a new round of meetings, this time including bilaterals with Kamal Nath, Rob Portman, Peter Mandelson, Japanese trade minister Shoichi Nakagawa, and WTO director-general Pascal Lamy. Almost all these meetings took place in the winter garden of the Brazilian permanent representative's[49] residence, Mont-Riant. This was more than a gesture of recognition of Brazil's important role: the nineteenth-century *maison de campagne*, in Grand Saconnex, a municipality in the Canton of Geneva, is a beautiful venue, surrounded by parkland containing what one of my predecessors as representative to the GATT had once told me was "the biggest collection of pine trees in Switzerland." As a bonus, on a very clear day it offers a view of the snow-covered summit of Mont Blanc. And also, very conveniently, it is no more than ten minutes' drive from WTO headquarters. In fact, we quite often made use of our ambassadors' residences for WTO-related meetings: in addition to Geneva and Paris we would also use the buildings in Rome and London on numerous occasions.

On October 19 and 20 there were also meetings of the FIPS and a group I described in my notebook as the "expanded FIPS," which I suppose must have denoted the inclusion of Japan. I referred to the meetings as "frustrating and useful." They were frustrating because they did not yield any concrete result, and useful because they provided an incentive for the G20 to complete its proposal on market access by including the specific issue of sensitive products.[50] I also noticed with interest that the United States and the European Union were continuing to court Brazil, seeking to lure us toward their respective positions. Meanwhile, the G20 continued to attract the attention of the international media. One of the news items about the meetings on October 19 and 20 referred to the G20 as "the powerful group of developing countries led by Brazil." I concluded my notes on those meetings with a rather bittersweet reflection: "Internationally, adulation and respect. In Brazil, criticism and skepticism about our foreign policy."

My work on the Doha Round did not consist only of meetings abroad with trade or foreign ministers. There was also a domestic dimension to take care of. And, whenever possible, I had to try to maintain the unity of Mercosur, which was not always an easy proposition given the sometimes contradictory interests and radical positions of Argentina. It was important to try to ensure that Brazil's rising international profile neither made our neighbor jealous nor awakened any dormant rivalry. That had been part of the explanation for my decision—uncommon in the diplomatic milieu—to invite the trade secretary in the Argentine foreign ministry, Alfredo Chiaradía, to my bilateral with my Pakistani counterpart. I should point out that Chiaradía was always a good partner, even though during the course of the negotiations Argentina's position, especially on NAMA, would become increasingly rigid and difficult to accommodate, sometimes requiring Brazil to sacrifice some of its own objectives (though obviously not the fundamental ones). At one point in one of my meetings in Montevideo aimed at ensuring that Brazil's role in the Doha Round remained transparent as far as Mercosur was concerned (and, who knows, perhaps also allowing the Mercosur ministers to say that "we gave instructions to Amorim"), I wanted to hand over to Chiaradía so he could describe the evolution of the discussions in Geneva, especially in the context of the G20. He elegantly declined, however: "You speak, Celso," he said. "You're the one in the eye of the storm." Around that time, Argentina insisted that we enter into bilateral discussions on safeguard mechanisms (euphemistically known as "Competitive Adjustment Mechanisms" or, to use the Portuguese/Spanish acronym, MACs). The use of safeguards[51] was actually prohibited under the Treaty of Asunción.[52] This attempt to introduce safeguards into Mercosur by the "back door" aroused strong opposition both on the part of the Brazilian business sector and my fellow ministers in Brasilia. This made the coordination of the multilateral trade negotiations a more delicate operation. With Uruguay, and to a lesser extent Paraguay, harmonizing our respective positions was not a simple task. In the case of Montevideo there was dissatisfaction with Brazil's strategy of accommodating the interests of other developing countries (at the expense of a more aggressive posture aimed at opening up agricultural markets). Also, I sensed that even after the election of the left-leaning President Tabaré Vasquez, there was some lingering resentment following the episode surrounding the choice of the new WTO director-general. Moreover, Uruguay had previously played a prominent role in the old GATT negotiations, especially in the launching of the round that carried its name. During the Doha Round, however, Uruguay's role faded into the background, at least at ministerial level. As for Paraguay, its positions were in principle similar to those of Uruguay, but at the ministerial meetings our differences with Asunción were eased by broader political interests and our good relationship with Paraguayan foreign minister Leila Rachid. Leila recognized the value of our leadership in the multilateral arena and the efforts we were making, both bilaterally and in the context of Mercosur, on issues such as the "asymmetries" and the FOCEM.[53]

Pascal's triangle

In Brazil, trade negotiations have traditionally been conducted by the foreign ministry. In the early part of President Lula's first term of office there were periodic attempts to challenge Itamaraty's leadership of the Doha Round negotiations, but they fizzled out in the wake of Cancún. The agricultural lobby recognized the importance of our work on vital issues such as subsidies (including our victories in the cotton and sugar disputes)[54] and also on market access. Our technical staff in Geneva liaised closely with Brazil's agricultural producers, as reflected by the well-prepared proposals they produced. And most Brazilian industrialists saw in Itamaraty's leadership a bulwark against the kind of rash openings to imports that were favored by other ministries in Brasilia (our textiles producers were a major exception, as they were always dreaming of the FTAA or a bilateral agreement with the EU). In the finance ministry there were those who strongly favored unilateral trade liberalization on economic grounds (essentially to combat inflation by allowing competition from cheaper imported products). Several sectors of Brazilian manufacturing had already been badly shaken by the greater competitiveness of countries such as China. Therefore, although it was necessary to flatter certain individual egos—which is what I tried to do, for example, through presentations to the Chamber of Foreign Trade (CAMEX),[55] chaired by the Minister for Development, Industry, and Trade—it was not difficult to obtain endorsement for the strategy Itamaraty was pursuing. The role of President Lula himself was also very important in that respect. In October and November 2005 he convened at least two meetings at the Planalto, during which he accepted my recommendations. I should make clear, indeed, that even without entering into the technical minutiae, Lula was fully aware of what was at stake in the Doha Round and listened carefully to my explanations, including with regard to what I would later describe, particularly after

Hong Kong, as "Pascal's triangle."[56] That was the pun with which I tried to encapsulate the principal axes of the negotiations and the "variable geometry" of the alliances that formed around them. I will return to this subject later in the narrative. Lula had already given his full support to our actions in the FTAA and the WTO, despite the pressure from the most powerful countries (in the face of which, it must be said, some of my fellow ministers in the Brazilian government were more pliable). The president knew the Doha Round negotiating process would sooner or later obligate us to make concessions likely to displease this or that part of our industrial or agricultural sector. But he understood the value of the agreement we were seeking to achieve, which would strengthen what could be described as "trade multilateralism." For the president to reject protectionism (a stance that would perhaps have been natural on the part of a former leader of a metalworkers' union) was nevertheless surprising, and confirmed his remarkable degree of political intuition. Having overcome the initial problems with the trade minister, Luiz Fernando Furlan, and the agriculture minister, Roberto Rodrigues, the remaining differences still to be addressed concerned the finance ministry, which favored a more rapid reduction in our industrial tariffs (to be "bound" in the WTO)[57] so as to contribute to macroeconomic stability. I do not know to what extent this stance was encouraged by contact between our finance minister, Antonio Palocci, and his counterparts in developed countries, but I was aware that Palocci spoke frequently with the British chancellor of the exchequer, Gordon Brown, an active supporter of liberalization. At one point technicians in our finance ministry had considered unilaterally reducing rates on some manufactured goods, which, apart from its effect on our industry, would obviously have weakened our hand when trying to extract concessions on, for example, agricultural subsidies. But that was another specific point on which I had Lula's backing. Overall, therefore, in the run-up to Hong Kong, things on the home front were relatively quiet.

On October 27, the European Union presented its revised offer on agriculture, which included the issue of market access. The next day, there was a video conference—of the FIPS, I think, although it might have been the G4. Based on the analyses already carried out by Itamaraty technicians (especially the department dealing with agriculture, headed by the diplomat Flávio Damico) we were able to show that the EU proposal on access to its agricultural markets fell far short of what was demanded by the G20 (and obviously also by the US and the Cairns Group). Employing some numerical sleight of hand,[58] the European Commission tried to show that its proposal would constitute a significant opening, not far from the average level of reductions requested by the G20. The United States and Australia, without prior consultation with us, had reached conclusions almost identical to ours. And so the European attempt to "gloss over" the reality of their proposal—and to make the other parties look intransigent in rejecting it—did not work. With its figures clearly unsustainable, over the course of the negotiations the EU eventually stopped insisting on them. To my dismay, however, the Brazilian TV news programs merely repeated the European perspective, apparently totally ignorant of our own analysis. In my notes the following day, in a brief reference to the video conference I mentioned only the importance of maintaining the unity of the G20 (probably out of concern about India's permanent tendency to lean toward less ambitious proposals on access to agricultural markets):[59] "In that respect I think the EU has made an error of judgment by presenting very aggressive objectives in relation to NAMA and services. But it will obviously continue trying to separate us from India and from other developing countries."

President Lula's participation in WTO issues was not limited to the support he offered me within the government. He also had frequent meetings and phone conversations with other world leaders on the subject. On October 25, for example, he wrote to several European presidents and prime ministers with whom he had already established a personal or political relationship. Coincidentally they were also the leaders of countries that were adopting more inflexible positions on agriculture, thereby severely limiting the scope for progress in the negotiations. Conscious as I was that our battle was one in which public opinion played an important role, I decided that the content of the letters should be reproduced in Itamaraty press releases.[60] President Lula sent letters on the Doha Round to President Jacques Chirac of France; President Carlo Azeglio Ciampi of Italy; Prime Minister José Luis Rodríguez Zapatero of Spain; and Prime Minister José Sócrates of Portugal. He also wrote to the president of the European Commission, José Manuel Durão Barroso. Lula referred in the letters to the G20 proposals and the step taken by the United States in proposing a ceiling on domestic subsidies. He urged European leaders to submit, through the EU, a proposal on access to agricultural markets that would encourage Washington to improve its offer on subsidies. That, in turn, would encourage moves from the developing countries on NAMA and services. An interesting detail of the letters was Lula's preventive refutation of allegations employed by the EU to justify its reluctance to make significant concessions. Those allegations were based on supposed concerns for poor countries that were the recipients of trade preferences. On the subject of the letters I wrote the following: "It is a political gesture designed to show that: (1) Lula has a grasp of the issues; (2) he and I are in tune with each other; and (3) we're not dumb [in relation to the attempts to manipulate other developing countries]." I added: "For my part, I sent a long e-mail to the Zambian minister, Dipak Patel, the coordinator of the LDCs, with whom I developed a good relationship at the G20 meetings in India and Pakistan." In keeping him abreast of the latest developments and the positions Brazil had been taking, my intention was to maintain the spirit of cooperation that had characterized the previous meetings and to guard against any attempt, particularly on the part of the Europeans, to co-opt the LDCs.

The notebook entries that appear in the above paragraphs were written on October 27. The next entry, on November 7, was written during a flight to London, where I was due to have a number of meetings (some of them very significant) related to the Round. Before that there were other important commitments, including a trip to New York to attend a ministerial meeting of the Security Council to study the report on the assassination of Lebanese prime minister Rafic Hariri.[61] On the subject of the trade negotiations there was a video conference (or possibly just a conference call) with the interlocutors I referred to subsequently in my notes as "the usual suspects." I remember that the conversation in question included a few moments of acrimony and ended rather abruptly, with Peter Mandelson saying he needed to leave because of another commitment. The EU trade commissioner was obviously upset by an observation I had made about the EU's self-interested approach to the issue of the alleged difficulties that a greater opening on agriculture would pose for the developing countries (members of the ACP) that enjoyed trade preferences in the European market. Somewhat histrionic demonstrations of irritation were a Mandelson trademark, and would feature again at the Hong Kong Ministerial Conference. That same day I had a conversation with Rob Portman in which we discussed the sensitive issue of the tying together by Washington of two different questions: the extension of the Generalized System of Preferences (GSP)[62] and the ever-contentious issue of intellectual property. Taking advantage of the constructive dialogue we had developed, I said to Portman that it would be helpful if the dispute could be resolved before the visit by President Bush to Brazil in November, just after the Summit of the Americas in Mar del Plata. Although time was short, the USTR assured me he would give the matter due attention. And indeed, the next day, he informed me that he had taken the initiative of holding a meeting involving representatives of eight or nine different US government departments, so as to begin a process that could potentially terminate the unilateral investigation of patents and the GSP. According to my notes, Portman took that action based upon: "(1) our cooperation in the search for negotiated solutions to cases such as that of [the pharmaceutical company] Abbott [involving compulsory licensing for the production of medicines]; and (2) the good coordination between us so far during the Round."

"Everything will have to be decided with a certain amount of political intuition"

Before my departure for London, the Summit of the Americas took place in Mar del Plata, and Bush visited Brazil. The FTAA was a prominent theme in both events, particularly the former. Given the obvious strategic relationship between the various negotiations, I think it is appropriate to transcribe the numbered points about the FTAA that I wrote on a piece of paper during the debates at the summit, intended to help Lula when he made his speech. As it turned out, he read out the points almost word for word.

1. The debate on trade can't be ideological; it has to be based on practical considerations;
2. For Brazil, it makes no sense to focus on free trade while there are still massive agricultural subsidies that "tilt the playing field";
3. Hence the priority we give to the WTO, where those issues can effectively be addressed;
4. There is no single model for trade relations. In the FTAA, before Miami 2003, issues were being discussed that went far beyond trade (rules for investment, government procurement, etc.), limiting the space for policies on industry, technology, etc.. That's why we proposed—and achieved—a redefinition of the basis for the negotiations;
5. Brazil (and Mercosur) has been negotiating agreements with other developing countries, taking fully into account the asymmetries and sensitivities of the less advanced countries. The same principle should govern hemispheric negotiations;
6. We're willing to continue this discussion, but we can't set artificial deadlines that won't be complied with and will only cause political friction. We would therefore prefer to assess the situation after Hong Kong, in the light of what takes place there, especially with regard to the subsidies.

Although moderate compared with the attitudes of Kirchner and Chávez, our position left no doubt about our unwillingness to return to the hemispheric negotiations without knowing what the next stages of the multilateral negotiations might bring. To avoid direct confrontation, Brazil was adopting an attitude toward the FTAA that might be described as "neither resuscitate it nor bury it," but the rather technical formulation of the points read by Lula made clear our position and was another factor leading to the FTAA's gradual disappearance from the scene. Its definitive "burial" took place with the closure of the offices of its secretariat in Puebla, Mexico, in 2008. In my notes written during the flight to the UK, a couple of hours before landing at Heathrow airport, I wrote: "In London I will be dealing with the WTO (G4) again. Then there will be meetings [in various formats] in Geneva. The moment of truth is approaching. How far will [the US and the EU] move on agriculture? And where will our limits be on NAMA and services? Everything will have to be decided with a certain amount of political intuition."

"With a certain amount of political intuition"? I am surprised I felt it necessary to write those words. I knew very well that I would not be making decisions in a political and economic vacuum. The meetings at the Planalto, and Lula's attitude in general, had given me leeway to take initiatives, but I also knew that any step too far on my part would incur the wrath of both the business sector and the media. I was already accustomed to harsh criticism in response to some of my initiatives toward Mercosur, and there was sure to be a parallel in this case. The presentation of the US and EU offers, although insufficient, meant the pressure was back on Brazil and India, particularly in relation to NAMA. Brazil would be the main target, as New Delhi was relatively comfortable in the field of industrial products. As part of its macroeconomic policy India had already reduced tariffs to average levels that were lower than ours. If we made no move and simply waited for improved offers from the US and EU, we would probably be accused of obstructing the progress of the Round. In a game in which perceptions were always important, we would run the risk of losing the moral high ground. I therefore prepared myself to make an offer that would be conditional upon advances in agriculture (subsidies and market access) and also—very important—subject to the approval of our Mercosur partners. My use of the words "political intuition" referred above all to the impossibility of knowing precisely what effect our tariff cuts would have on each and every sector of Brazilian industry. Obviously I had some idea of what might happen, based on technical studies conducted in conjunction with various government departments, and conversations with the private sector. But to some extent our offer would be a leap in the dark. I emphasized this fact in my presentation at the G4 meeting. Interestingly, a similar situation would arise during the fateful week in July 2008, when I had to make a judgment about how far we could go on the so-called "anti-concentration" clauses.[63] In both cases, in addition to the specific gains and losses, my approach also took into account Brazil's interest in strengthening the multilateral trading system and in avoiding pressures to become involved in FTAA-style negotiations, which I considered structurally disadvantageous. There was also the fact that I saw in the WTO, which Brazil had been involved in creating, a pillar of a rules-based world order. These considerations shaped my approach at the G4 meeting in London and, as I will describe later, in Geneva in July 2008. The same considerations also guided me in moments when I thought I should not collude with maneuvers aimed at pressuring Brazil—and the developing countries in general—into accepting an unbalanced deal, as would be the case in Hong Kong and also, in 2007, in Potsdam. And so, when making a concession, or when "turning the tables" in the face of an unacceptable imposition, I adopted this attitude with a full awareness of my responsibilities. One consequence of the leadership role Brazil had adopted since Cancún was that we could not hide behind the positions of other countries or groups (although of course that did not prevent us from making use of a group's position to strengthen our own). Strictly speaking, the reflections in the preceding sentences could have been inserted anywhere in this narrative. I chose to place them here because it seemed appropriate to give an idea of the background to Brazil's "offer," during the London meeting of the G4, of a "coefficient of 30" with regard to tariff reductions on industrial products.[64]

"Un négociateur redoubtable"

Before the G4 meeting, my visit to London began with a conversation with Tony Blair at 10 Downing Street, the house that is both the British prime minister's residence and office. Despite having previously been ambassador to the United Kingdom for a little over a year, I had never previously stepped through the doorway of that famous address. It was with some curiosity, therefore, that I waited to meet the head of Her Majesty's Government. With this somewhat unusual gesture of receiving the foreign minister of a developing country, I think Blair intended to indicate the importance of the Doha Round to the British government. He had probably been encouraged to do so by my negotiating partner Peter Mandelson, one of his closest associates in the Labour Party and a former member of the cabinet. It what turned out to be a friendly but short conversation, the prime minister appealed to Brazil's "constructive spirit," clearly having in mind our position on industrial tariffs. I told him that any effort toward liberalization in that area could only be justified, economically and politically, by real gains in agriculture. I added that a good European offer on AMA was essential, not only because it would provide a direct boost to the exports of developing countries but also because it would be the major determinant of how far the US would go in reducing their domestic subsidies. Blair assured me that the European Union had room (whether economic or political, I was not sure) to improve its offer on agriculture, but that in order to do so it "needed to show that it had gained something." That "something," of course, would be a concession from us on industrial tariffs. Unfortunately, at the meeting later that evening, Blair's expectations regarding the EU's flexibility—or rather, the expectations he aroused in me—were to prove unfounded.

The G4 meeting took place in a large and dimly lit room at India House, an old building in the district of Aldwych, close to the City (London's famous financial district) and home to the London School of Economics (where I had been a postgraduate student). In the days of the British Empire the building had housed the India Office, and after decolonization it was made available to the Indian government, which used it as a cultural center. Seated at the negotiating table with Kamal Nath, Rob Portman, and Peter Mandelson, I made the offer that had been agreed with President Lula. Mandelson, who had been making further demands with regard to NAMA, appeared to react with a mixture of indifference and hostility. My gesture, which my advisors and I considered bold, and which had required long and arduous explanations to our Argentine partners and some sectors of our industry, seemed to have no positive impact whatsoever. To this day I am not sure if Mandelson's attitude was calculated so as to avoid renewed pressure with regard to the EU offer on agriculture,[65] or if he genuinely did not realize, because of insufficient technical knowledge, just how significant a step I was taking. Until then, Brazil, like other developing countries, had refused to base any offer in the area of industrial products upon a harmonizing formula. We had previously argued for an approach based upon a linear cut, also involving safeguards and flexibilities. The meeting at India House ended in a serious and somber mood that did not go unnoticed by the Brazilian journalists huddled outside the door in the cold and wet London night. A similar atmosphere persisted throughout the broader meeting—a kind of mini-ministerial—that took place the following day in Geneva. The "failure" was the subject of various newspaper reports. The *International Herald Tribune*, which always gives a lot of space to international economic issues, ran a front-page story featuring a number of quotes from Mandelson and me. The headline was "Brazil and the European Union trade barbs in Geneva."

I do not think I could be described as a naive negotiator. Indeed, the criticisms sometimes aimed at me by my US and European interlocutors were generally based on quite the opposite perception. Once, in a dialogue between Lula and Jacques Chirac during a state visit to Brazil by the French president, I felt obligated to explain why I was intervening in the part of the conversation that concerned the WTO. Chirac knew me as the foreign minister who accompanied Lula in discussions on combating hunger or political dialogues about Iraq and global governance, but I had no reason to believe he was aware of my role in the trade negotiations. No sooner had I started my explanation, however, than Chirac interjected: "*Je le sais, et un négociateur redoutable*." Despite this reputation for being a tough or even intransigent negotiator, and certainly not a credulous one, I was baffled by Mandelson's attitude, which was so different from what Blair had led me to expect. The surprise was even greater because of the well-known proximity between the prime minister and the European trade commissioner, who had been close collaborators during the emergence and consolidation of New Labour. During that period Mandelson had become known in the British media (and also by some of his opponents within the Labour Party) as the "Prince of Darkness," in reference to the methods he employed. But neither that unflattering image nor the accusations against him regarding real-estate transactions did anything to diminish his intimacy with the prime minister. Therefore, discounting the possibility that the two of them were colluding to deceive me (my paranoia did not stretch quite that far), there seemed to be no explanation for Mandelson's cold response.

Still in the shadow cast by Mandelson's behavior, I later wrote: "What can explain the gap between Mandelson's inflexibility and the picture painted by Blair? In retrospect—with the help of Lamy, whom I spoke to at length—I can see there is an issue of timing. [According to Lamy] Europe will be able to move forward [on agriculture], but not yet. For that to happen, we must make moves now—although that's precisely what I already did, albeit with conditions attached! [In the same conversation] Lamy said Mandelson had been 'hurt' (*meurtri*) by my criticism." So as to dispel the bad atmosphere of the London and Geneva meetings, I thought I should resume the dialogue with Mandelson. I wanted, among other things, to maintain a balance between the moves the different sides were making, because around the same time Rob Portman was visiting India on his way to an APEC meeting. Although on agriculture their respective positions were far apart, the possibility of an Indo-US *entente* on services and industrial goods (though the latter was less likely) would potentially leave Brazil in an isolated position in the G4, obligating us to make a corresponding move. I also believed it was essential to carry out a more detailed assessment of what results could be obtained at the Hong Kong Ministerial Conference, which by then was only one month away. Brazil and the EU had stated their positions loudly and clearly, but there was no point in carrying on with accusations and counter-accusations all the way until December. I therefore accepted the EU trade commissioner's invitation to another meeting, although I suggested it should take place not in Brussels but in Rome.

"Agriculture lies . . ."

Before describing my meeting with Mandelson at the Palazzo Pamphilj on November 12, I will reproduce what I wrote in my notebook that same day about the previous negotiations in Geneva: "*Agriculture lies*: I think that would make a very good title for a book about the agricultural negotiations. I allowed myself to make that joke at the press conference after the mini-ministerial meeting. 'Agriculture lies' were actually the first two words of a G20 statement, although they weren't chosen deliberately to suggest the negotiating positions of our partners were disingenuous. They were just the start of a sentence in which we said, for the umpteenth time, that agriculture was at the heart of the Round ('Agriculture lies at the center . . .'). I couldn't resist the play on words. *Agriculture lies* really could be title of our manifesto. After the press conference there were still lots of journalists wanting to speak to me. I made further statements, which were given a high profile in the *International Herald Tribune* and the *Financial Times*. I called for advances on the part of the European Union without which there could be no movement from the developing countries 'in one month, or in two months, or in two years.' Friday's *New York Times* [November 11] used my quote in their editorial."

That same editorial went on to give the developing countries the following advice: "Stand firm; don't give way on industrial [goods] and services as long as the Europeans don't make any move on agriculture." Of course the *New York Times* was not saying that out of kindness or sympathy for our goals; instead it was a sign of a battle going on in the US against the agricultural lobby, which had already been evident at the time of our victory in the cotton dispute. Even the *Economist*, which generally did not have much sympathy for our position, praised our attitude, albeit only implicitly, by suggesting we should maintain our firm stance: "Nothing is better than too little," it said. I also mentioned in my notes that the positive coverage of our position by the foreign media had been noticed in Brazil, which had the effect of strengthening my position in relation to other ministers, certain business sectors, and the national media. My notes reflected my concern, perhaps exaggerated, that despite the support of the president, my strategy on the Doha Round might still be challenged.

I must begin my account of the Rome meeting with Peter Mandelson with an anecdote. I already mentioned how I tried to put our embassies to good use by creating a favorable setting for negotiations. The EU trade commissioner, a man of refined sensitivities with an added dash of theatricality, had been dazzled by our premises in Paris (both the ambassador's residence and the embassy), and had been unable to contain himself when he set eyes on the main room of the ambassador's residence in Geneva, which is not particularly large but is decorated with early nineteenth-century *grotteschi* frescoes inspired by the discoveries at Pompeii. He had joked that he wanted to do a complete tour of the world's Brazilian embassies because "each one's more stunning than the one before." So I had suggested to one of my colleagues that we should take Mandelson to the Palazzo Pamphilj, the late-Renaissance/early Baroque architectural jewel that is the residence of our ambassador in Rome. It turned out to be a good idea. Talking on his cell phone with Tony Blair as he wandered through the rooms of the palace, Mandelson was ecstatic when he saw the Cortona gallery, its name deriving from its ceiling frescoes created by the Italian Baroque painter.

After the mutual accusations in the press and the harsh words that had marked the meetings in London and Geneva, it was important to restore the level of dialogue. Mandelson had suggested a meeting on the previous Thursday in Brussels, but I felt the institutional setting of the European Commission might further increase the excessively technical character of the discussion as originally conceived by his aides. Knowing Mandelson would be visiting Italy on the Friday, I invited him to breakfast on Saturday morning. The rooms of the palace, once home to the Pamphilj family (which produced at least one pope), created a propitious environment, further enhanced by the sunlight streaming in from the Piazza Navona through the large windows. It was the perfect setting in which to seek some sort of understanding, however limited, in the run-up to Hong Kong. The meeting included an "exchange in good faith," as they say in the WTO, of the numbers the two delegations were working with, along with an analysis of what they signified. We compared our respective calculations and cleared up certain misunderstandings, although we were not aiming to arrive at an agreement right there and then. The meeting lasted for more than four hours (four and a half, in fact, according to the Brazilian journalists who had traveled from Geneva and were in one of the adjacent lounges). The first hour was devoted to political analysis of the situation. With apparent frankness, Mandelson referred to the constraints upon his role as commissioner, emphasizing the limits placed on the negotiations by the EU Common Agricultural Policy (CAP).[66] For my part I spoke of the resistance I was facing from certain industrial sectors, and above all from our principal partner in Mercosur, Argentina. I sought to clarify the implications of the "coefficient of 30" for Brazilian industry, showing how it would open up markets as well as significantly consolidating previous steps taken toward trade liberalization.[67]

As usual, we also discussed our respective analyses of how flexible the other two partners in the G4 might be. As I had done in my conversation with the British prime minister, I tried to make Mandelson see that the European offer on market access would certainly influence the US position on domestic support, which was a central issue for us. From our point of view, therefore, an analysis of the European proposal could not be limited merely to counting tons of beef and comparing the figure with the presumed value of our imports of auto parts. When it came to liberalizing agricultural trade, the conclusion from our discussions was basically the following: there was no chance of reforming the CAP, but in reality the red lines were more like red "bands." Therefore, according to Mandelson, there was some scope for negotiation. I wondered, in fact, if that was what Tony Blair had been referring to during our conversation in Downing Street. Mandelson still did not leave room for much optimism, however. He explained that any opening that went beyond a small reduction in the number of sensitive products would only occur after January, and even then it was doubtful. Referring to the probable reactions on the part of certain EU member states, Mandelson said he hoped not to find himself in a position where he could not "make progress" at a later date, when there had also been progress on other aspects of the Round. He also showed interest and even surprise at some of the numbers we presented on industrial tariffs, though I do not know if that was sincere or just part of the mood of *détente* we were both keen to create. Our shared conclusion was that we needed to decide on the level of ambition of our goals in Hong Kong. It would be necessary, therefore, to hold another G4 meeting. I said I would keep Pascal Lamy informed of our intentions.

From Rome I returned to Brasilia, and two days later I went to Montevideo for the Mercosur ministerial meeting on the Doha Round. The vital thing there was to win support, or at least tacit acceptance, for the bold proposal I had made in London on the coefficient of 30. I did feel I had the backing of our partners, even though Argentina gave its assent with the proviso that the coefficient of 30 was the absolute limit. I would hear much the same thing from FIESP a few days later. At the Mercosur meeting I also said there needed to be a "generous attitude" toward the Least Developed Countries on the issue of market access, and on that point too I left the meeting confident that I had my colleagues' endorsement.

After a TV interview and a CAMEX meeting in which I brought the other ministers up to date with my recent movements, I flew back to Geneva for meetings of the G4 and the G4+2 (denoting the inclusion of Japan and Australia), in addition to the inevitable bilaterals. As always, I also made a point of meeting the permanent representatives of the G20 countries. In notes written shortly before the G4 meeting, I anticipated it would be "probably the last opportunity for the ministers from the main players to outline what can be achieved in Hong Kong." I also referred to the expression used at the time by Geneva negotiators to denote the level of ambition at the forthcoming ministerial conference: "less than full modalities." But even I was not sure what that meant exactly, apart from that we would not be arriving at precise figures. At most we would be able to agree on concepts broad enough to accommodate opposing interests and diverse sensitivities. It was obvious that there had been a general lowering of expectations with regard to Hong Kong, although no one thought that should affect the level of ambition of the Round as a whole. It was necessary, in other words, to look further ahead, to a "Hong Kong II." And indeed, as it turned out, the Geneva meetings brought nothing new. I tried to suggest, in the G4 (or possibly G4+2) meeting, that we should decide on a "basket" of issues to be discussed and studied before Hong Kong (export subsidies; relationship between overall tariff cuts and market access; development issues; NAMA and services). It was not really a new idea, merely an attempt to focus attention, but not even that modest methodological proposal was accepted. We agreed to have another meeting in early December, although I had my doubts about how useful it would be.

"Africa and Brazil are closer than ever"

Soon after the meeting in Geneva, I headed for Arusha, the Tanzanian city at the foot of Kilimanjaro that on October 23 would be hosting an extraordinary meeting of the African Union on the subject of trade. Having offered a "ride" to Pascal Lamy, we picked him up in Geneva and he traveled with me in the presidential aircraft on the last leg of the long flight to East Africa. It was a rare opportunity for an informal conversation with the WTO director-general. We talked mostly about questions of procedure rather than the actual substance of the Doha Round, but for me it was still an extremely valuable opportunity to get an idea of how the coordinator of the negotiations intended to proceed. Our *tête-à-tête* in the private cabin of the plane was photographed by my press secretary Ricardo Tavares (now ambassador in Rome). The inclusion of Arusha in my itinerary was a clear demonstration of Brazil's determination to obtain a positive result in the Round and to maintain our active cooperation with the various groups of developing countries. As well as participating in the formal meeting—at which I gave a short speech, immediately after Lamy—I offered a lunch for a group of African trade ministers. Among the ten or so ministers who attended were those from Tanzania, Angola, Ghana, and Zambia (Dipak Patel, the coordinator of the LDCs), along with the African Union trade commissioner. We discussed various topics of interest to the less developed or most vulnerable countries, such as the erosion of tariff preferences and duty-free, quota-free market access (DFQF) for the LDCs. I wanted to foster an atmosphere of trust that would be conducive to continuing cooperation with those countries around common objectives. I left with the feeling that the meeting had achieved its objective, and later wrote in my notebook: "Thanks to President Lula, but also because of the work I have been developing, Africa and Brazil are closer than ever."

My trip to the heart of Africa, possible only because I was able to use the presidential aircraft, was far from an isolated case. It was part of a concerted effort to achieve closer ties with the groups of developing countries that in the past had tended to be distrustful of initiatives such as that of the G20. Before the July Framework of 2004, I had had similar meetings with the G90 in Georgetown, Guyana, and Port Louis, Mauritius. This commitment to strengthening relations with countries geographically distant from Brazil (with some exceptions) would be amply rewarded at the Hong Kong Ministerial Conference.

Back in Brazil, I had plenty to keep me busy. There were the Paraguayan claims regarding the Itaipu dam and power plant;[68] the negotiations with Argentina on the Competitive Adjustment Mechanism (MAC); and the Mercosur summit, including developments with regard to the Community of South American Nations (CASA).[69] My time back "home" was brief, however, and was also interrupted by a trip down to Puerto Iguazú for the commemorations of the twentieth anniversary of the Brazil-Argentina agreements.[70] At the start of December I set off again for Geneva for another round of meetings, the last ones before Hong Kong. I had low expectations regarding what might actually be achieved in those conversations. I was aware that the finance ministers of some countries, led by British chancellor of the exchequer Gordon Brown, were considering some kind of initiative with regard to the Doha Round. But I struggled to see how, without a detailed knowledge of the trade issues being discussed, they would be able to do anything other than issue exhortations.

Spurred on by me and to some extent also by the finance minister, Antonio Palocci, Lula decided to call Tony Blair. The president essentially said to the British prime minister that the negotiators had exhausted all the possibilities and there was not much prospect of the finance ministers making progress either. It was therefore essential, Lula said, for the "leaders" to take up the reins of the negotiations. Blair, who at that time held the presidency both of the G7/G8 and the European Union, would be the person best placed to bring those leaders together. Lula, for his part, said he would be willing to participate in any meeting that might take place. Blair's reaction was positive but cautious. He asked if such a summit would replace the meeting of finance ministers that was being arranged by Gordon Brown. He was audibly relieved when Lula said that, as he saw it, the two gatherings would be separate. I attributed Blair's concerns to the long-running rivalry between him and the chancellor over the leadership of the Labour Party. Lula suggested to Blair a format similar to that of Gleneagles (although naturally without Russia, which was not a WTO member). Besides South Africa, he said, a less developed African country could also participate. In my own initial suggestion to Lula, I had left it open as to whether the summit would take place before or after Hong Kong. But Lula strongly favored the former in his conversation with Blair, reiterating his availability to take part "at any time." Blair concluded the call by assuring Lula that he shared his concerns and that he would be in touch again soon. Given the succession of impasses that had characterized the most recent meetings of trade ministers, a summit of leaders did seem to have the potential to introduce a new dynamic that might unblock the negotiations. And yet, if it did not succeed, there was also a risk that it might prove politically damaging for some of the heads of government involved. The ability to take risks, however, is one of the attributes expected of a leader.

"They don't represent the developing countries"

On my way to Geneva, via Paris, I wrote some notes about the two meetings I was about to attend (G4 and G4+2). My lack of optimism was apparent: "[The meeting] doesn't promise significant progress, only advances on procedural issues, clarification of concepts, etc.. Even the idea of drawing up a list of items on which there could be some progress has been left to one side. The WTO continues to give Brazil a high profile on the international stage, but it's very time-consuming and has brought little in the way of results." I arrived at the meeting armed with a series of questions that in my view would potentially contribute to clarifying various topics. The questions concerned export subsidies, domestic support, agricultural market access, NAMA, services, and issues of interest to the Least Developed Countries—the usual themes, in other words. But I tried to formulate them in a manner that might encourage some conceptual advances. For example, regarding export subsidies, I posed the question: "Is it possible to establish a date in the near future by which export subsidies can be eliminated, bearing in mind the parallel need to eliminate other kinds of trade-distorting government support?" In relation to domestic support, I asked: "Is it possible to agree to cuts in the overall levels of domestic support that will actually entail real, effective cuts, provided that the appropriate conditions are met in the other pillars of the agricultural negotiations?" I prepared various additional questions about other aspects of the negotiations or, in some cases, questions that involved more than one area.Frustratingly, however, my questions were not sufficient to spark a thoroughgoing discussion. In fact the only tangible result of the Geneva meeting was a preliminary understanding on the so-called "development package" (a group of items of interest to the LDCs). One section of my notes reads as follows: "No concrete progress was achieved on any of the central issues of the Round, including agriculture. My relationship with the European commissioner is still difficult, partly because of the differences of position but also because of his hypersensitivity. [Mandelson] chose Brazil and the G20 as the prime targets for his attacks, taking on the role Zoellick played after Cancún. They are not just criticisms of our positions or our proposals, but attempts to invalidate our role, such as: 'They don't represent the developing countries.' At the end of a somewhat heated discussion, I pointed out this rather unfair ploy. I don't remember my precise words, but they made Mandelson rather upset.[71] My relationship with Portman, on the other hand, is excellent. He visited me at Mont-Riant [the Brazilian ambassador's residence] after the meetings. The firm attitude Brazil has been adopting in relation to market access is in line with the USTR's own interests. But what will happen when I have to turn my guns on the Americans' insufficient offer on domestic subsidies? Some advisors tell me the US government is interested, for economic (fiscal) reasons, in cutting spending on subsidies—I hope that's true! In this complex chess game, with multiple players, the US has interests convergent with those of the EU (and contrary to ours) on industrial goods and on services, but so far our tactical alliance on agriculture has held firm. The other member of this central quartet, my Indian colleague Kamal Nath, is always unpredictable. On agriculture, his protectionist approach ends up helping the Europeans. On services, he plays a more offensive game than we do, especially with regard to 'Mode 4' and outsourcing,[72] but his proposals are not as ambitious as those of the developed countries. Whereas Brazil needs to defend the interests of the G20 as a whole, India tends to pursue its own interests."

While I was attending the G4+2[73] meeting, which consumed almost all of one day, President Lula called me. He wanted to follow up on his conversation with Blair. I asked the Itamaraty secretary-general, Samuel Pinheiro Guimarães, to arrange a phone call with, among others, President Bush. At my request the relevant preparatory work was carried out the very next day, in Geneva, by Roberto Azevêdo, with the assistance of Antonio Simões. I was pleased that the president was so clearly taking an interest in the negotiations. In part this was due to his labor union background and instinctive solidarity with the poor and disadvantaged. Sometimes I had to alert Lula to the ways in which the Europeans (especially the French) tried, on the political level, to manipulate the positions of poor countries (especially African ones), aiming to separate Brazil and the other members of the G20 from the LDCs and other countries with "vulnerable" economies. Although I was absolutely committed to the efforts to arrange a summit on the Doha Round, I could see that realistically there was not much chance of it happening before Hong Kong. And even afterwards, such a high-level event would face problems. To announce a summit in advance of the ministerial conference would have the immediate effect of diminishing the importance of Hong Kong. But if a summit were to take place in the new year, the United Kingdom—our most likely partner in the undertaking, given its liberalizing position on agriculture—would no longer hold the presidency of either the G7 or the European Union.[74]

On December 7, Lula called Bush. The US president welcomed the idea of a summit, but said that because of the lack of time and the "political conditions" (he did not elaborate), it could only take place early in the new year. The suggestion was picked up by the US media and given quite a lot of coverage. The *New York Times* devoted an editorial to it. Declarations attributed to the USTR, and an announcement on the State Department website, gave the idea some momentum. As usual whenever I was in Brazil and Lula had a scheduled phone conversation with a foreign leader, I was present in the room with him, listening in. And so I was pleased to hear Bush praise the "leadership" I had been showing in the run-up to Hong Kong. The US president clearly also recognized my unusual dual role. His exact description of me to Lula, in his distinctive Texan drawl, was "your trade-slash-foreign minister."

"You seem to hold the key to these negotiations"

On December 9, after a Mercosur meeting in Montevideo, the most important aspect of which was an agreement with Paraguay on payments for energy from Itaipu, I headed for Hong Kong via São Paulo and Johannesburg. On the flight to South Africa I went over some aspects of the strategy I intended to adopt at the ministerial conference. Over the previous weeks and months the negotiations had focused on domestic support, access to agricultural markets, and NAMA. The paucity of the European offer on agricultural market access meant there was no prospect, in the short term, of the US making a significant offer on domestic subsidies. My attempt to break this impasse by demonstrating our own flexibility on industrial tariffs, at the meetings in London and Geneva, had not been successful. The Americans had at least been kind enough to describe our gesture as "interesting"; the Europeans, probably due to their limited scope to make any corresponding move on agriculture, had simply dismissed it. The "grand bargain," resting on three pillars—domestic support, market access in agriculture (AMA), and industrial tariffs (NAMA)—was not going to happen. Therefore, to save the conference from complete failure, it would be necessary to focus on certain "deliverables" (i.e. partial results, but with concrete significance). With this in mind, I decided that our principal goal in Hong Kong should be the elimination of all forms of export subsidies by a specific date. But I was aware that other aspects of the negotiations, both "offensive" and "defensive" from Brazil's perspective, could not be ignored.

On December 11, in my hotel in the territory that used to be a British colony but is now a "special administrative region" of China, I wrote in my notebook: "These few lines will probably be the only ones I'm able to write this week, which is going to be a mixture of unfolding drama, jostling interests, and media exposure. . . . There won't be any definite results here. We all know that. Lula has planted the seed of political dialogue at the highest level. It's up to me to create the conditions for that dialogue to begin on an appropriate basis. But I have to be humble. However much I do—and I'll have to do a lot—I can't forget I'm just a cog in the machine. Brazil has taken flight, but it has also become the favorite target of the defenders of the status quo. Technical rigor, political audacity, and intense coordinating efforts in the G20, and beyond, will be crucial in these coming days."

The Hong Kong Ministerial Conference was scheduled for December 13–18. The two days before the official opening were frenetic. There were bilaterals with Kamal Nath, Mandelson, and Portman; a trilateral with the latter two; a meeting of the G4+2; and a lot of contact with the media, including a live interview with CNN. Rob Portman was very friendly. Obviously he wanted to prolong, as far as possible, the US-Brazil "alliance" in the face of the European Union. Such was his desire to extract concessions on AMA that he advised me not to "use up all your ammunition" on the issue of services. One moment when we were alone together, the USTR commented that Mandelson seemed obsessed with the Brazilian offer on NAMA, and how to get us to improve it. "I don't know what you guys did," Portman said, in his Midwestern accent, "but now you seem to hold the key to these negotiations." In the trilateral meeting with Mandelson and Portman, the main topic was the final date for the elimination of export subsidies (which were used mainly by European Union) and the related issues of food aid and export credits (mostly used by the US). I wrote later: "It's good that we're present during a discussion between the two major players, since it gives us a comfortable (and possibly useful) role as mediator." The fact that the United

States, the European Union, and Brazil were meeting in this format (without India, Japan, or Australia, and also without the director-general) reinforced our weight in the negotiations. Nevertheless, I was worried that this "privileged" position might give the impression that I had been co-opted by the two commercial superpowers.

On December 13 I coordinated a meeting of the G20 and also spoke one-to-one with the trade ministers of several countries, including South Africa (Mandisi Mpahlwa) and China (Bo Xilai). As part of our outreach strategy I also met my friend Clement Rohee, the Guyanese trade minister, who was the "facilitator" for the so-called "development package," a group of topics of particular interest to the LDCs and other small and vulnerable economies. In the same vein I coordinated a meeting of the G20 with other groups of developing countries. In the evening there was the first "Green Room on Development, Agriculture and NAMA," an informal gathering chaired by the director-general that was aimed at moving toward consensus. The day had begun with breakfast with Brazilian cabinet colleagues. Besides Furlan and Rodrigues, the agrarian development minister, Miguel Rossetto, also participated. I spoke at length with Rossetto, who had legitimate concerns about the effects of trade liberalization on family agriculture. For a long time, in fact, I had been trying to secure recognition for that particular issue in the face of the more aggressive liberalizing stance adopted by Brazil's powerful and highly competitive agribusiness. Essentially Rossetto's concerns were very similar to those that had inspired the creation of the G33, the group formally led by Indonesia but in which India exerted a strong influence. As the G20 itself was a heterogeneous group, including countries that were members of Cairns Group (competitive in agriculture) and others that were part of the G33 (more defensive), I was able to make the argument that my colleague's concerns had already been taken into account, albeit in a general rather than specific way, by the G20 proposals.[75] Moreover, however vigorously we defended the right to give financial support to small farmers in Brazil, we would never be able to compete with the treasuries of the richest countries. It would therefore be unwise for us to adopt an essentially defensive position. Probably on the basis of my argument, Rossetto advised me to "concentrate your fire" on the export subsidies.

The Hong Kong conference had a bit of everything, from periods of high tension during the negotiations to moments when we had to devote our energies to dealing with the media. The press published "profiles" of the principal negotiators on a daily basis. The exposure was constant. Gone were the days of Cancún, when the media attention had been focused almost exclusively on the representatives of Washington and Brussels (and I had resorted to unconventional tactics to attract the spotlight toward Brazil and the G20, such as calling a press conference while the plenary meeting was still in progress). The whirl of meetings in Hong Kong became even more intense as the conference neared its end. Several times, particularly in the last two days, the Green Room, which also became known as the "Chairman's Consultative Group" (CCG), continued its discussions through the night. Three or four hours sleep per night was the most we could hope for. On the flight back to Johannesburg, I wrote in my notebook that the results attained had been "reasonable": duty-free, quota-free access to both developed and developing countries' markets for the LDCs, which they had long been seeking;[76] a text on agriculture that consolidated the progress made so far (especially on export subsidies and domestic support), and that would serve, in theory, as a basis for further advances; and chapters on NAMA and services that did not create major problems for Brazil. On industrial tariffs, we even managed to introduce the concept of "proportionality," meaning that cuts to tariffs in the area of manufactured goods should not be out of proportion with the tariff reductions in agriculture. I was perfectly conscious that the value of this "concession" was only relative: its litmus test would come only when we eventually arrived at the "hard core" of the negotiations. But the concept of proportionality would at least serve as additional protection against the excessive ambitions of the developed countries.

The final date

As expected, the most heated discussions were those concerning agricultural issues, principally in relation to the final date[77] for the elimination of all forms of export subsidy. I had chosen this topic as one capable of producing a concrete result that would be of genuine interest to the media and the public. That is indeed what happened, as I will describe later. It also proved possible to obtain positive formulations, albeit not precisely quantified, with regard to domestic support, both in terms of a cut to overall tariffs (the term used was "Overall Trade-Distorting Support" (OTDS)), in relation to which we managed to establish the concept of effective cuts, and also with regard to disciplines inside the so-called "boxes."[78] As regards special products and special safeguards for developing countries, the language adopted seemed to be satisfactory to the G33 members.

Because of its concrete impact on agricultural trade and also its symbolic value (the total elimination of a form of trade distortion is not something that happens often), the question of the final date was the one that attracted the most attention and also sparked the greatest controversy. Initially the European Union did not want to set any date for the abolition of those subsidies and intended to leave the decision until the moment when the modalities were adopted. The G20, the United States, and most of the other countries (except for the G10)[79] took the position that export subsidies should come to an end in 2010. It was up to the G20, and to a large extent Brazil, to take command of this battle, which was to result in overflowing meeting rooms and intense media interest. An important development was a meeting between the G20 and the G90, from which emerged a document in which virtually all the developing countries called for the end of export subsidies in 2010. The most dramatic moment in the forging of this alliance actually took place away from the media spotlight, in a restricted-access area of the Hong Kong Convention Centre. We had convened a meeting between some of the more active members of the G20 and the coordinators of the various groups that made up the G90. But, as it turned out, the gathering was attended by virtually every delegate from every country in the G20 and G90. Hordes of developing country representatives swept into the meeting room. Visually, it was if the "wretched of the earth," to use Frantz Fanon's famous expression, had taken over the WTO, which had been (in the days of the GATT) and to a significant degree still was an Anglo-Saxon gentlemen's club, or at least wanted to be. This demonstration of Brazil's ability to bring together both "emerging" and very poor countries, competitive economies and those dependent upon the concession of trade preferences by the rich countries, surprised the media and also many delegations, particularly the European Union. It had become impossible to claim that the "elimination of all forms of export subsidy" was just a G20 banner, of little interest to the less developed countries with more vulnerable economies.

When the Green Room met again on the subject of agriculture, on the third or fourth day of the conference, the clamor for the establishment of a final date could not be ignored. The Europeans resisted as much as they could. The compromise solution was to set 2013 as the deadline. But that was not enough to resolve the differences. A new battle erupted in the Green Room, where Brazil, accompanied by some other countries, continued to fight for the inclusion of a reference to 2010 as an intermediary stage by which a substantial proportion of the subsidies should be eliminated. This was not a mere whim on our part. We were well aware that if all or even the bulk of the subsidies were to remain in force until close to the deadline, it was actually unlikely that they would be eliminated by the agreed date. The effect of setting an intermediary date for the elimination of a substantial part of the subsidies would lend credibility to the commitment. After numerous verbal skirmishes, including a moment in the early hours of the morning of the last day when I threatened to abandon the meeting, we were able to agree on a text in which it was stated that a significant amount of the subsidies would be eliminated by the mid-way point of the implementation period (which just so happened to be 2010). But there were several clashes before we reached that point. Peter Mandelson said time and again that for the European Commission it was a "point of honor" that the year 2010 should not be mentioned. His attitude probably derived from the uncompromising position of France. It is worth noting that over the course of that long nocturnal battle, almost all our allies succumbed one by one to the rigid European approach, whether due to sheer tiredness or because they had other priorities. But in direct opposition to Mandelson's stance, it was a "point of honor" for the G20 to ensure 2010 *was* referred to in the text. That was the approach I took—but the only delegate who offered me determined support throughout that long night was the agriculture minister of South Africa, Angela Thoko Didiza, a friendly and energetic matron-like figure who reminded me of the foreign minister, my friend Nkosazana Zuma. Gradually, thanks to the persistence of the director-general, who obstinately insisted that an agreement had to be reached, other supporters did re-emerge, particularly from African countries such as Nigeria and Senegal. Among the South Americans who participated in the Green Room, Argentina had the same position as Brazil but for some unknown reason was not very forceful in defending it. I imagined that the new Argentine foreign minister, my friend Jorge Taiana, having until recently been in the field of human rights, did not yet feel totally at ease with the specifics of trade negotiations. But it was also possible that, even back then, Buenos Aires was already planning to save its ammunition for its defensive struggle on industrial goods. With the rising tide in favor of the reference to the date in question, the EU trade commissioner was eventually forced to abandon his initial "take it or leave it" attitude, which had been typical of European arrogance in the context of the Doha Round.

At one point in the early morning, when the resistance to Mandelson seemed to have crumbled, I seriously considered abandoning the meeting. I had no wish to be complicit in an attitude of complacency or subservience toward the intransigence of Brussels. I departed from the meeting room, leaving my collaborators in a state of some puzzlement (as I found out later). But I had not thought through the possible consequences of what I was doing. I had not decided whether, when it came to the formal meeting in the late afternoon, I would seek to "block" any eventual consensus or just "put down a marker" with a speech denouncing the Europeans' inflexibility. Nor could I be sure how well my departure would go down in Brazil. Pondering these issues as I walked through the waiting room on the way to the restroom, I came across Japanese trade minister Shoichi Nakagawa. He seemed oblivious to the unfolding crisis and spoke to me about a different subject (the issue of duty-free, quota-free, if I remember rightly). Although Nakagawa's attitude suggested a total lack of a sense of opportunity, I listened to him out of courtesy. No sooner had he finished speaking than Rob Portman appeared, insisting that I return to the meeting room.[80] According to the USTR, in the few minutes I had been absent, a text had begun to be drafted—upon his initiative and with Lamy's support—that included, albeit in a far from clear way, our vision of "progressivity" toward the elimination of subsidies. I returned to the fray, and indeed made another intervention or two. When the meeting was suspended at about 9 a.m., it seemed that we had reached a solution, although there were still ambiguities. Back at the hotel about an hour later, after a sleepless night, I received a call from Lamy. Mandelson, he said, had backtracked and decided he could not accept a reference to 2010 "under any circumstances." Apparently the commissioner had mentioned internal conflicts in the EU, and even claimed he could not afford to give the impression he was "still taking orders" from his former boss Tony Blair, who was among our allies on the issue (not only because of the UK's free-trade vocation but also due to British opposition to the level of spending on the EU Common Agricultural Policy (CAP)). That was the moment when I suggested the term "half-period" (referring to the half-way point between the first and the last year of the phasing-out process) as a way of alluding to the date without mentioning it explicitly.[81] Lamy accepted the suggestion.

"I would never let you down"

I got a few hours' sleep before the afternoon meetings, without knowing what exactly lay ahead. When I woke up, I had a light meal and then went to rejoin the battle. On the way to the convention center I received another call, this time from the chair of the conference, the affable but not very firm John Tsang, Hong Kong's secretary for commerce, industry and technology. He asked if I would accept an alternative formulation that Mandelson had come up with. He implied (or at least I inferred) that he was also speaking on behalf of the Chinese trade minister, Bo Xilai. But in my view the wording of this new proposal by the EU was absolutely meaningless. It was along the lines of "eliminate a substantial part [of the export subsidies] before the final date." I politely told Tsang I could not agree with such "slyness." I added that I did not wish to create a problem for him as chair, but deliberately also left an element of doubt about the attitude I would adopt. Because WTO decisions are adopted by consensus, the slightest degree of uncertainty about Brazil's position would have given Tsang pause for thought. I continued on my way to the G20 meeting, which would be followed by the plenary session with the heads of delegation. At the meeting, I began by telling the other members of the group (very few of whom had participated in the Green Room) about what had taken place during the night and the early hours of the morning. While I was in the middle of my explanation, I was handed a document that had just been produced by the WTO Secretariat under the director-general's authority. I immediately saw that the formulation I had proposed to Lamy remained intact. It was an enormous relief. The director-general's preservation of my compromise formulation on the timeframe for the elimination of export subsidies—along with the previously mentioned advances with regard to domestic support and special products (which I described to my audience as "modest but not insignificant")—allowed me, as coordinator, to recommend that the G20 accept the director-general's draft.

Bolstered by the unanimous support of the G20, and by expressions of appreciation and even some applause, I set off for a press conference accompanied by the ministers of India, Argentina, Chile, Zimbabwe, and Tanzania: a varied group quite representative of the G20 as a whole. The G20 meeting was also marked by emotional moments. In addition to the applause, there were warm words of support and also an apology from Kamal Nath for having abandoned me at a critical moment during the last session of the Green Room. Kamal's words were: "I know you think I have let you down, but I want you to know I would never let you down." There was also a kind note from my faithful friend Leila Rachid, in which the Paraguayan minister said I had achieved the status of "universal citizen" and that the Doha Round could henceforth be known as the "Amorim Round."

The game is never won until the final whistle blows, however. When I was on my way to the meeting of the heads of delegation, Clodoaldo Hugueney called to inform me, in a rather alarmed tone, that something "very serious" was happening. It concerned Venezuela, represented at the ministerial conference by the minister for food, a member of the military (if I remember rightly), who had a very limited grasp of the issues. Apparently the Venezuelan minister intended to object to the adoption of the draft declaration, thereby destroying the fragile and indeed uncertain consensus (the position of the EU, at this stage, was still unknown). In substantive terms his concerns were little different from those of the G33 or our own agrarian development ministry, but in his case they were expressed with such stridency and anti-capitalist rhetoric that there was little room for negotiation. I went to speak to the Cuban delegation (always more reasonable and less prone to isolation than the Venezuelans) to see if they might be able to dissuade the representatives of Caracas from creating an impasse that would lead the conference to total collapse. I pointed out that the draft declaration that was set to be approved contained several aspects that represented real gains for developing countries (including the poorest ones), and that a rupture at that late stage would not be well received by, among others, the countries of Africa and the Caribbean. The head of the Venezuelan delegation, however, was unmovable. He had received direct instructions from Chávez and could only change position with the president's explicit permission. Fearing the worst, I decided to call President Lula. It was late afternoon in Hong Kong, and therefore quite early in the morning in Brazil. And it was a Sunday. But, when I was in the meeting of heads of delegation, Lula returned my call. I asked him to get in touch with Chávez. Not long afterwards, the Venezuelan minister came to find me. In our earlier conversation I had been forthright in expressing my concerns not only about the fate of the conference but also about the unity both of Mercosur (it was a period in which Venezuela's entry into the bloc was beginning to be discussed) and the G20 (of which Venezuela was a member). He seemed to accept some of my points, although I imagined his newfound flexibility was due less to their intrinsic merits than to the likelihood that he had already received a message from Caracas in the wake of Lula's call to Chávez. And yet later, during the plenary session, I still had to listen rather anxiously to a stern oration from the Venezuelan minister in which the words "rejection" (*rechazo*) and "demands" (*exigencias*) featured prominently. At the end of his soliloquy I was therefore somewhat surprised, and hugely relieved, that he nevertheless did not object to the emerging consensus. And so Brazil had just prevented the WTO Hong Kong Ministerial Conference from being torpedoed by one of our own allies in the G20. It is a fact the majority of delegates are still unaware of to this day.

"I want to give you a gift—the pen I used to sign away the export subsidies"

When things had calmed down, Rob Portman came over to the area where the Brazilian delegation was seated. He invited me to go with him to meet his family, who were nearby in the hall. His wife and children were very well dressed, as if they were about to go to the Sunday service at their local church back home. In introducing me to them, he made a point of describing me not only as a professional whom he admired but also as a friend. The "happy ending" to the ministerial conference also had other pleasant moments. I recorded some of them in I the notes I wrote during the flight from Johannesburg to São Paulo: "The pen I'm using to write these lines . . . was given to me by the director of the agriculture section of the European Commission, a friendly Galician by the name of José Manuel Silva Rodríguez, better known by his nickname Cookie (or might that be Kuki?). As we were saying goodbye, at the end of the last meeting of heads of delegation, he said to me: 'I want to give you a gift—the pen I used to sign away the export subsidies.'" According to the declaration we had just signed, those subsidies would come to an end in 2013. As we now know, however, that supposedly final date would end up being postponed indefinitely. But Silva Rodríguez's gesture was still significant, as well as charming. It came as I was still recovering from hours and indeed days of rapidly changing emotions. The comment I wrote, perhaps a little over-sentimental, was: "Friendship and mutual respect can transcend differences of position."

From the broader perspective of Brazilian foreign policy, Hong Kong would strengthen our leadership role and earn us even greater respect. One important consequence was the deepening of relations with other developing countries, especially in Africa. On the sidelines of the conference I had a meeting with the ministers of the "Cotton-4," the four African countries most affected by US (and, though less overtly, European) subsidies: Benin, Burkina Faso, Mali, and Chad. I subsequently asked the director of Itamaraty's economic department, Roberto Azevêdo, to visit all four countries. A few months later, the countries' agriculture ministers (and their counterpart from Togo) would come to Brazil for meetings at Embrapa.[82] During that meeting in Hong Kong, the original purpose of which had been to coordinate our negotiating positions, we decided to initiate a technical cooperation program whose most significant aspect was the support for a model farm in Mali where, years later, I would find myself picking samples of cotton alongside President Amadou Touré. As result of the time I spent with South African trade minister Angela Thoko Didiza, who participated with me in the battle of the Green Room and with whom I was able to exchange a few ideas during the flight from Hong Kong to Johannesburg, the SADC[83] countries would be invited to Brazil in 2006 to attend an event on family agriculture organized by the agrarian development ministry. Later, at the instigation of President Lula, Embrapa would stage an event in Brasilia aimed at promoting agricultural cooperation with Africa; an impressive number (about forty) of the continent's agriculture ministers would attend.

The notes I wrote on the journey back from Hong Kong to Brazil contain comments on the behavior of some of the delegations, and of the director-general. For example: "The Chinese delegation, headed by Bo Xilai,[84] had a discreet role. Rumor has it that they even allowed themselves to be used by the Europeans, in the period when Lamy had gone to get some sleep, so that a *corrigendum* could be inserted into the declaration without the reference to the elimination of a substantial part of the export subsidies "by the end of the first half of the implementation period." According to second-hand reports (I was not able to confirm their veracity), when Lamy came back, he refused go along with the maneuver. Lamy, for me, was a towering figure at the conference, not only on account of his competence and his sheer capacity for work, but also because of the dignity and firmness he displayed. On the penultimate and last mornings, having spent the preceding nights embroiled in the Green Room, I went to bed feeling very discouraged because of the negative pressures exerted by the European Union. Based on previous experience, [I feared that those pressures] would eventually prevail in the final texts to be issued by the secretariat. But on both occasions, to my surprise, [my fears were unfounded]. Of all the participants, Lamy made the biggest contribution to the balanced outcome of the conference."

The prominence given to Brazil by the international media[85] had a positive impact within the government, strengthening the leadership position of Itamaraty in the trade negotiations. And in the Brazilian media there were favorable comments on the role of our delegation. The most significant was a column by Clóvis Rossi in the *Folha de São Paulo* entitled "The Statesman."[86] The superlative adjectives that appeared in some articles were echoed by cabinet colleagues at a reception hosted by President Lula on the day I arrived back in Brasilia. The minister in charge of regional development, Ciro Gomes (who, incidentally, had run for president in the 2002 elections won by Lula) and the controller-general (later to become defense minister), Waldir Pires, were particularly lavish in their praise. Vice President José Alencar, although less inclined toward extravagant praise, nevertheless proffered a number of positive adjectives. Later I learned via the Itamaraty secretary-general, Samuel Pinheiro Guimarães, that at a cabinet meeting before I arrived, agriculture minister Roberto Rodrigues and also President Lula himself had been very complimentary about my efforts in Hong Kong. A sign of Lula's enthusiasm had been his announcement that he intended to attend the World Economic Forum in Davos, in January, in order to "talk about poverty and the WTO."

FROM HONG KONG TO GENEVA

"It's impressive how engaged Lula is!"

As it turned out, domestic commitments prevented Lula from going to Davos. But his personal involvement with WTO issues would continue through his contact with the leaders of the major powers. From a personal perspective, 2005 ended in triumph. Or rather in relative triumph, given that the positive results obtained at Hong Kong were restricted to certain specific points (although undeniably important ones). Furthermore, those advances would only translate into concrete gains if corresponding progress was made in the others areas of the Round. The mantra, as ever, was "nothing is agreed until everything is agreed." Nevertheless, I made Hong Kong the subject of an article I wrote in the *Folha de São Paulo* on December 26, and of the speech I gave to a get-together of Brazilian ambassadors at the start of the new year. I also continued to receive positive feedback from the business sector. I heard through one of my collaborators, for example, that the steel industry magnate Jorge Gerdau had said I had "harnessed ideology to the national interest." Coming from one of Brazil's leading businesspeople, that was high praise indeed.

Although Hong Kong had brought one stage of the Doha Round to a close, the arduous negotiation process continued. The "next stop" was the by-now traditional meeting of some ministers in Davos, convened this time by my old acquaintance Joseph Deiss, the Swiss economy minister who had been a victim of Bob Zoellick's abrasive temperament in one of the Green Room meetings preceding the adoption of the July Framework in 2004. Also scheduled were meetings of the G6, G4, and G20, along with a public panel discussion to be chaired by Christine Ockrent, a well-known presenter on French TV and wife of Médecins Sans Frontières co-founder and future French foreign minister Bernard Kouchner. Unfortunately, a few days before the scheduled meetings, the European trade commissioner returned to an aggressive tone, expressing harsh criticism of Brazil and India. Although by now accustomed to Mandelson's outbursts, the main purpose of which was to bolster his credentials among the EU members states, I felt obliged to respond and persuaded my Indian colleague to do likewise.

Before departing for Davos I had a meeting with President Lula in which I encouraged him to maintain the political momentum aimed at pushing the negotiations forward. In particular I insisted that he should call the German chancellor, Angela Merkel, to discuss with her the suggestion he had made to Tony Blair and George W. Bush, before Hong Kong, about a "mini-summit" on the Doha Round. In fact there was an opportunity coming up in the near future for a discussion among leaders, albeit not with a great number of heavyweight participants, in the form of the summit of the Progressive Governance Network[87] in South Africa. Lula called Merkel and also President Thabo Mbeki on January 26. In his conversation with the German chancellor, Lula described the results achieved in Hong Kong as "modest," and emphasized the importance of the Doha Round for the "poorest countries." He conveyed his impression that the negotiators had "reached their limit" and that now the desired results could only be achieved if leaders themselves intervened, in the form of an "emergency summit." Merkel made a brief comment about Germany being interested in the issue of industrial goods "now that progress has been achieved on agricultural subsidies." As for the idea of the summit, Merkel was reticent. Without discarding the idea altogether, she noted that there would be an alternative opportunity to meet at the European Union, Latin America and the Caribbean summit set to take place in May in Vienna. Lula nevertheless insisted that there should be an "extraordinary meeting of the G8 with the WTO G20." He assured Merkel that if such a meeting were to take place, Brazil would be willing to make concessions so as to move toward an agreement in which the "main winners should be the poor countries." Merkel said she had noted Lula's position and suggestions, and that she would discuss the matter internally with her EU colleagues, but then she immediately changed subject and started talking about an IAEA Board of Governors' resolution on Iran. In his phone conversation with Thabo Mbeki, the same day, Lula said to the South African president that he was making calls to some of the G8 leaders to discuss how to follow up on the Hong Kong conference. He repeated the suggestion of a high-level "G8 plus G20" meeting on the subject of the Doha Round. Pointing out that various important figures with an interest in the subject would be present at the forthcoming Progressive Governance Summit, including the WTO director-general himself, Lula proposed that the working breakfast already scheduled for February 12 should be used as an opportunity for an in-depth discussion on the Doha Round. Mbeki readily agreed and said he would make the necessary arrangements.[88] At the time, after reading the transcripts of these conversations, I wrote in my notebook the following comment: "It's impressive how engaged Lula is!"

The Davos meetings produced nothing very substantial. I think I did reasonably well in the panel discussion, which was an opportunity for little "public diplomacy."[89] I also participated in an informal exchange of views on the next steps to be taken in the negotiations, which took place in what might be described as a "G3+1" format (EU, US, Brazil + WTO director-general). In summary, no progress was made in Davos (indeed, every year was the same in that respect), but nor did the Europeans, as I had feared on account of Mandelson's strident statement a few days earlier, make headway with their attempt to change the terms of the discussion and push agriculture into the background. Both at the big events and in the discussions held by smaller groups, agriculture continued to be the dominant theme, although there was a more or less general recognition that other issues such as industrial goods (NAMA) and services also needed to be addressed. "We didn't go backwards" was my observation, reflecting my concern with preserving the results of Hong Kong. I also noted that the G3+1 meeting was useful in that it established a methodology for the discussions.

Meanwhile, the idea of a summit seemed to make some headway. It was mentioned by UK chancellor of the exchequer Gordon Brown at a meeting I attended in Davos on economic issues (not specifically on the Doha Round). Naturally I expressed my support for the idea. The possibility of the summit had also been raised during the G3+1. On that occasion Mandelson pointed out, reasonably enough, that the summit would have to be "one-shot operation." The heads of government could not afford to waste their energies on a meeting that did not produce results, because a failure at the highest level would make it even more difficult to resume the negotiations afterwards. There was also the issue of who would attend. A "G8 Plus" format would include Chirac and Berlusconi, whose interventions were hardly likely to contribute to a positive outcome. According to my notes, Pascal Lamy suggested that Durão Barroso, the president of the European Commission, could be the European interlocutor (not an idea that would go down well with Mandelson, I imagined). There were still doubts, however, about Barroso's capacity to take decisions on crucial issues. Overall, my impression was that Davos marked a small improvement in the mood between the principal negotiators. We agreed that new meetings in various formats (G6, G4, or G3+1) would take place in March. In the meantime there would be a discussion of WTO issues during the Progressive Governance Summit in South Africa. From Davos I departed for Geneva and then London, donning my hat of foreign minister *strictu sensu* in order to participate, as the only representative of Latin America, in a conference on Afghanistan.

"My people tell me that you don't want an agreement..."

Our communications on the subject of the Doha Round continued during February. The most important of all these endeavors was the attempt to forge a "tactical alliance" with the United Kingdom, aimed at pushing the negotiations forward. It was a joint effort based partly upon the discussions between Lula and Blair at the Progressive Governance Summit in South Africa. London not only wanted to see a reduction in spending on the EU Common Agricultural Policy but also had an intrinsic interest in promoting free trade. More specifically, the UK anticipated that there were substantial gains to be made in the area of services (the country having long ago lost its primacy in manufacturing to Germany, now the industrial powerhouse of Europe). In pursuing this commercial *entente cordiale* with the UK, I took advantage of a previously scheduled meeting in Paris with President Chirac, on the efforts to combat world hunger, in order to travel to London on February 24. Two days earlier I had received a visit in Brasilia from a special envoy of the British prime minister, who had come with a message for President Lula. I knew the visitor only by his formal title, Lord Levy, though I noticed he persisted in calling me by my first name. He was a slightly odd character, who I must say did not inspire a great deal of confidence, but apparently he enjoyed a very close relationship with Tony Blair and evidently felt able to speak on his behalf. For some time Levy had been performing the role of Blair's special envoy to the Middle East. Regarding the WTO, he said little about any of the important topics, but he did stress the importance of the meeting I was due to have in London with the prime minister's chief of staff, Jonathan Powell. He also pointed out that by entering into a direct dialogue with Brazil, the British government was acting outside the mandate of the European Commission and even, strictly speaking, transgressing its rules. Perhaps that explained why my meeting with Powell would be taking place not at 10 Downing Street but at the more discreet location of Admiralty House. For my part, I reciprocated this desire for little or no publicity: in my diary I see that the page for February 24 contains nothing more than the times of my arrival in and departure from London.

Hong Kong, as I said, had made possible important advances on issues of interest to Brazil and other developing countries, and yet the ministerial conference had hardly touched upon what I referred to as the "grand bargain" of the Doha Round. In the forthcoming conversations with the British government I saw, perhaps over-optimistically, an opportunity to dissolve the blockages that were holding back the negotiations. At the time, with the help of my aides, I was trying to come up with a creative way of producing an offer that would be attractive to the European Union without having the devastating impact on our industry that across-the-board trade liberalization would no doubt cause. Mulling over the technical aspects during the flight to

London via Paris, I committed some of my thoughts to paper. I began with the observation that the limits imposed both by FIESP and Mercosur/Argentina (a coefficient of 30 as the bottom line) left little room to explore the possibility of a formula for concessions on manufactured goods that might elicit a reciprocal concession on the part of the EU. I wrote: "All I can do is try to see if, independently of the coefficients, products that are of interest to the Europeans could [receive more favorable treatment] and be excluded from the flexibilities (or be subject to more limited flexibilities). It is also the case that some of those [flexibilities] will have to be reserved . . . for products from China, such as textiles and footwear, so as to protect or industry from having to compete with them.[90] The other issue I will have to explain in London is that we find ourselves in a complex situation that does not consist of a straightforward deal between two parties . . . but a triangular game in which what Brazil (or the G20) needs from Europe is a concession in AMA that will in turn lead the United States to substantially reduce, in effective terms, its domestic subsidies. For that to happen I don't think it's sufficient to come up with gestures such as those made by Europe on agricultural market access through quotas, which will be of little benefit to the Americans. It will be necessary to achieve something closer to a formula cut in agricultural tariffs. Only a movement of that kind, which will also have an indirect positive impact on tariff reductions by other countries (India and China, for example)[91] will be able to provide the Americans with the kind of gains in market access that they consider necessary in order to make it politically viable for them to reduce their overall domestic subsidies and also accept the disciplines.[92] Any conversation with the EU on reciprocal concessions is incomplete without the United States. . . . And so that obviously places limits on my dialogue with Powell. However, if I can get a concrete idea of what the Europeans consider to be the minimum concession on our part [on industrial goods], moving from the logic of the coefficients to the logic of the products (as the Europeans have been doing with us on agriculture), I will be able to see if it is possible to advance toward an agreement (which will always depend also on the US)." My reflections included a note of caution: "This is a Development Round. The EU and US demands cannot disregard the basic needs of developing countries—recognized, for example, by Article 24 of the Hong Kong Declaration." And I added: "I don't want to be seen as someone who is acting behind the backs of the G20 or the broader group of countries we formed alliances with in Hong Kong."

With Powell I would also need to test the water with regard to the proposed summit. Tony Blair's envoy had told me in Brasilia that the prime minister was still favorable toward the idea, in principle, but that he would only want to go ahead with the summit "when it's fairly certain that advances can be made." At that stage I myself was beginning to have doubts about whether the meeting of leaders could realistically take place. Presumably there would be resistance to overcome, especially from the French. Also, Blair would need the support of Merkel—and that in turn raised the issue, again, of an offer on industrial goods to attract the Germans. In the notes I made before my conversation with Blair's chief of staff, I went as far as to draw a little diagram—a triangle representing Brazil, the European Union, and the United States, with arrows denoting their respective demands. In retrospect, the biggest flaw in my thinking, which I had no way of fully appreciating at the time, was to underestimate the impact that special products (SP) and the Special Safeguard Mechanism (SSM),[93] championed by India, could have on the outcome of negotiations. In summary, the situation I attempted to capture pictorially was that Brazil's demands toward the EU were in the areas of domestic support and market access for agricultural products, while the EU's demands toward Brazil concerned market access for industrial goods. What the EU was demanding from the US, meanwhile, was in the area of domestic support (so as to compensate for the reductions in subsidies the EU itself would have to implement as part of the reform of the CAP). As for what the US wanted from the EU, it principally had to do with access to agricultural markets. Brazil was making significant demands of the US in terms of domestic support, while the US was seeking to extract concessions from us on access to markets for industrial products. There was not enough space in the diagram for some of the other significant aspects of the triangular interplay, such as the demands with regard to services that both the US and the EU were making of Brazil. Nor could I fit in the Europeans' concerns about "geographical indications."[94] But I was convinced that if we were able to elicit some movement along the vectors of the diagram, substantive progress could be made. In that spirit, I set off for Admiralty House.

Although strictly speaking my conversation with Jonathan Powell could not be characterized as a negotiation—partly because of the concerns Lord Levy had previously referred to—it nevertheless yielded some positive results. It was on the basis of that meeting that, with the assistance of my aides, I was able to draw up a Lula-Blair joint statement on the subject of the Doha Round, issued during the president's state visit to the UK about ten days later. The statement was considered "strong and positive" by our permanent representative in Geneva, Clodoaldo Hugueney, who was not someone inclined to indulge in insincere praise. It expressed the shared opinion that Hong Kong had produced positive results (on development issues and the time limit for the elimination of export subsidies) but had not made progress with regard to the modalities. The statement called on the WTO members to improve their offers on agriculture (market access and domestic support), and also on NAMA and services. It emphasized—and this was important from our point of view—that the concessions to be made by the developing countries should be proportionate and in accordance with the principle of differential treatment. Lula and Blair also reiterated the importance of holding a summit of leaders, and declared their willingness to consult with their counterparts in that regard.

During Lula's state visit in March, Jonathan Powell gave a further indication of his trust in our negotiating abilities. This second meeting with Blair's chief of staff took place at 10 Downing Street, the day after the state banquet offered by Queen Elizabeth II, and gave rise to the idea that I could meet with Angela Merkel, considered by Powell to be the key figure in shaping the European position. Quite apart from Germany's considerable economic weight, Chancellor Merkel was the only leader able to exert influence over President Jacques Chirac of France. It soon became evident that Powell must have mentioned the idea to Blair very soon afterwards. When Lula sat down with Blair for a "private conversation" (at which I was also present, in contravention of British protocol) and the subject of the Round came up, the British prime minister said he would call the *Bundeskanzlerin* to suggest that she receive me in Berlin.

Before describing my meetings in Berlin, I would like to mention a curious episode from my visit to London. At the state banquet at Buckingham Palace, I was seated between Camilla Parker Bowles[95] and the prime minister. After we had taken our places, the Duchess of Cornwall (the title Camilla had received upon being accepted into the royal family—and, incidentally, one that for a long time I had been unaware of, despite having been Brazil's ambassador in London in 2002-03) turned to me and struck up a conversation that must have lasted about half an hour. To her left was President Lula, who had been engaged in conversation by Her Majesty the Queen. I suppose Camilla was merely following the rigid protocol of state occasions in London by devoting her attention to me so that Lula was free to talk to the head of state. As a result, however, I was unable to take the opportunity for what would have been a less formal conversation with Blair. And the frustration was tinged with discomfort: I did not want the prime minister to think I was yet another foreign diplomat dazzled by the chance to exchange a few words (or, in this case, considerably more) with the duchess, at the expense of a more substantive discussion with a powerful politician. Fortunately (and this too must have been part of the protocol), the duchess eventually turned her attentions very deliberately to Lula, which allowed me to have a brief but interesting chat with Blair. The prime minister got straight to the point: "So, my people tell me that you don't want an agreement [on the Doha Round]." To which I replied: "Not true, Prime Minister." Blair stated his own desire for progress: "Not many people want to move forwards—perhaps only Lula and me." He continued: "And for that to happen, we need to move some way from the current negotiating positions." I commented briefly on my conversation with Powell, indicating that there might be some additional flexibility on our part with regard to manufactured goods (a slightly lower coefficient had been mentioned at one point), as long as there were corresponding moves on agriculture. But, I added, because of the realities of our industrial sector and also Mercosur, there were certain limits we simply could not go beyond. Blair made an observation that provided an outline of how he might be able to proceed, although obviously he could not afford to give the impression that he had taken it upon himself to negotiate on behalf of the European Commission (or, worse, behind its back). He said he would be able to give a message to the EC along the lines of "I think Brazil would accept X or Y." But in order to do so, he added, he would need a "sign" during Lula's stay in London. The sign was duly provided in the joint statement, issued less than twenty-four hours afterwards. Blair concluded his comments on WTO-related matters by saying he would be able to convince Bush to participate in a summit if it were scheduled at a "convenient moment" for the US president. The prime minister then kindly made reference to a subject he knew was very dear to me: "Brazil has to be part of the Security Council. I'll persuade Washington of that."

On March 13 I woke up in snow-covered Berlin. While waiting to meet Chancellor Merkel, I thought about the points I wanted to raise. The rough notes I made reflected my intention not to take a purely technical approach: "(a) importance of Round for poorer countries, strengthening prospects for prosperity and peace, including containment of terrorism; (b) very brief description of current situation [in the Doha Round] and our willingness to do our bit, in accordance with [the principle of] proportionality; (c) role of Germany, above all in Europe and especially with regard to France—show we need to go beyond immediate interests, such as Chirac's with regard to agriculture." On the flight back to São Paulo in the early hours of February 14, I recorded my impressions of the meetings in Berlin: "I'm probably the first Brazilian official to have had a meeting with the new German chancellor. . . . My hosts were impeccable, from the two or three police cars providing an escort, and the diplomat playing the liaison role, to the Brazilian flag flying at government headquarters between those of Germany and the European Union. And all this for a visit that was arranged at the last minute and had a very specific purpose. I'd been told Merkel only had fifteen minutes to spare, but we ended up talking for about half an hour (and did so in English, which was definitely another advantage) . . . She was friendly and smiling, attentive without being over-formal, and seemed genuinely interested in the conversation. She showed a willingness to engage with the subject, including with regard to her difficult neighbor. Talking of which, Chirac is arriving in Berlin today for his first formal meeting with the new German cabinet. Perhaps the most interesting point was the connection Merkel herself made between the Doha Round and global governance. It's a perception that favors the idea, promoted by Lula, that the leaders need to participate more in the trade negotiations. Like other heads of government, the *Kanzlerin* naturally doesn't want to go to a summit unless there's a reasonable degree of certainty that it's going to be successful."

My conversation with the chancellor followed a brief dialogue with two of her advisors, mainly concerning Iran. On that particular subject I argued that the sooner the Iranian nuclear program stopped being the concern of the Security Council and was passed back to the IAEA, the better for all concerned. I also highlighted the role that countries such as South Africa and Brazil could play. My notes continue: "Afterwards, I had a productive meeting with the German "sherpa,"[96] Bernd Pfaffenbach. I told him what movements would be necessary in order to achieve the steps the chancellor had agreed to take. Like his boss, Pfaffenbach seemed to realize the importance of a quick and positive result [in the Doha Round], especially for the developing countries. Based on some background information about him in the notes that had been prepared by our Berlin embassy, I told Pfaffenbach I was delighted to be meeting "the most influential public servant in Germany." That went down well, needless to say. But it was the meeting with Merkel that made the trip really worthwhile.

The aides accompanying me on these visits—my chief of staff, Maria Nazareth Farani Azevêdo, and my press secretary, Ricardo Neiva Tavares—were enthusiastic about the way events had unfolded. Neiva Tavares pointed out the highly unusual nature of a situation in which "the British prime minister calls the German chancellor to ask her to receive a Brazilian foreign minister." He also noted the way in which the British attitude toward my participation in the meetings had changed. Based on the British (and also, generally, European) model in which a cabinet minister with their own specific area of authority does not necessarily have a very close, personal relationship with the head of government, Blair's aides had not been keen on my accompanying Lula in his "private" meeting with Blair, and originally had not even wanted me to meet Jonathan Powell. But the fluidity of my conversation with the prime minister at the Buckingham Palace banquet made things much easier in that respect. Indeed, during the meal, it was Blair himself who said: "I think you should come to the private meeting between me and Lula." To which I replied: "It's your call, Prime Minister." While on the subject of Blair, I should mention that I was impressed by how closely he was following the Doha Round negotiations. He knew, for example, about a very long phone conversation I had had with the EU trade commissioner at the end of February. What that also showed, of course, was that the relationship between Blair and Peter Mandelson remained a very close one.

"The most pleasant place in the world"

Before I left London there were meetings in the G3, G4 and G6 formats, organized by Mandelson at Carlton Gardens.[97] And in the period after Lula's state visit to the UK, meetings with "the usual suspects" continued at a frenetic pace but with limited results. At the end of March, after a visit to Chile and an IBSA meeting in Rio de Janeiro, I met again with Mandelson, Portman, and Lamy, this time at the Copacabana Palace hotel in Rio. I do not remember if Kamal Nath was unable to attend or if the idea was to see what advances could be made through an exchange of views in a slightly less formal context. It was on that occasion that we began to study tables of figures in order to try to work out what would be the real impact of different formulas and coefficients on tariffs and subsidies. Seated beneath the verdant canopy of the hotel's exuberant pergola on a sunny day, Mandelson commented that we were in "the most pleasant place in the world." The welcoming and at times light-hearted ambience did not prove sufficient to produce any real progress. It was, however, conducive to Portman indicating that he would accept, in theory, a significantly lower ceiling for total US domestic subsidies—which is to say a bigger "Overall Reduction of Trade-Distorting Domestic Support" (OTDS)—than any he had previously spelled out. In a bilateral meeting at the apartment the US delegation was using as their office, the USTR referred to a hypothetical ceiling ("if everything else falls into place") of $13 billion USD. But he very quickly backtracked. Checking his notes, he realized that such an offer would not actually be consistent with the figures he had in front of him—or, in other words, with the official limit for his negotiating position. Somewhat embarrassed, he asked me not to mention his slip, which would have had the potential to get him into trouble with the US agricultural lobby. Years later, when Portman was no longer USTR, I would hear from one of our mutual contacts that he had been very grateful for my discretion. In 2011 Portman would be elected as senator for Ohio and his name would even be suggested as a possible Republican vice presidential candidate. When I was no longer foreign minister, I visited him in his office on Capitol Hill. He received me with great courtesy. As far as I know, he has never again been directly involved in issues related to international trade. The figure mentioned that day by Portman was never officially accepted by the US, but it stayed in my mind as a possible indicator of the outer boundary of Washington's "tolerance." The only other noteworthy episode in the period after my trip to London was an altercation between Lamy and Mandelson, when the European trade commissioner responded indignantly to an opinion expressed by the WTO director-general about how the EU could proceed in certain areas of the agriculture negotiations: "Stick to your job as WTO director-general," said Mandelson.[98]

Immediately after the meetings in Rio de Janeiro, I was obliged to dedicate myself to an issue that, for various reasons, I considered something of an unwanted distraction. Brazil was due to take an important decision about the system of digital TV it would adopt. The technical experts had a clear preference for the Japanese system, a fact Tokyo was already aware of thanks to their active (and occasionally inconvenient) ambassador in Brasilia. In return for its business, the Brazilian government wanted the provider country to make commitments in terms of investment and technology transfer. Designated by President Lula to head a mission to the Japanese capital with those specific objectives, I did what I could, and indeed received some praise for my efforts, but obviously our negotiating position was weakened by the fact that our preference had been leaked beforehand. My two main interlocutors were the Japanese economy and communications ministers, with whom I had long and, to some extent, productive meetings. Spurred by the prospect of clinching a good deal, Prime Minister Junichiro Koizumi received me and my delegation (which included two other cabinet ministers) with great courtesy. During my visit to Tokyo I did also discuss the WTO, because Japanese trade minister Shoichi Nakagawa insisted on meeting me. Nakagawa, who expressed his appreciation of my negotiating role, was anxious for information on the latest developments in the G3/G4. He was particularly interested in the theme of trade liberalization in the area of services (and so we did not discuss, for example, Tokyo's intransigence with regard to the major barriers to trade it had erected around certain products, most notably rice). On the flight back to Brazil I noted down my concerns about the way the negotiations were going: "I will have to revisit our tactics with regard to the WTO. In my conversation with the president before leaving for Tokyo [on May 6 or 7], I explained the outlines of a possible agreement, and what steps would be necessary to get there. (…) Lula was anxious to make sure we would coordinate with Argentina. Although he usually leaves such tactical details to my discretion, he indirectly suggested that I should go to Buenos Aires [with that purpose]. (…) Another conversation with the British will also be needed in order to achieve any progress. In the midst of so much political confusion (in Europe and South America),[99] is there really any chance of another Lula-Blair initiative, something like a new edition of the joint statement that was issued in London, but this time with some approximate figures? Clearly I was succumbing to pessimism in the face of the meager results achieved by the negotiations going on in Geneva among senior officials, and by the meetings of ministers such as those that had taken place recently in London and in Rio.

Over the following months my attention was focused mostly on South America, particularly the actions of the recently elected government of Evo Morales in Bolivia. During a dinner in Geneva at the residence of the US permanent representative to the WTO (I was invited by Rob Portman so that I could meet his newly installed successor as USTR, Susan Schwab), I received a phone call from Lula's chief of staff, Dilma Rousseff, who informed me that Morales's government had just nationalized the assets of Petrobras in Bolivia. I was obliged to cut short what would have been a series of conversations on the subject of the Doha Round, on the margins of an informal meeting of ministers called by the WTO director-general to assess the state of the negotiations, and return to Brazil as quickly as possible. I did still have time, however, to chair a G20 meeting and to have lunch with Lamy. I later learned from my collaborators that nothing very important had happened at the informal meeting of ministers. A few days afterwards, Bolivia again demanded our attention while I was accompanying Lula at a European Union, Latin America and the Caribbean (EU-LAC) summit in Vienna. Indeed, I was so preoccupied by our troubled relations with our neighbor that I found it very difficult to pay attention to the conversation between Lula and Chancellor Merkel (their first face-to-face meeting) that took place over breakfast on May 12. I do remember, however, that the Doha Round was one of the main issues they discussed. As might be expected, Merkel insisted on greater openness on our part with regard to industrial goods, and said very little about whatever she had been able to extract from Chirac on agriculture. This was one of the occasions when I noticed there was a certain amount of confusion over concepts. As far as I could tell, Merkel took "coefficient of 30" to mean "tariff ceiling." She assumed, therefore, that when we were talking about a coefficient of 30 we were indicating that the tariff we would apply on industrial goods of particular interest to Germany, such as capital goods and automobiles (or auto parts), was 30%.[100] Lula also met with Blair during the EULAC summit, but the fog swirling into my mind from the Bolivian *altiplano* made it almost impossible for me to follow their conversation. All I know is that a new joint statement was not forthcoming.

In June, Lula and Bush had phone conversations on the subject of the Round. They again reiterated their shared willingness to "do more" in order to reach an agreement, but there were no concrete proposals. The idea of a summit of leaders received little attention, perhaps because of the forthcoming G8+5 summit in St. Petersburg in July. Rob Portman's replacement by Susan Schwab—an economist from an academic background, and previously a trade negotiator in the specific area of textiles[101] —was also unhelpful. The personal familiarity and trust that build up between individual negotiators, even when they hold conflicting positions, are vital in order for the process not to suffer disruptions. I had gone to great efforts to build up that trust with Bob Zoellick[102] and, less arduously, with Portman. Although I would go on to develop a friendly working relationship with Susan, at that time she was "new on the block." Although a good technician, she had hardly any experience of negotiations with such a significant political component as the Doha Round. Some of my interlocutors had the impression that Schwab was "scared"—terrified, in fact—by the possibility of becoming the first USTR to achieve a result during negotiations and subsequently have it rejected by the US Congress. Although an extremely thorough professional with a profound knowledge of her *métier* (or at least part of it), she lacked both the strategic vision of Zoellick and the political skills of Portman. Inevitably, therefore, she was less inclined toward bold gestures, which are occasionally indispensable if effective progress is to be made.

"They can't fool Grandpa Celso"

During a trip to Geneva, where I made a speech on behalf of Brazil at the first session of the recently established UN Human Rights Council (which constituted something of an "upgrade" of the old UN Commission on Human Rights), I had dinner with Lamy. The WTO director-general was still hopeful that we would be able to advance the negotiations, mainly because he perceived President Bush as being keen to reach an agreement. "In spite of everything else, he's a free-trader. And he wants to leave a legacy. His assistants, who've got their eyes on the [US mid-term] elections in November, are more cautious." On the subject of elections, it was around this time that an interview with Mandelson caught my eye. Commenting on the prospects for the Round, the European commissioner said that if progress were not achieved in the very short term, there would be potential complications further down the line. To justify his concerns Mandelson mentioned the coming elections in Brazil and the US (in that order). It was the first time during my many years of involvement in trade-related matters that the political process in Brazil had ever been depicted as having a significant bearing on multilateral negotiations in the GATT or the WTO. "That's what I call playing in the big league!" was what I wrote in my notebook, perhaps a little over-enthusiastically.

So as not to lose the habit, I also took advantage of my time in Geneva to meet with the permanent representatives of the other G20 countries. Basically I issued an appeal for unity, which I sensed was under threat from the sheer diversity of individual interests represented within the group. My notes, written very soon after the meeting, illustrate this almost permanent concern on my part: "I had a meeting with G20 ambassadors. No surprises. I called for unity, emphasizing that without it we would not have reached the point where we now stood. This is true both for the countries with offensive interests and those with defensive concerns. The countries that are also members of the G33 again asked for support and understanding. What I tried to convey to the others [i.e. those whose agriculture is more competitive] was that, at the end of the day, gaining access to the markets of other developing countries is not our main aim. More than a negotiation between liberalizers and protectionists within the G20, this was an attempt to find a reasonable solution to the issues of 'special products' and 'special safeguards,' and thereby allow the Round to be concluded."

In Geneva I had the pleasure of the company of my daughter, Anita, and two of my grandchildren, Yasemin and Omar. Their presence certainly lightened the load imposed by the grueling and at times sterile discussions. At one point when I was setting off for a round of meetings that promised to be strenuous, my daughter suggested that I should receive an "invigorating massage" from a friend of hers, an Ayurvedic practitioner. My granddaughter, who was eight years old, asked her mother why I needed such a massage. Anita replied that it was to ensure I was well rested and full of energy, and therefore unlikely to be "fooled" by my interlocutors. Yasemin immediately declared: "They can't fool Grandpa Celso." Nothing could have been more invigorating than that.

I returned to Geneva at the end of June for meetings of the WTO Trade Negotiations Committee. This was the occasion on which I had my first bilateral meeting with the new USTR, Susan Schwab (not counting the purely social occasion when Portman had introduced her). She invited me to dinner at the InterContinental hotel. It was basically an opportunity to get to know each other. We gave our respective assessments of the state of the negotiations and reiterated our intentions and concerns, which essentially were the same as before: the US demands on NAMA in relation to Brazil, and our goals in the area of US domestic support. It is very likely that we discussed ways to force the Europeans to open their markets for agricultural products. I also had other bilaterals, including with Peter Mandelson. I attended a dinner for trade ministers from developing countries at the invitation of Kamal Nath, and a dinner for heads of delegation (not limited to any particular category of countries) organized by his Pakistani counterpart Humayun Khan. I also found time to chair meetings of the G20 with the LDCs and with the coordinators of other groupings of developing countries, plus a meeting of the G20 itself.

It was during one of those G20 meetings—at Mont-Riant, the residence of our permanent representative—that Mandelson passed me a handwritten note that read as follows: "Celso, it's clear that the coming days/weeks are do or die. After that, the Round will be a lost cause and we'll all have to bow down before United States, who'll use their TPA[103] weapon. I think the European Union and the G20 are much closer together now, certainly with regard to AMA average cuts, and we have to resolve the issue of sensitive products (I'll have to look at that point myself). On domestic support, we have to make the US lower their OTDS to $15 billion USD. On NAMA it will be a battle, I know. But if we don't manage to make our positions converge, we'll be staring into the abyss. Do you think our people—the permanent representatives in Geneva—can work together next week, so as to make it possible for the ministers themselves to get together, perhaps in a conference call? Peter." I do not remember how I replied. But Mandelson's note, leaving aside the trickery, showed that the alliances had been changed around. At the Hong Kong Ministerial Conference and in the weeks preceding it, the US had been on our side with regard to export subsidies and had been counting on us to apply pressure on the EU with regard to market access. Now, however, the focus was on domestic support, which in accordance with my famous triangular diagram, brought Brazil (and the G20) closer to the EU. And the divergences on industrial tariffs were unlikely to be resolved through a simple "battle." But to a large extent the EU trade commissioner's note, although largely inspired by self-interest, was a correct description of the power play at that particular moment.

In early July I received a visit in Brasilia from the new UK foreign secretary, Margaret Beckett. In March, during Lula's state visit to London, she and I had signed a joint agreement on sustainable development and climate change. The visit—Beckett's first trip outside Europe in her new role—was another step in the consolidation of what was in some ways a special relationship between Brazil and Britain. Although officially trade was not part of her portfolio, Beckett nevertheless publicly praised Brazil's leadership role in the WTO. (And on the subject of the enlargement of the Security Council, the foreign secretary was even more emphatic in her support. She even went so far as to ask a rhetorical question: "Why Britain and not also Brazil?") Our conversation took place on July 3. The next day, I accompanied the president to Caracas for the ceremony marking Venezuela's accession to Mercosur (an agreement that would take some years to be ratified). A few days later, in Bahia, there was the Conference of Intellectuals from Africa and the Diaspora (CIAD). Our foreign policy was therefore in an effervescent phase as I headed off again to Europe to resume the conversations on the Doha Round.

During the flight to London, I wrote: "We'll be arriving in about one hour. I'll have a little bit of time to relax before meeting with my collaborators in preparation for the meeting with Mandelson and his team. This will be the last bilateral before St. Petersburg, which is where the leaders of the G8 and five "emerging" countries (as well as a representative of Africa, I believe) will be discussing ways to unlock the Round. The ideal thing in St. Petersburg would be a meeting in a reduced format (G4 or G5),[104] but I don't think that will be possible. Last Friday [July 6], talking on the phone with Susan Schwab [I spoke to Kamal Nath on the same day], I said that what we could expect from the presidents/prime ministers in the G8+5, apart from positive indications of flexibility (principally from Bush), was an instruction to their trade ministers to go to Geneva and not leave until a deal has been done. The next day, during an interview in which [Schwab] spoke in a slightly unpleasant manner about the need for openings on the part of 'the Chinas, Indias, and Brazils of the world,' the young and relatively insecure USTR repeated what I had said almost word for word: '[The ministers] have to come back [from Geneva] with the job done.' But is that going to be possible?"

"Man, I know you have two hats"

My meeting with Mandelson was nothing more than an exchange of perceptions of how things were going. On July 17, the "G8+5+1" (the "+1" being the Republic of the Congo, which held the presidency of the African Union at the time) took place in St. Petersburg. The day began with a bilateral between Lula and Bush. It was an expanded meeting in the sense that both presidents were accompanied by various advisors. On the American side, Secretary of State Condoleezza Rice and USTR Susan Schwab were both present. Without either the time or the inclination to indulge in formalities, Bush got straight to the point: "WTO. We're going to do more. We're prepared to do more." This affirmation, however, depended on concessions being made by the other parties, especially the Europeans. There was also a clear expectation with regard to the "Chinas, Indias, and Brazils" that the USTR had referred to, although the president expressed it more tactfully. This was one of the occasions on which Bush's genuine liking for Lula was quite evident. The Texan cowboy and the São Paulo metalworker shared a marked preference for directness and informality, although it did not prevent Bush from asking a rather provocative question: "So, this guy Evo Morales—he confiscated all your assets, right?" Lula, of course, refused to take the bait. At some point the conversation on the WTO gave way to political themes (Bolivia, Venezuela, Security Council reform). Lula very deliberately prefaced some of his comments with references to me: "Just like I said to Celso . . ." or "What I sometimes say to Celso is . . ." Encouraged by this, I offered an observation of my own on the political subject the two presidents were discussing. Before I could explain the basis upon which I was intervening in the conversation, Bush removed any need to do so: "Man, I know you have two hats," he told me.

At the expanded G8 summit, I watched as Lula made two interventions.[105] The first was on one of his favorite themes at that time: ethanol, biodiesel, and H-Bio. The other focused exclusively on the WTO. He used a well-structured text, with several points that were forcefully made. Lamy, who also attended the meeting, said he was moved by Lula's words. As for Jacques Chirac—who had already interrupted the WTO director-general's speech, rather impolitely—he waited for Lula to finish but then responded in less than gentlemanly fashion. Although also offering warm words of friendship and admiration, the French president was indelicate in depicting what he referred to as Lula's "negotiating principle": "What's mine is mine, and what's yours is negotiable." It was, needless to say, an inversion of reality. This rare show of bad manners from the French president, whose conduct was usually that of a *grand seigneur*, did not go unnoticed. Lamy and Schwab commented on it later when I traveled with them on a US Air Force plane to Geneva, where we would have a G4 dinner with the director-general. That particular journey was not without complications, by the way, as the combined incompetence of the Russian and US bureaucracies almost prevented us from boarding the plane in time. In notes written on July 18, I concluded that the G8 summit had fulfilled its role. The inclusion of the subject of the WTO in the discussions, at Lula's insistence, had allowed almost all the leaders present to declare the importance of flexibility (including their own) in order to conclude the Doha Round. The principal exception was Chirac, who conspicuously sat on his own, drawing attention to his isolation with a series of gestures and facial expressions that bordered on the unbalanced. Even President Sassou Nguesso of the Republic of the Congo, a country still economically dependent on France, referred to the importance of the Round without echoing Chirac's dire warnings about the "harmful consequences" of an agreement for the poorest countries.

The trip on the USAF plane was comfortable. In the "lounge" I sat next to Susan Schwab and opposite Lamy. Nearby were the USTR's closest advisors and the two chiefs of staff—Lamy's (Arancha Gonzalez) and mine (Ambassador Maria "Lelé" Nazareth). Susan was overflowing with kind words for me, referring for example to my "extraordinary diplomatic skills." Alluding to Bush's reference to my two hats, the USTR also said: "Condi and I often grumble that we have to share you, Celso." Such kindness, though pleasing to hear, did not obscure the fact that the differences between our positions were very substantial. Indeed, they would essentially consign us to a state of antagonism, albeit one in which the asperities were smoothed by politeness and friendly gestures. In fact I was making a deliberate effort to maintain a fluid and frequent dialogue with Susan, in order to balance the "complicity" Mandelson was trying to develop with me (and, I should add, with Kamal). In the G6 meeting at WTO headquarters in the early evening of July 17, I did what I could to prevent Susan from becoming isolated. Considering our own objectives, it seemed counterproductive at that stage to force the USTR into an extremely defensive position. That is why, unlike Kamal and Mandelson, I did not take the numbers contained in the G20 proposal on access to agricultural markets as a parameter, knowing as I did that they were nowhere near sufficient to satisfy the US ambitions.[106] But there was a reason why the European commissioner and the Indian trade minister were insisting on those particular figures. Both had an interest in starting from a relatively low base, such as that in the G20 proposal. For the Europeans, this step in the direction of the G20 was a tactical move: the European Commission could then concentrate its defensive efforts on the area of sensitive products (where, also, many of our own priorities lay). As for Nath, more than a question of solidarity with the G20, he wanted to guarantee that the base from which the tariff reductions to be made by the developing countries would be calculated remained a low one. For my part, although keen not to move away from the G20 proposals (which were also ours, after all), at that particular moment I thought it was much more important to obtain some flexibility on the part of the US with regard to domestic support than to try to back the Americans into a corner on the issue of market access.

On the flight back to Brazil, after an eight-day trip that had taken in Salvador (CIAD), London, Porto (just one night), St. Petersburg, Geneva and Paris, my reflections focused mostly on the Doha Round. I was already preparing myself to go back again to Geneva four days later for the meetings of the G6 that would precede the broader ministerial meetings of the WTO at the end of the month. There had been doubts about whether these meetings would actually go ahead. If they did not, the negotiations would effectively have to be postponed almost indefinitely. I noticed that the perception in the media, including in Brazil, was that the eventual fixing of the dates for those ministerial meetings, as a result of the discussions at the G8, represented a victory for Brazil and was a tribute to our persistence. It seemed to me that the upcoming series of meetings constituted the last chance for an agreement in the short or medium term. Pascal Lamy had told me that, with regard to the key issues, he was considering proposing some numerical markers while also allowing a certain amount of leeway. As for my own relationship with Lamy at that time, I wrote: "The fact is that I have been able to maintain a privileged relationship with my main interlocutors. . . . Lamy always listens to me . . . with a certain degree of deference, not only with regard to Brazil's or the G20's position but also about how to structure the meetings, etc.. This time, in our short phone conversation before the G8+5+1, immediately after the G8 summit itself, I advised him to take a firm stance in relation to the time-limit of one month [in order to achieve a "breakthrough"]. I suggested that he take the rhetorical show of willingness [expressed at the G8 by the US and others] as a sign of real political engagement. The announcement by the main leaders (Bush, Lula, Singh, and—with limitations—Barroso)[107] of their willingness to be more flexible helped give [the negotiations] a new impulse."

Looking back at certain episodes during the summit, I recorded in my notes what Putin had said when, with the discussion having turned to the Doha Round, he invited Lula to speak immediately after the interventions by Chancellor Angela Merkel (very brief) and the WTO director-general: "And, as we're dealing with trade, I must give the floor to Lula." I do not know if the president of the Russian Federation—which was still in the process of accession to the WTO—was aware of just how correct his perception was. The truth is that the Round would almost certainly not have been discussed to the same extent at the summit had it not been for Lula's efforts in putting it at the center of the agenda. Given that the way forward was uncertain, and indeed that the resumption of the negotiations might be postponed indefinitely, it would be true to say that we had achieved our objective in preventing the Doha Round from being overlooked in the midst of so many other pressing concerns (such as climate change and the energy crisis). The question now was whether we could turn "Pascal's triangle" into what the Brazilian economist Paulo Nogueira Batista Jr. had flatteringly referred to as "Amorim's triangle." The former, to persist with the geometric metaphor, was equilateral, but the latter, crucially, was isosceles: its shortest side represented, in my mind, the relatively smaller concessions to be made by the developing countries. A couple of days later I wrote: "A major problem for us, in addition to the actual substance of the negotiations, is how to achieve an . . . understanding attitude on the part of Argentina regarding the agriculture-NAMA relationship.[108] Quite apart from the substantive difficulties, we'll have to tread carefully when it comes to the jealousy of those who feel they've been left out of the negotiations."

On July 22 I found myself heading back to Geneva yet again. The few days I had spent in Brasilia were devoted to the preparations for the Mercosur summit about to take place in Argentina, and to the situation in Lebanon. On the latter issue I had a number of phone conversations with the UN secretary-general and with those of my interlocutors who were most closely involved, such as Condoleezza Rice and Abdullah Gül.[109] I felt a little guilty that, for the first time as foreign minister, I would not be present at a Mercosur summit. But my absence was also a sign of the priority I was giving, with the president's support, to the Doha Round. I managed to get some rest during the flight, with the help of a sleeping pill, and my energies were further restored by a good breakfast. As was my habit on long flights, I spent the last couple of hours writing notes about what lay ahead: "In Geneva there will be the next stage of the negotiations. We are reaching a point at which there is not much to discuss. The positions are well known, the arguments have been made, and the lines drawn. . . . [Ultimately] it will be up to Lamy to propose something that he judges to be fair and/or acceptable, on the basis of what he already knows and also any flexibility he detects over the coming days. Essentially I can see two possible scenarios, one more ambitious than the other [entailing bigger or smaller concessions along the main axes of the Round]. But it's going to be difficult—especially if the US insists, as they have been doing, on disproportionate concessions on the part of the developing countries. . . . In fact the US wants smaller cuts to [their] domestic subsidies but substantial reductions in our [industrial] tariffs. For our part, the biggest problem will be to ensure, even in an ambitious scenario, that we don't fall below a coefficient of 20 when it comes to tariffs on industrial goods.[110] But even that will be difficult to sell . . . to the Brazilian industrial lobby and, above all, to our Argentine partners. Strictly speaking, [in the final calculations] the practical difference between a coefficient of, say, 20 or 22, and another of 18 or 19—which might just satisfy the Europeans—will not be very large. But the question is also psychological, and one of fairness [in relation to what we will receive in exchange] (a concept that isn't worth much in trade negotiations)."

My writing was interrupted, oddly enough, by a memory that suddenly came back to me regarding Sergey Lavrov. About a year earlier I had spoken with the Russian foreign minister about his country's accession to the WTO. The two of us had maintained an excellent relationship ever since the days when we had served together on the Security Council. On that particular occasion, however, Lavrov complained during our conversation that Russia had agreed the terms of its accession to the WTO with every country in South America except Brazil.[111] I chose to reply to him with a question: what would he think if, with regard to any international issue, I told him that Brazil had come to agreements "with every country in Eastern Europe, apart from Russia?" Given the superpower syndrome that Russian diplomats still tended to suffer from, I do not know if my friend quite understood my allusion to the fact that Brazil represents half of our subcontinent in terms of territory, population, and GDP. Since he did not respond, I guess he had some idea of what I was getting at. In fact I had shared this little anecdote with Susan Schwab in St. Petersburg (there was no more appropriate location in which to do so, apart from Moscow perhaps). The USTR, who at the time was wading through the negotiations for Russia's entry into the WTO, found it highly amusing.

Back to my notes. I think the following was written when I was alone in my daughter's apartment in Geneva (she was out at work and my grandchildren were at school) on July 23, the day after a G6 meeting: "What a day. The whole time was taken up with a futile reiteration of positions, and ended up with everyone realizing—and Lamy declaring—that the negotiations would have to be suspended. To use the term our ambassador Clodoaldo Huguеney is so fond of, the "monkey"[112] was definitely the US, to the relief (and indeed, to some extent, satisfaction) of the Europeans and the Indians. [On the subject of the impasse] Australia and Brazil together stated (during the meeting of ministers, which took place without advisors present) our fears and apprehensions, while the Japanese minister, probably not fully realizing what was going on,[113] said nothing more than 'I trust Pascal.'" My reference to an outstandingly bad day also had to do with the situation in Lebanon, where thousands of Brazilian citizens living there were endangered by Israeli bombing. On that subject, at various moments in the midst of the G6 meeting I had to speak on the phone with my usual interlocutors (including at least one long conversation with President Lula).

"It's important not to let failure become a habit"

The next day, July 24, I woke up with a feeling of disquiet, but also still with a certain amount of hope. I wrote: "If the Americans show some flexibility [in meetings later that day], the game will continue. . . . Otherwise, the suspension [of the negotiations] is inevitable. The question is, will it be possible to prevent a 'suspension' turning into a collapse? And even if we can avoid that scenario, will it be possible to prevent attentions from turning to bilateral or regional agreements? That would be very bad for us and . . . for the multilateral trading system. I can always denounce the 'inflexibility of the rich countries' [at the meeting of the WTO Trade Negotiations Committee (TNC), scheduled for that afternoon]—but what would be the point of that? The next few hours will be decisive." As it turned out, however, nothing "decisive" happened in the following hours, and the scenario I feared did indeed come to pass, although obviously I did not yet know what the full consequences would be.

Also that morning, before another G6 meeting that Lamy had arranged largely at my insistence, I received a visit at Mont-Riant from Susan Schwab and the US secretary of agriculture, Mike Johanns. Perhaps their intention in coming to see me was to demonstrate that the United States was still committed to reaching an agreement. During the conversation, Susan practically invited herself to go to Brazil. We arranged to meet in Rio de Janeiro the following weekend, when I returned from a trip to Adana in Turkey to meet Brazilian refugees from the violence in Lebanon. The G6 meeting proved to be nothing more than a formality. During the TNC, in which Lamy confirmed that the negotiations would indeed be suspended, Kamal and Mandelson were very critical of the US, explicitly blaming the Americans for the impasse. For my part, although I did argue that the breakdown was due largely to issues related to domestic support (and therefore, implicitly, the US), I tried to be more careful in my use of words. Again I wanted to avoid giving the impression that we were ganging up on Washington. I said that each of us had our own difficulties, but that the blockage with regard to domestic subsidies meant that potential flexibilities elsewhere (including our own, on NAMA) could not even be tested. In my speech, in which I employed some deliberately emotive language, I made clear my sadness at the situation we found ourselves in. Looking back over the recent history of the GATT/WTO system, I said it was rare indeed to reach a consensus on conceptual aspects, as we had done in this case, and yet be so glaringly incapable of reaching an agreement when it came to the numbers. Unknowingly giving a foretaste of what I would say two years later, in 2008, after the "great failure of July," I said we had failed our political leaders, who had instructed us to be more flexible (I was referring specifically to the G6), and had also let down all those tens of millions of people (especially the poor) who had placed their hopes in our negotiating capacity. Referring to the ongoing situation in Lebanon—and, implicitly, to the inaction of the UN Security Council in that context—I said that our failure in Geneva was further damaging the reputation of multilateralism. My speech—made off the cuff, without notes, which naturally increased its impact—was much appreciated. The representative of Pakistan came to tell me that he would have applauded had it not been contrary to WTO protocol. Mike Johanns, probably relieved that my attack on the US position had been less fierce than he feared, came up and complemented me on "a statesman's speech."

On the morning of July 25, before setting off to Adana via Istanbul, I requested a meeting with Lamy. I wanted to discuss the prospects for the coming weeks and months. I got the impression during our conversation that the WTO director-general did not have a definite plan. We spoke a little about the "numbers," especially those concerning domestic support. Probably based on what Susan had told him in their one-to-one "confessional," Lamy indicated that the US was still being inflexible. The minimum amount they would consider for OTDS, he said, was $19 billion USD (well above the $13 billion Rob Portman had let slip during that moment of "candor" in Rio). Lamy was very interested to hear that Schwab would shortly be visiting me in Brazil, and suggested I should tell her that a proposal based on the figure of $19 billion was simply unacceptable. He also talked a little about some of the assumptions contained in the July Framework that might perhaps need to be revised, particularly the flexibilities with regard to special products (I seem not to have recorded whether Lamy was suggesting an upward or a downward adjustment, but I assume he was thinking of "accommodating" the US). I responded by reiterating what I had said during the G6 meeting: to "reopen" the July Framework at this stage would be a huge risk. If something really needed to be done to accommodate a specific situation, it was preferable to do it "in practice" rather than "in theory." To do otherwise would be to raise the prospect of what Lamy himself, and indeed all the negotiators, most feared: the unraveling[114] of the negotiations as a whole. Lamy requested the assistance of Brazil, as the coordinator of the G20, in finding formulas that could overcome the difficulties in relation to special products (the target of criticism particularly from the US), but agreed that the divergences on that particular issue (or on "special safeguards") were not the main cause of the impasse. Nevertheless, those twin aspects of the theme of access to the markets of developing countries were providing a pretext for the Americans not to advance on the issue of domestic support. (In retrospect it is interesting to note that the dynamic between domestic support, on the one hand, and SP and the SSM, on the other, was largely responsible for the failure in July 2008.)

In my conversation with the director-general, I insisted that the political implications of the potential collapse of the Doha Round had to be made clear. Wishing to highlight the threat to the multilateral system that such an outcome would pose, I said would follow Lamy's example and call Kofi Annan. It was important that the UN secretary-general should convey his concerns about the stalemate in the WTO to the person who ultimately held the key to unlock the negotiations: President George W. Bush. I also suggested to Lamy that he should take advantage of his position as the world's most senior official in the area of international trade by calling all the relevant leaders, especially Bush and Singh. I remember one of the exact phrases I used: "It's important not to let failure become a habit." Without any pretence that I was saying anything new, I stated my perception that the WTO was at a crossroads: it could either retain its status as the principal global forum for trade negotiations, or it could become merely a subsidiary to bilateral agreements, an entity its members might turn to sporadically if, for example, they needed to resolve a dispute or receive a waiver.[115] It is curious to note that as I write these lines, eight years later, this scenario continues to loom over the negotiators.

I arrived in Rio from Turkey on July 29, and very soon afterwards went to meet Susan Schwab. Following the impasse at the G6 meeting in Geneva, and in the midst of doom-laden media reports on the state of the Doha Round, our conversation served as a sign of continuing engagement on the part of two of the principal participants. Indeed, when speaking to the media about her forthcoming trip to Brazil, Susan had presented it in precisely those terms. Our conversation took place at the Copacabana Palace hotel on a Saturday. It served to clarify certain points, which at the time I described in my notebook as follows: "(1) the United States is still willing to negotiate . . . rather than simply blame the other parties, as it did after Cancún for example; (2) any schedule for future meetings will have to take into account the need for substantive progress by January or February 2007, in order to prepare the ground for the extension of the TPA; (3) the degree of flexibility the US is willing to reveal is still nowhere near enough to set in motion the 'virtuous circle' that would be necessary in order to conclude the Round." The conversation with Susan was friendly, however, and indeed reflected the healthy state of the Brazil-US dialogue as a whole at that time, our various differences notwithstanding. Back in Brasilia, I continued my efforts to revive the Round. After several phone conversations, including one with Pascal Lamy, I decided to initiate the necessary procedures in order to convene a meeting of the G20 in September. Lamy had already said he would attend, which would help attract the ministers and other officials (from the EU and the US) I intended to invite.

As usual, nothing very significant happened during the month of August. But the G20 meeting did indeed take place in September, in Rio de Janeiro. A surprisingly large number of trade ministers from developing countries attended. Indeed, some countries that had distanced themselves somewhat from the group in the period immediately after Cancún, under pressure from the US, had now rejoined it. Therefore, in Rio, I had the pleasure of welcoming back Peru and Ecuador. Coordinators from other groups of developing countries were also present: the "Cotton-4" from Africa, the African, Caribbean and Pacific Group (ACP), the Least Developed Countries (LDCs), and the G33. On September 9, a Saturday, there were meetings of ministers in different formats: G20 "only," G20 with the WTO director-general, and G20 with the coordinators of the other groups. On the Sunday, in the presence of the other coordinators, there was a meeting between the G20, the European trade commissioner, the USTR, and the Japanese trade minister (who more or less invited himself to attend). More than anything else, this succession of discussions represented an important effort to revive the negotiations after they had come to a shuddering halt in Geneva in July. In my brief opening statement I highlighted the significance of the occasion, which I chose to portray as the result of efforts not only on my part but also by Kamal Nath. I stressed that if the negotiations were to be relaunched, it must not be done at the expense of the progress previously achieved. I also issued a reminder that "development" lay at the very heart of the Doha Round. I highlighted the contribution the G20 and other groups of developing countries had made to the advances achieved since Cancún, especially the establishment in Hong Kong of a date for the total elimination of export subsidies and other forms of financial support that distorted exports of agricultural products. I reminded the audience of some of the most important causes that we had been advocating: effective cuts in domestic subsidies; proportionality between the concessions to be made by developing countries with regard to industrial goods and those by the developed countries on agricultural products; and the need for differential treatment when it came to "special products" and "special safeguards." In the press conference I stressed that the developing countries represented at the meeting regarded the failure of the Round as "unthinkable." I also stressed how vital it was for the G20 to remain united and to continue acting in a purposeful way.

"The patient is still in hospital but is no longer in intensive care"

The meetings in Rio served, above all, to show that the Doha Round was still alive and that the G20 remained at the center of negotiations. When I convened the event, I knew it would be regarded with skepticism in some quarters. There was also the risk of a mediocre attendance, which would have been sure to provoke criticism. As it turned out, the number of participants exceeded even my most optimistic hopes. What took place in Rio de Janeiro on that September weekend was the biggest trade-related story in the global media at that time. The trade ministers of the most powerful developed countries converged on the city. The Japanese minister flew most of the way around the world to be there. Some of the ministers from developing countries could hardly contain their enthusiasm. The Philippine trade minister, for example, said the Rio meetings would be remembered as the "resurrection" of the Doha Round. I was slightly more modest in my choice of metaphor, telling a group of journalists that the results obtained could be summarized as: "The patient is still in hospital but is no longer in intensive care."

Soon after the end of the Rio meetings, I set off for Havana for a summit of the "Non-Aligned Movement" and, before that, a ministerial meeting of the G15, a group of developing countries that had come together in the 1980s to pursue a "dialogue" with the G7. The G15 had lost much of its initial impetus due to the indifference of the world's biggest economic powers toward its demands, and also the difficulty of organizing the still-novel and unfamiliar notion of South-South cooperation projects. In any case, I took advantage of the occasion to stress how the G20 was performing its role in pragmatic fashion but without losing sight of its guiding principles with regard to world trade. From Havana I traveled on to New York, where I met up with President Lula for the opening of the UN General Assembly.

An episode that took place at the UN illustrates how the Doha Round was always one of our uppermost concerns. On September 19, in a small room situated behind the main General Assembly Hall, while we were waiting for the opening of the General Debate,[116] there was a brief encounter between the men who would be making the first two speeches: the presidents of Brazil and the United States. After exchanging greetings with Lula, Bush turned to speak to me. He asked if I was still "wearing two hats," and how the Doha Round was going. I told him I thought there needed to be a bolder gesture from Washington, especially with regard to domestic support. "Oh, same old story," the US president said, already turning to walk away, "it's always Bush's fault." No, Mister President," I replied, "we want it to be Bush's *achievement*. We want it to be the 'Bush Round.'" I momentarily considered mentioning the "Kennedy Round" of GATT negotiations in the 1960s, but decided the comparison might seem irreverent. Bush, in his folksy way, gave my face a couple of gently affectionate slaps and then moved on to greet the officials gathered in the corner of the room. Later I wrote: "It wasn't exactly an episode that fills me with pride, but if my little bit of flattery serves to stir the vanity of the US president, to even the smallest degree, it will have been worthwhile."

During that same General Assembly, I attended a working breakfast organized by the foreign ministers of Norway and France. It was aimed at addressing one of those issues that political analysts tend to describe as "soft" but is by no means of only secondary importance: foreign policy and health. On my way to the meeting I recalled that during my time as permanent representative to the WTO I had been involved with an important issue connected with that particular theme: pharmaceutical patents and their impact on the price of medicines in poor countries. I remembered in particular the resistance I had put up against the attempts by the chairman of the WTO Council, Stuart Harbinson—born in Hong Kong, but as British as an actor in the Royal Shakespeare Company—to arbitrate (certainly not in our favor) a text between two different proposals on TRIPS and health that were part of the declaration to be presented before the Doha Ministerial Conference in 2001. My tough approach[117] made it possible to reverse the unfavorable situation that, for reasons too complex to explain here, we were faced with at the time in Geneva. What also came to mind was the moment in Doha when the "facilitator" of the negotiations, the Mexican minister Luis Ernesto Derbez, said he wanted to have a meeting just with me and the US delegate. I objected to the idea, saying I would not enter the room without an African delegate also being present. But then the African representative in question, a minister or ambassador from Cameroon, declared: "We feel represented by Brazil." That was one of the episodes that contributed to my growing conviction that Brazil could indeed conduct itself with firmness in the negotiations, and defend not only its own interests but also those of a large number of developing countries. The incident took place in 2001. Brazil did indeed take on that leadership role in 2003, in Cancún. And it was consolidated in 2005, in Hong Kong.

In contrast to the corresponding period the year before, in the run-up to Hong Kong, nothing very important happened in the last few months of 2006 as far as the Doha Round was concerned. The work being done in Geneva carried on, of course, but the role of Brazilian ministers, or at least my own involvement, was very limited. South America (mainly questions such as natural gas, with Bolivia, or the Itaipu hydroelectric plant, with Paraguay) demanded almost all my attention. And there was also the campaign to re-elect President Lula, in which I chose to participate to a greater extent than would normally be expected of a foreign minister (for which I received a lot of criticism, in fact). There were a couple of trade-related phone conversations, but no significant move was made before the mid-term elections in the United States in early November. On November 22 I went to Montevideo to attend an event to commemorate the twentieth anniversary of the launch of the Uruguay Round. It was organized by former Uruguayan foreign minister Sergio Abreu, my counterpart when I had been foreign minister under Itamar Franco. As well as being a friendly gesture toward our neighbors, my participation in this event allowed me to repeat some messages in support of the Round. It also gave me an opportunity to meet again with Pascal Lamy. The WTO director-general still had the same doubts he had expressed to me four months earlier in Geneva: uncertainties about how the US would behave on the issue of domestic support, and skepticism about Indian flexibility on special products. We commented on the new Democratic leaders in Congress who would be sure to have an influence on the negotiations. The future president of the powerful Agriculture Committee in the House of Representives, Collin Peterson of Minnesota, was closely linked to the agricultural lobbies that defended the US subsidies. In the Senate, Lamy thought the situation "won't be so bad." Overall, it was not the most encouraging of assessments. The director-general also spoke about the still-uncertain sequence of events that would take place with regard to the Farm Bill and the TPA. These were dry subjects, and ones with which I would now need to refamiliarize myself. Being a trade negotiator is, I am told, a bit like being a pilot: you cannot afford to get out of practice. In my case, when the rhythm of Doha Round-related work slowed, as it did for a few months after that intense weekend of G20 activity in Rio in September 2006, and I concentrated hard on other subjects, I did indeed get the feeling that I was beginning to "forget" the WTO.

"Celso doesn't even need to call me"

On January 3, 2007, two days after the inauguration ceremony that marked the start of President Lula's second term of office, I made a lightning trip to New York for a meeting with USTR Susan Schwab. It was, as the press reported, a "talk about talks." Susan and I were both anxious, for different reasons, to resume contact. A few days later, during a very brief vacation on the coast of the northeastern Brazilian state of Bahia, my rest was twice interrupted by WTO-related phone calls: one from Susan, the other from Peter Mandelson. During these conversations we made plans for future meetings—starting in Davos, where after a few months of calm the trade ministers' activities would return to the rhythm of the pre-Hong Kong period.

On January 23 I went to Paris to attend a conference on the reconstruction of Lebanon. From there I flew to Zurich, and then on by car to Davos. Before the trip I wrote in my notebook that the work of the WTO was probably about to intensify. The indications that this was happening were not always positive, however. Newspapers including the *Financial Times* and Brazil's *Valor Econômico* referred to the possibility of a deal between the United States and the European Union. In my notes I observed with a certain amount of optimism that even such a scenario would be less unfavorable than the situation in 2003 before Cancún, because after the July Framework and the Hong Kong Ministerial Conference "the starting point now is different." Still, one of my missions in Davos would be to make clear that there could be no agreement without the G20. Before leaving Brazil, between a visit from my old acquaintance Didier Opertti, former Uruguayan foreign minister and now executive secretary of ALADI,[118] and a phone call from Prime Minister Fouad Siniora of Lebanon, which seemed to me to be an appeal for help, I received a call from Susan. She was anxious, above all, to try to ensure she would not come under disproportionate pressure at the Davos meetings. The *Financial Times* reported that, in the bilateral negotiations with the European Union, the United States had indicated it was willing to consider a ceiling of $17 billion USD for OTDS, which was below not only the minimum it had accepted publicly ($22 billion) but also the figure Susan had referred to as the limit in her "confessional" with Lamy in July ($19 billion). But this was still a long way from the figure of $13 billion that Rob Portman had briefly let slip in Rio, which corresponded approximately with the G20 proposal of between $12 and 13 billion. In terms of average cuts to tariffs on agricultural products, the European Union's offer was now very close to the figure of 54% previously proposed by the G20. But, as I pointed out in an interview with Brazilian journalist Clóvis Rossi, the problem was the large number of "sensitive products" (which would not be subject to the formula cuts), and the lack of clarity about how they would be dealt with. Something similar was happening with the supposed US offer on domestic support. In addition to the overall reduction being insufficient, there was no precise indication of the disciplines that would be imposed on the programs of the "blue box," so there was a lot of leeway for tampering with the overall limit. Nor was it clear whether there would be ceilings for each product so as to avoid a situation in which subsidies were simply moved across from one side to the other ("box shifting"). My phone conversation with Susan did not shed much light on these issues. As for the EU proposal, what I was hearing from Geneva, and from Mandelson, was consistent with the report in the *Financial Times*.

In Davos, neither the bilateral nor the plurilateral discussions got down to the fine details. I arrived in the Swiss ski resort, where the sanatorium in Thomas Mann's classic *The Magic Mountain* was situated, at about 9 p.m.. The snow-covered surroundings and the sub-zero temperatures caused me to retire briefly to bed to try to get warm under the covers, but soon I received the message that President Lula, who had flown direct from Brazil, wanted to have dinner with me. The idea was that we would look through the paperwork for the next day: the text of a lecture on combating world hunger, a meeting with CEOs, and a discussion on Latin America in which the recently elected president of Mexico, Felipe Calderón, would also participate. As so often, however, Lula barely glanced at the papers, and would end up largely improvising during his speeches. The president just wanted some company and an opportunity to talk about recent events—in particular a meeting of the monetary policy committee of Brazil's Central Bank, whose conservative stance was causing him some discomfort. I participated in Lula's bilateral meetings with Prime Minister Tony Blair and Chancellor of the Exchequer (already chosen as Blair's successor later in the year) Gordon Brown. In both conversations the Doha Round was the main theme. Lula displayed the same impressive degree of engagement as ever, linking the results of the trade negotiations with the fight against global poverty and, indirectly, terrorism. Lula also participated in a restricted meeting on the WTO, coordinated by Blair, at which Pascal Lamy was present. During that particular meeting Lula said very little, instead handing over to me. He emphasized to those present that I had the authority to close the deal: "Celso doesn't even need to call me." Although this explicit demonstration of the president's confidence in me was flattering, and probably would have increased my stature in the eyes of my cabinet colleagues who were present, I had doubts about whether it was a good negotiating tactic. In fact, what Lula had said would prevent us from employing the tactic (often used in negotiations, whether to buy time or dissuade others from exerting pressure) of saying we needed to pause to consult our country's highest authority. But still, it came as a useful indication of Brazil's engagement and optimism at a moment when the principal objective was to breathe new life into the Doha Round.

Engagement and optimism were also the mood of a meeting of trade ministers organized by the head of Switzerland's Federal Department of Economic Affairs, Doris Leuthard, who would eventually become a good friend despite our differences of position (the small Alpine country, not a member of the EU, was very protectionist in agriculture and very demanding of other countries in seeking access to their markets for manufactured goods and services). Similarly positive sentiments were expressed later that day in a public discussion between some of the principal negotiators, a kind of political-diplomatic "reality show" very much in keeping with the usual Davos style. The EU representative, Peter Mandelson, confirmed an average cut in AMA close to what the G20 had proposed, although he left doubts as to how the move would be implemented. The USTR, for her part, was more cautious, not committing herself to any specific figures with regard to the reduction in OTDS.

After those meetings I went to Geneva, where I had the Sunday to rest and to have internal meetings with my delegation. On the Monday, January 29, I attended a meeting with the permanent representatives of the G20 countries, followed by a meeting between them and the EU trade commissioner. The attention I was giving to the G20, even in the absence of the trade ministers, was not a mere public relations ploy. It was part of an exercise in transparency, aimed at fostering a sense of involvement on the part of the members of the group, who otherwise would have been distant onlookers. These meetings also served to remove doubts and alleviate anxieties arising from the suspicion, which could never be entirely eradicated, that the members of the G20 who were at the forefront of the negotiations (above all Brazil and India, as members of the G4) might be cooking up a deal behind the backs of the other members. In Geneva I also had separate meetings with Mandelson and Schwab, just to confer on certain aspects of the negotiation process. Both meetings took place at the residence of the Brazilian permanent representative—a not insignificant detail in the context of the careful choreography surrounding the negotiations. At the end of the day we had a discussion *à trois*. As for the other member of our quartet, Kamal Nath, I had met with him in Davos. On the morning of January 30, over breakfast, Lamy and I swapped impressions of how the Round was going. During that conversation, as in the ones with Peter and Susan the day before, the attitude of India—or, more specifically, of Kamal himself—was one of the main topics. I had to tread a fine line between, on the one hand, my personal relationship with Kamal and the Brazil-India strategic alliance, and on the other, the need to inject forward momentum into the negotiating process as a whole. We were rather concerned not only by the problems India raised in the G4, the broader meetings, and sometimes in bilateral conversations, but also by Kamal's own interventions, which tended to be vague or even, so it seemed, deliberately aimed at muddying the waters. The overall impression was that India, deep down, did not actually want a successful conclusion to the Doha Round, although of course, if that was indeed the case, Kamal would never admit it. My discomfort at the thought that I was participating in conversations behind Kamal's back was assuaged by the knowledge that he too had separate meetings with the other two members of the G4 on quite a regular basis. It was essential for the mutual trust between Kamal and me not to be lost. But his restless nature, which frequently led him to consult his tablet computer in the middle of conversations, and his reluctance to stay for more than the minimum possible time in any one place, made it difficult to enter into a deeper dialogue. To get around this problem I made frequent phone calls to Kamal in New Delhi, or sometimes spoke instead to our mutual contacts among the permanent representatives in Geneva, but doubts about Kamal's underlying objectives lingered in my mind.

"And you'll have to put aside your little South American problems"

I concluded my notes on the cycle of meetings by briefly "updating" my analysis of the personalities of Mandelson and Schwab, and of their positions in the negotiations. My earlier impression of the EU trade commissioner as a wily political fox had been confirmed. But, far from being a "cold" negotiator, he was prone to frequent shows of great irritation (whether spontaneous or calculated, it was impossible to say). At the same time, however, I also found him open, intellectually, to points of view different from his own, particularly when the conversation was in private. As for Susan (who, like Peter, was keen to express appreciation of her dialogue with Brazil and was trying to get me "on her side"), she revealed a certain degree of disorientation, the result of the difficult position she occupied, subject to conflicting pressures from the other negotiators and the politicians in the US Congress. Back in Brazil, on January 31, I conducted the swearing-in ceremony for the new Itamaraty undersecretaries, and took part in a long meeting conducted by Lula's chief of staff, Dilma Rousseff, on the risks and opportunities arising from cooperation with the United States in the field of ethanol production, ahead of the forthcoming trip to Brazil by President Bush. In the early morning of February 1, before breakfast, I noted down an observation Mandelson had made during our bilateral in Geneva. Near the end of our conversation, in an amiable tone, the EU trade commissioner had said more or less the following: "Well, Celso, it's clear now what each of us must do. I have to keep the member states in line with my proposal—or perhaps even a slightly better one—on [agricultural] market access. Susan, meanwhile, will have to convince her politicians in the US Congress to significantly reduce their ridiculous domestic subsidies. As for you, you'll have to put aside your little South American problems and devote yourself full time to concluding the Round." To which I replied, jokingly: "I don't get paid what Pascal Lamy does, you know." But in fact my conclusion in the wake of the latest meetings was that I should indeed try to find a way of spending more time on WTO matters. My first step in that direction was to arrange an internal meeting at Itamaraty for an overview of the "state of play" with regard to the trade negotiations.

Throughout the month of February, contrary to Mandelson's recommendation, I devoted myself mostly to South American issues (with a particular emphasis on Bolivia, whose president visited Brazil for long and laborious discussions about the price of gas). The subject of the Doha Round was not forgotten, however. My diary entries refer to WTO-related phone conversations (one each with the other members of the G4, and one with Lamy) and to a conference call with Mandeslon and Schwab. But it was not until March, in Geneva, that I had my next face-to-face meetings with my "favorite partners." On that flight to Switzerland (finally aboard an FAB Legacy made by Embraer,[119] a much more comfortable plane than my previous one), Roberto Azevêdo told me about his recent conversations with senior officials from the European Union, the US, and India, in preparation for the ministerial-level meetings I was due to have. On February 4 I arrived in Geneva from Georgetown, Guyana, where I had accompanied the president at a summit of the Rio Group, organized with the help of both funds and staff from Brazil. While we were in Guyana it was announced that we would recommence the building of the bridge over the Takutu river, a project very important for our South American/Caribbean neighbor and indeed for the two countries' bilateral relations.

All the meetings in Geneva took place on February 5 at Mont-Riant, the residence of the Brazilian permanent representative. The initial idea had been to start with a "trilateral" (Peter, Susan, and I), but the USTR insisted on first having a bilateral with me, which lasted about half an hour. And so the day's commitments began at 7:15 a.m., not quite in keeping with fine diplomatic tradition. Although I tended to wake up early (and still do), I was used to setting aside the first couple of hours of my day for reading or for making by notebook entries. But I could not say no to my over-anxious American negotiating partner. Right after the trilateral I had a meeting with Kamal Nath—a *tête-à-tête* followed by a broader meeting, including our respective aides, that extended all the way through the lunch hour. In fact Kamal and I were together for almost four hours in all, which was certainly a record. We covered almost the whole Doha Round agenda, from OTDS to special products, and also addressed issues related to manufactured goods and services, which we had hardly ever spoken about before. We agreed, to a large extent, on most of the subjects that came up. Kamal left at about 3 p.m., and Mandelson arrived not long afterwards for a bilateral that lasted a couple of hours. Once again he made demands about our industrial tariffs. For my part I insisted that the issue of sensitive products in agriculture should also be addressed. And, as always during my bilaterals with the European trade commissioner, we commented on the behavior of the other two members of the G4. To finish off the long working day (which had also included a brief chat with Brazilian journalists), I received the WTO director-general for what turned out to be quite a thorough discussion. Strangely, however, I see that in my notebook and diary there is no mention of a meeting in the G4 format that day.

Traveling back to Brazil on board the Legacy, about an hour and a half before landing, I wrote: "Advances? Yes. Especially in the attitude of Kamal, who has begun to think in more specific terms and to be less negative. . . . With Peter, the conversation was useful, especially [our] joint analysis of Susan Schwab's behavior and the political constraints that reduce her room for maneuver. Susan didn't say anything that constituted a backward step, but nor did she demonstrate, in concrete terms—i.e. that could be translated into numbers—a willingness to move forward. [The USTR] recognizes that the United States has to 'do more' on domestic support, but avoids going anywhere near precise figures and indeed says that will only happen 'when we're sure what moves the others will make.' And so we're stuck in a vicious circle, which . . . will be difficult to break out of." In those same notes I speculated about whether the forthcoming meeting between Lula and Bush, scheduled as part of the latter's visit to Brazil the following weekend, might give rise to an opportunity to extract some specific details on Washington's position. Among US trade negotiators there was a widely shared perception that the offer made by the US in late 2006, known as the "October Offer," was simply "pocketed" by the other negotiating partners, who offered nothing in return. Although certainly an exaggeration, this made the US disinclined to make the "first move" in the next phase of the negotiations. Fears about possible reactions in Congress served to further entrench this defensive approach. From my conversation with Mandelson I also gathered that the European Union was not about to make any further move on AMA. And without that, it would be impossible to elicit forward steps from the Americans—unless Brazil itself made some additional gesture in relation to industrial tariffs. For my part, I actually thought the latter was feasible. The impact on our industry of reducing the coefficient by a few points would be less significant than it might appear at first glance. Perhaps, if we tried, we could indeed lower the coefficient—although there was no way we could go below 20, which is what the European Union wanted. In technical meetings the European Commission insisted on a coefficient close to 18, which was politically impossible for us to accept. To a layman—which is what I would have been, were it not for the constant briefings by my advisors—this numerology might seem excessive. However, in addition to the actual practical impact of tariff reductions, it was also necessary to consider what was known in the jargon of the GATT/WTO as their "optical aspect," i.e. how they were likely to be perceived by public opinion. And when it came to perceptions, a coefficient below 20 could be presented as a "gain" extracted by the EU, which would not be the case with a coefficient of, say 22 or 23, even though the difference in terms of their practical impact would not be great, given the moderating factor of the "flexibilities."

On the basis of the latest series of meetings, I concluded that I needed to deepen my engagement with other blocs—especially the G33, which comprised developing countries with defensive concerns in agriculture, linked to food security and small farmers. This engagement would be essential if I wanted to have some influence (which I had not yet achieved, or at least not sufficiently) over the degree of flexibility on the part of the G20 with regard to special products and special safeguards for developing countries. In fact I was beginning to see more clearly that the issue of special products and special safeguards, although it lay outside my favorite triangular diagram, might become a deal-breaker for the negotiations as a whole, and also the cause of fissures within the G20. The principal outcome of the meetings was, as so often, the convening of the next ones. In this instance they were set to take place (in the G4 and G6 formats) about a month later, in New Delhi.

"We'll have to lock the negotiators in a room and throw away the key"

Four days after the meetings in Geneva, President George W. Bush arrived in Brazil. The day before, there was a state visit by the president of Germany, Horst Köhler, a former managing director of the International Monetary Fund who I remember had been overcome with emotion when he embraced Lula, the metalworker turned president, on the occasion of their first meeting in 2003.

My accommodation during Bush's stay in São Paulo was the extremely spacious penthouse suite of the Hilton hotel, which allowed me to receive visits from my two American counterparts, Secretary of State Condoleezza Rice and USTR Susan Schwab. In the notes I prepared for my dialogue with Condoleezza, "WTO" was followed by two question marks, which shows I was hesitant about raising the subject with her. I did not want to give the impression I was trying to "bypass" the USTR. At the same time, however, I thought it was important that the US government should not see the issue from a purely technical angle or through the prism of the special interests of this or that economic sector. I emphasized to the secretary of state the political importance of a WTO agreement for global stability (in fact it was 9/11 that had made it politically possible to launch the Doha Round on bases not very different from those of the resounding failure in Seattle).

Before describing the three meetings in São Paulo (Amorim-Rice, Lula-Bush, Amorim-Schwab, in that order), I would like to reproduce some notes that illustrate my doubts about how Brazil should pursue a cooperative relationship with the United States, including with regard to the other South American countries. Although the notes were probably written in preparation for my meeting with the secretary of state and are therefore predominantly political in tone, they are nevertheless relevant to some aspects of our trade relationships and had a bearing on our attitudes toward the WTO, including in relation to regional projects such as the FTAA. What I wrote was: "The temptation on the part of all Brazilian governments [since Joaquim Nabuco, it could be said][120] has always been to have a privileged relationship with the United States, one of the objectives being thereby to emphasize our superiority over our neighbors in South/Latin America. But today, the integration of South America is the priority of Brazilian foreign policy. . . . Brazil does not want the role of "surrogate" or "agent" of the United States in the region. We want, above all, to make South America stronger. . . . We can have partnerships with the United States that also benefit other countries in South/Latin America, but [those partnerships] have to be carefully calibrated." Those notes continue with some observations about actions that I thought might be useful in relation to Bolivia, such as the extension of the ATPDEA[121] or the inclusion of the country in the Millennium Challenge Account,[122] which were issues I would raise in my conversation with Condoleezza. But I myself had doubts about whether it was possible for a country to receive even limited and temporary help from the US without it becoming a mechanism for subsequent domination.

Both in my conversation with the secretary of state and in the dialogue between Bush and Lula, the term "strategic relationship" came up several times. We discussed several issues: the Middle East, trilateral cooperation involving countries in Central America, the Caribbean, and Africa; ethanol; and, naturally, Haiti. We exchanged views on the growing presence of China in Africa, an issue that seemed to be of particular concern to Condoleezza. Her eyes lit up when I suggested some kind of joint Brazil-US action in Africa to counterbalance what appeared to be the increasingly vast scale of Chinese involvement in the continent's affairs. (A few months later, in Washington, we would sign a memorandum on the strengthening of political institutions in Guinea Bissau.)[123] On the WTO, Rice responded to my points about the global political implications in a generic way. Speaking about the Doha Round after our aides had left the room, the secretary of state painted the US position in dramatic colors. She warned that if President Bush felt he was being put under unreasonable pressure, he might simply "walk out" of the negotiations. What she referred to as the president's "exasperation" reflected not only the resistance from Congress but also the fact that the main US lobbies were losing interest in the gains that could potentially be made. As I myself had observed on other occasions, especially in meetings in Davos, the multinational companies were not exerting much pressure to conclude the Round. They had already achieved most of what they wanted with regard to services and intellectual property, for example, during the Uruguay Round. Hence the US focus on what might be gained in terms of access to agricultural markets (AMA), including those of developing countries. I must admit, however, that these reflections were not fully formed at the time of the São Paulo meetings; it was only later that they would crystallize in my mind.

The main theme of the meeting between the two presidents was not the WTO but cooperation on ethanol production (the subject of an agreement I signed with the secretary of state). However, the Doha Round was uppermost in our minds, and would end up dominating the conversation that took place at the Hilton after our visit to a Petrobras terminal. In very similar terms to those Condoleezza had used, Bush repeated to Lula the warning that in an extreme scenario he would abandon the negotiations. But the message was not entirely negative. He said he still had a personal interest in reaching an agreement, although "the United States won't be able to make the first step." This was an indirect reference to the attitude the US attributed to its negotiating partners over the supposed "pocketing" of the American offer on OTDS the previous October. With a simple hand gesture, Lula invited me to respond. In a conciliatory manner, but still making clear the need for simultaneous moves from all the parties involved, I provided an overview of the state of the negotiations. Susan stepped into the conversation at this point to emphasize that she and I had been having "good discussions" on a bilateral level. She also indicated the advances that would be necessary from the US perspective. She spoke mainly about the issue of access to agricultural markets in the European Union, but she also mentioned the US interest in the liberalization of agricultural trade in developing countries, which would obviously be a move in the opposite direction from that of special products and special safeguards. I think it might have been at that moment that Lula said "We'll have to lock the negotiators in a room and throw away the key." The president was obviously thinking primarily of Susan and me, which introduced an element of embarrassment into the situation. Later, in the press conference, President Bush repeated Lula's words, although in general he spoke in a more optimistic tone than he had done during the meeting.

As it turned out, Susan and I were not forcibly detained. We did, however, have a working breakfast the next morning, a Saturday. It was a long meeting, in which I spent much of the time trying to reassure my interlocutor that she was not the target of a conspiracy ("they're all trying to back the United States into a corner"). This concern on the part of the USTR had become almost obsessive, and was the result of a degree of insecurity that Mandelson, Lamy, and I had long been aware of. My approach, unlike that of Mandeslson, was to seek to allay Susan's fears in the hope of inducing greater flexibility on her part. The USTR's distrustful posture also manifested itself in her habit of delegating important aspects of the negotiations to her aides, which made it more difficult for me and her other interlocutors to deal politically with the most controversial issues. Susan harbored certain expectations, which to me seemed excessive, in terms of access to agricultural markets in developing countries such as India and Indonesia. Domestic support and NAMA were naturally also mentioned during our breakfast meeting, but nothing really noteworthy was said on those issues. Her main concern at that time was the next ministerial meeting of the G33, scheduled to take place in ten days' time in Jakarta. She would not be present at the event, where she feared the US negotiating positions would be the target of attacks and accusations.

Stop-over in Jakarta

My diary records that on March 13 I spoke on the phone with Kamal Nath and Peter Mandelson. I made no notes about either conversation but I suppose we must have discussed the dialogues that had taken place during Bush's visit. In Mandelson's case the purpose of the call was also to get an idea of my intentions in relation to the forthcoming G33 meeting. On March 15 I set off for Indonesia via Norway, where I had a bilateral with my counterpart Jonas Store that focused mainly on political issues (despite his distinction, rare in Europe, of combining the positions of foreign and trade minister). Trade issues were never far away, however. The European trade commissioner called me again, this time about the Jakarta meeting. I gathered from our conversation that Mandelson had essentially invited himself to the event. Susan Schwab also phoned me to talk about Jakarta: she was still fretting about the supposed prospect of a host of countries ganging up on the US, but also hoped the meeting might provide her with "breathing space." For me it was obvious that a group of developing countries united by their defensive concerns in agriculture were unlikely to produce a statement the United States would enjoy reading. Realistically, the tormented USTR could only hope that the references to the US position would not be too negative and the criticisms not too bruising. I made the unusual step of suggesting to Susan that she should send a message to the G33, finding some way to indicate respect for the sensitivities of the group with regard to the issues dearest to them: special products (SP) and the Special Safeguard Mechanism (SSM). Susan liked the idea and said she would show me a draft before sending the text. Her email with the draft message arrived while I was in Paris, where I had to wait for a few hours for the connecting flight to Jakarta. I suggested just one small alteration: a sentence about the "contribution" the G33 could make to increasing access to agricultural markets should, I said, be placed at the end of the paragraph in which the USTR expressed her country's willingness to "do more" with regard to domestic subsidies. This demonstration of trust (and a certain amount of humility) on Susan's part was also indicative of her continuing disorientation. On the subject of her message I later wrote: "It is not what I would write on behalf of Brazil, but coming from the United States it will have a positive effect."

During the long flight from Paris to Jakarta, I had time to consider what my objectives should be upon arrival. I doubted that there would be favorable conditions in which to convince (or, more modestly, help convince) an amorphous group of countries, generally defensive in the agricultural arena, that it was in their interest to conclude the Doha Round. Unlike Brazil, most G33 members did not have a great interest in agricultural exports. It would not be easy to make them see, through force of argument, that in fact they had a potential that could be exploited if the export subsidies were eliminated and the rich countries' domestic support measures reduced "substantially." Nor it was self-evident that the greater liberalization of the rich countries' agricultural markets would be beneficial to the group members. Moreover, the argument—for me a very powerful one—that if the Round were not concluded the multilateral system would give way to bilateral or bi-regional arrangements, in which the rich countries would be more able to exert coercive pressure, would probably sound too abstract to most of the audience. I concluded my notes with the thought that probably the biggest benefit I could derive from taking part in the G33 meeting was a deeper personal understanding of the problems, interests, and concerns of member countries. And for me in my role as coordinator of the G20, which included several countries that were also members of the G33, that was already sufficient motivation to make the long journey. Mulling over these various factors, and already suffering the effects of jet lag, I disembarked from the plane in Jakarta.

The G33 had frequently been called upon to "simplify" or "rationalize" its demands with regard to special products, and indeed this was one of the stated aims of the meeting. It was not achieved, however. Special products constituted a category that had never been very clearly defined. Whenever Kamal Nath was asked to come up with a more specific description, he was in the habit of saying: "Special products are classified as special products because they are so defined by the government of a developing country." In Jakarta there was an attempt to limit the number of indicators that could be used to identify an SP, but as far as I could see it was not pursued with much conviction. In that respect the result was disappointing. The final statement, however, did adopt moderate language, and the speeches by President Susilo Yudhoyono, at the opening, and trade minister Mari Pangestu, at the end, gave greater emphasis to eliminating or reducing developed countries' subsidies than to securing privileged treatment for special products and special safeguards. In summarizing the conclusions from the meeting, Pangestu echoed something I myself had said during the working session. She emphasized how much the developing countries had to lose if the Doha Round failed. The participation of Pascal Lamy, Peter Mandelson and myself was helpful in fostering an atmosphere of moderation and balance. And I felt that my presence served to discourage Kamal Nath from some of his more extreme pronouncements. Pangestu treated me with special distinction (even though Brazil's status was merely that of an observer), offering me a prominent seat at the working dinner, the formal meeting, and even the press conference. Various factors had originally led me to accept the invitation to Jakarta, ranging from awareness that it was time to make important decisions regarding the Round to a desire to reciprocate Pangestu's attendance at the G20 meeting in Rio de Janeiro. The occasion gave me the opportunity to demonstrate engagement with the causes of the poorest countries. In that sense it contributed to the consolidation of Brazil's position of leadership (or, I should say, shared leadership). The conversations I had with Kamal, Mandelson, and Lamy helped me to see more clearly what would need to done in the coming weeks. As for Susan Schwab, who had not been invited and did not dare turn up on her own account, the fact that she sent the message (albeit without my suggested alteration) did have some positive impact. At the very least it helped dampen down the smoldering anti-American sentiments of that heterogeneous group.

I should also mention that I took advantage of the trip to Jakarta to have a meeting with President Susilo Yudhoyono. We not only discussed the Round but also spoke about various bilateral issues including biofuels and Embraer aircraft. I also presented the Indonesian president with an invitation from Lula to visit Brazil, which he received with obvious interest. In fact the invitation would lead to an exchange of visits between our two huge developing countries (both in terms of population and territory), which until then had virtually ignored each other apart from occasional coordination in international forums on environmental matters (forests). We even agreed upon a trilateral cooperation project for the benefit of East Timor. In summary, the long journey was tiring but useful. On the flight back to Brazil I looked ahead to some of the tasks that awaited me in the days and weeks ahead. I commented in my notebook on how little free time I had for some of the projects we had previously initiated (including one of my personal favorites, the IBSA group), and added: "But who knows, maybe things will be quieter from June onward?"[124] It was a reference to the possibility, ever present in my mind, that the Doha Round negotiations might come to a standstill. Psychologically, I was looking for a silver lining to the cloud of frustration that would come with failure.

"The Europeans will have to put their cards on the table"

A few days after my return from Jakarta, there was a ministerial reshuffle in Brasilia. Although my name had been mentioned in connection with another cabinet role, I was not included in the shake-up. President Lula himself told me that I had been considered (either by him or by his closest advisors; he did not elaborate) for the post of minister for development, industry and trade: "You just managed to escape," he joked. In fact that particular cabinet position went to Miguel Jorge, a São Paulo business executive and former journalist with whom I would go on to have quite a harmonious relationship (unlike with his predecessor). When the dust had settled after the ministerial changes, I set off for Washington. Twenty-four hours after my arrival, the president would join me, commencing his second official trip to the United States. I spent the first night at the official accommodation for guests of the government, Blair House, famous in WTO circles in Geneva for having been the place where the United States and the European Union made the agreement that provided the impetus for the conclusion of the Uruguay Round. All the work during Lula's visit, and indeed all the social side, would take place at Camp David, the US president's ranch-style residence about half an hour from Washington by helicopter.

Much of my time in Washington was spent in meetings with Condoleezza and Susan, aimed at preparing the ground for the dialogue between the two presidents (which would prove to be substantive and wide-ranging). I told the USTR about my latest Doha Round-related conversations, and what the next steps seemed likely to be. With Condi I also talked about the WTO, in addition to various political issues. This time there seemed to be none of the reticence on her part that had caused her, in São Paulo, to raise the prospect of the US walking away from the negotiations. Lula arrived on March 31. At Camp David, before the meetings started, we were driven in golf carts through the verdant fields. I was reminded of the descriptions of the ranch I had read in a book by Boutros Boutros-Ghali,[125] who had been there as Egypt's foreign minister for the signing of the Camp David Accords with Israel in 1978. It was Susan's job to drive me to the "cabin" where the Brazilian delegation would be staying (and to try to keep up with the secretary of state, who showed a liking for surprising speed at the wheel of her diminutive vehicle). The Doha Round was one of the issues on the agenda, along with ethanol, Cuba, the Middle East, Iran, and UN reform. Comments about the leaders of other countries in South America would also arise. In the written report of the meeting that was later produced by my aides, the WTO negotiations took up four paragraphs. Here is a selection of excerpts: "The US president introduced the theme of the Doha Round, drawing attention to [one of the] problems in the negotiations. 'Everyone wants exceptions,' he said [probably referring to what the Europeans considered sensitive products, and to the G33's special products in agriculture]. Nevertheless, [Bush] said he was 'anxious' for the Round to be concluded, adding that 'without the Doha Round there will be no fight against poverty.' [This was an obvious reference to the Lula-Chirac initiative, in which the US was not a participant.] Bush said Susan Schwab would announce that there were now thirty days[126] in which to reach a preliminary agreement with a view to finalizing the Round. . . . Bush recalled President Lula's words in São Paulo about the need for clarity in the demands for [or, from the US perspective, offers of] openings to trade: 'You have to put the numbers on the table.' For that to happen, Bush says it is necessary to establish what the other parties involved want [and what they themselves are willing to do]. 'I need to fully understand what the Europeans want.[127] I can't afford to get my country into trouble.' Bush said he perceived significant differences between the positions of Brazil and India. In response to that, President Lula mentioned Brazil's leadership role in the G20 and expressed his determination to 'get Prime Minister Singh to engage in the negotiations.'"

My aides' report of the meeting continues: "Minister Celso Amorim intervened to say that he and Susan would be going to India [for a G4/G6 meeting] and could address the issue [of India's immobility with regard to SP and the SSM]. He suggested that the presidents should telephone Prime Minister Singh to encourage him to . . . adopt 'a flexible position.' Condoleezza Rice said [this] option would be examined. Bush suggested that he and Lula should send a [joint] letter to the Indian PM. The Brazilian president noted that this might cause discomfort among other members of the G20, especially Argentina.[128] He said, however, that the idea of both presidents calling Singh seemed a good one. Bush noted that Singh's coalition was fragile. 'He doesn't have the autonomy to close the deal,' he said. Minister Amorim said the Indians did not wish to become isolated [a potentially positive factor]. Bush referred to [the difficulties in relation to] the US-India nuclear agreement, [but acknowledged] that in the case of the Doha Round there was less chance of adverse reactions in New Delhi. The US president pointed out that the Indian middle class is very numerous (more than 350 million people). 'With the agreement,' he added, 'India will be a big market for products from Brazil and the US.'"

With that last observation, Bush was trying to turn our eyes toward the Indian market and thereby also lure us toward his own position. In fact it was a position already held by much of Brazil's agribusiness sector, which took something of a dim view of our alliance with New Delhi. The report continues: "Bush reiterated that his main concern was with the European Union: 'The Europeans will have to put their cards on the table. . . . The EU promises and doesn't deliver. But the United States delivers what it promises.' President Lula commented that 'the decisions made by the United States have global importance' . . . and that he was 'extremely satisfied' with the American willingness to seek a solution in order to achieve progress in the negotiations within a time limit of thirty days."

Some of the colorful details of the Camp David dialogue did not appear in the official Itamaraty report. There was, for example, the Americans' constant concern with what Bush depicted as the other negotiating partners' tendency to "pocket" US offers and give nothing in return—a perception that contributed greatly to Washington's immobility. Nor does the report capture the US president's distinctively colloquial style. Commenting that Brazil had a lot of delicate work ahead, I remember Bush said: "Your minister will be in trouble." As for the European Union, he said it was necessary to "call their bluff." Commenting on India's position, Bush emphasized Brazil's role and implied we might exert some influence on Delhi:[129] "Many countries look at what Brazil does." Bush was of course referring to Brazil's political leadership role among developing countries. There was an element of deliberate flattery in this, although it was not always expressed in the most articulate way. As for Lula's comments during the meeting, the report mentions his perception (which I shared) that "[Prime Minister] Singh is different from Kamal" (i.e. more constructive). My overall impression from the Camp David talks was that although the US approach still fell short of what would be needed in order to unlock the negotiations, President Bush was becoming more proactive and indeed optimistic in relation to the Doha Round.[130] This, in turn, helped keep alive my own little flame of hope.

The dialogue between the two presidents, although generic and sometimes technically imprecise, was indicative of a mood of understanding. A similar mood prevailed, around that time, in my conversations with my European negotiating partner. There was as yet no sign that at the potentially decisive G4 meeting in June, the United States and European Union would actually form an unholy alliance against Brazil (and, by extension, India). The question still remains: what caused the two biggest blocs (the US can be considered a bloc on its own) to put aside, at least temporarily, their differences over OTDS and access to agricultural markets in order to focus instead on NAMA, turning their combined guns against us in a way not dissimilar to their behavior in Cancún in 2003? I still do not have a full explanation for the turnaround that was shortly to take place. At the time, however, I was already aware that with regard to industrial goods, the underlying tensions that placed us in opposition to both Washington and Brussels were bound to come to the surface sooner or later. Nor was I unaware of the narrowness of Washington's "comfort zone" when it came to domestic support, or that of

Brussels in relation to AMA. But over the preceding months it seemed both major players had been focused on gaining our support so as to extract concessions from the other one. In the case of the United States there had also been the attempt to involve us in their battle against the restrictions on agricultural products that the G33 wanted to maintain or indeed increase. In the aftermath of Camp David, and also following Mandelson's apparent vow of friendship during our most recent meeting in Geneva, I certainly did not foresee the change that lay ahead.

"Only Lula can make Singh smile"

A few days after the Camp David summit, on April 11, I started a two-day visit to India. This time I was wearing not two hats but three: that of foreign minister, which I used for the India-Brazil Joint Commission and for bilaterals with my counterpart Pranab Mukherjee, who had literally come out of hospital to see me (having suffered a minor accident a few days before); that of "security advisor," for the strategic dialogue I initiated with Mayankote Narayanan, national security advisor to the Indian prime minister, as had been agreed during the visit to Brazil by Prime Minister Manmohan Singh the year before; and that of minister responsible for the trade negotiations, in bilaterals with Kamal Nath and in meetings of the G4 and G6. During my stay in Delhi I was also received by the prime minister. On the subject of the Doha Round the most important conversation took place during a G4 working dinner on April 11. That is when we sketched out a provisional calendar of events and targets for the period from April to July, which we formally approved the next day. It was, above all, a demonstration of engagement and an indication of our shared recognition that, with some effort and political will, it would not be impossible to achieve a positive result in two or three months. The biggest problem this time, it seemed to me, was the issue of agricultural market access—specifically the distance between the Americans' excessive ambitions and the Indians' continuing sensitivities. At the heart of the matter were the special products (SP) and the Special Safeguard Mechanism (SSM), which would come to torment us and ultimately contribute to the implosion of the negotiations in July the following year. This was not to say, of course, that the other problems (OTDS, NAMA, AMA) had disappeared from the agenda; it was simply the case that the main preoccupation tended to change from meeting to meeting.

My conversation with the Indian prime minister deserves a separate mention. I wrote the following in my notebook: "I feel that [Manmohan Singh] has a real enthusiasm for the relationship with Brazil, for the IBSA group, and above all for President Lula. It would be no exaggeration to say that his face lit up when I told him that India's inclusion in the president's program of visits for 2007 was Lula's own idea (I have in my files a photo of the moment when I handed him Lula's letter—the PM has a beatific smile on his face).[131] We talked about various topics: social programs, renewable energy, Security Council reform, and bilateral trade (which we were hoping to raise from slightly more than $2 billion USD in 2007 to $10 billion in 2010). Singh, a renowned economist, referred to the late Celso Furtado, the Brazilian economist and intellectual who had been one of the world's leading thinkers in the field of development economics: 'I grew up with him,' he said. On the subject of the Doha Round, the prime minister [showing an understanding of the political tensions inevitably caused by our efforts to maintain the unity of the G20] expressed thanks for Brazil's understanding attitude toward 'Indian sensitivities.'" But, as if to distance himself from the more rigid positions of the trade minister, he added: "India wants to be part of the solution, not part of the problem." I thought it would not be appropriate for me to insist on firm deadlines or specific numbers. I merely emphasized the importance of the multilateral trading system for countries such as Brazil and India, and mentioned the potential gains for the poorest nations.

The rest of the month of April was dedicated to South America: discussions about UNASUR (the new name for the CASA);[132] issues related to energy integration; and presidential visits to Chile and Argentina. A reference to the Round appears in my notes in the context of those visits: "There are differences between the roles of Chile and Argentina (both in the G20) in the WTO. Chile, more liberal, would be ready to accept an agreement negotiated by Brazil [in the G4 or G6]. In fact, Santiago might favor even greater flexibility than Brazil [on industrial goods]. Argentina will tend to resist, for economic reasons connected with its efforts to reindustrialize, which are at the expense of its agriculture. [In addition, there are] historical-political reasons . . . connected with the country's loss of stature in the negotiations.[133] [Buenos Aires] will certainly want to make its voice heard." Even against this regional backdrop it was still impossible to let the global negotiations out of my sight.

In mid-May I went back to Geneva, where at the request of the Brazilian health minister, José Gomes Temporão, I spoke at the World Health Assembly on a subject related to the WTO: the use of compulsory licenses for the production and/or importation of medicines at costs lower than the prices charged by the big pharmaceutical companies holding the patents. Temporão was probably aware of my previous involvement with the subject. He also knew that the words of the foreign minister, who formally represents the State, would carry more weight than his own. And at that time it was far from being merely an abstract issue. We were in the process of issuing a license for the importation of generic versions of an anti-HIV drug, Efavirenz, as part of Brazil's successful and much-lauded program to combat AIDS.[134] From Geneva I went briefly to Paris for an OECD "outreach" session and a meeting of ministers at the Australian embassy (including a discussion in the

G6 format), before a short flight to Brussels for another gathering of what some commentators in the economic and financial media were now calling the "Big Four" of the WTO. I could not help thinking of the newsreels of my boyhood (*Movietones* and *Actualités Françaises*, among others), in the late 1940s and early 1950s, with their references to the "Big Four" powers at the time: the United States, France, the United Kingdom, and the Soviet Union. It was a distant reminder, as if any were necessary, that the membership of elite groups of nations is forever subject to change. So I had no illusions about the WTO quartet remaining unaltered, but the reference was in itself a tribute to the leadership Brazil and India had proved capable of providing. The G4 meeting in Brussels had earlier been the subject of a phone call from Bush to Lula, which took place while I was flying back to Brasilia from Ottawa (where I had made my first bilateral visit to Canada, reciprocating the visit to Brasilia by Canadian foreign minister Peter MacKay a few months earlier). Later, from the written account of the presidents' phone conversation, I learned that Bush was attributing "crucial importance" to the discussions set to take place in the Belgian capital. I commented in my notebook: "Let's see if the United States comes up with something concrete, rather than just putting pressure on India, the G20, and the G33!" My short time in Paris was not very productive. The meeting of about fifteen ministers at the Australian embassy, and the smaller G6 meeting, served primarily to "take the temperature" of countries that were not part of the inner circle of WTO members who were leading the negotiations. As for the OECD "outreach," it is primarily an opportunity for short and (if possible) incisive pronouncements. It is also an occasion when individual members of the EU can express, in a broader international forum, their opinions on trade-related issues.

"The world is on your shoulders"

Val-Duchesse is a castle on the outskirts of Brussels, surrounded by elegant French-style gardens, lush woodland, and small lakes. At that time, in late spring, the temperature was pleasant—as indeed, on the whole, was the atmosphere of the G4/G6 meeting. We were in the very place where, in 1957, the negotiations that created the European Common Market were completed. This fact was recorded by a bronze plaque in the entrance hall of the castle, which I took to be a good sign for the Doha Round.[135] The G4 discussions were mostly quite productive. We performed simulations with the various NAMA coefficients, which produced interesting comparisons between the potential consequences both for developing and developed countries. The combination of political and technical discussions, though sometimes a little heated, made it possible to see more clearly the scenarios likely to be produced by the various hypotheses.[136] There was a detailed discussion on a topic hardly discussed by ministers until that point: the special safeguards employed by rich countries (SSG[137]—not to be confused with the SSM (Special Safeguard Mechanism) demanded by India and other developing countries), which had arisen from the Uruguay Round. This was an area where protectionist mechanisms, particularly European ones, continued to operate to the detriment of exports from countries such as Brazil. The European Commission was certainly resistant to the idea of their elimination during the period in which the results of the Round were to be implemented, and yet this was starting to be considered a possibility. According to my notes, the crucial issue of the ceiling for US domestic subsidies was not examined in depth, but *ad laterem* conversations made me believe that the "landing zone" would be somewhere near $15 billion USD. To me it seemed that this figure, although higher than the one Rob Portman had let slip in Rio, would be just about acceptable from the G20's point of view, as long as it was accompanied by adequate disciplines to prevent tampering with the different categories of subsidies or products.[138] My notes on the meeting reflect a cautious optimism: "The Americans continue to apply pressure for greater market access [in agriculture], which in turn stirs the [aggressive] European attitude in relation to NAMA. But the shared perception that we might be reaching the finishing straight could lead to the ambitions becoming more reasonable on all sides. There will still be the thorny issue of special products (SP) and the Special Safeguard Mechanism (SSM). . . . But the talks do seem to be advancing, or at least seem not to be blocked." The most curious aspect of my notes was my apparent tranquility with regard to the analytical exercise that had been carried out in the area of NAMA. Looking back, this was perhaps a moment when my intuition failed me. Perhaps I should have sensed that the calm was a sign of the storm to come at the G4 meeting in Potsdam in July. But in the attitude of my interlocutors there was no indication that the two major players were shortly to join forces against us. In Brussels, Susan Schwab even went so far as to suggest that the "decisive meeting" in July should take place in Brazil. Her proposal obviously made the possibility of US-EU collusion seem even more remote, as it would not make sense for the USTR to choose our home ground to initiate an aggressive maneuver against Brazil. The only reason the meeting did not go ahead in Rio de Janeiro was because Kamal Nath and Peter Mandelson, citing logistical problems, insisted it should take place in Europe.

The next week was devoted almost entirely to our neighbors. But in early June I accompanied Lula on another visit to New Delhi. This time the president was awarded the Jawaharlal Nehru Award for International Understanding. On the way to India we made a stop-over in London, where the most important event was a soccer game between the national teams of Brazil and England to officially inaugurate the "new" (i.e. rebuilt) Wembley Stadium. The British official designated to accompany Lula at the game was the young Secretary of State for Environment, Food and Rural Affairs, my longstanding friend David Miliband. (I had also met David a few weeks earlier in Paris, when he told me he had chosen not to compete with Gordon Brown for the leadership of the Labour Party so as to avoid what he described as "blood-letting.")[139] My diary records that my stay in London also included a very long meeting (about four hours) with Susan Schwab, in which the US secretary of agriculture, Mike Johanns, also participated. According to my notes the meeting allowed me to glimpse, on the part of Johanns, some positive signs in the area of agriculture. On the other hand the difficulties regarding NAMA, an area in which the Americans were making increasing demands, seemed to be worsening. Schwab got in touch with me again not long afterwards, while I was accompanying Lula in bilateral meetings in Berlin on the eve of the G8+5 summit. These great efforts on the USTR's part to maintain a high level of understanding with Brazil, despite our differences, were in contrast to her behavior a few days later at the G4 ministerial meeting. In New Delhi the WTO also came up in conversations between Lula and Manmohan Singh, for which Kamal and I were also present. Again I had the distinct impression that the prime minister was more receptive to an agreement than his trade minister, who remained very difficult to pin down.

The G8+5 summit in Heiligendamm, a German seaside resort on the Baltic (which we reached by a combination of car, plane and helicopter), was the fourth such gathering in which Brazil had participated. Much of the meeting between the leaders, on the morning of June 8, focused on climate change. During lunch, Lula spoke about the WTO. Between events I was able to have a few brief conversations with some of the leaders present. Coincidentally, Tony Blair and Durão Barroso both hinted, separately, that I held "the key to the negotiations." Behind this ego-stroking there lay, of course, a deliberate and significant degree of pressure. In a tone that was jocular but, I thought, not without an element of provocation, the British prime minister (very soon to hand over to Gordon Brown) also told me: "The world is on your shoulders." Bush, for his part, showed me a table (a copy of which I had received from Schwab just a few minutes before) with ambitious numbers for NAMA and more modest figures for US agricultural subsidies. I politely declined the opportunity to engage in a discussion with the US president on such fine technical details: "Mister President, sir, I'm not going to negotiate with you. I would be intimidated. But I'll carry on discussing [the numbers] with Susan." This little verbal exchange took place while we were taking a walk along a path through linden trees between the venue for the working meeting and the main hotel building, where we were going to have lunch. I think it is appropriate here to transcribe an observation I wrote in my notebook at the end of the Heiligendamm summit, even though it does not directly concern the WTO: "In the G8, little by little, the idea of dialogue with major developing countries is becoming established. It is obvious, however, that [the rich countries] want to use the mechanism to pressure us on certain issues, such as intellectual property, investment, and climate obligations [all of which featured in the so-called Heiligendamm Process, which proved to be inconclusive]. At the same time, [these countries] seek to guard the important decisions for themselves."[140]

My next destination was Geneva, where on June 9, a Saturday, I met again with Peter Mandelson to discuss the Round. On the Monday I coordinated a long meeting of the G20 that covered a lot of ground, and which I felt was positive overall. At the end of the meeting, as was now traditional, the members of the G20 were joined by the representatives of the various groups of developing countries (the African group, the LDCs, the SVEs, etc.).[141] In addition to Kamal and myself, a large number of ministers were present, including those of Argentina (Jorge Taiana, always accompanied by Alfredo Chiaradía, secretary of commerce in the Argentine foreign ministry); Pakistan (Humayun Khan); Egypt (Rachid Mohamed Rachid); South Africa (Mandizi Mpalwa); Indonesia (Mari Pangestu, coordinator of the G33) and Tanzania (Basil Mramba). Some of the ministers spoke of the need to combine firmness with flexibility. More importantly, from the point of view of Kamal and myself, the other ministers reaffirmed their confidence in the "representatives of the group" in the G4. Indeed, that was the principal focus of the interventions made by the ministers representing South Africa, Egypt, Indonesia, and also Pakistan (which was noteworthy, given the well-known rivalry between Islamabad and New Delhi). The coordinators of the other groups of developing countries expressed similar sentiments. Some of the speakers specifically praised the "leadership" shown by Brazil (and, to a lesser extent, India). Showing that my long trip to Indonesia a few months before had not been in vain, Mari Pangestu thanked me effusively for attending the G33 meeting in Jakarta. The permanent representative of Benin, the coordinator of the Cotton-4, was full of praise for our initiative in having invited a delegation representing that group to Brazil. But there were also some discordant notes. The Bolivian delegate, Pablo Solón, referred to a "lack of transparency" in the negotiations. Rather than a direct criticism of India or Brazil, however, I think that was probably just a reprise of the familiar refrain on the part the countries that were not part of the smaller groups at the forefront of the G20. Nevertheless, in that context, Solón's words could have been misinterpreted. Anyway, his voice was an isolated one. As if to illustrate the intrinsic difficulties of coordinating an ideologically heterogeneous group, the Cuban representative, a senior diplomat in Geneva, launched an ardent—and, in that context, inappropriate—verbal attack against biofuels, a topic that had been addressed superficially, and positively, by Rachid Rachid. Jorge Taiana, although careful in his use of words, emphasized the elements that from an Argentine point of view made it difficult to reach an agreement. Despite these nuances, the meeting ended with a strong show of unity from the developing countries. The statement prepared by the permanent representatives, with a couple of small alterations proposed by Tanzania, was adopted without any significant problems. Later there was a press conference at WTO headquarters, which resulted in quite a lot of media coverage.

After the G20 there was a meeting of the NAMA-11, a group concerned about the pressure being placed on developing countries to open their markets for industrial goods). The NAMA-11 was of much lesser importance than the G20, and some of its members held such radical positions that they seemed not to want the Doha Round to produce any results whatsoever. Mari Pangestu, Humayun Khan, and I left the meeting feeling somewhat alarmed. Overall, however, despite some contradictory signs, these latest Geneva meetings with the developing countries gave encouragement to the efforts Kamal and I would shortly be making in the next stage of the negotiations.

Over the next three days I "took refuge" in the residence of the Brazilian ambassador in Paris, my very good friend Vera Pedrosa (who had previously served as undersecretary for political affairs, at the time—and to this day, I believe—the highest position any woman had occupied in Itamaraty). Over the course of my endless travels, certain places ended up becoming homes away from home. That was certainly the case with our ambassador's residence in Paris and with two addresses in Geneva: my daughter Anita's apartment in the Saint Jean neighborhood, and our permanent representative's charming and extremely comfortable residence, Mont-Riant, where indeed my wife Ana and I had lived for two extended periods. Once, between returning from India and setting off for Brussels, I entered "my" suite in the Paris residence to find, on the bedside table, the same book that I had not finished reading, and in the shower, the same bottle of shampoo I had bought during my previous visit. I took advantage of the interval before the G4 (potentially G6) meeting in Potsdam to devote myself to the detailed study of the dossiers on market access for agricultural products and industrial goods. With regard to agriculture I wanted to study not only the tariff reductions by "bands" but also the treatment of products declared to be "sensitive." What I hoped to do was to secure a reasonable increase in access to the developed countries' agricultural markets, particularly in the European Union. In the case of NAMA, I immersed myself in the tables that set out coefficients and flexibilities with regard to hypothetical tariff reductions in the various industrial sectors of greatest "defensive" interest to Brazil.

The choice of location for my "retreat" was not due to a desire to enjoy the attractions of *La Ville Lumière* but because the French capital was hosting a series of meetings of senior officials in preparation for Potsdam. Although as a minister I did not attend the meetings, at the end of each day spent poring over the tables of figures I was able to receive updates from the Brazilian delegates, headed by Roberto Azevêdo. I also took advantage of these "after hours" sessions to clear up any doubts that had arisen while sifting through the papers earlier in the day. Ever since my conversations with Tony Blair and Jonathan Powell a year before, I had been conscious that Brazil would need to make additional concessions on NAMA. More specifically, to use the WTO jargon, we would need to seek a "landing zone" below the coefficient of 30 (somewhere between 20 and 25, in fact). However, I was also convinced that we had to resist pressures to make excessive concessions without reciprocal moves (in proportional terms) from the rich countries on agriculture. I was very concerned that such concessions would potentially accelerate "deindustrialization" in Brazil (a process already taking place, according to many analysts), although the precise point on the scale of coefficients at which this would begin to occur was difficult to determine. I took the view that even if the Doha Round did not in the end live up to its "Development Round" billing, it must not be permitted to work *against* development. After my pause for reflection in Paris, I made another stop in Geneva to receive briefings on certain issues I had studied less intensively, such as services, before flying on to Germany.

At the end of the Second World War, the very hotel where our meeting would take place, the Schlosshotel Cecilienhof, had been the scene of one of the most important summits aimed at establishing the new world order. A pamphlet distributed during our meeting refreshed my memory of the details of that historic moment. The Potsdam Summit took place between July 17 and August 2, 1945. It was attended by Truman, Stalin, and Churchill (soon to be replaced by Clement Attlee after the Conservatives were defeated by Labour in the British general election). During the proceedings, Truman informed Stalin that the US had carried out a nuclear explosion that served as a test for the imminent attacks on Hiroshima and Nagasaki. The mood was generally tense and the leaders of the principal wartime allies would not meet again. It was not the best of omens for our meeting. And it was not only historical precedent that made the choice of location inauspicious.

The Schlosshotel Cecilienhof seemed not to have been refurbished since 1945. It might have been an elegant hotel in the first decades of the twentieth century, but now it was old and tired. The long corridors were reminiscent of a boarding school; the meeting rooms were cramped; and the bedrooms, although spacious, lacked modern comforts. My bathroom gave off an unpleasant smell that would probably have interfered with my (few) hours of sleep had I not been so exhausted at the end of each long and tense working day. The only attraction nearby was a castle that was once home to a prince in the Hohenzollern family; I believe it dated from the seventeenth or eighteenth century, but the possibility of visiting it failed to arouse my interest. On the first day I managed to have a morning walk in the field in front of the hotel, but the damp wind of a drab early summer in northern Europe made it less than enjoyable. Nor did the hotel's clientele generate a very cheerful atmosphere. Apart from the participants in the summit, most of the guests were senior citizens from other parts of Germany; there were no young people apart from a few children accompanying their grandparents, and no foreigners. In summary, it was a far cry from the vibrant atmosphere of the modern resorts frequented by the "jet set"—where international summits sometimes take place—and indeed from the warm, welcoming atmosphere of so many of the world's older hotels.

I arrived in Potsdam feeling politically and technically prepared for a clash likely to prove decisive for the fate of the Doha Round.[142] But with the unfortunate historical echoes and the generally rather depressing surroundings, it was difficult not to wonder if Potsdam was about to become another somber milestone: a kind of Cancún II, burying the hopes of overcoming the new division of the world, in terms of trade, between the rich North and the poor South. Such were my thoughts and feelings as I looked for the umpteenth time through the figures and tables I intended to use during the discussions.

Il Teatro

Potsdam was, in every respect, a disaster. Unlike Cancún, where at least we had been able to consolidate the G20, the meeting of the G4 that took place between June 19 and 21, 2007, brought nothing positive. There were unfavorable signs from the very start, during the private lunch on the first day. Peter Mandelson, with the silent connivance of Susan Schwab, proposed that the order in which we were going to deal with the main themes (the order that had also been followed at Val-Duchesse) should be changed. With an air of utmost innocence, the EU trade commissioner suggested that, "just for a change," we should start the discussions with NAMA, not agriculture. Naturally I said I was strongly against the idea, and my Indian colleague backed me up. The USTR stayed quiet, so Mandelson had to retreat. The substantive discussions, with the participation of two or three advisors on each side, began at 4 p.m. and went on until about 8:30. After a general presentation made in largely neutral terms by the US officials (at Val-Duchesse this task had fallen to Brazil), we started talking about agriculture. I made what I thought was a strong presentation on domestic support, incorporating the data I had been studying over the previous days. I was able to show that the United States' average total expenditure on OTDS over the preceding years had been around $11 or 12 billion USD—far below the figure the US negotiators were now proposing ($17 billion). It would make no sense to provide the Americans with a "cushion" of an extra $5 or 6 billion that would allow them to increase their subsidies in response, for example, to a fall in international prices. I also spoke about the disciplines in each of the "boxes" and the need for ceilings for each product so as to guarantee the credibility of the reductions. US agriculture secretary Mike Johanns complained at the end of the meeting, albeit in a friendly tone, about the "pressure" I was applying. The European agricultural expert, Jean-Luc Demarty, commented to Roberto Azevêdo that "Amorim was at his best." I see from my notes that at this point in the proceedings I still nurtured positive expectations, despite Mandelson's maneuvering. I was very aware, however, that the problems were a long way from being solved.

The meetings the next day basically covered AMA and NAMA. On access to agricultural markets, I insisted on the need for tariff cuts in the category of "sensitive" products, regardless of quotas. This, it seemed, infuriated the Europeans. The fact that the issue had not been discussed previously at ministerial level led Mandelson to say I was "moving the goalposts." But nor had we ever accepted that the "sensitive" products should be dealt with only by means of quotas. I remember I also said that the calculation for the quotas for the imports of those products should be based on a percentage of the actual levels of consumption in Europe (rather than merely increasing the figures established in the Uruguay Round, as the Europeans wanted). I also brought up the subject of the SSG, an anachronistic provision dating from the Uruguay Round that facilitated European agricultural protectionism. It was necessary, I said, to set a timeframe for their elimination. To my disappointment, my arguments on AMA received only discreet support from Susan Schwab and Mike Johanns, which was not consistent with the strong US interest in that particular area of the negotiations. I cannot say I already sensed collusion between the two major players, but the conspicuously low profile of the US negotiators was making me uneasy. My disquiet increased during the afternoon session, dedicated to the issue of industrial goods. It was a session in which Kamal Nath took an appropriate line, avoiding creating openings that went beyond the margins I had at my disposal.[143] Up until that point my expectation had been that after an initial discussion of each of the broad themes of the negotiations, we would go back to them and test the flexibilities so as to explore possible deals. My illusions were undone at the working dinner, at a restaurant appropriately called Il Teatro. During the meal, Mandelson and Schwab put me under constant pressure. I would certainly have suffered indigestion were it not for my habit of eating very lightly in the evening. They both bombarded me with hypothetical coefficients for tariff reductions on industrial goods that were significantly below the minimum I could reach. Kamal, again, adopted a correct approach, not seeking to facilitate the EU-US line of attack. I retired to my less than inviting quarters at the Schlosshotel, spoke briefly with my advisors, and went to bed feeling very concerned.

But worse was to come. The following day, the drama at Il Teatro would turn into a farce worthy of Pirandello. After a perfunctory working session in which we discussed, in a relatively normal atmosphere, peripheral issues that were not part of the "grand bargain," Mandelson began a summing up of the discussions of the previous day and also raised procedural questions such as the moment at which we should call Pascal Lamy and the Japanese minister to join us—which was only supposed to happen at the end of the meeting.[144] As I still fully expected that there would be a second round of discussions, I expressed my perplexity to the EU trade commissioner and asked him directly if he was already preparing a "soft landing" for a scenario of failure. Mandelson said merely that we could talk about that during lunch, an attitude that to me seemed stranger still. Moments later, the European commissioner and the USTR, backed by their respective agriculture experts, announced that it was pointless to continue with the negotiations. It was also around this point in the proceedings that Schwab and Mandelson launched into a bizarre dialogue aimed at establishing what I had said during dinner the night before. Three or four times the USTR asserted: "Celso said [such and such]." And each time, Mandelson disagreed: "No, Susan, Celso said [such and such]." It became so farcical that at one point I suggested I should leave the room so that the two of them could decide, in my absence, precisely what it was that I had said. Their shared objective, obviously, was to back me into a corner. Kamal, for his part, was mostly silent. Later I found out that the two of them had met up again the night before, after dinner at Il Teatro, to decide upon the scene they would stage during the morning session and lunch.

In the June 22 edition of the Brazilian financial newspaper *Valor Econômico*, its competent Geneva correspondent Assis Moreira transcribed the verbal ping-pong of questions and answers that took place between me and a group of journalists (Brazilian and foreign) in my room at the Schlosshotel after news of the impasse had been announced. This came about because, immediately after lunch, I had suggested to my Indian colleague that we needed to change the script of the scenario being developed by Mandelson and Schwab by calling a quick press conference. This, I said, was the only way to prevent their peculiar double-act from placing the blame for the impasse on Brazil and India (principally the former). Kamal agreed. Our respective analyses in the press conference were convergent, although we had not prepared our lines together beforehand.[145] Our initiative in speaking to the media—a lesson I had learned in Cancún—took the other two members of the G4 by surprise. They would have preferred the failure of the meeting to have followed the scenario they had delineated and hoped to control. The aggressive expressions used by Mandeslon and Schwab in conversations after the press conference made it clear that they had been caught off guard. Our decision to take the initiative by communicating the situation to the public, and not just behave reactively, produced positive results. Contrary to the expectations of the European Union and the United States, major newspapers such as the *Wall Street Journal* and the *International Herald Tribune* began their reports on the meeting in Potsdam with headlines that clearly attributed the failure to the impasses on the issue of agriculture.

The article in *Valor Econômico* quoted some of my analyses. For example it faithfully reproduced my perception that, just like at Cancún, the US and the EU had agreed upon a "comfort zone" for their respective difficulties: in the case of the Americans, an elevated ceiling for OTDS, with insufficient disciplines for the distortive subsidies; in the case of the Europeans, insignificant reductions in the barriers to the entry of agricultural products. In the same interview I said it would be totally unacceptable, for example, to allow the US to operate a level of cotton subsidies equal to or higher than that which the WTO Dispute Settlement Body had already described as causing "serious damage to Brazilian producers." I expressed my conviction that the representatives of the two most powerful economies had gone to Potsdam intending to put pressure on Brazil and India, and if possible to separate them from each other. I was sure that if Brazil had given way on industrial tariffs the guns would then have turned on India, in the expectation of isolating it on SP and the SSM. It was also possible, I said, that the Europeans and the Americans had hoped Brazil's longstanding demonstration of commitment to the success of the Round, given our preference for multilateral agreements over bilateral or regional ones, would lead us to make major concessions on NAMA. I pointed out in the interview that my responsibilities in the negotiations extended beyond Brazil's own interests (which in any case would not have been served by the outcome in Potsdam): "I could not make an agreement [that constituted] a betrayal of the interests of Brazilian industry, a betrayal of Mercosur, and a betrayal of the G20 countries." In effect I used my conversation with journalists to nip in the bud the fallacious version of events according to which Kamal and I were responsible for the impasse. I revealed what had happened at lunch, when both Mandelson and Susan, despite my obvious willingness to carry on with the negotiations, said it was "useless to continue." As I said to the journalists, it was at that moment that I had decided to take preventative action by denouncing the plot that was unfolding against us.

From Potsdam I went to Geneva, where on June 23 I had meetings with Pascal Lamy and the G20. I spoke several times on the phone with President Lula (the first conversation was while I was still in Potsdam), who firmly supported the position I had taken. However, Lula wanted to know the details, so that he could participate meaningfully in the conversations he was expecting to have with other leaders. As it turned out, after an unsuccessful attempt to organize a conference call between Lula, Blair, Merkel, and Barroso, the president ended up speaking only to Blair. There was a meeting of the Trade Negotiations Committee (TNC) of the WTO coming up. I strongly advised the director-general not to encourage ministers to attend, as it might only exacerbate the negative mood that had arisen in Potsdam. Good sense prevailed and the TNC meeting was attended only by permanent representatives; I learned later from ours, Clodoaldo Hugueney, that some forceful speeches were made. I also told Lamy that in my meeting with the G20 I intended to avoid conveying a negative message. I would have to be frank about the difficulties and the hostile maneuvers, but I would express the opinion that we should continue striving for a positive result. This was the approach that Lamy himself also favored.

Somewhat to my surprise, I received a phone call in the afternoon of June 23 from the USTR. In Potsdam, both she and Mandelson had indicated that they did not intend to go to Geneva, but they had probably changed their minds when they found out I was there. Schwab requested a meeting with me. I sent the message that I would be at Mont-Riant at 5 p.m.. Her aides tried briefly to get me to see her at her hotel instead, but did not insist. And so Susan came to speak to me on Brazil's "home ground." We sat together outside, just the two of us, in exactly the same spot where we had talked a year before in the wake of another impasse (but without the stagecraft of Potsdam). Overlooking the large park with its expanse of pine trees, with the peaks of the Alps visible in the distance, it seemed I was listening to a USTR completely different from the one I had encountered in Potsdam. Although in terms of their substance her positions were unchanged from those she had defended at the Cecilienhof, her tone was now conciliatory and she admitted to "mistakes and misunderstandings" (which she attributed mainly to Mandelson) in the way the meetings had been conducted. She listened to me patiently, neither agreeing explicitly nor contesting my version of events. In a way that did not correspond at all with the pressure exerted against me on NAMA, Susan now gave an unsustainable but nevertheless revealing interpretation of her (and, no doubt, Mandelson's) intentions: she said I had "embraced" the cause of India to the detriment of the negotiations. It was a distorted view that implied I had adopted a rigid attitude on industrial goods (an area in which my interlocutor was well aware of Brazil's sensitivities) merely to divert the pressure that would have been on India with regard to SP and the SSM. Faced with my obvious perplexity, Susan did not persist with this nonsensical explanation. She asked me what I would say to the idea of "discreet" meetings of our senior officials, aimed at exploring ways forward. With the wounds from Potsdam still raw I did not want to commit myself, but nor did I respond negatively. We parted with friendly words, agreeing that we had just had a "non-conversation" (i.e. one that would stay between the two of us) and that we would stay in touch.

I did not know exactly what had caused such a sudden change in the USTR's behavior, but no doubt it had something to do with the failure of the strategy she and Mandelson had adopted. They had pursued two objectives, one after the other, and not achieved either. They had not obtained the concessions they thought Brazil might make on NAMA (which would then have left India isolated with regard to SP/SSM). Nor, subsequently, had they managed to transmit to public opinion the message that the failure of the meeting was our fault. Susan had another concern, noticeable at more than one moment during our conversation: she did not want the impasse to be depicted as the result of a North-South conflict. I do not know if that—or perhaps a conversation with Bush, who still wanted a positive conclusion to the Round—was the explanation for such a marked change in her behavior in the space of two days. From my point of view the USTR's switch to a conciliatory approach served to confirm that the position I had adopted over the preceding days was the right one. In my eternal optimism I thought I could still see a light, albeit faint and flickering, at the end of the tunnel.

My short stay in Geneva ended with a meeting with Lamy, at his request, and a phone call from Peter Mandelson. Immediately after the conversation with the director-general, I spoke briefly to the journalists who cover the WTO. Asked if I had plans to meet again with Schwab or Mandelson in the near future, I said I did not anticipate taking the initiative in that respect. As agreed, I omitted to mention the conversation with the USTR that had already taken place, at her request, at Mont-Riant. I added, however, that I liked to consider myself a well-mannered person, and therefore if either of them telephoned me, I would not refuse to take the call. In the case of Mandelson, that is exactly what happened the following day. The European trade commissioner made three comments about Potsdam: (1) that the US had not been "convincing" on OTDS; (2) that the EU itself had not been convincing on AMA (an unexpected touch of humility, albeit probably insincere); (3) that the developing countries had not been convincing on access to their own markets (both industrial and agricultural). Mandelson also said that his conversations in Geneva had led him to conclude that "there is no market for" a level of OTDS above $14 billion on the part of the US ("I prefer $13 billion, but that's very difficult," he said). I should mention, *en passant*, that this statement from Mandeslon directly contradicted something one of the European negotiators had told a member of our delegation in Potsdam. An official who dealt with agriculture had admitted that in order to discourage the Americans from making demands on AMA, the EU would not press for a lower level of OTDS. With ostensible candor (indeed, it would have been touching had I not suspected he was being disingenuous), Peter told me that he found what I had said about NAMA on behalf of Brazil (i.e. my long analyses based on exhaustive study of the statistical data) to be more interesting than the briefings he received from his own aides in Brussels. As if nothing serious had happened in Potsdam, he airily proposed that we should meet in Lisbon in early July, on the eve of the EU-Brazil Strategic Partnership.[146]

On the flight back to Brazil, I had time to reflect on Potsdam and its aftermath. The attitudes toward Brazil on the part of Schwab and Mandelson had changed radically in a very short space of time. What could have caused them to come so quickly to conclusions so different from those they had expressed (in a manner that bordered on rude) a couple of days earlier? One reason might have been the atmosphere in Geneva, where it was quite possible they had encountered negative reactions to their attitude in Potsdam. In Susan's case I wondered if she had received new instructions from Bush. Similarly, Lula's phone conversation with Blair, based on the information I had passed on to him, would certainly have been reported to Mandelson and might have influenced his behavior. Another, simpler explanation was that a little time to think about the implications of a continued crisis in the negotiations had led the USTR and the European commissioner to seek an accommodation. Whatever the explanation, it was certain that both of them had exercised some degree of self-criticism. Besides that, as both of them knew, it would be impossible to carry forward the negotiations without Brazil's engagement. Other G20 countries such as South Africa and Argentina (not to mention Venezuela and Cuba) had positions far less flexible than ours. Furthermore, without our leadership, shared with India, there would be no way to contain the avalanche of grievances from the various groups of developing countries, which was something the two negotiators possibly sensed in the air in Geneva.

I took the view that, given our profound commitment to the Doha Round, I could not refuse the different forms of contact proposed by Mandelson and Schwab. And with the G4 now in a state of suspension, I also had to keep Kamal Nath informed. The other factor I could not ignore was that time was short. In our long conversation in Geneva, Lamy warned me that the coordinators of the negotiating groups, previously on the margins of the process, were likely to present their "papers" within ten days.[147] What surprised me most of all was the speed with which Schwab and Mandelson "re-engaged" with me. I remembered that after Cancún, four months went by before Zoellick tried to talk to me again on the subject of the Round. This time it was twenty-four hours in Susan's case, and forty-eight in Peter's. I wrote in my notebook: "We are now starting a new chapter." I did not know at the time, of course, that the story would ultimately have such a disastrous ending.

Five days after the events described above, there was a meeting of the Common Market Council of Mercosur, which is composed of foreign and finance ministers. During the dinner held on June 27, on the eve of the formal meeting, I gave the assembled ministers a detailed description of what had happened in Potsdam. As far as I could tell, they listened with great interest. Brazil's position was praised by almost everyone present. The sole exception was Uruguay's economics and finance minister, Danilo Astori, who for a long time had been complaining about Brazil's attitude (and mine, in particular) in not facilitating a trade agreement between Uruguay and the United States. For Astori, who did not excel when it came to diplomatic niceties, my presentation on Potsdam was a "waste of time." However, the Uruguayan foreign minister, Reinaldo Gargano, thanked me for my explanation and expressed his support for our position. So too did the Argentine foreign minister and finance minister, Jorge Taiana and Felisa Miceli (the latter even said she wished she could have made a recording of my speech). The feedback from Paraguayan foreign minister Rubén Ramirez was similarly positive. During the formal Mercosur meeting the next day, there were expressions of support for our actions in Potsdam from the representatives of the Mercosur Parliament and the Economic and Social Consultative Forum. The latter, a veteran Argentine trade unionist, was especially vehement. During the leaders' summit, which is usually attended by the associate members, President Michelle Bachelet of Chile, whom I had spoken to briefly beforehand, made a strong statement in support of Brazil in which she emphasized the way we were prioritizing the fight against agricultural protectionism. Bachelet's speech was particularly valuable because it signified an overruling of certain attitudes on the part of the Chilean permanent representative in Geneva, who along with a few of his counterparts from other countries (including Mexico)[148] had presented a "conciliatory" proposal on NAMA that went directly against Brazil's interests (and even more so those of Argentina, South Africa, etc.). After the collapse of the talks in Potsdam, the political support from our partners in Mercosur, including from associate members such as Chile, was very welcome indeed.

Papers fluttering in the air

In early July, I accompanied President Lula to Lisbon for a summit at which the EU-Brazil Strategic Partnership was officially launched. Several European leaders were present, including President Nicolas Sarkozy of France, Prime Minister José Luis Zapatero of Spain, and Prime Minister Romano Prodi of Italy. Chairing the event was Prime Minister José Sócrates of Portugal. The summit was useful in many ways, and was also a clear demonstration of the attraction President Lula exerted among the European leaders. The state of the multilateral trade negotiations was discussed in a general way, with the leaders reaffirming their commitment to the process, but Doha had to share the spotlight with other issues related to global governance and also specific questions concerning South America. Just before the summit, as arranged, I met with Mandelson. After the skirmishes of Potsdam the European trade commissioner now reverted to a friendly tone, adopting the air of a "neutral analyst" that he maintained in many of his conversations with me over the years. He said the greatest challenge now facing the Round was that of getting the Americans to re-engage. In stark contrast to his approach on the last occasion we had been together, he implied a degree of flexibility with regard to the European demands concerning NAMA, although he also declared, in typical style, that a coefficient higher than 22 would leave him in a "humiliating situation" in the eyes of the EU member states. Despite the pathetic tone, and the fact that obviously I could not rely on vague allusions, the European commissioner's words did signal some possibility of advancement. He seemed now to be more realistic about the kind of "exchange rate" between NAMA, OTDS, and AMA that might allow the negotiations to resume. Even with regard to the issues that were particularly sensitive from a European point of view, there seemed to be some inclination to move forward. Mandelson appeared to accept the need for change regarding the Uruguay Round special safeguards (SSG). In the case of sensitive products, he did not immediately reject my argument that a cut of around 30% (regardless of quotas) was necessary. Roberto Azevêdo and Clodoaldo Hugueney, meanwhile, had maintained "very discreet" communication with the USTR's staff and with officials at the US Department of Agriculture, during which they too had perceived reluctance on the part of Washington to return to the talks. I intended to call Susan Schwab at some point, but I did not want to do so before the end of the meetings due to take place in Geneva after the EU-Brazil summit in Lisbon and its follow-up in Brussels.[149] I had already scheduled meetings in Geneva with the G20/G90, Pascal Lamy, and Kamal Nath. One of my concerns upon arriving in Geneva would be the fact that in one or two weeks' time, the group coordinators at the WTO who were now leading discussions on the various main aspects of the Doha Round would be presenting the papers that would subsequently frame the discussions. These coordinators' texts, containing outlines of proposed agreements, would then be reviewed by the member states. I believed there needed to be some form of "intervention" at ministerial level if we wanted to advance sufficiently so as to be able to conclude the negotiations before the next US presidential election in November of the following year. At this stage I still believed that was possible, although obviously I recognized the enormous problems that lay ahead. I asked myself: were the Americans willing to engage in genuine negotiations, like those we had undertaken in the framework of the FIPS in July 2004? And should I encourage Lamy to take the initiative of calling a meeting with that objective? With these questions in mind I embarked upon the series of commitments I had arranged for myself in Geneva.

My first meeting, in the morning, was with Kamal Nath. After that, I met with the G20/G90. In the late afternoon, at WTO headquarters, I spoke with Lamy. Kamal and I exchanged information about our recent conversations. He had been to Washington in the context of an India-US Joint Commission. His comments by and large confirmed the impression of American reticence toward a resumption of talks that I had already received from Mandelson, Hugueney, and Azevêdo. The US trade negotiators were apparently concerned about getting into political trouble with Congress and the farm lobby. I told Kamal about my conversation with the European commissioner in Lisbon. I said that both Mandelson and I thought it was a good idea to return to a faster pace of consultations, potentially in various different formats but not necessarily (or at least not for the time being) in that of the G4, which as an instrument for negotiation had been damaged by what happened at Potsdam. Contrary to what appeared to me to be his natural inclination toward procrastination, Kamal said he was interested in participating in such consultations, even before the end of July. Indeed, he telephoned Lamy, in my presence, to tell him we had discussed a possible program of work and that I would be conveying the details of "our ideas" in my meeting with the director-general later that day.

The meeting with the permanent representatives of the G20 countries was very positive, at least according to my assessment at the time. All the speakers began their comments with words of praise for Brazil's position and for our efforts to maintain the group dynamic and keep the negotiations on track. My conversation with Pascal Lamy focused on procedural issues. I said I was concerned about a "dangerous disengagement" on the part of the ministers, as a result of which the negotiations were being left to permanent representatives and senior officials who did not have the power to take decisions. I also referred to what I saw as the risk of the "papers" being left "fluttering in the air" for a long time. Lamy assured me he was determined to ensure the papers would be presented in the week beginning July 16 and that they would already contain specific numbers (or at least bands of numbers). He said he would think about my concerns and even mentioned the possibility of ministerial-level consultations in August. Meanwhile, the telephone contact between the ministers continued. On July 9, in Brasilia, I received a call from Susan Schwab. I spoke with Peter Mandelson the next day. Also on July 10, the new British prime minister, Gordon Brown, called Lula. Although I have no written record of the content of those conversations, they demonstrated a shared willingness to intensify the dialogues. Despite the failure of what had been expected to be the decisive meeting in Potsdam, none of the principal players wanted to say the game was over.

From July 15–17, I was in New Delhi for an IBSA meeting. It was there that I heard by phone (from either Hugueney or Azevêdo) about the papers presented by the chairs (or coordinators) of the agriculture and NAMA groups in Geneva. My initial reaction, before the relevant experts had studied the details, was not entirely negative. In notes written on the flight back from Delhi to Paris, after descriptions of my meetings with Prime Minister Singh and other senior Indian officials, I observed that: "We're going to have to do some pleading, but if we can manage to push the numbers to the very edge of each band, it won't be so bad." I stayed no time at all in Paris, instead catching a TGV from the airport to Brussels in order to meet again with the EU trade commissioner. My conversation with Mandelson was friendly and indeed good humored, but on the most important issues there was nothing new. Earlier in the day, while I was still traveling, Roberto Azevêdo had had conversations with Mandelson and with the European commissioner for agriculture that he described as "not very productive." Nevertheless, Mandelson and I agreed that we should give a positive sign to the media. As for the substance of the negotiations, we agreed that our "senior officials" should sit down together again in Geneva to try to solve the conundrum of the quotas. Essentially, when it came to the quotas, there was a technical problem in addition to the Europeans' protectionist maneuvers. While the level of consumption across the EU, which should serve as the basis for the calculation of quotas, was measured by sector (beef, for example), the possible amount of imports under the quotas would have to take into account the tariff classifications of each product, which were much more specific ("boneless beef," for example). Therefore, in order to establish the import quotas for products designated as "sensitive" (the rules for the delimitation of these products were another headache), it was necessary to translate percentages of domestic consumption, measured overall by sector, into absolute quantities (weights, in tonnes) in accordance with tariff lines. It is interesting to note, however, that despite all the difficulties we continued to make progress in the technical discussions about issues that had previously been considered out of bounds. From the political point of view, Mandelson and I agreed that the engagement displayed by Washington was only "lukewarm." The European commissioner therefore insisted that Lula should telephone Bush, given that Blair (who used to have the US president's ear) "is no longer around."

After a good night's sleep in a pleasant hotel on the edge of the Place du Grand Sablon, close to the historic center of Brussels, I set off for Geneva. There, I attended another meeting of G20 ambassadors, as I wanted to make my presence felt and to encourage the group to remain united. I also visited the director-general, this time with three objectives: (1) to convey criticisms—not only mine, but also from the other members of the G20—about the "papers," especially the one on NAMA; (2) to assess, together with him, the respective positions of the main players (we would share the perception that the US position remained ambiguous); and (3) to discuss the process we should follow from that point onward. I expressed my concern, albeit only indirectly, that given the current pace at which the conversations were taking place, and that they mostly involved only permanent ambassadors and senior officials, it would not be possible to conclude the negotiations by October, the point at which the proximity of the US elections would make it more difficult to arrive at an agreement. Pascal, however, seemed unworried in that respect. The most interesting part of this latest brief visit to WTO headquarters was my meeting with the developing countries, which I managed to rearrange at very short notice, with the help of Clodoaldo, so that not only the G20 were present but also the representatives of other groups (African group, LDCs, ACP, SVEs, etc.). Our frank and open dialogue helped me realize that the complaints and concerns about the "chairman's text" on NAMA were widely shared. The meeting was also an opportunity to discuss the prospects of producing a common declaration on the part of all the developing countries. I suggested that while this declaration should contain the criticisms that needed to be made in response to various elements of the proposed text, it should not reject it entirely. In other words, the declaration should be worded in such a way as to allow the negotiations to continue. India's permanent representative expressed the argument, which I agreed with, that the main beneficiary of a radical attitude on the part of all the developing countries would actually be the US—a view that prevailed over the desire of Argentina and some other countries to give full vent to their anger over the contents of the chairman's proposals on NAMA.[150] If we were indeed able to produce a statement that represented the positions of such a vast group of countries, we would be sending an important political signal. It would help refute the thesis (which was still being propounded, especially by Washington) that India and Brazil had acted selfishly in Potsdam, ignoring the interests of the majority of developing countries. From the narrower perspective of Brazil's own interests, my own analysis at this point was that the situation had shifted slightly in our favor. On the basis of the official numbers that I had been shown (and others I was able to deduce from what I had been hearing from the delegates and the secretariat), it seemed to me that a level of OTDS close to the minimum proposed in the chairman's text on that particular issue ($13 billion USD), and a coefficient at the upper end of the range proposed by the text on NAMA (23), would constitute an acceptable deal. It was still necessary to obtain more specific commitments in relation to access to agricultural markets in the rich countries, especially the European Union. I knew that getting there was not going to be easy. To boost our chances of obtaining a reasonable deal, I continued to stress how important it was for the developing countries to remain united.

"The Doha Round saved you"

While these developments were taking place in Geneva and in the capitals of our principal partners, Brasilia was plunged into a new political crisis. This time the focus was the Ministry of Defense, due to a series of problems related to civil aviation that were suddenly aggravated by a tragic accident involving a TAM aircraft at Congonhas airport in São Paulo.[151] The biggest of the ongoing headaches was a labor dispute involving air traffic controllers (formally attached to the Ministry of Defense), which had caused what the Brazilian media referred to as an "aerial blackout." These factors combined to put enormous pressure (in my view unfair) on the defense minister, Waldir Pires. During my morning walk—a habit I had adopted, at my wife's insistence, on the rare days when I was in Brasilia—I bumped into the veteran journalist Pedro Rogério (previously a presenter on Globo, Brazil's main TV network, but at this time the director of another network). "This time it's going to happen," he said, referring to media speculation that I might replace Waldir (who, by the way, was one of the cabinet colleagues I was closest to). The columnist Tereza Cruvinel brought up the issue with my press officer Ricardo Tavares. Tereza warned me, through Ricardo, that I should not accept the post of defense minister if I was offered it—first because it would be an enormously problematic role,[152] and second because I was, as she put it, "the foreign affairs man." For a few days, speculation surrounding my name appeared in newspaper articles and blogs, most of them claiming to have received information from "sources in the Planalto."[153] According to some of these commentators, I was "Lula's preferred choice" for the defense job because he had "full confidence" in me. Although not totally insensitive to such flattery, I was not at all keen to confront the chaos of Brazil's civil aviation, the result of a longstanding lack of resources and a confused tangle of overlapping administrative structures. Nor would I feel comfortable abandoning the various foreign policy projects that were still ongoing. Furthermore, to deal with the civil aviation situation (which at the time seemed more urgent than any of the purely military issues) would require someone with a distinctly managerial profile. I conveyed my concerns directly to the president. More by his facial expressions than what he actually said, Lula seemed to agree. So I asked him a direct question: "You mean I can rest easy, President?" Lula's reply was equally direct: "Yes, you can." Later—and perhaps this is the most interesting part of the story from the point of view of the broader narrative—a person journalists might refer to as a "well-informed source" told me with conviction: "The Doha Round saved you."[154]

In Geneva, the discussions regarding the declaration to be made by the "G110" (the G20 combined with the G90, G33, etc., with some overlap) had been completed successfully, thanks to the good work of Azevêdo and Hugueney (although I also closely followed the negotiations about the text). Again Brazil was taking the role of leader of the developing countries, while also exercising a moderating and constructive influence so as to increase the chances of reaching an overall agreement. The attention I was giving to developing countries, in addition to South America, was not limited to the context of the Doha Round. For some time I had been thinking about how to give political impetus to the discussions aimed at establishing trade agreements between Mercosur, SACU,[155] and India. Mercosur had already negotiated separate arrangements with SACU and India that were limited in their scope (framework and fixed preference agreements). One of my plans (shared by the foreign ministers of South Africa and India, though not so much by those countries' trade ministers) was to bring the three blocs (India alone constituted a bloc) together as one huge economic zone of the "South." It was an ambitious idea that, despite some modest steps, did not ultimately come to fruition. President Lula himself, always true to his vision of a "new economic and political geography," was very keen on the idea of a G20 summit that would be attended by the political leaders of the group of developing countries that had come into being in the WTO (not the G20 of leaders of major powers that would be formed in the wake of the global financial crisis). "But it wouldn't be to deal just with agriculture, or even trade," Lula said. Various factors, from differing political priorities to the practical difficulty of finding a date convenient for all, meant the idea never got off the ground. Around this time, alongside the pleasing progress in Geneva with the G110 declaration, there was a positive development on the domestic front in the form of a speech in the Senate by a former Brazilian president, José Sarney. The speech, in which Sarney reflected upon what had happened at Potsdam, was full of praise for Brazil's international role. He even went so far as to say: "Celso Amorim is one of the best foreign ministers in our history." Personal gratification aside, the former president's sentiments were particularly valuable because one of our major problems at that time was that of trying to secure ratification by Congress of Venezuela's accession to Mercosur. In that regard Sarney himself had been singled out for criticism by President Hugo Chávez as a conservative representative of Brazil's old political class. It was reassuring to know that our neighbor's inopportune outbursts had not tainted the views of an influential leader in the Senate.

During the rest of July there were no meetings between the ministers of the G4. Nevertheless, I see that among the main points in my preparations for a lecture at Brazil's diplomatic institute, I wrote: "Conclude Doha Round (optimism)." The following months were filled with intense diplomatic activity centered on Latin America, including presidential trips to Mexico and Central America. I was also still dealing with the approval by Congress of Venezuela's entry into Mercosur. This was an issue that led me to visit Caracas for a conversation long into the night with President Chávez, in which I tried to convince him that it was important to respect the differences between countries' economic systems and that such differences did not necessarily prevent effective and mutually supportive cooperation. This was also the period in which the first problems with Ecuador arose, especially the friction between Petrobras and the government of Rafael Correa. The situation required me to make a trip to Quito for a long (and ultimately fruitless) dialogue with the Ecuadorian president. There was also an IBSA summit in Pretoria, where (as we later found out) a representative of China approached President Mbeki with a view to becoming the fourth member of the group. (A few years later a similar development would take place, with South Africa becoming the fifth member of the BRIC countries.) From Pretoria, President Lula set off on an African tour that would help consolidate Brazil's presence on the continent. And in the midst of all these activities, state visits to Sweden, Denmark, Norway, and Finland, plus a presidential trip to Spain, were among the other events that added not only color but also a business/economic dimension to our intense diplomatic schedule. With the exception of a brief reference to an attempted phone call by Prime Minister Gordon Brown to Lula, in which the WTO was one of the subjects due to be discussed (the conversation did not take place in the end), my notes contain no reference at all to the Doha Round until early November, when in a section dedicated largely to a bilateral visit to Berne (which coincided with a trip by Lula to Zurich, where Brazil was announced as the host nation for the soccer World Cup in 2014) I alluded to meetings with Lamy and the permanent representatives of the G20 countries. The purpose of the latter was to "warm up our engines" ahead of a ministerial-level G20 meeting that was set to take place on November 15. Regarding my breakfast meeting with the WTO director-general, I wrote: "Despite Lamy's confidence in the Genevan process [i.e. the discussions between the negotiators], I'm increasingly convinced that some kind of external impulse will be necessary, which at this point—given the well-known difficulties on the part of the ministers most involved in the negotiations [i.e. those present at Potsdam]—has to come from the leaders themselves." Rereading those lines, I note two things: first, in political terms, nothing had changed since July, i.e. the aftermath of Potsdam; and second, the relations between Mandelson and Schwab, on one side, and Kamal and me, on the other, remained strained, even though they had not had any direct contact for more than three months. To these two observations I should perhaps add a third: that by this time, with the prospect of reaching an agreement at our level becoming increasingly distant, I was just about ready to "throw in the towel." And my hope that the "leaders" would have greater success proved, sadly, to be unfounded.

On November 15 I attended a ministerial meeting of the G20 in Geneva, my only commitment during a brief trip to Europe. In the forty-eight hours or so preceding the meeting, I spoke personally to some of the ministers of the G20 countries, encouraging them to participate. I asked Kamal to do the same with our Asian counterparts. As for how the meeting went, during the flight back to Brazil I wrote the following: "With the G20 meeting we definitely scored a goal. Six or seven ministers attended [including, much to my satisfaction, Jorge Taiana of Argentina], along with various deputy ministers and other [senior] officials from the national capitals. We managed to send a message that was forceful but constructive, and also [presented ourselves] as critics of the delays and procrastination. In other words [our statement] said that the G20 wants the Round [to be concluded] and wants it now! The participation of other groups of developing countries, although restricted to their permanent representatives in Geneva, was also positive. Very significant was the intervention by the permanent representative of Mauritius, one of the countries initially skeptical about our alliance [given its economic dependence upon European trade preferences]. He said the sense of unity among the group [G20 + G90] was being expressed in increasingly concrete terms. In fact, the nuances that exist . . . did not cause friction at any point. . . . The representative of Uruguay, whose economy is highly competitive in agriculture . . . felt compelled to praise the constructive intervention by the Indonesian minister (and G33 coordinator), Mari Pangestu. Kamal and I, in our speeches, were very much in tune. It will be difficult this time for the press to repeat their favorite headlines ('Divisions among developing countries' or 'Brazil and India block advances'). . . . Overall, the attitude . . . was constructive and proactive."

The Doha Round was not mentioned again in my notebook before the end of 2007. Before moving on to the events of 2008, which culminated in the "great failure of July," I would like to reproduce a section of a lecture I gave on the subject of the diplomatic legacy of Rui Barbosa at a conference in Rio de Janeiro on Brazilian foreign policy, ten days before the G20 meeting.[156] Before an audience made up largely of intellectuals and academics in the field of international relations, I tried to include in my lecture an explanation of my motives and expectations with regard to the Doha Round, linking them with the importance the Lula government (following a tradition that goes all the way back to Rui Barbosa) attached to the world's multilateral institutions. I will quote three paragraphs:

> We are at a crucial moment. The negotiations have been going on for almost six years. World leaders continue to express support for the conclusion of the Round. It is essential that developing countries maintain their cohesion. At the same time, we have to show positive vision and a willingness to negotiate.
>
> We will continue working to achieve results that are ambitious and that satisfy our interests. The subsidies that distort agricultural trade have the effect of exporting hunger and poverty. The developed countries need to recognize that these issues cannot be pushed aside indefinitely. . . .
>
> Without the WTO, international trade would be a hostage of unilateralism and of pernicious policies that do not respect any rules and tend to favor only the strongest and the most privileged. It is no exaggeration to say that without the WTO, international trade would be subject to the law of the jungle.

"Last year we had a window of opportunity. Now we have a window of necessity."

The date on which the Doha Round returned to occupy my time was January 19, 2008. My notebook refers to a phone call a few days before from Peter Mandelson, whom I had not spoken to "for more than two months." Thinking about what lay ahead in the next couple of weeks, I wrote: "In Davos, it's going to be WTO, WTO, WTO." I arrived in Zurich on January 24, and traveled on from there to the Alpine resort where by now I had become a *habitué*. A curious thing happened a few minutes before landing. Through one of the windows on the left-hand side of the FAB Legacy (in which I was accompanied by my wife Ana, Ambassador Maria Nazareth, and my aide

Nilo Ditz) I saw a Swiss Air Force fighter jet, no more than fifty meters away. It was so close that I could clearly see the gray helmet the pilot was wearing. Our aircraft was obviously being "escorted" to its destination. I noted: "This kind of honor is usually reserved for heads of state. Did the pilots mistake me for someone else, or does Switzerland have fighter aircraft to spare?"

Davos, as usual, was an intensely busy few days. There were bilaterals, working breakfasts and lunches, round-table discussions, and interviews (both one-to-ones and press conferences). The subject, almost constantly, was the WTO. I met with my principal interlocutors (Schwab, Mandelson, Nath, Lamy) and also Australia's new trade minister, Simon Crean (a true believer in trade liberalization who would play a role in future events). It seemed that attitudes had evolved in a positive direction. Lamy and Mandelson, from different perspectives, showed some understanding of the need to make the flexibilities in NAMA broader than those proposed in the "chairman's text" produced the previous July. This issue—very important for Mercosur, given the differences between the industrial structures of the members of the bloc—was now coming up for the first time in meetings with the European commissioner and the USTR, besides the director-general. In other words it was being dealt with not only by ambassadors and senior officials but by the ministers themselves. The enlargement of the margins for including items in the flexibilities would, in theory, be helpful in overcoming the reticence of Argentina in relation to a possible agreement. The USTR, for her part, now seemed less negative and elusive than during our last few meetings in 2007. Overall, however, the attitudes of my interlocutors still did not inspire a great deal of confidence. My observation at the time was: "Among the main players, Kamal Nath is now the most reluctant [to engage in the negotiations so as to conclude the Round]. But Susan is not far behind. They seem almost to work as a duo, reinforcing each other's negativity." Indeed, that is precisely what would happen about six months later in Geneva. In my conversations with both of them I tried to use the looming financial crisis (although at that point it was still confined to the US real-estate market) as an extra reason to push the negotiations forward. "When the patient has a fever, the medicine might be bitter but it's absolutely necessary," was one of the things I remember saying. Of the other phrases I came up with in Davos, the one that made the biggest splash was: "Last year we had a window of opportunity. Now we have a window of necessity." This *boutade* ended up being repeated not only by Swiss trade minister Doris Leuthard but also by Peter Mandelson when he and I were taking part in a panel discussion at which the media were also present. Both had the good grace to acknowledge the original author.

Soon after Davos, back in Brazil, I went to the headquarters of the Federation of Industries of the State of São Paulo (FIESP). I spoke to the president,

Paulo Skaff, and some of the directors. They asked me about Venezuela's accession to Mercosur and mentioned their desire to see progress in the negotiations between Mercosur and the European Union (which had stalled, I should point out, because of the priority both blocs were giving to the Doha Round). Curiously, they seemed simply to have forgotten the reservations they had expressed years earlier when an EU-Mercosur deal had been on the horizon. An alternative explanation is that such doubts had since been rendered irrelevant by the increasing number of mergers and associations between Brazilian and foreign companies. On the subject of the Doha Round, Roberto Azevêdo was in regular contact with various senior figures at FIESP, including Carlos Cavalcanti. The mood during my own conversations with the representatives of São Paulo's industrial base was reasonably warm. Although I knew there would be complaints when the time came to implement the tariff cuts, the meeting with FIESP served to confirm my impression that it would not be too difficult to secure Brazilian industry's acceptance for the kind of deal that, at that stage, seemed still to be possible if we were able to widen the margins of flexibility with regard to the most sensitive products.

After the meeting at FIESP, the Doha Round disappeared again from my diary. In February, apart from being busy with South American affairs, I embarked on a long tour of several Middle Eastern countries, aimed at following up on the Annapolis Conference,[157] and also made an exploratory trip to Asia, passing through Hanoi and Singapore. The Round resurfaced in March in the form of worryingly negative pronouncements by the agriculture ministers of some European Union countries. These were followed by pessimistic statements on the part of the EU trade commissioner himself. My impression was that Mandelson was addressing his remarks at the European public, issuing a warning about the implications if the Round failed. The United States, meanwhile, was adopting a more aggressive posture by making a series of new demands, now in the area of services. On March 2 I referred in my notes to a letter I had received a few days before from the USTR, written in a high-handed style reminiscent of earlier periods in our bilateral commercial relationship. Even before the technical experts had analyzed the contents of the letter, I had the distinct impression from its tone that Washington's attitude was not going to facilitate a rapid conclusion of the Round. The "window of necessity" therefore seemed already to be closing. The thought occurred to me that we should increase our own demands in services so as to achieve greater balance. But in services it was not easy to find areas where our "offensive" interests were clearly greater than our "defensive" concerns. The most we could do was present proposals that might "inconvenience" our interlocutors. We carried out some analytical exercises along those lines, but developments in other areas of the negotiations meant we were not able to test our hypothesis. March continued to be dominated by

South American matters: an extraordinary summit of the Rio Group in the wake of a Colombian attack on a FARC base situated in Ecuadorian territory; an OAS consultation meeting on the same subject; and Brazil's efforts to mediate the internal conflict in Bolivia between La Paz and the *Media Luna*.[158] In the midst of these episodes, Durão Barroso came to Brasilia with the aim of strengthening the EU-Brazil Strategic Partnership. Of course he also took the opportunity to put pressure on me, including with regard to the Doha Round. "You're a very tough negotiator," complained the European Commission president, who had previously been Portuguese prime minister and, in the first half of the 1990s, my counterpart as foreign minister. In his conversation with Lula, Durão Barroso pointed to three elements responsible for what he gratifyingly described as "Brazil's new position in the world": the economy, the social programs, and diplomacy. What Barroso seemed not to realize was that firmness in negotiations, for example in those that had led to the creation of the G20 and the positive outcome in Hong Kong with regard to export subsidies, was an integral part of our successful diplomacy.

In April, when accompanying President Lula at an UNCTAD meeting in Ghana, I met with Pascal Lamy and Kamal Nath. I also took advantage of the presence of several trade ministers to chair a G20 meeting. This was an occasion on which I could clearly see the great unwillingness of some countries (particularly Argentina and South Africa) to conclude the Round. They took the view that the process would ultimately be too "costly" for developing countries because of the concessions they would have to make on NAMA and services. This perception was reinforced at the time by the generally high prices of agricultural products, which had already caused the rich countries to reduce their agricultural subsidies. In doing so, of course, they were removing one of the principal incentives for developing countries to engage in the negotiations. Now that they were enjoying high prices, US farmers did not need to be subsidized to the same extent as before. Indeed, the figures for OTDS being considered in the negotiations were actually significantly higher than the average amount spent on US agricultural subsidies over the preceding years. Although obviously the situation was temporary (it would change, for example, if there was a drop in Chinese demand), it was nevertheless the case that in the prevailing circumstances the developing countries' efforts to reduce their industrial tariffs, so as to obtain reciprocal concessions in relation to agricultural subsidies, seemed to have less practical purpose than before. Their own concessions might be seen, in fact, as little more than a show of "good behavior" aimed at strengthening the multilateral institution of the WTO. They were efforts, therefore, that various developing countries were now unwilling to make.

On May 13, after an IBSA ministerial meeting in South Africa and refueling stops for the Legacy in São Tomé and Libya, I received Susan Schwab for a working dinner at the Palazzo Pamphilj, the elegant residence of our ambassador in Rome. I had chosen the Palazzo as the venue not only because of the propitious surroundings it offered but also because Rome was a convenient stop-over on the journey that would take me to Yekaterinburg, Russia, for the first formal ministerial meeting of the BRIC countries.[159] My conversation with Susan was extensive and frank. I deliberately left the fine details for the next day, when we would be meeting again and our technical experts would be present. I told the USTR about Brazil's reservations regarding the suggestion, circulating at the time in Geneva, that the negotiations should move on to a "horizontal" process in which the main themes would be discussed simultaneously. My main concern at that stage was to ensure that the negotiations did not undermine the integrity of Mercosur as a customs union.[160] I can no longer remember the technical arguments on which we based our position, but they must have been convincing because they were eventually taken on board, to some extent, during the negotiations in Geneva. Although Schwab seemed impressed by my determination to protect the unity of Mercosur, and expressed interest in continuing our dialogue on the issue, she gave no sign that she was ready to accept my position. Leaving aside the details, a subsequent article in *Valor Econômico* included a quote from me that adequately expressed the message I wanted to convey: "They want to charge a high price for a Round that's losing value all the time."

In early June, after the first ministerial meeting of the BRICs in Russia, and a summit in Brasilia at which UNASUR was officially established, I turned my attentions back to the Doha Round and met again with Pascal Lamy and Susan Schwab. My choice of venue, again, was our ambassador's residence in Rome. My conversation with the WTO director-general focused, as usual, on procedural issues. Throughout the negotiations I endeavored to maintain a relationship of trust with Lamy, who for his part always expressed appreciation for Brazil's role. Our conversations were rarely limited to one specific point. The director-general appreciated my analyses and liked to share his own with me. What else could explain his willingness to travel to Rome on the eve of a meeting in Paris (in which we would both participate), if not the desire for a quieter conversation away from both the media spotlight and the attentions of other ministers? Lamy also clearly recognized Brazil as an influential participant that not only defended its own positions and those of the other G20 members, but also wanted to help propel the negotiations toward a positive conclusion. In return, Lamy tried to come up with solutions that took into account our difficulties with regard to NAMA. He did so, for example, with the text produced the previous year by the chair of the NAMA group, in which our proposals regarding the need to maintain Mercosur's common external tariff were subsequently incorporated, albeit "in brackets."[161] The issue of NAMA also dominated my conversation with Schwab, which followed the meeting with Lamy and continued over lunch. The USTR continued to push for a result in NAMA that was simply too ambitious from our point of view. But she avoided taking a confrontational approach, and proposed that our technical experts should meet for more detailed conversations in the coming weeks. On the issue of access to agricultural markets in developed countries (i.e. the European Union and Japan, mainly), the US and Brazilian positions were generally convergent. Potsdam, in that tense, had been an "outlier" motivated by a momentary US-EU alliance; a fleeting relapse into the old pre-Cancún syndrome that would not be repeated.[162] As the discussions became more focused, however, frictions did arise. This was the case, for example, with the double taxation levied on imports of ethanol into the United States. It was a situation that violated the basic principle that there should be no other barrier to importation apart from the tariff (leaving aside the issue of sensitive products, for which there are quantitative restrictions offset by quotas). More than once Brazil had considered taking the subject to the WTO Dispute Settlement Body, before deciding it was more prudent, above all for tactical reasons, to seek a negotiated solution in the context of the Round. The issue would be addressed in parallel discussions in July, and would potentially be the subject of a separate agreement if we were able to make progress on its central aspects. As always, the USTR and I had differing approaches to the question of access to agricultural markets in developing countries (special products and the Special Safeguard Mechanism), though in this case the divergence was caused less by Brazil's own situation than by our role as coordinator of the G20.

From Rome I traveled to Paris, for the annual meeting of the OECD. Much of my time there was devoted to the WTO. As the third speaker in the plenary "outreach" session, I made a brief address in which I railed against the rich countries' agricultural subsidies. I pointed to the global food shortage and the devastating effects of the subsidies on local production in poor countries such as São Tomé and Haiti, in which prime ministers had recently been overthrown amid popular protests stemming from the high price of imported rice.[163] Possibly stretching my rhetoric a little too far, I made an oblique reference to one of Charles Dickens' most famous works by referring to "a tale of two islands." I also coined the expression "riots for rice." After a working lunch chaired by French trade minister Christine Lagarde, who invited me to address the gathering "on any subject you want" (without my having requested to do so), I attended the traditional mini-ministerial at the Australian embassy and also had a few bilaterals (India, EU, Australia, Japan). The day ended with a dinner hosted by Susan Schwab that was also attended by Lamy, Mandelson, Simon Crean, and (as I put it in my notebook) "the furtive presence of Kamal Nath." Nothing particularly important was said during any of those discussions. During my stay in Paris I also met, at his request, with the French foreign minister, the friendly and media savvy Bernard Kouchner. He made a point of organizing our meeting as if it was a formal bilateral visit, with a guard of honor at Quai d'Orsay and an official car (with motorcycle outriders) to pick me up at the Château de la Muette (the OECD headquarters) and take me to my other meetings afterwards. For an hour or so the kinetic Kouchner and I discussed an array of subjects including Haiti, the BRICs, Lebanon, and Colombia. The Doha Round came up near the end of the conversation. I commented on the difficulties the French farmers caused for Brazil and indeed for the WTO itself, a bastion of the multilateral system to which the French claimed to attach great importance. "And they're no more than one per cent of the population," I said. "Two per cent," replied Kouchner. "And they're very violent," he added.

From Paris I went to Ljubljana for a meeting with the troika[164] of the European Union in the context of the EU-Brazil Strategic Partnership. The consultations there were essentially political, with the WTO and Doha hardly coming up at all. On the way back to Brazil I stopped in Geneva for a useful bilateral with the Swiss trade minister, Doris Leuthard, who had chaired various meetings in Davos earlier in the year. We had already become good friends, to the extent that she invited me (and my grandchildren) to a soccer game at the European Championship that was just getting underway in Switzerland. I think it was during our meeting, on June 7, that Doris really began to appreciate the efforts Brazil was making on NAMA so as to try to make possible a positive result (although those efforts still fell short of Swiss ambitions in that area). For my part, I was careful to "go easy" on my interlocutor when it came to agriculture. Although still very protectionist in that area (it was said that the per capita income of Swiss cows was higher than that of humans in many countries), Switzerland was not a militant voice on issues such as OTDS and the disciplines of the "blue box." I considered it advantageous to try to maintain Berne's not particularly aggressive position on NAMA (after all, the Swiss were the famous formula that we had accepted, albeit unwillingly). If we were to reach a final, conclusive stage of the negotiations, we would certainly need the support (or at least the understanding) of some developed countries, such as Norway and Switzerland. After a few commitments back in Brazil, I set off on a trip to three countries in the Maghreb and also Cape Verde. On the return flight, during a brief stop again in Cape Verde, I spoke to Roberto Azevêdo, who was in Geneva, about the latest talks on the Round. Azevêdo was particularly focused on our efforts to ensure that the special methodology for Mercosur would be incorporated into the implementation of the NAMA formula. He said the negotiations were proving very tough, but also that a phone call I had made the previous day to Susan Schwab seemed to have had a positive impact. The US negotiator in Geneva, Peter Allgeier (who had been an incorrigible free-trade fundamentalist at the time of the FTAA negotiations) was apparently being somewhat more flexible in the wake of my call. I finished my notes on my conversation with Roberto with the following observation: "If the discussions move forward now, we'll have a ministerial in mid-July. Before that, we'll have to work very hard with our partners and also our Argentine friends." On the last leg of the flight home, I made an addition to those notes that clearly reflected my anxiety: "At various moments during this journey I had to address the subject of the Round, whether with Roberto Azevêdo and Clodoaldo or with Lamy. The prediction now is that there will be a ministerial meeting on July 21. It will be the last chance."

"Closer than ever to an agreement"

Before the ministerial meeting, the next opportunity for positive steps was the G8+5 summit in Toyako, Japan, from July 7–9. The dominant theme, however, was not the WTO but climate change. The Round came up mainly in bilateral meetings Lula had with George W. Bush and Gordon Brown, in which I also participated. The US president, already nearing the end of his time in office, appeared uninterested. He hardly participated at all in the debate the world's "major economies" conducted on the subject of global warming, limiting himself to a very brief intervention that appeared to contain a degree of self-pity (although it could also be interpreted as arrogance or indifference). In a valedictory tone, he told the leaders present that they would soon "be free of the great polluter." In fact, although Bush would not participate in another G8, his final appearance on the multilateral stage would be at the G20 world leaders' summit following the collapse of Lehman Brothers. During his meeting with Lula, Bush made a few generic statements in defense of the Round. Showing none of the enthusiasm (genuine or otherwise) he had displayed in previous dialogues, Bush avoided entering into any substantive issues, claiming it would not be appropriate for the presidents to discuss technical details. His implicit message seemed to be: "I'd like the Round to be concluded—but don't go thinking I'll make any concessions you want, just because my time as president is ending." He was, nevertheless, still warm in his personal interaction with his interlocutors, liberally distributing his usual kisses and playful face-slaps, and calling me and Lula's interpreter, Sérgio Ferreira, by our first names. Susan Schwab was also there at the meeting, probably expecting to have time for a structured conversation with me. That was not possible, however, given the typically hectic nature of the summit and my obligation, as "sherpa," to stay by Lula's side.

Gordon Brown, for his part, emphasized Brazil's central role in the negotiations. At Lula's request I explained to the British prime minister our difficulties concerning the so-called NAMA "sectorials"[165] and also the latest invention that the European negotiators had pulled out of their hat: the concept of "anti-concentration" in the application of the flexibilities. What the EU essentially intended to do through this new mechanism was prevent the flexibilities (which every developing country was entitled to) from becoming concentrated in one particular industrial sector. The main purpose of the idea was to help German automobile producers to access markets abroad. Brown tried to get us to come up with the precise number we could offer for the coefficient, but naturally we resisted. Toward the end of the conversation he lavished praise (which, as so often, masked a certain amount of deliberate pressure) on Brazil: "You will be the heroes," he said, looking forward to a positive outcome. Lula and Brown adopted a joint statement aimed at generating momentum ahead of the ministerial meeting scheduled for July 21. According to the text, we were "closer than ever to an agreement." However, the statement also warned that "the window of opportunity to reach this agreement [is] small and [is] closing." The two leaders stated that "after months of hard work and very detailed negotiations,"[166] the time had come for political decisions. So as to reinforce the message, the statement placed the Doha Round squarely in the context of the wider efforts to combat economic crises, specifically mentioning the food shortages suffered by the poorest countries. Any mention of the specific problems hindering the negotiations was carefully avoided. The original version of the joint statement, presented to us by the British sherpa, had contained certain points that we were uncomfortable with. When I expressed my objections the British prime minister promptly retreated, thereby making clear that the priority as far as he was concerned was to arrive at a joint statement with the Brazilian president on the Doha Round.

Following the G8+5, I accompanied Lula on visits to Hanoi, Jakarta, and Dili (East Timor). It was the beginning of what had the potential to be our own "pivot to Asia," focused on cooperation and trade. We returned to Brasilia on July 13, a Sunday. On the Monday morning I left for Rio de Janeiro to attend a meeting of ministers of the Mercosur countries, specially convened to discuss the "revised papers" presented by the coordinators in Geneva.[167] My task at this meeting (which I referred to in my notebook as "almost impossible") was to convince our Argentine partners that it was still possible, at least in theory, to arrive at a positive agreement, as long as unreasonable demands were left to one side. I knew Uruguay and Paraguay would criticize the text on agriculture, particularly the facilities granted to the developing countries that were net food importers. I thought my best tactic would be to avoid coming to very precise conclusions. The main thing, with regard to Uruguay and Paraguay, was simply to fulfill our obligation to be transparent. In the notes I wrote before the meeting, I referred to my wish to have a separate bilateral with Taiana. Although I have no written record of the meeting, and memory can often play tricks, I am reasonably sure it did take place. Allow me at this point to refer back to Lula's meeting in Toyako with Gordon Brown, because it is relevant to the attitudes displayed by Buenos Aires and the way we dealt with them. In Japan the British prime minister had at one point suggested he could "help" in encouraging Argentina to move forward by raising the issue of the country's official debt with the Paris Club of creditor countries. I took the initiative of responding directly, saying I did not think it was a good idea to link the issues of trade and debt. Brown had depicted his idea as a potential "stimulus" rather than an exertion of pressure, but for me it was obvious that the line between the two was blurred.

On the day of the Mercosur meeting, I received a call from Peter Mandelson. The next day Susan Schwab also telephoned me. I have no notes about either call, but they indicate the developing mood of nervousness in the run-up to the ministerial meeting. I set off for Geneva convinced that this would be the last chance to conclude the Doha Round, at least for the foreseeable future. I wrote during the flight: "If we don't do it now, political factors will mean we have to wait for another two or three years." Little did I know that the wait would in fact end up being much longer, extending all the way to the present day. I was troubled by the idea that if no result were achieved in the short term, Lula and I would be out of the game, given that the president's second term of office was going to expire at the end of 2010. Although very aware that I could not let such considerations affect my behavior in the tough negotiations to come, it saddened me to think that our legacy, after such enormous efforts, might be restricted to the rebalancing of forces we had achieved through the creation of the G20, and the unprecedented degree of cohesion among developing countries in the ambit of the WTO. Apart from that, we had managed to fight our way out of a bad deal in Cancún. But overall, it was not very much.

"A straight road to success and a winding path to failure"

The first two legs of the long journey from Rio to Geneva in the FAB Legacy were up to the northeastern city of Natal and then across the Atlantic to Cape Verde. I spent much of the time immersed in the arduous task of digesting the information prepared by our technical experts on the texts presented by the coordinators (or chairs). It was neither light nor enjoyable reading, and various points were still unclear. I hoped I would be able to clarify them in the meetings of the Brazilian delegation that would take place upon arrival. During the flight I made a summary of what I believed were the necessary conditions for reaching a deal: (a) within the margins proposed by the chair of the agriculture group, the rich countries had to advance to the maximum limit of their offers (which in theory would not be difficult, since the figures in question would be attainable without a great deal of effort from the starting point of the measures currently in place—particularly in the case of domestic support; (b) the rich countries would also need to show some moderation with regard to their goals—particularly on NAMA, where even in the less ambitious scenarios (from the rich countries' point of view) the developing countries would still be taking on commitments more onerous than those that had been under consideration until recently; (c) reasonable solutions had to be found for the questions that lay on the margins of what I regarded as the "grand bargain," among which I highlighted tariff ceilings for agricultural products (a particularly sensitive issue for Japan); SP and the SSM for developing countries; and issues of particular concern to countries that had only recently joined the WTO, such as China. At this point I still did not fully appreciate the central importance of SP/SSM, which would become evident during the exhaustive consultations and discussions in Geneva. I had long been aware that those issues were sensitive from the point of view of India and the other members of the G33 (indeed, that was part of the reason why I had made the long trip to Jakarta the year before), but I believed the problem could be solved if there was sufficient political will.

I concluded my brief written analysis with two considerations—one of them my own, the other from Jagdish Baghwati, a renowned American economist of Indian origin. Baghwati was a specialist in international trade who believed it was vital not to "overload the negotiations." An advocate of free trade and the multilateral system, he was also a fierce opponent of bilateral agreements, which he saw as responsible for the fragmentation of international trade. Ever since the Uruguay Round, Baghwati had been opposed the inclusion in the WTO agenda of topics that were not, strictly speaking, commercial in nature, such as TRIMs and TRIPS. He and I had participated together in a few discussions, during which the points on which we disagreed were always less significant than our areas of convergence. We were both firm supporters of multilateralism in trade matters, but his vision of how the developing countries should behave in cutting industrial tariffs was different from mine. Paradoxically, in relation to agriculture, Baghwati seemed to favor a protectionist attitude on the part of certain developing countries, including to the point of accepting measures such as SP/SSM that were, strictly speaking, exceptions to free trade.[168] In spite of these nuances, I thought Baghwati's concern about the overloading of the negotiations was absolutely pertinent. For my part, perhaps over-simplifying slightly, I made the following observation, which I would later return to in my address to the WTO Trade Negotiations Committee (TNC): "It could be . . . said that there is a straight road to success and a winding path to failure."

I arrived in Geneva on the morning of July 18, a Friday. After receiving some briefings from the experts, I had my first bilateral with Kamal Nath, described in my notes as my "comrade in arms." Very soon afterwards, however, the Indian trade minister had to interrupt his stay at WTO headquarters in order to return to New Delhi to cast his vote in defense of the government of Prime Minister Singh, which was facing a motion of no confidence arising from India's nuclear energy negotiations with the United States. Although he would not be absent for long, Kamal was nevertheless going to miss the G20 meeting on the Monday (July 21). Nor would he be able to participate in the Green Room set to take place over the first few days—and his absence from that process was, at least in theory, already a hindrance to progress. Although the Indian permanent representative and other senior officials were very competent, none of them would actually take a decision (not even a provisional one) in the absence of the minister. During our conversation, Kamal exuded pessimism. Also, as usual, he came up with a mish-mash of arguments on several different issues, some of them regarding the content of the negotiations and others on purely procedural matters. He said he was unhappy with several points in the revised papers, including those on NAMA and SP. He also referred to the uncertainty about what might happen in the US Congress, even if an agreement were reached. Moreover, there would soon be a new administration in Washington, whose objectives we obviously could not know in advance.

Kamal's argument about the US Congress was valid, up to a point. In the absence of a TPA[169] there was a genuine risk that if we reached a deal, the members of Congress might subsequently try to alter its terms in favor of certain US interest groups. In such a scenario the other WTO members would have to sit down again with the US to renegotiate what had already been agreed, and most probably make concessions beyond what was, in theory, their bottom line. One of the justified obsessions in every trade negotiation—and the Doha Round was no exception—is to avoid "negotiating twice." That was precisely what would happen if Congress did indeed decide to amend an eventual agreement. However, it was a risk most of the countries involved in the negotiations were willing to take. At that juncture, for those WTO members committed to achieving a successful conclusion to the Round, there was no other option but to rely on the ability of the US government to "force through" the approval of whatever modalities came to be agreed in Geneva.

Kamal and I agreed about the patent lack of balance between the demands being made by the developed countries and the concessions they themselves were prepared to make. I must admit that at this point, when I saw the various problems listed one by one, my own certainty that we needed to conclude the Round in the short term began to waver. In Brazil, however, unlike in India, there was a great deal of pressure aimed at opening up the agricultural markets of the developed countries. In fact this pressure was also directed at the agricultural markets of the developing countries, but so far we had been able to prevent our agricultural lobby from undermining the solidarity of the G20. To be fair, I should admit that even some of the advocates of a more aggressive position did understand the importance of the alliance we had been consolidating ever since Cancún, which had allowed us to obtain successive advances principally in the area of subsidies but also with regard to market access. I had to take into account this strong Brazilian interest in the liberalization of agricultural trade (with certain exceptions, such as the defenders of family agriculture, whom I respected and tried to accommodate). For this reason, among others, I was impelled toward finding a multilateral solution, in the ambit of the WTO, that would satisfy the "appetite" of our farmers. If this proved impossible, the impulses toward bilateral agreements with the United States and the European Union would gain strength, which would put us in a much less favorable negotiating situation. Therefore—and this is a factor that distanced us from India—a failure pure and simple, without any prospect of resuming the negotiations, was simply not an option (unless, that is, we were faced with the prospect of an extremely unbalanced outcome). Kamal and I agreed to do everything possible to maintain the unity of positions between Brazil and India. Carrying out those good intentions, however, would prove more difficult than I imagined.

The next day, a Saturday, I met with Pascal Lamy. My notes, written beforehand, indicate the general message I intended to convey to the director-general, and I imagine I largely stuck to it. My main point was that, within the parameters that had been established by the chairs and were now contained in the revised papers, we needed to find the most "development-friendly" solutions. After all, the official name of the Round was the "Doha Development Agenda." It was already going to be difficult for the developing countries to stay within those parameters. Pressure was building, for example, for developing countries to accept an agreement on NAMA, based on the Swiss Formula, with a coefficient much lower than the one we had proposed before Hong Kong. The "blueprint" I intended to present to Lamy included a bigger cut to OTDS, stricter disciplines with regard to subsidies by product, and some improvement in quotas for sensitive products in AMA. Above all, however, I insisted that the developed countries' demands in NAMA should not be excessive. As for Mercosur's position, I intended to argue that the figures proposed for the formula coefficient and the flexibilities[170] would not easily be accepted by Argentina, a fact I could not ignore. Additional demands regarding anti-concentration would be highly problematic given their potential to seriously upset the internal balance of Mercosur. And of course there were myriad other issues that I did not have time to raise in my short conversation with Lamy. My greatest fear, in the event of an impasse, was that there would be a temptation to repeat the pre-Cancún scenario by resorting to a text drawn up by the director-general, which would then be presented to the negotiators on the very last day with the message of "take it or leave it." Personally I trusted Lamy, whose conduct in Hong Kong had been beyond reproach, but I knew the pressure for an unbalanced solution (from our point of view) might prove irresistible. At the end of the notes I made before my conversation with the director-general, there is a comment that shows that, despite Brazil's specific interests, I was not willing to accept an agreement at any price: "Although [a firm attitude of refusal] might mean I get crucified by our agribusiness, we must be prepared for another Cancún."

The Saturday and Sunday were filled with bilaterals. I met with, among others, Peter Mandelson, Susan Schwab, and the trade ministers of Japan, China, South Africa, and Egypt (the last three all influential members of the G20). I also spoke to the trade minister of Burkina Faso, one of the poorest African countries and a member of the Cotton-4. I attended several plurilateral meetings involving various groups of developing countries. The most substantial of these was with the G20, which issued a statement reiterating our wish for the Round to be concluded and emphasizing the importance of agriculture.[171] On the Monday, July 21, the first meeting of the TNC took place.

As on other occasions, the conference unfolded in different formats. The TNC was the setting for the initial presentation by the director-general, and would also be where any formal decisions were announced. The TNC also served as a platform for speeches aimed at the "wider public." In my own address, for example, as well as referring to issues of specific interest to Brazil, I tried also to convey some political messages. I began my speech, some of which was improvised, by recalling a metaphor used by the late Arthur Dunkel, director-general of the old GATT and the chair of the TNC during the Uruguay Round. In one of his many public exhortations to the negotiators, he had compared our endeavors to an ascent of Mount Everest. I admitted to my audience that at the time, with the playful irreverence of a young ambassador, I had asked whether, as we were in Geneva, it might not be wiser to aim for the summit of Mont Blanc instead (meaning, of course, that perhaps we should lower our expectations slightly). I then introduced into my speech a third peak, the so-called "*Mont Blanc des Anglais*." It was said that mischievous Genevans were in the habit of pointing out this smaller mountain to unsuspecting tourists (the "*Anglais*") and telling them it was Mont Blanc (when in fact, as so often, Europe's highest peak remained shrouded in cloud). The risk we now faced, I said, was that some members would point to Everest but merely offer *Mont Blanc des Anglais*. I stressed the importance of achieving a result aimed at "promoting development." I said that for the sake of the "credibility and relevance" of the WTO itself, it was crucial to re-establish confidence in the organization at "this critical moment that the international economy is going through." Referring to the food crisis, I stressed that "eliminating or substantially reducing the subsidies" would be a decisive factor in preventing any increase in world hunger and poverty. I reiterated that I had come to Geneva with a "willingness to conclude the negotiations on the agriculture and NAMA modalities," so as then to make it possible to conclude the Doha Round by the end of 2008. Reminding my audience of Brazil's "central interest" in the multilateral trading system, I quoted the words of President Lula, who had often declared that "Brazil will do its part, as long as the others—especially the rich countries—do theirs." I commented upon the imbalance, as I saw it, between the texts on agriculture and NAMA. I made sure, naturally, that my point was forcefully conveyed: "Reading the text on agriculture, we can conclude that, despite all the efforts, the text has been based on the logic of accommodating exceptions rather than seeking ambition. Almost thirty paragraphs are devoted to establishing specific exceptions for certain countries. The text on NAMA, on the other hand, is based on the logic of forcing developing countries out of their 'comfort zone.'" I summarized the essence of my thoughts (which I had already conveyed to Lamy) about how it would be possible to conclude the Round: "We have no time for play-acting. We must advance by the most direct route possible. . . . Whenever we have the choice, [we must] choose the most pro-development option. After all, this is the Development Round. By doing so . . . we will have a straight road to success. The alternative is a winding path to failure." I finished my address by calling on the negotiators not to hold back possible concessions and wait for their partners to make the first move. "Of course you can always wait until the last minute to use your bargaining chip, but the last minute might already be too late."

"*Nous n'avons pas un* '**deal**'"

The director-general quickly set up a Green Room consisting of about thirty countries. Unlike in Hong Kong, however, Lamy would conduct the most important negotiations in a restricted group consisting only of the by now traditional G4 (EU, US, Brazil, India) plus Australia, Japan and—a significant new arrival—China.[172] The idea behind this new grouping was that a consensus among the "big seven" would, in principle, have a high chance of being accepted by the WTO members as a whole. The Green Room would effectively function as an intermediary body. As always, this implicit delegation of negotiating power did not take place without tensions arising. Several countries initially spoke out against the creation of the smaller group, but eventually acknowledged that there was no other practical way of trying to make progress. On the Wednesday, the "G7" met for the first time in the director-general's office. This "consultation," as it was officially referred to, carried on until the early hours of Thursday morning. We would meet again in this format on various occasions in the days that followed, right up until Tuesday, July 29. I think it was at the end of the first meeting, after long group discussions and one-to-one conversations ("confessionals"), that Lamy gave me the impression that he was about to throw in the towel: "*Nous n'avons un pas un* 'deal,'" he told me, in the *franglais* typical of the WTO. If I remember rightly, that moment came at the end of my own long confessional with the director-general. I urged Lamy not to give up on an agreement. My appeal was echoed by other members of the G7. Later that day there was a difficult Green Room meeting at which unhappiness with the small-group format was forcefully expressed ("It's not producing results.") But, in the end, the thirty or so countries called on the G7 to carry on trying to achieve an agreement on the basic elements of the negotiations. Virtually the same scene would be repeated one or two days later. The essence of the negotiations consisted of our old friends AMA, NAMA, OTDS (with disciplines), special products (SP), and the Special Safeguard Mechanism (SSM). Included in NAMA were the flexibilities, anti-concentration, and sectorials.

My next notebook entry was written on July 27. Totally immersed in the endless discussions of that crucial week, there were days when I did not manage to write a single word. The meetings were initially supposed to end on the Friday, July 25, but they were extended in a desperate attempt to salvage the Round. The negotiations were difficult from the very start, the air thick with mutual accusations that seemed to indicate a desire on the part of several members—above all the developed countries—to protect themselves before the finger of blame was pointed in their direction. The European Union and the United States were quick to complain of the "intransigence" of the big developing countries, especially Brazil, India, and China. This blatant distortion of the facts provoked me at one point into a rhetorical outburst in which I recalled the famous saying by Goebbels, Nazi Germany's chief propagandist, that if a lie is big enough and repeated sufficiently often, people will start accepting it as the truth. My words were taken out of context and widely reported by the international media, provoking an avalanche of criticism. In Brazil, however, there were also positive reactions, such as an article by Mauro Santayana in the *Jornal do Brasil*. The episode did not have any repercussions for the negotiations themselves, which continued in an intense rhythm, but it would be something of an understatement to say the general mood in Geneva was not favorable.[173]

Based on what he had heard both in the meetings and the confessionals, Lamy sketched out some numerical proposals for each of the main areas of the negotiations. His succinct suggestions fitted on a single piece of paper, which he presented to the G7 when the consultations resumed on the Friday. With regard to the sectorials, his formulation was essentially discursive, without precise figures. Unsurprisingly, the director-general's proposal provoked strong reactions. Such heated responses were part of the ever-present "theatrical" dimension of such negotiations, aimed essentially aimed at securing an advantageous position in the ensuing discussions. In the case of India, however, the problem at this particular moment was genuinely serious. Kamal Nath was the first person to reject the director-general's suggestions. He expressed complete disagreement with the approach Lamy had taken toward SP[174] and the SSM. The margins Kamal was seeking for the products he wanted to be considered as SP were much broader than those proposed on Lamy's piece of paper. Kamal rejected the director-general's proposal that the application of the SSM should be conditional upon clear evidence that imports of the product in question had increased significantly in relation to the year before. His pretext was that the Indian government did not have the technical capability to provide such evidence.[175] Mandelson also reacted negatively to Lamy's piece of paper, saying that the numbers the director-general had presented for NAMA, particularly on anti-concentration, were insufficient. I cannot remember the European trade commissioner's choice of words, but the thrust of his message was that the proposal was a non-starter. The ministers representing Japan and China spoke next. From differing perspectives they also criticized the director-general's suggestions, and were quite outspoken on certain points. Chinese trade minister Chen Deming—whom I had spoken to at the Brazilian ambassador's residence a couple of days before, and who seemed willing to be an active participant in the negotiations—was particularly concerned about the NAMA sectorials and about market access for agricultural products. China also wanted to take advantage of the SSM to curb any increase in imports of those products that had recently been negotiated as part of the terms for the country's accession to the WTO. As for Japan's trade minister, Akira Amari, always backed by his colleague the agriculture minister, he was fighting against the imposition of ceilings for tariffs (tariff capping) on agricultural products, above all in the case of rice.[176]

When it was my turn to speak, I decided to make a bold move. The day before, my collaborators had been involved in lengthy technical consultations with experts in various ministries in Brasilia. More importantly, I myself had briefed President Lula on the state of play in Geneva. So I felt I was on very firm ground as far as the home front was concerned. On that basis I started by telling my G7 negotiating partners there were various points in the proposal that I did not like. I explained that, for reasons that were more or less the opposite of those given by Mandelson, the paragraph on NAMA, particularly the part on anti-concentration, was difficult for Brazil to accept. As for agriculture, I said the figure proposed for OTDS was higher than we had expected.[177] I declared, however, that I would be willing to "swallow" the proposal, despite its shortcomings, if that helped us reach a deal. My attitude caught the other participants by surprise, as I knew it would, and changed the dynamics of the meeting. My sentiment was echoed by Simon Crean and Susan Schwab (though in her case with certain restrictions), which in turn caused Mandelson to reconsider his previous opinion that Lamy's proposal was unacceptable. The Chinese and Japanese ministers, for their part, stayed relatively quiet at this stage. The fact that both they needed interpreters limited their ability to keep up with the discussions. At this point the only clearly dissonant voice continued to be that of Kamal Nath. However, over the hours and days that followed, Schwab, already dissatisfied with the numbers for SP/SSM, and frustrated with what she saw as a lack of precision with regard to the NAMA sectorials, began shifting position. Eventually the USTR would form an alliance of convenience with Kamal Nath, with the shared aim of suspending the negotiations.[178] This marriage of opposites only became explicit on the last day when, in the midst of a G7 meeting in which some of us (including the director-general himself) were still searching for a way out of the impasse, Kamal and Susan began discussing the dates and times of their respective flights out of Geneva. It was a pathetic scene. Curiously, given that Mandelson and I had been involved in perhaps the most heated exchange so far (concerning NAMA), the European commissioner and I found ourselves united, along with the well-intentioned Australian minister, in pushing for an agreement based on Lamy's proposals.[179] European Commission officials, together with our own (and some help from the Australians and the WTO Secretariat), were instructed to seek alternatives that might make the proposals on SP/SSM acceptable to the United States on the one hand, and to China and India on the other.[180] Something similar, *mutatis mutandis*, was attempted in relation to the NAMA sectorials. The feeling at this stage was that, despite the difficulties, China would probably accept a compromise solution so as to avoid being left isolated. But, essentially, the game was already up. Kamal's intransigence in refusing to consider any formula that differed in the slightest from his own initial proposal, and Susan's inability or unwillingness to make concessions on agricultural subsidies (without sufficient compensation, as she saw it, in NAMA or in access to agricultural markets), together defeated all attempts at reconciliation. After much wailing and gnashing of teeth, which carried on until the Tuesday, July 29, (far beyond the planned duration of the TNC) Lamy officially announced that the negotiations had collapsed.

"Amorim's prediction"

It was not an easy decision for Brazil to accept Lamy's proposal. The discussions preceding the session in which the director-general presented his piece of paper had made clear that if we wanted to reach an agreement, we would have to make a concession on anti-concentration. The day before, Roberto Azevêdo had told me, based on conversations with Brasilia, that a rate of 15% would be bearable. Lamy himself had previously suggested 20%.[181] It was not a very big difference. As for the flexibilities, Lamy's proposal was that they should be applicable to 14% of the tariff lines and 16% of the total value of trade. These were actually very close to the numbers demanded by Brazil so as to accommodate the difficulties of the Mercosur members as a whole. Lamy's suggested coefficient for the tariff reduction formula was the same as had been proposed in the earlier "revised paper": 20. This figure, accompanied by the flexibilities, would not represent a disastrous degree of opening for Brazil's industrial sector. In São Paulo, the staff at FIESP who were closely following the negotiations indicated that they could "live with" such an outcome. In these circumstances, even though we were obviously making sacrifices, I believed it made sense to accept the package.

Peter Mandelson's thought process must have been similar, even though his specific interests were different from mine. For the European Union, the multilateral trading system was valuable in itself. Back in the days of the Uruguay Round, the European Economic Community (the predecessor to the EU), with a legal system different from that of the United States, had been strongly in favor of the establishment of the WTO as a solid institution to replace the GATT (which had been merely an agreement, and a provisional one at that). Like Brazil, the EU saw the WTO as a system for the resolution of disputes that would inhibit the use of unilateral measures such as the notorious Section 301 of the US Trade Act, which Washington frequently resorted to using. Although Brussels was not in principle averse to bilateral trade agreements (indeed, the EU has signed several of them over the years), it did not want to see world trade become fragmented. In that respect the EU's stance was very different from that of the US, which generally seemed ambivalent about such a prospect. Mandelson could reasonably assume that Lamy's proposal, although it certainly did not meet all his objectives, would be sufficiently attractive from the point of view of the EU member countries. With regard to agriculture, for example, with a cap on OTDS and disciplines on US domestic subsidies, the Europeans would be able to claim they had to some degree "leveled the playing field" with regard to domestic support (counterbalancing the reduction in European subsidies as part of the ongoing reform of the CAP). In NAMA, with a coefficient relatively close to his initial target (15), and with the incorporation (to some extent) of anti-concentration as a factor that would "moderate" the flexibilities, the EU trade commissioner would be able to present the industrial producers in Germany (and some other countries) with a concrete gain. Naturally, over the course of the negotiations, Mandelson also hoped to make similar gains in the areas of services and (with smaller chances of success) geographical indications.[182]

As for Susan Schwab, I already mentioned her apparent perception that the concessions her interlocutors were demanding in the area of OTDS would not be accepted by Congress, given that, as she saw it, the US had been offered insufficient concessions in return. Apart from what the US might still be able to obtain in services, Washington's focus was mainly on issues related to market access. In relation to manufactured goods, the topic of "sectorials" (vigorously opposed by China, and to a lesser extent by Brazil and India) was the main priority. Since there was a general understanding that we would not be dealing with precise numbers for sectorials at that stage (modalities), I thought it should be possible to phrase a text on the subject in such a way that it would be sufficiently ambiguous to accommodate the ambitions of the Americans while still being acceptable to the Chinese. Of course the problem would reappear when we moved to the next stage of negotiations (scheduling). But, to borrow an expression from my Anglo-Saxon friends, I believed we could cross that bridge when we came to it. As for agriculture, the Americans had traditionally trained their sights both on the markets of developed countries (Europe and Japan) and those of the less competitive developing countries such as India, China, and Indonesia. But, over the previous two and a half years (since Hong Kong), the US seemed to have been focusing more on the latter than the former. In one of my several bilaterals with the USTR after Lamy had presented his paper, Schwab complained about virtually every aspect of the negotiations and seemed very agitated about the "concessions" she had already made. But at that point she had still not given up entirely on a deal. It would be difficult, after all, to accept responsibility for a failure, even if the blame would be shared to some extent with India. In that same meeting, the USTR expressed the hope that "Brazil could help, by convincing the G33 to make a move."

As for India, Kamal Nath seemed to have played his cards badly. It was reasonable for New Delhi to expect its negotiating partners to take into account India's well-known sensitivities in relation to small-scale agriculture and food security. Consistent with our own government's policy vis-à-vis family agriculture within Brazil, to a certain extent we had been supportive of India's position on rural development and food security. In doing so we had sometimes incurred the displeasure both of our Mercosur partners and our own agribusiness. But my impression at that point in the negotiations was that Kamal was expecting to get everything he wanted without making any concessions whatsoever. In other words I perceived (and still do, in retrospect) that Kamal imagined his six interlocutors, faced with the prospect of India "vetoing" a potential agreement, would cave in to his demands. Despite initial backing from the G33, the overall support for India's positions was less solid than Kamal had expected. The coordinator of the G33, Mari Pangestu, would later confess that she regretted having aligned herself with India's radical positions that ultimately contributed to the collapse of the negotiations.[183] Some G33 countries, especially the poorest ones, had hoped to obtain advantages in other areas of the negotiations (such as "duty-free, quota-free"). Therefore, although supportive of Kamal's radical proposals (partly because they were not fully aware of their precise contents, partly because they did not grasp the dynamics of the negotiations as a whole), the majority of LDCs that were members of the G33 were not attracted by the option of abandoning the process altogether, which at one point Kamal had openly suggested. When Kamal later admitted to me that he had proposed breaking off the negotiations, he said the vehement response on the part of the smaller G33 countries was that he must not do so. Perhaps it was discomfort following that reaction that led Kamal to propose that he and I should meet with Pangestu and the director-general, so that with "the help of Brazil" it might be possible to close the gap between the G33 and the United States.

Uncomfortable with so many requests for help, I said to Lamy, when we were alone together, that although I was absolutely committed to trying to break the impasse, I did not want to get involved in the discussion suggested by Kamal until the director-general had consulted Schwab and Mandelson. My fear at that moment was that even a well-intentioned effort to bring the parties closer together might be used as a pretext, by either the US or the EU, to reopen other aspects of the package. These efforts on my part to keep the negotiations on the rails, and the confidence displayed by Kamal in asking me to continue the *démarches* in relation to SP/SSM, clearly disprove the idea that Brazil "abandoned" India (a notion propagated for a while in certain quarters, and unfortunately given credence even by reputable analysts such as Baghwati). The almost desperate appeals for our help in solving the impasse, from Mari Pangestu in particular, were further evidence that our concerns and objectives were widely shared by the developing countries, including at least some of the LDCs. As well as the tactical error of overestimating the strength of his hand, there is also another factor that probably had an influence on Kamal's behavior. Within a few months there were going to be state elections in India, in which his ambition to become chief minister of Madhya Pradesh would hang in the balance. The economy of that important Indian state, it is relevant to mention, consists largely of small farmers.[184]

In the wake of the official declaration that the negotiations had collapsed, all the participants had their own version of events. Some of them, including the director-general himself, attempted to smooth over the failure. This was not my own approach. Leaving the meeting room in which the last Green Room had taken place, I went down the stairs in the Centre William Rappard, the old GATT headquarters (which in the interwar years had housed the Secretariat of the International Labor Organization), and spoke to the journalists who were waiting eagerly for news and reactions. With my emotions still running high, I improvised a little speech in which I expressed doubts about the viability of preserving whatever progress we had made. I added: "I share the wish [to preserve those advances], but . . . it doesn't depend on us. Life goes on. We have the food crisis. We will have other crises. Other concerns will arise. [Groups with] protectionist interests . . . will look closely at what we had agreed [in principle], which at times represented a leap of faith. . . ." Commenting upon my "poignant words" in a book published in 2009,[185] Paul Blustein referred to the financial crisis triggered by the bankruptcy of Lehman Brothers, and pointed out: "With astounding swiftness, Amorim's prediction came true about the onset of 'other crises' that would overshadow the failure of the WTO's July 2008 meeting."

I spent one more day in Geneva, and did not duck the opportunity to give further interviews. Speaking to *Newsweek*, I lamented the narrowness of vision displayed by the trade negotiators, dependent as they were on their various domestic lobbies, and went so far as to suggest, paraphrasing the former French prime minister Georges Clemenceau,[186] that the "trade negotiations are too important to be left to the trade ministers." In that same interview—and in another, with the *Financial Times*—I predicted (rather too optimistically, as it turned out) that it would take three or four years to put together another package capable of producing an agreement. I told the British newspaper that the suggestion that we could resume the discussions if they were restricted to individual issues (an idea the journalist attributed to Susan Schwab) was "wishful thinking." I also pointed to the very real risk of the fragmentation of the international trading system, and stated that bilateral agreements would always be only a "second best" option, incapable of dealing with central issues such as agricultural subsidies.

FROM GENEVA TO . . .

"Argentina is *your* problem, Celso!"

I returned to Brasilia on July 31. My low spirits were exacerbated by the unexpected drizzle (it was the "dry season" in that part of Brazil). Also unusual was the fact that only two people were waiting for me at the air base where the Legacy landed: Ambassador Ruy Nogueira, the most senior of the Itamaraty undersecretaries, and Cecilia Neiva Tavares, the wife of my press officer. In the afternoon I gave President Lula a detailed account of what had happened in Geneva. The next day, I received a visit from the Indonesian trade minister, Mari Pangestu. After that, I accompanied Lula on a two-day visit to Buenos Aires. On our first day in the Argentine capital the president held discussions with about twenty "heavyweights" from the Brazilian business sector, in preparation for a meeting with their Argentine counterparts. The FIESP president, Paulo Skaff, praised the fluid and constant dialogue in Geneva between the Brazilian delegation and the representatives of Brazilian industry who had also made the trip to Switzerland. Skaff expressed total support for the position Itamaraty had adopted. While Lula and President Cristina Kirchner[187] were having a private meeting, I had conversations with the foreign minister, Jorge Taiana, and some of the most senior Argentine economic officials. To my great surprise I realized that they all seemed to share a misperception of the impact on industrial tariffs of the application of the Swiss Formula with a coefficient of 20, accompanied by the flexibility margins proposed by Lamy on his piece of paper. Taiana, whom I had met on a number of occasions both before and during the most recent phase of the negotiations, anxiously took me by the arm and led me to the trade secretary (whose position was linked to the finance ministry rather than the foreign ministry), requesting that I explain to his colleague what the real impact of the tariff cuts in Lamy's proposal would be. I said to the trade secretary that, with the flexibilities, the tariff on automobiles (a sector of particular interest to Argentina) would not fall to 14 or 15%, as he thought, but would in fact be 23 or 24%. His surprise was genuinely disconcerting. Brazil had always been careful to accommodate Argentine concerns. The excruciating discussions we had held with our WTO partners and the secretariat about the widening of the flexibilities had to a large extent been based upon those considerations. During the most recent negotiations in Geneva I had often mentioned Argentina's difficulties in NAMA. And, every time, the response from my interlocutors had been along the lines of: "Argentina is *your* problem, Celso!" I was very aware that if we had been able to conclude the modalities in the July meetings in Geneva, when it came to the final phase of the negotiations (the actual scheduling of concessions) Brazil would probably have had to "foot the bill" by leaving out of the flexibilities certain tariff lines that were of interest to us. The lack of knowledge on the part of a senior Argentine economic official was perplexing. Who or what would have led one the individuals primarily responsible for Argentine industrial policy to base the country's negotiating positions on absolutely false premises? And what might have been the specific interests of that person, who apparently had not even provided the foreign minister himself with an adequate briefing? It was difficult not to ponder such intriguing questions, although the answers (whatever they were) were already becoming irrelevant as the Doha Round discussions lost impetus in the wake of the "great failure of July" and eventually slipped into a state of profound lethargy.

On August 2, before we left for Argentina, I had persuaded President Lula to phone Bush. It was not a long discussion. Essentially the call was aimed at making sure Washington remained engaged in the negotiations, which seemed a feasible goal at the time. In fact it was Lamy who had suggested to me, before I left Geneva, that Lula should speak to the US president. Our efforts to keep things moving proceeded over the next few days. On August 5 Lula called Manmohan Singh to emphasize the importance Brazil continued to attach to the Round. The response from the Indian prime minister (who, it must be said, was always easier to reconcile than his trade minister) was vaguely encouraging. That same day, Kamal called me, saying he was willing to keep up a dialogue with Brazil in order to try to break the impasse. I also received a visit from Egyptian trade minister Rachid Mohamed Rachid, my G20 colleague, whose attitude was always sensible and cooperative. But the subject of our conversation—and this in itself indicated that Doha was already on the way to becoming lost in the broader panorama of trade issues—was the possibility of quickly concluding a trade deal between Egypt and Mercosur. At some point I spoke to Lamy, who was in New Delhi trying to gain India's support for further negotiations. I also received a call from Susan Schwab. This intense burst of telephone diplomacy was picked up by the international media. On August 13, referring to President Lula's presence (without me) at the opening ceremony of the Olympic Games in Beijing, *Le*

Monde reported under the headline "President Lula and Pascal Lamy move heaven and earth" that "never has there been so much talk about trade at the Olympics." The same article contained excerpts from an interview I had recently given to the French newspaper. In that interview, apart from lamenting the specific losses for Brazil from the breakdown of the negotiations, I highlighted our geopolitical vision, including our conviction that the multilateral trading system was essential in order to try to achieve greater balance in contemporary world affairs. I added that bilateral agreements, as a supposed alternative, offered no hope of solving the problems of the poor countries because they would not remove the agricultural subsidies that did those countries so much harm. In response to a question about the prospects for resuming the negotiations, I said that if we were able to restart them quickly, it might just be possible to "continue where we left off." If not, I said, all the *acquis* would be lost. At the end of the section in my notebook in which I recorded these events, my comments reflected my faint hopes: "Will it be possible to build a bridge between Delhi and Washington? Susan seemed bewildered, and Kamal, although saying he is willing to talk, continues to jumble arguments in his usual style. Today . . . [the British prime minister] will talk to Lula [in Beijing]. But, as Joseph Stalin . . . once asked about the pope [Pius XII], how many divisions does Gordon Brown have?"

At the end of August, I visited Australia and New Zealand. As I noted at the time, the most important aim during the trip was to see what could be done to help the ailing Doha Round ("the patient some of us have been trying to revive"). Australia, which led the Cairns Group and had played quite a significant role in the July Framework as a member of the FIPS, remained an ardent defender of the Round. As previously mentioned, the Australian trade minister, Simon Crean, was a true believer in the multilateral trading system. New Zealand, for its part, proudly considered itself a "good citizen" in international affairs, and had traditionally taken quite an active role in the WTO with regard to agriculture. In the case of both countries my trip naturally also included discussions about bilateral and global political issues. On August 24, before leaving for Canberra, I spoke again with Lamy. He had just returned from Washington, which had been his destination immediately after India—a travel schedule that indicated where in the world the main problems lay. The director-general said he was "moderately hopeful" about the chances of resuming the negotiations. For my part I was hoping to meet Kamal Nath in an intermediary location along my route back from Oceania (perhaps Dubai). Given that a face-to-face conversation is always more useful than a phone call, I thought a meeting with Kamal would allow me to ascertain if it was worth continuing with the efforts to resuscitate the Round. In the end the meeting did not take place, due to Kamal's "pressing commitments" of a political nature in Madhya Pradesh. Before those long days in Geneva in late July, I had said that my estimate of the probability of successfully concluding the Round in the short term was "sixty percent." Now, in the aftermath of our failed attempts, it was no more than ten percent. But I still believed, or wanted to believe, that it was worth having "one last try."

"It won't be easy to go the last mile"

In the first week of October, Peter Mandelson left his post as EU trade commissioner. He had been chosen by Gordon Brown for a senior role in the Labour government, which was being buffeted both by the economic situation and its own internal disputes. I would not meet again with Mandelson during the rest of my time at the helm of Itamaraty, although we would speak on the phone later in the year, shortly before the summit convened by the US president to deal with the global financial crisis.[188] The next time I would see Peter was at a seminar in São Paulo in the early months of 2011, between leaving my post as foreign minister (at the end of Lula's second term of office) and my appointment as defense minister by President Dilma Rousseff. On that occasion we reminisced about our joint efforts in Geneva aimed at saving the Round, and Peter presented me with a copy of his recently published memoirs, *The Third Man*. Inside the front cover was a handwritten dedication: "To Celso Amorim, united for the common good."

On October 13, 2008, I flew to Delhi to accompany Lula at yet another IBSA summit. Both the president and I attached great importance to the India-Brazil-South Africa forum, knowing that like so many other foreign policy initiatives that we had launched, the tripartite grouping was a "tender plant" that needed to be "watered daily."[189] I arrived in the Indian capital a day and a half before Lula so as to have time to meet with the foreign minister, Pranab Mukherjee, and of course Kamal Nath. I was still seeking to revive the ailing Doha Round. I had therefore asked my aides, headed by Roberto Azevêdo, to hold preparatory talks with the relevant Indian officials. The main issue at this stage was the Special Safeguard Mechanism (SSM), which was where the biggest obstacle to the resumption of negotiations lay (the closely related issue of special products did not seem quite so problematic). According to my notes, much of my time with Kamal was spent on a very generic discussion of the global financial crisis and the political situation in the US. In a business seminar that we both attended, just before our private meeting, Kamal voiced his support when I called for a reform of the international financial/monetary system. Indeed, my journalist friends (yes, I do have a few!) who were present informed me later that, at a stage in the proceedings when I was not in the room, Kamal had been quite outspoken, suggesting that the entire existing architecture should be replaced by a "WFO," with the "F" standing for "financial."

During my meeting with Kamal, I chose to go along with his evident desire to talk about generalities rather than specifics. I felt a conversation of that nature might lift the mood between us, which was still rather heavy in the wake of the events of July in Geneva. I had actually decided, partly on the basis of advice from my collaborators, that we should divide our efforts with the Indians into two separate stages. Before the local elections, in which Kamal would be running for the position of chief minister in his state of Madhya Pradesh, the work would have to be discreet and technical, not aiming at any concrete conclusions. During the pre-election period India would not be receptive to proposals offering anything less than absolute protection for the country's small farmers. But after the elections there would at least be the possibility of arriving at a more realistic understanding. Of course it would not be easy, given the array of agricultural products covered by India's protectionist concerns. When I explained my reasoning to Kamal, he agreed and said he was willing to work on that basis, even though we would have very little time between the Indian elections and the change of government in the United States. He also agreed with the idea of a three-way conversation involving Susan Schwab, for which we set an approximate date in the second week of November.[190]

Kamal also offered me a private dinner, which seemed a good opportunity to extend our conversation. Indeed, it proved conducive to what Spanish speakers refer to as a *sinceramiento*. Kamal complained, gently, about my behavior during the clashes in July, alleging that I had left him "alone." I tried to explain the position I had adopted in Geneva, reminding him of how thorny and divisive issues such as SP and the SSM were for the G20. Most importantly, I tried to contextualize and counterbalance Kamal's complaint by reminding him of the frequent occasions—in the G7 in Geneva and also in previous G4/G6 meetings—when he had admitted, in my presence, that he was willing to be flexible on NAMA, the most sensitive issue for Brazil, as long as he obtained the result he wanted on SP/SSM. Nevertheless, I conceded to Kamal that maybe I should have made clear to him, immediately after Lamy's presentation in Geneva, that I had been willing to accept the contents of the director-general's "piece of paper." Then again (and this was a point I probably did not make during the dinner), for me and the rest of the Brazilian delegation in Geneva, the little time available between the director-general tabling his proposal and the G7 meeting had been entirely taken up by consultations and calculations (above all concerning anti-concentration).

Kamal confessed to me during our dinner that his real political ambition, if successful in the forthcoming state elections, was to become leader of the Congress Party at the national level. If the party (whose president was Sonia Gandhi, with whom Kamal apparently had close links) succeeded in maintaining its majority in Parliament, he would then automatically become prime minister. As Kamal memorably put it: "I don't intend to stay very long in Bhopal" (referring to the state capital of Madhya Pradesh, best known for the terrible accident at the Union Carbide chemical plant in 1984, which claimed thousands of lives).

From Delhi I set off on a short tour of Africa that included Maputo (where I accompanied the president on a bilateral visit), Harare, and Lusaka. In Zimbabwe I found myself having delicate talks both with the ageing leader (or, as many see him, dictator), Robert Mugabe, and representatives of the opposition (including its most prominent figure, Morgan Tsvangirai, who struck me as politically fragile and highly dependent on his supporters in the United Kingdom). I also met with former South African president Thabo Mbeki, who had been given the role of mediator in Zimbabwe's intractable crisis by the SADC.[191] I managed to overcome a mild stomach upset with the help of numerous cups of black tea, which I must admit was virtually the only thing I drank in a country that, tragically, was about to suffer a serious outbreak of cholera. (The main preoccupation during my visit, however, was the looming prospect of widespread hunger, due to a decrease in both the planting and harvesting of food crops.)

In Zambia I was able to recuperate at our ambassador's residence following a series of commitments that had been quite intense (but much less problematic politically than my schedule in Zimbabwe). Following a suggestion from my wife Ana, whom I spoke to regularly during such trips, I called Clóvis Rossi of the *Folha de São Paulo*, who was in Madrid at the time. I intended to convey my impressions of Zimbabwe and talk about Brazil's actions aimed at assisting in the alleviation of the country's political crisis. Essentially I was taking preventative action, all too aware that the Brazilian press might criticize my presence alongside "another African dictator." The veteran journalist listened attentively but soon changed the subject, telling me about the latest developments in the financial crisis. I subsequently made a point of watching the TV news that evening, and therefore found out about the decision by President Bush, apparently encouraged by Sarkozy and Durão Barroso, to convene, before the end of November, a summit in Washington of developed and developing countries aimed at addressing the crisis. According to the *Washington Post*, Brazil would be among the countries invited. Rossi, in fact, had taken the opportunity to ask me who would be in charge of Brazil's preparations for the event: the finance ministry or Itamaraty? I told him it would naturally be the former, given that the subject was essentially economic-financial. That same day, however, President Lula called me to request that I help prepare the speech that he would be making at the opening of the meeting of the "financial" G20[192] (at ministerial level) on November 8 in São Paulo, which to some extent would constitute a preparation for the Washington summit. I noticed later, with a sense of gratification, that he had included in his address a reference to the conclusion of the Doha Round, "no longer as an opportunity, but as a necessity." About ten days earlier, in late October, we had convened a meeting of Mercosur foreign ministers, finance ministers, and central bank governors, at which we made sure the Doha Round was not forgotten. Given Argentina's well-known resistance to everything concerning the Round, that was no mean feat. As I saw it, the prospect of a summit in Washington on economic and financial matters, involving the leaders of the world's largest economies, reopened the possibility of discussions on the WTO at the highest level. This prospect, although remote, rekindled my hopes.

Around this time, returning from a trip to Tehran (the first of the several journeys that culminated in the 2010 declaration on Iran's nuclear program),[193] I stopped for a couple of days in Geneva. One of my meetings there was with Roberto Azevêdo, who had recently taken over from Clodoaldo Hugueney as Brazil's permanent representative to the WTO. Roberto told me the prevailing mood among the negotiators was one of "strong pessimism." On November 4 (the day of the US presidential election, in which Barack Obama was victorious) I met with Pascal Lamy. The director-general was less pessimistic than I was about the position the Democrats might take on the Doha Round. He nevertheless agreed with me that it was essential to seek advances before the Bush administration came to an end in early January. That same day I also spoke to the Australian trade minister, Simon Crean, who for some reason happened to be visiting the WTO headquarters. I told both Lamy and Crean that, in my view, the declaration that would emerge from the meeting of leaders in the new G20 format needed to contain more than a merely *pro forma* reference to the Doha Round. My opinion, with which they both expressed agreement, was that the declaration should contain "clear instructions" for the trade ministers, based upon the work conducted in Geneva in July. Those instructions, I said, should also establish a clear time limit for results to be achieved. My Australian colleague, who seemed to be actively involved in the preparation of the documents for the summit, promised to incorporate my suggestions into the project his prime minister would take to Washington. During my brief stay in Geneva I unequivocally declared Brazil's support for Lamy continuing in his role as WTO director-general, even before he had made any official statement on the matter. The reason I did so was to quash the rumors that I myself might be a candidate for the position. In that respect my declaration had the desired effect.

At my suggestion, Lula had proposed to Bush that Lamy should be invited to the G20 summit. More or less at the same time, I had made the same suggestion to the US treasury secretary, Henry Paulson, with whom I had had a frank and positive dialogue on trade-related issues when he visited me in Brazil in 2007. The invitation to Lamy was not forthcoming, however. This seemed to suggest that the Doha Round might end up being little more than a footnote in the leaders' declaration. For my part I continued to take a keen interest in the preparatory discussions, receiving regular updates from Azevêdo's successor as Itamaraty's undersecretary for economic affairs, Pedro Carneiro de Mendonça. Along with the representative from the finance ministry (also a diplomat, by the way), Mendonça was one of our two sherpas during the preparations for the event. (During the summit itself, this role would be played by our ambassador in Washington, Antonio Patriota.)

On my way back from Geneva to Brazil, where I would spend only two days before heading off with the president to Rome and then Washington, the Legacy made its usual stop in Cape Verde. I took the opportunity to phone Patriota. I wanted not only to hear his insights about Obama's victory but also to discuss my earlier suggestion to Paulson that Lamy should be present at the summit. Patriota told me he had recently met with the treasury secretary, who had in fact already spoken to the director-general. What Lamy apparently had told Paulson, however, was that he was unsure whether he should attend the summit. This was a big surprise for me, as in my long conversation with Lamy the day before, he had said nothing to suggest any hesitation on his part. When I thought back, however, I did remember Lamy had said it might be "advantageous" for him "not to attend the leaders' meeting" (or words to that effect). At that moment, however, it had seemed he was just thinking aloud about the scenario of not being invited so as to prepare himself psychologically for that possibility. It was also possible that Lamy had had second thoughts on account of his bid to be re-elected as director-general and a desire not to make any waves that might hinder that ambition. Whatever the explanation, there was something not quite clear about Lamy's motives. But still, I took heart from the fact that the director-general had agreed with me about the need for the leaders' declaration to include an "appeal" on the subject of the Doha Round along with unambiguous instructions to the negotiators.

When I learned that the format of the summit would be "one plus one"—i.e. leaders to be accompanied by just one minister—I myself began to have doubts about whether my presence in Washington was a good idea. It was natural, after all, that Lula's companion at an event convened to discuss the financial crisis should be the finance minister, Guido Mantega. But such was the president's insistence that I too should make the trip, the choice was taken out of my hands. As it turned out, the margins of the summit offered opportunities for several bilateral conversations on Doha Round-related topics. More interesting still was the chance to contribute to the interventions Lula made during the summit, one of which, during lunch, specifically concerned the WTO. I was also able to monitor the negotiations leading to the drafting of the leaders' declaration, the final version of which, contrary to my earlier fears, largely said what I had hoped it would about the Round.[194] Even if indirectly, my participation also helped strengthen the presence of Itamaraty as it assumed, for the first time in many years, a prominent role in an international meeting whose primary focus was financial. This role was reinforced by the joint interviews I gave with Mantega, in accordance with an explicit instruction from the president.

A subheading on the front page of the *Washington Post* conveyed the extent of the change that the G20 leaders' summit represented. According to my notes, it read: "At beginning of summit, emerging nations show strength: Brazil, China and India rise, in turnaround of diplomatic power." Though "excluded" from the "ball" (or at least its main set piece) by the one-plus-one format, I still had a parallel schedule of engagements. While Lula and Mantega were at the banquet in the White House, I attended a dinner hosted by Secretary of State Condoleezza Rice on the eighth floor of the State Department. For Condoleezza it was a mixture of farewell party and birthday celebration. It was a thoroughly pleasant occasion, not only because of the interesting conversation but also the good music played by a quartet composed entirely of the secretary of state's friends. As the society columns might have said in times gone by, it was "an exclusive gathering," the guest list definitely not having been based on standard protocol. Not all of the foreign ministers who had accompanied their leaders to Washington were present, and there were very few senior US government officials (the national security advisor, Stephen Hadley, was among the exceptions). Perhaps because my gray hair made her feel obliged to grant me special treatment, Condoleezza insisted that I sit immediately to her right. The secretary of state and I entered into a lively discussion on the prospects for organizing a G20 of foreign ministers that she suggested the two of us could co-chair. But unfortunately the Bush administration had too little time left for us to put the idea into practice.

Afterwards, when listing in my notebook the people who were present at Condoleezza's *soirée*, I almost forgot Susan Schwab. It would have been an unforgivable omission, and certainly one with a Freudian explanation. In fact, on the day of the summit itself, the USTR came to talk to me in the comfortable and stylish hotel suite where I was staying in the Georgetown neighborhood. Despite her friendly tone I could discern no signs of progress toward a resumption of the negotiations. Susan still seemed to be a hostage of the US lobbies—especially the National Association of Manufacturers (NAM), which was pressing for immediate results with regard to the "sectorials." As I saw it, the only way to address that issue (a sensitive one for Brazil, but even more so for China) was to start with generic concepts from which it would then be possible to move on to specific negotiations at a later stage, after the "modalities." In principle Susan did not disagree with me, but she clearly lacked the political clout that would have allowed her to stand up to the "special interest groups." And as her boss in the White House freely confessed his lack of knowledge of (or interest in) the details, quite apart from demonstrating political fatigue, the overall prospects were not encouraging. As I wrote in my notebook: "Even though now we have the [new] instructions from the leaders . . . it won't be easy to go the last mile."

During the flight back to Brazil I enumerated the results of the Washington summit: "(1) Consolidation of the G20, instead of the G8, as the decision-making body on financial issues (especially those concerning the IMF and the Bank World); (2) coordination of proactive policies to stimulate the economy; (3) the need for greater international oversight of financial operations; (4) change to the 'institutional architecture,' with greater participation by developing countries; [and last but not least] (5) engagement [of the leaders] in concluding the Doha Round by the end of the year, with clear instructions to ministers and [explicit] willingness of heads of government to closely follow the process."

"Get real!"

Late November was devoted to South American issues. Among them was an unfolding crisis connected with a hydroelectric dam project that the Brazilian Development Bank (BNDES) had funded in Ecuador. The dispute, which also involved a Brazilian construction company, had led the country's president, Rafael Correa, to initiate arbitration proceedings against the bank. The BNDES had made disbursements strictly in accordance with the contractual clauses, but now Ecuador was withholding the repayments. Ecuador's course of action, highly unusual and utterly inappropriate, had the potential to undermine the "Covenant on Reciprocal Credits," an essential element of the credit system put in place by ALADI.[195] This in turn was an indispensable tool for international financial operations within South America. The episode led me, with Lula's consent, to temporarily recall our ambassador from Quito. But there were also more positive events, such as a Mercosur-ASEAN meeting in Brasilia on November 24 (the same day as a cabinet meeting at Granja do Torto, at which the president asked me to be one of the principal speakers, alongside Mantega, on the subject of the international financial crisis). The meeting between Mercosur and the Southeast Asian bloc originated from an initiative on my part that had promptly received the backing of the Singaporean trade minister, George Yeo. It was the result, more directly, of a broader FEALAC conference the year before (which had been somewhat lacking in purpose, in my opinion).[196] Broadening the relationship between Mercosur and other groups of developing countries was a directive I myself had issued, and one I was committed to putting into action.

At the end of November, I revisited Doha (the capital of Qatar, that is) for the United Nations Conference on Financing for Development. In my short speech during the plenary session, the Doha Round was one of four main points. I emphasized recent statements from representatives of some of the poorest countries in which they had asserted that the gains they could make from a positive conclusion to the Round would outweigh any increase in development assistance they might receive in the years ahead. This, I said, indicated an increased level of maturity on the part of the so-called LDCs. I pointed out that we had come very close to a conclusion in Geneva in July, and said that progress in the negotiations would only be possible if the rich countries did not try to wrest additional concessions from the developing ones. During my stay in Doha—in the midst of bilateral meetings with Arab and African leaders or foreign ministers, and a "retreat"-style collective discussion organized by the UN secretary-general—I had breakfast with WTO director-general Pascal Lamy (as so many times before) and encouraged him to try to organize the meeting of trade ministers (foreseen in the leaders' joint statement at the Washington summit) as soon as possible.

On the way back to Brazil I stopped in Geneva, where on December 1 I attended a lunch with Catherine Ashton, the new EU trade commissioner. A compatriot of her predecessor, Peter Mandelson, Ashton also shared with him a political background in the Labour Party. She was a member of the UK parliament's upper chamber, the House of Lords, where her official title was Baroness Ashton of Upholland.[197] My first impressions of Ashton were positive: she seemed calm, objective, and secure—very different from her predecessor, but perhaps also without his distinctive intellectual spark. I took advantage of my background knowledge of the UK—where I had been a young diplomat and postgraduate student in the late 1960s, and then ambassador for a little over a year between 2002 and 2003—to strike up a less formal relationship with the new European commissioner, who was very receptive. Brazil and the EU were now closer together as a result of the circumstances in which the negotiations had broken down in July. Moreover, in the context of the debates around trade, we had a longstanding special relationship with London. My conversation with Ashton—which was especially opportune given that a date for the ministerial meeting, December 13, had been announced just after my meeting with Lamy in Doha—confirmed that, despite differences on specific issues, we were on the same wavelength about the need to conclude the Doha Round. At the end of the lunch, Ashton and I gave a joint interview to the press, which served to underline our convergent positions. Also in Geneva, at Azevêdo's suggestion, I organized meetings (including a lunch) on December 2 with some permanent representatives, including the chairs of the agriculture and NAMA negotiating groups, and also with the president of the WTO General Council. My impression from those dialogues was that some progress had been made at the technical level but that there were still significant difficulties. New Zealand's permanent representative, the chair of the agriculture group, confessed to me that the paper he anticipated producing would be "far from ideal." The coordinator of the NAMA group, the Swiss permanent representative, was even less precise. The Japanese ambassador, who seemed to be new to Geneva, referred to the "mantra" he said he was hearing all the time: "Get real!"

I arrived back in Brasilia late at night on December 2. The next day, at noon, I attended a hearing in the Chamber of Deputies. I faced several questions concerning the crisis with Ecuador. This time, given the firm line we had taken, the opposition deputies were unable to allege that the government was being too "lenient" with one of our left-leaning South American partners, but they still took the opportunity to criticize our policy of pursuing closer ties with the countries in the "Bolivarian axis." Toward the end of that week I spent almost the whole of one working day on the phone, immersed in delicate conversations about the Round. I received a call from Peter Mandelson, newly installed as the member of the British cabinet responsible for industrial and trade strategy.[198] My former collaborator and sparring partner continued to take a great interest in the negotiations, and wanted to hear about the latest developments. I myself took the initiative of calling Kamal Nath and the Chinese trade minister, Chen Deming, as I was worried about US insistence regarding the "sectorials" issue and believed it required coordination between the three biggest "emerging" powers. I also had three separate phone conversations with the director-general, each time at his request. Again these were efforts to "save" the Round, which had hit the rocks in Geneva and was now in danger of sinking completely. It was essential to conclude the "modalities," but the latest developments in the United States were not positive. Both Republican and Democrat representatives in Congress, including the respected Max Baucus and Charles Rangel, had recommended in a letter to President Bush that he should not accept the July package. I did not know who was trying to convince whom, but it was certainly the case that quite apart from the ever-restive farm lobby, the US industrial interests represented by the NAM were very dissatisfied. Susan Schwab had not been able to recruit the power of the Executive in confronting those lobbies even when Bush had "a bullet in the chamber" (to use a Brazilian expression), so now that he was a lame duck, shortly to depart the scene, the prospects looked bleak indeed. The panorama in Geneva was not very encouraging either. On the same day as the first of my three conversations with Lamy, the chair of the NAMA group threatened to add an appendix to the paper that would have been highly problematic from Brazil's point of view. Alerted by our representative in Geneva, I managed to prevent that from happening by speaking firmly to Lamy and also sending a forthright message to the chair himself. During this episode we acted alongside China and India—a degree of coordination that, as I noted at the time, would have to be maintained in order to rescue the negotiations. At the same time, I emphasized to the director-general that any attempt to reopen the July package (which he had suggested doing, so as to carry out a *réequilibrage* of its various elements) would inevitably lead to changes being made to other parts of the documents, which would ultimately produce the general "unraveling" scenario that the negotiators most feared. During the last of the three phone conversations with Lamy, on the evening of December 7, he outlined his plan of action (*schéma*) for the remainder of the pre-Christmas period. He said he would ask the ministers of the most active WTO members to set aside the dates of December 18 and 19 for a meeting. I said nothing, but could not help thinking it was very unwise to choose dates so close to the end-of-year vacation. In the intervening period of ten days or so, Lamy planned to have a series of phone calls and video conferences with the ministers, and also consultations in Geneva with "senior officials" through which he hoped to achieve progress on the most difficult issues. An earlier plan had been to hold the ministerial meeting sooner, on December 13 and 14, but Lamy now believed that was unfeasible, "given the US attitude on the sectorials and, to a certain extent, the position of India on the SSM." It was interesting to hear Lamy imply, through the order in which he mentioned the issues and the emphasis he used for the two sets of questions, that Washington's stance was a more serious problem than that of Delhi. Also significant, in my opinion, was the statement released by the director-general in which he referred in a relatively optimistic tone to the latest papers presented by the chairs of the agriculture and NAMA groups. In the text, Lamy warned of the risk of "excessive ambitions," the exact term I myself had used frequently in interviews and speeches when referring to the developed countries' attitude (and that of the US in particular) with regard to the NAMA sectorials.

I warned Lamy about the risk, implicit in his *schéma*, of the negotiations becoming divided into segments consisting of separate groups of countries, a scenario that could cause difficulties in the future. I particularly disagreed with his view that the NAMA sectorials were an issue primarily concerning the US and China. It was quite possible that an agreement on that subject between Washington and China would be unsatisfactory for other countries, including Brazil. But I said I understood his attempt to "delay the agony," and that I shared his hope that the Obama administration might give some kind of positive sign and thereby reduce the negative political impact of the letter sent by the congressional representatives. Immediately after my conversation with the director-general, I called Roberto Azevêdo again in order to reiterate the importance of coordination with India and China. In the somewhat confused picture that was now emerging, we had to avoid a situation in which, if there was some progress on the SSM, the US then laid the blame for an eventual failure at the door of the emerging countries. After all, it was Washington that would be committing a "breach of faith" by changing the order of the negotiations, bringing the NAMA sectorials forward into the modalities phase. The understanding had always been that the negotiations on the sectorials would be left until afterwards.[199] That evening, I wrote the following: "I'm starting to have doubts about the usefulness of these desperate efforts to save the Round. Only yesterday I sent Undersecretary Pedro Carneiro de Mendonça and two aides to Buenos Aires. I did so because of a dramatic appeal made (informally) by one of our neighbor's negotiators: 'Brazil must not leave Argentina alone.' We have worked very hard on the political, diplomatic, and technical planes in order to conclude the Round, but we can't allow a final result that is bad for us." I concluded these reflections the following day: "It's obvious that the prospect of concluding the 'modalities' by the end of the year is increasingly remote. And therefore the WTO will go into a state of limbo. . . . In Brazil, [what that means is] the pressures for bilateral agreements will increase, even if the financial crisis serves to sound a note of caution."

"An unpleasant sense of *déjà vu*"

I left again for Geneva on December 10, though this time the reason for my trip was to speak on behalf of Brazil at the Human Rights Council on the occasion of the sixtieth anniversary of the Universal Declaration of Human Rights. Inevitably, however, the Doha Round found a way into my schedule. On December 11 I spoke on the phone with Kamal Nath and Simon Crean. Later that day I had a long conversation with Lamy in the meeting room that forms part of the director-general's offices at WTO headquarters. (That same meeting room, by the way, had become known at some point in the past as the "Green Room," because it was the venue for the restricted meetings that preceded the broader formal discussions. The same name was subsequently applied to the consultation process that normally precedes meetings of the TNC, either at the level of senior officials or ministers.[200] On the morning of December 12, so as not to lose the habit, I met with the permanent representatives of the G20 countries. Rather than try to summarize what took place during this short period in Geneva, I will reproduce the following section from my notes: "And the WTO? Well, to cut a long story short, I learned this morning that Lamy was going to announce that it was no longer possible to convene a ministerial meeting. In our long conversation yesterday in the famous Green Room, and [later] by phone, I suggested that [Lamy] should get some of the most involved ministers together to carry out a joint assessment of the situation. But Lamy preferred the shorter route. In my [media] interviews today and yesterday, I expressed the opinion that the responsibility [for this latest setback/failure] lies fundamentally with United States, because of their excessive ambitions in NAMA/sectorials. Yesterday I said that, given the attitudes of the [US] negotiators and the letter from the members of Congress, the only thing that can reverse the situation is some kind of sign from the president-elect, Barack Obama. I added that the leaders shouldn't try to hide behind the formalities of the handover [of power]. [In that respect] I recalled that in 2002 Lula cooperated with Cardoso on a difficult issue concerning the crisis in Venezuela.[201] Reuters and some of the other foreign media reported the thrust of my message. And the *Estado de São Paulo* came up with the headline 'Amorim blames Obama for impasse.'" Between this point and the end of 2008 there was no let-up in the rhythm of diplomatic activity: the South/Latin American "multi-summits" (Mercosur, UNASUR, CALC);[202] a bilateral visit to Brazil by Cuban president Raúl Castro; and meetings in Rio de Janeiro between Lula and Sarkozy, to which the latter came in the dual capacity of French and (temporary) EU president. On December 14, contemplating the long working days that still lay ahead of me before the end of the year, I lamented: "All of this would be less tiring if the Doha Round gave me something to celebrate."

The Round would appear again in my diary about six weeks later, because of the now traditional events in Davos at the end of January. The dominant theme there, of course, was the financial crisis. The discussions on the WTO took place in that context. During one of the panel discussions I referred to protectionism as a "contagious disease." My expression was quoted by various newspapers, and one of them, the *Boston Globe*, even elected it "phrase of the day." But, of course, my pronouncements on the theme were not limited to this *mot d'esprit*. I said the tendency we were witnessing was not merely "ad hoc protectionism," motivated by the need or desire to "shield" a specific sector of the economy. It was instead, I said, reminiscent of the kind of economic nationalism that had prevailed in the 1930s. I referred, without naming names, to recent statements by European leaders, such as "I will help the automobile industry as long as it invests in my country," and "[a certain bank] should not be lending money outside this country."[203] In another European country, I pointed out, the government had launched a campaign calling on consumers to "sell your old foreign cars and buy a new car [that is produced here]." Faced with such an approach, I asked during one of the discussions, could the developing countries really be expected not to react? And given that they did not have huge financial reserves to draw upon, the way the developing countries could react, I said, was by raising their tariffs. My main aim, in fact, was to challenge the importance attached to the so-called "monitoring" of tariff barriers erected by poor countries while the financial subsidies and the direct support practiced by the rich countries were ignored. In the various meetings that focused on the WTO, I emphasized that the member states should collectively still concentrate their efforts on trying to achieve a swift conclusion to the Doha Round. I was particularly critical of the idea, which was beginning to circulate, that guidelines (such as the so-called "sunset clauses")[204] were now needed in order to provide orientation about what kind of protectionist measures were "permitted" (i.e. which of them would be considered consistent with the norms of the WTO). On the one hand these guidelines could (and probably would) allow for a certain degree of "creative interpretation," which could entail limitations on the freedom of WTO members, especially the developing countries, to make use of their "policy space" (in this case the gap, in many instances quite considerable, between the bound tariff and the one actually applied). But on the other hand, paradoxically, they could actually encourage the use of protectionist measures, provided that they stayed within certain parameters. The argument that the Round needed to be concluded ended up prevailing in the Davos discussions, but did not have any positive practical consequences in the face of Kamal Nath's threat to "return to the Hong Kong text" (implying the abandonment of the conceptual advances made in the preceding two and a half years—and there had indeed been some) and the absence of the United States at the political level. Taking advantage of the forum that Davos provides, I took part in two symbolic acts: I signed, with Kamal, a joint statement on the wrongful seizure at Amsterdam airport of medicines from India that were being transported to Brazil;[205] and I had a quick meeting with Kamal and the South African trade minister, Mandisi Mpahlwa, aimed at relaunching the idea of a Mercosur-SACU-India agreement. The usual bilateral meetings (with the European trade commissioner, the Australian minister, and the WTO director-general) completed my trade-related commitments. I also participated in a working lunch entitled "Brazil: the new power broker," at which I was one of the keynote speakers. I began my speech by drawing attention to the title: "If this event had been taking place just a few years ago," I said, "it would have been called 'Brazil, the sleeping giant,' or at best, imitating Stefan Zweig, 'Brazil, country of the future.'"

By this point the pace of the discussions concerning the Doha Round had slowed considerably. In truth, they lacked concrete content. They had become what are known in the diplomatic jargon as mere "talks about talks." About a month later I gave President Sarkozy a letter from Lula that addressed several international issues ahead of the next G20 summit, due to take place in London. The ongoing financial crisis was one of the main topics. In that part of the letter, referring to the recrudescence of protectionism, Lula underlined the urgent importance of the Round. It was, he wrote, "crucial in order to increase market access for products from developing countries, especially the poorest countries." Lula did not neglect to mention that Sarkozy himself, during his visit to Brazil, had emphasized how important it was for the leaders themselves to participate in the "final" negotiations. In his letter the president also widened the focus of his arguments to cover the reform of global governance, a subject apparently dear to Sarkozy. The reference to Doha made clear that despite the Round having slipped into a state of lethargy, it was certainly not a dead issue as far as Brazil was concerned. In late March, Lula received a visit from Gordon Brown. In addition to the strictly financial topics (special drawing rights, revolving fund, resources for the IMF. etc.), Lula addressed the issue of protectionism, "criticized by all, but [widely] practiced, albeit covertly." He took advantage of the opportunity to emphasize the importance of resuming the negotiations, "because the poorest countries will be the ones most affected by the recession [and by a failure to conclude the Round]." Brown agreed with Lula on the importance of the Round and said he was determined to "convince the United States and India," but added that the new USTR appointed by Obama, Ron Kirk, seemed inclined to review the entire negotiation, disregarding the advances of the preceding years and starting again almost from scratch.[206] But, Brown said, if Washington were to accept the agreement on the existing basis, India would probably do so too, "because after April the [Indian general] election will be out of the way." But the British prime minister soon tempered these somewhat optimistic words with observations about the serious difficulties Obama was facing in Congress. I intervened in the discussion at this point to mention something Pascal Lamy had told me a few days earlier in Geneva. The WTO director-general had already spoken to the new USTR, I said, and it was indeed the case that Kirk intended to undertake a full review of the entire negotiation, which he had told Lamy would take "at least six months." I added that the "mistake" on the part of the US government was to treat the Doha Round and free trade purely as elements in a traditional commercial bargaining process, rather than as part of a countercyclical policy that would put the global economy back on its feet. Brown expressed the view that the Democrats would not approve the Round unless the issues of labor and environmental standards were introduced. I recalled the discussions regarding labor standards that I had taken part in at the Seattle Ministerial Conference in 2001, where initial indications of possible success were soon extinguished amid the general debacle. I said we should not reopen the negotiations with regard to the advances achieved prior to the July impasse. I added, however, that with regard to social issues, including labor rights, it might be possible to come up with a formula consisting of a separate declaration, without legal obligations but pointing the way forward to future understandings, rather like the model used in Marrakesh in relation to the environment.

During the previous weekend I had participated in a forum in Brussels entitled "How to make multilateralism work?" The main event was a discussion involving the president of the World Bank, my old interlocutor and sparring partner Bob Zoellick; the minister of state[207] in the UK's Foreign and Commonwealth Office, Mark Malloch-Brown; and the Commonwealth secretary-general (and former UN colleague of mine), Kamalesh Sharma. The subject was the financial crisis, but the questions from the moderator and the audience shifted the discussion toward the issues of trade and protectionism. The opinions Zoellick and I (and also the British minister) expressed were surprisingly convergent, reminiscent more of the cooperation between us at the time of the July Framework than the battles surrounding the FTAA. On the sidelines of the event I also spoke with the World Bank president about ways to increase South-South trade. Zoellick's thinking had evidently evolved a great deal, leading him to an appreciation of the importance of relations between developing countries.[208] We discussed the possibility of World Bank guarantees for South-South trade, which had been seriously affected by the credit crunch. The former USTR did not reject the idea but mentioned certain practical difficulties that he was "trying to get around." Also during my stay in Brussels, I paid a visit to the president of the European Commission, José Manuel Durão Barroso, who told me he continued to believe that the Round could be revived, and that Brazil's role was crucial. I could not help remembering the occasion when Durão Barroso had told me I was a "very tough" negotiator, and not meant it as a compliment. I would hear a similar description from another heavyweight interlocutor in Brussels, Javier Solana, the EU high representative for foreign affairs and security policy, but this time it was meant much more positively. After praising Brazil's foreign policy and President Lula's central position in its formulation and implementation, Solana referred to my own role and said: "Don't underestimate your own credibility and influence. People see you as a tough negotiator, but they respect you."

In the United States there was very little sign of any change in attitudes toward the Doha Round. At a meeting between Lula and Obama at the White House on March 14, the issue was addressed only in a superficial way. Reacting to President Lula's expression of hope regarding the resumption of the multilateral trade talks, the US president came up with a couple of vague comments and then gave the floor to his economic advisor, Larry Summers, a former collaborator of President Clinton. But Summers seemed to be stuck in a mental framework of old concepts dating from the end of the Uruguay Round and the launch of the FTAA, about fifteen years before. Not present on this occasion was the new USTR, Ron Kirk, whose appointment would be confirmed by the Senate shortly afterwards. My first contact with him would be in April, when I was in London for meetings parallel to the second G20 summit (the same day on which Obama said of Lula, "This is my man"). Kirk phoned me from Washington, basically as a gesture of courtesy, but during our conversation he also brought up the subject of the Round. Formerly the mayor of Dallas, Kirk was a friendly and extrovert African American with the air of a successful businessman. Our initial conversation was so relaxed that I allowed myself to give him a little piece of advice in reference to his *curriculum vitae* (the details of which he had been keen to tell me): "If you want to conclude Doha, use your experience as a politician more than your experience as a lawyer."

At this stage, because of the international financial crisis, the discussions with Sarkozy and his advisors on global governance, the first BRICs summit, and the recurring issues involving our neighbors, the space in my diary for the Doha Round was very limited. But in various speeches I made on global economic issues, including at the UN Conference on the World Financial and Economic Crisis and its Impact on Development, held in New York on June 26, I always made a point of mentioning the need to conclude the negotiations. It was this need that also took me to Paris for another meeting of the OECD, where the other attendees included Ron Kirk, Catherine Ashton, Rob Davies (the new South African trade minister; a white politician with a background in his country's old Communist Party); and Kamal Nath's replacement as India's trade minister, Anand Sharma (previously the minister of state[209] in the country's foreign ministry). Both in my short speech at the OECD and in brief comments I made during the traditional mini-ministerial at the Australian embassy, I emphasized the importance of not becoming sidetracked by new proposals that diverged from the texts that had been on the table the previous July in Geneva. Other countries, particularly the United States, revealed their intention to use the possible resumption of the negotiations in order to try to gain additional concessions. Ron Kirk, who came across as a politician with little patience for technical details, said he was willing to "go ahead" but did not specify under what conditions. The continued pressure on China, Brazil, and India led me to speak out against the singling out of those countries, which I described as totally unfair. The Australian embassy was located in a spacious penthouse with views of the Eiffel Tower. During the discussion there were numerous generic references to the importance of the WTO, mixed with reiterations of the difficulties and expressions of dissatisfaction with the texts that were the result of many years of painstaking work. It was as if some of the members of the WTO were reverting to their initial negotiating positions. Although the line-up of individuals was new, for me the meeting was like a flashback to the first mini-ministerials I had participated in, four or five years earlier, during which esoteric issues such as the AVEs emerged as seemingly insurmountable obstacles. I was overcome by an unpleasant sense of *déjà-vu*, which made me feel even more despondent.

The most significant indication that the Doha Round was no longer considered one of the leaders' primary concerns was its very low profile at the G8+5 summit in L'Aquila, Italy. My notes on the summit refer only to the issue of climate change (which effectively took over the summit, and the attention of the media) and Iran, which was the main topic in a meeting between Lula and Obama. The Round did make an appearance in the joint declaration,[210] and Lula alluded to it in one of his pronouncements. But in the years that Brazil had been participating in these summits, ever since Gleneagles in 2005, this was the first time the Round had been almost off the radar during the discussions. It was becoming increasingly clear that the world leaders, with few exceptions, now treated the Round like an old and very sickly person at a party: an inconvenient presence they preferred to ignore.

Only in September, at a WTO mini-ministerial convened by Anand Sharma, did I again devote some attention to the subject that had absorbed so much of my time over the previous ten years.[211] I already knew Sharma well. He was a mild-mannered and contemplative man. He always spoke very softly, as if he wanted to avoid giving the impression that he was trying to impose his point of view. It was certainly not the case, however, that he lacked convictions. His temperament and personality were very different from those of his agitated predecessor. In his previous capacity as deputy foreign minister, Sharma had represented his country at IBSA events in Brazil or South Africa (the foreign ministers themselves having been elderly men disinclined to embark on frequent long trips abroad). As for this particular mini-ministerial, I asked myself what might have motivated Sharma to convene it. Even at the height of the negotiations India had never been very proactive in terms of hosting meetings (staging just one G20 event, apart from the restricted G4/G6 occasions). My guess was that with the Indian elections out of the way, Sharma might now be thinking he could begin the negotiations "for real." He probably also wanted to erase the bad impression the majority of WTO members, including many developing countries, would have had after witnessing India's role in the disaster of July 2008. Although India's substantive positions were largely unchanged, there was at least a new style, and that in itself was positive. It would be difficult to disagree, however, that it was too little too late.

The first two days of my stay in India were devoted to an IBSA ministerial meeting (which was a success, with various projects underway) and bilaterals of a political nature with Indian officials including the new foreign minister, S. M. Krishna (the successor to Pranab Mukherjee, who had been appointed as finance minister and would later be elected as president, a high-profile though largely ceremonial role). The WTO mini-ministerial meeting in Delhi served to stimulate discussion of topics that had been dormant for a long time. The prevailing mood was one of caution, as no-one wanted to play the role of killjoy after the Indian minister's well-intentioned efforts to revive the talks about the Round (even if they were only "talks about talks"). Not wanting to be an exception to this general show of good behavior, I avoided leveling accusations at any of my fellow participants. I did make clear, however, that I saw no possibility of real progress in the negotiations while one country (I was referring to the United States) insisted on changing the balance of the July 2008 package (which, strictly speaking, had received some "retouches" from the group coordinators in Geneva at the end of 2008). Some of the ministers present, such as South Africa's Rob Davies and China's Chen Deming, openly agreed with me. Others (generally the representatives of the developed countries) seized upon the idea that a "horizontal" discussion, which would go beyond the "modalities" and include topics such as services and trade facilitation (an issue now resurfacing for the first time since Cancún), might prove so advantageous that it could bring the United States back to the negotiating table. Those who held this view also believed "adjustments" would be necessary in the approach to NAMA, particularly the introduction of more explicit references to "sectorials." Blunt, voluble Ron Kirk had little time for the fine details (although his confessed liking for the game of poker suggested a tactical mind behind the outer demeanor). Obama's USTR kept saying simply that the package in its present form would never be accepted by the US Congress. His position, expressed with blithe disregard for diplomatic subtleties, threw cold water over those in the room who believed a resumption of the negotiations in the short term was still possible. I myself was no longer one of them. My main hope at this stage was that at the next G20 summit, scheduled to take place in a few weeks' time in Pittsburgh, the principal leaders, especially Obama, would somehow be inspired to come up with something new. In the absence of any rational grounds for optimism, it seemed I was beginning to succumb to magical thinking.

In the interval between a courtesy visit to Prime Minister Manmohan Singh and a "restricted meeting" of the heads of delegation, some of us accepted an invitation to drinks at the official residence[212] of our restless former negotiating partner, Kamal Nath, in a very salubrious neighborhood in New Delhi. After failing in his bid to be elected as chief minister of Madhya Pradesh, Kamal was now minister for road transport and highways (a very specific portfolio that, as he himself told us, did not include India's vast railway network, which was the concern of a separate ministry). I do not know if Kamal's new role constituted a promotion, though quite possibly it had the potential to bring him votes in some future election. Kamal was relaxed and in very good humor, although I wondered if in general he was enjoying himself in his new position as much as he had done as trade minister. One thing was for sure, however: he now had fewer opportunities to create havoc on the international plane! Manmohan Singh, for his part, was very affectionate when I visited him with the other ministers. He held me by one arm and came very close to embracing me—which, given his reserved nature, was a significant demonstration of warmth, and one that did not go unnoticed by my fellow ministers. We exchanged friendly words and he hinted that he would soon resume the discussions with the leaders of Brazil and South Africa about the dates for the next IBSA summit, which had been postponed because of Singh's ill health. Anand Sharma also had the good idea of inviting Rob Davies and me for breakfast, which proved to be a propitious occasion. Besides offering the opportunity for the three countries to coordinate their positions ahead of mini-ministerial, it was useful in other respects. Sharma, Davies, and I agreed to further increase our efforts in the field of trilateral cooperation. At my suggestion we had a photograph taken together and issued a joint press release.

While in Delhi, Ron Kirk and I arranged that he would visit me in Brazil two weeks later. I still had some hope of convincing the USTR of the merits of taking the July 2008 package as a basis for resuming the Doha negotiations. Recalling the conversation between Lula and Gordon Brown, in which I had participated, I thought a "sweetener" in the form of a non-binding declaration on labor standards might help. But the timing was especially cruel. I had just told the press that within the next two weeks Brazil would prepare its list of retaliatory actions in the context of the cotton dispute with the US. If that schedule was maintained, the list might be announced just as the USTR arrived in Brazil. I wrote in my notebook: "For the sake of basic good manners I will have to extend that period." I knew from experience that if the situation was reversed, my US counterpart would not feel similarly constrained.[213] But let me return to the ministerial meeting in Delhi. As always, I tried to be as well prepared as possible from the technical point of view. One of my aides had informed me of a study by a highly reputable US research institution according to which, if the parameters of the previous year (the July 2008 package) were maintained, Brazil would be among the countries undergoing the greatest degree of opening to trade.[214] I did not fail to mention these figures at the meeting, but unfortunately I think they had little impact on the new USTR.

On September 17, Ron Kirk arrived at my office at Itamaraty in Brasilia. Extrovert and well practiced in rhetoric, the former mayor of Dallas, whose background was as a lawyer and politician, did not seem at ease in his new role. Kirk was not inclined to pore over minutiae and was impatient with WTO-style negotiations, full of acronyms and subtleties that are frequently incomprehensible. He was guided, above all, by political instinct. And his instinct seemed to be telling him that the proposed agreement that was on the table regarding the "modalities" would not be able to win the votes or the support of the US business sector. He had neither the strategic mind of Zoellick nor the inclination toward compromise shown by Rob Portman. Even though he appeared to have more political clout than Susan Schwab, he did not exhibit the determination of a true negotiator in pursuit of an agreement. In my brief notes about our meeting (which included a lunch in the Sala Bahia, the coziest and most pleasant of the dining rooms at Itamaraty), I wrote that despite our differences over the Doha Round and the cotton dispute, "rarely has a meeting with a USTR been so free of tensions." That was the case even though I also voiced Brazil's criticisms over the unfair treatment of our ethanol in the United States, where it was subject to double taxation. Kirk chose not to address any of the areas of conflict, instead concentrating on the proposal for a "new bilateral agreement" on economic cooperation. It was not clear to me if the USTR understood the limits imposed on bilateral trade agreements by Brazil's membership of the Mercosur customs union. Either way, I accepted the challenge of seeking some kind of understanding, perhaps a framework agreement that would facilitate reciprocal business missions and investment (without commitments with regard to rules, or any dispute-resolution mechanism). This would not be inconsistent with Mercosur. I stressed the latter point both to Kirk himself and the media, as I was acutely aware of the importance of not arousing distrust on the part of the other Mercosur members. My new interlocutor (the fourth USTR I had dealt with during the Lula government)[215] was obviously not interested in discussing the Round. As soon as the two of us were alone together, between the meeting in my office and lunch, I tried to raise the subject, hoping to explore some new idea that might enable us to think "outside the box." I suggested it might be useful to set aside the bolder US ambitions in NAMA and instead seek a political declaration that met the longstanding US demands (notably when the Democrats were in power) regarding labor standards (which I preferred to denominate as "social issues"). My reasoning was based on the fact that, with the progress Brazil had made in recent years on workers' rights, and the Lula government's prioritizing of social issues, the subject was no longer as sensitive for us as it had been in the past. Although misconceived ideas such as that of "social dumping"[216] could not be accepted, it would probably be possible to arrive at some kind of compromise, particularly as Brazil's business sector had begun complaining constantly about "unfair competition" from Chinese products made by workers receiving extremely low wages (or, worse, by child laborers or prisoners). To move in that direction it would obviously be necessary to change the political alliances that Kirk's Republican predecessors had established. It was a risky ploy, although perhaps it offered the prospect of rescuing the Round. But Kirk did not buy into my idea. I am not even sure he fully understood it. Our conversation was friendly, but nothing practical came out of it, apart from the somewhat vague commitment to seek a bilateral cooperation agreement that would boost trade and investment without damaging Mercosur.

"They are not well informed—they don't read the *Estado de São Paulo*"

Toward the end of 2009, my meetings and telephone conversations regarding the Doha Round became few and far between. The number of references to the subject in my notebook decreased accordingly. The next WTO ministerial conference, in Geneva at the end of November, was a low-key affair. During the preceding weeks my focus was mainly on the issue of the Iranian nuclear program and the bizarre situation of President Manuel Zelaya of Honduras, who had been deposed and expelled from the country but returned soon afterwards (possibly with the intention of provoking a popular uprising, which did not take place) and ended up taking refuge in the Brazilian embassy in Tegucigalpa. The WTO director-general had told me in the run-up to the Geneva conference that it would be "uneventful," and he was proved right. Indeed, compared with previous ministerial conferences, it was remarkably lacking in interest. I nevertheless took the opportunity to have some bilateral meetings (the most interesting of which was with Turkey's trade minister) and to convene, by now almost in ritual fashion, a meeting between the G20 and the other groups of developing countries. The G20 approved by consensus a document that would later serve as an inspiration for those other groups: a simple clarification of which countries were adversely affected by the paralysis of the negotiations and which were actually benefiting from the situation. The United States repeated its list of demands, again pointing the finger at the "big emerging nations," particularly China, India, and Brazil. In my speech, about half of which was improvised, I emphasized that it was unreasonable to expect the developing countries to make "additional concessions" unilaterally. Some of my audience inferred from my inclusion of the word "unilateral" that I thought further concessions could be made as long as there was reciprocity on the part of the developed countries. I saw no reason to deny that was the case.

On the margins of the WTO ministerial conference, in addition to the meetings of the developing countries, there were two other noteworthy events: the approval of the "modalities" of the São Paulo Round of the GSTP,[217] and the first ever SACU-Mercosur-India ministerial meeting. I took the opportunity to tease the developed countries by declaring to the media: "The North has ground to a halt but the South is moving." It was some small consolation. At this stage the leaders had not yet completely given up on concluding the Round. In a letter from Lula to Obama, dated November 26, there was a paragraph on the negotiations in the midst of other subjects such as Iran, Honduras, and climate change. In addition to a reference to the previously mentioned study about Brazil's significant degree of opening to trade, Lula urged Obama to work toward concluding the Round and to leave aside proposals that would only serve to unbalance the package and "do away with all the previous efforts." After that, the Round did not appear again in my notes before the end of 2009.

Curiously, my role in the Doha Round negotiations, from Cancún onward, was cited by the magazine *Foreign Policy* (or, more specifically, the journalist and author David Rothkopf) as one of the reasons for describing me in October 2009 as "the world's best foreign minister." This unexpected accolade did not go completely unnoticed by the Brazilian press, although it generated little comment. Shortly after Rothkopf had written the piece in question, a journalist from the conservative newspaper *O Estado de São Paulo* conducted a long interview with me on various aspects of foreign policy. At the end of the interview he asked me why, in my opinion, I had been accorded such high praise. I answered without hesitation: "It's because they [the editors of *Foreign Policy*] are not well informed—they don't read the *Estado de São Paulo*." The journalist later reproduced most of my answers to his questions with reasonable accuracy, but unsurprisingly chose to leave out that final comment.

Nothing indicates more clearly the Doha Round's retreat into the background than its almost total absence from my schedule in Davos at the end of January 2010. My commitments that month were dominated by other issues. Foremost among them was the humanitarian catastrophe in Haiti following the earthquake of January 12. A few days after the tragedy I had visited Port-au-Prince, much of the city reduced to rubble, and then traveled on to Montreal for a conference aimed at coordinating the humanitarian operations. Brazil had made a huge investment in Haiti in the financial, human, and indeed emotional sense. Eighteen Brazilians lost their lives in the earthquake. Most of them were military personnel, but they also included the deputy special representative of the UN secretary-general, Luiz Carlos da Costa (whom I had known well in my time at the UN), and the selfless humanitarian worker Zilda Arns. The agony of the families of the Brazilian victims was almost nothing alongside the brutal enormity of the cataclysm for the Haitian people. It was inevitable that Haiti would be my main focus in Davos. I took part in a round-table discussion aimed at coming up with new ideas about how to help the country (alongside, among others, former US president Bill Clinton), and a working dinner convened by the director of the World Food Programme. I took advantage of meetings on trade-related issues, such as the one convened by the Swiss minister Doris Leuthard, to emphasize the urgent need for measures—such as duty-free, quota-free market access—that would benefit the small but populous island, the only country in the Americas qualifying as a member of the Least Developed Countries (LDCs). During a brief stay in Paris on the way to Geneva and Davos, I announced to the director-general of UNESCO a contribution of $400,000 USD to an emergency education program in Haiti.

The other issues I focused on in January included disarmament (in Paris I attended an event organized by a private foundation, Global Zero) and Iran, which was a subject already looming large in my conversations with foreign ministers and leaders. Looking back, it is curious to see how I referred to the Round in my notebook following a conversation with Pascal Lamy in The Posthorn, a hotel in Davos where we were both staying: "As for Doha, a subject people [now] only refer to with a justified ironic smile, I have little to say. My conversation with Lamy . . . seemed to give [the director-general] some pointers ahead of the "stock-taking" scheduled for March. [On that occasion] Lamy will attempt to gather together the issues so that the leaders can take decisions at the next G20 summits [in 2010] (Toronto and Seoul). It's either that or nothing." My final comment was: "Everything will depend on Obama." Despite the almost total non-existence of new ideas, at least my friend Pascal seemed to have appreciated our conversation: "*Finalement, j'ai eu la chance d'une conversation agréable et utile*," he said.

In February I returned to Europe, this time to Madrid, for consultations with Catherine Ashton (no longer the EU trade commissioner, having been promoted to the role of High Representative for Foreign Affairs and Security Policy) and Miguel Angel Moratinos, the foreign minister of Spain, which at that time held the presidency of the European Council. The dominant themes were political, with the Iranian nuclear program at the center of our discussions. But we also spoke about the prospects for a resumption of negotiations between Mercosur and the European Union (given that the WTO was now in a state of paralysis). Almost a year earlier, on the margins of a meeting of Portuguese ambassadors in Lisbon, I had mentioned to Durão Barroso that a free trade agreement between the two regions had become more "attractive," since it had the potential, among other things, to "stir up" US interest in the Doha Round. During Barroso's time as Portuguese foreign minister, he and I had been the main proponents of a formal understanding between the two blocs in 1994. Later that year the Mercosur foreign ministers signed a memorandum with European Commission president Jacques Delors. At that time, the purpose as far as I was concerned was to construct a counterweight to the FTAA, the creation of which seemed inevitable. For Europe the main goal was not to "lose" South America (or its most dynamic part), in an economic sense, to the United States. Now, in 2010, the idea returned to me, but with the main purpose of luring the North American giant back to the multilateral trade negotiations. But I do not remember if I broached the subject exactly in those terms in my conversations with Ashton and Moratinos, or in a separate meeting with Prime Minister José Luis Rodríguez Zapatero.

My conversations with the Spanish prime minister and foreign minister left me with no illusions about the viability or indeed the usefulness of such an agreement at a moment when Europe's economies and governments were being ravaged by the crisis. The idea that there might be a political and financial conspiracy against European governments of the left or center-left arose in my dialogue with Zapatero, who pointed out to me that Goldman Sachs had denounced the "covering up" of economic data regarding the Greek economy, after having itself been complicit it that accounting maneuver. Moratinos was even more explicit, alleging there was a deliberate attempt underway to use financial speculation as a means of undermining Europe's socialist and social-democratic governments. The perpetrators, he said, "have names and addresses." Faced with such a bleak picture, even though I was being pressured by the Brazilian media to seek a trade deal with the Europeans, I asked myself in my notebook: "Will an agreement really be in Mercosur's interests when Europe is in such a debilitated state?" But I also asked: "Might the disenchantment with the euro make the Europeans less arrogant and dictatorial than in the past [perhaps offering better conditions for negotiations]?" But I soon concluded I would not feel at ease in conducting those negotiations, if indeed they came to be relaunched. Unlike in the Doha Round, where the gains arising from the cutting of agricultural subsidies would be very concrete, I could see no great benefits in an agreement with the Europeans in the current circumstances. My dialogues in Madrid were almost entirely political in nature; economic issues arose mainly as a background explanation for the crisis faced by the European governments with which, in theory, the Lula administration had most affinity. I suppose my brief musing about a bi-regional agreement probably had to do with the constant criticism from the Brazilian media and some business interests regarding our alleged abandonment of an agreement with Brussels and our supposedly ill-conceived "bet" on the WTO.

Over the following two months I hardly focused at all on the Doha Round or on any subject even loosely connected to it. I devoted my attention principally to Iran, the organization of the BRIC and IBSA "macro-summits" in Brasilia, and a trip to Washington for a meeting convened by Obama on nuclear security. For some reason (probably a trip to another South American country), however, the WTO director-general was in Brasilia on April 17, a Saturday. Lamy came to my office, where he was photographed with me and—curious premonition—Roberto Azevêdo, who was then still Brazil's permanent representative in Geneva but would later become the Frenchman's successor at the helm of the WTO. I also invited Lamy to my house, where we chatted about the main issues of the moment (from our perspective at least) such as the ongoing Brazil-US cotton dispute. And of course, eventually, we spoke a little about the Round. Lamy told me that "not much" could be achieved at the first G20 summit of the year, in Toronto in June, but that he still had "hopes" for the one afterwards, in Seoul in November. The latter summit, he pointed out, would be taking place after the US mid-term elections and also (though whether he said this out of conviction or politeness, I was not sure) after the presidential election in Brazil. However, he still thought it important that at the Toronto summit there should be some kind of declaration, "like at L'Aquila," in support of concluding the Round. I chose not to mention that the L'Aquila declaration had achieved precisely nothing. Before we parted, I parodied the restaurant reviews in the Michelin guides by playfully asking Lamy to evaluate the conversation we had just had: "*Est-ce qu'il vaut le détour*?" At some point during our meeting, Lamy spoke to the press. Asked what had brought him to Brasilia, my friend graciously said he had come to seek my "wisdom." Needless to say, the remark was not published.[218]

In September 2010, I went to Geneva for a meeting of the International Institute for Strategic Studies on regional and global security situation, an invitation that had arisen from my participation in the Tehran Declaration.[219] I was pleased to have the opportunity for yet another breakfast with Pascal

Lamy, this time at Mont-Riant. Amid the general skepticism the director-general was still committed to eliciting from the leaders some kind of gesture that would serve to push the Round forward. "Maybe Lula could say something in Seoul?" he suggested, a little hesitantly, as if a statement from the Brazilian president (who had not attended the Toronto summit and was about to leave office) would be sufficient to change the course of events. Of course the leading actor in this play was the US president. Interestingly, Obama—a Democrat, and therefore, one was entitled to expect, a supporter of multilateralism—was much less receptive to suggestions from a former labor union leader from the Third World than his Republican predecessor had been, although his public words of praise for Lula (which were not without an element of condescension) probably gave the opposite impression. I suggested to Lamy that, together with Zoellick and Kamal, we should write an article in support of the Round in the *International Herald Tribune*. After all, the four of us (plus the Australian Mark Vaile, who had disappeared from the political scene due to health problems) had been responsible for the July Framework, which in 2004 had relaunched the negotiations after the Cancún debacle. This was another idea that failed to get off the ground.

In the speech I gave on behalf of Brazil at the UN General Assembly (Lula had decided not to attend because of the forthcoming presidential election), amid references to the Tehran Declaration, the coup in Honduras, and climate change, I made sure I mentioned the international financial crisis and the risk of protectionism on the part of the rich countries. This was probably the last time I referred to the Doha Round in a global forum before I left office at the end of the year. I said the developed countries had not shown the necessary commitment to global economic stability, because they continued to "let themselves be guided by parochial interests." I added: "Nowhere is this more evident than in the Doha Round of negotiations in the WTO. A balanced solution to this negotiating process, which has lasted for almost ten years, would promote economic expansion and the development of the poorest countries. . . . After all, poor countries are the greatest victims of the narrow and selfish view that still prevails in international trade." Strong words of this kind were not usually heard from a minister of a moderate country such as Brazil. As expected, they had no effect.

"The rest is (not) history"

I would be tempted to end this narrative with the expression "the rest is history," were it not for the fact that "history" is probably too grand a word for the disjointed movements of the WTO during 2010. It was a year in which ambitions were lowered, if not altogether abandoned, and the emphasis was primarily on avoiding the kind of protectionist backsliding that becomes more attractive in times of recession. With the negotiations paralyzed,

Brazil would again come to measure the importance of the WTO in terms of the efficacy and fairness of its dispute settlement mechanism. We resorted to it in relation to the implementation of the panel on cotton. As the United States still refused to comply with the findings of the panel, which had been ratified by the WTO Dispute Settlement Body (DSB), Brazil requested authorization to take retaliatory measures. The details are worth describing. Brazil decided to make use of an option that had been made available, in certain circumstances, by the Marrakech Agreements.[220] We sought and obtained authorization to suspend the privileges the United States enjoyed under the TRIPS Agreement, which involves sensitive areas such as patents and copyrights (and thereby powerful US lobbies such as the pharmaceutical laboratories and the Motion Picture Association). In the event, the mere threat of retaliation was sufficient. Although not complying fully with the DSB decisions, the US backed off and became more amenable to a solution that Brazil regarded as partially satisfactory.[221]

This episode illustrates how provisions desperately pursued by certain countries can sometimes backfire. Ironically, during the Uruguay Round it was the developed countries—especially the United States—that had insisted on the possibility of this kind of "retaliation," as they wanted to give "teeth" to the provisions of the new agreements on TRIPS and services (i.e. guarantee their enforceability) by being able to take punitive measures in the area of goods, which was much more sensitive for developing countries. The developing countries resisted this new instrument as much as they could, but by late 1991 it was clear that the inclusion of cross-retaliation was inevitable.[222]

At the end of 2010, Lula's second term of office came to an end, and so did my time at the helm of Itamaraty. I left the stage and from that point onward became merely a spectator, watching the drama unfold from the gallery. And in the Doha Round the drama (or the comedy) seemed now to be taking place in slow motion. In 2013 the WTO came "under new management" following the election of the intelligent and skillful Brazilian diplomat Roberto Azevêdo to the position of director-general when Pascal Lamy's second term came to an end. That same year, the renewed efforts to revive the negotiations would culminate in the so-called "Bali Package." This time the WTO members preferred not to face the asperities of the negotiations that would have been necessary in order to reach an ambitious, wide-ranging agreement. They decided instead to focus primarily on a specific issue (trade facilitation), complemented by political understandings (subject to posterior negotiations) with regard to other areas, including agriculture. Time will tell if this route is more promising than the one that had been pursued before the "great failure" of July 2008. The biggest question, in my view, is whether this new, piecemeal approach can deliver on the objectives that originally inspired the Doha Development Agenda.

As for Brazil, the mental, physical, and political efforts we made in pursuing a successful conclusion to the Doha Round were not motivated only by the prospect of economic benefits, although potentially they were very significant. We were also seeking to strengthen the WTO by providing it with solid foundations consisting of fairer relations between its members. Our profound conviction was that development—not only free trade—needed to be recognized as one of the essential pillars of a more equal and cohesive world order. Our efforts stemmed from a world view that was also reflected in many other aspects of the foreign policy pursued by the two governments of President Lula—from the creation of UNASUR to our embrace of other continents and regions, such as Africa and the Arab world. Our endeavors also included the attempt to reform the UN Security Council, and the creation of groups such as the BRICs and IBSA. All these initiatives were inspired by the conception of a world order less subject to hegemony and areas of influence; an order in which unilateral actions (in trade or in the use of military force) become increasingly rare, and in which nations can base their relations on balanced and predictable rules that are not imposed by any single country (or group of countries) but agreed multilaterally.

Though I continue to reject the accusation, often heard during the Lula years, that our initiatives on the world stage were "ideological," I would freely admit that they were to some degree utopian. Then again, if politics is not to be limited to the raw pursuit of narrow self-interest, utopias are indispensable. Without them we are inevitably consigned to role of mere spectators, watching the unfolding of history without ever helping to write it.

September 2014[223]

NOTES

1. Not to be confused with the G20 of major economies, a grouping that first acquired its present high profile in the aftermath of the 2008 financial crisis and has held annual summits since then. The G20 that emerged in the context of the WTO negotiations consists of developing countries that have a particularly strong interest in the issue of trade in agricultural products. Its creation, at the WTO Ministerial Conference in Cancún in 2003, is described in my book *Breves narrativas diplomáticas*, available in Portuguese (Benvirá, 2013) and Spanish (Taeda, 2014).

2. This episode, and other aspects of the Doha Round, are covered in my book *Conversas com jovens diplomatas*, published in Portuguese (Benvirá, 2011).

3. The Potsdam and Geneva conferences, in 2007 and 2008 respectively, are covered in *Conversas com jovens diplomatas*. The WTO negotiations of 2003–04 are described in *Breves narrativas diplomáticas*.

4. The "July Framework" (2004) refers to an understanding on the basic elements of the agricultural negotiations. Initially agreed by the US, the EU, Brazil, India, and Australia (known as the "Five Interested Parties" or FIPS), it was subsequently endorsed by the WTO Council.

5. Although a relatively small country, New Zealand was an active participant in the agricultural negotiations. Its permanent representative in Geneva, Tim Groser (later to become

trade minister), was the chairman of the WTO committee on agriculture at the time of the July Framework.

6. The Cairns Group was formed during the Uruguay Round, at a meeting in the Australian city from which it gets its name. It is composed of countries with a particular interest in increasing their agricultural exports. Australia coordinates the group. The role of the Cairns Group in the MTN was to some extent overshadowed by the creation of the G20.

7. Regarding Japan's participation, I must mention a remark made during a visit to Brasilia by a group of Japanese parliamentarians. One of them said to one of my colleagues: "Please explain something to me. In international trade, Japan is big, Brazil is small. In the WTO, Brazil is big, Japan is small. How is that possible?"

8. Amorim, Celso. *Breves narrativas diplomáticas* (Chapter 4).

9. In 1973, Ulysses Guimarães, the leader of the "tolerated opposition," presented his candidature for the presidency of Brazil. He knew he was sure to lose, as the election was going to take place by means of an electoral college controlled by the military. However, his campaign opened the way for the landslide victory by the Movimento Democrático Brasileiro (MDB) in the parliamentary elections of 1974, generally considered a milestone in the slow process of Brazilian redemocratization.

10. It was thanks to the active interest on the part of Yeo, as Singapore's foreign minister, that on August 22, 2007, I was able to organize a breakfast meeting of Mercosur and ASEAN ministers on the sidelines of a meeting of the Forum for East Asia-Latin America Cooperation (FEALAC). Another, similar meeting took place in Brasilia in November 2008.

11. The conversation is described in detail at the end of the third chapter of *Breves narrativas diplomáticas*.

12. A more detailed explanation of these "boxes" appears both in *Conversas com jovens diplomatas* and *Breves narrativas diplomáticas*.

13. Note that the Special Safeguard Mechanism is often referred to (including in WTO documents) as "Special Safeguard Measures." I have opted to use the former denomination throughout the narrative.

14. NAMA refers to all products not covered by the Agreement on Agriculture. In other words, in practice, it includes manufactured goods, fuels, mining products, fish and fish products, and forestry products. In practice, manufactured goods (often referred to in the narrative, a little imprecisely, as "industrial goods") were the main focus of the NAMA negotiations.

15. Trade facilitation had been one of four topics of particular interest to the developed countries. The other three (investment, government procurement, and competition policy) were abandoned in the wake of the revolt by developing countries at the Cancún Ministerial Conference in 2003.

16. The circumstances of my meeting with Zoellick in Davos are described in some detail in *Breves narrativas diplomáticas*, in the chapter on the FTAA. What I gathered from my discussion with him, essentially, was that even if we had made the concessions Washington was seeking in the area of intellectual property, we would not have obtained the market opening we were seeking for our agricultural goods (particularly sugar).

17. I had appointed Adhemar Bahadian, Brazil's consul general in Buenos Aires, as Brazil's "senior official" for the FTAA negotiations. In this capacity he was, together with Peter Allgeier, co-chair of the negotiating group at sub-ministerial level.

18. The dispute is described in some detail in a footnote at the end of the third chapter of *Conversas com jovens diplomatas*.

19. Bob Zoellick left office on February 22, 2005. Rob Portman took over as USTR on May 17.

20. The European Commission (EC) is the executive body of the European Union (EU), and in that capacity takes charge of trade negotiations.

21. The Organization for Economic Cooperation and Development (OECD) essentially comprises developed countries, joined in recent decades by some developing countries such as Mexico, Chile, and South Korea. Some "emerging" countries are often invited to the OECD's annual meeting, and their representatives have the opportunity to address the gathering. At the meeting in 2005, I highlighted the importance of agriculture—in particular the need to address agricultural subsidies—for the success of the Doha Round. I also spoke about the AVEs issue.

It was also on that occasion that the new USTR, Rob Portman, referred to agriculture as the "engine" of the Round, repeating the expression I had used in Mombasa.

22. An informal mechanism of Latin American and Caribbean countries, created in the 1980s. See also note 13 in the narrative on Brazil and the Middle East.

23. The United Nations Conference on Trade and Development, established in 1964.

24. At a critical moment in the negotiations between Mercosur and the European Union, in 2004, I attended a meeting at the Federation of Industries of the State of São Paulo (FIESP) at which it was very clear that, as well as dissatisfaction with the EU's offers on agriculture, much of the Brazilian industrial sector had significant fears regarding the EU's demands in the area of manufactured goods. Unlike the current version of what happened during those negotiations, which is that they "stalled" due to unwillingness on the part of Itamaraty or inflexibility on the part of Argentina, the real reason for the deadlock was the paucity of the EU's offer on agriculture.

25. Given that Brazil was part of a customs union with the other Mercosur countries, negotiations aiming at trade liberalization had to be conducted jointly with them. This circumstance would become another cause for complaint on the part of some sectors of our industry, and a constant target for criticism by the Brazilian media, based on the mistaken idea that Brazil was being held back by its partners.

26. That meeting—a "compressed" mini-ministerial, organized every year by Australia—was the one in Paris that I mentioned earlier, which produced nothing very significant apart from the agreement on AVEs.

27. The Bharatiya Janata Party (BJP), founded in 1980, is an Indian political party with Hindu nationalistic tendencies. In elections held during April and May 2004, the BJP lost power. Prime Minister Atal Bihari Vajpayee was succeeded by Manmohan Singh of the Congress Party. Ten years later the BJP would return to power under the leadership of Narendra Modi.

28. The General Agreement on Tariffs and Trade (GATT) was created in 1947. Its scope was limited basically to trade in goods. Toward the end of the Uruguay Round the "contracting parties" of the GATT agreed to create a new and broader international organization, the WTO.

29. The "Millennium Round" was proposed by European commissioner Leon Brittan. The idea was essentially to address in a broader context the negotiations previously "mandated" by the Marrakesh Agreement on agriculture and services. In theory that would facilitate concessions on the part of the European Union with regard to agricultural trade.

30. TRIPS is the acronym for Trade-Related Aspects of Intellectual Property Rights; TRIMs refers to Trade-Related Investment Measures. There were agreements on both during the Uruguay Round. "Implementation" is an "umbrella" category that arose from the implementation (or lack thereof) of decisions adopted during the Uruguay Round. Many of these issues were of special interest to developing countries. Although the implementation issue aroused great controversy in the run-up to Seattle, it lost much of its political appeal during later negotiations.

31. There had of course been previous attempts at coordination among developing countries, including in the GATT era. One example was the initiative led by Ambassador Paulo Nogueira Batista, along with representatives of India and Yugoslavia, at the time of the launching of the Uruguay Round. But its scope and impact, in practice, were more limited.

32. There was never any effective coordination within the G20 on the issues of NAMA and services, but the interconnections between the different areas of the Doha Round negotiations meant it was important for the ministers from the developing countries to at least communicate informally on those issues. Those conversations allowed me to "take the pulse" of the various delegations, which in turn helped me to conduct the discussions in smaller groups.

33. Mackintosh-Smith, Tim. *The Hall of a Thousand Columns* (John Murray, 2006).

34. More idealistic still was the IBSA meeting that also took place earlier that day in Delhi, at which discussions regarding a trilateral free-trade agreement were initiated.

35. The Brazilian Network for the Integration of Peoples (REBRIP), created in 1998, is a network of NGOs, labor unions, social movements, and associations carrying out work connected with regional integration and trade. REBRIP was especially active in the FTAA and Doha Round negotiations.

36. In the GATT and then later the WTO, the group formed by the four largest developed economies (the United States, the European Union, Japan, and Canada) played a central role in monitoring the negotiations. Most of the issues brought to broader forums were "pre-negotiated" by this so-called "Quad." From 2004, and especially in 2005, this role was exercised by the G4, composed of the US, the EU, Brazil, and India.

37. Although our proposal focused on tariff reductions to be made by developed countries, there would be an implicit impact on the developing countries because they would have to take the concessions by the developed countries as the basis for their own tariff reductions (even if with a moderating factor).

38. "*Tout flatteur vit aux dépens de celui qui l'écoute.*"

39. The emphasis on "disciplines" was meant to avoid maneuvers by the rich countries that would reduce the size of the reductions to their domestic support. These maneuvers (or manipulations) included "box shifting" and "product shifting." The former essentially consisted of moving the subsidies from one box to another (e.g. from the amber to the blue box). The latter involved transferring the financial support from one product to another. In both cases the rich countries would potentially thwart the objective of the reduction while still being able to say they had complied with their overall commitment.

40. The G33 is a group of developing countries concerned with the impact of trade liberalization on their own agricultural production. It is formally led by Indonesia but strongly influenced by India. The G90 is an alliance of developing countries that includes members of the African Union, the African, Caribbean and Pacific Group (ACP), and the Least Developed Countries (LDCs). The G90 emerged as a strong grouping at the Cancún Ministerial Conference in 2003.

41. Technical proposals were produced by the permanent representatives of the G20 countries in Geneva after the Bhurban meeting. They were adopted by the G20 ministers following an informal mini-ministerial ("Flüela Group") convened by the United States in Zurich on October 10, 2005.

42. I am grateful to my aide Antonio Simões for his precise recollection of the quote, which he mentioned in the context of the visit to Brazil by President Bush. The visit took place shortly after the Summit of the Americas in Mar del Plata, the occasion on which the FTAA was effectively buried.

43. This notebook entry reveals a near-obsessive anxiety about my imagined lack of technical expertise. Somehow I must have been able to get by, however, because Peter Mandelson, himself one of the most combative negotiators, remarked in his book *The Third Man* (Harper Press, 2010) that I had an irritatingly detailed knowledge of the dossiers. His exact words were: "The Brazilian foreign minister lived up to his international reputation for having a tough, and sometimes emotional, negotiating style, coupled with a forensic grasp of his brief."

44. The Farm Bill is a comprehensive piece of legislation approved by the US Congress every five years on average. Its provisions on the subsidies (domestic support) proved to be one of the most contentious issues in the different phases of the negotiations. The Farm Bill in force in 2005 had been passed in 2002.

45. Before becoming USTR, Rob Portman had served as a congressman for Ohio.

46. India advocated greater openness in the market for services, especially in so-called "Mode 4," the category in which persons of one WTO member are present in the territory of another for the purpose of providing a service. Indian interest in services, especially outsourcing (e.g. telecommunications and IT), has increased in recent years.

47. The meeting was attended by the ministers responsible for trade issues in the governments of Australia, Brazil, Canada, China, Egypt, the European Union, India, Hong Kong, Japan, Kenya, South Korea, Malaysia, Rwanda, South Africa, and the United States.

48. From time to time the United States resuscitated groups whose composition best served their interests at that particular moment. This was the case both with the Flüela Group and the FIPS.

49. Permanent representatives to international organizations (such as the WTO in Geneva and the UN in New York) normally also have the more formal title of "ambassador." Throughout this book the two terms are used interchangeably.

50. The concept of "sensitive products" referred to agricultural goods that had not been subject to tariff cuts in the Uruguay Round. The very limited market access the developed countries (especially the members of the European Union and members of the so-called G10, which included Japan, Switzerland, and Norway) were offering with regard to these products was limited to quotas under the heading of "minimum access." How to broaden that access was one of the most difficult issues to arise during the entire Doha Round. It occupied ministers' attention particularly in the run-up to the Potsdam meeting in 2007.

51. The term "safeguards" refers to a mechanism—permitted by the old GATT and, with some restrictions, by the WTO—through which a country protects its market from the "disruption" that would be caused by a surge of imports in circumstances *other than* the use of unfair trade practices (e.g. dumping, or subsidies) by the exporting country. It is natural that in a customs union purporting to bring about deeper economic integration, such trade-restrictive measures are not permitted.

52. The treaty through which Mercosur was founded in 1991.

53. In the context of Mercosur, "asymmetries" refers essentially to the differences in levels of development between member countries. The Mercosur Structural Convergence Fund (FOCEM), which became operational in 2006, is aimed at financing infrastructure projects in the smaller economies and less developed regions of the bloc. The creation of the fund, to which Brazil makes a more than proportional contribution, was one of the ways we found to placate the grievances of Uruguay and Paraguay about differential treatment.

54. The cotton dispute between Brazil and the United States is described in some detail in a footnote in Chapter 3 of *Conversas com jovens diplomatas*. The sugar dispute pitched Brazil (together with Thailand and Australia) against the European Union with regard to the latter's export subsidies for its sugar industry.

55. The Chamber of Foreign Trade (CAMEX) is composed of the Minister for Development, Industry, and Trade (who coordinates its activities), the presidential chief of staff, the foreign minister, the finance minister, the Minister for Agriculture, Livestock and Supply, the Minister for Planning, Budget and Management, and the Minister for Agrarian Development.

56. My pun was taken up by the Brazilian economist Paulo Nogueira Batista Jr. in an article entitled "Commercial Geometry," published in the *Folha de São Paulo* on July 13, 2006. Batista Jr. referred to a hypothetical "Amorim's triangle," which would represent a more favorable outcome for Brazil. He was skeptical about the chances of such an outcome being achieved, however.

57. A "bound" tariff is one that a country formally commits to during negotiations. It becomes a legal obligation for the country subsequently to adhere to the bound tariff. An "applied" tariff is one that is currently in place: it can be (and frequently is) lower than the bound tariff.

58. According to our calculations, corroborated by the US and Australian technicians, the average cut in European tariffs would have been between 38 and 39%. According to the EC, the reduction would have been 46%, much closer to that sought by the G20 (54%).

59. Although it was taken for granted that developing countries should receive more favorable treatment with regard to tariff cuts, it was still the case that the smaller the cuts on the part of the developed countries in the area of agriculture, the lower would be the starting point from which to calculate the concessions to be made by the developing countries. India, therefore, always concerned with protecting its not very efficient agricultural sector, had a vested interest in avoiding significant tariff reductions on the part of the developed countries.

60. Press Release on the WTO Doha Round: Letters from President Luiz Inácio Lula da Silva (25/10/2005). *Resenha de Política Exterior do Brasil*, no. 97, 2005.

61. See the narrative on Brazil and the Middle East.

62. The Generalized System of Preferences was designed to allow developing countries to have privileged access to developed countries' markets on a non-reciprocal basis, so as to facilitate their economic growth. Under the GSP, developed countries—including the members of the EU, the US, Switzerland, Canada, Norway, and Japan—granted preferential tariff treatment to some products from developing countries.

63. The concept of anti-concentration was developed by the Brussels technicians as a way of restricting the use of the flexibilities that had been negotiated by the developing countries when

it came to reducing their industrial tariffs. The European aim, in essence, was to prevent developing countries from shielding entire industrial sectors (automobile production, for example) from tariff cuts.

64. Although reasonably familiar with the calculations of the potential impacts of tariff reductions when different coefficients were applied, I would find it difficult to explain what exactly the "coefficient of 30" signified, in mathematical terms, in accordance with the so-called "Swiss Formula" for NAMA. Indeed, these numbers were a source of much confusion. From conversations with heads of government I could tell that the coefficient was frequently taken to denote a tariff ceiling that would be applied generically to all tariffs, or as a percentage reduction. Perhaps this confusion stemmed entirely from the intrinsic complexity of the issue, though the possibility cannot be discounted that negotiators also sometimes made deliberate use of the lack of clarity in order to defend their own positions.

65. Brazil was not alone in criticizing the inadequacy of the European offer. In a study presented to Congress, the US government stated that: "The EU's 'level of ambition' in market access does not reach that of the G-20 or the United States. A major criticism of EU's agricultural proposal is the fact that [it does not] provide an inducement for developing countries such as Brazil, Thailand, or other G-20 members to make concessions in non-agricultural market access or services." *CRS Report for Congress: WTO Doha Round: Agricultural Negotiating Proposals* (November 9, 2005).

66. The Common Agricultural Policy (CAP), introduced in 1962, comprises a system of agricultural subsidies and other programs. It has undergone several changes over the years, aimed mainly at reducing its cost.

67. Roughly speaking, the coefficient of 30 meant, in Brazil's case, that if there were no flexibilities, the tariffs on the most sensitive products would be reduced from 35 to 16%, a considerable change. But applying the flexibilities provided for developing countries in the model favored by Brazil (reduction by half in the case of 10% of the tariff items), this 19% decrease would become a 9.5% decrease. The tariff on imported motor vehicles, for example, would be reduced from 35 to 25.5%.

68. The Itaipu hydroelectric dam, on the border between Brazil and Paraguay, near the Iguazu Falls, was a major project developed during the years of military government in Brazil. The initial agreement for its construction was made in 1973. Itaipu became operational in 1984, and at the time was the largest hydroelectric dam in the world. It has since given rise to several disputes concerning, for example, the price Brazil paid for the use of that part of the energy that belongs to Paraguay, the value of the debts the binational company Itaipu Binacional owes to Brazil, and whether or not Paraguay has the right to sell energy to third countries.

69. One of the flagships of Brazilian policy aimed at South American integration, the CASA was formally established in 2004. Later, in 2008, it evolved into UNASUR. Every country in South America is a member of UNASUR (as was also the case with the CASA).

70. The Iguazu agreements, signed by presidents José Sarney of Brazil and Raúl Alfonsin of Argentina, marked the political rapprochement between Brasilia and Buenos Aires in the context of the democratization of both countries following the years of military rule. The agreements became a cornerstone of Brazil-Argentina relations and led ultimately to the creation of Mercosur.

71. His reply, if I remember rightly, was: "You are so rude, Celso!" It is possible, therefore, that my choice of words had been slightly abrasive.

72. See note 46.

73. The G4 plus Japan and Australia.

74. The reader may be slightly confused by the use the terms G7 and G8. Essentially, the G8, which included Russia, dealt with broad political questions. The G7, which comprised the largest market economies, was focused on questions of an economic nature. In this case, given that Russia had not yet acceded to the WTO, the G7 was the relevant group. Even so, there were often gray areas. For example, as I describe later in this narrative, during a G8+5 summit in Saint Petersburg, President Putin chaired a meeting on trade!

75. On one occasion, in explaining to President Lula the position of India on agriculture, I remember I came up with a comparison: "Try to imagine an enormous Ministry of Agrarian Development."

76. For Brazil, this was a small but highly symbolic concession. Calculations at the time indicated that our total annual trade with the LDCs was slightly less than $1 billion USD, of which Brazilian imports accounted for only $30 million. The later attempts to apply DFQF unilaterally were unsuccessful because of resistance from the industrial lobby in Congress, in spite a political commitment on the part of President Lula at an UNCTAD meeting of in Accra in 2008.

77. During more than one period when I was permanent representative to the United Nations (in New York and Geneva), I dealt with disarmament issues, including the implementation of Article VI of the Treaty on the Non-Proliferation of Nuclear Weapons (NPT), which concerns the total elimination of those weapons. Later, when dealing with the Doha Round, a parallel inevitably formed in my mind between that goal and the elimination of export subsidies. Though I knew the comparison was somewhat far-fetched, the attempt to set a "final date" for the abolition of those most trade-distorting of all subsidies nevertheless had a certain symbolic value, as well as proving useful in practical terms.

78. The biggest conceptual gain in relation to reductions in overall domestic support was the consolidation of the term "effective cuts," which helped do away with the idea that the reductions might be limited to those that, in the jargon of the WTO, would merely be "cutting water." The latter referred to reductions in the overall *permitted* amount of subsidies and did not necessarily lead to reductions in the subsidies *currently in place* at the time of the agreement.

79. The G10, a group formed in the context of the discussions on agriculture, had what could be described as a protectionist bent. It was composed of Bulgaria, Taiwan, South Korea, Iceland, Israel, Japan, Liechtenstein, Mauritius, Norway, and Switzerland.

80. This episode is described, with more grace than I could ever manage, by Paul Blustein in his book *Misadventures of the Most Favored Nations: Clashing Egos, Inflated Ambitions, and the Great Shambles of the World Trade System* (Public Affairs, 2009). It is one of the few genuinely readable books on the subject of the Doha Round.

81. The text of the declaration reads: ". . . 6. 6. We agree to ensure the parallel elimination of all forms of export subsidies and disciplines on all export measures with equivalent effect to be completed by the end of 2013. This will be achieved in a progressive and parallel manner, to be specified in the modalities, so that a substantial part is realized *by the end of the first half* of the implementation period." (My italics.)

82. The Brazilian Agricultural Research Corporation (Embrapa), founded in 1973, is a world leader in its field. One of its main achievements was to produce a variety of soybean that would grow in the tropics. It also played an important role in researching different varieties of cotton that would be more resistant to plagues.

83. The Southern African Development Community (SADC) is an intergovernmental organization that seeks to encourage cooperation and social and economic integration among its fifteen member countries, which include South Africa, Angola, Mozambique, Namibia, Tanzania, Zambia, Botswana, and Zimbabwe.

84. China's trade minister, Bo Xilai, came across as a strong personality, very aware of his influential position in the power structure. It that respect he was unlike the Chinese foreign ministers I had come into contact with, who were mostly career diplomats and behaved more like typical bureaucrats. The son of one of the leaders of Chinese revolution, Bo was often depicted as being representative of the more orthodox tendency in the Communist Party that still followed the teachings of Mao Tse-tung. But that certainly did not tally with my impression of him, which was based partly on his conduct in the WTO. He struck me as being genuinely committed to the process of opening China to trade and to the ongoing process of integrating the country into the global economy.

85. One example was an article in the French newspaper *La Tribune* on December 19, 2005, which emphasized my role in forming "an eclectic coalition, a group of developing countries that denounced the developed nations' contempt for the poor." The article ended with a quote from a French diplomat, according to whom: "It is ironic that the [Brazilian] minister managed, by himself, through his declarations, to save the United States and demonize the European Union. [The EU], he said, 'does not run the world,' and 'should understand that it needs to adapt to the rest of the world, not the other way round.'"

86. Rossi, Clóvis. "*O homem de Estado*" (*Folha de São Paulo*, December 18, 2005).

87. A forum created upon the initiative of Tony Blair and New Labour (with Peter Mandelson as one of the initial driving forces), the Progressive Governance Network was aimed at bringing together socialist and social-democratic leaders of both developed and developing countries. Lula had already participated in one of its meetings during a visit to London. The countries invited to the meeting in South Africa in February 2006 were: Argentina, Brazil, Canada, the Czech Republic, Chile, Ethiopia, Hungary, New Zealand, Poland, South Africa, South Korea, Spain, Sweden, and the UK. The WTO director-general also attended.

88. The setting for the breakfast discussion of the Doha Round would be the Didimala Game Lodge in the South African savannah about an hour and a half from Johannesburg, the venue chosen to host the summit. Although originally conceived as a forum for leaders, on this occasion, given the subject of the breakfast discussion, it included other interlocutors such as Mandelson, Lamy, and me. Nothing very significant happened. But, as on so many other occasions, the discussion helped maintain the overall political momentum. The same could be said of the bilateral meeting that took place between Lula and Blair, at which the EU trade commissioner and I were also present.

89. Among the audience was one of the world's most famous Brazilian writers, the best-selling author Paulo Coelho. I can only suppose he was there in support of his compatriot.

90. As previously mentioned, the assumption was that the flexibilities in the use of the formula would be restricted to 5% of the total tariff lines (in the case of full use of the formula) or 10% of the total (if the flexibility was limited to 50% of the reduction resulting from the application of the formula). In that way, even some of the products considered "sensitive" would have to undergo tariff reductions to some extent.

91. The reduction by formula on the part of the European Union and other developed countries, although modified by the system of bands, would impact upon the reductions made by the developing countries, even though the latter (due to the principles of special and differential treatment) would always be smaller. Obviously I did not take into account the opposite effect of the special products (SP) and the Special Safeguard Mechanism (SSM), which would be among the principal causes of the impasse of July 2008.

92. "Disciplines" refers to measures aimed at preventing the practices through which countries would significantly reduce or nullify the impact of tariff cuts by tampering with the numbers or with types of subsidies. The most common practices of this kind were known in the WTO as "box shifting" and "product shifting." See also note 39.

93. According to the WTO glossary, the terms "Special Safeguard Measures" and "Special Safeguard Mechanism" are used to describe precisely the same type of proposed mechanism.

94. The WTO's glossary describes geographical indications as "place names (or words associated with a place) used to identify products (for example, 'Champagne,' 'Tequila,' or 'Roquefort') that have a particular quality, reputation or other characteristic because they come from that place."

95. The second wife of Prince Charles, the eldest child and heir apparent of Queen Elizabeth II.

96. Curiously, a "sherpa" is not only a Nepalese mountain guide and porter, but also a personal representative of a head of state or government who does the work of preparing the items to be discussed at a forthcoming summit. The term is used most frequently in the context of G8 summits.

97. Carlton Gardens, a building in central London belonging to the British Crown, is where Charles de Gaulle had his headquarters during the Second World War. It is also the official residence of the British foreign secretary, although the recent occupants of that position have tended to use the building only for meetings and other engagements. During my first visit to London as foreign minister, under President Itamar Franco, I was received at Carlton House by Douglas Hurd, foreign secretary under Prime Minister John Major.

98. Although I seem to have made very few notes with regard to the Copacabana Palace meeting, I recall that the European trade commissioner was particularly anxious to obtain concessions from Brazil in the form of tariff reductions on industrial goods. In his aforementioned memoirs *The Third Man*, Mandelson states that at the time of the Copacabana Palace meeting he was concerned about how much emphasis Tony Blair was putting on CAP reform. According to Mandelson, the effect of the British prime minister's approach was to "encourage

the Brazilians . . . to hold back on any serious move regarding their tariff barriers, thinking they could squeeze yet more out of me."

99. In the South American context, "confusion" referred principally to a looming crisis in our relations with Bolivia over the issue of natural gas. But there were also other issues that were causing me concern: the dispute between Argentina and Uruguay over the *papeleras*; the always unpredictable attitudes of our friend Hugo Chávez; and Paraguay's eternal complaints (some of them justified) with regard to the Itaipu power plant. I must admit I cannot remember what European political "confusion" I was referring to.

100. Given the complex details of trade negotiations, this kind of misapprehension was not uncommon. This left a lot of room for ministers and experts (not only senior but also middle-echelon ones) to find ways of imposing the views of the interest groups they had links to.

101. Schwab's past experience held a certain symbolic significance for veterans of the GATT. Given the great technical complexity of the negotiations in area of textiles, the term "textile negotiator" was used more broadly to describe someone who had an extensive knowledge of the details but did not necessarily possess a broader vision of the political context.

102. I am sure the efforts were mutual.

103. The Trade Promotion Authority (TPA) is a legal instrument by which the US Congress authorizes the Executive to negotiate trade agreements. Those agreements would then be approved or rejected as a whole, rather than being subject to amendments. This procedure was also known as "fast track." The TPA then in place was due to expire in 2007, which in theory put a time limit on the ability of the Executive to accept an agreement in the context of the Doha Round. This factor could be used (as it had been in the past) by the US to try to force through deals that were favorable to Washington.

104. The G4 will be familiar to readers by now. The G5, with the inclusion of China, would only really become established from 2008 onward. At this point in the narrative, in mid-2006, I am not sure if in my mind the possible fifth participant would have been Beijing or Tokyo. Another possibility—more likely, in fact—is that I was thinking that in addition to the four leaders, the director-general of the WTO could also participate.

105. Unlike the majority of foreign ministers, I acted as a "sherpa" for President Lula at most summits (my South African counterpart played the same role, as did, I believe, the Mexican foreign minister). The sherpas did not stay in the same room as the leaders but listened to their conversations via an audio link. At certain summit venues we were also able to see what was going on, separated from the leaders only by a glass screen. The leaders' meeting in St. Petersburg took place in just such an "aquarium." I remember that in the rush to keep up with the president, I lost a pair of glasses.

106. As previously mentioned, access to the agricultural markets of the EU and some developing countries was a major US goal in the negotiations.

107. Prime Minister Manmohan Singh of India, and European Commission president José Manuel Barroso. The latter sought to speak on behalf of the European countries as a whole, but he did not have the same weight as the elected leaders directly representing their countries at the summit.

108. At the Hong Kong Ministerial Conference, Brazil was one of the countries—alongside South Africa and Argentina—that fought hardest for the inclusion of the concept of "proportionality" between the concessions potentially to be made with regard to market access for agricultural (AMA) and non-agricultural (NAMA) products. We also made sure that this point was included in the Lula-Blair joint statement. We did fear, however, that if this argument were taken to extremes, it might cause the negotiations to break down.

109. See the narrative on Brazil and the Middle East.

110. In my conversations with Jonathan Powell I had mentioned, purely speculatively and without any commitment (and, of course, subject to what progress would be made in the areas of interest to us), a coefficient of 22.5. But officially we still adhered to the "coefficient of 30."

111. A country that is not a member of the WTO has to negotiate its accession to it by means of concessions to pre-existing members.

112. The metaphor, often used by Brazilian trade negotiators, comes from a card game for children. The cards all have a picture of an animal on them and there are two cards for each animal—apart from the black monkey, of which there is only one. The idea of the game is to

match the cards, which is obviously possible in every case apart from that of the black monkey. In the trade negotiations, the monkey is the country whose positions are perceived as preventing agreement—and therefore, in the eternal game of apportioning blame, the loser.

113. In the G6 meetings, the Japanese ministers (both trade and agriculture) were the only ones who needed simultaneous interpretation, which consisted of an interpreter whispering in the minister's ear so as not to disrupt the discussion. Although the Japanese interpreters (who were always women, by the way) were very competent, misunderstandings arose on more than one occasion. In July 2008, when Lamy interrupted a tense meeting to say he would commence the "confessionals" (referring to the procedure in which the director-general consulted the principal negotiators separately, one by one), the puzzled Japanese minister said: "He's going to call the professionals?"

114. The "unraveling" metaphor is quite often used by WTO negotiators when there is a risk of previous advances becoming undone.

115. A waiver is when, in special circumstances, a WTO member is granted permission not to comply with specific commitments.

116. The General Debate is the annual meeting of heads of state and government at the beginning of the General Assembly session. It is usually the first debate of the session. It takes place in the General Assembly Hall at the United Nations Headquarters in New York.

117. Months later, the Indian permanent representative, Shri S. Narayanan, expressed to me his regret at not having taken a similarly firm line on certain issues of interest to his country. His self-deprecating exclamation was: "I do not have your stature, sir!"

118. The Latin American Integration Association (ALADI) was created by the Treaty of Montevideo in 1980, replacing the Latin American Free Trade Association (ALALC). The trade agreements made under the aegis of ALADI include the one that brought Mercosur into being.

119. Flying in a Brazilian-made "E-Jet" (a particular line of Embraer aircraft) was obviously a source of pride as well as physical comfort. Incidentally, the dispute between Embraer and the Canadian company Bombardier had taken up much of my time during my second period as Brazil's permanent representative in Geneva (1999–2001).

120. Joaquim Nabuco (1849–1910) was a Brazilian politician, diplomat, and author who served as our first ambassador in Washington (1905–1910). A strong supporter of a close Brazil-US alliance, Nabuco was the main force behind the convening of the third Pan American Conference in Rio de Janeiro in 1906.

121. The Andean Trade Promotion and Drug Eradication Act (ATPDEA): a system of trade preferences granted by the United States to Bolivia, Peru, Ecuador and Colombia, created in 2002 to replace the Andean Trade Preferences Act of 1991. Its stated goal was to discourage the production of narcotics in those countries by offering tariff exemptions for Andean products in the US market.

122. A US government development assistance program, launched in 2004, which dispensed significant funds.

123. The secretary of state and I signed the memorandum on March 30, at Camp David, during a working visit by Lula to the United States. Guinea Bissau's ambassador in Washington was present at the ceremony.

124. Two very important meetings were scheduled for the month of June: the G8+5 Summit in Heiligendamm, and a G4/G6 ministerial (which ended up taking place in Potsdam). At the time I wrote those notes, the prospects did not look good.

125. Boutros-Ghali, Boutros. *Egypt's Road to Jerusalem: A Diplomat's Story of the Struggle for Peace in the Middle East* (Random House, 1997).

126. I never understood what Bush meant with that reference to "thirty days." But, as will be seen, Lula later repeated it. I suppose they both simply wanted to emphasize the urgent need for progress in the negotiations.

127. In fact, apart from the issue of "geographical indications," which was not at the center of the discussions at that time, the EU itself did not have any specific demands with regard to the US. The Europeans simply wanted the US to reduce its OTDS in response to the cuts in farming subsidies the EU would be making as part of the ongoing process of CAP reform. The

biggest difference between the EU and the US was the former's resistance on the issue of agricultural market access (AMA).

128. Lula had always attached importance to coordinating with Argentina in the WTO negotiations, maybe even to a greater extent than I did. It is hard to see, however, how a joint letter written with the US president would affect Buenos Aires.

129. The official name of India's capital city is, of course, New Delhi. But among diplomats, especially in multilateral forums, it is usually referred to simply as Delhi.

130. In the joint statement issued at the end of President Lula's visit to Camp David, one paragraph was devoted to the Doha Round. It reads as follows: "The Heads of State reaffirmed global economic growth and development as the main objectives of the Doha Round of the World Trade Organization (WTO). They underscored the importance of continuing to constructively engage negotiators, which facilitated the resumption of the negotiations. The Presidents pledged to work together toward a successful conclusion, taking advantage of the window of opportunity opened in 2007. They emphasized that the agreement should be ambitious and balanced, with a view to both an appreciable increase in market access and in global trade flows, and a significant reduction in global poverty rates."

131. Singh's smile on that occasion was especially significant because the Indian leader tended to maintain a countenance of great serenity and sobriety. Once, following an IBSA meeting in Brasilia, South African president Thabo Mbeki remarked to me that "only Lula can make Singh smile."

132. The Portuguese/Spanish acronym for the Community of South American Nations.

133. During the Uruguay Round, Argentina was one of the most active members of a small group (along with, among others, the US, the European Economic Community, Australia, and New Zealand) that did not include Brazil.

134. One of the most eloquent parts of my speech at the World Health Assembly, made on May 15, was as follows: "This time, not even those who are usually critical of any form of government action on socio-economic issues can deny that the measure taken by Brazil was unassailable on both moral and legal grounds. Some of [those critics] have expressed concern about its negative impact on investment. But here we need to ask: what kind of investment? Not investment in the production of medicines. And certainly not in research and development aimed at new technological advances—because we all know those activities are restricted to the headquarters of the big pharmaceutical companies, or their subsidiaries in other developed countries. And in any case, no economic consideration should prevent measures aimed at saving tens of millions of human lives."

135. The same logic, but this time based on negative historical precedent, surely made Potsdam an inauspicious choice of location for the G4 meeting the following month. I will elaborate on this later in the narrative.

136. The discussions at Val-Duchesse covered the main vectors of the negotiations in systematic fashion. Therefore, in addition to the themes mentioned in the text, there were also sessions on the subjects of services, rules (particularly anti-dumping), etc.

137. The special safeguards (SSG) were intended to provide an additional protection mechanism in agriculture and were used mainly by the Europeans, in addition to the "general" safeguards that were the subject of a different agreement. I have always wondered what the "G" in the acronym stands for. I remember speculating at the time of the Uruguay Round that the third letter might have been added simply to avoid the grisly echoes "SS" would have. I have not yet heard a better explanation.

138. These maneuvers, whose technical details lie beyond the scope of this narrative, were known in the WTO jargon as "box shifting" and "product shifting." See also note 39.

139. David Miliband (whose father, the left-leaning intellectual and author Ralph Milliband, had been my thesis supervisor at the LSE about forty years earlier) became foreign secretary not long afterwards. A few years later, when Labour was no longer in power, he fought and lost a battle with his younger brother, Ed Miliband, for the leadership of the party.

140. After Heiligendamm there were two more summits with a similar format: in Japan in 2008, and in Italy in 2009. The difficulties in agreeing an agenda in advance between the G8 and "the rest" (to borrow Fareed Zakaria's expression), along with the rise of the G20 leaders' summit in the wake of the explosion of the financial crisis, led to the abandonment of this

format, which nevertheless did have certain merits and could perhaps have evolved in a more positive direction. In 2010, while I was still foreign minister, Brazil itself gave up on such G8 "plus" gatherings, which in retrospect was perhaps a mistake.

141. The acronym SVEs refers to "Small and Vulnerable Economies," such as the small islands of the Caribbean and the Pacific. In the informal setting of the WTO, unlike in the UN, there were no regional groups as such. The main exception was that of the African members, although the countries of CARICOM would occasionally meet. The Latin American countries had met in the past (in the old GATT), but this practice was discontinued with the emergence of subject-oriented groups such as the G20.

142. I believe it was my performance at Potsdam that elicited Peter Mandelson's aforementioned reference to my supposedly "forensic" grasp of the dossiers in his memoirs *The Third Man*. I should also mention an article by Larry Elliott in the *Guardian* ("Deal or no deal: Big Four hold last-ditch talks so save Doha"), written at the beginning of the Potsdam meeting, which set the scene with great clarity and also memorably referred to Peter as a "spinmeister."

143. My appreciation for Kamal's attitude was increased by the knowledge that India had fewer difficulties than Brazil with regard to NAMA. That was because India had unilaterally lowered its industrial tariffs in the early 1990s as part of the liberalization policy pursued by Manmohan Singh as finance minister.

144. As will be clear by now, the WTO director-general was a far from constant presence at the G4 meetings. At times when the negotiating aspect of the meetings predominated over mere evaluation (although it is difficult to separate the two), the tendency, particularly on the part of Mandelson and Schwab, was to dispense with Lamy's participation. As for the Japanese trade minister, he was already accustomed to playing a lesser role in the inner circle of the negotiations.

145. Kamal's acquiescence would not have been based only on solidarity, although I do think that was one of his motives. He would have been very aware that although the guns of our "adversaries" were turned against Brazil, when the time came to apportion blame there would be no shortage of negative references to India with regard to SP/SSM. Indeed, that was precisely the case in the dialogue I had with Susan after the meeting, which is described later in the narrative.

146. The strategic partnership between the European Union and Brazil was an initiative on the part of Brussels, following a proposal made by European Commission president José Manuel Durão Barroso during a visit to Brasilia on May 31, 2006. The partnership came into being at the Lisbon Summit on July 4, 2007.

147. The traditional practice in the WTO (and its predecessor, the GATT) had been for negotiations among its members to be conducted on the basis of a "paper" prepared by the coordinator ("chair") responsible for the topic in question. But there was a loss of trust in that approach after the failure of the attempt at Cancún (2003) to use a document prepared by the president of the WTO General Council. The "July Framework" agreed in 2004 was the work of the FIPS, without a preprepared script drawn up by a supposedly neutral coordinator. Nor were the discussions within the G4 (or, by extension, the G6) based on papers produced by a chair. But following the impasse of July 2006, the director-general prepared to reintroduce the traditional procedure, although it remained "on hold" while the G4/G6 negotiations were in progress. In the immediate aftermath of the Potsdam fiasco, the chairs, with their papers, re-emerged.

148. Chile, like Mexico, is a member of the G20. These two countries, both of which had undergone processes of unilateral trade liberalization, acted independently on issues other than agriculture, such as services and NAMA.

149. The "second half" of the meeting between Brazil and the European Union, in Brussels, was hosted by the president of the European Commission. The focus was mainly on biofuels. There were also meetings between Brazilian ministers and their EC counterparts to discuss the various projects through which our strategic partnership would take shape in practical terms.

150. This constructive position of on the part of the Indian permanent representative contrasted with the attitudes of Indian trade minister Kamal Nath, who generally took every opportunity to express skepticism about the chances of achieving a positive conclusion to the negotiations. Although this might seem odd, differences in attitude (or with regard to tactical

and procedural matters) between a country's trade minister and its representative at the WTO in Geneva were not uncommon.

151. On July 17, 2007, a TAM Airbus overran the runway when attempting to land at Congonhas, an airport situated in urban São Paulo. A total of 199 people lost their lives (all 187 who were in the aircraft, and 12 on the ground).

152. Tereza actually used a favorite Brazilian idiom, describing the very difficult role of defense minister at that time as a "pineapple" (*abacaxi*). The idea behind the expression is that pineapples are troublesome to peel.

153. "Planalto" refers to the presidential palace in Brasilia.

154. Years later, ironically, I was invited to be defense minister by President Dilma Rousseff and accepted the role. By that time, fortunately, Nelson Jobim had dealt with the problems described above, and more importantly, had put an end to the anomaly of Brazil's civil aviation falling into the remit of the Brazilian Air Force.

155. The Southern African Customs Union (SACU) is a customs union of five southern African countries: Botswana, Lesotho, Namibia, South Africa, and Swaziland.

156. Rui Barbosa (1849–1923) was an emblematic Brazilian politician and diplomat, widely respected for his progressive positions and advocacy of the principle of juridical equality among states. He played a very important role at the Hague Conference of 1907. My lecture was entitled "*A diplomacia multilateral do Brasil: Um tributo a Rui Barbosa*." It was part of the second National Conference on Foreign Policy and International Politics, which took place in Rio de Janeiro on November 5, 2007. It was published later that year by FUNAG, under the same title.

157. See the narrative on Brazil and the Middle East.

158. The expression *Media Luna* refers to the eastern region of Bolivia where opposition to the government of Evo Morales was concentrated. The name comes from the crescent shape made by the four contiguous departments that constitute the region.

159. Previously the BRICs had met only in New York, on the sidelines of the UN General Assembly.

160. In simplified terms, in the context of the negotiations, the nature of a customs union (particularly one made up of developing countries, and still under construction) meant that a greater number of items would have to be subject to flexibilities. Because a sensitive product for one Mercosur member was not necessarily sensitive for another (although of course there was a significant degree of convergence), the only way to accommodate all the member countries' flexibilities without breaking the principle of the common external tariff was to increase, within reasonable limits, the number of goods eligible to receive favorable treatment.

161. During the process of drawing up texts in the WTO, if a certain point is "in brackets" it means it is still under discussion and has not yet been agreed upon.

162. Even at Potsdam there were no substantive changes of position on AMA. It was just that the guns were turned against different targets.

163. Largely on account of subsidized imported rice, countries such as the two mentioned above were led in times of oversupply to give up on their own, more costly, production of rice or other crops that might be a substitute for it.

164. Originally a Russian word used metaphorically to designate the three-pronged leadership of the Soviet Union, "troika" normally designates the coordinating body of a group of countries. In most cases the troika includes the country chairing the entity at a given moment, the immediately preceding chair, and the incoming one. In the narrative, Slovenia was the chair of the EU at that point, hence the meeting in Ljubljana.

165. With regard to NAMA, in addition to the formula for tariff reductions it was also foreseen that "sectorial" negotiations, by product group, would take place. This was of particular interest to the US, which hoped to gain advantages from the "sectorials" that it could not obtain through the formula. For Brazil and other developing countries, such as China, this prospect was highly problematic. It was one of the issues (though not the main one) that would ultimately make it impossible to reach an agreement.

166. In fact, the hard work had indeed produced considerable advances toward the establishment of numbers (or bands of numbers) for the main aspects of the "modalities."

167. The revised versions of the papers were the outcome of discussions at the WTO between the negotiators and the chairs (or coordinators) of the various groups, each of which dealt with a separate area of the negotiations. At this stage I remember that certain issues, such as that of the flexibilities to be granted to Mercosur, led me to have very long telephone conversations with the director-general.

168. It is important to note that in the case of the Special Safeguard Mechanism (SSM), India and other countries did not merely want safeguards so as to manage the risks arising from the liberalization imposed by tariff cuts, but also to create an additional layer of protection by raising their tariffs on agricultural products to levels higher than those established during the Uruguay Round. This is why the G20 never managed to produce anything other than generic formulations regarding the SSM.

169. Trade Promotion Authority: see note 103.

170. During the course of the negotiations we discovered that, within certain limits, the widening of the flexibilities served our interests better than the maintenance of a high coefficient. This point is covered in greater detail in *Conversas com jovens diplomatas*, Chapter 7.

171. The statement issued by the G20 at the meeting on July 20 emphasizes that: "It will be necessary to achieve effective cuts in Overall Trade-Distorting Domestic Support (OTDS), taking into account changes in . . . world prices." The statement stresses the importance of "disciplines" in order, *inter alia*, to avoid the concentration of subsidies on just a few products (cotton is mentioned specifically). As for export subsidies, "the timeframe agreed in Hong Kong for the elimination of all export subsidies must be respected." The statement continues: "Developed countries should produce results that correspond to the Doha Mandate with regard to a substantial improvement in market access, and the Hong Kong Mandate with regard to balance between agriculture and NAMA (paragraph 24). The formula for tariff cuts must be ambitious, particularly in the highest band; and the minimum average cut of 54% must be respected, in line with the G20 proposal. The limits on tariff capping must be effective. . . ." The statement also emphasizes "the vital role of special products ('SPs') in dealing with food security, rural development, and the subsistence concerns of developing countries, and also of the special safeguard mechanism ('SSM')." In reproducing this G20 statement, as in a handful of other cases during this book, I did not have access to the original text in English. Instead I used the Portuguese translation in the official Itamaraty records, which was obviously then "retranslated" back into English. There might therefore be some very minor discrepancies, but the essence of the original text has certainly been maintained in every case.

172. After a long period of introspection following its admission to the WTO, China was beginning to show signs of wanting to act in a manner commensurate with the size of its economy. China's presence in the group also guaranteed that if an agreement was reached, Beijing would comply with it. China was targeted with demands by the developed countries, particularly the US, both with regard to manufactured goods and agricultural products.

173. A detailed reconstruction of these meetings in Geneva in July 2008 appears in Paul Blustein's *Misadventures of the Most Favored Nations* (Chapter 13). For an account written in the immediate aftermath of the events (and to some extent still in the heat of the moment), see *Conversas com jovens diplomatas* (Chapter 7).

174. In addition to special products, which would be subject to smaller tariff reductions than those arising from the formula, the G33 had managed to create an additional category of so-called "super specials." These products would be subject to no tariff reductions whatsoever. On this issue the debate focused on establishing the maximum percentage of products or tariff lines that could be classified as super-specials.

175. One of Kamal's arguments was that in India there were several points of entry for these products, and that the central government did not have reliable statistics on the basis of which it could accurately measure the overall increase in imports and act quickly enough to remedy the negative impact on the country's farmers.

176. In some cases the tariffs imposed by Japan were tantamount to a ban on imports. Tariffs of between 200% and 600% were not uncommon, and for certain types of rice they could even exceed 1,000%!

177. The G20 proposal was to adopt the minimum limit proposed by the earlier "revised text," i.e. $13 billion USD. Lamy's paper stipulated a ceiling of $14.5 billion, which was a

compromise between the upper and lower ends of the range. Before negotiations began, Susan Schwab announced that if the main US demands in other areas were met, she might accept a figure of $15 billion, but no lower. All these figures were higher than the actual average OTDS over the preceding two or three years (approximately $11 billion). This signified, on the one hand, that Washington acknowledged it could not return to the astronomical levels of OTDS of previous years, which had reached or even exceeded $20 billion, but on the other hand that there would be no reduction in comparison with the immediately preceding years.

178. To some extent Schwab's change of position can be attributed to her contact during the preceding weekend with the US industrial and agricultural lobbies, represented in Geneva by, respectively, the National Association of Manufacturers (NAM) and the Farm Bureau. But there were also deeper reasons involving Susan's own personality, the end of President Bush's time in office, and fear of a hostile reaction in Congress.

179. At one point during the G7 discussions, when Susan Schwab tried to play down the significance of a suspension of the negotiations, as if she was unaware how serious the implications were, Mandelson referred to her behavior as "disgraceful."

180. In Mandelson's *The Third Man*, his description of the proceedings, although briefer, is very similar to mine. Referring to the intransigence of Schwab and Nath, he says: "Celso Amorim and I, with the support of Pascal Lamy, tried every way we could think of to get through the impasse, but the two sides were simply unwilling to compromise any further."

181. The anti-concentration percentages refer to the minimum number of tariff lines, within a category of products, that would be subject to an integral cut in accordance with the formula (i.e. those that would not benefit from the flexibilities). The higher the percentage, the less scope there would be to "concentrate" the flexibilities in a single category of products (e.g. the automotive industry).

182. As previously mentioned, the expression "geographical indications" refers to names of places used to identify products that originated from those places and have specific characteristics (e.g. "Champagne," "Tequila," "Roquefort"). In the WTO negotiations on the issue, Brazil adopts an intermediate position while the US, Australia and Argentina are radically opposed to the very concept of geographical indications.

183. Mari Pangestu, Indonesia's mild-mannered trade minister, came from an academic background. Although she had some experience of trade negotiations, having taking part in ASEAN agreements with Japan and South Korea, she was probably not yet accustomed to the asperities and manipulation that were so typical of political conflicts within the WTO. Pangestu visited me in Brasilia on August 1, soon after the collapse of talks in Geneva. On that occasion she told me she had been very upset about the impasse on the issue of special products. She said that as coordinator of the G33 she felt she had been used for the benefit of radical positions. After her visit, in response to a message I sent to her through our ambassador in Jakarta, Pangestu admitted that although she was unhappy about the failure of the negotiations, she was unable to gather together her G33 partners in order to undertake technical studies (as Lamy had requested) because most of them were now imbued with the radicalism that Kamal had proved so adept at instilling and exploiting.

184. I was certainly anxious to maintain both Brazil's strategic alliance with India and the unity of the G20, but the weak point of our shared position always lay in the area of SP/SSM. Even then, however, we tried until the last moment to find a solution. Had we been able to accommodate New Delhi, it is difficult to say whether or not the United States would have returned to a more positive position. The burden of isolation is always a heavy one, and the mutually comforting relationship that Susan and Kamal created in Geneva certainly helped them maintain their respective positions. But, ultimately, the ability to stick to an isolated negotiating position is one of the characteristics of the great powers.

185. Blustein, Paul. *Misadventures of the Most Favored Nations* (Public Affairs, 2009).

186. Georges Clemenceau (1841–1929), prime minister of France for two periods in the first two decades of the twentieth century, is believed to have said: "War is too important to be left to the generals."

187. Cristina Kirchner was president of Argentina from 2007 to 2015, succeeding her late husband Néstor Kirchner, who had occupied the role between 2003 and 2007.

188. I will return to the subject of this summit later in this section.

189. In the late 1940s, just after the Second World War and the downfall of the dictatorship of Getúlio Vargas, the Brazilian politician João Mangabeira used this metaphor to refer to the country's fragile young democracy.

190. With regard to the USTR, however, Kamal and I agreed that her "excessive demands" in other areas of the negotiations, especially the NAMA "sectorials," made it difficult to envisage resuming the negotiations.

191. The Southern Africa Development Community (SADC) is a regional economic community comprising fifteen member states.

192. Reminder: this G20 of major economies, which emerged in the aftermath of the 2008 financial crisis, should not be confused with the G20 that has appeared throughout this narrative, i.e. the group of developing countries that came together in the context of the WTO in 2003.

193. See the narrative on the Tehran Declaration.

194. After calling on the countries not to adopt protectionist measures, Paragraph 13 of the G20 leaders' joint statement directly addresses the subject of the Doha Round: "Further, we shall strive to reach an agreement this year on modalities that leads to a successful conclusion to the WTO's Doha Development Agenda with an ambitious and balanced outcome. We instruct our Trade Ministers to achieve this objective and stand ready to assist directly. We also agree that our countries have the largest stake in the global trading system and therefore each must make the positive contributions necessary to achieve such an outcome."

195. See also note 118.

196. The Forum for East Asia-Latin America Cooperation (FEALAC) was born out of a joint initiative between Singapore and Chile in 1999, aimed at encouraging interaction, promoting political dialogue, and increasing cooperation.

197. In the British system of titles and forms of address (which is so obscure and complicated that it is virtually incomprehensible even to the British themselves), "Baroness" is the title given to women who have been chosen to be members of the House of Lords.

198. Mandelson's full title at the time was Secretary of State for Business, Enterprise and Regulatory Reform.

199. Paragraph 16 of the Ministerial Declaration at the WTO Ministerial Conference in Hong Kong (2005) stated the following: "In furtherance of paragraph 7 of the NAMA Framework, we recognize that Members are pursuing sectoral initiatives. To this end, we instruct the Negotiating Group to review proposals with a view to identifying those which could garner sufficient participation to be realized. Participation should be on a non-mandatory basis."

200. As I happened to discover while reading the famous biography *The Life of Samuel Johnson* by James Boswell, the term was originally used to refer to the anteroom in a theater where the actors would wait immediately before entering the stage. In one of the sections of the book, Boswell describes Johnson's fondness for frequenting the "green rooms" of eighteenth-century London theaters. The idea of being "behind the scenes" is obviously also present in the usage of the expression in the context of the WTO decision-making process.

201. At the end of 2002, the outgoing Brazilian president, Fernando Henrique Cardoso, and his imminent successor, Lula, agreed to send a petrol tanker to Venezuela to "break" the "lock-out" on the part of the Venezuelan state-owned oil company (PDVSA) that was aimed at destabilizing the government of President Hugo Chávez.

202. In December 2008, Brazil hosted the first Latin American and Caribbean Summit on Integration and Development (CALC). It was the first ever meeting of Latin American and Caribbean heads of state and government not to have been co-sponsored by powers from outside the region. All 33 countries in the Americas, with the exception of the US and Canada, participated. The second CALC summit, in Mexico in 2010, saw the beginning of the process of convergence between the CALC and the Rio Group, which together would form the Community of Latin American and Caribbean States (CELAC).

203. The statement on the automobile industry was made by Sarkozy. The idea that a particular bank should not be lending abroad was proposed in the UK, in specific reference to the Bank of Scotland. The country in which the public were implored to buy locally produced cars was Spain. All three references are based on memory, but I am quite confident of their accuracy.

204. "Sunset clause" has been a common expression in the WTO ever since the GATT era. It denotes the date until which a measure or policy not in line with the general rules is permitted to remain in place.

205. ". . . Ministers Amorim and Nath expressed grave concern at the decision to seize goods of a strategic nature for public health, traded between developing countries in full compliance with international disciplines. The decision also represents a serious step backward from the principle of universal access to medicines, and is contrary to the spirit of Resolution 2002/31 of the Human Rights Commission. . . ." These were the words of the Itamaraty press release (January 21, 2009) condemning the seizure of a shipment of Losartan Potassium at Amsterdam airport. The seizure was not only contrary to the basic rules of freedom of transit in international trade but also the Doha Declaration on TRIPS and public health. After long and fruitless protests in Brussels, Brazil formally requested the opening of consultations under the auspices of the WTO Dispute Settlement Body, as stated in a later press release dated May 12, 2010.

206. The attentive reader will notice that, from a very different starting point, the new USTR's intentions coincided with what would have been the consequences (in my opinion) of Kamal Nath's radical attitude.

207. In the United Kingdom and some other countries that follow the British tradition, the title "minister of state" denotes a deputy minister. This often leads to confusion, since in most countries of the "Latin world," especially the former French colonies, *Ministre d'État* is a title reserved for the most important ministers, the ones who constitute a kind of "inner cabinet." In Brazil, where we are always very generous with titles, an equivalent denomination is used for any member of the cabinet.

208. In the past, commenting on Brazilian doubts about the FTAA, even before Lula's inauguration as president, the then USTR had said something to the effect that if Brazil did not want to negotiate a trade deal that included the US, it should go and negotiate with Antarctica instead.

209. In India, as in the ex-metropole, a "minister of state" is a deputy minister.

210. "7. We . . . are committed to seek an ambitious and balanced conclusion to the Doha Development Round in 2010, consistent with its mandate, building on the progress already made, including with regard to modalities. . . . In order to fill in the remaining gaps in the negotiations as soon as possible, we instruct our Ministers in charge of trade to explore immediately all possible avenues for direct engagement within the WTO and to meet prior to the Pittsburgh Summit." (Joint Declaration: promoting the global agenda, G8 and G5 Summit, July 8-10, 2009, L'Aquila)

211. About three years during my second spell as Brazil's permanent representative in Geneva, followed by seven (by this point in the narrative) as foreign minister under Lula.

212. Not Kamal's private home with the spectacular ruin in the backyard, mentioned much earlier in this narrative.

213. Back in 1985, Washington had chosen September 7 to announce unilateral retaliation against Brazil because of aspects of our policy at the time on information technology. Not only is September 7 our Independence Day, but that year it was also just one or two days before a scheduled visit to the US by our science and technology minister, Renato Archer. Thankfully the visit was cancelled. My role at the time was that of Archer's international advisor.

214. I was referring to a paper published by the Peterson Institute for International Economics in 2009, later incorporated into a book entitled *Figuring out the Doha Round* (2010). According to one of its tables, Brazil, together with India, would be making the largest reduction in bound tariffs. Of course the reduction would have been much less significant when it came to applied tariffs, but even then, in terms of percentage points, greater than that which the US or the EU was due to make.

215. Just as a reminder, as Lula's foreign minister I also dealt with Bob Zoellick, Rob Portman and Susan Schwab. When I had been foreign minister under President Itamar Franco in the 1990s, the USTR was Mickey Kantor, a lawyer who exuded a certain nervous tension, expressed through his habit of constantly clicking his fingers. But as head of the economic department in Itamaraty or as permanent representative in Geneva, I also had contact with three other USTRs: Clayton Yeutter, Carla Hills, and Charlene Barshefsky. Out of all of them, Ron Kirk seemed least at ease in the role. His character was much more suited to the work of a US

secretary of commerce—a business-promotion role—than to that of a trade negotiator in the traditional sense.

216. The idea of social dumping, much discussed in the run-up to the Seattle Ministerial Conference in 2001, represented a widening of the concept of anti-dumping aimed at allowing the use of trade-restrictive measures. Apart from depending on subjective and arbitrary evaluations, the idea of social dumping was also based on a misconception in that the essence of dumping consists of selling a product in a foreign market at a price lower than those charged in the domestic market of the producer country.

217. The final protocol of the São Paulo Round of the Global System of Trade Preferences among Developing Countries (GSTP) would be signed on December 15, 2010, on the margins of the Mercosur summit in the Brazilian city of Foz do Iguaçu. The agreement represented the conclusion of a cycle of negotiations launched in 2004 in São Paulo, during the XI UNCTAD. The signatory countries agreed to grant each other a preference margin of 20% on the tariff applied to 70% of the total list of products. The agreement was signed by eleven developing countries: the members of Mercosur, Cuba, Egypt, India, Indonesia, Malaysia, Morocco, and South Korea.

218. Pascal Lamy often expressed appreciation for the role of Brazil—and, by extension, my own individual efforts—in the Doha negotiations. In an article he wrote in July 2014 (*L'Organisation Mondiale de Commerce, nouveaux enjeux, nouveaux défis*), for example, the former director-general referred to the increasing participation of developing countries in the trade negotiations, and stated that: "On the plane of international trade negotiations, this economic reactivation of nonalignment has been driven mainly by Brazil. It was on the occasion of the WTO Ministerial Conference in Cancún, in 2003, that Brazil took the initiative of bringing together the G20 in response to a restricted draft agreement on agriculture between the European Union and the United States." Lamy alluded to the diverse interests of the countries that made up the group, which consisted of "emerging powers such as India, China and South Africa, and less commercially dynamic countries such as Bolivia and Tanzania." According to Lamy, the G20 allowed Brazil, over the course of several years, to establish itself as a powerful player in the Doha Round. The former director-general commented on the coming together of the G20 and the G90, whose interests were not identical but who "shared certain orientations." He continued: "This movement on the part of Brazil is the result of the strategy developed by Celso Amorim, Foreign Minister under President Lula from 2003 to 2010. . . . During Amorim's time, Brazil was a significant force; since then, its influence has declined progressively."

219. See the first of the three narratives in this book.

220. The "option" mentioned here is commonly known as "cross-retaliation," i.e. the right WTO members have—if authorized by the organization's relevant bodies—to "withdraw concessions" in areas covered by the different agreements that constitute the Uruguay Round package. For instance, a member incurring a violation in the area of "goods" may face retaliation in the areas of services or TRIPS (and vice versa).

221. Washington did not meet all our expectations in terms of adjusting its practices (subsidies for US cotton farmers) to the WTO findings. In compensation, it offered to pay an indemnity to the Brazilian producers. Part of the amount paid, in accordance with our request, goes to Brazilian technical assistance programs for the countries of the Cotton-4.

222. In effect, the right to "cross-retaliate" was invoked twice in WTO disputes: first by Ecuador against the EU, in the case of bananas; and second by Brazil against the US, in the cotton dispute. When this mechanism was introduced into what came to be the Marrakesh agreements, I was Brazil's permanent representative in Geneva. During the very last stages of the negotiation of the "Draft Final Act," I argued that if such a compelling instrument were finally adopted (as indeed it would be), it should work both ways—not only from intellectual property and services to goods, but also from goods to intellectual property and services. The discussion on this issue took place during a meeting that went on long into the night in what used to be the USTR's offices in Geneva. Also sitting at the table were Warren Lavorel, the US chief negotiator; Hugo Paemen, representing the European Economic Community; and Anwarul Hoda of India. My proposal, which I made on the spur of the moment, took everyone by surprise. Hoda, my ally in the discussions, did not seem to understand it fully, but nevertheless did not object. I suppose neither Lavorel nor Paemen thought it would ever work the way I

envisaged, and that the possibility of resorting to cross-retaliation against TRIPS or services in response to a violation related to trade in goods was a purely theoretical one. Since all they wanted was to ensure that cross-retaliation found its way into the agreement, they finally accepted my proposal.

223. English translation completed in October 2016.

Index

Printed in Great Britain
by Amazon